Fodor's 2012

SOUTHERN CALIFORNIA

Fodor's Travel Publications   New York, Toronto, London, Sydney, Auckland

www.fodors.com

Excerpted from *Fodor's California 2012*

FODOR'S SOUTHERN CALIFORNIA 2012

Editors: Maria Teresa Hart, Matthew Lombardi

Writers: Cindy Arora, Tanvi Chheda,Cheryl Crabtree, Alene Dawson, Maren Dougherty, Maria Hunt, Amanda Knoles, Elline Lipkin, Lea Lion, Susan MacCallum-Whitcomb, Christine Pae, Reed Parsell, Laura Randall, Natasha Sarkisian, Sharon Silva, AnnaMaria Stephens, Claire Deeks van der Lee, Christine Vovakes, Sura Wood, Bobbi Zane, **Editorial Contributors:** Bethany Beckerlegge, Heidi Johansen, Claire Deeks van der Lee

Production Editors: Carolyn Roth, Evangelos Vasilakis, Carrie Parker, Anna Birinyi
Maps & Illustrations: David Lindroth and Mark Stroud, *cartographers;* Bob Blake, Rebecca Baer, *map editors;* William Wu, *information graphics*
Design: Fabrizio La Rocca, *creative director;* Guido Caroti, *art director;* Tina Malaney, Nora Rosansky, Chie Ushio, Jessica Walsh, *designers;* Melanie Marin, *associate director of photography*
Cover Photo: (Encinitas, San Diego County): Ty Milford/Masterfile
Production Manager: Angela L. McLean

COPYRIGHT

ISBN 978–0–679–00962–7

ISSN 1543–1037

SPECIAL SALES

This book is available at special discounts for bulk purchases for sales promotions or premiums. Special editions, including personalized covers, excerpts of existing books, and corporate imprints, can be created in large quantities for special needs. For more information, write to Special Markets/Premium Sales, 1745 Broadway, MD 3-1, New York, NY 10019, or e-mail specialmarkets@randomhouse.com.

AN IMPORTANT TIP & AN INVITATION

Although all prices, opening times, and other details in this book are based on information supplied to us at press time, changes occur all the time in the travel world, and Fodor's cannot accept responsibility for facts that become outdated or for inadvertent errors or omissions. So **always confirm information when it matters,** especially if you're making a detour to visit a specific place. Your experiences—positive and negative—matter to us. If we have missed or misstated something, **please write to us.** Share your opinion instantly through our online feedback center at fodors.com/contact-us.

PRINTED IN SINGAPORE

10 9 8 7 6 5 4 3 2 1

CONTENTS

MAPS

ABOUT THIS BOOK

Our Ratings

At Fodor's, we spend considerable time choosing the best places in a destination so you don't have to. By default, anything we recommend in this book is worth visiting. But some sights, properties, and experiences are so great that we've recognized them with additional accolades. Orange **Fodor's Choice** stars indicate our top recommendations; black stars highlight places we deem **Highly Recommended;** and **Best Bets** call attention to top properties in various categories. Disagree with any of our choices? Care to nominate a new place? Visit our feedback center at www.fodors.com/feedback.

Hotels

Hotels have private bath, phone, and TV, and do not offer meals unless we specify that in the review. We always list facilities but not whether you'll be charged an extra fee to use them.

> For expanded hotel reviews, visit **Fodors.com**

Restaurants

Unless we state otherwise, restaurants are open for lunch and dinner daily. We mention dress only when there's a specific requirement and reservations only when they're essential or not accepted—it's always best to book ahead.

Credit Cards

We assume that restaurants and hotels accept credit cards. If not, we'll note it in the review.

Budget Well

Hotel and restaurant price categories from ¢ to $$$$ are defined in the opening pages of the respective chapters. For attractions, we always give standard adult admission fees; reductions are usually available for children, students, and senior citizens.

Listings
- ★ Fodor's Choice
- ★ Highly recommended
- ✉ Physical address
- ✛ Directions or Map coordinates
- ☎ Telephone
- 🖷 Fax
- ⊕ On the Web
- ✎ E-mail
- ✇ Admission fee
- ☉ Open/closed times
- Ⓜ Metro stations
- ⊟ No credit cards

Hotels & Restaurants
- 🏨 Hotel
- ⇥ Number of rooms
- ⌂ Facilities
- ¶⦶ Meal plans
- ✗ Restaurant
- ⌕ Reservations
- ⌂ Dress code
- ⤵ Smoking

Outdoors
- 🏌 Golf
- ⛺ Camping

Other
- ☾ Family-friendly
- ⇨ See also
- ✉ Branch address
- ☞ Take note

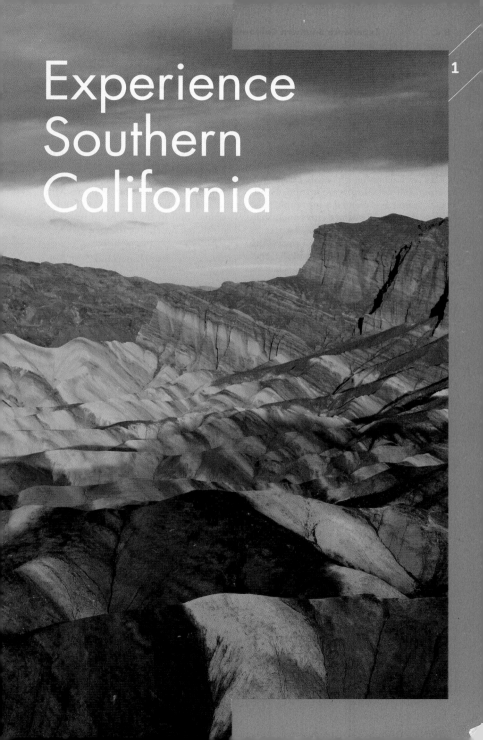

Experience
Southern
California

WHAT'S NEW IN SOUTHERN CALIFORNIA

Foodie's Paradise

Great dining is a staple of the California lifestyle, and a new young generation of chefs is challenging old ideas about preparing and presenting great food. Food-truck frenzy has created a moveable feast across the state. Esteemed chefs and urban foodies follow the trucks on Twitter as they move around cities 24/7 purveying delicious, cheap, fresh meals. In L.A., chef Roy Choi started the movement when he began serving up his Korean/Mexican Pacman burgers from his Kogi BBQ truck. In SoCal, you can find food-laden trucks at sports and entertainment venues, near parks and attractions, and on busy roads and boulevards—and the ensuing lines of hungry patrons.

California chefs continue to shop locally for produce and farmer-sourced meat. Tender Greens (with locations in Hollywood and Pasadena) sets the bar high by serving hand-raised produce from an Oxnard farm; grain-fed, hormone-free beef; hand-raised chickens; and line-caught tuna.

State of the Arts

California's beauty-obsessed citizens aren't the only ones opting for a fresh look these days: its esteemed art museums are also having a bit of work done.

Following a trend set by the Getty Villa in L.A., Long Beach's Museum of Latin American Art doubled its exhibition space. The Museum of Contemporary Art in San Diego (MCASD Downtown) has expanded into new digs, and the Palm Springs Museum of Art has morphed into a world-class showcase for contemporary work. The L.A. County Museum of Art keeps expanding its Wilshire Boulevard campus; the latest addition is the Renzo Piano–designed Resnick Pavilion, which will hold special exhibits.

Kid-ding Around

California's theme parks work overtime to keep current and attract patrons of all ages. Legoland California Resort leads the pack by adding Star Wars to Miniland and two new attractions to Sea Life. Coming soon to the Carlsbad resort is a Lego-theme hotel, due to open 2013.

Captain EO, a 3-D film starring Michael Jackson, is back at Disneyland. *Star Tours: The Adventures Continue*, also 3-D, has a new look, and World of Color in Disney California Adventure Park, presents an outdoor light and water show.

All Aboard

Riding the rails can be a satisfying experience, particularly in California where the distances between destinations can run into the hundreds of miles. You can save money on gas and parking, avoid freeway traffic, and see some of the best the state has to offer.

The best trip is on the luxuriously appointed Coast Starlight, a long-distance train with sleeping cars that runs between Seattle and Los Angeles, passing some of California's most beautiful coastline as it hugs the beach. For the best surfside viewing, get a seat or a room on the left side of the train and ride south to north from San Diego to Oakland.

Amtrak has frequent Pacific Surfliner service between San Diego and Los Angeles, and San Diego and Santa Barbara. These are coach cars, but many of the trains have been upgraded and are comfortable and convenient, especially if you plan to get off and on the train at several destinations, such as Anaheim (near Disneyland), downtown Los Angeles, coastal Ventura, and Santa Barbara.

WHEN TO GO

Because they offer activities indoors and out, the top California cities rate as all-season destinations. Ditto for Southern California's coastal playgrounds. Dying to see Death Valley? It's best appreciated in spring, when desert blooms offset its austerity and temperatures are still manageable. Yosemite is ideal in the late spring because roads closed in winter are reopened, the summer crowds have yet to arrive, and the park's waterfalls—swollen with melting snow—run fast. Snowfall makes winter peak season for skiers in Mammoth Mountain, where runs typically open around Thanksgiving. (They sometimes remain in operation into June.)

Climate

It's difficult to generalize much about the state's weather beyond saying that precipitation comes in winter and summers are dry in most places. As a rule, inland regions are hotter in summer and colder in winter, compared with coastal areas, which are relatively cool year-round. As you climb into the mountains, seasonal variations are more apparent: winter brings snow (at elevations above 3,000 feet), autumn is crisp, spring can go either way, and summer is sunny and warm, with only an occasional thundershower in the southern part of the state.

Microclimates

Mountains separate the California coastline from the state's interior, and the weather can sometimes vary dramatically within a 15-minute drive. Day and nighttime temperatures can also vary greatly. In August, Palm Springs' thermometers can soar to 110°F at noon, and drop to 75°F at night. Temperature swings elsewhere can be even more extreme.

Forecasts
National Weather Service (⊕ *www.wrh.noaa. gov*).

WHAT'S WHERE

The following numbers refer to chapters.

2 San Diego. San Diego's historic Gaslamp Quarter has charm—but it's big-ticket animal attractions like SeaWorld and the San Diego Zoo that pull in visitors.

3 Orange County. The real OC is a diverse destination with premium resorts, first-rate restaurants, strollable waterfront communities, and kid-friendly attractions.

4 Los Angeles. Go for the glitz of the entertainment industry, but stay for the rich cultural attributes and myriad communities of people from different cultures.

5 The Central Coast. Three of the state's top stops—swanky Santa Barbara, Hearst Castle, and Big Sur—sit along the scenic 200-mi route.

6 Channel Islands National Park. Only 60 mi northwest of Los Angeles, this park seems worlds away.

7 Monterey Bay Area. Postcard-perfect Monterey, exclusive Carmel, and surfer paradise Santa Cruz share this gorgeous stretch of coast.

8 The Inland Empire. The San Bernardino Mountains provide seasonal escapes at Lake Arrowhead and Big Bear Lake, and the Temecula Valley will challenge your ideas of "California Wine Country."

9 Palm Springs and the Desert Resorts. Golf on some of the West's finest courses, lounge at some of its most fabulous resorts, and experience the simple life at primitive desert parks.

10 Joshua Tree National Park. Proximity to major urban areas—as well as world-class rock climbing—help make this one of the most visited national parks in the United States.

11 The Mojave Desert. Material pleasures are in short supply, but Mother Nature's stark beauty more than compensates.

12 Death Valley National Park. America's second-largest national park isn't just vast—it's beautiful.

13 The Central Valley. Travelers along Highway 99 will enjoy attractions like Fresno's Forestiere Underground Gardens and the wineries of Lodi.

14 The Southern Sierra. Sawtooth mountains and deep powdery snowdrifts combine to create the state's premier skiing conditions.

15 Yosemite National Park. The views immortalized by photographer Ansel Adams are still camera-ready.

16 Sequoia and Kings Canyon National Parks. Ancient redwoods towering above jagged mountains will take your breath away.

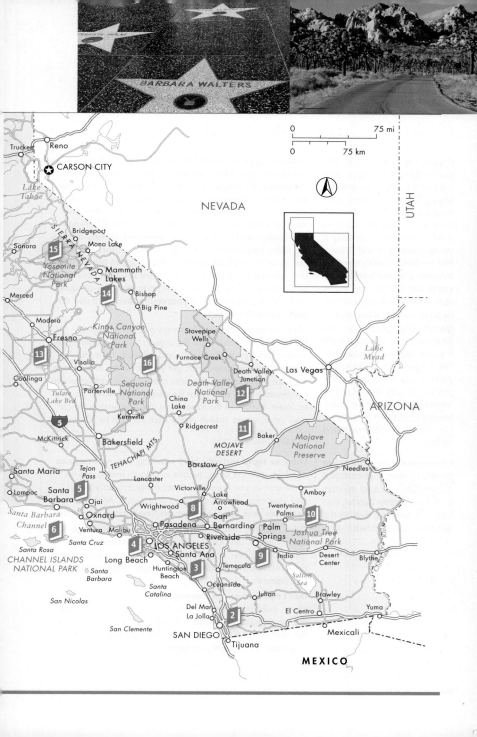

SOUTHERN CALIFORNIA PLANNER

Flying In

Around Los Angeles, LAX, the world's fifth-busiest airport, gets most of the attention—and not usually for good reasons. John Wayne Airport (SNA), about 25 mi south in Orange County, is a solid substitute—especially if you're planning to visit Disneyland or Orange County beaches. Depending on which part of L.A. you're heading to, you might also consider Bob Hope Airport (BUR) in Burbank (close to Hollywood and its studios) or Long Beach Airport (LGB), convenient if you're catching a cruise ship. The smaller size of these airports means easier access and shorter security lines. Another advantage is that their lower landing costs often attract budget carriers (like Southwest and JetBlue).

Convenience is the allure of San Diego's Lindbergh International Airport (SAN), located minutes from the Gaslamp Quarter, Balboa Park and Zoo, Sea World, and the cruise-ship terminal.

Driving Around

Driving may be a way of life in California, but it isn't cheap (gas prices here are usually among the highest in the nation). It's also not for the fainthearted; you've surely heard horror stories about L.A.'s freeways, but even the state's scenic highways and byways have their own hassles. For instance, on the dramatic coastal road between San Simeon and Carmel, twists, turns, and divinely distracting vistas frequently slow traffic; in rainy season, mudslides can close the road altogether. ⚠ **Never cross the double line when driving these roads. If you see that cars are backing up behind you on a long two-lane, no-passing stretch, do everyone (and yourself) a favor and use the first available pullout.**

On California's notorious freeways other rules apply. Nervous Nellies must resist the urge to stay in the two slow-moving lanes on the far right, used primarily by trucks. To drive at least the speed limit, get yourself in the middle lane. If you're ready to bend the rules a bit, the second (lanes are numbered from 1 starting at the center) lane moves about 5 mi faster. But avoid the far-left lane (the one next to the carpool lane), where speeds range from 75 mph to 90 mph.

SOCAL DRIVING TIPS

Use your signal correctly. Here signaling is a must. Because of all the different lanes, people may try to merge into the same spot as you from three lanes away. Protect yourself and your space by always using your signal. And don't forget to turn your signal off when the lane change is complete.

Drive friendly. Here's how to avoid causing road rage: don't tailgate. Don't flail your arms in frustration. Don't glare at the driver of the car you finally have a chance to pass. And above all, don't fly the finger. Road rage is a real hazard.

Don't pull over on the freeway. Short of a real emergency, never, ever, pull over and stop on a freeway. So you took the wrong ramp and need to huddle with your map—take the next exit and find a safe, well-lighted public space to stop your car and get your bearings.

FAQ

I'm not particularly active. Will I still enjoy visiting a national park? Absolutely, the most popular parks really do have something for everyone. Take Yosemite. When the ultrafit embark on 12-hour trail treks, mere mortals can hike Cook's Meadow—an easy 1-mi loop that's also wheelchair accessible. If even that seems too daunting, you can hop on a free shuttle or drive yourself to sites like Glacier Point or the Mariposa Grove of Giant Sequoias.

What's the single best place to take the kids? Well, that depends on your children's ages and interests, but for its sheer smorgasbord of activities, San Diego is hard to beat. Between the endless summer weather and sites such as SeaWorld, the San Diego Zoo, and Legoland (about 30 minutes away), California's southernmost city draws families in droves.

Once you've covered the mega-attractions, enjoy an easy-to-swallow history lesson in Old Town or the Maritime Museum. Want to explore different ecosystems? La Jolla Cove has kid-friendly tidal pools and cliff caves, while Anza-Borrego Desert State Park is a doable two-hour drive east. That said, there are kid-friendly attractions all over the state—your kids are going to have to try really hard to be bored.

California sounds expensive. How can I save on sightseeing? If you're focusing on the big cities, consider taking a pass—a Go Card Pass (☎ 800/887–9103 ⊕ www.gocardusa.com) that is. Sold in one-day to one-week versions, they're priced from $55 and cover dozens of tours and attractions in San Diego and L.A. CityPass (☎ 888/330–5008 ⊕ www.citypass.com) includes admission and some upgrades for main attractions in Hollywood and Southern California. Many museums set aside free-admission days. Prefer the great outdoors? An $80 America the Beautiful annual pass (☎ 888/275–8747 ⊕ www.nps.gov) admits you to every site under the National Park Service umbrella. Better yet, depending on the property, passengers in your vehicle get in free, too.

Any tips for a first-time trip into the desert? The desert's stark, sun-blasted beauty will strip your mind of everyday clutter. But it is a brutal, punishing place for anyone ill-prepared. So whether it's your first or 15th visit, the same dos and don'ts apply. Stick to a state or national park. Pick up pamphlets at its visitor center and *follow the instructions* they set out. Keep your gas tank full. Bring lots of water and drink at least two gallons a day—even if you're not thirsty. Wear a hat and sunscreen, and don't expect to move too fast at midday when the sun is kiln-hot.

I'm not crazy about spending 14 nights in hotels. Any alternatives? If you want to pretend you're lucky enough to live in California, try a vacation or time-share rental. Aside from providing privacy (a boon for families and groups), a rental lets you set your own schedule and cook at your leisure (you'll save money, plus it's a great excuse to stock up on that fine California produce!). In terms of coverage, geographically and pricewise, HomeAway (⊕ www.homeaway.com) is a good place for house hunting. It lists more than 4,000 condos, cottages, beach houses, ski chalets, and villas. *For more information on Southern California trip planning, see the Essentials sections in each chapter and the Travel Smart Southern California chapter at the back of the book.*

SOUTHERN CALIFORNIA TODAY

The People

California is as much a state of mind as a state in the union—a kind of perpetual Promised Land that has represented many things to many people. In the 18th century, Spanish missionaries came seeking converts. In the 19th, miners rushed here to search for gold. And, in the years since, a long line of Dust Bowl farmers, land speculators, Haight-Ashbury hippies, migrant workers, dot-commers, real estate speculators, and would-be actors has come chasing their own dreams.

The result is a population that leans toward idealism—without necessarily being as liberal as you might think. (Remember, this is Ronald Reagan's old stomping ground.) And despite the stereotype of the blue-eyed, blond surfer, California's population is not homogeneous either. Ten million people who live here (more than 28% of Californians) are foreign born—including former Governor Schwarzenegger. Almost half hail from neighboring Mexico; another third emigrated from Asia, following the waves of Chinese workers who arrived in the 1860s to build the railroads and subsequent waves of Indochinese refugees from the Vietnam War.

The Politics

What's blue and red and green all over? California: a predominantly Democratic state with an aggressive "go green" agenda. When he left office in 2010 (before his marital scandal broke involving "another woman"), Governor Arnold Schwarzenegger left a legacy of pushing a number of environmental initiatives including controls on gas emissions. Democratic Governor Jerry Brown, who was elected to the office for the second time in 30 years on a promise to clean up the financial mess created under Schwarzenegger, is moving his predecessor's green agenda ahead with policies that make California the greenest state in the nation supporting more green construction, wind farms, and solar panels.

The Economy

Leading all other states in terms of the income generated by agriculture, tourism, and industrial activity, California has the country's most diverse state economy. Moreover, with a gross state product of more than $2 trillion, California would be one of the top 10 economies *in the world* if it were an independent nation. But due to its wealth ($61,000 median household income) and productivity, California took a large hit in the recession that began in 2007. This affected all levels of government from local to statewide and resulted in reduction of services that Californians have long taken for granted.

But the Golden State's economic history is filled with boom and bust cycles—beginning with the mid-19th-century gold rush that started it all. Optimists already have their eyes on the next potential boom: high-tech and bio research, "green companies" focused on alternative energy, renewables, electric cars, and the like.

The Culture

Cultural organizations thrive in California. San Francisco—a city with only about 775,000 residents—has well-regarded ballet, opera, and theater companies, and is home to one of the continent's most noteworthy orchestras. Museums like San Francisco Museum of Modern Art (SFMOMA) and the de Young also represent the city's ongoing commitment to the arts. Art and culture thrive farther south in San Diego as well. Balboa Park alone holds 15 museums, opulent gardens, and three performance venues, in addition to the San Diego Zoo. The Old Globe Theater

and La Jolla Playhouse routinely originate plays that capture coveted Tony Awards in New York.

But California's *real* forte is pop culture, and L.A. and its environs are the chief arbiters. Movie, TV, and video production have been centered here since the dawn of the 20th century. Capitol Records set up shop in L.A. in the 1940s, and this area has been instrumental in the music industry ever since. And while these industries continue to influence national trends, today they are only part of the pop culture equation. Web sites are also a growing part of that creativity—Facebook, YouTube, and MySpace are California creatures.

The Parks and Preserves

Cloud-spearing redwood groves, snow-tipped mountains, canyon-slashed deserts, primordial lava beds, and a seemingly endless coast: California's natural diversity is staggering—and efforts to protect it started early. The first national park here was established in 1890, and the National Park Service now oversees 30 sites in California (more than in any other state). When you factor in 278 state parks—which encompass underwater preserves, historic sites, wildlife reserves, dune systems, and other sensitive habitats—the number of acres involved is almost as impressive as the topography itself.

Due to encroaching development and pollution, keeping these natural treasures in pristine condition is an ongoing challenge. For instance, Sequoia and Kings Canyon (which is plagued by pesticides and other agricultural pollutants blown in from the San Joaquin Valley) has been named America's "smoggiest park" by the National Parks Conservation Association, and the Environmental Protection Agency has designated it as an "ozone non-attainment area with levels of ozone pollution that threaten human health."

The Cuisine

California gave us McDonald's, Denny's, Carl's Jr., Taco Bell, and, of course, In-N-Out Burger. Fortunately for those of us with fast-clogging arteries, the state also kick-started the organic food movement. Back in the 1970s, California-based chefs put American cuisine on the culinary map by focusing on freshly prepared seasonal ingredients.

Today, this focus has spawned the "locavore" or sustainable food movement—followers try to only consume food produced within a 100-mi radius of where they live, since processing and refining food and transporting goods over long distances is bad for both the body and the environment. This isn't much of a restriction in California, where a huge variety of crops grow year-round. Some 350 cities and towns have certified farmers' markets—and their stalls are bursting with a variety of goods. California has been America's top agricultural producer for the last 50 years, growing more fruits and vegetables than any other state. Dairies and ranches also thrive here, and fishing fleets harvest fish and shellfish from the rich waters offshore.

QUINTESSENTIAL
SOUTHERN CALIFORNIA

The Beach

California's beach culture is, in a word, legendary. Of course, it only makes sense that folks living in a state with a 1,264-mi coastline (a hefty portion of which sees the sun upward of 300 days a year) would perfect the art of beach-going. True aficionados begin with a reasonably fit physique, plus a stylish wardrobe consisting of flip-flops, bikinis, wet suits, and such. Mastery of at least one beach skill—surfing, boogie boarding, kayaking, Frisbee tossing, power walking, or soaking up some rays—is also essential. As a visitor, though, you need only a swimsuit and some rented equipment for most sports. You can then hit the beach almost anywhere, thanks to the California belief in coastal access as a birthright. The farther south you go, the wider, sandier, and sunnier the beaches become; moving north they are rockier and foggier, with colder and rougher surf.

The Automobile

Americans may have a love affair with the automobile, but Californians have an out-and-out obsession. Even when gas prices rev up and freeway traffic slows down, their passion burns as hot as ever. You can witness this ardor any summer weekend at huge classic- and custom-car shows held statewide. Even better, you can feel it yourself by taking the wheel. Drive to the sea following Laguna Canyon Road to Laguna Beach; trace an old stagecoach route through the mountains above Santa Barbara on Highway 154; track migrating whales up the coast to Big Sur; or take 17-Mile Drive along the precipitous edge of the Monterey Peninsula. Glorious for the most part, but authentically congested in some areas in the south, Highway 1 runs almost the entire length of the state.

Californians live in such a large and splashy state that they sometimes seem to forget about the rest of the country. They've developed a distinctive culture all their own, which you can delve into by doing as the locals do.

The Unusual

Maybe the constantly perfect weather or the looming threat of earthquakes makes Southern Californians a little crazy. Whatever the reason, many have a pronounced appetite for the unusual, the off-center, even the bizarre. Witness the Integratron, a domed time machine with UFO landing strip, near Joshua Tree National Park (itself filled with natural oddities). Or San Luis Obispo's Madonna Inn, where you can sleep in a faux-cave and stir pink sugar into your coffee. Marta Becket performs solo in her Amargosa Opera House outside Death Valley National Park, where Scotty's Castle stands in pointless Moorish-style splendor way out in the desert. Idiosyncratic creations large and small litter the Southern California landscape— many of them designed to attract visitors, others simply personal expressions.

The Outdoors

One of California's greatest assets—the mild year-round weather enjoyed by most of the state—inspires residents to spend as much time outside as they possibly can. To be sure, they have a tremendous enthusiasm for every imaginable outdoor sport, and, up north especially, fresh-air adventures are extremely popular (which may explain why everyone there seems to own at least one pair of hiking boots). But, overall, the California-alfresco creed is more broadly interpreted. Indeed, the general rule when planning any activity is "if it can happen outside, it will!" *Plein-air* vacation opportunities include dining on patios, decks, and wharves; shopping in street markets or elaborate open-air malls; hearing almost any kind of music at moonlight concerts; touring the sculpture gardens that grace major art museums; and celebrating everything from gay pride to garlic at outdoor fairs.

SOUTHERN CALIFORNIA TOP ATTRACTIONS

San Diego

(A) San Diego is a thoroughly modern metropolis set on the sunny Pacific, filled with tourist attractions (think the Balboa Park, Zoo, SeaWorld, and Legoland) and blissful beaches. But this is also a city steeped in history—in 1769 Spaniards established a settlement here near Old Town, site of the first Spanish outpost and now a state park dedicated to illustrating San Diego's raucous early days. The city's rousing downtown dining and entertainment district, the Gaslamp Quarter, is a contemporary recreation of bawdy Stingaree of the late 1800s.

Channel Islands National Park

(B) This five-island park northwest of Los Angeles is a remote but accessible eco escape. There are no phones, no cars, and no services—but there are more than 2,000 species of plants and animals (among them blue whales and brown pelicans), plus ample opportunities for active pursuits. On land, hiking tops the itinerary. Underwater preserves surround the park, so snorkeling, scuba diving, fishing, and kayaking around lava tubes and natural arches are other memorable options.

Los Angeles

(C) Tinsel Town, Lala Land, City of Angels: L.A. goes by many names and has many personas. Recognized as America's capital of pop culture, it also has highbrow appeal with arts institutions like the Getty Center, the Geffen Contemporary at MOCA, Walt Disney Concert Hall, the Norton Simon Museum, and Huntington Library. But you can go wild here, too—and not just on the Sunset Strip. Sprawling Griffith Park, Will Rogers State Historic Park, and Malibu Lagoon State Beach all offer a natural break from the concrete jungle.

Palm Springs and Beyond

(D) Celebrities used to flee to the desert for rest, relaxation, a few rays of sun, and to indulge in some high jinks beyond the

watchful eyes of the media. You don't have to spend much time in Palm Springs to realize those days are *long* gone. In this improbably situated bastion of Bentleys and bling, worldly pleasures rule. Glorious golf courses, tony shops and restaurants, decadent spa resorts—they're all here. Solitude seekers can still slip away to nearby Joshua Tree National Park or Anza-Borrego Desert State Park.

Death Valley

(E) On the surface, a vacation in Death Valley sounds about as attractive as a trip to hell. Yet for well-prepared travelers, the experience is more awe-inspiring than ominous. Within the largest national park in the contiguous United States you'll find the brilliantly colored rock formations of Artists Palette, the peaks of the Panamint Mountains, and the desolate salt flats of Badwater, 282 feet below sea level. You can't get any lower than this in the West-

ern Hemisphere—and, in summer, you can't get much hotter.

Yosemite National Park

(F) Nature looms large here, both literally and figuratively. In addition to hulking Half Dome, the park is home to El Capitan (the world's largest exposed granite monolith, rising 3,593 feet above the glacier-carved valley floor) and Yosemite Falls (North America's tallest cascade). In Yosemite's signature stand of giant sequoias—the Mariposa Grove—even the trees are Bunyanesque. Needless to say, crowds can be super-size.

SOUTHERN CALIFORNIA TOP EXPERIENCES

Hit the Road

Kings Canyon Highway, Tioga Pass, 17-Mile Drive, and the grand Pacific Coast Highway: California has some splendid and challenging roads. Most of these are well-traveled paths, but if you venture over the Sierras by way of Tioga Pass (through Yosemite in summer only), you'll see emerald green meadows, gray granite monoliths, and pristine blue lakes—and very few people.

Ride a Wave

Surfing—which has influenced everything from fashion to moviemaking to music—is a quintessential California activity. You can find great surf breaks in many places along the coast between Santa Cruz and San Diego. But one of the best places to try it is Huntington Beach. Lessons are widely available. If you're not ready to hang 10, you can hang out at "Surf City's" International Surfing Museum or stroll the Surfing Walk of Fame.

Think Globally, Eat Locally

Over the years California cuisine has evolved from a mere trend into a respected gastronomic tradition: one that pairs local, often organic or sustainable, ingredients with techniques inspired by European, Asian, and, increasingly, Indian and Middle Eastern cookery.

Embrace Your Inner Eccentric

California has always drawn creative and, well, eccentric people. And all that quirkiness has left its mark in the form of oddball architecture that makes for some fun sightseeing. Begin by touring Hearst Castle—the beautifully bizarre estate William Randolph Hearst built above San Simeon. Scotty's Castle, a Moorish confection in Death Valley, offers a variation on the theme, as does Marta Becket's one-woman Amargosa Opera House.

Get Reel

In L.A. it's almost obligatory to do some Hollywood-style stargazing. Cue the action with a behind-the-scenes tour of one of the dream factories. (Warner Bros. Studios' five-hour deluxe version, which includes lunch in the commissary, is just the ticket for cinephiles.)

Other must-sees include the Kodak Theatre, permanent home to the Cirque du Soleil and Academy Awards; Grauman's Chinese Theatre, where celebs press feet and hands into cement for posterity's sake; Hollywood Boulevard's star-paved Walk of Fame; and the still-iconic Hollywood sign.

People-Watch

Opportunities for world-class people-watching abound in California. Just stroll the century-old boardwalk in time-warped, resiliently boho Santa Cruz. Better yet, hang around L.A.'s Venice Boardwalk, where chain-saw jugglers, surfers, fortune-tellers, and well-oiled bodybuilders take beachfront exhibitionism to a new high (or low, depending on your point of view). The result is pure eye candy.

GREAT ITINERARIES

SOUTHERN CALIFORNIA DREAMING

Los Angeles, Palm Springs, and San Diego

Day 1: Arrival/Los Angeles

As soon as you land at LAX, make like a local and hit the freeway. Even if L.A.'s top-notch art, history, and science museums don't tempt you, the hodgepodge of art-deco, beaux-arts, and futuristic architecture begs at least a drive-by. Heading east from Santa Monica, Wilshire Boulevard cuts through a historical and cultural cross-section of the city. Two stellar sights on its Miracle Mile are the encyclopedic Los Angeles County Museum of Art and the fossil-filled La Brea Tar Pits. Come evening, the open-air Farmers Market and its many eateries hum. Hotels in Beverly Hills or West Hollywood beckon, just a few minutes away.

Day 2: Hollywood and the Movie Studios

Every L.A. tourist should devote at least one day to the movies and take at least one studio tour. For fun, choose the special-effects theme park at Universal Studios Hollywood; for the nitty-gritty, choose Warner Bros. Studios. Nostalgic musts in half-seedy, half-preening Hollywood include the Walk of Fame along Hollywood Boulevard, the celebrity footprints cast in concrete outside Grauman's Chinese Theatre, and the 1922 Egyptian Theatre (Hollywood Boulevard's original movie palace). When evening arrives, the Hollywood scene boasts a bevy of trendy restaurants and nightclubs.

Day 3: Beverly Hills and Santa Monica

Even without that extensive art collection, the Getty Center's pavilion architecture, hilltop gardens, and frame-worthy L.A. views would make it a dazzling destination. Descend to the sea via Santa Monica Boulevard for lunch along Third Street Promenade, followed by a ride on the historic carousel on the pier. The buff and the bizarre meet on the boardwalk at Venice Beach (strap on some Rollerblades if you want to join them!). Rodeo Drive in Beverly Hills specializes in exhibitionism with a heftier price tag, but voyeurs are still welcome.

Day 4: Los Angeles to Palm Springs

Freeway traffic permitting, you can drive from the middle of L.A. to the middle of the desert in a couple of hours. Somehow in harmony with the harsh environment, midcentury "modern" homes and businesses with clean, low-slung lines define the Palm Springs style. The city seems far away, though, when you hike in hushed Tahquitz or Indian Canyon; cliffs and palm trees shelter rock art, irrigation works, and other remnants of Agua Caliente culture. If your boots aren't made for walking, you can always practice your golf game or indulge in some sublime or funky spa treatments at an area resort instead.

Day 5: The Desert

If riding a tram up an 8,516-foot mountain for a stroll or even a snowball fight above the desert sounds like fun to you, then show up at the Palm Springs Aerial Tramway before the first morning tram leaves (later, the line can get discouragingly long). Afterward stroll through the Palm Springs Art Museum where you can see a shimmering display of contemporary studio glass, an array of enormous Native American

baskets, and significant works of 20th-century sculpture by Henry Moore and others.

Day 6: Palm Springs to San Diego
South through desert and mountains via the Palms to Pines Highway on your way to San Diego, you might pause in the Temecula Valley for lunch at a local winery. Otherwise go straight for the city's nautical heart by exploring the restored ships of the Maritime Museum at the waterfront downtown. Victorian buildings—and plenty of other tourists—surround you on a stroll through the Gaslamp Quarter, but the 21st century is in full swing at the quirky and colorful Horton Plaza retail and entertainment complex. Plant yourself at a downtown hotel and graze your way through the neighborhood's many restaurants and nightspots.

Day 7: San Diego Zoo and Coronado
Malayan tapirs in a faux-Asian rain forest, polar bears in an imitation Arctic—the San Diego Zoo maintains a vast and varied collection of creatures in a world-renowned facility comprised of meticulously designed habitats. Come early, wear comfy shoes, and stay as long as you can stand the sea of children. Boutique-y Coronado—anchored by the gracious Hotel Del Coronado—offers a more adult antidote. Tea, cocktails, or perhaps dinner at the Del makes a civilized end to an untamed day.

Day 8: SeaWorld and Old Town
Resistance is futile: you're going to Sea-World. So what if it screams commercial? This humongous theme park, with its walk-through shark tanks and killer-whale shows, also screams fun. Surrender to the experience and try not to sit in anything sticky. Also touristy (but with genuine historical significance), Old Town drips with Mexican and early Californian heritage. Soak it up in the plaza at Old Town San Diego State Historic Park; then browse the stalls and shops outside the park at Bazaar del Mundo and San Diego Avenue.

Day 9: La Jolla to Laguna Beach
Positioned above an idyllic cove, La Jolla invites lingering. So slow down long enough to enjoy its chic shop-lined streets, sheltered beaches, and cultural institutions like the low-key Birch Aquarium at Scripps and the well-curated Museum of Contemporary Art. At Mission San Luis Rey, in Oceanside, and Mission San Juan Capistrano, you can glimpse life as it was during the Spanish missionary days. Once a haven for artists, Laguna Beach still abounds with galleries. Its walkable downtown streets would abut busy Main Beach Park if the Pacific Coast Highway didn't run through the middle of town.

Day 10: Catalina Island

Having spent so much time looking at the ocean, it's high time you got out *on* it—a quick excursion to Catalina, 75 minutes from the coast, will do the trick. Get an early start, catching the boat from Newport Beach, then use the day to explore this nostalgia-inducing spot. The harbor town of Avalon has a charming, retro feel, while the island's mountains, canyons, and coves are ideal spots for outdoor adventures. Take the 4:30 boat back to the mainland and overnight in Anaheim.

Day 11: Disneyland

Disney's original park is a blast even without kids in tow. So go ahead: skirt the lines at the box office—advance-purchased ticket in hand—and storm the gates of the Magic Kingdom. You can cram the highlights into a single day if you arrive at opening time with a strategy already mapped out. Alternatively, you can spend your final full day next door at Disneyland's sister park, California Adventure, which is a fitting homage to the Golden State. In either case, cap your holiday with a nighttime toast at Downtown Disney.

TIPS

❶ No matter how carefully you plan your movements to avoid busy routes at peak hours, you will inevitably encounter heavy traffic in L.A., Orange County, and San Diego.

❷ Allow yourself twice as much time as you think you'll need to negotiate LAX.

Day 12: Departure/Los Angeles

Pack up your Mouseketeer gear and give yourself ample time to reach the airport. Without traffic the 35-mi drive from Anaheim to LAX *should* take about 45 minutes. But don't count on it.

SOUTH-OF-THE-BORDER FLAVOR

From Cal-Mex burritos to Mexico City–style tacos, Southern California is a top stateside destination for experiencing Mexico's myriad culinary styles.

Many Americans are surprised to learn that the Mexican menu goes far beyond Tex-Mex (or Cal-Mex) favorites like burritos, chimichangas, enchiladas, fajitas, and nachos—many of which were created or popularized stateside. Indeed, Mexico has rich, regional food styles, like the complex *mole* sauces of Puebla and Oaxaca and the fresh *ceviches* of Veracruz, as well as the trademark snack of Mexico City: tacos.

In Southern California, tacos are an obsession, with numerous blogs and Web sites dedicated to the quest for the perfect taco. They're everywhere—in ramshackle taco stands, roving taco trucks, and strip-mall taquerias. Whether you're looking for a cheap snack or a lunch on-the-go, SoCal's taco selection can't be beat. But be forewarned: there may not be an English menu. Here we've noted unfamiliar taco terms, along with other potentially new-to-you items from the Mexican menu.

THIRST QUENCHERS

Spanish for "fresh water," *agua fresca* is a nonalcoholic Mexican drink made from fruit, rice, or seeds that are blended with sugar and water. Fruit flavors like lemon, lime, and watermelon are common. Other varieties include *agua de Jamaica*, flavored with red hibiscus petals; *agua de horchata*, a cinnamon-scented rice milk; and, *agua de tamarindo*, a bittersweet variety flavored with tamarind. If you're looking for something with a little more kick, try a *Michelada*, a beer that has been enhanced with a mixture of lime juice, chili sauce, and other savory ingredients. It's typically served in a salt-rimmed glass with ice.

1

DECODING THE MENU

Ceviche—Citrus-marinated seafood appetizer from the Gulf shores of Veracruz. Often eaten with tortilla chips.

Chile relleno—Roasted poblano pepper that is stuffed with ingredients like ground meat or cheese, then dipped in egg batter, fried, and served in tomato sauce.

Clayuda—A Oaxacan dish similar to pizza. Large corn tortillas are baked until hard, then topped with ingredients like refried beans, cheese, and salsa.

Fish taco—A specialty in Southern California, the fish taco is a soft corn tortilla stuffed with grilled or fried white fish (mahimahi or wahoo), pico de gallo, and shredded cabbage.

Gordita—"Little fat one" in Spanish, this dish is like a taco, but the cornmeal shell is thicker, similar to pita bread.

Mole—A complex, sweet sauce with Aztec roots made from more than 20 ingredients, including chiles, cinnamon, cumin, anise, black pepper, sesame seeds, and Mexican chocolate. There are many types of mole using various chiles and ingredient combinations, but the most common is *mole poblano* from the Puebla region.

Quesadilla—A snack made from a fresh tortilla that is folded over and stuffed with simple fillings like cheese, then toasted on a griddle. Elevated versions of the quesadilla may be stuffed with sautéed *flor de calabaza* (squash blossoms) or *huitlacoche* (corn mushrooms).

Salsa—A class of cooked or raw sauces made from chiles, tomatoes, and other ingredients. Popular salsas include *pico de gallo*, a fresh sauce made from chopped tomatoes, onions, chiles, cilantro, and lime; *salsa verde*, made with tomatillos instead of tomatoes; and *salsa roja*, a cooked sauce made with chiles, tomatoes, onion, garlic, and cilantro.

Sopes—A small, fried corn cake topped with ingredients like refried beans, shredded chicken, and salsa.

Taco—In Southern California, as in Mexico, tacos are made from soft, palm-sized corn tortillas folded over and filled with meat, chopped onion, cilantro, and salsa. Common taco fillings include *al pastor* (spiced pork), *barbacoa* (braised beef), *carnitas* (roasted pork), *cecina* (chile-coated pork), *carne asada* (roasted, chopped beef), *chorizo* (spicy sausage), *lengua* (beef tongue), *sesos* (cow brain), and *tasajo* (spiced, grilled beef).

Tamales—Sweet or savory corn cakes that are steamed, and may be filled with cheese, roasted chiles, shredded meat, or other fillings.

Torta—A Mexican sandwich served on a crusty sandwich roll. Fillings often include meat, refried beans, and cheese.

THE ULTIMATE ROAD TRIP

CALIFORNIA'S LEGENDARY HIGHWAY 1

by Cheryl Crabtree

One of the world's most scenic drives, California's State Route 1 (also known as Highway 1, the Pacific Coast Highway, the PCH) stretches along the edge of the state for nearly 660 miles, from Southern California's Dana Point to its northern terminus near Leggett, about 40 miles north of Fort Bragg. As you travel south to north, the water's edge transitions from long, sandy beaches and low-lying bluffs to towering dunes, craggy cliffs, and ancient redwood groves. The ocean changes as well; the relatively tame and surfable swells lapping the Southern California shore give way to the frigid, powerful waves crashing against weatherbeaten rocks in the north.

Ft. Bragg
Mendocino

SONOMA COUNTY

Point Reyes National Seashore

MARIN COUNTY

Sacramento

Marin Headlands

San Francisco

Santa Cruz

17-Mile Drive

Monterey
Carmel

Big Sur

Fresno

Hearst San Simeon State Historical Monument

San Luis Obispo

Santa Barbara

Santa Monica
Los Angeles
Long Beach

HIGHWAY 1 TOP 10

- Santa Monica
- Santa Barbara
- Hearst San Simeon State Historical Monument
- Big Sur
- Carmel
- 17–Mile Drive
- Monterey
- San Francisco
- Marin Headlands
- Point Reyes National Seashore

CALIFORNIA 1

For more information, please see our Highway 1 features in The Central Coast, and the Monterey Bay Area.

Give yourself lots of extra time to pull off the road and enjoy the scenery

STARTING YOUR JOURNEY

You may decide to drive the road's entire 660-mile route, or bite off a smaller piece. In either case, a Highway 1 road trip allows you to experience California at your own pace, stopping when and where you wish. Hike a beachside trail, dig your toes in the sand, and search for creatures in the tidepools. Buy some artichokes and strawberries from a roadside farmstand. Talk to people along the way (you'll run into everyone from soul-searching meditators, farmers, and beatniks to city-slackers and working-class folks), and take lots of pictures. Don't rush—you could easily spend a lifetime discovering secret spots along this route.

To help you plan your trip, we've broken the road into two regions (Santa Monica to Big Sur and Carmel to San Francisco); each region is then broken up into smaller segments—many of which are suitable for a day's drive. If you're pressed for time, you can always tackle a section of Highway 1, and then head inland to U.S. 101 or I-5 to reach your next destination more quickly.

WHAT'S IN A NAME?

Though it's often referred to as the Pacific Coast Highway (or PCH), sections of Highway 1 actually have different names. The southernmost section (Dana Point to Oxnard) is the Pacific Coast Highway. After that, the road becomes the Cabrillo Highway (Las Cruces to Lompoc), the Big Sur Coast Highway (San Luis Obispo County line to Monterey), the North Coast Scenic Byway (San Luis Obispo city limit to the Monterey County line), the Cabrillo Highway again (Santa Cruz County line to Half Moon Bay), and finally the Shoreline Highway (Marin City to Leggett). To make matters more confusing, smaller chunks of the road have additional honorary monikers.

Just follow the green triangular signs that say "California 1."

HIGHWAY DRIVING

- Rent a convertible. (You will not regret it.)
- Begin the drive north from Santa Monica, where congestion and traffic delays pose less of a problem.
- Mind your manners on the freeway. Don't tailgate or glare at other drivers, and don't fly the finger.
- If you're prone to motion sickness, take the wheel yourself. Focusing on the landscape outside should help you feel less queasy.
- If you're afraid of heights, drive from south to north so you'll be on the mountain rather than the cliff side of the road.

San Diego

WORD OF MOUTH

"Unlike most East Coast or Midwest big cities, you will be surprised that [in San Diego] the actual traffic Downtown is much less difficult. . . . The actual Downtown area is quite small. Downtown (or Hillcrest, my favorite) is close to Balboa Park (and its zoo), to the bay, to the ocean, etc."

—d_claude_bear

WELCOME TO SAN DIEGO

TOP REASONS TO GO

★ **Beautiful beaches:** San Diego's shore shimmers with crystalline Pacific waters rolling up to some of the prettiest stretches of sand on the West Coast.

★ **Good eats:** Taking full advantage of the region's bountiful vegetables, fruits, herbs, and seafood, San Diego's chefs surprise, dazzle, and delight diners with inventive California-colorful cuisine.

★ **History lessons:** The well-preserved and reconstructed historic sites in California's first European settlement help you imagine what the area was like when explorers first arrived.

★ **Stellar shopping:** Horton Plaza, the Gaslamp Quarter, Seaport Village, Coronado, Old Town, La Jolla . . . no matter where you go in San Diego, you'll find great places to do a little browsing.

★ **Urban oasis:** Balboa Park's 1,200 acres contain most of San Diego's museums and its world-famous zoo.

1 **Downtown.** San Diego's Downtown area is delightfully urban and accessible, filled with walkable A-list attractions like the Gaslamp Quarter, Horton Plaza, and the harbor.

2 **Balboa Park.** San Diego's cultural heart is where you'll find most of the city's museums and its world-famous zoo.

3 **Coronado.** Home to the Hotel Del, this island-like peninsula is a favorite celebrity haunt.

4 **Harbor and Shelter Islands and Point Loma.** Yachts and resorts, fast-food shacks and motels— plus gorgeous views of Coronado and the Downtown skyline.

5 **Mission Bay and SeaWorld.** Home to 27 mi of shoreline, this 4,600 acre aquatic park is San Diego's monument to sports and fitness.

6 **Old Town.** California's first permanent European settlement is now preserved as a state historic park.

7 **La Jolla.** This luxe, blufftop enclave fittingly means "the jewel" in Spanish. Come here for fantastic upscale shopping and unspoiled stretches of the coast.

GETTING ORIENTED

Exploring San Diego may be an endless adventure, but there are limitations, especially if you don't have a car. San Diego is more a chain of separate communities than a cohesive city, and many of the major attractions are miles apart. Walking is good for getting an up-close look at how San Diegans live, but true Southern Californians use the freeways that crisscross the county. Interstate 5 runs a direct north–south route through the coastal communities from Orange County in the north to the Mexican border. Interstates 805 and 15 do much the same inland. Interstate 8 is the main east–west route. Routes 163, 52, and 94 serve as connectors.

2

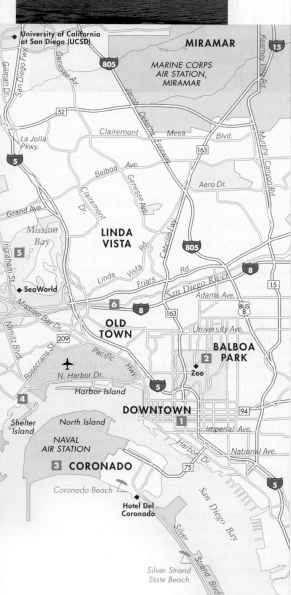

University of California at San Diego (UCSD)

805

MIRAMAR

15

MARINE CORPS AIR STATION, MIRAMAR

Kearney Villa Rd.

Gilman Dr.

San Diego Fwy.

Genesee Av.

52

Jacob Dekema Freeway

Clairemont Mesa Blvd.

163

La Jolla Pkwy.

5

Balboa Ave.

Genesee Ave.

Aero Dr.

Murphy Canyon Rd.

Grand Ave.

Clairemont Dr.

LINDA VISTA

Cabrillo Fwy.

Mission Bay

5

Ingraham St.

SeaWorld

Linda Vista Rd.

Friars Rd.

San Diego River

Adams Ave.

8

15

6

8

163

BUS 8

Mission Bay Dr.

OLD TOWN

209

University Ave.

BALBOA PARK

Nimitz Blvd.

Rosecrans St.

Pacific Hwy.

N. Harbor Dr.

Harbor Island

5

2

Zoo

4

Shelter Island

North Island

DOWNTOWN

1

94

Imperial Ave.

NAVAL AIR STATION

3 **CORONADO**

75

Harbor Dr.

National Ave.

5

Coronado Beach

Hotel Del Coronado

San Diego Bay

Silver Strand Blvd.

Silver Strand State Beach

Updated by Claire Deeks van der Lee, with Maren Dougherty, Maria Hunt, Amanda Knoles, Christine Pae, AnnaMaria Stephens, and Bobbi Zane

San Diego is a big California city—second only to Los Angeles in population—with a small-town feel. It also covers a lot of territory, roughly 400 square mi of land and sea. To the north and south of the city are 70 mi of beaches. Inland, a succession of chaparral-covered mesas are punctuated with deep-cut canyons that step up to savanna-like hills, separating the coast from the arid Anza-Borrego Desert.

The San Diego area, the birthplace of California, was claimed for Spain by explorer Juan Rodríguez Cabrillo in 1542 and eventually came under Mexican rule. You'll find reminders of San Diego's Spanish and Mexican heritage throughout the region—in architecture and place-names, in distinctive Mexican cuisine, and in the historic buildings of Old Town.

In 1867 developer Alonzo Horton, who called the town's bay front "the prettiest place for a city I ever saw," began building a hotel, a plaza, and prefab homes on 960 Downtown acres. The city's fate was sealed in 1908, when President Theodore Roosevelt's Great White Fleet sailed into the bay. The U.S. Navy, impressed by the city's excellent harbor and temperate climate, decided to build a destroyer base on San Diego Bay in the 1920s. The newly developed aircraft industry soon followed (Charles Lindbergh's plane *Spirit of St. Louis* was built here). The military, which operates many bases and installations throughout the county (which, added together, form the largest military base in the world), continues to contribute to the local economy.

PLANNING

GETTING HERE AND AROUND

If you're going to drive around San Diego, study a map before you hit the road. The freeways are convenient and fast most of the time, but if you miss your turnoff or get caught in commuter traffic, you'll experience a none-too-pleasurable hallmark of Southern California living—freeway madness.

The San Diego Trolley, which runs south to San Ysidro, has expanded north from Old Town to beyond Mission San Diego and San Diego State University; commuter Coaster trains run frequently between Downtown San Diego and Oceanside, with convenient stops in the charming coastal towns of Solana Beach, Encinitas, and Carlsbad; and the bus system covers almost all of the county.

The Sprinter offers commuter train service between Oceanside and Escondido. Making connections to see the various sights can be daunting, however. Since the coast is itself a major attraction, consider staying there if you're carless. The great distances between sights render taxis too expensive for general transportation, although cabs are useful for getting around once you're in a given area. Old Town Trolley Tours has a hop-on, hop-off route of popular spots around the city.

AIR TRAVEL

The major airport is San Diego International Airport, called Lindbergh Field locally. The airport's three-letter code is SAN. Major airlines depart and arrive at Terminal 1 and Terminal 2; commuter flights identified on your ticket with a 3000 sequence flight number depart from a third commuter terminal. A red shuttle bus provides free transportation between terminals.

Airport San Diego International Airport (☎ *619/400–2400* ⊕ *www.san.org*).

Airport Transfers Access Shuttle (☎ *619/282–1515* ⊕ *www.accessshuttle. net*). **San Diego Transit** (☎ *619/233–3004, 800/568–7097 TTY and TDD* ⊕ *transit.511sd.com*). **Cloud 9 Shuttle/SuperShuttle** (☎ *800/974–8885* ⊕ *www.cloud9shuttle.com*).

BUS AND TROLLEY TRAVEL

San Diego County is served by a coordinated, efficient network of bus and rail routes that includes service to Oceanside in the north, the Mexican border at San Ysidro, and points east to the Anza-Borrego Desert. Under the umbrella of the Metropolitan Transit System, there are two major transit agencies: San Diego Transit and North County Transit District (NCTD). The bright-red trolleys of the San Diego Trolley light-rail system serve Downtown San Diego, Mission Valley, Old Town, South Bay, the U.S. border, and East County. The trolley system connects with San Diego Transit bus routes.

Bus and Trolley Contacts North County Transit District (☎ *800/266–6883* ⊕ *www.gonctd.com*). **San Diego Transit** (☎ *619/233–3004, 800/568–7097 TTY and TDD* ⊕ *transit.511sd.com*). **Transit Store** (✉ *102 Broadway, Downtown* ☎ *619/234–1060*).

CAR TRAVEL

When traveling in the San Diego area, it pays to consider the big picture to avoid getting lost. Water lies to the west of the city. To the east and north, mountains separate the urban areas from the desert. Interstate 5, which stretches from Canada to the Mexican border, bisects San Diego. Interstate 8 provides access from Yuma, Arizona, and points east. Drivers coming from Nevada and the mountain regions beyond can reach San Diego on I–15. During rush hour there are jams on I–5 and on I–15 between I–805 and Escondido.

TAXI TRAVEL

Taxi stands are at shopping centers and hotels; otherwise you must call and reserve a cab. The companies listed below do not serve all areas of San Diego County. If you're going someplace other than Downtown, ask if the company serves that area.

Taxi Companies Orange Cab (☎ 619/291-3333 ⊕ www.orangecabsandiego. com). **Silver Cabs** (☎ 619/280-5555 ⊕ www.sandiegosilvercab.com). **Yellow Cab** (☎ 619/444-4444 ⊕ www.driveu.com).

TRAIN TRAVEL

Amtrak serves Downtown San Diego's Santa Fe Depot with daily trains to and from Los Angeles, Santa Barbara, and San Luis Obispo. Connecting service to Oakland, Seattle, Chicago, Texas, Florida, and points beyond is available in Los Angeles. Amtrak trains stop in San Diego North County at Solana Beach and Oceanside.

Coaster commuter trains, which run between Oceanside and San Diego Monday–Saturday, stop at the same stations as Amtrak plus others. The Sprinter runs between Oceanside and Escondido with many stops along the way.

Information Amtrak (☎ 800/872-7245 ⊕ www.amtrak.com). **Coaster** (☎ 619/233-3004 ⊕ www.sdcommute.com). **Metrolink** (☎ 800/371-5465 ⊕ www.metrolinktrains.com).

TOURS

Recommended Tours/Guides DayTripper (☎ 619/299-5777 or 800/679-8747 ⊕ www.daytripper.com). **San Diego Scenic Tours** (☎ 858/273-8687 ⊕ www.sandiegoscenictours.com). **Secret San Diego** (☎ 619/917-6037 ⊕ www.wheretours.com).

Boat Tours H&M Landing (☎ 619/222-1144 ⊕ www.hmlanding.com). **Hornblower Cruises & Events** (☎ 619/234-8687 or 800/668-4322 ⊕ www.hornblower.com). **Flagship Cruises and Events** (☎ 619/234-4111 or 800/442-7847 ⊕ www.flagshipsd.com).

Bus and Trolley Tours Centre City Development Corporation Downtown Information Center (☎ 619/235-2222 ⊕ www.ccdc.com). **Gray Line San Diego** (☎ 800/331-5077 ⊕ www.sandiegograyline.com). **Old Town Trolley Tours** (☎ 619/298-8687 ⊕ www.trolleytours.com).

Walking Tours Coronado Walking Tours (☎ 619/435-5993 ⊕ coronadowalkingtour.com). **Gaslamp Quarter Historical Foundation** (☎ 619/233-4692 ⊕ www.gaslampquarter.org). **Offshoot Tours** (☎ 619/239-0512 ⊕ www.balboapark.org). **Urban Safaris** (☎ 619/944-9255 ⊕ www.walkingtoursofsandiego.com).

VISITOR INFORMATION

City Contacts San Diego Convention & Visitors Bureau (☎ 619/232-3101 ⊕ www.sandiego.org). **San Diego Convention & Visitors Bureau International Visitor Information Center** (✉ 1040⅓ W. Broadway, at Harbor Dr., Downtown ☎ 619/236-1212 ⊕ www.sandiego.org). **San Diego Visitor Information Center** (☎ 800/827-9188 ⊕ www.infosandiego.com).

San Diego County Contacts California Welcome Center Oceanside (☎ 760/721–1101 or 800/350–7873 ⊕ www.oceansidechamber.com). **Carlsbad Convention & Visitors Bureau** (☎ 800/227–5722 ⊕ www.visitcarlsbad.com). **Coronado Visitor Center** (☎ 619/437–8788 ⊕ www.coronadovisitorcenter.com). **Encinitas Chamber of Commerce** (☎ 760/753–6041 ⊕ www.encinitaschamber.com). **Promote La Jolla, Inc.** (☎ 858/454–5718 ⊕ www.lajollabythesea.com).

2

EXPLORING SAN DIEGO

DOWNTOWN

Nearly written off in the 1970s, today Downtown San Diego is a testament to conservation and urban renewal. The turnaround began with the revitalization of the Gaslamp Quarter Historic District and massive redevelopment that gave rise to the Horton Plaza shopping center and the San Diego Convention Center, as well as to elegant hotels, upscale condominium complexes, and trendy restaurants and cafés. Like many modern U.S. cities, Downtown San Diego's story is as much about its rebirth as its history.

Although many consider Downtown to be the 16½-block Gaslamp Quarter, it actually comprises eight neighborhoods, also including East Village, Little Italy, and Embarcadero. Considered the liveliest of the bunch, Gaslamp's Fourth and Fifth avenues are peppered with trendy nightclubs, swanky lounge bars, chic restaurants, and boisterous sports pubs.

Nearby, the most ambitious of the Downtown projects is East Village, encompassing 130 blocks between the railroad tracks up to J Street, and from 6th Avenue east to around 10th Street. Sparking the rebirth of this former warehouse district was construction of the San Diego Padres' baseball stadium, PETCO Park. As the city's largest Downtown neighborhood, East Village is continually broadening its boundaries with its urban design of redbrick cafés, spacious galleries, rooftop bars, sleek hotels, and warehouse restaurants.

There are reasonably priced ($4–$7 per day) parking lots along Harbor Drive, Pacific Highway, and lower Broadway and Market Street. Most restaurants offer valet parking at night, but beware of fees of $15 and up.

EXPLORING DOWNTOWN

Embarcadero. The bustle of Embarcadero comes less these days from the activities of fishing folk than from the throngs of tourists, but this waterfront walkway—comprised of Seaport Village and the San Diego Convention Center—remains the nautical soul of the city. There are several seafood restaurants here, as well as sea vessels of every variety—cruise ships, ferries, tour boats, and Navy aircraft carriers.

On the north end of the Embarcadero at Ash Street you'll find the **Maritime Museum.** South of it, the **B Street Pier** is used by ships from major cruise lines—San Diego has become a major cruise-ship port, both a port of call and a departure point. The cavernous Cruise Ship Terminal has a cruise-information center. The occasional sight of several massive vessels lined up side-by-side is unforgettable, but note that security is tight on embarkation days, and only passengers with tickets are allowed in the cruise terminal on such occasions.

Tickets for harbor tours and whale-watching trips are sold at the foot of Broadway Pier. The terminal for the Coronado Ferry lies just beyond, between Broadway Pier and B Street Pier. One block south of Broadway Pier at Tidelands Park is Military Heritage Art, a collection of works that commemorate the service of the U.S. military.

Lining the pedestrian promenade between the Cruise Ship Terminal and Hawthorn Street are 30 "urban trees" sculpted by local artists. Docked at the Navy pier is the decommissioned USS *Midway*, now the home of the San Diego Aircraft Carrier Museum.

The pleasant Tuna Harbor Park offers a great view of boating on the bay and across to any aircraft carriers docked at the North Island naval base.

The next bit of seafront greenery is a few blocks south at **Embarcadero Marina Park North,** an 8-acre extension into the harbor from the center of Seaport Village. It's usually full of kite fliers, in-line skaters, and picnickers. Seasonal celebrations, including San Diego's Parade of Lights, the Port of San Diego Big Balloon Parade, the Sea and Air Parade, and the Big Bay July 4 Celebration, are held here and at the similar **Embarcadero Marina Park South.**

Providing a unique shopping experience, **Seaport Village** covers 14 acres of waterfront retail stores, restaurants, and cafés.

The **San Diego Convention Center,** on Harbor Drive between 1st and 6th avenues, is a waterfront landmark designed by Canadian architect Arthur Erickson. The backdrop of blue sky and sea complements the building's nautical lines. The center often holds trade shows that are open to the public, and tours of the building are available.

Gaslamp Quarter Historic District. When the move for Downtown redevelopment gained momentum in the 1970s, there was talk of bulldozing the Gaslamp's Victorian-style buildings and starting from scratch. (The district has the largest collection of Commercial Victorian–style buildings in the country.) History buffs, developers, architects, and artists formed the Gaslamp Quarter Council, however, and gathered funds from the government and private benefactors to clean up and preserve the quarter, restoring the finest old buildings and attracting businesses and the public back to its heart. Their efforts have paid off. Former flophouses have become choice office buildings, and the area is filled with hundreds of trendy shops, restaurants, and nightclubs. ■ TIP➔ Although there is metered street parking throughout Downtown, a spot can be difficult to find. One alternative is to park in the Horton Plaza parking structure, where you can get three free hours with validation.

William Heath Davis House. The oldest wooden house in San Diego houses the Gaslamp Quarter Historical Foundation, the district's curator. Before Alonzo Horton came to town, Davis, a prominent San Franciscan, had made an unsuccessful attempt to develop the waterfront area. In 1850 he had this prefab saltbox-style house, built in Maine, shipped around Cape Horn and assembled in San Diego (it originally stood at State and Market streets). Audio-guided or brochure-guided

Be sure to enjoy a walk along San Diego's lovely waterfront sometime during your visit.

museum tours are available with museum admission. Regularly scheduled two-hour walking tours of the historic district leave from the house on Saturday at 11 and cost $10. If you can't time your visit with the weekly tour, a self-guided tour map is also available for purchase for $2. ⊠ *410 Island Ave., at 4th Ave., Gaslamp Quarter* ☎ *619/233–4692* ☞ *$5* ☼ *Tues–Sat 10–5, Sun 12–4.*

(No. 631). The Romanesque-revival **Keating Hotel** (⊠ *432 F St., at 5th Ave., Gaslamp Quarter*) was designed by the same firm that created the famous Hotel Del Coronado. At the corner of 4th Avenue and F Street, peer into the Hard Rock Cafe, which occupies a restored turn-of-the-20th-century tavern with a 12-foot mahogany bar and a spectacular stained-glass domed ceiling.

The section of G Street between 6th and 9th avenues is a haven for galleries; stop in one of them to pick up a map of the Downtown arts district. Just to the north, on E and F streets from 6th to 12th avenues, the evolving Urban Art Trail has added pizzazz to drab city thoroughfares by transforming such things as trash cans and traffic controller boxes into works of art. For additional information about the historic area, call the **Gaslamp Quarter Association** (☎ *619/233–5227*) or log on to their Web site (⊕ *www.gaslamp.org*). ⊠ *614 5th Ave.*

International Visitor Information Center. Located across from Broadway Pier, this office is a great resource. ■ **TIP→ Need to feed the meter? A change machine is located inside the visitor center.** ⊠ *1040 W. Broadway, at Harbor Dr., Embarcadero* ☎ *619/236–1212* ⊕ *www.sandiego.org* ☼ *June–Sept., daily 9–5; Oct.–May, daily 9–4.*

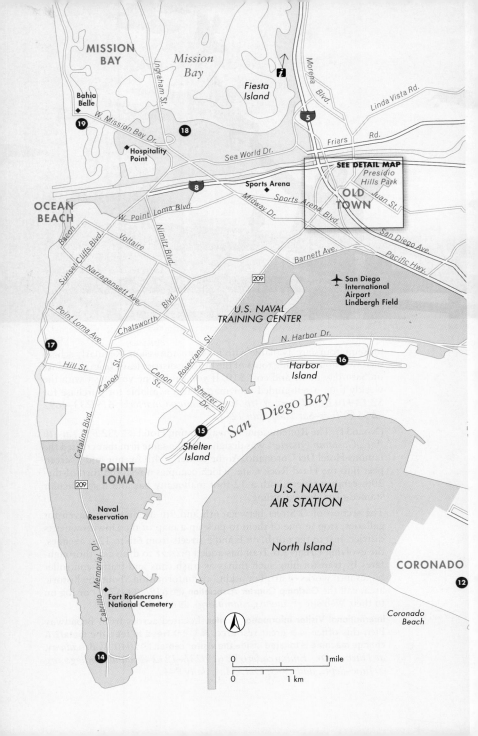

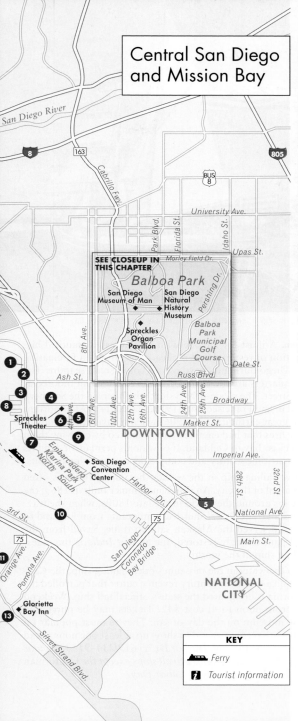

Central San Diego and Mission Bay

KEY

🚢 *Ferry*

🛈 *Tourist information*

The *Star of India*, the oldest active sailing ship in the world, still occasionally plies San Diego Bay.

Maritime Museum. A must for anyone with an interest in nautical history, this collection of restored and replica ships affords a fascinating glimpse of San Diego during its heyday as a commercial seaport. The museum's headquarters are the *Berkeley*, an 1898 ferryboat moored at the foot of Ash Street. The steam-driven ship, which served the Southern Pacific Railroad in San Francisco until 1958, played its most important role during the great earthquake of 1906, when it saved thousands of people from the fires that had engulfed San Francisco by carrying them across San Francisco Bay to Oakland. It now holds permanent exhibits on West Coast maritime history and complementary rotating exhibits.

The oldest active sailing ship in the world, the *Star of India*, is often considered a symbol of the city. An iron windjammer built in 1863, the ship made 21 trips around the world in the late 1800s, when she traveled the East Indian trade route, shuttled immigrants from England to New Zealand, and served the Alaskan salmon trade. Saved from the scrap yard and painstakingly restored, the *Star of India* is the oldest active iron sailing ship in the world.

You can take to the water in the museum's other sailing ship, the *Californian*. This replica of a 19th-century revenue cutter that patrolled the shores of California is designated the state's official tall ship. Weekend sails, typically from noon to 4, cost $42. Tickets may be purchased online or at the museum on the day of sail. They're most popular on sunny days, when it's recommended to show up at least one hour ahead of desired departure. ⊠ *1492 N. Harbor Dr.* ☎ *619/234–9153* ⊕ *www. sdmaritime.org* ⌨ *$14 includes entry to all ships except the* Californian ☉ *9–8, until 9 pm Memorial Day to Labor Day.*

Fodor'sChoice
★

Fodor's Choice
★

Museum of Contemporary Art San Diego (MCASD). At the Downtown branch of the city's contemporary art museum, explore the works of international and regional artists in a modern, urban space that is easily accessible via San Diego's trolley system. In January 2007, the museum expanded its galleries across the street in a superb juxtaposition of old and new. The Jacobs Building—formerly the baggage building at the historic Santa Fe Depot—features large gallery spaces, high ceilings, and natural lighting, giving artists flexible spaces to create large-scale installations. MCASD showcases both established and emerging artists in rotating exhibitions, as well as permanent, site-specific commissions by Jenny Holzer and Richard Serra. Free cell phone audio tours and Podcasts are available for most exhibits; if you don't have an iPod with you, the museum will lend you one. ■TIP➔ Admission is good for seven days, and includes both the Downtown and La Jolla locations. ✉ *1100 and 1001 Kettner Blvd., Embarcadero* ☎ *858/454–3541* ⊕ *www.mcasd.org* 🎟 *$10; ages 25 and under are free, free 3rd Thurs. of the month 5–7* ⊙ *Thurs.–Tues. 11–5, 3rd Thurs. until 7. Closed Wed.*

Fodor's Choice
★

San Diego Aircraft Carrier Museum. After 47 years of worldwide service, the retired USS *Midway* began a new tour of duty on the south side of the Navy pier in 2004. Launched just after the end of World War II, the 1,001-foot-long ship was the largest in the world for the first 10 years of its existence. Now it serves as the most visible landmark on the north Embarcadero and as a floating interactive museum—an appropriate addition to the town that is home to one-third of the Pacific fleet and the birthplace of naval aviation. Starting on the hangar deck, a free audio tour guides you through the massive ship while offering insight from former sailors. Through passageways and up and down ladder wells, you'll get to see how the *Midway*'s 4,500 crew members lived and worked on this "city at sea." While the entire tour is impressive, you'll find yourself saying "wow" when you step out onto the 4-acre flight deck—not only the best place to get an idea of the ship's scale, but also one of the most interesting vantage points for a view of the bay and the city skyline. An F-14 Tomcat jet fighter is just one of many incredible aircraft on display. There are free guided tours of the bridge and primary flight control, known as "the Island," departing every 10 minutes from the flight deck. Many of the docents stationed throughout the ship served in the Navy, some even on the *Midway*, and are eager to answer questions or share stories. The museum also offers multiple flight simulators for an additional fee, climb-aboard cockpits, and interactive exhibits focusing on naval aviation. There is a gift shop and a café with pleasant outdoor seating. This is a wildly popular stop, with most visits lasting several hours. ⚠ Despite significant efforts to provide accessibility throughout the ship, some areas can only be reached via fairly steep steps; a video tour of these areas is available on the hangar deck. ✉ *910 N. Harbor Dr., Embarcadero* ☎ *619/544–9600* ⊕ *www.midway.org* 🎟 *$18* ⊙ *Daily 10–5, last admission 4 pm.*

☾ **Seaport Village.** On a prime stretch of waterfront that spreads out across 14 acres connecting the harbor with hotel towers and the convention center, the three bustling shopping plazas of Seaport Village are designed to reflect the New England clapboard and Spanish Mission architectural styles of early California. A ¼-mi boardwalk that runs along the bay and 4 mi of paths lead to specialty shops—everything from a kite store and swing emporium to a shop devoted to hot sauces—as well as snack bars and restaurants, many with harbor views; there are more than 60 in all. Seaport Village's shops are open daily 10 to 9; a few eateries open early for breakfast, and many have extended nighttime hours, especially in summer. Restaurant prices here are high and the food is only average, so your best bet is to go elsewhere for a meal. Live music can be heard daily from noon to 4 at the main food court. Additional free concerts take place every Sunday from 1 to 4 at the East Plaza Gazebo. If you happen to visit San Diego in late November or early December, you might be lucky enough to catch Surfing Santa's Arrival and even have your picture taken with Santa on his wave. Every year in April catch the Seaport Buskers Fest, featuring a wide array of street performers.

The **Seaport Village Carousel** has 54 animals—lots of horses plus a giraffe, dragon, elephant, dog, and others—hand-carved and hand-painted by Charles Looff in 1895. (This is a replacement for Seaport Village's previous historic carousel, also a Looff, which was sold in 2004.) Tickets are $2. Strolling clowns, balloon sculptors, mimes, musicians, and magicians are also on hand throughout the village to entertain kids. ⊠ *849 W. Harbor Dr., Embarcadero* ☎ *619/235–4014 office and events hotline* ⊕ *www.seaportvillage.com.*

OFF THE
BEATEN
PATH

Hillcrest. Northwest of Balboa Park, Hillcrest is San Diego's center for the gay community and artists of all types. It truly is one of the city's most interesting neighborhoods. University, 4th, and 5th avenues are filled with cafés, a superb collection of restaurants (including many outstanding ethnic eateries), and boutiques (among which are several indie bookstores selling new and used books along 5th below University).

Westfield Horton Plaza. This Downtown shopping, dining, and entertainment mecca fronts Broadway and G Street from 1st to 4th avenues and covers more than six city blocks. Designed by Jon Jerde and completed in 1985, Westfield Horton Plaza is far from what one would imagine a shopping center—or city center—to be. A collage of colorful tile work, banners waving in the air, and modern sculptures, Westfield Horton Plaza rises in uneven, staggered levels to five floors; great views of Downtown from the harbor to Balboa Park and beyond can be had here.

Macy's and Nordstrom department stores anchor the plaza, and an eclectic assortment of more than 130 clothing, sporting-goods, jewelry, book, and gift shops flank them. Other attractions include the country's largest Sam Goody music store, a movie complex, restaurants, and a long row of take-out ethnic food shops and dining patios on the uppermost tier—and the respected San Diego Repertory Theatre below ground level. In 2008 the **Balboa Theater**, contiguous with the shopping center, reopened its doors after a $26.5 million renovation. The historic 1920s theater seats 1,400 and offers live arts and cultural performances throughout the week.

The mall has a multilevel parking garage; even so, lines to find a space can be long. ■ TIP➔ **Entering the parking structure on G Street rather than 4th Avenue generally means less traffic and more parking space.** Parking validation is complimentary whether you spend a bundle or just window-shop. Validation machines (open 7 am–9 pm) throughout the center allow for three hours' free parking; after that it's $8 per hour (or $2 per 15-minute increment). If you use this notoriously confusing fruit-and-vegetable–themed garage, be sure to remember at which produce level you've left your car. If you're staying Downtown, the Old Town Trolley Tour will drop you directly in front of Westfield Horton Plaza. ⊠ *324 Horton Plaza, Gaslamp Quarter* ☎ *619/238–1596* ⊕ *www. westfield.com/hortonplaza* ☉ *Weekdays 10–9, Sat. 10–8, Sun. 11–7.*

CORONADO

Although it's actually an isthmus, easily reached from the mainland if you head north from Imperial Beach, Coronado has always seemed like an island and is often referred to as such. Located just 15 mi east of Downtown San Diego, Coronado was an uninhabited sandbar until the late 1800s; it was named after Mexico's Coronados Islands.

As if freeze-framed in the 1950s, Coronado's quaint appeal is captured in its old-fashioned storefronts, well-manicured gardens, and charming Ferry Landing Marketplace. Today's residents, many of whom live in grand Victorian homes handed down for generations, can usually be seen walking their dogs or chatting with neighbors in this safe, non-gated community. Naval Air Station North Island was established in 1911 on Coronado's north end, across from Point Loma, and was the site of Charles Lindbergh's departure on the transcontinental flight that preceded his famous solo flight across the Atlantic. Coronado's long relationship with the U.S. Navy and its desirable real estate have made it an enclave for military personnel; it's said to have more retired admirals per capita than anywhere else in the United States.

Coronado is accessible via the arching blue 2.2-mi-long San Diego–Coronado Bay Bridge, which handles some 68,000 cars each day. The view of the harbor, Downtown, and the island is breathtaking, day and night. Until the bridge was completed in 1969, visitors and residents relied on the Coronado Ferry, which today has become quite popular with bicyclists, who shuttle their bikes across the harbor and ride Coronado's wide, flat boulevards for hours.

San Diego's Metropolitan Transit System runs a shuttle bus, No. 904, around Coronado; you can pick it up where you disembark the ferry and ride it out as far as Silver Strand State Beach. Bus No. 901 runs daily between the Gaslamp Quarter and Coronado.

You can board the ferry, operated by **Flagship Cruises and Events** (☎ *619/234– 4111, 800/442–7847 in CA* ⊕ *www.flagshipsd.com*), at the Broadway Pier on the Embarcadero in Downtown San Diego; you'll arrive at the Ferry Landing Marketplace in Coronado. Boats depart every hour on the hour from the Embarcadero and every hour on the half hour from Coronado, daily 9–9 from San Diego (9–10 Friday and Saturday), 9:30–9:30 from Coronado (9:30–10:30 Friday and Saturday); the fare is $4.25 each way. Service to Coronado also departs from the convention center every other hour. Buy tickets at the Broadway Pier, 5th Ave. Landing, or the Ferry Landing Marketplace. The company also offers water-taxi service weekdays 9 am–9 pm, Friday and Saturday until 11 pm. The fare is $7 per person. Call ☎ *619/235–8294* to book.

EXPLORING CORONADO

Coronado Museum of History and Art. The neoclassical First Bank of Commerce building, constructed in 1910, holds the headquarters and archives of the Coronado Historical Association, a museum, the Coronado Visitor Center, the Coronado Museum Store, and Tent City Restaurant. The collection celebrates Coronado's history with photographs and displays of its formative events and major sights. Two galleries have permanent displays, while a third hosts traveling exhibits. For information on the town's historic houses, pick up a copy of the inexpensive *Promenade Through the Past: A Brief History of Coronado and Its Architectural Wonders* at the museum gift shop. The book traces a 60-minute walking tour of the architecturally and historically significant buildings that surround the area. The tour departs from the museum lobby on Wednesday at 10:30 am and costs $10 (reservations required). ⊠ *1100 Orange Ave., Coronado* ☎ *619/435–7242* ⊕ *www.coronadohistory.org* ⊠ *$4 suggested donation* ☉ *Weekdays 9–5, weekends 10–5.*

☾ ★ **Ferry Landing Marketplace.** This collection of shops at Ferry Landing is on a smaller scale than the Embarcadero's Seaport Village, but you do get a great view of the Downtown San Diego skyline. Located along San Diego Bay, the little shops and restaurants resemble the gingerbread domes of the Hotel Del Coronado. If you want to rent a bike or in-line skates, stop in at **Bikes and Beyond** (⊠ *1201 1st St., #122, Coronado* ☎ *619/435–7180*). ⊠ *1201 1st St., at B Ave., Coronado* ☎ *619/435–8895.*

Fodor'sChoice ★ **Hotel Del Coronado.** One of San Diego's best-known sites, the hotel has been a National Historic Landmark since 1977. It has a colorful history, integrally connected with that of Coronado itself. The Hotel Del, as natives call it, was the brainchild of financiers Elisha Spurr Babcock Jr. and H. L. Story, who saw the potential of Coronado's virgin beaches and its view of San Diego's emerging harbor. The hotel opened in 1888, just 11 months after construction began.

The Del's distinctive red-tile roofs and Victorian gingerbread architecture have served as a set for many movies, political meetings, and extravagant social happenings. It's speculated that the Duke of Windsor may have first met Wallis Simpson here. Eleven presidents have been guests of the Del, and the film *Some Like It Hot*—starring Marilyn Monroe, Jack Lemmon, and Tony Curtis—used the hotel as a backdrop.

Broad steps lead up to the main, balconied lobby, which is adorned with grand oak pillars and ceiling and opens out onto a central courtyard and gazebo. To the right is the cavernous **Crown Room,** whose arched ceiling of notched sugar pine was constructed without nails. A lavish Sunday brunch is served here from 9:30 to 1. During the holidays, the hotel hosts Skating by the Sea, an outdoor beachfront ice-skating rink open to the public.

Although the pool area is reserved for hotel guests, several surrounding dining patios make great places to sit back and imagine the scene during the 1920s, when the hotel rocked with good times. To the right, the Windsor Lawn provides a green oasis between the hotel and the

Continued on page 53

BALBOA PARK
SAN DIEGO'S CULTURAL HEART

Acres of lush gardens, dozens of top attractions, and stunning architecture . . . no trip to San Diego is complete without a visit to Balboa Park.

SAN DIEGO'S TREASURE TROVE

Overlooking downtown and the Pacific Ocean, San Diego's sprawling, 1,200-acre Balboa Park is one of the world's great urban green spaces. It's home to most of the city's museums (so many that it's been dubbed "the Smithsonian of the West"), the Tony Award-winning Globe Theatre, and the world-famous San Diego Zoo.

The incredibly varied landscape here includes collections of palm trees, arid areas dotted with sagebrush and cactus, ornate rose gardens . . . and a canyon. Balboa Park was formally established as "City Park" in 1868, though much of the development that you see here today—including the lovely Spanish Renaissance style architecture—was a result of the 1915 Panama-California Exposition.

San Diegans spend years exploring this local treasure. And even though you'll just be scratching the surface, a visit here should definitely be on your itinerary.

(Above) Casa del Prado; (Previous page) The Alcazar Garden.

BEST BETS

Here at Balboa Park's attractions sorted by interest. *Numbers correspond with map and photo/descriptions on next page.*

ARTS AFICIONADOS
Globe Theatre, 7
Museum of Photographic Arts, 24
San Diego Art Institute, 20
San Diego Museum of Art, 14
SDAI: Mus. of the Living Artist, 27
Spanish Village Art Center, 18
Spreckels Organ Pavilion, 16
Timken Museum of Art, 21

ARCHITECTURE BUFFS
Bea Evenson Fountain, 3
Cabrillo Bridge, 5
California Building and Tower, 6
Casa de Balboa, 22
House of Charm, 26
House of Hospitality, 8

CULTURAL EXPLORERS
Centro Cultura de la Raza, 29
House of Pacific Relations, 9
Mingei International Mus., 28

HISTORY JUNKIES
Museum of San Diego History, 25
San Diego Museum of Man, 6
San Diego Nat. History Mus., 19
Veterans Mus., 30

NATURE LOVERS
Alcazar Garden, 1
Botanical Building, 4
Japanese Friendship Garden, 10
Inez Grant Parker Mem. Rose Garden, 11
Palm Canyon, 12

SCIENCE & TECHNOLOGY GEEKS
Reuben H. Fleet Science Ctr., 23
San Diego Air and Space Mus., 33
San Diego Automotive Mus., 32

KIDS OF ALL AGES
San Diego Zoo, 15
Carousel, 2
Miniature Railroad, 17
San Diego Model Railroad Mus., 13
San Diego Hall of Champions, 34
Marie Hitchcock Puppet Theater, 31

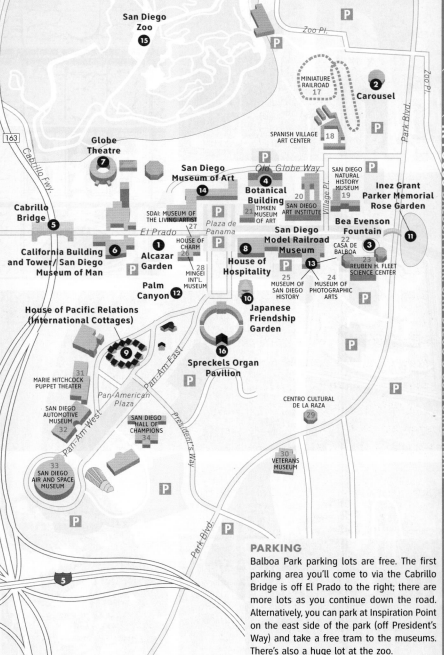

San Diego Zoo 15

MINIATURE RAILROAD 17

Carousel 2

SPANISH VILLAGE ART CENTER 18

163

Globe Theatre 7

San Diego Museum of Art 14

Old Globe Way

San Diego Museum of Art 4

SAN DIEGO NATURAL HISTORY MUSEUM 19

Inez Grant Parker Memorial Rose Garden

Cabrillo Fwy.

Cabrillo Bridge 5

SDAI: MUSEUM OF THE LIVING ARTIST 27

Botanical Building

TIMKEN MUSEUM OF ART 21

20

SAN DIEGO ART INSTITUTE

Bea Evenson Fountain

El Prado

Plaza de Panama

San Diego Model Railroad Museum 8

22 CASA DE BALBOA

3

11

California Building and Tower / San Diego Museum of Man

Alcazar Garden 1

HOUSE OF CHARM 26

House of Hospitality

13

REUBEN H. FLEET SCIENCE CENTER 23

Palm Canyon 12

28 MINGEI INT'L. MUSEUM

25 MUSEUM OF SAN DIEGO HISTORY

24 MUSEUM OF PHOTOGRAPHIC ARTS

House of Pacific Relations (International Cottages)

Japanese Friendship Garden 10

Pan-Am East

9

Spreckels Organ Pavilion 16

MARIE HITCHCOCK PUPPET THEATER 31

Pan-American Plaza

CENTRO CULTURAL DE LA RAZA 29

SAN DIEGO AUTOMOTIVE MUSEUM 32

Pan-Am West

SAN DIEGO HALL OF CHAMPIONS 34

President's Way

30 VETERANS MUSEUM

SAN DIEGO AIR AND SPACE MUSEUM 33

Park Blvd.

5

PARKING

Balboa Park parking lots are free. The first parking area you'll come to via the Cabrillo Bridge is off El Prado to the right; there are more lots as you continue down the road. Alternatively, you can park at Inspiration Point on the east side of the park (off President's Way) and take a free tram to the museums. There's also a huge lot at the zoo.

16

14

21

TOTUS MUNDUS AGIT HISTRIONEM

Old Globe Theatre

7

12

8

19

TIPS AND TOP ATTRACTIONS

Balboa Park's immense size and myriad attractions all but require a premeditated plan of attack. Here are a few resources for planning a successful visit:

Your First Stop. Before your visit, be sure to call the Balboa Park Visitors Center (619/239–0512) or visit their Web site (www.balboapark. org) for more information.

Fueling Up. The park is filled with dining options; you'll find everything from hot dog stands to fine dining at The Prado (in the House of Hospitality), which is also home to the Balboa Park Food and Wine School (www. balboawinefood.com).

Free Tuesdays. Most of the park's museums offer free admission for residents of San Diego County one Tuesday each month (on a rotating schedule); call ahead for more information.

TOP ATTRACTIONS

Balboa Park is filled with amazing sights, but these are a few of our favorites.

❶ **Alcazar Garden.** Modeled after the grounds of Spain's Alcazar Castle, this lush spot's tiled fountains, formal boxed gardens, and shady pergola encourage lingering.

❷ **Carousel.** All but two of the hand-carved animals on the park's 1910 carousel are originals.

❸ **Bea Evenson Fountain.** A favorite of barefoot children, this fountain in the Plaza de Balboa shoots cool jets of water 50 feet.

❹ **Botanical Building.** Sunlight streams through this graceful redwood-lath structure onto more than 2,000 orchids, ferns, and other tropical plants.

❺ **Cabrillo Bridge.** The park's official (and pedestrian-friendly) gateway soars 120 feet above the canyon floor.

❻ **California Building and Tower/San Diego Museum of Man.** The dramatic tower flanking the glittering dome of this 1915 structure is a San Diego icon. Inside is the park's highly respected anthropological institution.

❼ **Globe Theatre.** Founded in 1935 and modeled after Shakespeare's original, this Tony Award-winning theatre stages productions throughout the year.

❽ **House of Hospitality.** The park's visitor center is inside this intricately detailed landmark, originally built for the 1915 Panama-California Exposition and rebuilt in 1990.

❾ **House of Pacific Relations (International Cottages).** Originally built for the 1935 California Pacific Exposition, each of these 32 cottages represents a different country and hosts festive cultural events.

❿ **Japanese Friendship Garden.** The serenity of this peaceful Japanese-style garden—replete with walking paths, cherry trees, a Koi pond, and a traditional teahouse—is well worth the small admission price.

⓫ **Inez Grant Parker Memorial Rose Garden.** This gorgeous garden contains 125 varieties of roses...and more than 1,750 individual bushes.

⓬ **Palm Canyon.** Wander the winding paths of this shadowy canyon to see 450 tropical palms representing 58 different species.

⓭ **San Diego Model Railroad Museum.** The world's largest operating model railroad museum is exhilarating for kids and adults alike.

⓮ **San Diego Museum of Art.** The region's oldest and largest art museum holds an impressive collection—ranging from old masters to contemporary artists.

⓯ **San Diego Zoo.** More than 4,000 rare and endangered animals reside at this zoo, famous for its natural habitats and progressive conservation efforts.

⓰ **Spreckels Organ Pavilion.** A civic organist has performed free Sunday concerts on this outdoor 4,530-pipe organ since 1917.

Numbers correspond with photos and the map on the previous page.

LIONS AND TIGERS AND PANDA BEARS: THE WORLD FAMOUS SAN DIEGO ZOO

The San Diego Zoo, on a hilly 100-acre corner of Balboa Park, is one of the park's treasures. Operated by the nonprofit Zoological Society of San Diego, the conservation-focused zoo features more than 4,000 rare and endangered animals.

Occupying natural habitats rather than being cooped up in cages, they represent some 800 species from around the planet. While the zoo's adorable pandas get top billing, there are plenty of other cool creatures to see here, from teeny-tiny mantella frogs to larger-than-life African elephants.

STAR ANIMAL ATTRACTIONS

Polar Bear Plunge: Check out the agile swimmers from the underwater viewing room.

Orangutan and Siamang Exhibit: Arboreal orangutans and siamangs—each with their own distinct and vocal personality—swing around in a rain forest ecosystem.

Owens Rain Forest Aviary: San Diego has some of the largest free-flight aviaries in the world, including this one featuring 200 birds from the Southeast Asian jungle.

Gorilla Exhibit: Observe the complex social dynamics of gorillas in this unique natural habitat, which simulates an African rain forest. Nearby you'll find pygmy chimpanzees, or bonobos, thought to be the most intelligent primates after humans.

Koala Exhibit: The zoo has the largest number of koalas outside Australia.

Monkey Trails: This elaborate exhibition is like venturing deep into African and Asian forests. From a safe distance, you can spy on monkeys, elusive clouded leopards, rare albino hippos, and venomous snakes.

(Above) Hippo underwater at the San Diego Zoo

PANDA-MONIUM
The zoo currently has three pandas (on loan from China) at its Giant Panda Research Station and has had five successful panda births. The bears you'll likely see during your visit are Bai Yun ("White Cloud"); Gao-Gao ("Big-Big"), a rambunctious rescued bear; and Yun Zi ("Son of Cloud").

ZOO TIPS
If you want to see it all, give it a full day. To experience everything the zoo has to offer—or most of it, anyway—you'll need at least five hours.

Do your homework: Check the zoo's Web site for details on unique events like the summertime Nighttime Zoo, themed sleepover parties, and sunrise strolls, as well as info on admission deals.

Avoid ticket lines: Purchase and print tickets online using the zoo's Web site.

Picnic before (or after) your visit: The zoo doesn't allow any outside food. There's a wide variety of food available for purchase inside the zoo—but prices are steep.

Prioritize: When you arrive, grab a park map and plot your route (or, better yet, plan ahead with the interactive map on the zoo's Web site).

Wear comfortable shoes: Even if you utilize the zoo's aerial trams, buses, and moving walkways, you'll still be hoofing it quite a bit.

GETTING AROUND THE ZOO
The Skyfari, an aerial gondola lift, offers a bird's-eye view of the grounds and quick transportation. A double-decker, open-roof guided tour bus provides a narrated overview of much of the property; express buses stop at five points in the zoo every 20 minutes. Of course, you can also walk everywhere—just be aware that the terrain is occasionally hilly, and the zoo is *huge*.

PRACTICALITIES
✉ 2920 Zoo Dr.
☎ 619/234-3153, 888/697-2632 giant panda hotline
🌐 www.sandiegozoo.org
💲 $40 includes zoo, Children's Zoo, and animal shows, plus guided bus tour, unlimited express bus rides, and Skyfari Aerial Tram rides; zoo free for children under 12 in Oct.; $76 pass good for admission to zoo and San Diego Zoo Safari Park within 5 days
💳 AE, D, MC, V
🕐 July–Sept., daily 9–9; Oct.–June, daily 9–dusk; Children's Zoo and Skyfari ride generally close 1 hr earlier.

SAN DIEGO ZOO SAFARI PARK
About 45 minutes north of the zoo, the 1,800-acre San Diego Wild Animal Park is an extensive wildlife sanctuary where animals roam free—and guests can get up close and personal in escorted caravans and on backcountry trails. *See listing in this chapter.*

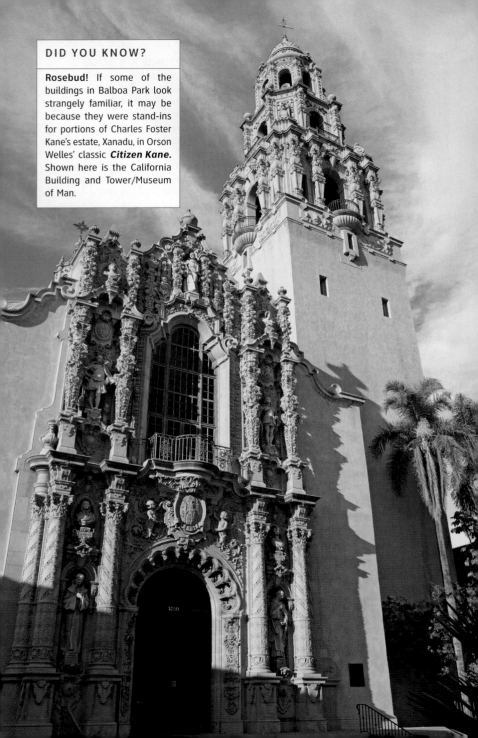

beach. Behind the pool area, an attractive shopping arcade features a classic candy shop as well as several fine clothing and accessories stores. ■ **TIP➜ Even if you don't happen to be saying at the Del, gazing out over the ocean while enjoying a drink at the Sun Deck Bar and Grill makes for a great escape. If it's chilly, the fire pits and sofa seating are very inviting.**

The History Gallery displays photos from the Del's early days, and books elaborating on its history and that of Kate Morgan, the hotel's resident ghost, are sold along with logo apparel and gifts in the hotel's 15-plus shops. In early 2008 the Del unveiled $150 million in luxury enhancements, including 78 new cottages and villas, a signature restaurant, a wine room, and a spa. The resort recently published a new book titled *Building the Dream: The Design and Construction of the Hotel Del Coronado*. Tours of the Del are available Tuesday and Friday at 10:30, Saturday and Sunday at 2, and cost $15. Reservations are required through the **Coronado Visitor Center** (✉ *1100 Orange Ave., Coronado* ☎ *619/437–8788* ⊕ *www.coronadovisitorcenter.com*), which is open weekdays 9–5, weekends 10–5 year-round. ✉ *1500 Orange Ave., Coronado* ☎ *619/435–6611* ⊕ *www.hoteldel.com*.

Orange Avenue. Coronado's business district and its villagelike heart, this is surely one of the most charming spots in Southern California. Slow-paced and very "local" (the city fights against chain stores), it's a blast from the past, although entirely up to date in other respects. The military presence—Coronado is home to the U.S. Navy Sea, Air and Land (SEAL) forces—is reflected in shops selling military gear and places like McP's Irish Pub, the unofficial SEALs headquarters and a family-friendly stop for a good, all-American meal. Many clothing boutiques, home-furnishings stores, and upscale restaurants cater to visitors with deep pockets, but you can buy plumbing supplies, too, or get a genuine military haircut at Crown Barbers.

Bay Books. Peruse a selection from the huge magazine collection while sipping a latte at the sidewalk café of Bay Books, San Diego's largest independent bookstore. ✉ *1029 Orange Ave., Coronado* ☎ *619/435–0070*.

HARBOR AND SHELTER ISLANDS AND POINT LOMA

The populated outcroppings that jut into the bay just west of Downtown and the airport demonstrate the potential of human collaboration with nature. Point Loma, Mother Nature's contribution to San Diego's attractions, has always protected the center city from the Pacific's tides and waves. It's shared by military installations, funky motels and fast-food shacks, stately family homes, huge estates, and private marinas packed with sailboats and yachts. Newer to the scene, Harbor and Shelter islands are landfill. Created out of sand dredged from the San Diego Bay in the second half of the past century, they've become tourist hubs—their high-rise hotels, seafood restaurants, and boat-rental centers looking as solid as those anywhere else in the city.

San Diego's myriad coastal trails and paths provide great views of natural and man-made wonders alike.

EXPLORING HARBOR AND SHELTER ISLANDS AND POINT LOMA

Cabrillo National Monument. This 160-acre preserve marks the site of the first European visit to San Diego, made by 16th-century explorer Juan Rodríguez Cabrillo (circa 1498–1543)—historians have never conclusively determined whether he was Spanish or Portuguese. Cabrillo, who had earlier gone on voyages with Hernán Cortés, landed at this spot, which he called San Miguel, in 1542. Today the site, with its rugged cliffs and shores and outstanding overlooks, is one of the most frequently visited of all the national monuments.

Fodor's Choice ★

The **visitor center** presents films and lectures about Cabrillo's voyage, the sea-level tide pools, and migrating gray whales. **Interpretive stations** have been installed along the walkways that edge the cliffs. The moderately steep **Bayside Trail,** 2½-mi round-trip, winds through coastal sage scrub, curving under the cliff-top lookouts and taking you ever closer to the bay-front scenery. You cannot reach the beach from this trail and must stick to the path to protect the cliffs from erosion and yourself from thorny plants and snakes—including rattlers. You'll see prickly pear cactus and yucca, black-eyed Susans, fragrant sage, and maybe a lizard or a hummingbird. The climb back is long but gradual, leading up to the **Old Point Loma Lighthouse.**

The western and southern cliffs of Cabrillo National Monument are prime whale-watching territory. A sheltered **viewing station** has wayside exhibits describing the great gray whales' yearly migration from Baja California to the Bering and Chukchi seas near Alaska. High-powered telescopes help you focus on the whales' waterspouts. More accessible sea creatures can be seen in the **tide pools** at the foot of the monument's western cliffs. Drive north from the visitor center to Cabrillo Road on the left, which winds down to the Coast Guard station and the shore. ✉ *1800 Cabrillo Memorial Dr., Point Loma* ☎ *619/557–5450* ⊕ *www.nps.gov/cabr* ⌦ *$5 per car, $3 per person entering on foot or by bicycle* ☉ *Park daily 9–5.*

Harbor Island. Restaurants and high-rise hotels dot the inner shore of this 1½-mi-long man-made peninsula adjacent to the airport. The bay's shore is lined with pathways, gardens, and scenic picnic spots.

Tom Ham's Lighthouse. On the west point, this restaurant has a U.S. Coast Guard–approved beacon shining from its tower. ✉ *2150 Harbor Island Dr., Harbor Island* ☎ *619/291–9110* ⊕ *www.tomhamslighthouse.com.*

Island Prime and C-level Lounge. On the east end point, this lounge offers a killer view of the Downtown skyline. ✉ *880 Harbor Island Dr., Harbor Island* ☎ *619/298–6802* ⊕ *www.cohnrestaurants.com* ✉ *Harbor Island Dr., Harbor Island.*

Shelter Island. This reclaimed peninsula now supports towering palms, a cluster of resorts, restaurants, and side-by-side marinas. The center of San Diego's yacht-building industry, boats in every stage of construction are visible in Shelter Island's yacht yards. A long sidewalk runs past boat brokerages to the hotels and marinas that line the inner shore, facing Point Loma. On the bay side, fishermen launch their boats and families relax at picnic tables along the grass, where there are fire rings and permanent barbeque grills. Within walking distance is the huge Friendship Bell, given to San Diegans by the people of Yokohama, Japan, in 1960 and the Tunaman's Memorial, a statue commemorating San Diego's once-flourishing fishing industry. ✉ *Shelter Island Dr., Shelter Island.*

★ **Sunset Cliffs.** As the name suggests, the 60-foot-high bluffs on the western side of Point Loma south of Ocean Beach are a perfect place to watch the sun set over the sea. To view the tide pools along the shore, use the staircase off Sunset Cliffs Boulevard at the foot of Ladera Street.

The dramatic coastline here seems to have been carved out of ancient rock. The impact of the waves is very clear: each year more sections of the cliffs are posted with caution signs. Don't ignore these warnings—it's easy to lose your footing and slip in the crumbling sandstone, and the surf can be extremely rough. The small coves and beaches that dot the coastline are popular with surfers drawn to the pounding waves and neighborhood locals who name and claim their special spots. The homes along the boulevard—pink stucco mansions beside shingled Cape Cod–style cottages—are fine examples of Southern California luxury. ✉ *Sunset Cliffs Blvd., Point Loma.*

MISSION BAY AND SEAWORLD

Mission Bay Park is San Diego's monument to sports and fitness. This 4,600-acre aquatic park has 27 mi of shoreline including 19 of sandy beach. Playgrounds and picnic areas abound on the beach and low grassy hills of the park. On weekday evenings joggers, bikers, and skaters take over. In the daytime, swimmers, water-skiers, anglers, and boaters—some in single-person kayaks, others in crowded power-boats—vie for space in the water. One Mission Bay caveat: swimmers should note signs warning about water pollution; on occasions when heavy rains or other events cause pollution, swimming is dangerous.

EXPLORING MISSION BAY AND SEAWORLD

Belmont Park. The once-abandoned amusement park between the bay and Mission Beach Boardwalk is now a shopping, dining, and recreation complex. Twinkling lights outline the **Giant Dipper,** an antique wooden roller coaster on which screaming thrill-seekers ride more than 2,600 feet of track and 13 hills (riders must be at least 4 feet, 2 inches tall). Created in 1925 and listed on the National Register of Historic Places, this is one of the few old-time roller coasters left in the United States. The **Plunge,** an indoor swimming pool, also opened in 1925, and was the largest—60 feet by 125 feet—saltwater pool in the world at the time (it's had freshwater since 1951). Johnny Weismuller and Esther Williams are among the stars who were captured on celluloid swimming here. Other Belmont Park attractions include a video arcade, a submarine ride, bumper cars, a tilt-a-whirl, and an antique carousel. Belmont Park also has the most consistent wave in the county at the **Wave House,** where the FlowRider provides surfers and bodyboarders a near-perfect simulated wave on which to practice their skills. The rock wall challenges both junior climbers and their elders. ⊠ *3146 Mission Blvd., Mission Bay* ☎ *858/488–1549, 858/228–9300 for pool* ⊕ *www. belmontpark.com* ☏ *$6 for roller coaster, other rides cost $2 to $5, or buy a full-day unlimited ride package $22.95 for 50" and over, $15.95 for under 50"; pool $7 for one-time entry* ⊙ *Park opens at 11 daily, ride operation varies seasonally; pool weekdays noon–4 pm, and 8–10 pm, weekends noon–8 pm.*

SeaWorld San Diego. One of the world's largest marine-life amusement parks, SeaWorld is spread over 189 tropically landscaped bay-front acres—and it seems to be expanding into every available square inch of space with new exhibits, shows, and activities. The biggest attraction in its 40 years of existence opened in 2004: **Journey to Atlantis** involves a cruise on an eight-passenger "Greek fishing boat" down a heart-stopping 60-foot plunge to explore a lost, sunken city. After-this journey serenaded by dolphins calls, you view a 130,000-gallon pool, home to exotic Commerson's dolphins, a small black-and-white South American species known for speed and agility.

The majority of SeaWorld's exhibits are walk-through marine environments. Kids get a particular kick out of the **Shark Encounter,** where they come face-to-face with sand, tiger, nurse, bonnethead, black-tipped, and white-tipped reef sharks by walking through a 57-foot clear acrylic tube that passes through the 280,000-gallon shark habitat. The hands-on **California Tide Pool** exhibit gives you a chance to get to know San Diego's indigenous marine life. At **Forbidden Reef** you can feed bat rays and go nose-to-nose with creepy moray eels. At **Rocky Point Preserve** you can view bottlenose dolphins, as well as Californian sea otters. At **Wild Arctic,** which starts out with a simulated helicopter ride to a research post at the North Pole, beluga whales, walruses, and polar bears can be viewed in areas decked out like the wrecked hulls of two 19th-century sailing ships. **Manatee Rescue** lets you watch the gentle-giant marine mammals cavorting in a 215,000-gallon tank. Various **freshwater and saltwater aquariums** hold underwater creatures from around the world. And for younger kids who need to release lots of energy, **Sesame Street Bay of Play at SeaWorld**, opened in 2008, is a hands-on fun zone that features three family-friendly Sesame Street–theme rides.

SeaWorld's highlights are its large-arena entertainments. You can get front-row seats if you arrive 30 minutes in advance, and the stadiums are large enough for everyone to get a seat in the off-season. Introduced in 2006 and starring the ever-beloved Shamu the Killer Whale, **Believe** features synchronized whales and brings down the house. **Blue Horizons,** new in 2010, combines dolphins, pilot whales, tropical birds, and aerialists in a spectacular performance.

Another favorite is *Sesame Street Presents: Lights, Camera, Imagination!* in 4-D, a new film that has Cookie Monster, Elmo, and other Sesame Street favorites swimming through an imaginary ocean and flying through a cinematic sky. **Clyde and Seamore's Sea Lions LIVE,** the sea lion and otter production, also is widely popular.

Not all the shows are water-oriented. **Pets Rule!** showcases the antics of more-common animals like dogs, cats, birds, and even a pig. One segment of the show actually has regular house cats climbing ladders and hanging upside down as they cross a high wire. The majority of the animals used in the show were adopted from shelters.

The **Dolphin Interaction Program** gives guests the chance to interact with SeaWorld's bottlenose dolphins in the water. The 1-hour experience (20 minutes in the water), during which visitors can feed, touch, and give behavior signals, costs $190. A less expensive treat ($42 adults, $38 children) is the 1-hour **Penguin Experience Tour,** which gets you up close and personal with these cute, cold-weather creatures.

Shipwreck Rapids, SeaWorld of San Diego's first adventure ride, offers plenty of excitement—but you may end up getting soaked. For five minutes, nine "shipwrecked" passengers careen down a river in a raftlike inner tube, encountering a series of obstacles, including several waterfalls. There's no extra charge, making this one of SeaWorld's great bargains—expect long lines. Those who want to head to higher ground might consider the **Skytower,** a glass elevator that ascends 265 feet; the views of San Diego County are especially spectacular in early morning and late evening. The **Bayside Skyride,** a five-minute aerial tram ride located on the west side of the park, travels across Mission Bay. Combined admission for the Skytower and the tram is $6. The San Diego 3-for-1 Ticket ($129 for adults, $99 for children ages 3 to 9) offers five consecutive days of unlimited admission to SeaWorld, the San Diego Zoo, and the San Diego Wild Animal Park. This is a good idea, because if you try to get your money's worth by fitting everything in on a single day, you're likely to end up tired and cranky. Many hotels, especially those in the Mission Bay area, also offer SeaWorld specials that may include rate reductions or two days' entry for the price of one. ⊠ *500 SeaWorld Dr.,* *near west end of I–8, Mission Bay ☎ 800/257–4268 ⊕ www.seaworld. com ⚏ $69.99 adults, $61.99 kids; parking $12 cars, $8 motorcycles, $17 RVs and campers; 1-hr behind-the-scenes walking tours $13 extra adults, $11 extra kids ⊙ Daily 10–dusk; extended hrs in summer.*

OLD TOWN

San Diego's Spanish and Mexican roots are most evident in Old Town, the area north of Downtown at Juan Street, near the intersection of interstates 5 and 8, which was the site of the first European settlement in Southern California. Although Old Town was largely a 19th-century phenomenon, the pueblo's true beginnings took place much earlier and on a hill overlooking it, where soldiers from New Spain established a military outpost in May 1769. Two months later Father Junípero Serra established the first of the California's missions, San Diego de Alcalá.

On San Diego Avenue, the district's main drag, art galleries and expensive gift shops are interspersed with tacky curio shops, restaurants, and open-air stands selling inexpensive Mexican pottery, jewelry, and blankets. The Old Town Esplanade on San Diego Avenue between Harney and Conde streets is the best of several mall-like affairs constructed in mock Mexican-plaza style. Shops and restaurants also line Juan and Congress streets. Bazaar del Mundo, a much-loved collection of shops holding handmade arts and crafts is at 4133 Taylor Street.

Access to Old Town is easy thanks to the nearby Transit Center. Ten bus lines stop here, as do the San Diego Trolley and the Coaster commuter rail line. Two large parking lots linked to the park by an underground pedestrian walkway ease some of the parking congestion, and signage leading from I–8 to the Transit Center is easy to follow.

EXPLORING OLD TOWN

⟳ **Fiesta de Reyes.** North of San Diego's Old Town Plaza lies the area's
Fodor's Choice unofficial center, built to represent a colonial Mexican square. This col-
★ lection of shops and restaurants around a central courtyard in blossom with magenta bougainvillea, scarlet hibiscus, and other flowers in season reflect what it might have looked like in the early California days, from 1821 to 1872, complete with shops stocked with items reminiscent of that era. More than a dozen shops are open, and there are also three restaurants, including **Casa de Reyes,** serving Mexican food. If you are lucky, you might catch a mariachi band or folklorico dance performance on the plaza stage—check the Web site for times and upcoming special events. This area, formerly operated as Plaza del Pasado, and, before that, Bazaar del Mundo, was rechristened as Fiesta de Reyes in mid-2009. ⊠ 2754 Calhoun St., Old Town ☎ 619/297–3100 ⊕ www. fiestadereyes.com ⊙ Shops 10–9 daily.

Heritage Park. A number of San Diego's important Victorian buildings are the focus of this 7.8-acre park, up the Juan Street hill near Harney Street. The buildings, moved here and restored by Save Our Heritage Organization, include Southern California's first synagogue, a one-room Classical Revival structure built in 1889 for Congregation Beth Israel. The most interesting of the park's six former residences might be the

Sherman Gilbert House, which has a widow's walk and intricate carving on its decorative trim. It was built for real-estate dealer John Sherman in 1887 at the then-exorbitant cost of $20,000—indicating just how profitable the booming housing market could be. All the houses, some of which may seem surprisingly colorful, do in fact accurately represent the bright tones of the era. Management of the park was recently transferred to a hospitality firm, and renovation of the buildings is underway. For visitors looking to stay overnight in a historic setting, four of the houses should be converted into "The Inns at Heritage Park" during the lifespan of this book. The park remains open during this process, with the synagogue and Senlis Cottage open to visitors daily from 9 to 5. The McConaughy House hosts the Old Town Gift Emporium, a gift shop specializing in Victorian porcelain dolls (Thurs.– Tues. 10–5). ⊠ *2455 Heritage Park Row, Old Town* ☏ *619/819–6009* ⊕ *www.heritageparksd.com.*

Ⓒ
Fodor's Choice
★
Old Town San Diego State Historic Park. The six square blocks on the site of San Diego's original pueblo are the heart of Old Town. Most of the 20 historic buildings preserved or re-created by the park cluster around **Old Town Plaza,** bounded by Wallace Street on the west, Calhoun Street on the north, Mason Street on the east, and San Diego Avenue on the south. The plaza is a pleasant place to rest, plan your tour of the park, and watch passersby. San Diego Avenue is closed to vehicle traffic here.

Some of Old Town's buildings were destroyed in a fire in 1872, but after the site became a state historic park in 1968, reconstruction and restoration on the structures that remained began. Seven of the original adobes are still intact. The tour pamphlet available at Robinson-Rose House gives details about all the historic houses on the plaza and in its vicinity; *a few of the more interesting ones are noted below.* Several reconstructed buildings serve as restaurants or as shops purveying wares reminiscent of those that might have been available in the original Old Town; Racine & Laramie, a painstakingly reproduced version of San Diego's first (1868) cigar store, is especially interesting. The noncommercial houses are open daily 10–5 (until 4 in winter); none charges admission, though donations are appreciated. Free tours depart daily from the Robinson-Rose House at 11 and 2. ■ TIP➔ The covered wagon in Old Town Plaza makes for a great photo opportunity.

Also worth exploring in the plaza area are the free **Dental Museum, Mason Street School, Wells Fargo History Museum, First San Diego Courthouse, Casa de Machado y Silvas Commercial Restaurant Museum,** and the **Casa de Machado y Stewart.** Ask at the visitor center for locations.

Robinson-Rose House. This house on Wallace Street facing Old Town Plaza was the original commercial center of Old San Diego, housing railroad offices, law offices, and the first newspaper press. Built in 1853 but in ruins at the end of the 19th century, it has been reconstructed and now serves as the park's visitor center and administrative headquarters. It contains a model of Old Town as it looked in 1872, as well as various historic exhibits. Just behind the Robinson-Rose House is a replica of the Victorian-era Silvas-McCoy house, originally built in 1869. ⊠ *4002 Wallace St., Old Town* ☏ *619/220–5422.*

TIP SHEET: SEAWORLD SAN DIEGO

Who Will Especially Love This Park?

The park, on 180 tropically land-scaped acres, caters to adults and kids of all ages. The Sesame Street Bay of Play—for toddlers less than 42 inches tall—is a two-acre area with familiar television characters, live performances, Sesame Street rides, and interactive educational exhibits like the California Tide Pool.

What's This Really Gonna Cost?

In addition to tickets, you'll need to pay $12 for parking. Meals are about $6–$20 per person. There are also additional fees for Bayside Skyride ($4) and Skytower ($4); you can buy a combo ticket for both for $6. SeaWorld offers a broad range of public and private tours and animal interaction experiences, which start at $13 per person for a one-hour Behind-the-Scenes tour and run up to $190 per person for the Dolphin Interaction Program.

TOP 5 ATTRACTIONS:

Believe: This multimedia Shamu show blends killer whale behaviors with theatrical set pieces, music, and choreography. For an additional $28–$42, you can Dine with Shamu.

Penguin Encounter: Enjoy a close-up look at 250 penguins represent-ing five species—including the only successful emperor penguin breed-ing colony outside Antarctica.

Shark Encounter: This 280,000-gal-lon tank is home to 12 shark species that swim above and around you as you walk through a clear acrylic tube.

Wild Arctic: Board a simulated jet helicopter, and disembark at a realistic Arctic research station with beluga whales, polar bears, walruses, and seals.

Blue Horizons: Super-intelligent bottlenose dolphins and pilot whales perform alongside birds and acro-bats for huge crowds in this spec-tacular show.

TIPS:

Cool Down: If it's hot when you visit, be sure to ride Journey to Atlantis, a cruise on an eight-pas-senger Greek ship that plunges 60 feet to the lost city—creating a nice, refreshing splashdown.

Up, Up and Away: Don't miss the Bayside Skyride over Mission Bay. It's an extra $4, but well worth the time and money—you'll get a great overview of the park and surround-ing area.

Get Good Seats: Arrive at shows at least 30 minutes early to get front-row seats.

Save Some Cash: Look for Sea-World specials at Mission Bay area hotels; some offer reduced rates and/or two-days-for-the-price-of-one admission deals. Be sure to ask when you book.

Elmo's Flying Fish, in SeaWorld's Sesame Street Bay of Play.

Acrobatic dolphins perform in SeaWorld's Dolphin Discovery show.

Cosmopolitan Hotel and Restaurant. On Mason Street, at the corner of Calhoun Street, is the Cosmopolitan Hotel and Restaurant, once one of the prettiest haciendas in San Diego. Built in 1829 by a Peruvian, Juan Bandini, the house served as Old Town's social center during Mexican rule. Albert Seeley, a stagecoach entrepreneur, purchased the home in 1869, built a second story, and turned it into the Cosmopolitan Hotel, a way station for travelers on the daylong trip south from Los Angeles. It later served as a store and a factory.

Seeley Stable. Seeley Stable, next door to the Cosmopolitan building, became San Diego's stagecoach stop in 1867, and was the transportation hub of Old Town until near the turn of the 19th century, when trains became the favored mode of travel. The stable houses a collection of horse-drawn vehicles, some so elaborate that you can see where the term "carriage trade" came from. Also inside are Western memorabilia, including an exhibit on the California vaquero, the original American cowboy, and a collection of Native American artifacts. ⊠ *2630 Calhoun St., Old Town.*

Casa de Estudillo. The Casa de Estudillo was built on Mason Street in 1827 by San Diego's first County Assessor, Jose Antonio Estudillo, in collaboration with his father, the commander of the San Diego Presidio, José Maria Estudillo. The largest and most elaborate of the original adobe homes, it was occupied by members of the Estudillo family until 1887. It was purchased and restored in 1910 by sugar magnate and developer John D. Spreckels, who advertised it in bold lettering on the side as "Ramona's Marriage Place." Spreckels's claim that the small chapel in the house was the site of the wedding in Helen Hunt Jackson's

Old Town
San Diego

popular novel *Ramona* had no basis; that didn't stop people from coming to see it, however. ⊠ *4001 Mason St., Old Town.*

San Diego Union Museum. The San Diego Union Museum is in a New England–style, wood-frame house prefabricated in the eastern United States and shipped around Cape Horn in 1851. The building has been restored to replicate the newspaper's offices of 1868, when the first edition of the *San Diego Union* was printed. ⊠ *2602 San Diego Ave., Old Town* ⊠ *4002 Wallace St., Old Town* ☎ *619/220–5422* ⊕ *www.parks.ca.gov.*

Presidio Park. The hillsides of the 40-acre green space overlooking Old Town from the north end of Taylor Street are popular with picnickers, and many couples have taken their wedding vows on the park's long stretches of lawn, some of the greenest in San Diego. You may encounter enthusiasts of the sport of grass-skiing, gliding over the grass and down the hills on their wheeled-model skis. ■ TIP→ **Grab a cardboard box to try grass-sledding the low-tech way.** It's a nice walk from Old Town to the summit if you're in good shape and wearing the right shoes—it should take about half an hour. You can also drive to the top of the park via Presidio Drive, off Taylor Street.

If you do decide to walk, look in at the **Presidio Hills Golf Course** on Mason Street. It has an unusual clubhouse that incorporates the ruins of Casa de Carrillo, the town's oldest adobe, constructed in 1820. At the end of Mason Street, veer left on Jackson Street to reach the **presidio ruins,** where adobe walls and a bastion have been built above the foundations of the original fortress and chapel. Archaeology students from San Diego State University who excavated the area have marked off the early chapel outline, although they reburied the artifacts they uncovered in order to protect them. Also on-site are the 28-foot-high **Serra Cross,** built in 1913 out of brick tiles found in the ruins, and a bronze **statue of Father Serra.** Take Presidio Drive southeast and you'll come to the site of **Fort Stockton,** built to protect Old Town and abandoned by the United States in 1848. Plaques and statues also commemorate the Mormon Battalion, which enlisted here to fight in the battle against Mexico. ⊠ *1 block north of Old Town San Diego State Historic Park, Old Town.*

★ **Thomas Whaley House Museum.** Thomas Whaley was a New York entrepreneur who came to California during the gold rush. He wanted to provide his East Coast wife with all the comforts of home, so in 1857 he had Southern California's first two-story brick structure built, making it the oldest double-story brick building on the West Coast. The house, which served as the county courthouse and government seat during the 1870s, stands in strong contrast to the Spanish-style adobe residences that surround the nearby historic plaza and marks an early stage of San Diego's "Americanization." A garden out back includes many varieties of Old Garden roses from before 1867, when roses were first hybridized. The place is perhaps most famed, however, for the ghosts that are said to inhabit it. Starting at 7 pm, admission is by guided tour offered every half hour with the last tour departing at 9:30 pm. The nighttime tours are geared more toward the supernatural aspects of the house than the daytime self-guided tour. ⊠ *2476 San Diego Ave., Old Town* 🖼 *619/297–7511* ⊕ *www.whaleyhouse.org* 🖼 *$6 before 5 pm, $10 after 5* ☉ *Sept.–May, Sun.–Tues. 10–5, Thurs.–Sun. 10–9:30; June–Aug., daily 10–9:30.*

LA JOLLA

La Jollans have long considered their village to be the Monte Carlo of California. Its coastline curves into natural coves backed by verdant hillsides dotted with homes worth millions. Although La Jolla is a neighborhood of the city of San Diego, it has its own postal zone and a coveted sense of class; the ultrarich from around the globe own second homes here—the seaside zone between the neighborhood's bustling Downtown and the cliffs above the Pacific has a distinctly European flavor—and old-monied residents maintain friendships with the visiting film stars and royalty who frequent the area's exclusive luxury hotels and private clubs. The town has a cosmopolitan air that makes it a popular vacation resort.

To reach La Jolla from I–5, if you're traveling north, take the La Jolla Parkway exit, which veers into Torrey Pines Road, and turn right onto Prospect Street. If you're heading south, get off at the La Jolla Village Drive exit, which also leads into Torrey Pines Road.

Prospect Street and Girard Avenue, the village's main drags, are lined with expensive shops and office buildings. Through the years the shopping and dining district has spread to Pearl and other side streets. Although there is metered parking on the streets, parking is otherwise hard to find.

EXPLORING LA JOLLA

Birch Aquarium at Scripps. The largest oceanographic exhibit in the United States, maintained by the Scripps Institution of Oceanography, sits at the end of a signposted drive leading off North Torrey Pines Road. More than 60 tanks are filled with colorful saltwater fish, and a 70,000-gallon tank simulates a La Jolla kelp forest. A special exhibit on sea horses features several examples of the species, plus mesmerizing sea dragons and a sea horse nursery. Besides the fish themselves, attractions include a gallery based on the institution's ocean-related research, and interactive educational exhibits on a variety of environmental issues. ⊠ *2300 Expedition Way, La Jolla* ☎ *858/534–3474* ⊕ *www.aquarium.ucsd.edu* ☜ *$12, parking free for 3 hrs* ☼ *Daily 9–5, last ticket sold at 4:30.*

La Jolla Caves. It's a walk of 145 sometimes slippery steps down a tunnel to Sunny Jim, the largest of the caves in La Jolla Cove and the only one reachable by land. This is a one-of-a-kind local attraction, and worth the time if you have a day or two to really enjoy La Jolla. The man-made tunnel took two years to dig, beginning in 1902; later, a shop was built at its entrance. Today La Jolla Cave Store, a throwback to that early shop, is still the entrance to the cave, which was named Sunny Jim after a 1920s cartoon character. The shop sells jewelry and watercolors by local artists. ⊠ *1325 Coast Blvd. S, La Jolla* ☎ *858/459–0746* ⊕ *www. cavestore.com* ☜ *$4* ☼ *Daily 10–5.*

La Jolla Cove. This shimmering blue inlet is what first attracted everyone
FodorśChoice to La Jolla, from Native Americans to the glitterati; it's the secret to the
★ village's enduring cachet. You'll find the cove—as locals always refer to it, as though it were the only one in San Diego—beyond where Girard Avenue dead-ends into Coast Boulevard, marked by towering palms that line a promenade where people strolling in designer clothes are as common as Frisbee throwers.

Smaller beaches appear and disappear with the tides, which carve small coves in cliffs covered with ice plants. Pathways lead down to the beaches. Keep an eye on the tide to avoid getting trapped once the waves come in. A long layer of sandstone stretching out above the waves provides a perfect sunset-watching spot. Be careful, these rocks can get slippery.

An underwater preserve at the north end of La Jolla Cove makes the adjoining beach the most popular one in the area. On summer days, when water visibility reaches up to 20 feet, the small beach is covered with blankets, towels, and umbrellas, and the lawns at the top of the stairs leading down to the cove are staked out by groups of scuba divers, complete with wet suits and tanks. The **Children's Pool,** at the south end of the park, has a curving beach protected by a seawall from strong currents and waves. Since the pool and its beach have become home to an ever-growing colony of Harbor seals, it cannot be used by swimmers. It is however the best place on the coast to view these engaging creatures.

■ TIP➜ Take a walk through Ellen Browning Scripps Park, past the groves

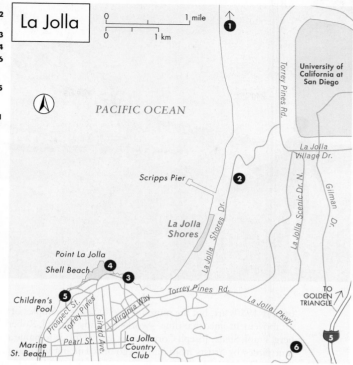

La Jolla

PACIFIC OCEAN

University of
California at
San Diego

La Jolla
Village Dr.

Scripps Pier

La Jolla
Shores

Point La Jolla

Shell Beach

Children's
Pool

Marine
St. Beach

Pearl St.

La Jolla
Country
Club

Torrey Pines Rd.

La Jolla Pkwy.

TO
GOLDEN
TRIANGLE

of twisted junipers to the cliff's edge. Perhaps one of the open-air shelters overlooking the sea will be unoccupied, and you can spread your picnic out on a table and enjoy the scenery. ⊹ *From Torrey Pines Road, turn right on Prospect, then right on Coast Blvd. The park is located at the bottom of the hill* ⊕ *www.sandiego.gov/lifeguards/beaches/cove.shtml.*

Mount Soledad. La Jolla's highest spot can be reached by taking Nautilus Street to La Jolla Scenic Drive South, and then turning left. Proceed a few blocks to the park, where parking is plentiful and the views are astounding, unless the day is hazy. The top of the mountain is an excellent vantage point from which to get a sense of San Diego's geography: looking down from here you can see the coast from the county's northern border to the south far beyond Downtown. ⊠ *6905 La Jolla Scenic Dr. S, La Jolla.*

Fodor'sChoice   **Museum of Contemporary Art, San Diego.** The oldest section of La Jolla's
   ★   branch of San Diego's modern art museum was originally a residence, designed by Irving Gill for philanthropist Ellen Browning Scripps in 1916. In the mid-1990s, the compound was updated and expanded by architect Robert Venturi, who respected Gill's original geometric structure and clean, mission-style lines while adding his own distinctive touches. The result is a striking contemporary building that looks as though it's always been here. California artists figure prominently in the museum's permanent collection

A surfer prepares to head out before sunset at La Jolla's Torrey Pines State Beach and Preserve.

of post-1950s art, but the museum also includes examples of every major art movement since that time—works by Andy Warhol, Robert Rauschenberg, Frank Stella, Joseph Cornell, and Jenny Holzer, to name a few. Important pieces by artists from San Diego and Tijuana were acquired in the 1990s. The museum also gets major visiting shows. Museum admission is good for seven days at both the La Jolla and Downtown locations. Free exhibit tours are offered weekends at 2. ⊠ *700 Prospect St.* ☎ *858/454–3541* ⊕ *www.mcasd.org* ✉ *$10, ages 25 and under are free, free 3rd Thurs. of the month 5–7* ⊗ *Thurs.–Tues. 11–5, Closed Wed.*

Fodor'sChoice
★
Torrey Pines State Natural Reserve. *Pinus torreyana,* the rarest native pine tree in the United States, enjoys a 1,700-acre sanctuary at the northern edge of La Jolla. About 6,000 of these unusual trees, some as tall as 60 feet, grow on the cliffs here. The park is one of only two places in the world (the other is Santa Rosa Island, off Santa Barbara) where the Torrey pine grows naturally. The reserve has several hiking trails leading to the cliffs, 300 feet above the ocean; trail maps are available at the park station. Wildflowers grow profusely in spring, and the ocean panoramas are always spectacular. When in this upper part of the park, respect the various restrictions. Not permitted: picnicking, smoking, leaving the trails, dogs, alcohol, or collecting plant specimens.

You can unwrap your sandwiches, however, at Torrey Pines State Beach, just below the reserve. When the tide is out, it's possible to walk south all the way past the lifeguard towers to Black's Beach over rocky promontories carved by the waves (avoid the bluffs, however; they're unstable). **Los Peñasquitos Lagoon** at the north end of the reserve is one of the many natural estuaries that flow inland between Del Mar and Oceanside. It's a good place to watch shorebirds. Volunteers lead guided nature walks at 10 and 2 on most weekends. ⊠ *N. Torrey Pines Rd. exit off I–5 onto Carmel Valley Rd. going west, then turn left (south) on Coast Hwy. 101, La Jolla* ☎ *858/755–2063* ⊕ *www.torreypine.org* 🎫 *Parking $10* ☉ *Daily 8–dusk.*

WHERE TO EAT

San Diego's unbeatable sunny and warm weather combined with gorgeous ocean views and the abundance of locally grown produce make it a satisfying place to be a chef or a diner. While most of the top restaurants offer seasonal California cuisine, San Diego also boasts excellent examples of ethnic cuisines available at all prices. Local specialties include fish tacos and spiny lobster.

While "Appropriate Dress Required" signs are sometimes displayed in the entrances to restaurants, this generally means nothing more than clean and reasonably neat clothing. Meal prices in San Diego have caught up with those of other major metropolitan areas, especially in districts like La Jolla, the Gaslamp Quarter, and Coronado, where high rents and popularity with the tourists lead to more expensive entrées. Reservations are always a good idea; we mention them only when they're essential or not accepted.

Use the coordinate (✛ A1) at the end of each listing to locate a site on the corresponding map.

WHAT IT COSTS					
	¢	$	$$	$$$	$$$$
Restaurants	under $10	$10–$17	$18–$24	$25–$35	over $35

Prices are for a main course at dinner, excluding 8.75% tax.

CORONADO AND SOUTH BAY

$$$$ ✕ **1500 Ocean.** The fine-dining restaurant at Hotel Del Coronado offers
AMERICAN a memorable evening that showcases the best organic and naturally raised ingredients the region has to offer. Chef Brian Sinnott, who honed his technique in San Francisco, presents sublimely subtle dishes such as chilled king crab with compressed Asian pear salad; wild prawns with kale, smoked bacon, and shelled beans; and Kurobuta pork tenderloin with creamy polenta. The interior, at once inviting and elegant, evokes a posh cabana, while the terrace offers ocean views. An excellent international wine list and equally clever desserts and artisanal cheeses complete the experience. ⊠ *Hotel Del Coronado, 1500 Orange Ave., Coronado* ☎ *619/522–8490* ☉ *No lunch* ✛ *D6.*

$$$ ✕ **Chez Loma.** A favorite with guests at nearby Hotel Del Coronado, this
FRENCH restaurant is tucked away on a side street. Chez Loma is located in a former private home with plenty of windows, attractive lighting, and an upstairs Victorian parlor where coffee and dessert are served. The more elaborate dishes among the carefully prepared French bistro menu are *boeuf bourguignon*, rack of lamb with balsamic marinade, and roasted salmon in

a horseradish crust. The solid selection of desserts includes classics like chocolate soufflé and crème caramel. A specially priced early dinner menu, and two choices of fixed-price menus for $40 or $45 offer more value than the à la carte selections. ✉ *1132 Loma Ave., Coronado* ☎ *619/435–0661* ⊕ *www.chezloma.com* ⊗ *No lunch, closed Mondays* ✛ *D6.*

DOWNTOWN

¢　✗ **Bread on Market.** The baguettes at this artisanal bakery near the
CAFÉ　PETCO Park baseball stadium are every bit as good as the ones you'd buy in Paris. Focaccia and other superior loaves are the building blocks for solid sandwiches, which range from the turkey special with honey mustard and cranberry sauce to a vegan sandwich with locally grown avocado. The menu extends to a daily soup, a fruit-garnished cheese plate, and an appetizing Mediterranean salad. If you have a sweet tooth, try the peanut butter and chocolate-chip cookies, coconut macaroons, and biscotti with hazelnut and chocolate. ✉ *730 Market St., East Village* ☎ *619/795–2730* ⊕ *www.breadonmarket.com* ⊗ *No dinner* ✛ *E5.*

$　✗ **Café Chloe.** The intersection of 9th and G is now the meeting point for
FRENCH　San Diego's café society, thanks to the superchic and friendly Café Chloe.
Fodor's Choice　Surrounded by luxury high-rises, hotels, and boutiques, this pretty, Pari-
★　sian spot is frequented by the area's residents for breakfast, lunch, dinner, and weekend brunch. Start the day with whole-wheat pancakes and sour-cherry sauce; lunch on smoked trout and apple salad or a casserole of macaroni, pancetta, and Gorgonzola; or enjoy duck confit or steak frites for dinner. Enjoy wines by the glass, imported beers, and coffee with desserts like seasonal fruit tarts or chocolate pot de crème. It's a lovely place to spend the afternoon. ✉ *721 9th Ave., East Village* ☎ *619/232–3242* ✛ *E5.*

$$$　✗ **Candelas.** The scents and flavors of imaginative Mexican cuisine with a
MEXICAN　European flair permeate this handsome, romantic restaurant and nightspot in the shadow of San Diego's tallest residential towers. Candles glow everywhere around the small, comfortable dining room. There isn't a burrito or taco in sight. Fine openers such as black bean soup and watercress salad with bacon and pistachios give way to main courses like local lobster stuffed with mushrooms, jalapeño peppers, and aged tequila; or tequila-flamed jumbo prawns over creamy, seasoned goat cheese. The adjacent bar pours many elegant tequilas and has become a popular, often jam-packed nightspot. They also serve a Mexican-style breakfast on weekends. ✉ *416 3rd Ave., Gaslamp Quarter* ☎ *619/702–4455* ✛ *H2.*

$$　✗ **Jsix.** Creative and carefully prepared seafood reigns on this menu that
AMERICAN　reflects the diverse flavors found along the West Coast from Mexico
Fodor's Choice　to Washington. Chef Christian Graves favors fresh, light fare, using
★　sustainably raised seafood such as the tarragon and Dijon mussels and seared albacore with avocado puree. Nonseafood options include vegetarian butternut squash ravioli, chicken and dumplings, and pork chop with apple-brandy butter sauce. The cheeses, salami, and house-made pickles are excellent. Desserts are made with equal care, and the bar boasts cocktails made with seasonal fruit. The eclectic decor includes blown-glass pendant lights, a series of culinary paintings by a local artist, and a dramatically backlighted bar. ✉ *616 J St., Gaslamp Quarter* ☎ *619/531–8744* ⊕ *www.jsixrestaurant.com* ✛ *H3.*

2

$$$ ╳ **Oceanaire Seafood Room.** Engineered to recall an ocean liner from
SEAFOOD   the 1940s, Oceanaire is a bit put-on but admirable for the long bar
serving classic cocktails, oysters, and sashimi, and a carefully prepared
menu of up to 25 daily "fresh catches," with many specialties ranging
from convincing Maryland crab cakes and oysters Rockefeller to richly
stuffed California sole, a luxurious one-pound pork chop, and irresist-
ible hash brown potatoes. Executive chef Sean Langlais creates a daily
menu that may include the deliciously hot, spice-fired "angry" pink
snapper. Service is a casual thing in San Diego, which makes the pro-
fessional staff here all the more notable. ⊠ *400 J St., Gaslamp Quarter*
🕾 *619/858–2277* ⊕ *www.theoceanaire.com* ☽ *No lunch* ⊹ *H3.*

$$ ╳ **Searsucker.** The much-hyped first restaurant of *Top Chef* finalist Brian
AMERICAN Malarkey opened in summer 2010 in the middle of the Gaslamp Quar-
ter. Since then it has maintained its buzz, attracting patrons with its fun
urban decor and experimental dishes like swordfish with drunken cherries and beef cheeks over goat cheese dumplings. The flavor combinations are mostly successful, particularly when paired with comfort-food
sides like bacon grits and grilled asparagus. Chef Malarkey adds to the
lively vibe when he makes his rounds to chat with diners. ⊠ *611 5th*
Ave., Gaslamp Quarter 🕾 *619/233–7327* ⊕ *www.searsucker.com* ⊹ *H2.*

¢ ╳ **The Tin Fish.** On the rare rainy day, the staff takes it easy at this eatery
SEAFOOD   less than 100 yards from the PETCO Park baseball stadium (half of
its 100-odd seats are outdoors). Musicians entertain some evenings,
making this a lively spot for dinners of grilled and fried fish, as well as
seafood burritos and tacos. The quality here routinely surpasses that
at grander establishments. Service hours vary with the day of the week
and whether it's baseball season or not, but generally Tin Fish is open
from 11 am to 10 pm Sunday through Thursday and until midnight on
weekends. ⊠ *170 6th Ave., Gaslamp Quarter* 🕾 *619/238–8100* ⊕ *www.*
thetinfish.net ⬧ *Reservations not accepted* ⊹ *H3.*

LITTLE ITALY

$ ╳ **Buon Appetito.** This charmer serves old-world-style cooking in a casual
ITALIAN   but somewhat sophisticated environment. Choose a table on the breezy
sidewalk or in a room jammed with art and fellow diners. Baked eggplant *all'amalfitana*, in a mozzarella-topped tomato sauce, is a dream
of a dish (in San Diego, tomato sauce doesn't get better than this). Consider also sea bass in mushroom sauce, hearty seafood cioppino, and
expert osso buco paired with affordable and varied wines. The young
Italian waiters' good humor makes the experience fun. ⊠ *1609 India*
St., Little Italy 🕾 *619/238–9880* ⊹ *E5.*

$$ ╳ **Po Pazzo.** An eye-catching creation from leading Little Italy restaura-
ITALIAN   teurs Joe and Lisa Busalacchi, Po Pazzo earns its name, which means
"a little crazy," by mixing a lively bar with a restaurant serving mod-
ern Italian fare. A steak house with an accent, this stylish eatery offers
attractive salads and thick cuts of prime beef, as well as a top-notch
presentation of veal chops Sinatra style with mushrooms, tomatoes, and
onions; and Sicilian rib-eye steak that defines richness. ⊠ *1917 India*
St., Little Italy 🕾 *619/238–1917* ⊹ *E5.*

BEST BETS FOR SAN DIEGO DINING

With hundreds of restaurants to choose from, how will you decide where to eat? We've selected our favorite restaurants by price, cuisine, and experience in the Best Bets list below. In the first column, Fodor's Choice properties represent the "best of the best" in every price category. Bon appétit!

HOTEL DINING

Jsix, $$, p. 68
Nine-Ten, $$$, p. 76

OUTDOOR DINING

1500 Ocean, $$$$, p. 67
Café Chloe, $, p. 68
Osteria Romantica, $, p. 76

Fodor's Choice★

Bread & Cie, ¢, p. 71
Café Chloe, $, p. 68
Cucina Urbana, $, p. 71
George's at the Cove, $$$$, p. 76
Jsix, $$, p. 68
Nine-Ten, $$$, p. 76
Ortega's Bistro, $, p. 74
Sushi on the Rock, $, p. 77

Best By Price

¢

Bread & Cie, p. 71
El Zarape, p. 71

$

Café Chloe, p. 68
Cucina Urbana, p. 71
Ortega's Bistro, p. 74
Sushi on the Rock, p. 77

$$

Jsix, p. 68
Searsucker, p. 69
Sushi Ota, p. 75

$$$

Nine-Ten, p. 76

$$$$

1500 Ocean, p. 67
George's at the Cove, p. 76

Best By Cuisine

AMERICAN

Jsix, $$, p. 68
Nine-Ten, $$$, p. 76
Searsucker, $$, p. 69

ASIAN

Sushi on the Rock, $, p. 77
Sushi Ota, $$, p. 75

CAFÉS

Bread & Cie, ¢, p. 71
Café Chloe, $, p. 68

ITALIAN

Cucina Urbana, $, p. 71

LATIN/MEXICAN

El Zarape, ¢, p. 71
Ortega's Bistro, $, p. 74

PIZZA

Cucina Urbana, $, p. 71

SEAFOOD

Oceanaire Seafood Room, $$$, p. 69

Best By Experience

BRUNCH

Bread & Cie, ¢, p. 71
Café Chloe, $, p. 68
Nine-Ten, $$$, p. 76

BUSINESS MEALS

George's at the Cove, $$$$, p. 76
Oceanaire Seafood Room, $$$, p. 69

DINING WITH KIDS

Ortega's Bistro, $, p. 74
Rimel's Rotisserie, $, p. 76

GOOD FOR GROUPS

Oceanaire Seafood Room, $$$, p. 69

ROMANTIC

Chez Loma, $$$, p. 67
George's at the Cove, $$$$, p. 76
Whisk'n'ladle, $$, p. 77

SINGLES SCENE

JRDN at Tower 23, $$, p. 75
George's at the Cove, $$$$, p. 76
Oceanaire Seafood Room, $$$, p. 69

TRENDY

Jsix, $$, p. 68
Searsucker, $$, p. 69

WATER VIEWS

George's at the Cove, $$$$, p. 76
JRDN at Tower 23, $$, p. 75
Marine Room, $$$$, p. 76

WINE LISTS

1500 Ocean, $$$$, p. 67
George's at the Cove, $$$$, p. 76

UPTOWN

$ ✕ **Bombay Exotic Cuisine of India.** Notable for its elegant dining room
INDIAN   with a waterfall, Bombay employs a chef whose generous hand with
raw and cooked vegetables gives each course a colorful freshness reminiscent of California cuisine, though the flavors definitely hail from
India. Try the tandoori lettuce-wrap appetizer and any of the stuffed
kulchas (a stuffed flatbread). The unusually large selection of curries
may be ordered with meat, chicken, fish, or tofu. The curious should
try the *dizzy noo shak*, a sweet and spicy banana curry. Try the family-
style tasting menu, which includes appetizer, tasting portions of four
entrées, naan, and mango mousse dessert for $29 per person. ⊠ *Hill-
crest Center, 3960 5th Ave., Suite 100, Hillcrest* ☎ *619/297–7777*
⊕ *www.bombayrestaurant.com* ✛ *E4.*

¢   ✕ **Bread & Cie.** There's a brisk East Coast air to this artsy urban bakery
CAFÉ   and café known for being one of San Diego's first and best artisanal
Fodor'sChoice   bread bakers. Owner Charles Kaufman is a former New Yorker and
★   filmmaker, who gave Bread & Cie a sense of theater by putting bread
ovens imported from France on center stage. The mix served from
daybreak to sunset includes warm focaccia covered in cheese and vegetables, crusty loaves of black olive bread, gourmet granola with Mediterranean yogurt, bear claws, and first-rate cinnamon rolls. Lunch on
house-made quiche; paninis filled with pastrami, turkey, and pesto;
or Brie and honey, washed down with tea, coffee, upscale soft drinks,
beer, or wine. ⊠ *350 University Ave., Hillcrest* ☎ *619/683–9322* ✛ *E4.*

$ ✕ **Cucina Urbana.** Proprietor Tracy Borkum transformed the former Lau-
ITALIAN   rel into a casual and stylish Cal-Italian spot that's quickly become one
Fodor'sChoice   of the most popular tables in town. Weathered wood treatments, boho
★   floral tablecloths covered in butcher paper, and creamy vinyl barrel
chairs wrapped in burlap signal the sea change. Nothing on the dinner
menu is more than $20 and diners can pop into the retail wine room,
select a bottle, and drink it with dinner for just a $7 corkage fee. The
ricotta gnocchi bathed in brown butter and fried sage are the best yet;
fried squash blossoms sing; and polenta boards mixed tableside are
creative and satisfying. The best entrées include a pork Milanese with
artichoke salad, and short rib pappardelle. Sit at the cozy bar and watch
the chefs turn out bubbly, thin-crust pizzas topped with wild mushroom
and taleggio cheese or pancetta, fried egg, and potatoes, or find a spot
at the main bar for a clever cocktail crafted from seasonal fruit and Italian liqueurs. ⊠ *505 Laurel St., Banker's Hill* ☎ *619/239–2222* ⊕ *www.
sdurbankitchen.com* ⟡ *Reservations essential* ✛ *E5.*

¢   ✕ **El Zarape.** There's a humble air to this cozy Mexican taqueria, but
MEXICAN   one bite of the signature scallop tacos and you'll realize something special is happening in the kitchen. Inside the satiny corn tortilla, seared
bay scallops mingle with tangy white sauce and shredded cheese. Or
perhaps you'll prefer sweet pieces of lobster meat in oversize quesadillas; burritos filled with chiles rellenos; or the original beef, ham, and
pineapple Aloha burrito. No matter, nearly everything is fantastic at
this busy under-the-radar eatery that's part of a developing independent
restaurant row in University Heights. Mexican beverages, including the
sweet-tart hibiscus-flower drink *Jamaica* and the cinnamon rice drink

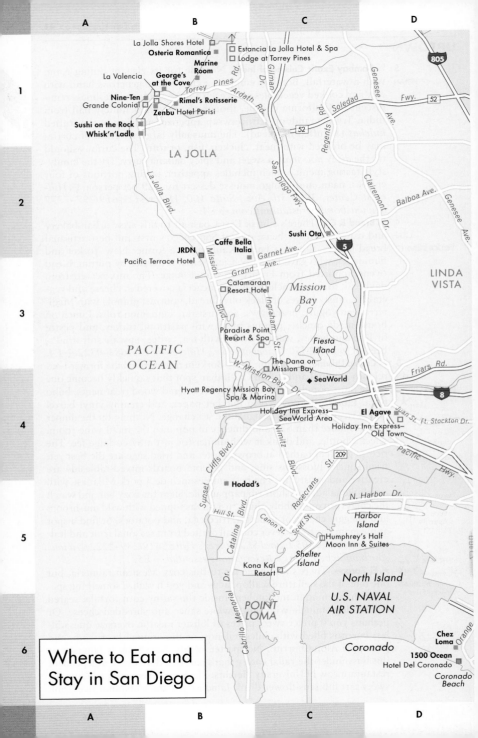

Where to Eat and Stay in San Diego

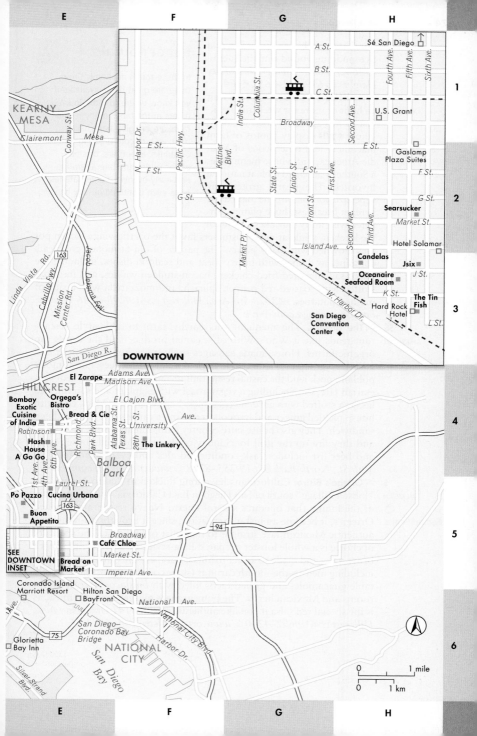

horchata, and house-made flan and rice pudding round out the menu. ✉ *4642 Park Blvd., University Heights* ☎ *619/692–1652* ✛ *E4.*

$ ✕ **Hash House A Go Go.** Expect to wait
AMERICAN   an hour or more for weekend breakfast at this splashy Hillcrest eatery, whose walls display photos of farm machinery and other icons of Middle America, but whose menu takes a Southern-accented look at national favorites. The nearly grotesquely supersize portions are the main draw here; at breakfast, huge platters carpeted with fluffy pancakes sail out of

the kitchen, while at noon customers favor the overflowing chicken pot pies crowned with flaky pastry. The parade of old-fashioned good eats continues at dinner with hearty meat and seafood dishes, including the grand sage-flavored fried chicken, bacon-studded waffles, and meatloaf stuffed with roasted red pepper, spinach, and mozzarella with a side of mashed potatoes. ✉ *3628 5th Ave., Hillcrest* ☎ *619/298–4646* ⊕ *www. hashhouseagogo.com* ✛ *E4.*

$$ ✕ **The Linkery.** The menu at this earthy farm-to-table-style restau-
AMERICAN   rant reads like a Who's Who of seasonal produce and the area's top organic farms. House-made sausages such as chicken-mushroom and *kaisekreiner* (spicy Vienna-style pork sausage with cheese) and smoky poblano pork lend the casual restaurant its name, but there's lots of vegetarian fare, too, including a vegan roast with eggplant and squash, and lasagna stuffed with garden vegetables. Entrées include black cod with house-pickled ginger and haricots verts, and a ranch-style ham-and-egg sandwich. They also house-cure country ham, Italian coppa, and lardo, and they fire up the grill for Sunday cookouts. The well-chosen wine and beer list includes cask-conditioned ales and even mead. ✉ *3794 30th St., North Park* ☎ *619/255–8778* ⊕ *www.thelinkery.com* ✛ *F4.*

$ ✕ **Ortega's Bistro.** Californians have long flocked to Puerto Nuevo, the
MEXICAN   "lobster village" south of San Diego in Baja California. When a member
☺   of the family that operates several Puerto Nuevo restaurants opened
Fodor's Choice   Ortega's, it became an instant sensation, since it brought no-nonsense,
★   authentic Mexican fare straight to the heart of Hillcrest. The specialty of choice is a whole lobster prepared Baja-style and served with superb beans, rice, and made-to-order tortillas, but there are other fine options, including melt-in-the-mouth carnitas (slow-cooked pork), made-at-the-table guacamole, and grilled tacos filled with *huitlacoche* corn mushrooms and Mexican herbs. The pomegranate margaritas are a must, as is the special red salsa if you like authentic spice. ✉ *141 University Ave., Hillcrest* ☎ *619/692–4200* ⊕ *www.ortegasbistro.com* ✛ *E4.*

BEACHES

$$
ITALIAN

✕ **Caffe Bella Italia.** Contemporary northern Italian cooking as prepared in Italy is the rule at this simple dinner-only restaurant near one of the main intersections in Pacific Beach. The menu presents Neapolitan-style macaroni with sausage and artichoke hearts in spicy tomato sauce, pizzas baked in a wood-fired oven, linguine with clams, mussels, white fish and salmon, plus formal entrées like chicken breast sautéed with Marsala wine and mushrooms and slices of rare filet mignon tossed with herbs and topped with arugula and Parmesan shavings. Impressive daily specials include beet-stuffed ravioli in creamy saffron sauce. ✉ *1525 Garnet Ave., Pacific Beach* ☎ *858/273–1224* ⊕ *www.caffebellaitalia. com* ⊗ *No lunch* ✛ *B2.*

¢
AMERICAN
☺

✕ **Hodad's.** No, it's not a flashback. The 1960s live on at this fabulously funky burger joint. Walls are covered with license plates, and the amiable servers with tattoos. Still, this is very much a family place, and Hodad's clientele often includes toddlers and octogenarians. Huge burgers are the thing, loaded with onions, pickles, tomatoes, lettuce, and condiments, and so gloriously messy that you might wear a swimsuit so you can stroll to the beach for a bath afterward. The minihamburger is good, the double bacon cheeseburger is breathtaking (and artery-clogging), as are the onion rings and seasoned potato wedges. ✉ *5010 Newport Ave., Point Loma* ☎ *619/224–4623* ✛ *B4.*

$$
AMERICAN

✕ **JRDN.** With some 300 seats, this ocean-facing restaurant, pronounced Jordan, in the beach-chic boutique-style Tower23 Hotel might seem overwhelming, but the seating is divided between a long, narrow outdoor terrace and a series of relatively intimate indoor rooms. Chef David Warner presents modern steakhouse fare including chops and steaks with sauces of the diner's choosing, lightened with lots of seasonal produce and a raw bar menu. Weekend brunch and lunch have a similar appeal, with dishes like blue-crab eggs Benedict with citrus hollandaise, eggplant panini sandwich, or a salad of smoked tri-tip over spinach and fingerling potatoes. On Friday and Saturday the bar is the place to see and be seen in Pacific Beach for under-30 types, and it's jammed after 9. Just note that the hotel only serves breakfast to guests during the week. ✉ *723 Felspar St., Pacific Beach* ☎ *858/270–5736* ✛ *B3.*

$$
JAPANESE

✕ **Sushi Ota.** Wedged into a minimall between a convenience store and a looming medical building, Sushi Ota initially seems less than auspicious. Still, San Diego–bound Japanese businesspeople frequently call for reservations before boarding their trans-Pacific flights. Look closely at the expressions on customers' faces as they stream in and out of the doors, and you can see the eager anticipation and satisfied glows that are products of San Diego's best sushi. Besides the usual California roll and tuna and shrimp sushi, sample the specialties that change daily such as sea urchin or surf clam sushi, and the soft-shell crab roll or the *omakase* tasting menu. Sushi Ota offers the cooked as well as the raw. There's additional parking behind the mall. It's hard not to notice that Japanese speakers get the best spots, and servers can be abrupt. ✉ *4529 Mission Bay Dr., Pacific Beach* ☎ *858/270–5670* ⊕ *www.sushiotamenu. info* ⌂ *Reservations essential* ⊗ *No lunch Sat.–Mon.* ✛ *C2.*

LA JOLLA

$$$$
AMERICAN
Fodor's Choice
★

✕ **George's at the Cove.** An extensive makeover brought an updated look to this eternally popular restaurant overlooking La Jolla Cove. Hollywood types and other visiting celebrities can be spotted in George's California Modern, the sleek main dining room with its wall of windows. Simpler, more casual preparations of fresh seafood, beef, and lamb reign on the new menu chef Trey Foshee enlivened with seasonal produce from local specialty growers. Give special consideration to succulent roasted chicken with escarole, local swordfish with prosciutto-wrapped gnocchi, and cider-glazed Niman Ranch pork chops. For more informal dining and a sweeping view of the coast, try the rooftop Ocean Terrace. ✉ *1250 Prospect St., La Jolla* ☎ *858/454–4244* ⊕ *www. georgesatthecove.com* ⌕ *Reservations essential* ✛ *B1.*

$$$$
FRENCH

✕ **Marine Room.** Gaze at the ocean from this venerable La Jolla Shores mainstay and, if it's during an especially high tide, feel the waves race across the sand and beat against the glass. Long-running chef Bernard Guillas takes a bold approach to combining ingredients. Creative seasonal menus score with "trilogy" plates that combine three meats, sometimes including game, in distinct preparations. Exotic ingredients show up in a variety of dishes, including Bengali cashew-spiced prawns, sesame-peppered ahi tuna, and a rack of lamb with violet mustard. ✉ *2000 Spindrift Dr., La Jolla* ☎ *866/644–2351* ⊕ *www.marineroom.com* ✛ *B1.*

$$$
AMERICAN
Fodor's Choice
★

✕ **Nine-Ten.** Many years ago, the elegant Grande Colonial Hotel in the heart of La Jolla "village" housed a drugstore owned by actor Gregory Peck's father. In the sleekly contemporary dining room that now occupies the space, acclaimed chef Jason Knibb serves satisfying seasonal fare at breakfast, lunch, and dinner. At night the perfectly executed menu may include tantalizing appetizers like Jamaican jerk pork belly or lamb sugo. The kitchen's creative flair comes through with dishes such as duck breast with pickled Swiss chard and ginger, and short ribs with smoked shiitake mushroom puree. Delicious desserts include spiced crumb cake with butternut ice cream and caramelized bacon. ✉ *910 Prospect St., La Jolla* ☎ *858/964–5400* ⊕ *www.nine-ten.com* ✛ *B1.*

$
ITALIAN

✕ **Osteria Romantica.** The name means "Romantic Inn," and with a sunny location a few blocks from the beach in La Jolla Shores, the look suggests a trattoria in Positano. The kitchen's wonderfully light hand shows up in the tomato sauce that finishes the scampi and other dishes, and in the pleasing Romantica salad garnished with figs and walnuts. Savory pasta choices include lobster-filled *mezzelune* (half moons) in saffron sauce, and wonderfully rich spaghetti *alla carbonara*. The breaded veal cutlets crowned with chopped arugula and tomatoes is a worthy main course. The warm, informal service suits the neighborhood. ✉ *2151 Ave. de la Playa, La Jolla* ☎ *858/551–1221* ⊕ *www. osteriaromantica.com* ✛ *B1.*

$
AMERICAN
☾

✕ **Rimel's Rotisserie.** An affordable option in often-pricey La Jolla, this comfy spot sometimes serves seafood caught that morning by fishermen who work for the owner. Other than market-priced "fresh catches" and the $25 grass-fed filet mignon from the owner's Home Grown meat shop, most items come in under $12, such as grilled mahimahi tacos (served with rice, beans, and a powerful green chili-garlic salsa),

The quality of the food complements the spectacular views at George's at the Cove.

grain-fed chicken grilled on a mesquite-fire rotisserie, and "steaming rice bowls" that actually are plates spread with jasmine rice, wok-cooked vegetables, and grilled seafood with a variety of vegetables. This is one of La Jolla's better choices for families. ✉ *1030 Torrey Pines Rd., La Jolla* ☎ *858/454–6045* ⊕ *www.rimelsrestaurants.com* ✢ *B1.*

$
JAPANESE
Fodor's Choice
★

✕ **Sushi on the Rock.** This popular California-style sushi spot now operates just from its newest location, which boasts a patio with an ocean view. The restaurant opens at 11:30 am daily, though it gets busy around 5 with people wanting to nail a seat for the daily happy hour from 5 to 6:30 pm. There's something fun about Sushi on the Rock, from the young friendly sushi chefs to the comically named specialties, like the Slippery When Wet roll featuring tempura shrimp, eel, crab, and cucumber. Loads of original rolls include the Barrio Roll stuffed with fried white fish and spicy tomato salsa, the Ashley Roll that pairs seared tuna with soft-shell crab and tangy whole-grain mustard sauce, and the Bruce Lee with spicy crab, tuna, and avocado. Also try the Japanese-inspired dishes including pot stickers, Asian-style Caesar salad, and lobster mac-and-cheese. ✉ *1025 Prospect St., La Jolla* ☎ *858/459–3208* ⊕ *www.sushiontherock.com* ✍ *Reservations not accepted* ✢ *B1.*

$$
SEAFOOD

✕ **Whisk'n'ladle.** Whisk'n'ladle has earned national acclaim with its combination of casual comfort and a menu of ever-changing local fare. Appetizers include dishes like warm spinach salad with grilled butternut squash and seared scallops with caramelized endive. Larger plates feature black ink risotto and wild steelhead trout with Moroccan spices. By all means request a patio table when reserving at this hip, popular eatery that doubles as a fashion show of some of La Jolla's ladies who lunch. And the bar is worth a visit, too, with its original menu of cocktails like the tamarind margarita, passion-fruit vanilla mimosa, and pomegranate mojito. ⊠ *1044 Wall St., La Jolla* ☎ *858/551–7575* ⊕ *www.whisknladle.com* ✢ *B1.*

$$ ✕ **Zenbu.** There's a cool California vibe to this cozy, moodily lighted
ASIAN sushi-and-seafood restaurant that serves some of the freshest fish in town and attracts a Who's Who of La Jolla. Restaurateur Matt Rimel runs a commercial fishing company and uses his connections to bring varied seafood from all over the world that excels, whether raw or cooked. Seasonal specialties include buttery *otoro* tuna belly and local sea urchin fresh from its spiny shell. Sushi, which can be pricey, ranges from simple nigiri to beautiful sashimi plates and original rolls like Salmon Spider, which combines soft-shell crab with fresh salmon. Cooked dishes run from noodle bowls and grass-fed Montana prime sirloin seared at the table on a hot stone, to whole fried rockfish or spicy "dynamite" lobster. ⊠ *7660 Fay Ave., La Jolla* ☎ *858/454–4540* ⊕ *www.rimelsrestaurants.com* ☾ *No lunch* ✢ *B1.*

OLD TOWN

$$$ ✕ **El Agave.** A Mexico City native brings authentic regional Mexican fare
MEXICAN to an otherwise touristy area. Be sure to try quesadillas filled with mushrooms and manchego cheese; grilled shrimp bathed in bright, smoky guajillo chili sauce; and chicken in a slow-simmered mole sauce. Try one of the more than 2,000 tequilas, which make El Agave the largest "tequileria" in the United States. The collection includes artisanal tequilas dating to the 1930s and some infused with jalapeño chilies. ⊠ *2304 San Diego Ave., Old Town* ☎ *619/220–0692* ⊕ *www.elagave. com* ✢ *D4.*

WHERE TO STAY

When you make reservations, ask about specials. Many hotels promote discounted weekend packages to fill rooms after convention and business customers leave town. Since the weather is great year-round, don't expect substantial discounts in winter. That being said, you can find affordable rooms in even the most expensive areas. If an ocean view is important, request it when booking, but be aware that it will cost significantly more. You can save on hotels and attractions by visiting the San Diego Convention & Visitors Bureau Web site (⊕ *www.sandiego.org*) for a free Vacation Planning Kit with a Travel Value Coupon booklet.

Use the coordinate (✢ A1) at the end of each listing to locate a site on the corresponding map.

WHAT IT COSTS				
¢	**$**	**$$**	**$$$**	**$$$$**
Hotels	under $100	$100–$200	$201–$300	$301–$400	over $400

Prices are for a standard double room in high (summer) season, excluding 10.5% tax.

CORONADO

For expanded reviews, visit Fodors.com.

$$$ ⚙ **Coronado Island Marriott Resort.** Near San Diego Bay, this snazzy hotel
☾ has rooms with great Downtown skyline views. **Pros:** spectacular views;
on-site spa; close to water taxis. **Cons:** not in downtown Coronado;
difficult to find. ✉ *2000 2nd St., Coronado* ☎ *619/435–3000, 800/543–
4300* ⊕ *www.marriotthotels.com/sanci* ⇆ *273 rooms, 27 suites* ⚿ *In-
room: a/c, Wi-Fi. In-hotel: restaurant, bar, pool, tennis court, gym, spa,
water sports, parking* ✛ *E6.*

$$$ ⚙ **Glorietta Bay Inn.** The main building on this property is an Edward-
ian-style mansion built in 1908 for sugar baron John D. Spreckels.
Pros: great views; friendly staff; close to beach. **Cons:** mansion rooms
are small; lots of traffic nearby. ✉ *1630 Glorietta Blvd., Coronado*
☎ *619/435–3101, 800/283–9383* ⊕ *www.gloriettabayinn.com* ⇆ *100
rooms* ⚿ *In-room: a/c, kitchen, Wi-Fi. In-hotel: pool, parking* ✛ *E6.*

$$$ ⚙ **Hotel Del Coronado.** The Victorian-styled "Hotel Del," situated along
☾ 28 oceanfront acres, is as much of a draw today as it was when it
Fodor's Choice opened in 1888. **Pros:** romantic; on the beach; hotel spa. **Cons:** some
★ rooms are small; expensive dining; public areas are very busy. ✉ *1500
Orange Ave., Coronado* ☎ *800/468–3533, 619/435–6611* ⊕ *www.
hoteldel.com* ⇆ *757 rooms, 65 suites, 43 villas, 35 cottages* ⚿ *In-room:
a/c, Wi-Fi. In-hotel: restaurant, bar, pool, gym, spa, beach, water sports,
children's programs, business center, parking* ✛ *D6.*

DOWNTOWN

For expanded reviews, visit Fodors.com.

$ ⚙ **Gaslamp Plaza Suites.** On the National Register of Historic Places,
this 10-story structure a block from Horton Plaza was built in 1913
as one of San Diego's first "skyscrapers." **Pros:** historic building; good
location; well priced. **Cons:** books up early; smallish rooms. ✉ *520
E St., Gaslamp Quarter* ☎ *619/232–9500, 800/874–8770* ⊕ *www.
gaslampplaza.com* ⇆ *12 rooms, 52 suites* ⚿ *In-room: a/c, Wi-Fi. In-
hotel: bar, parking* ⓞ*Breakfast* ✛ *H2.*

$$$ ⚙ **Hard Rock Hotel.** Self-billed as a hip playground for rock stars and
Fodor's Choice people who just want to party like them, the Hard Rock Hotel is con-
★ veniently located near PETCO Park overlooking glimmering San Diego
Bay. **Pros:** central location; great scene; luxurious rooms. **Cons:** pricey
drinks; some attitude. ✉ *207 5th Ave., Gaslamp Quarter* ☎ *619/702–
3000, 866/751–7625* ⊕ *www.hardrockhotelsd.com* ⇆ *244 rooms, 176
suites* ⚿ *In-room: a/c, Internet, Wi-Fi. In-hotel: restaurant, bar, pool,
gym, spa, business center, parking* ✛ *H3.*

$$ ⚙ **Hilton San Diego Bayfront.** This modern 30-story hotel overlooking San
Diego Bay isn't a typical Hilton. **Pros:** close to the convention center;
new rooms. **Cons:** awkward layout; pricey drinks. ✉ *1 Park Blvd.,
Downtown* ☎ *619/564–3333* ⊕ *www.hiltonsdbayfront.com* ⇆ *1,160
rooms, 30 suites* ⚿ *In-room: a/c, Wi-Fi. In-hotel: restaurant, bar, pool,
gym, spa, parking, some pets allowed* ✛ *E5.*

BEST BETS FOR SAN DIEGO LODGING

Fodor's offers a selective listing of quality lodging experiences. Here we've compiled our top recommendations. The very best properties—in other words, those that provide a particularly remarkable experience in their price range—are designated in the listings with a Fodor's Choice logo.

Fodor's Choice★

Catamaran Resort Hotel, $$$, p. 84

Grande Colonial, $$, p. 83

Hard Rock Hotel, $$$, p. 79

Hotel Del Coronado, $$$, p. 79

Hotel Solamar, $$, p. 81

Lodge at Torrey Pines, $$$$, p. 83

Best By Price

$

The Dana on Mission Bay, p. 84

$$

Grande Colonial, p. 83

Hotel Solamar, p. 81

$$$

Catamaran Resort Hotel, p. 84

Hard Rock Hotel, p. 79

Hotel Del Coronado, p. 79

Pacific Terrace Hotel, p. 84

Paradise Point Resort & Spa, p. 84

$$$$

La Valencia, p. 83

Lodge at Torrey Pines, p. 83

Best By Experience

BEST BEACH

Catamaran Resort Hotel, $$$, p. 84

Hotel Del Coronado, $$$, p. 79

La Jolla Shores Hotel, $$$, p. 83

Paradise Point Resort & Spa, $$$, p. 84

BEST POOL

Hotel Solamar, $$, p. 81

Hyatt Regency Mission Bay Spa & Marina, $$$, p. 84

La Valencia, $$$$, p. 83

BEST FOR ROMANCE

Hotel Del Coronado, $$$, p. 79

Hotel Parisi, $$, p. 83

Hotel Solamar, $$, p. 81

The Lodge at Torrey Pines, $$$$, p. 83

BEST SPA

Estancia La Jolla Hotel & Spa, $$, p. 83

Sè San Diego, $$, p. 81

BEST VIEWS

Hilton San Diego Bayfront, $$, p. 79

Hyatt Regency Mission Bay Spa & Marina, $$$, p. 84

MOST TRENDY

Sè San Diego, $$, p. 81

$$ **Fodor's Choice** ★ ⌂ **Hotel Solamar.** For its first entry onto San Diego's hotel scene, the Kimpton boutique hotel chain renovated an old warehouse, hitting the right notes with striking, high style. **Pros:** great restaurant; attentive service; upscale rooms. **Cons:** busy valet parking; bars are crowded on weekends. ⊠ *435 6th Ave., Gaslamp Quarter* ☎ *619/531–8740, 877/230–0300* ⊕ *www.hotelsolamar.com* ⇌ *217 rooms, 16 suites* ⅏ *In-room: a/c, Wi-Fi. In-hotel: restaurant, bar, pool, gym, parking, some pets allowed* ✛ *H3.*

> **BUDGET LODGING**
>
> When booking your hotel, it pays to make reservations directly with the property—you'll often get the best rate.

$$ ⌂ **Sè San Diego.** This Dodd Mitchell–designed hotel sets a new standard for luxury digs in San Diego. **Pros:** new rooms; centrally located; luxury amenities. **Cons:** expensive parking; sliding glass doors in bathrooms provide limited privacy. ⊠ *1047 5th Ave., Downtown* ☎ *619/515–3000* ⊕ *www.sesandiego.com* ⇌ *181 rooms, 37 suites, 20 condos, 3 penthouses* ⅏ *In-room: a/c, Wi-Fi. In-hotel: restaurant, bar, pool, gym, spa, parking, some pets allowed* ✛ *H1.*

$$ ⌂ **U.S. Grant.** Stepping into the regal U.S. Grant not only puts you in the lap of luxury, but also back into San Diego history; the 100-year-old building is on the National Register of Historic Sites. **Pros:** modern rooms; great location; near shopping and restaurants. **Cons:** small elevators; the hotel's many special events can make for a hectic atmosphere. ⊠ *326 Broadway, Downtown* ☎ *619/232–3121, 800/237–5029* ⊕ *www.luxurycollection.com/usgrant* ⇌ *270 rooms, 47 suites* ⅏ *In-room: a/c, Internet, Wi-Fi. In-hotel: restaurant, bar, gym, parking* ✛ *H1.*

HARBOR ISLAND, SHELTER ISLAND, AND POINT LOMA

For expanded reviews, visit Fodors.com.

$ ⌂ **Holiday Inn Express–SeaWorld Area.** In Point Loma near the West Mission Bay exit off I–8, this is a surprisingly cute and quiet lodging option despite proximity to bustling traffic. **Pros:** near SeaWorld; free breakfast; good service. **Cons:** not a scenic area; somewhat hard to find. ⊠ *3950 Jupiter St., Point Loma* ☎ *619/226–8000, 800/320–0208* ⊕ *www.seaworldhi.com* ⇌ *69 rooms, 2 suites* ⅏ *In-room: a/c, Wi-Fi. In-hotel: pool, laundry facilities, parking* ⅋ *Breakfast* ✛ *C4.*

$$ ⌂ **Humphrey's Half Moon Inn & Suites.** This sprawling South Seas–style resort has grassy open areas with palms and tiki torches. **Pros:** water views; near marina; nightlife on property. **Cons:** vast property; not centrally located. ⊠ *2303 Shelter Island Dr., Shelter Island* ☎ *619/224–3411, 800/542–7400* ⊕ *www.halfmooninn.com* ⇌ *128 rooms, 54 suites* ⅏ *In-room: a/c, kitchen, Wi-Fi. In-hotel: restaurant, bar, pool, gym, laundry facilities, business center, parking* ✛ *C5.*

$$ ⌂ **Kona Kai Resort.** This 11-acre property blends Spanish and Mediterranean styles. **Pros:** quiet area; near marina; water views. **Cons:** not centrally located; small rooms. ⊠ *1551 Shelter Island Dr., Shelter Island* ☎ *619/221–8000, 800/566–2524* ⊕ *www.resortkonakai.com* ⇌ *124 rooms, 5 suites* ⅏ *In-room: a/c, Wi-Fi. In-hotel: restaurant, bar, pool, gym, spa, beach, parking* ✛ *C5.*

Hotel Del Coronado

Hard Rock Hotel

OLD TOWN AND VICINITY

For expanded reviews, visit Fodors.com.

$ ⊞ **Holiday Inn Express–Old Town.** Already an excellent value for Old Town, this cheerful property throws in such perks as a free breakfast buffet. **Pros:** good location; hot Continental breakfast. **Cons:** smallish rooms; few nightlife options. ⊠ *3900 Old Town Ave., Old Town* ☎ *619/299–7400, 800/465–4329* ⊕ *www.hioldtownhotel.com* ⤳ *125 rooms, 2 suites* ♿ *In-room: a/c, Internet, Wi-Fi. In-hotel: pool, laundry facilities, parking* ⧓ *Breakfast* ✛ *D4.*

LA JOLLA

For expanded reviews, visit Fodors.com.

$$ ⊞ **Estancia La Jolla Hotel & Spa.** La Jolla's newest resort was once the site of a famous equestrian ranch, Blackhorse Farms, where Thoroughbreds were trained. **Pros:** upscale rooms; nice spa; landscaped grounds. **Cons:** spotty service; not centrally located. ⊠ *9700 N. Torrey Pines Rd., La Jolla* ☎ *858/550–1000, 877/437–8262* ⊕ *www.estancialajolla.com* ⤳ *200 rooms, 10 suites* ♿ *In-room: a/c, Wi-Fi. In-hotel: restaurant, bar, pool, gym, spa, parking* ⧓ *Breakfast* ✛ *B1.*

$$ ⊞ **Grande Colonial.** This white wedding cake–style hotel has ocean views
Fodor'sChoice and is in the heart of La Jolla village. **Pros:** near shopping; near beach;
★ superb restaurant. **Cons:** somewhat busy street. ⊠ *910 Prospect St., La Jolla* ☎ *858/454–2181, 800/826–1278* ⊕ *www.thegrandecolonial. com* ⤳ *52 rooms, 41 suites* ♿ *In-room: a/c, kitchen, Wi-Fi. In-hotel: restaurant, bar, pool, parking* ✛ *A1.*

$$ ⊞ **Hotel Parisi.** A Zen-like peace welcomes you in the lobby, which has a skylighted fountain and is filled with Asian art. **Pros:** upscale amenities; modern decor; centrally located. **Cons:** one-room "suites"; staff can be aloof. ⊠ *1111 Prospect St., La Jolla* ☎ *858/454–1511* ⊕ *www. hotelparisi.com* ⤳ *29 suites* ♿ *In-room: a/c, Wi-Fi. In-hotel: parking* ⧓ *Breakfast* ✛ *B1.*

$$$ ⊞ **La Jolla Shores Hotel.** One of the few San Diego hotels actually on the
☺ beach, La Jolla Shores is located at La Jolla Beach and Tennis Club. **Pros:** on beach; great views; quiet area. **Cons:** not centrally located; unrenovated rooms are dated. ⊠ *8110 Camino del Oro, La Jolla* ☎ *619/567–4601, 877/346–6714* ⊕ *www.ljshoreshotel.com* ⤳ *127 rooms, 1 suite* ♿ *In-room: a/c, kitchen, Internet. In-hotel: restaurant, bar, pool, tennis court, gym, beach, laundry facilities, parking* ✛ *B1.*

$$$$ ⊞ **La Valencia.** This pink Spanish-Mediterranean confection drew Hollywood film stars in the 1930s and '40s with its setting and views of La Jolla Cove. **Pros:** upscale rooms; views; near beach. **Cons:** expensive; lots of traffic outside. ⊠ *1132 Prospect St., La Jolla* ☎ *858/454–0771, 800/451–0772* ⊕ *www.lavalencia.com* ⤳ *82 rooms, 16 villas, 15 suites* ♿ *In-room: a/c, Wi-Fi. In-hotel: restaurant, bar, pool, gym, parking* ✛ *B1.*

$$$$ ⊞ **Lodge at Torrey Pines.** This beautiful Craftsman-style lodge sits on a
Fodor'sChoice bluff between La Jolla and Del Mar and commands a coastal view. **Pros:**
★ upscale rooms; good service; near golf. **Cons:** not centrally located; expensive. ⊠ *11480 N. Torrey Pines Rd., La Jolla* ☎ *858/453–4420,*

800/995–4507 ⊕ *www.lodgetorreypines.com* ⤴*164 rooms, 6 suites* ⅾ *In-room: a/c, kitchen, Internet, Wi-Fi. In-hotel: restaurant, bar, golf course, pool, gym, spa, parking* ✛ *B1.*

MISSION BAY AND THE BEACHES

For expanded reviews, visit Fodors.com.

$$$ 🖭 **Catamaran Resort Hotel.** Exotic macaws perch in the lush lobby of this
☾ appealing hotel on Mission Bay. **Pros:** recently upgraded rooms; spa;
Fodor'sChoice free cruises. **Cons:** not centrally located. ⊠ *3999 Mission Blvd., Mission*
★ *Beach* 🖀 *858/488–1081, 800/422–8386* ⊕ *www.catamaranresort.com*
⤴ *311 rooms, 50 suites* ⅾ *In-room: a/c, kitchen, Internet, Wi-Fi. In-
hotel: restaurant, bar, pool, gym, spa, beach, parking* ✛ *B3.*

$ 🖭 **The Dana on Mission Bay.** There's a modern chic feel to the earth-tone
lobby of this beach hotel, making it feel you've arrived somewhere
much more expensive. **Pros:** water views; two pools. **Cons:** slightly
confusing layout; not centrally located. ⊠ *1710 W. Mission Bay Dr.,
Mission Bay* 🖀 *619/222–6440, 800/445–3339* ⊕ *www.thedana.com*
⤴ *259 rooms, 12 suites* ⅾ *In-room: a/c, Wi-Fi. In-hotel: restaurant,
bar, pool, parking* ✛ *C3.*

$$$ 🖭 **Hyatt Regency Mission Bay Spa & Marina.** This modern and stunning
☾ property has many desirable amenities, including balconies with excel-
lent views of the garden, bay, ocean, or swimming pool courtyard (pools
have 120-foot waterslides, plus a smaller slide on the kiddie pool).
Pros: modern decor; eco-spa; water views. **Cons:** slightly hard to navigate surrounding roads; thin walls; not centrally located. ⊠ *1441 Quivira Rd., Mission Bay* 🖀 *619/224–1234, 800/233–1234* ⊕ *www.hyatt.
com* ⤴ *354 rooms, 76 suites* ⅾ *In-room: a/c, Internet, Wi-Fi. In-hotel:
restaurant, bar, pool, gym, spa, children's programs, business center,
parking* ✛ *C3.*

$$$ 🖭 **Pacific Terrace Hotel.** Travelers love this terrific beachfront hotel and
the ocean views from most rooms; it's a perfect place for watching
sunsets over the Pacific. **Pros:** beach views; large rooms; friendly ser-
vice. **Cons:** busy area; lots of traffic. ⊠ *610 Diamond St., Pacific Beach*
🖀 *858/581–3500, 800/344–3370* ⊕ *www.pacificterrace.com* ⤴ *61
rooms, 12 suites* ⅾ *In-room: a/c, Wi-Fi. In-hotel: pool, gym, laundry
facilities, parking* ❍*Breakfast* ✛ *B3.*

$$$ 🖭 **Paradise Point Resort & Spa.** The beautiful landscape of this 44-acre
☾ resort on Vacation Isle has been the setting for a number of movies.
Pros: water views; pools; good service. **Cons:** not centrally located;
summer minimum stays; motel-thin walls. ⊠ *1404 Vacation Rd., Mission Bay* 🖀 *858/274–4630, 800/344–2626* ⊕ *www.paradisepoint.com*
⤴ *462 cottages* ⅾ *In-room: a/c, Internet. In-hotel: restaurant, bar, pool,
tennis court, gym, spa, beach, parking* ✛ *C3.*

Lodge at Torrey Pines

Hotel Solamar

Hotel Solamar

Grande Colonial

Catamaran Resort Hotel and Spa

NIGHTLIFE AND THE ARTS

Downtown is the obvious neighborhood for party animals of all ages. Its streets are lined with sleek lounges, massive nightclubs, and quirky dive bars. The Gaslamp Quarter is party central, with the most bars and clubs located on its 16-block stretch. The late-night commotion is spreading to East Village, the area surrounding PETCO Park. A few neighborhoods on the outskirts of Downtown—Golden Hill, Hillcrest, and North and South Park, in particular—offer plenty of hip underground treasures for intrepid visitors.

The beach areas tend to cater to the casual and collegiate, though certain haunts have their share of former flower children and grizzled bikers. Hillcrest is the heart of San Diego's gay community, and home to loads of gay-popular bars. Coffeehouses are another important element of San Diego nightlife culture, especially for the under-21 set. Singer Jewel got her start in local coffee shops, and plenty of other acts have launched to fame from an active area music scene, including pop-punkers Blink-182 and Grammy-winning gospel group Nickel Creek. Locals rely on alt-weeklies like the *Reader* and *San Diego CityBeat*, as well as glossy monthlies like *San Diego* and *Riviera* magazines for nightlife info. You can't buy booze after 2 am, which means last call is around 1:30. Smoking is only allowed outside, and even then it can be tricky. And be sure to hail a taxi if you've tied one on—drunk driving laws in California are stringent. ■TIP→ All of San Diego's trendiest, flashiest, busiest clubs and bars have dress codes and require identification. Call ahead for details.

NIGHTLIFE

CASUAL BARS AND PUBS

LITTLE ITALY
Fodor'sChoice
★

The Waterfront. It isn't actually *on* the waterfront, but this was once the gathering spot for the Italian fishermen who used to live in the area. Now a local landmark, San Diego's oldest bar actually had an apartment building constructed around it rather than be torn down. It's also famous for its burgers, and it's still the hangout of some working-class heroes, even if most of the collars are now white. There's live jazz and blues many evenings. ✉ *2044 Kettner Blvd., Little Italy* ☎ *619/232–9656.*

COFFEEHOUSES

★

Brockton Villa Restaurant. This charming café overlooking La Jolla Cove has indoor and outdoor seating, as well as scrumptious desserts and coffee drinks; the beans are roasted in San Diego. It closes at 9 most nights. ✉ *1235 Coast Blvd., La Jolla* ☎ *858/454–7393.*

Fodor'sChoice
★

Extraordinary Desserts. This café lives up to its name, which explains why there's often a line here, even though it has ample seating. Paris-trained Karen Krasne turns out award-winning cakes, tortes, and pastries of exceptional beauty (many are decorated with fresh flowers). The Japanese-theme patio invites you to linger over yet another coffee drink. There is a second location in Little Italy. ✉ *2929 5th Ave., Hillcrest* ☎ *619/294–2132.*

CLOSE UP

Craft Beer Capital

San Diego claims to be the craft beer–making capital of the planet. What exactly *is* a craft beer? The term can include brews from small family-operated breweries—where you might get something different every time you go in for a sip of suds—to some fairly large, commercial operations that turn out standard (although still not mainstream) brews. Most craft brewmeisters started out as home beer makers, and the beer produced for sale reflects abundant creativity (and sometimes outright experimentation) in the use of grain, hops, and other things that go into a great glass of beer.

The brew culture continues to grow in San Diego, and enthusiasts are noticing. Escondido-based **Stone Brewing** (⊕ *www.stonebrew.com*) was declared the best brewery on the planet by readers of *Beer Advocate* magazine in 2009, and other San Diego breweries on the list are AleSmith (⊕ *www. alesmith.com*) and **O-Brien's Pub** (⊕ *www.obrienspub.net*) in Kearny Mesa. The largest and oldest of the San Diego craft brewers is **Karl Strauss Brewing** (⊕ *www.karlstrauss. com*), which operates a number of brew-pubs in the region.

So if you're looking for a cold one, you've come to the right place.

DANCE CLUBS

GASLAMP
QUARTER

★ **Ivy Nightclub.** A cavernous downstairs space with a decidedly naughty feel, this big-money, multilevel dance club in the Andaz San Diego hotel is one of the few places in town where you can bump and grind with sports stars and visiting celebs. ⊠ *600 F St., Gaslamp Quarter* ☎ *619/814–1000.*

On Broadway. This huge club in a former bank building used to be the hottest destination in town, but looks more and more like a dinosaur as the Gaslamp evolves around it. Still, on Friday and Saturday nights—the only nights it's open—scantily clad twentysomethings wait in a line that sometimes reaches around the block. Cover charges are steep and ordering drinks is a hassle, but the cool decor—marble floors, Greek columns, and original vault doors mixed with modern design elements—make it worth a visit, as do the computerized light shows, Leviathan sound system, and skilled DJs. ⊠ *615 Broadway, Gaslamp Quarter* ☎ *619/231–0011.*

★ **Stingaree.** In the posh Gaslamp Quarter, Stingaree occupies an old warehouse in the former red-light district. The owners spent approximately a gazillion dollars creating this smashing three-story space with translucent "floating" staircases and floor-to-ceiling water walls. There's a high-end restaurant and a dance club inside (the music tends to be of the Top 40 variety). Dress nicely—the air of exclusivity at this hangout is palpable, and to further prove the point, drinks are steep. ⊠ *454 6th Ave., at Island St., Gaslamp Quarter* ☎ *619/544–9500.*

GAY

Fodor's Choice
★
Baja Betty's. Although it draws plenty of gay customers, Baja Betty's is popular with just about everyone in the Hillcrest area. It's a low-key but elegant space with chandeliers and soft lighting, and it stocks more than 100 brands of tequila and mixes plenty of fancy cocktails. ⊠ *1421 University Ave., Hillcrest* ☎ *619/269–8510.*

Urban Mo's Bar and Grill. Mo's rounds up cowboys for line dancing and two-stepping on its wooden dance floor—but be forewarned, yee-haw-ers, it can get pretty wild on Western nights. There are also Latin, hip-hop, and drag revue, but the real allure is in the creative drinks ("Gone Fishing"—served in a fishbowl, for example) and the breezy patio where love (or something like it) is usually in the air. ⊠ *308 University Ave., Hillcrest* ☎ *619/491–0400.*

HIP LOUNGES AND TRENDY SINGLES BARS

Altitude Sky Lounge. This lounge, at the San Diego Marriott Gaslamp Quarter, occupies the hotel's 22nd-story rooftop. Location is everything—the views here (of the Downtown skyline and PETCO Park) will give you a natural high. ⊠ *660 K St., Gaslamp Quarter* ☎ *619/696–0234.*

Fodor's Choice
★
Ivy Rooftop and Ivy Nightclub. These two bars offer a chiller version of nightlife for Andaz San Diego visitors and hotel guests. Sink into a deep leather couch in the posh lobby Ivy Nightclub and Wine Bar or head to the spacious Ivy Rooftop, where you can swill cocktails poolside while gazing at gorgeous people or views of the city—both are abundant. ⊠ *600 F St., Gaslamp Quarter* ☎ *619/814–1000.*

★
JRDN. This contemporary lounge occupies the ground floor of Pacific Beach's chicest boutique hotel, Tower23. JRDN, pronounced "Jordan," captures both the laid-back personality of the neighborhood and the increasingly sophisticated sensibility of San Diego, with sleek walls of windows and an expansive patio overlooking the Pacific Beach boardwalk. ⊠ *723 Felspar St., Pacific Beach* ☎ *858/270–5736.*

JAZZ

Clay's La Jolla. Clay's is a new version of one of San Diego's most famous jazz venues, which closed in the mid-1990s, then returned five years later in a slightly different format. Perched on the top floor of the Hotel La Jolla, Clay's delivers an ocean view and a lineup of mostly jazz musicians (and the occasional small band) Thursday through Sunday. ⊠ *7955 La Jolla Shores Dr., La Jolla* ☎ *858/459–0541.*

Croce's. Restaurateur Ingrid Croce (widow of singer-songwriter Jim Croce) books superb acoustic-jazz musicians, among others, in this intimate dinner joint and jazz cave. Son A. J. Croce frequently performs here. ⊠ *802 5th Ave., Gaslamp Quarter* ☎ *619/233–4355.*

Humphrey's by the Bay. Surrounded by water, Humphrey's is the summer stomping ground of musicians such as the Cowboy Junkies and Chris Isaak. From June through September this dining and drinking oasis hosts the city's best outdoor jazz, folk, and light-rock concert series. The rest of the year the music moves indoors and with a lineup that includes first-rate jazz and blues. ⊠ *2241 Shelter Island Dr., Shelter Island* ☎ *619/224–3577.*

LIVE MUSIC CLUBS

Belly Up Tavern (✉ *143 S. Cedros Ave.* ☎ *858/481–8140* ⊕ *www. bellyup. com*), a fixture on local papers' "best of" lists, has been drawing crowds of all ages since it opened in the mid-'70s. The BUT's longevity attests to the quality of the eclectic entertainment on its stage. Within converted Quonset huts, critically acclaimed artists play everything from reggae and folk to—well, you name it.

Fodor'sChoice
★ **Casbah.** Near the airport, the Casbah is a small club with a national reputation for showcasing up-and-coming acts. Nirvana, Smashing Pumpkins, and the White Stripes all played the Casbah on their way to stardom. For more than two decades, it's been the unofficial head-quarters of the city's indie music scene. You can hear every type of band here—except those that sound like Top 40. ✉ *2501 Kettner Blvd., Middletown* ☎ *619/232–4355.*

★ **House of Blues.** This branch of the renowned chain of clubs is a cavernous space decorated floor to ceiling with colorful folk art from HOB's huge collection. There's something going on here just about every night of the week, and Sunday's gospel brunch is one of the most praiseworthy events in town. Can we get a hallelujah? ✉ *1055 5th Ave., Downtown* ☎ *619/299–2583.*

THE ARTS

Arts Tix. You can buy advance tickets, many at half price, to theater, music, and dance events at Arts Tix. ✉ *Horton Plaza, Gaslamp Quarter* ☎ *858/381–5595* ⊕ *www.sdartstix.com.*

DANCE

★ **California Ballet Company.** The company performs high-quality contemporary and classical works September–May. The *Nutcracker* is staged annually at the **Civic Theatre** ✉ *3rd Ave. and B St., Downtown.* Other ballets are presented at **Balboa Theatre** ✉ *868 4th Ave., Downtown* ☎ *619/570–1100, 858/560–6741.*

MUSIC

Fodor'sChoice
★ **Copley Symphony Hall.** The great acoustics here are surpassed only by the incredible Spanish baroque interior. Not just the home of the San Diego Symphony Orchestra, the renovated 2,200-seat 1920s-era theater has also hosted major stars like Elvis Costello and Sting. ✉ *750 B St., Downtown* ☎ *619/235–0804.*

La Jolla Music Society (☎ *858/459–3728*) presents internationally acclaimed chamber ensembles, orchestras, and soloists at Sherwood Auditorium, the Civic Theatre, Copley Symphony Hall, and the Stephen and Mary Birch North Park Theatre.

★ **San Diego Opera.** Drawing international artists, the opera's season runs January–April. Past performances have included *Die Fledermaus, Faust, Idomeneo,* and *La Bohème,* plus concerts by such talents as the late Luciano Pavarotti. ✉ *Civic Theatre, 3rd Ave. and B St., Downtown* ☎ *619/533–7000.*

San Diego Symphony Orchestra. The orchestra puts on special events year-round, including classical concerts and summer and winter pops. Nearly all concerts are held at Copley Symphony Hall; the Summer Pops series is held on the Embarcadero, beyond the San Diego Convention Center on North Harbor Drive. ⊠ *750 B St., Downtown* 🕾 *619/235–0804.*

★ **Spreckels Organ Pavilion.** This is the home of a giant outdoor pipe organ donated to the city in 1915 by sugar magnates John and Adolph Spreckels. The beautiful Spanish baroque pavilion hosts concerts by civic organist Carol Williams and guest organists on most Sunday afternoons and on most Monday evenings in summer. Local military bands, gospel groups, and barbershop quartets also perform here. All shows are free. ⊠ *Balboa Park* 🕾 *619/702–8138.*

THEATER

FodorsChoice **La Jolla Playhouse.** The playhouse crafts exciting and innovative produc-
★ tions under the artistic direction of Christopher Ashley, May through March. Many Broadway shows, such as *Tommy* and *Jersey Boys,* have previewed here before heading for the East Coast. The playhouse has three stages: the Mandell Weiss Theatre has the main stage, the Mandell Weiss Forum is a thrust stage, and the Sheila and Hughes Potiker Theatre is a black-box theater. ⊠ *University of California at San Diego, 2910 La Jolla Village Dr., La Jolla* 🕾 *858/550–1010.*

★ **Lamb's Players Theatre.** The theater's regular season of five productions runs from February through November. It also stages a musical, *Festival of Christmas,* in December. *An American Christmas* is the company's dinner-theater show at the Hotel Del Coronado. ⊠ *1142 Orange Ave., Coronado* 🕾 *619/437–0600.*

FodorsChoice **Old Globe Theatre.** The oldest professional theater in California presents
★ classics, contemporary dramas, and experimental works. The Globe has two sister theaters: the intimate Cassius Carter Centre Stage and the outdoor Lowell Davies Festival Theater. The Old Globe also mounts a popular Shakespeare Festival every summer at Lowell Davies. The recently opened Conrad Prebys Theatre Center merges the flagship Old Globe Theatre with a new, state-of-the-art multilevel facility. ⊠ *1363 Old Globe Way, Balboa Park* 🕾 *619/234–5623.*

Spreckels Theatre. A landmark theater erected in 1912, the Spreckels hosts comedy, dance, theater, and concerts. Good acoustics and old-time elegance make this a favorite local venue. ⊠ *121 Broadway, Downtown* 🕾 *619/235–9500.*

SPORTS AND THE OUTDOORS

BASEBALL

FodorsChoice Long a favorite spectator sport in San Diego, where games are rarely
★ rained out, baseball gained even more popularity in 2004 with the opening of PETCO Park, a stunning 42,000-seat facility in the heart of Downtown. In March 2006, the semifinals and the final game of the first-ever World Baseball Classic, scheduled to be a quadrennial event fielding teams from around the world, took place here.

San Diego Padres. The Padres slug it out for bragging rights in the National League West from April into October—they won the division in 2005 and 2006. Tickets are usually available on game day, but games with such rivals as the Los Angeles Dodgers and the San Francisco Giants often sell out quickly. For an inexpensive day at the ballpark, go for the $5 park pass (available for purchase at the park only) and have a picnic on the grass, while watching the play on one of several giant-screen TVs. ⊠ *100 Park Blvd., Downtown, San Diego* ☎ *619/795–5000, 877/374–2784* ⊕ *www.sandiegopadres.com.*

BEACHES

Water temperatures are generally chilly, ranging from 55°F to 65°F from October through June, and 65°F to 73°F from July through September. For a surf and weather report, call ☎ *619/221–8824.* San Diego's beaches are well maintained and very clean during summertime, when rainfall is infrequent. Beaches along San Diego county's northern cities are typically cleaner than ones farther south. Pollution is generally worse near river mouths and storm-drain outlets, especially after heavy rainfall. The weather page of the *San Diego Union-Tribune* includes pollution reports along with listings of surfing and diving conditions.

Lifeguards are stationed at city beaches from Sunset Cliffs up to Black's Beach in the summertime, but coverage in winter is provided by roving patrols only. Pay attention to signs listing illegal activities; undercover police often patrol the beaches. Smoking and alcoholic beverages are completely banned on city beaches. Drinking in beach parking lots, on boardwalks, and in landscaped areas is also illegal. Certain beaches also prohibit skateboarding. Fires are allowed only in fire rings or elevated barbecue grills. Although it may be tempting to take a starfish or some other sea creature as a souvenir from a tide pool, it upsets the delicate ecological balance and is illegal, too.

Finding a parking spot near the ocean can be hard in summer, but for the time being, unmetered parking is at all San Diego city beaches. Del Mar has a pay lot and metered street parking around the 15th Street beach.

Beaches are listed geographically, south to north.

CORONADO

Silver Strand State Beach. This quiet Coronado beach is ideal for families. The water is relatively calm, lifeguards and rangers are on duty year-round, and there are places to rollerblade or ride bikes. Three day-use parking lots provide room for more than 1,000 cars. RV sites at a state campground ($50 by the beach, $35 inland) are available by reservation (☎ *800/444–7275* ⊕ *www.reserveamerica.com*). Foot tunnels under Route 75 lead to a bay-side beach that has great views of the San Diego skyline. Across from the beach are the Coronado Cays, an exclusive community popular with yacht owners and celebrities, and the Loews Coronado Bay Resort. **Best for:** camping, families, long walks, swimming. **Amenities:** lifeguard year-round, camping facilities, food concessions open in summer, grills/fire pits, parking ($10), picnic tables, showers, toilets. ⊠ *From San Diego–Coronado Bridge, turn left onto Orange Ave., which becomes Rte. 75, and follow signs, Coronado* ☎ *619/435–5184.*

Ⓒ **Coronado Beach.** With the famous Hotel Del Coronado as a backdrop,
★ this stretch of sandy beach is one of San Diego County's largest and
most picturesque. It's perfect for sunbathing, people-watching, or Frisbee. Exercisers include Navy SEAL teams as well as the occasional
Marine Recon unit, who do training runs on the beaches in and around
Coronado. Parking can be difficult on the busiest days. There are plenty
of restrooms and service facilities, as well as fire rings on the north end.
Best for: families, long walks, swimming. **Amenities:** lifeguard year-
round, grills/fire pits at north end, parking (free on street), picnic tables,
playground, showers, toilets. ✉ *From the San Diego–Coronado bridge,
turn left on Orange Ave. and follow signs, Coronado.*

POINT LOMA

Sunset Cliffs. One of the more secluded beaches in the area, Sunset Cliffs
is popular with surfers and locals. A few miles long, it lies beneath the
jagged cliffs on the west side of the Point Loma peninsula. At the south
end of the peninsula, near Cabrillo Point, tide pools teeming with small
sea creatures are revealed at low tide. Farther north the waves lure
surfers and the lonely coves attract sunbathers. Stairs at the foot of
Pescadero and Bermuda avenues provide beach access, as do some cliff
trails, which are treacherous at points. There are few facilities. A visit
here is more enjoyable at low tide; check the local newspaper for tide
schedules. **Best for:** couples/romance, scenic drives, scenic views, tide
pools. **Amenities:** parking in lots and on street, picnic tables. ✉ *Take
I–8 west to Sunset Cliffs Blvd. and head west, Point Loma.*

MISSION BAY AND BEACHES

Ocean Beach. Much of this mile-long beach is a haven for volleyball players, sunbathers, and swimmers. The area around the municipal pier at
the south end is a hangout for surfers and transients. The pier itself is
open to the public 24 hours a day for fishing and walking, and there's a
restaurant midpier. The beach is south of the channel entrance to Mission Bay. You'll find fire rings as well as plenty of casual places to grab
a snack on adjoining streets. Swimmers should beware of strong rip currents around the main lifeguard tower. There's a dog beach at the north
end where Fido can run leash-free. During the summer there can be as
many as 100 dogs running in the sand. For picnic areas and a paved
path, check out Ocean Beach Park across from Dog Beach. **Best for:**
dogs, fishing pier, sunbathing, surfing, volley ball. **Amenities:** lifeguard
year-round, grills/fire pits, parking in lots and on street, picnic tables,
showers, toilets. ✉ *Take I–8 west to Sunset Cliffs Blvd. and head west;
a right turn off Sunset Cliffs Blvd. takes you to the water, Point Loma.*

Ⓒ **Mission Beach.** San Diego's most popular beach draws huge crowds
★ on hot summer days, but it's lively year-round. The 2-mi-long stretch
extends from the north entrance of Mission Bay to Pacific Beach. A
wide boardwalk paralleling the beach is popular with walkers, joggers, roller skaters, rollerbladers, and bicyclists. Surfers, swimmers, and
volleyball players congregate at the south end. Scantily clad volleyball
players practice on Cohasset Court year-round. Toward its north end,
near the Belmont Park roller coaster, the beach narrows and the water
becomes rougher. The crowds grow thicker and somewhat rougher as

Experts and beginners alike head to La Jolla for its excellent surfing.

well. For parking, you can try for a spot on the street, but your best bets are the two big lots at Belmont Park. **Best for:** accessibility, bicycling, boardwalk, families, volleyball. **Amenities:** lifeguard year-round, grills/fire pits, parking widely available at Belmont Park, picnic tables, showers, toilets. ⊠ *Exit I–5 at Grand Ave. and head west to Mission Blvd.; turn south and look for parking near roller coaster at West Mission Bay Dr., Mission Bay.*

Pacific Beach/North Pacific Beach. The boardwalk of Mission Beach turns into a sidewalk here, but there are still bike paths and picnic tables along the beach. Pacific Beach runs from the north end of Mission Beach to Crystal Pier. North Pacific Beach extends from the pier north. The scene here is particularly lively on weekends. There are designated surfing areas, and fire rings are available. Parking can be a challenge, but there are plenty of restrooms, showers, and restaurants in the area. **Best for:** couples/romance, nightlife, singles scene, surfing, swimming. **Amenities:** lifeguard year-round, grills/fire pits, parking in lots and on street, picnic tables, showers, toilets. ⊠ *Exit I–5 at Grand Ave. and head west to Mission Blvd. Turn north and look for parking, Mission Bay.*

Tourmaline Surfing Park. Year-round, this is one of the area's most popular beaches for surfing and sailboarding. Separate areas designated for swimmers and surfers are strictly enforced. There's a 175-space parking lot at the foot of Tourmaline Street that normally fills to capacity by midday. **Best for:** boating, surfing. **Amenities:** lifeguard year-round, parking in lots and on street, picnic tables, showers, toilets. ⊠ *Take Mission Blvd. north (it turns into La Jolla Blvd.) and turn west on Tourmaline St., Mission Bay.*

LA JOLLA

Windansea Beach. Named for a hotel that burned down in the late 1940s, Windansea Beach has increasingly gained notoriety due to its association with surfers. If the scenery here seems familiar, it's because Windansea and its habitués were the inspiration for Tom Wolfe's article "The Pump House Gang," about a group of surfers who protect their surf-turf from outsiders. The reef break here forms an unusual A-frame wave, making it one the most popular (and crowded) surf spots in San Diego County. Just below the parking lot is a palm-covered surf shack, constructed in 1946 and named a historical landmark in 1998. With its incredible views and secluded sunbathing spots set among sandstone rocks, Windansea is also one of the most romantic of West Coast beaches, especially at sunset. You can usually find nearby street parking. **Best for:** couples/romance, sunsets, surfing, solitude, tide pools. **Amenities:** lifeguard in summer, street parking. ⊠ *Take Mission Blvd. north (it turns into La Jolla Blvd.) and turn west on Nautilus St., La Jolla.*

Marine Street Beach. Wide and sandy, this strand often teems with sunbathers, swimmers, walkers, and joggers. The water is known as a great spot for bodysurfing, although the waves break in extremely shallow water and you'll need to watch out for riptides. **Best for:** body boarding, solitude, swimming. **Amenities:** lifeguard, street parking, picnic tables, showers and toilets near cove. ⊠ *Accessible from Marine St., off La Jolla Blvd., La Jolla.*

© **La Jolla Cove.**
Fodor'sChoice This shimmering blue inlet is what first attracted everyone ★ to La Jolla, from Native Americans to the glitterati; it's the secret to the village's enduring cachet. You'll find "the Cove"—as locals refer to it, as though it were the only one in San Diego—beyond where Girard Avenue dead-ends into Coast Boulevard, marked by towering palms that line a promenade where people strolling in designer clothes are as common as Frisbee throwers. A palm-lined park sits on top of cliffs formed by the incessant pounding of the waves. At low tide the pools and cliff caves are a destination for explorers. Divers, snorkelers, and kayakers can check out the underwater delights of the **San Diego–La Jolla Underwater Park Ecological Reserve.** The cove is also a favorite of rough-water swimmers. **Best for:** diving, long walks, scenic views, snorkeling, tide pools. **Amenities:** lifeguard year-round (reduced hours in winter), parking on side streets, picnic tables, showers, toilets. ⊠ *Follow Coast Blvd. north to signs, or take La Jolla Village Dr. exit from I–5, head west to Torrey Pines Rd., turn left, and drive downhill to Girard Ave.; turn right and follow signs, La Jolla.*

© **La Jolla Shores.** This is one of San Diego's most popular beaches, so get ★ here early on summer weekends. The lures are an incredible view of La Jolla peninsula, a wide sandy beach, an adjoining grassy park, and the gentlest waves in San Diego. In fact, several surf schools teach here, and kayak rentals are nearby. A concrete boardwalk parallels the beach. Arrive early to get a parking spot in the lot at the foot of Calle Frescota. **Best for:** boogie boarding, families, long walks, sunbathing, surfing, swimming. **Amenities:** lifeguard year-round, grills/fire pits, parking in lots and on side streets, picnic tables, playground, showers, toilets. ⊠ *8200 Camino del Oro, From I–5 take La Jolla Village Dr. west and* *turn left onto La Jolla Shores Dr.; head west to Camino del Oro or Vallecitos St., turn right, La Jolla.*

★ **Black's Beach.** The powerful waves at this beach, which is officially known as Torrey Pines City Park beach, attract world-class surfers, and its relative isolation appeals to nudist nature lovers (although by law nudity is prohibited) as well as gays and lesbians. Backed by cliffs whose colors change with the angle of the sun, Black's can be accessed from Torrey Pines State Beach to the north, or by a narrow path descending the cliffs from Torrey Pines Glider Port. Access to parts of the shore coincides with low tide. There are no lifeguards on permanent duty, although they do patrol the area between spring break and mid-October. Strong rip currents are common—only experienced swimmers should take the plunge. Storms have weakened the cliffs in the past few years; they're dangerous to climb and should be avoided. Part of the fun here is watching hang gliders and paragliders ascend from the Torrey Pines Glider Port atop the cliffs. **Best for:** solitude, sunbathing (nude), surfing. **Amenities:** lifeguard sometimes, parking available at the Torrey Pines Glider Port and La Jolla Farms. ⊠ *Take Genesee Ave. west from I–5 and follow signs to Torrey Pines Glider Port; easier access, via a paved path, available on La Jolla Farms Rd., but parking is limited to 2 hrs., La Jolla.*

DEL MAR

★ **Torrey Pines State Beach and Reserve.** One of San Diego's best beaches encompasses 2,000 acres of bluffs and bird-filled marshes. A network of meandering trails leads to the sandy shoreline below. Along the way enjoy the rare Torrey pine trees, found only here and on Santa Rosa Island, offshore. Guided tours of the nature preserve are offered on weekends. Torrey Pines tends to get crowded in summer, but you'll find more isolated spots heading south under the cliffs leading to Black's Beach. **Best for:** families, hiking, scenic views, sunbathing, swimming. **Amenities:** lifeguard year-round (reduced hours in winter), parking in two small lots, showers, toilets. ⊠ *Take Carmel Valley Rd. exit west from I–5, turn left on Rte. S21, Del Mar, California* ☎ *858/755–2063* ⊕ *www.torreypine.org* ☞ *Parking $10.*

Del Mar Beach. The numbered streets of Del Mar, from 15th north to 29th, end at a wide beach popular with volleyball players, surfers, and sunbathers. Parking can be a problem in town; there's metered parking along the beach, making it challenging to stay for more than a few hours. The portion of Del Mar south of 15th Street is lined with cliffs and rarely crowded. Leashed dogs are permitted on most sections of the beach year-round; from October through May, dogs may run free at Rivermouth, Del Mar's northernmost beach. During the annual summer meeting of the Del Mar Thoroughbred Club, horse bettors sit on the beach in the morning, working on the *Daily Racing Form* before heading across the street to the track. Food, hotels, and shopping are all within an easy walk of the beach. Because parking is at a premium, it's a great idea to bring a bike to cruise around the city before or after the beach. **Best for:** dogs, families, picnicking, swimming. **Amenities:** lifeguard year-round (reduced hours in winter), food concession at 17th Street, metered parking on streets, picnic tables, playground, showers, toilets. ⊠ *Take Via de* *la Valle exit from I–5 west to Rte. S21 (also known as Camino del Mar in Del Mar) and turn left, Del Mar, California.*

ENCINITAS

★ **Swami's.** The palms and the golden lotus-flower domes of the nearby Self-Realization Center temple and ashram earned this picturesque beach its name. Extreme low tides expose tide pools that harbor anemones, starfish, and other sea life. Remember to look but don't touch; all sea life here is protected. The beach is also a top surfing spot; the only access is by a long stairway leading down from the cliff-top Seaside Roadside Park, where there's free parking. On big winter swells, the bluffs are lined with gawkers watching the area's best surfers take on, and be taken down by, some of the best big waves in the county. Offshore, divers do their thing at North County's only underwater park, Encinitas Marine Life Refuge. **Best for:** diving, surfing, tide pools. **Amenities:** lifeguard year-round, parking, picnic tables, toilets. ⊠ *Follow Rte. S21 north from Cardiff, or Exit I–5 at Encinitas Blvd., go west to Rte. S21, and turn left, Encinitas, California.*

BICYCLING

On any given summer day **Route S21** (or Old Highway 101) from La Jolla to Oceanside looks like a freeway for cyclists. It's easily the most popular and scenic bike route around, never straying more than a quarter-mile from the beach. For more leisurely rides, **Mission Bay, San Diego Harbor,** and the **Mission Beach boardwalk** are all flat and scenic. For those who want to take their biking experience to the extreme, the **Kearny BMX** (⊠ *3170 Armstrong St.* ☎ *619/561–3824* ⊕ *www.kearnybmx.com*)has a dirt track where BMXers rip it up, racing three times a week, with time for practice beforehand.

Hike Bike Kayak San Diego offers a wide range of guided bike tours, from easy excursions around Mission Bay and Coronado Island to slightly more rigorous trips through coastal La Jolla. Mountain-biking tours are also available, and the company also rents bikes of all types (and can van-deliver them to your hotel). ⊠ *2246 Ave. de la Playa, La Jolla, San Diego* ☎ *858/551–9510, 866/425–2925* ⊕ *www.hikebikekayak.com.*

Holland's Bicycles. This great rental source on Coronado Island has a sister store (**Bikes and Beyond** ☎ *619/435–7180)* located at the ferry landing, so you can jump on your bike as soon as you cross the harbor from Downtown San Diego. ⊠ *977 Orange Ave., Coronado, San Diego* ☎ *619/435–3153* ⊕ *www.hollandsbicycles.com.*

Cheap Rentals Mission Beach is right on the boardwalk, this place has good daily and weekly prices for bike rentals, which include beach cruisers, tandems, hybrids, and two-wheeled baby carriers. ⊠ *3689 Mission Blvd., Mission Beach, San Diego* ☎ *858/488–9070, 800/941–7761* ⊕ *www.cheap-rentals.com.*

DIVING

FodorśChoice ★ Enthusiasts the world over come to San Diego to snorkel and scuba-dive off La Jolla and Point Loma. At La Jolla Cove you'll find the 6,000-acre **San Diego–La Jolla Underwater Park Ecological Preserve.** Because all sea life is protected here, it's the best place to see large lobster, sea bass, and sculpin (scorpion fish), as well as numerous golden garibaldi, the state marine fish. It's common to see hundreds of beautiful (and harmless) leopard sharks schooling at the north end of the cove, near La Jolla Shores, especially in summer. Farther north, off the south end of Black's Beach, the rim of **Scripps Canyon** lies in about 60 feet of water. The canyon plummets to more than 900 feet in some sections.

The HMCS *Yukon,* a decommissioned Canadian warship, was intentionally sunk off **Mission Beach** to create a diving destination. A mishap caused it to settle on its side, creating a surreal, M. C. Escher–esque diving environment. This is a technical dive and should be attempted by experienced divers only; even diving instructors have become disoriented inside the wreck. Another popular diving spot is **Sunset Cliffs** in Point Loma, where the sea life and flora are relatively close to shore. Strong rip currents make it an area best enjoyed by experienced divers. For recorded diving information, contact the **San Diego City Lifeguard Service** ☎ *619/221–8824.*

Ocean Enterprises Scuba Diving. Stop in for everything you need to plan a diving adventure, including equipment, advice, and instruction. ✉ *7710 Balboa Ave., Suite 101, Clairemont Mesa, San Diego* ☎ *858/565–6054* ⊕ *www.oceanenterprises.com.*

Scuba San Diego. This center is well regarded for its top-notch instruction and certification programs, as well as for guided dive tours of kelp reefs in La Jolla Cove, night diving at La Jolla Canyon, and unguided charter boat trips to Mission Bay's Wreck Alley or to the Coronado Islands (in Mexico, just south of San Diego). ✉ *Located at the San Diego Hilton Hotel, 1775 E. Mission Bay Dr., Mission Bay, San Diego* ☎ *619/260–1880* ⊕ *www.scubasandiego.com.*

FOOTBALL

San Diego Chargers. The Chargers fill Qualcomm Stadium from August through December and sometimes as late as January. Games with AFC West rivals the Oakland Raiders are particularly intense. ✉ *9449 Friars Rd., Mission Valley, San Diego* ☎ *858/874–4500 Charger Park, 877/242–7437 Season Tickets* ⊕ *www.chargers.com.*

GOLF

Southern California Golf Association. Search their Web site for detailed and valuable information on all clubs. ☎ *818/980–3630* ⊕ *www.scga.org.*

COURSES

Balboa Park Municipal Golf Course. Because it's in the heart of Balboa Park, this links is convenient for Downtown visitors. ✉ *2600 Golf Course Dr., Balboa Park, San Diego* ☎ *619/235–1184* ⊕ *www.balboaparkgolf. com* ⚑ *18 holes. 6267 yds. Par 72. Greens Fee: $40/$50* ☞ *Facilities:*

Driving range, putting green, pitching area, golf carts, pull carts, rental clubs, pro shop, golf academy/lessons, restaurant, bar.

★ **Coronado Municipal Golf Course.** Views of San Diego Bay and the Coronado Bridge from the front 9 make this course popular—it's difficult to get on unless you reserve a tee time, 8 to 14 days in advance, for an additional $60. ⊠ *2000 Visalia Row, Coronado, San Diego* ☎ *619/435–3121* ⊕ *www.golfcoronado.com* ⛳ *18 holes. 6590 yds. Par 72. Greens Fee: $30/$35. Reservations essential* ☞ *Facilities: Driving range, putting green, pitching area, golf carts, pull carts, rental clubs, pro shop, golf academy/lessons, restaurant, bar.*

★ **La Costa Resort and Spa.** There's an excellent golf school at this verdant location, which is one of the premier golf resorts in Southern California. After a full day on the links you can wind down with a massage, steam bath, and dinner at the resort. ⊠ *2100 Costa del Mar Rd., Carlsbad* ☎ *760/438–9111* ⊕ *www.lacosta.com* ⛳ *36 holes. North: 6608 yds., South: 6524 yds. North and South: Par 72. Greens Fee: $195/$205. Reservations essential* ☞ *Facilities: Driving range, putting green, pitching area, golf carts, caddies, rental clubs, pro shop, golf academy/lessons, restaurant, bar.*

Fodor's Choice **Park Hyatt Aviara Golf Club.** Designed by Arnold Palmer, this top-quality
★ course includes views of the protected adjacent Batiquitos Lagoon and the Pacific Ocean. The carts, which are fitted with GPS systems that tell you the distance to the pin, are included in the cost. ⊠ *7447 Batiquitos Dr., Carlsbad* ☎ *760/603–6900* ⊕ *www.golfaviara.com* ⛳ *18 holes. 7007 yds. Par 72. Greens Fee: $215/$235* ☞ *Facilities: Driving range, putting green, pitching area, golf carts, rental clubs, pro shop, golf academy/lessons, restaurant, bar.*

★ **Rancho Bernardo Inn and Country Club.** The course management here is JC Golf, which has a golf school as well as several other respected courses throughout Southern California that are open to guests of the Rancho Bernardo Inn. The restaurant here, El Bizcocho, serves one of the best Sunday brunches in the county. ⊠ *17550 Bernardo Oaks Dr., Rancho Bernardo* ☎ *858/675–8470* ⊕ *www.ranchobernardoinn.com* ⛳ *18 holes. 6631 yds. Par 72. Greens Fee: $100/$135* ☞ *Facilities: Driving range, putting green, golf carts, rental clubs, pro shop, golf academy/lessons, restaurant, bar.*

Fodor's Choice **Torrey Pines Golf Course.** One of the best public golf courses in the United
★ States, Torrey Pines was the site of the 2008 U.S. Open and has been the home of the Buick Invitational (now the Farmers Insurance Open) since 1968. The par-72 South Course receives rave reviews from the touring pros. Redesigned by Rees Jones in 2001, it's longer, more challenging, and more expensive than the North Course. Tee times may be booked from 8 to 90 days in advance at ☎ *877/581–7171* and are subject to an advance-booking fee ($43). A full-day or half-day instructional package includes cart, Greens Fee, and a golf-pro escort for the first 9 holes. ⊠ *11480 N. Torrey Pines Rd., La Jolla, San Diego* ☎ *858/452–3226, 800/985–4653* ⊕ *www.torreypinesgolfcourse.com* ⛳ *36 holes. South: 7227 yds., North: 6874 yds. North and South: Par 72. Greens Fee: South: $183/$229, North: $100/$125* ☞ *Facilities: Driving range, putting green, pitching area, golf carts, pull carts, caddies upon request in advance, rental clubs, pro shop, golf academy/lessons, restaurant, bar.*

SAILING AND BOATING

★ **Carlsbad Paddle Sports.** This shop handles kayak sales, rentals, and instruction for coastal North County. ⊠ *2002 S. Coast Hwy., Oceanside* ☏ *760/434–8686* ⊕ *www.carlsbadpaddle.com.*

Harbor Sailboats. You can rent sailboats from 22 to 41 feet long here for open-ocean adventures. The company also offers skippered charter boats for whale-watching, sunset sails, and bay tours. ⊠ *2040 Harbor Island Dr., Harbor Island, San Diego* ☏ *619/291–9568, 800/854–6625* ⊕ *www.harborsailboats.com.*

Seaforth Boat Rentals. Call here to arrange a charter for an ocean adventure or to rent a sailboat, powerboat, or skiff from their Mission Bay, Coronado, or Downtown San Diego locations. ⊠ *1641 Quivira Rd., Mission Bay, San Diego* ☏ *619/223–1681, 888/834–2628 reservations* ⊕ *www.seaforthboatrental.com.*

SURFING

★ **Surf Diva Surf School.** Check out clinics, surf camps, surf trips, and private lessons especially formulated for girls and women. Clinics and trips are for women only, but guys can book private lessons from the nationally recognized staff. ⊠ *2160 Ave. de la Playa, La Jolla, San Diego* ☏ *858/454–8273* ⊕ *www.surfdiva.com.*

Cheap Rentals Mission Beach. Many local surf shops rent both surf and bodyboards. Cheap Rentals Mission Beach is right on the boardwalk, just steps from the waves. They rent wet suits, bodyboards, and skimboards in addition to soft surfboards and long and short fiberglass rides. ⊠ *3689 Mission Blvd., Mission Beach, San Diego* ☏ *858/488–9070, 800/941–7761* ⊕ *www.cheap-rentals.com.*

Hansen's. A short walk from Swami's beach, Hansen's is one of San Diego's oldest and most popular surf shops. It has an extensive selection of boards, wet suits, and clothing for sale, and a rental department as well. ⊠ *1105 S. Coast Hwy. 101, Encinitas* ☏ *760/753–6595, 800/480–4754* ⊕ *www.hansensurf.com.*

SHOPPING

CORONADO

Fodor's Choice
★

Ferry Landing Marketplace. A staggering view of San Diego's Downtown skyline across the bay, a dozen boutiques, and a variety of restaurants all make a delightful place to shop while waiting for a ferry. Shops are open daily from 10 to 7. A **farmers' market** takes place on Tuesday from 2:30 to 6 pm, and several of the restaurants feature daily happy hours, with live music on Friday ⊠ *1201 1st St., at B Ave., Coronado* ☎ *619/435–8895* ⊕ *www.coronadoferrylanding.com.*

DOWNTOWN

★ **Seaport Village.** Quintessentially San Diego, this waterfront complex of more than 50 shops and restaurants has sweeping bay views, fresh breezes, and great strolling paths. Horse-and-carriage rides, an 1895 Looff carousel, and frequent public entertainment are side attractions. The Seaport is within walking distance of hotels, the San Diego Convention Center, and the San Diego Trolley, and there's also an easily accessible parking lot with two hours free with purchase validation. ⊠ *W. Harbor Dr. at Kettner Blvd., Embarcadero* ☎ *619/235–4014* ⊕ *www. spvillage.com.*

★ **Westfield Horton Plaza.** Within walking distance of most Downtown hotels, the open-air Horton Plaza is bordered by Broadway, 1st Avenue, G Street, and 4th Avenue. The multilevel shopping, dining, and entertainment complex is decorated with a terra-cotta color scheme and flag-draped facades. There are department stores, including Macy's and Nordstrom; fast-food counters; upscale restaurants; the Lyceum Theater; cinemas; a game arcade; and 130 other stores. Park in the plaza garage and validate your parking ticket at the validation machines in the mall; there's no purchase necessary and the validation is good for three free hours. ⊠ *324 Horton Plaza, Gaslamp Quarter* ☎ *619/238–1596* ⊕ *www.westfield.com/hortonplaza.*

GASLAMP QUARTER

Long a place where fine restaurants and clubs have catered to conventioneers and partying locals, the historic heart of San Diego has recently seen an explosion of specialty shops, art galleries, and boutiques take up residence in the Victorian buildings and renovated warehouses along 4th and 5th avenues. Some stores in this area tend to close early, starting as early as 5 pm. But a trip to the Gaslamp to shop is worth it. Here, you'll find the usual mall denizens as well as hip fashion boutiques and gift shops.

UPTOWN

Located north and northeast of Downtown, the Uptown area includes Hillcrest, North Park, South Park, Mission Hills, and University Heights. The boundaries between the neighborhoods tend to blur, but you'll find that each area has unique shops. Hillcrest has a large gay community and boasts many avant-garde apparel shops alongside gift, book, and music stores. North Park, east of Hillcrest, is a retro buff's paradise with many resale shops, trendy boutiques, and stores that sell a mix of old and new. University Avenue offers a mélange of affordably priced furniture, gift, and specialty stores appealing to college students, singles, and young families. South Park's 30th, Juniper, and Fern streets have everything from the hottest new denim lines to baby gear and craft supplies. The shops and art galleries in upscale Mission Hills, west of Hillcrest, have a modern and sophisticated ambience that suits the well-heeled residents just fine.

LA JOLLA

Known as San Diego's Rodeo Drive, La Jolla's chic boutiques, art galleries, and gift shops line narrow twisty streets that are often celebrity-soaked. Prospect Street and Girard Avenue are the primary shopping stretches, and North Prospect is chockablock with art galleries. The Upper Girard Design District stocks home decor accessories and luxury furnishings. Parking is tight in the village and store hours vary widely, so it's wise to call in advance. Most shops on Prospect Street stay open until 10 pm on weeknights to accommodate evening strollers. On the east side of I–5, office buildings surround the Westfield UTC mall, where you'll find department and chain stores.

SIDE TRIPS TO NORTH COUNTY

DEL MAR

23 mi north of Downtown San Diego on I–5, 9 mi north of La Jolla on Rte. S21.

Del Mar is best known for its quaint old section west of Interstate 5 marked with a glamorous racetrack, half-timber buildings, chic shops, tony restaurants, celebrity visitors, and wide beaches.

☾ ★ **Del Mar Fairgrounds.** The Spanish Mission–style fairground is the home of the **Del Mar Thoroughbred Club** (☎ 858/755–1141 ⊕ *www.dmtc. com*). Crooner Bing Crosby and his Hollywood buddies—Pat O'Brien, Gary Cooper, and Oliver Hardy, among others—organized the club in the 1930s, primarily because Crosby wanted a track near his Rancho Santa Fe home. Even now the racing season here (usually July–September, Wednesday–Monday, post time 2 pm) is one of the most fashionable in California. If you're new to horse racing, stop by the Plaza de Mexico where you'll find staff who can explain how to place a bet on a horse. The track also hosts free Four O'Clock Friday concerts following the races. Del Mar Fairgrounds hosts more than 100 different events each year, including the Del Mar Fair (San Diego County), which draws more than a million visitors annually, plus a number of horse shows. ✉ *2260 Jimmy Durante Blvd.* ☎ *858/793–5555* ⊕ *www.sdfair.com.*

WHERE TO EAT

$$$$ ✕ **Addison.** Sophisticated and stylish, Addison challenges many ideas
FRENCH about what fine dining is all about. The dining room and adjacent bar
Fodor's Choice feel Italian and clubby, with intricately carved dark-wood motifs, heavy
★ arches, and marble and wood floors. The tables, by contrast, are pure
white adorned with a single flower. William Bradley, one of San Diego's
most acclaimed rising star chefs, serves up explosive flavors in his four-
course prix-fixe dinners, such as Prince Edward Island mussels with
champagne sabayon and lemon verbena jus or foie gras de canard with
Le Puy lentils, port wine, and smoked bacon mousse. Entrées include
spring lamb *persille* (parsely and garlic topping) with pistachio pâté brisée
and caramelized garlic puree or perfectly cooked wild Scottish salmon
with sauce *vin jaune* (white wine from the Jura region of France), roasted
eggplant stick, and pine nuts. Acclaimed for its extensive wine collection,
Addison challenges vino lovers with a 160-page wine list. ✉ *5200 Grand
Del Mar Way* ☎ *858/314–1900* ⊕ *www.addisondelmar.com* ⌔ *Reservations essential* ◐ *Closed Sun. and Mon. No lunch.*

WHERE TO STAY

For expanded reviews, visit Fodors.com.

$$$$ ⊡ **Grand Del Mar.** Mind-blowing indulgence in serene surroundings sets
Fodor's Choice the Grand Del Mar apart from any other luxury hotel in the San Diego
★ area. **Pros:** ultimate luxury; secluded, on-site golf course. **Cons:** service can be slow; hotel is not on the beach. ✉ *5200 Grand Del Mar
Ct.* ☎ *858/314–2000 or 888/314–2030* ⊕ *www.thegranddelmar.com*
⌁ *218 rooms, 31 suites* ⌔ *In-room: Internet, Wi-Fi. In-hotel: 6 restaurants, bars, golf course, pools, tennis courts, gym, spa, children's
programs, business center, parking, some pets allowed.*

CARLSBAD

*6 mi from Encinitas on Rte. S21, 36 mi north of Downtown San Diego
on I–5.*

Once-sleepy Carlsbad, lying astride I–5 at the north end of a string of
beach towns extending from San Diego to Oceanside, has long been
popular with beachgoers and sun seekers. On a clear day in this village you can take in sweeping ocean views that stretch from La Jolla
to Oceanside by walking the 2-mi-long seawalk running between the
Encina power plant and Pine Street. En route, you'll find several stairways leading to the beach and quite a few benches. More recently, however, much of the attention of visitors to the area has shifted inland, east
of I–5, to LEGOLAND California and other attractions in its vicinity.

☾ **LEGOLAND California Resort.** The centerpiece of a development that
Fodor's Choice includes resort hotels and a designer discount shopping mall, offers
★ a full day of entertainment with more than 60 rides and attractions
for pint-size fun-seekers and their parents. The mostly outdoor experience is best appreciated by kids ages 2 to 12, who often beg to ride the
mechanical horses around the Royal Joust again and again or to take
just one more turn through the popular Jr. Driving School. Miniland
USA, an animated collection of U.S. cities and other areas constructed

TIP SHEET: LEGOLAND

Who will especially love this park?

LEGOLAND is especially tailored for families with kids 2–12—especially kids who love LEGOs.

What's This Really Gonna Cost?
In addition to tickets, you'll need to pay $12 for parking. Meals range from $3–$20 per person, and there's an extra charge for certain rides. Admission to LEGOLAND's adjacent SEA LIFE Aquarium is $20 for adults, $13 for children, and the Water Park costs $12—unless you purchase Hopper tickets good for admission to both parks ($89 adults; $77 kids and seniors).

Top 5 Attractions:
Lost Kingdom Adventure: Armed with a laser blaster, you'll journey through ancient Egyptian ruins in a desert roadster, scoring points as you hit targets.
Miniland U.S.A: This miniature, animated, interactive collection of U.S. icons was constructed out of 24 million Lego bricks!
Soak-N-Sail: Hundreds of gallons of water course through 60 interactive features including a pirate ship-wreck–themed area. You'll need your swimsuit for this one....
Dragon Coaster: Little kids love this popular indoor/outdoor steel roller coaster that goes through a castle. Don't let the name frighten you—the motif is more humorous than scary.
Volvo Driving School: Kids 6–13 can drive speed-controlled cars (not on rails) on a miniature road; driver's licenses are awarded after the course. Volvo Junior is the pint-sized version for kids 3–5.

Tips:
Don't Bring the Teens: Kids love LEGOLAND...but your older children will probably find it a bit juvenile.
Get a Hopper Ticket: The best ticket value is one of the Hopper Tickets that give you one admission to LEGOLAND plus Sea Life and the Water Park. These can be used on the same day or on different days.
Go Mid-week: Crowds are much lighter then—one Fodors.com user was able to see everything in four hours on a particularly quiet day!

entirely of LEGO bricks, captures the imaginations of all ages. Kids get a chance to dig for buried fossils on Dino Island, which holds the Dig Those Dinos paleontological play area as well as the Coastersaurus, a junior roller coaster. At the Fun Town Fire Academy, families compete at fire fighting by racing in a model fire truck and hosing down a simulated burning building. Also in Fun Town, besides the driving school, with miniature cars, is the Skipper School, with miniature boats. In Pirate Shores, kids cruise through pirate-infested waters past exploding volcanoes; Treasure Falls, a mini-flume log ride with a 12-foot soaking plunge; and Splash Battle, water-fight headquarters. Lost Kingdom Adventure, LEGOLAND'S first dark ride (meaning indoors), features the adventures of popular LEGO mini-figure Johnny Thunder battling the bad guys in an Egyptian temple with the help of riders using laser blasters to accumulate points and ultimately capture Sam Sinister and find the treasure. The Egyptian-theme Dune Raiders is a 30-foot-high slide with six side-by-side racing lanes. Also part of the mix are stage shows and restaurants with kid-friendly buffets. Buy a combination

A LEGOLAND model worker puts the finishing touches on the San Francisco portion of Miniland U.S.A.

park-hopper ticket to enjoy the adjacent Legoland Water Park and the Sea Life Aquarium for a full day of fun. ⊠ *1 LEGOLAND Dr. Exit I–5 at Cannon Rd. and follow signs east ¼ mi* ☎ *760/918–5346* ⊕ *www. legolandca.com* ⊠ *$69 adults, $59 kids; 1-day Hopper $89 adults, $79 kids; 2-day Hopper $99 adults, $89 kids; additional fees for some rides, parking $12, $15 for campers/RVs* ☼ *Closed Tues.–Wed., call for information.*

Ⓒ **Flower Fields at Carlsbad Ranch.** In spring the hillsides are abloom on this,

Fodor's Choice the largest bulb production farm in Southern California. Here, from

★ mid-March through mid-May, you can walk through fields planted with thousands of Giant Tecolote ranunculus—a stunning 50-acre display of color against the backdrop of the blue Pacific Ocean. Also to be seen are the rose gardens—including the miniature rose garden and the Walk of Fame garden, lined with examples of every All-American Rose Selection award-winner since 1940—and demonstration gardens created by artists who normally work with paint and easel. You can walk through a sweet-pea maze and a historical display of Paul Ecke poinsettias that were bred by the Ecke Nursery. Family activities include an open-air wagon drawn by an antique tractor ($5), LEGO Flower Garden, and kids' playground. The unusually large and well-stocked Armstrong Garden Center at the exit carries plants, garden accessories, and ranunculus bulbs. ⊠ *5704 Paseo del Norte, east of I–5* ☎ *760/431–0352* ⊕ *www. theflowerfields.com* ⊠ *$10* ☼ *Mar.–May, daily 9–6.*

2

OCEANSIDE

8 mi north of Carlsbad on Rte. S21, 37 mi north of Downtown San Diego on I–5.

Mission San Luis Rey. Known as the King of the Missions, it was built in 1798 by Franciscan friars under the direction of Father Fermin Lasuen to help educate and convert local Native Americans. Once a location for filming Disney's *Zorro* TV series, the well-preserved mission, still owned by the Franciscans, was the 18th and largest and most prosperous of California's missions. The *sala* (parlor), the kitchen, a friar's bedroom, a weaving room, and a collection of religious art convey much about early mission life. Retreats are still held here, but a picnic area, a gift shop, and a museum (which has the most extensive collection of old Spanish vestments in the United States) are also on the grounds, as are sunken gardens and the *lavanderia*, the original open-air laundry area. Tours are generally self-guided, although docent-led tours can be arranged in advance. The mission's retreat center has limited, inexpensive dormitory-style overnight accommodations. ⊠ *4050 Mission Ave.* ☎ *760/757–3651* ⊕ *www.sanluisrey.org* ⌲ *$4* ☉ *Daily 9-5.*

Fodor's Choice ★

ESCONDIDO

8 mi north of Rancho Bernardo on I–15, 31 mi northeast of Downtown San Diego on I–15.

San Diego Zoo Safari Park. An extension of the San Diego Zoo, 35 mi to the south, the 1,800-acre preserve in the San Pasqual Valley is designed to protect endangered species from around the world. Exhibit areas have been carved out of the dry, dusty canyons and mesas to represent the animals' natural habitats in various parts of Africa, the Australian rain forest, and Asian swamps and plains.

Fodor's Choice ★

The best way to see these preserves is to take the 45-minute, 2½-mi Journey into Africa bus tour. As you pass in front of the large, naturally landscaped enclosures, you can see animals bounding across prairies and mesas as they would in the wild. More than 3,500 animals of more than 400 species roam or fly above the expansive grounds. Predators are separated from prey by deep moats, but only the elephants, tigers, lions, and cheetahs are kept in isolation. Photographers with zoom lenses can get spectacular shots of zebras, gazelles, and rhinos. In summer, when the park stays open late, the trip is especially enjoyable in the early evening, when the heat has subsided and the animals are active and feeding. When the bus travels through the park after dark, sodium-vapor lamps illuminate the active animals.

The park is as much a botanical garden as a zoo, serving as a "rescue center" for rare and endangered plants. Unique gardens include cacti and succulents from Baja California, a bonsai collection, a fuchsia display, native plants, and protea. The park sponsors a number of garden events throughout the year, including a winter camellia show and a spring orchid show.

The **Lion Camp** gives you a close-up view of the king of beasts in a slice of African wilderness complete with sweeping plains and rolling hills.

As you walk through this exhibit, you can watch the giant cats lounging around through a 40-foot-long window. The last stop is a research station where you can see them all around you through glass panels.

The ticket booths at **Nairobi Village,** the park's center, are designed to resemble the tomb of an ancient king of Uganda. Animals in the **Petting Kraal** here affectionately tolerate tugs and pats and are quite adept at posing for pictures with toddlers. At the **Congo River Village** 10,000 gallons of water pour each minute over a huge waterfall into a large lagoon. **Hidden Jungle,** an 8,800-square-foot greenhouse, is a habitat for creatures that creep, flutter, or just hang out in the tropics. Gigantic cockroaches and bird-eating spiders share the turf with colorful butterflies and hummingbirds and oh-so-slow-moving two-toed sloths. **Lorikeet Landing,** simulating the Australian rain forest, holds 75 of the loud and colorful small parrots—you can buy a cup of nectar at the aviary entrance to induce them to land on your hand. Along the trails of 32-acre **Heart of Africa** you can travel in the footsteps of an early explorer through forests and lowlands, across a floating bridge to a research station, where an expert is on hand to answer questions; finally you arrive at Panorama Point for an up-close-and-personal view of cheetahs, a chance to feed the giraffes, and a distant glimpse of the expansive savanna where rhinos, impalas, wildebeest, oryx, and beautiful migrating birds reside. At **Condor Ridge,** the Safari Park, which conducts captive breeding programs to save rare and endangered species, shows off one of its most successful efforts, the California condor. The exhibit, perched like one of the ugly black vultures it features, occupies nearly the highest point in the park, and affords a sweeping view of the surrounding San Pasqual Valley. Also on exhibit here is a herd of rare desert bighorn sheep.

All the park's animal shows are entertainingly educational. The gift shops here offer wonderful merchandise, much of it limited-edition items. Rental camcorders, strollers, and wheelchairs are available. Serious shutterbugs might consider joining one of the special Photo Caravan Safari tours ($90–$150 plus park admission). You can also stay overnight in the park in summer on a Roar and Snore Sleepover (adults $140–$220, kids 8–11 $120–$160, plus admission). ✉ *15500 San Pasqual Valley Rd. Take I–15 north to Via Rancho Pkwy. and follow signs, 6 mi* ☎ *760/747–8702* ⊕ *www.sandiegozoo.org/wap* ☜ *$40 includes Journey into Africa tour and Conservation Carousel; $76 two-visit pass includes a 1-day pass to San Diego Zoo and Safari Park or two 1-day passes to either; parking $10* ☉ *Daily 9–dusk, later in summer (call ahead for closing time).*

Orange County and Catalina Island

WITH DISNEYLAND AND KNOTT'S BERRY FARM

WORD OF MOUTH

"Laguna Beach is a wonderful place to spend the weekend sunning and strolling through the many quaint galleries and shops."

—ECinSF

WELCOME TO ORANGE COUNTY AND CATALINA ISLAND

TOP REASONS TO GO

★ **Disney magic:** Walking down Main Street, U.S.A. with Cinderella's Castle straight ahead, you really will feel like you're in one of the happiest places on earth.

★ **Beautiful beaches:** Surf, swim, sail, or just relax on one of the state's most breathtaking stretches of coastline.

★ **Island Getaways:** Just a short hydrofoil away, Catalina Island feels 1,000 mi away from California. Wander around charming Avalon, or explore the unspoiled beauty of the island's wild interior.

★ **The fine life:** Some of the state's wealthiest communities are in coastal Orange County, so spend at least part of your stay here experiencing how the other half lives.

★ **Family fun:** Spend some quality time with the kids riding roller coasters, eating ice cream, fishing off ocean piers, and bodysurfing.

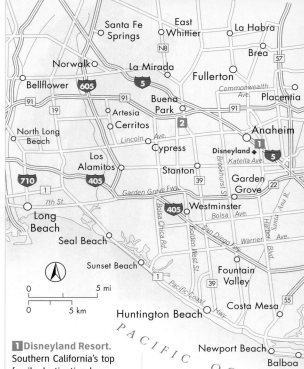

1 Disneyland Resort. Southern California's top family destination has expanded from the humble park of Walt Disney's vision to a megaresort with more attractions spilling over into Disney's California Adventure. But kids still consider it the happiest place on earth!

2 Knott's Berry Farm. Amusement park lovers should check out this Buena Park attraction, with thrill rides, the *Peanuts* gang, and lots of fried chicken and boysenberry pie.

3 Coastal Orange County. The OC's beach communities may not be quite as glamorous as seen on TV, but coastal spots like Huntington Beach, Newport Harbor, and Laguna Beach are perfect for chilling out in a beachfront hotel.

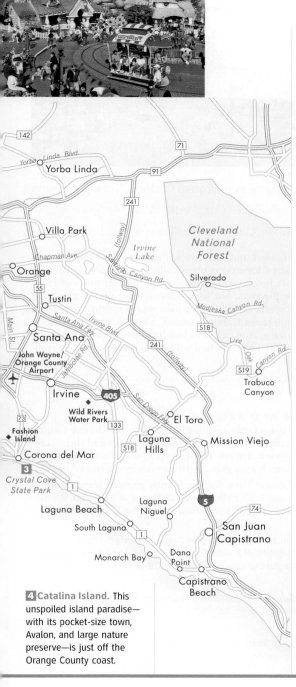

GETTING ORIENTED

3

Like Los Angeles, Orange County stretches over a large area, lacks a singular focal point, and has limited public transportation. You'll need a car and a sensible game plan to make the most of your visit. Try staying at a midpoint location such as Irvine or Costa Mesa, both equidistant from inland tourist attractions and the coast. These towns are less crowded than Anaheim and less expensive than the beach cities. Of course, if you can afford it, staying at the beach is always recommended.

Map Labels

142
Yorba Linda Blvd.
Yorba Linda
71
91
241
Villa Park
(tollway)
Irvine Lake
Cleveland National Forest
Chapman Ave.
Orange
Santa Ana Canyon Rd.
Silverado
55
Tustin
Modjeska Canyon Rd.
Santa Ana Fwy.
Irvine Blvd.
S18
Santa Ana
241 (tollway)
Live Oak Canyon Rd.
John Wayne/ Orange County Airport
Jamboree Rd.
S19
Irvine
405
Trabuco Canyon
Wild Rivers Water Park
133
El Toro
73
Laguna Hills
Mission Viejo
Fashion Island
S18
Corona del Mar
3
Crystal Cove State Park
1
Laguna Niguel
Laguna Beach
5
74
South Laguna
1
San Juan Capistrano
Monarch Bay
Dana Point
Capistrano Beach
Main St.
San Diego Fwy.

4 Catalina Island. This unspoiled island paradise—with its pocket-size town, Avalon, and large nature preserve—is just off the Orange County coast.

Updated by
Laura Randall

Few of the citrus groves that gave Orange County its name remain. This region south and east of Los Angeles is now ruled by tourism and high-tech business instead of farmers.

With its tropical flowers and palm trees, the stretch of coast between Seal Beach and San Clemente is often called the California Riviera. Exclusive Newport Beach, artsy Laguna, and the surf town of Huntington Beach are the stars, but lesser-known gems on the glistening coast—such as Corona del Mar—are also worth visiting. Offshore, meanwhile, lies gorgeous Catalina Island, a terrific spot for diving, snorkeling, and hiking. And despite a building boom that began in the 1990s, the area is still a place to find wilderness trails, canyons, green-belts, and natural parks.

PLANNING

GETTING HERE AND AROUND

Orange County's main facility is John Wayne Airport Orange County (SNA), which is served by 10 major domestic airlines and three commuter lines. Long Beach Airport (LGB) serves four airlines, including its major player, JetBlue. It's roughly 20–30 minutes by car from Anaheim.

Airport Bus and Prime Time Airport Shuttle provide transportation from John Wayne and LAX to the Disneyland area of Anaheim. Round-trip fares average about $27 per person from John Wayne and $17 to $32 from LAX.

Airport Information John Wayne Airport Orange County (✉ *MacArthur Blvd. at I-405, Santa Ana* ☎ *949/252-5200* ⊕ *www.ocair.com*). **Long Beach Airport** (✉ *4100 Donald Douglas Dr., Long Beach* ☎ *562/570-2600* ⊕ *www.longbeach. gov/airport*).

Shuttles Airport Bus (☎ *800/938-8933* ⊕ *www.airportbus.com*). **Prime Time Airport Shuttle** (☎ *800/262-7433* ⊕ *www.primetimeshuttle.com*).

BUS TRAVEL

The Orange County Transportation Authority will take you virtually anywhere in the county, but it will take time; OCTA buses go from Knott's Berry Farm and Disneyland to Huntington Beach and Newport

Beach. Bus 1 travels along the coast; buses 701 and 721 provide express service to Los Angeles.

Orange County Transportation Authority (OCTA) ☎ *714/636–7433* ⊕ *www. octa.net.*

CAR TRAVEL

The San Diego Freeway (I–405), the coastal route, and the Santa Ana Freeway (I–5), the inland route, run north–south through Orange County. South of Laguna I–405 merges into I–5 (called the San Diego Freeway south from this point). A toll road, the 73 Highway, runs 15 mi from Newport Beach to San Juan Capistrano; it costs $3.75–$5.50 (lower rates are for weekends and off-peak hours) and is usually less jammed than the regular freeways. Do your best to avoid all Orange County freeways during rush hours (6–9 am and 3:30–6:30 pm). Highway 55 leads to Newport Beach. The Pacific Coast Highway (Highway 1) allows easy access to beach communities and is the most scenic route.

FERRY TRAVEL

There are two ferries that service Catalina Island; Catalina Express runs from Long Beach (about 90 minutes) and from Newport Beach (about 75 minutes). Reservations are advised for summers and weekends.

TRAIN TRAVEL

When planning train travel, consider where the train stations are in relation to your ultimate destination. You may need to make extra transportation arrangements once you've arrived in town. Amtrak makes daily stops in Orange County at all major towns. Metrolink is a weekday commuter train that runs to and from Los Angeles and Orange County.

Information Amtrak ☎ *800/872–7245* ⊕ *www.amtrak.com.*
Metrolink ☎ *800/371–5465* ⊕ *www.metrolinktrains.com.*

For more information on Getting Here and Around, see Travel Smart Southern California.

RESTAURANTS

Much like L.A., restaurants in Orange County are generally casual, and you'll rarely see men in jackets and ties. However, at top resort hotel dining rooms, many guests choose to dress up.

Of course, there's also a swath of super-casual places along the beachfronts—fish-taco takeout, taquerias, burger joints—that won't mind if you wear flip-flops. Reservations are recommended for the nicest restaurants.

Many places don't serve past 11 pm, and locals tend to eat early. Remember that according to California law, smoking is prohibited in all enclosed areas.

HOTELS

Along the coast there's been a flurry of luxury resort openings in recent years; Laguna's Montage elevated expectations and was followed by the renovation of Dana Point's Ritz-Carlton and the debut of the Resort at Pelican Hill on the Newport Coast, among others.

As a rule, lodging prices tend to rise the closer the hotels are to the beach. If you're looking for value, consider a hotel that is inland along the I–405 freeway corridor.

In most cases, you can take advantage of some of the facilities of the high-end resorts, such as restaurants and spas, even if you aren't an overnight guest.

WHAT IT COSTS					
	¢	$	$$	$$$	$$$$
RESTAURANTS	under $10	$10–$15	$16–$22	$23–$30	over $30
HOTELS	under $90	$90–$120	$121–$175	$176–$250	over $250

Restaurant prices are for a main course at dinner, excluding sales tax. Hotel prices are for two people in a standard double room in high season, excluding service charges and tax.

VISITOR INFORMATION

The Anaheim-Orange County Visitor and Convention Bureau is an excellent resource for both leisure and business travelers and can provide materials on many area attractions. It's on the main floor of the Anaheim Convention Center.

The Orange County Tourism Council's Web site is also a useful source of information.

Contacts Anaheim-Orange County Visitor and Convention Bureau
✉ *Anaheim Convention Center, 800 W. Katella Ave., Anaheim* ☎ *714/765–8888*
⊕ *www.anaheimoc.org.* **Orange County Tourism Council**
⊕ *www.visitorangecounty.net.*

DISNEYLAND RESORT

26 mi southeast of Los Angeles, via I–5.

The snowcapped Matterhorn, the centerpiece of the Magic Kingdom, punctuates the skyline of Anaheim. Since 1955, when Walt Disney chose this once-quiet farming community for the site of his first amusement park, Disneyland has attracted more than 450 million visitors and thousands of workers, and Anaheim has been their host.

To understand the symbiotic relationship between Disneyland and Anaheim, you need only look at the $4.2 billion spent in a combined effort by the Walt Disney Company and Anaheim, the latter to revitalize the city's tourist center and run-down areas, the former to expand and renovate the Disney properties into what is known now as Disneyland Resort.

The resort is a sprawling complex that includes Disney's two amusement parks; three hotels; and Downtown Disney, a shopping, dining, and entertainment promenade. Anaheim's tourist center includes Angel Stadium of Anaheim, home of baseball's World Series Champion Los Angeles Angels of Anaheim; Arrowhead Pond, which hosts concerts and the hockey team the Anaheim Ducks; and the enormous Anaheim Convention Center.

GETTING THERE

Disney is about a 30-mi drive from either LAX or downtown. From LAX, follow Sepulveda Boulevard south to the I–105 freeway and drive east 16 mi to the I–605 north exit. Exit at the Santa Ana Freeway (I–5) and continue south for 12 mi to the Disneyland Drive exit. Follow signs to the resort. From downtown, follow I–5 south 28 mi and exit at Disneyland Drive. **Disneyland Resort Express** (☎ *714/978–8855* ⊕ *graylineanaheim.com*) offers daily nonstop bus service between LAX, John Wayne Airport, and Anaheim. Reservations are not required. The cost is $20 one-way for adults, $17 for children, for LAX, and $15 and $12 one-way for John Wayne Airport.

SAVING TIME AND MONEY

If you plan to visit for more than a day, you can save money by buying three-, four-, and five-day Park Hopper tickets that grant same-day "hopping" privileges between Disneyland and Disney's California Adventure. You get a discount on the multiple-day passes if you buy online through the Disneyland Web site.

A one-day Park Hopper pass costs $101 for anyone 10 or older, $91 for kids ages 3–9. Admission to either park (but not both) is $76 or $68 for kids 3–9; kids 2 and under are free.

In addition to tickets, parking is $15–$20 (unless your hotel has a shuttle or is within walking distance), and meals in the parks and at Downtown Disney range from $10 to $30 per person.

If you're staying in a hotel near the park, ask if any discount packages are available when you book.

If you think you'll only need a few hours at Knott's Berry Farm, you can save money by coming after 4 pm, when admission fees drop to $28. This deal is offered any day the park is open after 6.

A full-day pass for adults is $56.99; Southern California residents pay $46.99 and children three and older, up to 48 inches tall, are $24.99. Tickets can be purchased online and printed out ahead of time, to avoid waiting in line.

In addition to tickets, you'll need to pay $12 for parking. Meals are about $10–$14 per person. The Laser Tag attraction is an extra $10, and the Big Swing ride is an additional $5.

DISNEYLAND

↺
Fodor's Choice
★

Disneyland. One of the biggest misconceptions people have about Disneyland is that they've "been there, done that" if they've visited either Florida's mammoth Walt Disney World or one of the Disney parks overseas. But Disneyland, opened in 1955 and the only one of the kingdoms to be overseen by Walt himself, has a genuine historic feel and occupies a unique place in the Disney legend. There's plenty here that you won't find anywhere else: for example, Storybook Land, with its miniature replicas of animated Disney scenes from classics such as *Pinocchio, Alice in Wonderland,* and the Indiana Jones Adventure ride.

Characters appear for autographs and photos throughout the day; guidebooks at the entrances give times and places. You can also meet some of the animated icons at one of the character meals served at the three Disney hotels (open to the public). Belongings can be stored in lockers just off Main Street; purchases can also be sent to the package pickup desk, at the front of the park.

DISNEY LANDS
Neighborhoods for Disneyland are arranged in geographic order.

MAIN STREET, U.S.A.
Walt's hometown of Marceline, Missouri, was the inspiration behind this romanticized image of small-town America, circa 1900. The sidewalks are lined with a penny arcade and shops that sell everything from tradable pins to Disney-theme clothing and photo supplies. It opens half an hour before the rest of the park, so it's a good place to explore if you're getting an early start to beat the crowds (it's also open an hour after the other attractions close, so you may want to save your shopping for the end of the day). **Main Street Cinema** offers a cool respite from the crowds and six classic Disney animated shorts, including *Steamboat Willie*. There's rarely a wait to enter. Board the **Disneyland Railroad** here to save on walking; it tours all the lands, plus offers unique views of Splash Mountain and the Grand Canyon and Primeval World dioramas.

NEW ORLEANS SQUARE
A mini–French Quarter with narrow streets, hidden courtyards, and live street performances, this is home to two iconic attractions and the Cajun-inspired Blue Bayou restaurant. **Pirates of the Caribbean** now features Jack Sparrow and the cursed Captain Barbossa, in a nod to the blockbuster movies of the same name, plus enhanced special effects and battle scenes (complete with cannonball explosions). Nearby **Haunted Mansion** continues to spook guests with its stretching room and "doombuggy" rides (plus there's now an expanded storyline for the beating-heart bride). Its *Nightmare Before Christmas* holiday overlay is an annual tradition. This is a good area to get a casual bite to eat; the clam chowder in sourdough bread bowls, sold at the French Market Restaurant and Royal Street Veranda, is a popular choice.

FRONTIERLAND
Between Adventureland and Fantasyland, Frontierland transports you to the wild, wild West with its rustic buildings, shooting gallery, mountain range, and foot-stompin' dance hall. The marquee attraction, **Big Thunder Mountain Railroad,** is a relatively tame roller coaster ride (no steep descents) that takes the form of a runaway mine car as it rumbles past desert canyons and an old mining town. Tour the Rivers of America on the **Mark Twain Riverboat** in the company of a grizzled old river pilot or circumnavigate the globe on the **Sailing Ship Columbia,** though its operating hours are usually limited to weekends. You can also raft

---

DISNEY'S TOP ATTRACTIONS

Finding Nemo: Board a yellow submarine and view a 3-D animated adventure.

Haunted Mansion: A "doombuggy" takes you through a spooky old plantation mansion.

Pirates of the Caribbean: Watch buccaneers wreak havoc as you float along in a rowboat.

Space Mountain: This scary-but-thrilling roller coaster is indoors—and mostly in the dark!

Matterhorn Bobsleds: At the center of the Magic Kingdom, this roller coaster simulates bobsleds.

over from here to Pirate's Lair on **Tom Sawyer Island,** which now features pirate-theme caves, treasure hunts, and music along with plenty of caves and hills to climb and explore. If you don't mind tight seating, have a snack at the Golden Horseshoe Restaurant while enjoying the always-entertaining comedy and bluegrass show of Billy Hill and the Hillybillies. Children won't want to miss **Big Thunder Ranch,** a small petting zoo of real pigs, goats, and cows beyond Big Thunder Mountain.

CRITTER COUNTRY Down-home country is the theme in this shady corner of the park, where Winnie the Pooh and Davy Crockett make their homes. Here you can find **Splash Mountain,** a classic flume ride accompanied by music and appearances by Brer Rabbit and other characters from Song of the South. Don't forget to check out your photo (the camera snaps close-ups of each car just before it plunges into the water) on the way out. The patio of the popular Hungry Bear Restaurant has great views of Tom Sawyer's Island and Davy Crockett's Explorer Canoes.

ADVEN-TURELAND Modeled after the lands of Africa, Polynesia, and Arabia, this tiny tropical paradise is worth braving the crowds that flock here for the ambience and better-than-average food. Sing along with the animatronic birds and tiki gods in the **Enchanted Tiki Room,** sail the rivers of the world with joke-cracking skippers on **Jungle Cruise,** and climb the Disneyodendron semperflorens (aka always-blooming Disney tree) to **Tarzan's Treehouse,** where you can walk through scenes, some interactive, from the 1999 animated film. Cap off the visit with a wild jeep ride at **Indiana Jones Adventure,** where the special effects and decipherable hieroglyphics distract you while you're waiting in line. The kebabs at Bengal Barbecue and pineapple whip at Tiki Juice Bar are some of the best fast-food options in the park.

FANTASYLAND Sleeping Beauty Castle marks the entrance to Fantasyland, a visual wonderland of princesses, spinning teacups, flying elephants, and other classic storybook characters. Rides and shops (such as the princess-theme Once Upon a Time and Gepetto's Toys and Gifts) take precedence over restaurants in this area of the park, but outdoor carts sell everything from churros to turkey legs. Tots love the **King Arthur Carousel, Casey Jr. Circus Train,** and **Storybook Land Canal Boats.** This is also home to **Mr. Toad's Wild Ride, Peter Pan's Flight,** and **Pinocchio's Daring Journey,** classic, movie-theater-dark rides that immerse riders in Disney fairytales and appeal to adults and kids alike. The Abominable Snowman pops up on the **Matterhorn Bobsleds,** a roller coaster that twists and turns you up and around a made-to-scale model of the real Swiss mountain. Anchoring the east end of Fantasyland is **it's a small world,** a smorgasbord of dancing animatronic dolls, cuckoo clock–covered walls, and variations of the song everyone knows, or soon *will* know, by heart. A 2008 renovation added beloved Disney characters like Ariel from *Under the Sea* to the mix.

MICKEY'S TOONTOWN Geared toward small fry, this lopsided cartoonlike downtown, complete with cars and trolleys that invite exploring, is where Mickey, Donald, Goofy, and other classic Disney characters hang their hats. One of the most popular attractions is **Roger Rabbit's Car Toon Spin,** a twisting, turning cab ride through the Toontown of *Who Framed Roger Rabbit?*

BEST TIPS FOR DISNEYLAND

Buy entry tickets in advance. Many nearby hotels sell park admission tickets; you can also buy them through the Disney Web site. If you book a package deal, such as those offered through AAA, tickets are included, too.

The lines at the ticket booths can take more than an hour on busy days, so you'll definitely save time by buying in advance, especially if you're committed to going on a certain day regardless of the weather.

Come midweek. Weekends, especially in summer, are a mob scene. A winter weekday is often the least crowded time to visit.

Plan your times to hit the most popular rides. If you're at the park when the gates open, make a beeline for the top rides before the crowds reach a critical mass. Another good time is the evening, when the hordes thin out somewhat, and during a parade or other show. Save the quieter attractions for midafternoon.

Look into Fastpasses. These passes allow you to reserve your place in line at some of the most crowded attractions (only one at a time). Distribution machines are posted near the entrances of each attraction. Feed in your park admission ticket, and you'll receive a pass with a printed time frame (generally up to 1–1½ hours later) during which you can return to wait in a much shorter line.

Plan your meals to avoid peak mealtime crowds. Start the day with a big breakfast so you won't be too hungry at noon, when restaurants and vendors get swarmed. Wait to have lunch until after 1.

If you want to eat at the **Blue Bayou** in New Orleans Square, it's best to make reservations in person as soon as you get to the park. Another (cheaper) option is to bring your own food. There are areas with picnic tables set up for this. And it's always a good idea to bring water and a few nonmeltable snacks with you.

Check the daily events schedule online or at the park entrance. During parades, fireworks, and other special events, sections of the parks clog with crowds. This can work for you or against you. An event could make it difficult to get around a park—but if you plan ahead, you can take advantage of the distraction to hit popular rides. The Web site also lists rides that are closed for repairs or renovations, so you know what to expect before you go.

Send the Teens Next Door: Disneyland's newer sister park, California Adventure, features more intense rides suitable for older kids (Park Hopper passes include admission to both parks).

You can also walk through **Mickey's House** to meet and be photographed with the famous mouse, take a low-key ride on **Gadget's Go Coaster,** or bounce around the fenced-in playground in front of **Goofy's House.**

TOMOR-ROWLAND   This popular section of the park underwent a complete refurbishment in 1998 and has continued to tinker with its future, adding and enhancing rides regularly. One of the newest attractions, **Finding Nemo's Submarine Voyage,** updates the old Submarine Voyage ride with the exploits of Nemo, Dory, Marlin, and other characters from the Pixar film. Try

DID YOU KNOW?

Apparently, the plain purple teacup in Disneyland's Mad Tea Party ride spins the fastest— though no one knows why.

to visit this popular ride early in the day if you can and be prepared for a wait. The interactive **Buzz Lightyear Astro Blasters** lets you zap your neighbors with laser beams and compete for the highest score. Hurtle through the cosmos on **Space Mountain,** refurbished in 2005 or check out mainstays like the futuristic **Astro Orbiter** rockets, **Innoventions,** a self-guided tour of the latest toys of tomorrow, and **Honey, I Shrunk the Audience,** a 3-D film featuring Rick Moranis. Disneyland Monorail and Disneyland Railroad both have stations here. There's also a video arcade and dancing water fountain that makes a perfect playground for kids on hot summer days.

Besides the eight lands, the daily live-action shows and parades are always crowd-pleasers. **Fantasmic!** is a musical, fireworks, and laser show in which Mickey and friends wage a spellbinding battle against Disneyland's darker characters. ■TIP➔ Arrive early to secure a good view; if there are two shows scheduled for the day, the second one tends to be less crowded. A fireworks display sparks up Friday and Saturday evenings. Brochures with maps, available at the entrance, list show and parade times.

DISNEY'S CALIFORNIA ADVENTURE

♻ **Disney's California Adventure.** The sprawling 55-acre Disney's California
★ Adventure, right next to Disneyland (their entrances face each other), pays tribute to the Golden State with four theme areas. In 2007 the park began a major five-year overhaul aimed at infusing more of Walt Disney's spirit throughout the park.

New attractions include World of Color, a nighttime water-effects show and Toy Story Mania!, an interactive adventure ride hosted by Woody, Buzz Lightyear, and friends, which opened in 2008. Ariel's Undersea Adventure and a 12-acre section called Cars Land based on the Pixar film are also in the works. ⊠ *Disneyland Dr. between Ball Rd. and Katella Ave., Anaheim* ☎ *714/781–4565* ⊕ *www.disneyland.com* ☉ *Hrs vary.*

DISNEY LANDS

GOLDEN STATE   Celebrate California's history and natural beauty with nature trails, a winery, and a tortilla factory (with free samples). The area of Condor Flats has **Soarin' Over California,** a spectacular simulated hang-glider ride over California terrain, and the **Redwood Creek Challenge Trail,** a challenging trek across net ladders and suspension bridges. **Grizzly River Run** simulates the river rapids of the Sierra Nevadas; be prepared to get soaked. The Wine Country Trattoria is a great place for a relaxing outdoor lunch.

HOLLYWOOD   With a main street modeled after Hollywood Boulevard, a fake blue-
PICTURES   sky backdrop, and real soundstages, this area celebrates California's
BACKLOT   most famous industry. **Disney Animation** gives you an insider's look at the work of animators and how they create characters. **Turtle Talk with Crush** lets kids have an unrehearsed talk with computer-animated Crush, a sea turtle from *Finding Nemo.* The Hyperion Theater hosts **Aladdin—A Musical Spectacular,** a 45-minute live performance with terrific visual effects. ■TIP➔ Plan on getting in line about half an hour in advance: the show is well worth the wait. On the latest film-inspired ride, **Monsters, Inc. Mike & Sulley to the Rescue,** you climb into taxis and

travel the streets of Monstropolis on a mission of safely returning Boo to her bedroom. A major draw for older kids is the looming **Twilight Zone Tower of Terror,** which drops riders 13 floors.

A BUG'S LAND Inspired by the 1998 film *A Bug's Life,* this section skews its attractions to an insect's point of view. Kids can spin around in giant takeout Chinese food boxes on **Flik's Flyers,** and hit the bug-shaped bumper cars on **Tuck and Roll's Drive 'Em Buggies.** The short show *It's Tough to Be a Bug!* gives you a 3-D look at insect life.

PARADISE PIER This section re-creates the glory days of California's seaside piers. If you're looking for thrills, the **California Screamin'** roller coaster takes its riders from 0 to 55 mph in about four seconds and proceeds through scream tunnels, steeply angled drops, and a 360-degree loop. **Mickey's Fun Wheel,** a giant Ferris wheel, provides a good view of the grounds at a more leisurely pace. There's also carnival games, a fish-theme carousel, and Ariel's Grotto, where future princesses can dine with the mermaid and her friends (reservations a must).

OTHER ATTRACTIONS

Downtown Disney. Downtown Disney is a 20-acre promenade of dining, shopping, and entertainment that connects the Disneyland Resort hotels and theme parks. Restaurant-nightclubs here include the **House of Blues,** which spices up its Delta-inspired ribs and seafood with various live music acts on an intimate two-story stage. At **Ralph Brennan's Jazz Kitchen** you can dig into New Orleans–style food and music. Sports fans gravitate to **ESPN Zone,** a sports bar–restaurant–entertainment center with American grill food, interactive video games, and 175 video screens telecasting worldwide sports events.

There's also an **AMC** multiplex movie theater with stadium-style seating that plays the latest blockbusters and, naturally, a couple of kids' flicks. Promenade shops sell everything from Disney goods to antique jewelry; don't miss **Vault 28,** a hip boutique that sells one-of-kind vintage and couture clothes and accessories from Disney, Betsey Johnson, and other designers. ✉ *Disneyland Dr. between Ball Rd. and Katella Ave., Anaheim* ☎ *714/300–7800* ⊕ *www.disneyland.com* ✉ *Free* ☉ *Daily 7 am–2 am; hrs at shops and restaurants vary.*

WHERE TO EAT

$$$ ╳**Anaheim White House.** Several small dining rooms are set with crisp
ITALIAN linens and candles in this flower-filled 1909 mansion. The northern Italian menu includes steak, rack of lamb, and fresh seafood. Try the Gwen Stefani Ravioli, lobster-filled pasta on a bed of ginger and citrus. A three-course prix-fixe "express" lunch, served weekdays, costs $22. ✉ *887 S. Anaheim Blvd., Anaheim* ☎ *714/772–1381* ☉ *No lunch weekends.*

$$ ╳**Catal Restaurant & Uva Bar.** Famed chef Joachim Splichal of L.A.'s
MEDITERRANEAN Patina empire takes a more casual approach at this bi-level Mediterranean spot—with tapas breaking into the finger-food territory. At the Uva (Spanish for "grape") bar on the ground level you can graze on olives and Spanish ham, choosing from 40 wines by the glass. Upstairs, Catal's menu spans paella, rotisserie chicken, and salads. ✉ *1580 S. Disneyland Dr., Suite 103, Anaheim* ☎ *714/774–4442.*

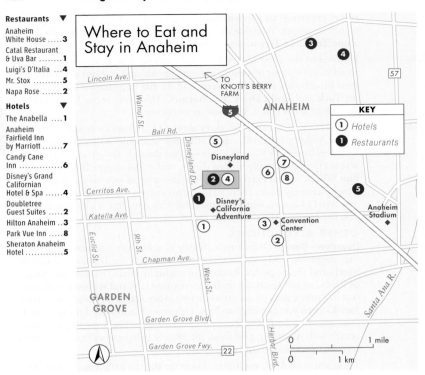

Where to Eat and
Stay in Anaheim

KEY
① *Hotels*
❶ *Restaurants*

$ — ITALIC — **✕ Luigi's D'Italia.** Despite the simple surroundings—red vinyl booths and plastic checkered tablecloths—Luigi's serves outstanding Italian cuisine: spaghetti marinara, veal Parmesan, homemade pizza, and other classics. Kids will feel right at home here; there's even a children's menu. It's an easy five-minute drive from Disneyland, but less crowded and expensive than many restaurants adjacent to the park. ✉ *801 S. State College Blvd., Anaheim* ☎ *714/490–0990.*

$ — AMERICAN — **✕ Mr. Stox.** Intimate booths and linen tablecloths create a sophisticated, old-school setting at this family-owned restaurant. Prime rib, Maryland crab cakes, and fresh fish specials are excellent; the pasta, bread, and pastries are made in-house; and the wine list is wide-ranging. ✉ *1105 E. Katella Ave., Anaheim* ☎ *714/634–2994* ⊘ *No lunch weekends.*

$$$$ — AMERICAN — ★ **✕ Napa Rose.** In sync with its host hotel, Disney's Grand Californian, this restaurant is done in a lovely Arts and Crafts style. The contemporary cuisine here is matched with an extensive wine list (600 bottles on display). For a look into the open kitchen, sit at the counter and watch the chefs as they whip up signature dishes such as Gulf of California rock scallops in a sauce of lemon, lobster, and vanilla and spit-roasted prime rib of pork with ranch-style black beans. The four-course $85 prix-fixe menu changes weekly. ✉ *Disney's Grand Californian Hotel, 1600 S. Disneyland Dr., Anaheim* ☎ *714/300–7170.*

WHERE TO STAY

For expanded reviews, visit Fodors.com.

¢ 🏨 **The Anabella.** This Spanish Mission–style hotel on the convention center campus is a good value. **Pros:** attentive service; landscaped grounds; pet-friendly rooms. **Cons:** some say the room walls are thin; it's a bit removed from the action. ⊠ *1030 W. Katella Ave., Anaheim* 🕿 *714/905–1050, 800/863–4888* 📠 *714/905–1054* ⊕ *www.anabellahotel.com* 🛏 *358 rooms, 124 suites* ☖ *In-room: Wi-Fi. In-hotel: restaurant, bar, pool, gym, spa, laundry facilities, parking.*

¢ 🏨 **Anaheim Fairfield Inn by Marriott.** Attentive service and proximity to Disneyland (a 10-minute walk away) make this high-rise hotel a big draw for families. **Pros:** free off-site parking with shuttle; close to many restaurants; the lobby offers fruit-infused drinking water and a TV showing Disney movies. **Cons:** small pool abuts the parking lot; lack of green space. ⊠ *1460 S. Harbor Blvd., Anaheim* 🕿 *714/772–6777, 800/228–2800* 📠 *714/999–1727* ⊕ *www.marriott.com* 🛏 *467 rooms* ☖ *In-room: Wi-Fi. In-hotel: restaurant, pool, laundry facilities, parking.*

$$ 🏨 **Candy Cane Inn.** One of the Disneyland area's first hotels (deeds were ★ executed Christmas Eve, hence the name), the Candy Cane is one of Anaheim's most relaxing properties. **Pros:** proximity to Disneyland; friendly service; well-lighted, landscaped property. **Cons:** rooms and lobby are on the small side; all rooms face parking lot. ⊠ *1747 S. Harbor Blvd., Anaheim* 🕿 *714/774–5284, 800/345–7057* 📠 *714/772–5462* ⊕ *www.candycaneinn.net* 🛏 *171 rooms* ☖ *In-room: Wi-Fi. In-hotel: pool, spa, laundry facilities, parking* 🍽 *Breakfast.*

$$$ 🏨 **Disney's Grand Californian Hotel & Spa.** The newest of Disney's Anaheim Fodor's Choice hotels, this Craftsman-style luxury property has guest rooms with views ★ of the California Adventure park and Downtown Disney. **Pros:** large, gorgeous lobby; direct access to California Adventure. **Cons:** the self-parking lot is across the street from the hotel; standard rooms are on the small side. ⊠ *1600 S. Disneyland Dr., Anaheim* 🕿 *714/956–6425* 📠 *714/300–7701* ⊕ *www.disneyland.com* 🛏 *901 rooms, 44 suites, 50 villas* ☖ *In-room: Internet. In-hotel: restaurant, bar, pool, gym, children's programs, parking.*

$$ 🏨 **Doubletree Guest Suites.** This upscale hotel near the Convention Center ★ caters to business travelers and families alike. **Pros:** huge suites; elegant lobby; within walking distance of a variety of restaurants. **Cons:** some say the hotel seems far-removed from Disneyland; pool area is small. ⊠ *2085 S. Harbor Blvd., Anaheim* 🕿 *714/750–3000, 800/215–7316* 📠 *714/750–3002* 🛏 *50 rooms, 202 suites* ☖ *In-hotel: restaurant, pool, spa, laundry facilities, parking* 🍽 *Breakfast.*

$$ 🏨 **Hilton Anaheim.** Next to the Anaheim Convention Center, this busy Hilton is one of the largest hotels in Southern California with a restaurant and food court, cocktail lounges, a full-service gym, and its own Starbucks. **Pros:** friendly efficient service; great seasonal kids' programs. **Cons:** huge size can be daunting; $14 fee to use health club. ⊠ *777 Convention Way, Anaheim* 🕿 *714/750–4321, 800/445–8667* 📠 *714/740–4460* ⊕ *www.anaheim.hilton.com* 🛏 *1,572 rooms, 93 suites* ☖ *In-hotel: restaurant, bar, pool, gym, parking.*

¢ ⊡ **Park Vue Inn.** This bougainvillea-trimmed two-story Spanish-style inn is one of the closest hotels you can find to Disneyland's main gate. **Pros:** easy walk to Disneyland and many restaurants; good value. **Cons:** all rooms face the parking lot; some complain about early-morning street noise. ⊠ *1570 S. Harbor Blvd., Anaheim* ☎ *714/772–3691, 800/334–7021* 🖷 *714/956–4736* ⊕ *www.parkvueinn.com* 🛏 *76 rooms, 8 suites* ⚒ *In-hotel: pool, gym, spa, laundry facilities, parking.*

$$ ⊡ **Sheraton Anaheim Hotel.** If you're hoping to escape from the commercial
★ atmosphere of the hotels near Disneyland, consider this sprawling replica of a Tudor castle. **Pros:** large, attractive lobby; game room; spacious rooms with comfortable beds. **Cons:** confusing layout; hotel sits close to a busy freeway and is not within walking distance of Disneyland. ⊠ *900 S. Disneyland Dr., Anaheim* ☎ *714/778–1700, 800/325–3535* 🖷 *714/535–3889* ⊕ *www.starwoodhotels.com* 🛏 *460 rooms, 29 suites* ⚒ *In-room: Wi-Fi. In-hotel: restaurant, bar, pool, gym, laundry facilities, parking.*

SPORTS

Los Angeles Angels of Anaheim. Pro baseball's Los Angeles Angels of Anaheim play at Angel Stadium of Anaheim. An "Outfield Extravaganza" celebrates great plays on the field, with fireworks and a geyser exploding over a model evoking the California coast. ⊠ *2000 Gene Autry Way, East Anaheim, Anaheim* ☎ *714/940–2000* ⊕ *www.angelsbaseball.com.*

Anaheim Ducks. The National Hockey League's Anaheim Ducks, winners of the 2007 Stanley Cup, play at Honda Center. ⊠ *Formerly Arrowhead Pond, 2695 E. Katella Ave., East Anaheim, Anaheim* ☎ *714/704–2400* ⊕ *ducks.nhl.com.*

KNOTT'S BERRY FARM

25 mi south of Los Angeles, via I–5, in Buena Park.

🕄 **Knott's Berry Farm.** The land where the boysenberry was invented (by cross-
★ ing red raspberry, blackberry, and loganberry bushes) is now occupied by Knott's Berry Farm. In 1934 Cordelia Knott began serving chicken dinners on her wedding china to supplement her family's income. Or so the story goes. The dinners and her boysenberry pies proved more profitable than husband Walter's berry farm, so the two moved first into the restaurant business and then into the entertainment business.

The park is now a 160-acre complex with 100-plus rides, dozens of restaurants and shops, and even a brick-by-brick replica of Philadelphia's Independence Hall. Although it has some good attractions for small children, the park is best known for its roster of awesome thrill rides. And, yes, you can still get that boysenberry pie (and jam, juice—you name it). ⊠ *8039 Beach Blvd.* ✛ *Between La Palma Ave. and Crescent St., 2 blocks south of Hwy. 91* ☎ *714/220–5200* ⊕ *www.knotts.com.*

PARK NEIGHBORHOODS

BOARDWALK Not-for-the-squeamish thrill rides and skill-based games dominate the scene at **Boardwalk.** Go head over heels on the **Boomerang** roller coaster, then do it again—backward. The **Perilous Plunge,** billed as the world's tallest, steepest, and—thanks to its big splash—wettest thrill ride, sends riders down an almost-vertical chute. Windseeker, opening in late 2011, whisks passengers on an unforgettable gondola ride 300 feet above the park. Boardwalk is also home to a string of test-your-skill games that are fun to watch whether you're playing or not, and Johnny Rockets, the park's newest restaurant.

CAMP SNOOPY It can get gridlocked on weekends, but small fry love this miniature High Sierra wonderland where the *Peanuts* gang hangs out. They can push and pump their own mini-mining cars on **Huff and Puff,** zip around a pint-size racetrack on **Charlie Brown Speedway,** and hop aboard **Woodstock's Airmail,** a kids' version of the park's Supreme Scream ride. Most of the rides here are geared toward kids only, leaving parents to cheer them on from the sidelines. **Sierra Sidewinder,** a roller coaster that opened near the entrance of Camp Snoopy in 2007, is aimed at older children with spinning saucer-type vehicles that go a maximum speed of 37 mph.

FIESTA VILLAGE Over in **Fiesta Village** are two more musts for adrenaline junkies: **Montezooma's Revenge,** a roller coaster that goes from 0 to 55 mph in less than five seconds, and **Jaguar!,** which simulates the motions of a cat stalking its prey, twisting, spiraling, and speeding up and slowing down as it takes you on its stomach-dropping course. There's also **Hat Dance,** a version of the spinning teacups but with sombreros, and a 100-year-old Dentzel Carousel, complete with an antique organ and menagerie of hand-carved animals.

GHOST TOWN Clusters of authentic old buildings relocated from their original mining-town sites mark this section of the park. You can stroll down the street, stop and chat with a blacksmith, pan for gold (for a fee), crack open a geode, check out the chalkboard of a circa-1875 schoolhouse, and ride an original Butterfield stagecoach. Looming over it all is **GhostRider,** Orange County's first wooden roller coaster. Traveling up to 56 mph and reaching 118 feet at its highest point, the park's biggest attraction is riddled with sudden dips and curves, subjecting riders to forces up to three times that of gravity. On the Western-theme **Silver Bullet,** riders are sent to a height of 146 feet and then back down 109 feet. Riders spiral, corkscrew, fly into a cobra roll, and experience overbanked curves. The **Calico Mine** ride descends into a replica of a working gold mine. The **Timber Mountain Log Ride** is a worthwhile flume ride, especially if you're with kids who don't make the height requirements for the flumes at Disneyland. Also found here is the park's newest thrill ride, the **Pony Express,** a roller coaster that lets riders saddle up on packs of "horses" tethered to platforms that take off on a series of hairpin turns and travel up to 38 mph. Don't miss the **Western Trails Museum,** a dusty old gem full of Old West memorabilia, plus menus from the original chicken restaurant, and Mrs. Knott's antique button collection. **Calico Railroad** departs regularly from Ghost Town station for a round-trip tour of the park (bandit holdups notwithstanding).

WILD WATER WILDERNESS Just as its name implies, this section is home to **Big Foot Rapids,** a splash-fest of white-water river rafting over towering cliffs, cascading waterfalls, and wild rapids. Don't miss the visually stunning show at **Mystery Lodge,** which tells the story of Native Americans in the Pacific Northwest with lights, music, and beautiful images.

Knott's Soak City Water Park is directly across from the main park on 13 acres next to Independence Hall. It has a dozen major water rides; the latest is **Pacific Spin,** an oversize waterslide that drops riders 75 feet into a catch pool. There's also a children's pool, 750,000-gallon wave pool, and funhouse. Soak City is open daily after Memorial Day; weekends only after Labor Day.

WHERE TO EAT AND STAY

$ ✕ **Mrs. Knott's Chicken Dinner Restaurant.** Cordelia Knott's fried chicken
AMERICAN   and boysenberry pies drew crowds so big that Knott's Berry Farm was built to keep the hungry customers occupied while they waited. The restaurant's current incarnation (outside the park's entrance) still serves crispy fried chicken, along with fluffy biscuits, corn, mashed potatoes, and Mrs. Knott's signature chilled cherry-rhubarb compote. The wait, unfortunately, can be two-plus hours on weekends; another option is to order a bucket of the same tasty chicken from the adjacent takeout counter and have a picnic at the duck pond next to Independence Hall across the street. ⊠ *Knott's Berry Farm Marketplace Area, 8039 Beach Blvd.* ☎ *714/220–5080.*

$$$$ ✕ **Pirate's Dinner Adventure.** During this interactive pirate-theme dinner
AMERICAN   show, 150 actors/singers/acrobats (some quite talented) perform on a galleon while you eat a three-course meal. Food—barbecue pork, roast chicken, salad, veggies, rice, and unlimited soda and coffee—is mediocre and seating is tight, but kids love making a lot of noise to cheer on their favorite pirate, and the action scenes are breathtaking. ⊠ *7600 Beach Blvd.* ☎ *866/439–2469.*

$$ ☐ **Knott's Berry Farm Resort Hotel.** Knott's Berry Farm runs this con-
venient high-rise hotel on park grounds. **Pros:** easy access to Knott's Berry Farm; plenty of kids' activities; basketball court. **Cons:** lobby and hallways can be noisy and chaotic. ⊠ *7675 Crescent Ave.* ☎ *714/995–1111, 866/752–2444* 🖷 *714/828–8590* ⊕ *www.knottshotel.com* ⤶ *320 rooms* ⚷ *In-room: Internet. In-hotel: restaurant, bar, pool, tennis court, gym, laundry facilities, parking.*

THE COAST

Running along the Orange County coastline is scenic Pacific Coast Highway (Highway 1, known locally as PCH). Older beachfront settlements, with their modest bungalow-style homes, are joined by posh new gated communities. The pricey land between Newport Beach and Laguna Beach is where Laker Kobe Bryant, novelist Dean Koontz, and a slew of Internet and finance moguls live.

Though the coastline is rapidly being filled in, there are still a few stretches of beautiful, protected open land. And at many places along the way you can catch an idealized glimpse of the Southern California lifestyle: surfers hitting the beach, boards under their arms.

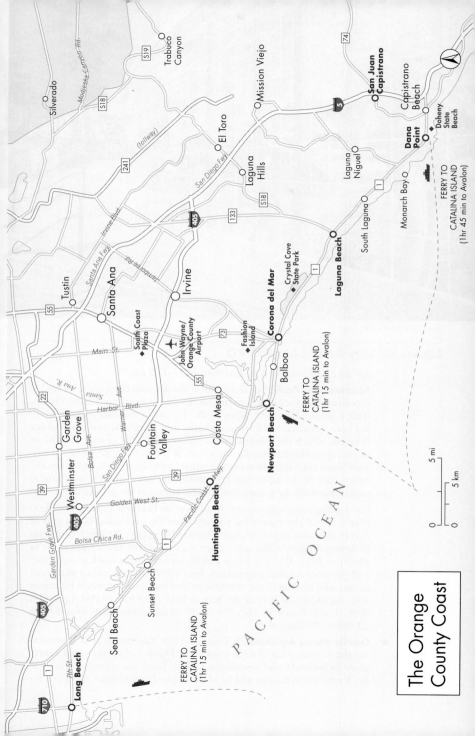

The Orange County Coast

PACIFIC OCEAN

5 mi
5 km
0
0

Long Beach
Seal Beach
Sunset Beach
Huntington Beach
Garden Grove
Westminster
Fountain Valley
Costa Mesa
Tustin
Santa Ana
South Coast Plaza
John Wayne/Orange County Airport
Irvine
Main St.
Harbor Blvd.
Warner Ave.
Bolsa Ave.
Golden West St.
Bolsa Chica Rd.
Garden Grove Fwy.
San Diego Fwy.
Santa Ana R.
7th St.
Pacific Coast Hwy.

Newport Beach
Balboa
Corona del Mar
Fashion Island
Crystal Cove State Park
Laguna Beach
South Laguna
Monarch Bay
Laguna Niguel
Dana Point
Capistrano Beach
Doheny State Beach
San Juan Capistrano
Mission Viejo
Laguna Hills
El Toro
Silverado
Trabuco Canyon

Santa Ana Fwy.
San Diego Fwy.
Irvine Blvd.
Jamboree Rd.
Modjeska Canyon Rd.
(tollway)

FERRY TO CATALINA ISLAND (1hr 15 min to Avalon)
FERRY TO CATALINA ISLAND (1hr 15 min to Avalon)
FERRY TO CATALINA ISLAND (1hr 45 min to Avalon)

710
1
405
22
39
55
241
405
133
S18
S18
73
55
39
1
1
5
74
S19

A mural at Huntington Beach.

LONG BEACH AND SAN PEDRO

About 25 mi southeast of Los Angeles, I–110 south.

Aquarium of the Pacific. Sea lions, nurse sharks, and octopuses, oh my!—this aquarium focuses primarily on ocean life from the Pacific Ocean, with a detour into Australian birds. The main exhibits include lively sea lions, large tanks of various sharks and stingrays, and ethereal sea dragons, which the aquarium has successfully bred in captivity. Most impressive is the multimedia attraction, *Whales: A Journey With Giants*. This panoramic film shows in the aquarium's Great Hall, and when the entire core of the aquarium goes dark, you suddenly feel as if you're swimming with the giants. Ask for showtimes at the information desk.

For a nonaquatic experience, head over to Lorikeet Forest, a walk-in aviary full of the friendliest parrots from Down Under. Buy a cup of nectar and smile as you become a human bird perch. Be sure to say hello to newest resident Ollie, a sea otter rescued off the Santa Cruz coast as a baby in 2010. If you're a true tropical animal lover, book an up-close-and-personal Animal Encounters Tour ($90) to learn about and assist in care and feeding of the animals; or find out how aquarium functions with the extensive Behind the Scenes Tour ($34.95). ✉ *100 Aquarium Way, Long Beach* ☎ *562/590–3100* ⊕ *www.aquariumofpacific.org* ⊠ *$24.95* ⊙ *Daily 9–6.*

★ **Cabrillo Marine Aquarium.** Dedicated to the marine life that flourishes off the southern California coast, this Frank Gehry–designed center gives an intimate and instructive look at local sea creatures. Head to the Exploration Center and S. Mark Taper Foundation Courtyard for kid-friendly interactive exhibits and activity stations. Especially fun is the "Crawl In" aquarium, where you can be surrounded by fish without getting wet. ■TIP→ From March through July the aquarium orga-nizes a legendary grunion program, when you can see the small, silvery fish as they come ashore at night to spawn on the beach. After visiting the museum, you can stop for a picnic or beach stroll along Cabrillo Beach. ✉ *3720 Stephen M. White Dr., San Pedro, Los Angeles* ☎ *310/548–7562* ⊕ *www.cabrilloaq.org* ✍ *$5 suggested donation, parking avail-able in adjacent lot at reduced rate of $1 for museumgoers* ☉ *Tues.–Fri. noon–5, weekends 10–5.*

Queen Mary. The reason to see this impressive example of 20th-century cruise ship opulence is because it's the last of its kind. And there's a saying among staff members that the more you get to know the *Queen Mary,* the more you realize she has an endearing personality to match her wealth of history.

The beautifully preserved ocean liner was launched in 1934 and made 1,001 transatlantic crossings before finally berthing in Long Beach in 1967. It has gone through many periods of renovations since, but in 1993, the RMS Foundation took over ownership and restored its origi-nal art deco style. Delaware North Companies took over management in 2009 with plans to continue restoration and renovation of the ship.

On board, you can take one of 12 tours, such as the informative Behind the Scenes walk or the downright spooky Haunted Encounters tour. (Spir-its have been spotted in the pool and engine room.) You could stay for dinner at one of the ship's restaurants, listen to live jazz in the original first-class lounge, or even spend the night in one of the wood-paneled rooms.

The ship's neighbor, a geodesic dome originally built to house Howard Hughes's *Spruce Goose* aircraft, now serves as a terminal for Carnival Cruise Lines, making the *Queen Mary* the perfect pit stop before or after a cruise. And anchored next to the *Queen* is the *Scorpion,* a Rus-sian submarine you can tour for a look at Cold War history. ✉ *1126 Queens Hwy., Long Beach* ☎ *877/342–0738* ⊕ *www.queenmary.com* ✍ *Tours $24.95–$32.95, includes a self-guided audio tour* ☉ *Call for times and frequency of guided tours.*

HUNTINGTON BEACH

40 mi southeast of Los Angeles, I–5 south to I–605 south to I–405 south to Beach Blvd.

Once a sleepy residential town with little more than a string of rugged surf shops, Huntington Beach has transformed itself into a resort des-tination. The town's appeal is its broad white-sand beaches with often-towering waves, complemented by a lively pier, shops, and restaurants on Main Street and a growing collection of luxurious resort hotels.

A draw for sports fans and partiers of all stripes is the U.S. Open pro-fessional surf competition, which brings a festive atmosphere to town each July. There's even a Surfing Walk of Fame, with plaques set in the sidewalk around the intersection of PCH and Main Street.

ESSENTIALS

Visitor and Tour Information **Huntington Beach Conference and Visitors Bureau** ⊠ *301 Main St., Suite 208* ☎ *714/969–3492, 800/729–6232* ⊕ *www.surfcityusa.com.*

EXPLORING

Huntington Pier. Huntington Pier stretches 1,800 feet out to sea, well past the powerful waves that made Huntington Beach reach for the title of "Surf City U.S.A." A farmers' market is held on Friday; an informal arts fair sets up most weekends. **Ruby's** (☎ *714/969–7829* ⊕ *www.rubys. com*). At the end of the pier sits Ruby's, part of a California chain of 1940s-style burger joints.

Pierside Pavilion. The Pierside Pavilion has shops, restaurants, and bars with live music. The best surf-gear source is **HSS Pierside** (☎ *714/841– 4000*), next to the pier, staffed by true surf enthusiasts. ⊠ *PCH across from Huntington Pier.*

International Surfing Museum. Just up Main Street from the pier, the International Surfing Museum pays tribute to the sport's greats with the Surfing Hall of Fame, which has an impressive collection of surfboards and related memorabilia. They've even got the Bolex camera used to shoot the 1966 surfing documentary *The Endless Summer.* ⊠ *411 Olive St.* ☎ *714/960–3483* ⊕ *www.surfingmuseum.org* ▱ *Free, $1 suggested donation for students, $2 for adults* ⊙ *Year-round weekdays noon–5, Tuesdays until 9, weekends 11–6.*

★ **Bolsa Chica Ecological Reserve.** This impressive reserve beckons wildlife lovers and bird-watchers with a 1,180-acre salt marsh where 321 out of Orange County's 420 bird species—including great blue herons, snowy and great egrets, and brown pelicans—have been spotted in the past decade. Throughout the reserve are trails for bird-watching, including a comfortable 1½-mi loop. Free guided tours depart from the walking bridge the second Saturday of each month at 10 am. ⊠ *Entrance on PCH 1 mi south of Warner Ave., opposite Bolsa Chica State Beach at traffic light* ☎ *714/846–1114* ⊕ *www.bolsachica.org* ▱ *Free* ⊙ *Daily dawn–dusk.*

WHERE TO EAT

$$$
SEAFOOD

✕ **Duke's.** Oceanfront vistas and fresh-caught seafood reign supreme at this homage to surfing legend Duke Kahanamoku, which is a prime people-watching spot right at the beginning of the pier. Choose from several fish-of-the-day selections—many Hawaiian—prepared in one of eight ways. Or try the crispy coconut shrimp or seven-spice ahi tuna. Duke's mai tai is not to be missed. ⊠ *317 PCH* ☎ *714/374–6446* ⊕ *www.dukeshuntington.com.*

$
AMERICAN

✕ **Lou's Red Oak BBQ.** You won't find any frills at Lou's Red Oak BBQ— just barbecue pork, grilled linguica, rotisserie chicken, and a lot of beef. Try the tri-tip (either as an entrée or on a toasted bun smothered with garlic butter) or a Hawaiian teriyaki plate to get into the surfing spirit. ⊠ *21501 Brookhurst St.* ☎ *714/965–5200* ⊕ *www.lousbbq.com.*

SPORTS AND THE OUTDOORS

BEACHES **Huntington City Beach.** This beach stretches for 3 mi north and south of the pier from Bolsa Chica State Beach to Huntington State Beach on the south. The beach is most crowded around the pier; amateur and professional surfers brave the waves daily on its north side. ☎ *714/536–5281* ⊕ *www.ci.huntington-beach.ca.us.*

Huntington State Beach. As you continue south, Huntington State Beach parallels Pacific Coast Highway. On the state and city beaches there are changing rooms, concessions, lifeguards, Wi-Fi, and ample parking; the state beach also has barbecue pits. ☎ *714/536–1454* ⊕ *www.parks. ca.gov/?page_id=643.*

Bolsa Chica State Beach. At the northern section of the city, Bolsa Chica State Beach has barbecue pits and RV campsites and is usually less crowded than its southern neighbors. ☎ *714/846–3460* ⊕ *www.parks. ca.gov/?page_id=642.*

SURFING **Corky Carroll's Surf School.** Corky Carroll's Surf School organizes lessons, weeklong workshops, and surfing trips. ☎ *714/969–3959* ⊕ *www. surfschool.net.*

Dwight's. You can rent surf- or boogie boards at Dwight's, one block south of the pier. ☎ *714/536–8083.*

NEWPORT BEACH

6 mi south of Huntington Beach, PCH.

Newport Beach has evolved from a simple seaside village to an icon of chic coastal living. Its ritzy reputation comes from megayachts bobbing in the harbor, boutiques that rival those in Beverly Hills, and spectacular homes overlooking the ocean.

Newport is said to have the highest per-capita number of Mercedes-Benzes in the world; inland Newport Beach's concentration of high-rise office buildings, shopping centers, and luxury hotels drive the economy. But on the city's Balboa Peninsula, you can still catch a glimpse of a more innocent, down-to-earth beach town scattered with tackle shops and sailor bars.

ESSENTIALS

Visitor and Tour Information Newport Beach Conference and Visitors Bureau ✉ *110 Newport Center Dr., Suite 120* ☎ *949/719–6100, 800/942–6278* ⊕ *www.visitnewportbeach.com.*

EXPLORING

Balboa Pavilion. The Balboa Pavilion, on the bay side of the peninsula, was built in 1905 as a bath- and boathouse. Today it houses a restaurant and shops and it serves as a departure point for harbor and whale-watching cruises. Look for it on Main Street, off Balboa Boulevard. Adjacent to the pavilion is the three-car ferry that connects the peninsula to Balboa Island. In the blocks around the pavilion you can find restaurants, beachside shops, and the small **Fun Zone**—a local kiddie hangout with a Ferris wheel and a nautical museum. On the other side of the narrow peninsula is **Balboa Pier.** On its end is the original branch of Ruby's, a 1940s-esque burger-and-shake joint.

Balboa Peninsula. Newport's best beaches are on Balboa Peninsula, where many jetties pave the way to ideal swimming areas. The most intense bodysurfing place in Orange County and arguably on the West Coast, known as the **Wedge,** is at the south end of the peninsula. Created by accident in the 1930s when the Federal Works Progress Administration built a jetty to protect Newport Harbor, the break is pure euphoria for highly skilled bodysurfers. ■TIP→ Since the waves generally break very close to shore and rip currents are strong, lifeguards strongly discourage visitors from attempting it—but it sure is fun to watch an experienced local ride it.

Fashion Island. Shake the sand out of your shoes to head inland to the ritzy Fashion Island outdoor mall, a cluster of arcades and courtyards complete with koi pond, fountains, and a Venetian-style carousel—plus some awesome ocean views. Although it doesn't have quite the international-designer clout of South Coast Plaza, it has the luxe department store Neiman Marcus and expensive spots like L'Occitane, Kate Spade, Ligne Roset, and Michael Stars. Chains, restaurants, and the requisite movie theater fill out the rest. ⊠ *410 Newport Center Dr., between Jamboree and MacArthur Blvds., off PCH* ☎ *949/721–2000* ⊕ *www. shopfashionisland.com.*

★ **Newport Harbor.** Newport Harbor, which shelters nearly 10,000 small boats, may seduce even those who don't own a yacht. Spend an afternoon exploring the charming avenues and surrounding alleys. Within Newport Harbor are eight small islands, including Balboa and Lido. The houses framing the shore may seem modest, but this is some of the most expensive real estate in the world. Several grassy areas on primarily residential Lido Isle have views of Newport Harbor.

Balboa Island. Balboa Island is a sliver of terra firma in Newport Harbor whose quaint streets are tightly packed with impossibly charming multimillion-dollar cottages. The island's main drag, Marine Avenue, is lined with equally attractive cafés and shops.

Newport Harbor Nautical Museum. This museum, in the Balboa Fun Zone (a small, historic amusement park), has exhibits on the history of the harbor as well as of the Pacific as a whole. There's a fleet of ship models, some dating to 1798; one is made entirely of gold and silver. Another fun display is a touch tank holding local sea creatures. A new exhibit features simulated and submersion experiences through live feeds from underwater archeological sites and a replicated yacht race. ⊠ *600 E. Bay Ave., Newport Beach* ☎ *949/675–8915* ⊕ *www.nhnm.org* ☜ *$4* ☽ *Call for hours.*

★ **Orange County Museum of Art.** Modernist paintings and sculpture by California artists and cutting-edge as well as international contemporary works can be found at this museum. Works by such key California artists as Richard Diebenkorn, Ed Ruscha, Robert Irwin, and Chris Burden are included in the collection. The museum also displays some of its digital art, Internet-based art, and sound works in the Orange Lounge, a satellite gallery at South Coast Plaza; free of charge, it's open the same

Riding the waves at Newport Beach.

hours as the mall. ⊠ *850 San Clemente Dr.* ☎ *949/759–1122* ⊕ *www. ocma.net* ☞ *$12* ☾ *Wed. and Fri.–Sun. 11–5, Thurs. 11–8.*

WHERE TO EAT

$$$
SEAFOOD
✕ **The Cannery.** This 1920s cannery building still teems with fish, but now they go into dishes on the eclectic Pacific Rim menu rather than being packed into crates. Settle in at the sushi bar, dining room, or patio before choosing between sashimi, bouillabaisse, or oven-roasted Chilean sea bass prepared with an Asian twist. The menu includes a selection of steaks, ribs, and seafood. Fodor's readers recommend the crème brûlée for dessert. ⊠ *3010 Lafayette Rd.* ☎ *949/566–0060* ⊕ *www.cannerynewport.com.*

$
AMERICAN
✕ **3-Thirty-3.** If there's a nightlife "scene" to be had in Newport Beach, this is it. This swank and stylish eatery attracts a convivial crowd—both young and old—for midday, sunset, and late-night dining; a long list of small, shareable plates heightens the camaraderie. Pair a cocktail with Chinese-spiced lollipop lamb chops or chicken satay while you check out the scene, or settle in for a dinner of Kobe flatiron steak or potato-crusted halibut. ⊠ *333 Bayside Dr.* ☎ *949/673–8464* ⊕ *www.3thirty3nb.com.*

WHERE TO STAY

For expanded reviews, visit Fodors.com.

$$$
🏨 **Balboa Bay Club and Resort.** Sharing the same frontage as the private Balboa Bay Club where Humphrey Bogart, Lauren Bacall, and the Reagans hung out, this hotel has one of the best bay views around. **Pros:** exquisite bayfront views; comfortable beds; romantic. **Cons:** service is helpful but can be slow; not much within walking distance. ⊠ *1221 W.*

Coast Hwy. ☎ *949/645–5000, 888/445–7153* ⊕ *www.balboabayclub. com* ⌫ *150 rooms, 10 suites* ♿ *In-room: Wi-Fi. In-hotel: restaurant, bar, gym, spa, some pets allowed.*

SPORTS AND THE OUTDOORS

BOAT RENTALS   **Balboa Boat Rentals.** You can tour Lido and Balboa isles by renting kayaks ($15 an hour), sailboats ($45 an hour), small motorboats ($65 an hour), and electric boats ($75–$90 an hour) at Balboa Boat Rentals. You must have a driver's license, and some knowledge of boating is helpful; rented boats must stay in the bay. ⊠ *510 E. Edgewater Ave.* ☎ *949/673–7200* ⊕ *www.boats4rent.com.*

BOAT TOURS   **Catalina Passenger Service.** Located at the Balboa Pavilion, this company operates 90-minute daily round-trip passage to Catalina Island for $68. Call first; winter service is often available only on weekends. ⊠ *400 Main St.* ☎ *949/673–5245* ⊕ *www.catalinainfo.com.*

GOLF   **Newport Beach Golf Course.** This par-59 executive course is lighted for night play. Rates start at $17. Reservations are accepted up to one week in advance, but walk-ins are accommodated when possible. ⊠ *3100 Irvine Ave.* ☎ *949/852–8681* ⊕ *www.npbgolf.com.*

SPORTFISHING   **Davey's Locker.** In addition to a complete tackle shop, Davey's Locker operates sportfishing trips starting at $40, as well as private charters and, in winter, whale-watching trips for $30. ⊠ *Balboa Pavilion, 400 Main St.* ☎ *949/673–1434* ⊕ *www.daveyslocker.com.*

CORONA DEL MAR

2 mi south of Newport Beach, via Hwy. 1.

A small jewel on the Pacific Coast, Corona del Mar (known by locals as "CDM") has exceptional beaches that some say resemble their majestic Northern California counterparts. South of CDM is an area referred to as the Newport Coast or Crystal Cove—whatever you call it, it's another dazzling spot on the California Riviera.

ESSENTIALS

Visitor and Tour Information Newport Beach Conference and Visitors Bureau ⊠ *110 Newport Center Dr., Suite 120, Newport Beach* ☎ *949/719–6100, 800/942–6278* ⊕ *www.visitnewportbeach.com.*

EXPLORING

Corona del Mar State Beach. This beach is actually made up of two beaches, Little Corona and Big Corona, separated by a cliff. Facilities include fire pits, volleyball courts, a restaurant, restrooms, and parking. ■TIP➔ **Two colorful reefs (and the fact that it's off-limits to boats) make Corona del Mar great for snorkelers and for beachcombers who prefer privacy.** Also, parking in the lot is a steep $15, $25 on holidays, but you can often find a spot on the street on weekdays. ☎ *949/644–3151* ⊕ *www.parks.ca.gov.*

Fodor'sChoice ★   **Crystal Cove State Park.** Midway between Corona del Mar and Laguna, stretching along both sides of Pacific Coast Highway, Crystal Cove State Park is a favorite of local beachgoers and wilderness trekkers. It encompasses a 3½-mi stretch of unspoiled beach and has some of

A whimbrel hunts for mussels at Crystal Cove State Park.

the best tide-pooling in southern California. Here you can see starfish, crabs, and other sea life on the rocks. The park's 2,400 acres of back-country are ideal for hiking, horseback riding, and mountain biking, but stay on the trails to preserve the beauty. Environmental camping is allowed in one of the three campgrounds. Bring water, food, and other supplies; there's a pit toilet but no shower. Open fires and pets are forbidden. Parking costs $10.

Inside the park, the **Crystal Cove Historic District** holds a collection of 46 handmade historic cottages (14 of which are available for overnight rental), decorated and furnished to reflect the 1935–55 beach culture that flourished here. On the sand above the high tide line and on a bluff above the beach, the cottages offer a funky look at beach life 50 years ago. ☎ 949/376–8762 ☎ 949/494–3539 ⊕ *www.crystalcovestatepark. com* ☉ *Daily 6–dusk.*

Crystal Cove Promenade. Further adding to Orange County's overwhelming supply of high-end shopping and dining is Crystal Cove Promenade, which might be described as the toniest strip mall in America. The storefronts of this Mediterranean–inspired center are lined up across the street from Crystal Cove State Park, with the shimmering Pacific waters in plain view. There is plenty of sidewalk and courtyard seating at this center that is both a regional destination and dog-friendly neighborhood hangout for the lucky locals.

LAGUNA BEACH

Fodor's Choice
★

10 mi south of Newport Beach on Hwy. 1, 60 mi south of Los Angeles, I–5 south to Hwy. 133, which turns into Laguna Canyon Rd.

Even the approach tells you that Laguna Beach is exceptional. Driving in along Laguna Canyon Road from the I–405 freeway gives you the chance to cruise through a gorgeous coastal canyon, large stretches of which remain undeveloped. You'll arrive at a glistening wedge of ocean, at the intersection with PCH.

Laguna's welcome mat is legendary. For decades in the mid-20th century a local booster, Eiler Larsen, greeted everyone downtown. (There's now a statue of him on the main drag.) On the corner of Forest and Park avenues you can see a 1930s gate proclaiming, "This gate hangs well and hinders none, refresh and rest, then travel on." A gay community has long been established here; until relatively recently, this was quite the exception in conservative Orange County. The Hare Krishnas have a temple where they host a Sunday vegetarian feast, environmentalists rally, artists continue to gravitate here—there seems to be room for everyone.

There's a definite creative slant to this tight-knit community. The California plein air art movement coalesced here in the early 1900s; by 1932 an annual arts festival was established. Art galleries now dot the village streets, and there's usually someone daubing up in Heisler Park, overlooking the beach. The town's main street, Pacific Coast Highway, is referred to as either South Coast or North Coast Highway, depending on the address. From this waterfront, the streets slope up steeply to the residential areas. All along the highway and side streets, you'll find dozens of fine art and crafts galleries, clothing boutiques, jewelry shops, and cafés.

ESSENTIALS

Visitor and Tour Information Laguna Beach Visitors Bureau ⊠ *252 Broadway* ☎ *949/497–9229, 800/877–1115* ⊕ *www.lagunabeachinfo.org.*

EXPLORING

Main Beach Park. Laguna's central beach gives you a perfect slice of local life. A stocky 1920s lifeguard tower marks Main Beach Park, at the end of Broadway at South Coast Highway. A wooden boardwalk separates the sand from a strip of lawn. Walk along this, or hang out on one of its benches, to watch people bodysurfing, playing sand volleyball, or scrambling around one of two half-basketball courts. The beach also has children's play equipment, picnic areas, restrooms, and showers. Across the street is a historic Spanish Renaissance movie theater.

Laguna Art Museum. The Laguna Art Museum displays American art, with an emphasis on California artists from all periods. Special exhibits change quarterly. ■TIP➔ The museum, along with galleries throughout the city, stays open until 9 for Art Walk on the first Thursday of each month (⊕ *www.firstthursdaysartwalk.com*). A free shuttle service runs from the museum to galleries and studios. ⊠ *307 Cliff Dr.* ☎ *949/494–8971* ⊕ *www.lagunaartmuseum.org* ☲ *$12* ⊙ *Daily 11–5.*

WHERE TO EAT

¢
VEGETARIAN

✕**Café Zinc & Market.** Families flock to this small Laguna Beach institution for well-priced breakfast and lunch. Try the signature quiches or poached egg dishes in the morning, or swing by later in the day for healthy salads, quesadillas, lasagna, or one of their pizzettes. The café also has great artisanal cheese and gourmet goodies to go, and your four-legged friends are welcome in the outdoor patio area. ⊠ *350 Ocean Ave.* ☎ *949/494–6302* ⊕ *www.zinccafe.com* ☉ *No dinner.*

$$$$
AMERICAN
★

✕**Studio.** In a nod to Laguna's art history, Studio has food that entices the eye as well as the palate. You can't beat the location, on a 50-foot bluff overlooking the Pacific Ocean—every table has an ocean view. And because the restaurant occupies its own Craftsman-style bungalow, it doesn't feel like a hotel dining room. The menu changes daily to reflect the finest seafood and the freshest local ingredients on hand. You might begin with Kumamoto oysters or slow-roasted pork belly with sautéed Napa cabbage before moving on to rack of lamb or wild Alaskan salmon scaloppine. The wine list here is bursting, with nearly 2,000 labels. ⊠ *Montage Hotel, 30801 S. Coast Hwy.* ☎ *949/715–6420* ⊕ *www.studiolagunabeach.com* ⌕ *Reservations essential* ☉ *Closed Mondays. No lunch.*

WHERE TO STAY

For expanded reviews, visit Fodors.com.

$$$
★

🏨 **Hotel Casa del Camino.** This historic Spanish-style hotel was built in 1927 and was once a favorite of Hollywood stars. **Pros:** breathtaking views from rooftop lounge; personable service; close to beach. **Cons:** decor a bit dated; frequent on-site events can make hotel busy and noisy. ⊠ *1289 S. Coast Hwy.* ☎ *949/497–2446, 888/367–5232* ⊕ *www.casacamino.com* ⤳ *26 rooms, 10 suites* ⌂ *In-room: Wi-Fi. In-hotel: restaurant, bar, gym, parking, some pets allowed.*

$$$$
Fodor's Choice
★

🏨 **Montage Resort & Spa.** Laguna's connection to the Californian plein air artists is mined for inspiration at this head-turning, lavish hotel. **Pros:** top-notch service; idyllic coastal location; special programs for all interests, from art to marine biology. **Cons:** pricey; food inconsistent given the prices. ⊠ *30801 S. Coast Hwy.* ☎ *949/715–6000, 888/715–6700* ⊕ *www.montagelagunabeach.com* ⤳ *190 rooms, 60 suites* ⌂ *In-room: a/c, Wi-Fi. In-hotel: restaurant, bar, pool, gym, spa, beach, water sports, children's programs, parking.*

NIGHTLIFE AND THE ARTS

Laguna Playhouse. The Laguna Playhouse, dating to the 1920s, mounts a variety of productions, from classics to youth-oriented plays. ⊠ *606 Laguna Canyon Rd.* ☎ *949/497–2787* ⊕ *www.lagunaplayhouse.com.*

SPORTS AND THE OUTDOORS

BEACHES

There are a handful of lovely beaches around town besides the Main Beach.

1,000 Steps Beach. 1,000 Steps Beach, off South Coast Highway at 9th Street, is a hard-to-find locals' spot with great waves. There aren't really 1,000 steps down (but when you hike back up, it'll certainly feel like it).

Wood's Cove. Wood's Cove, off South Coast Highway at Diamond Street, is especially quiet during the week. Big rock formations hide lurking

Looking for shells on Laguna Beach, one of the nicest stretches of sand in Southern California.

crabs. Climbing the steps to leave, you can see a Tudor-style mansion that was once the home of Bette Davis.

HIKING **Laguna Coast Wilderness Park.** For some of the area's best hiking, Laguna Coast Wilderness Park is spread over 19 acres of fragile coastal territory, including the canyon. The trails are great for hiking and mountain biking and are open daily, weather permitting. Docent-led hikes are given regularly; call for information. ☎ *949/923–2235* ⊕ *www. lagunacanyon.org.*

WATER SPORTS **Hobie Sports.** Because its entire beach area is a marine preserve, Laguna Beach is ideal for snorkelers. Scuba divers should head to the Marine Life Refuge area, which runs from Seal Rock to Diver's Cove. Rent bodyboards at Hobie Sports. ✉ *294 Forest Ave.* ☎ *949/497–3304* ⊕ *www.hobie.com.*

DANA POINT

10 mi south of Laguna Beach, via PCH.

Dana Point's claim to fame is its small-boat marina tucked into a dramatic natural harbor and surrounded by high bluffs.

ESSENTIALS

Visitor and Tour Information Dana Point Chamber of Commerce. The Dana Point Chamber of Commerce offers a useful visitor's guide. ☎ *949/496–1555* ⊕ *danapoint-chamber.com.*

Dana Point Harbor. This harbor was first described more than 100 years ago by its namesake, Richard Henry Dana, in his book *Two Years Before the Mast.* At the marina are docks for private boats and yachts, marine-oriented shops, restaurants, and boat and bike rentals. In early

March the **Dana Point Festival of Whales** celebrates the passing gray whale migration with concerts, 40-foot-long balloon whales on parade, films, sports competitions, and a weekend street fair. ☎ *949/472–7888, 888/440–4309* ⊕ *www.festivalofwhales.org* ☎ *949/923–2255* ⊕ *www.danapointharbor.com.*

Doheny State Beach. At the south end of Dana Point, Doheny State Beach is one of Southern California's top surfing destinations, but there's a lot more to do within this 61-acre area. Divers and anglers hang out at the beach's western end, and during low tide, the tide pools beckon both young and old. You'll also find five indoor tanks and an interpretive center devoted to the wildlife of the Doheny Marine Refuge.

There are food stands and shops, picnic facilities, volleyball courts, and a pier for fishing. The beachfront campground here is one of the most popular in the state with 120 no-hookup sites that rent for $30–$35 per night; essential reservations from **Reserve America** (☎ *800/444–7275*).

■**TIP**➔ Be aware that the waters here periodically do not meet health standards established by California (warning signs are posted if that's the case). ☎ *949/496–6172, 714/433–6400 water quality information* ⊕ *www.dohenystatebeach.org.*

WHERE TO EAT

$ ✕**Luciana's Ristorante.** This intimate family-owned eatery serves simply
ITALIAN prepared, tasty Italian food. Try one of the homemade soups or gnocchi classico—Grandma's homemade potato dumplings with marinara sauce. If you don't have a reservation, be prepared to wait at the bar with a glass of one of the many reasonably priced Italian wines, chatting with the predominantly local clientele. ✉ *24312 Del Prado Ave.* ☎ *949/661–6500* ⊕ *www.lucianas.com* ☯ *No lunch.*

$ ✕**Wind & Sea.** An unblocked marina view makes this a particularly great
AMERICAN place for lunch or a sunset dinner. Among the entrées, the macadamia-crusted mahimahi and the shrimp-stuffed halibut with lobster sauce stand out. On warm days, patio tables beckon you outside, and looking out on the Pacific might put you in the mood for a retro cocktail like a mai tai. ✉ *34699 Golden Lantern St.* ☎ *949/496–6500* ⊕ *www.windandsearestaurants.com.*

WHERE TO STAY

For expanded reviews, visit Fodors.com.

$$$ ⊡ **Blue Lantern Inn.** Combining New England–style architecture with
★ a Southern California setting, this white-clapboard B&B rests on a bluff overlooking the harbor and ocean. **Pros:** gas fireplaces; amazing harbor views from Room 304; afternoon wine and cheese; breakfast buffet. **Cons:** nearby restaurant can be noisy; understaffed compared to larger resorts. ✉ *34343 St. of the Blue Lantern* ☎ *949/661–1304, 800/950–1236* ⊕ *www.bluelanterninn.com* ⤵ *29 rooms* ⌂ *In-room: Internet. In-hotel: gym, parking* ¶⊙¶*Breakfast.*

$$$$ ⊡ **Ritz-Carlton, Laguna Niguel.** Take Ritz-Carlton's top-tier level of service
Fodor's Choice coupled with an unparalleled view of the Pacific and you're in the lap
★ of complete luxury at this opulent resort. **Pros:** beautiful grounds and views; luxurious bedding; seamless service. **Cons:** some rooms are small for the price; culinary program has room to grow. ✉ *1 Ritz-Carlton*

Dr. ☎ *949/240–2000, 800/240–2000* ⊕ *www.ritzcarlton.com* ➵ *363 rooms, 30 suites* ⚡ *In-room: Internet, Wi-Fi. In-hotel: restaurant, bar, pool, tennis court, gym, spa, beach, children's programs, parking.*

SPORTS AND THE OUTDOORS

Dana Wharf Sportfishing & Whale Watching. Dana Wharf Sportfishing & Whale Watching runs charters and whale-watching excursions from early December to late April. Tickets cost $29; reservations are required. ⊠ *34675 Golden Lantern St.* ☎ *949/496–5794* ⊕ *www.danawharf.com.*

SAN JUAN CAPISTRANO

5 mi north of Dana Point, Hwy. 74, 60 mi north of San Diego, I–5.

San Juan Capistrano is best known for its historic mission, where the swallows traditionally return each year, migrating from their winter haven in Argentina, but these days they are more likely to choose other local sites for nesting. St. Joseph's Day, March 19, launches a week of fowl festivities. After summering in the arches of the old stone church, the swallows head south on St. John's Day, October 23. Charming antiques stores, which range from pricey to cheap, line Camino Capistrano.

If you arrive by train, which is far more romantic and restful than battling freeway traffic, you'll be dropped off across from the mission at the San Juan Capistrano depot. With its appealing brick café and preserved Santa Fe cars, the depot retains much of the magic of early American railroads. If driving, park near Ortega and Camino Capistrano, the city's main streets.

ESSENTIALS

Visitor and Tour Information **San Juan Capistrano Chamber of Commerce and Visitors Center** ⊠ *31421 La Matanza St.* ☎ *949/493–4700* ⊕ *www.sanjuanchamber.com.*

EXPLORING

Fodor'sChoice ★ **Mission San Juan Capistrano.** This mission, founded in 1776 by Father Junípero Serra, was one of two Roman Catholic outposts between Los Angeles and San Diego. The Great Stone Church, begun in 1797, is the largest structure created by the Spanish in California. Many of the mission's adobe buildings have been preserved to illustrate mission life, with exhibits of an olive millstone, tallow ovens, tanning vats, metal-working furnaces, and the padres' living quarters. The gardens, with their fountains, are a lovely spot in which to wander. The bougainvillea-covered Serra Chapel is believed to be the oldest church still standing in California and is the only building remaining in which Fr. Serra actually led Mass. Mass takes place daily at 7 am in the chapel. ⊠ *Camino Capistrano and Ortega Hwy.* ☎ *949/234–1300* ⊕ *www.missionsjc.com* 🎟 *$9* ☉ *Daily 8:30–5.*

CATALINA ISLAND

Fodor'sChoice ★ Just 22 mi out from the L.A. coastline, across from Newport Beach and Long Beach, Catalina has virtually unspoiled mountains, canyons,

Mission San Juan Capistrano.

coves, and beaches; best of all, it gives you a glimpse of what undeveloped Southern California once looked like.

Water sports are a big draw, as divers and snorkelers come for the exceptionally clear water surrounding the island. The main town, Avalon, is a charming, old-fashioned beach community, where yachts bob in the crescent bay. Wander beyond the main drag and find brightly painted little bungalows fronting the sidewalks, with the occasional golf cart purring down the street.

Perhaps it's no surprise that Catalina has long been a destination for filmmakers and movie stars. In its earlier past, however, the island also sheltered Russian fur trappers (seeking sea-otter skins), pirates, gold miners, and bootleggers (carrier pigeons were used to communicate with the mainland).

In 1919, William Wrigley Jr., the chewing-gum magnate, purchased a controlling interest in the company developing Catalina Island, whose most famous landmark, the Casino, was built in 1929 under his orders. Because he owned the Chicago Cubs baseball team, Wrigley made Catalina the team's spring training site, an arrangement that lasted until 1951.

In 1975, the Santa Catalina Island Conservancy, a nonprofit foundation, acquired about 86% of the island to help preserve the area's natural flora and fauna, including the bald eagle and the Catalina Island fox. These days the conservancy is restoring the rugged interior country with plantings of native grasses and trees. Along the coast you might spot oddities like electric perch, saltwater goldfish, and flying fish.

GETTING HERE AND AROUND

FERRY TRAVEL   Two companies offer ferry service to Catalina Island. The boats have both indoor and outdoor seating and snack bars. Excessive baggage is not allowed, and there are extra fees for bicycles and surfboards. The waters around Santa Catalina can get rough, so if you're prone to seasickness, come prepared.

Catalina Express makes an hour-long run from Long Beach or San Pedro to Avalon and a 90-minute run from Dana Point to Avalon with some stops at Two Harbors. Round-trip fares begin at $68.50, with discounts for seniors and kids. On busy days, a $15 upgrade to the Commodore Lounge, when available, is worth it. Service from Newport Beach to Avalon is available through Catalina Passenger Service. Boats leave from Balboa Pavilion at 9 am (in season), take 75 minutes to reach the island, and cost $68 round-trip. Return boats leave Catalina at 4:30 pm. Reservations are advised in summer and on weekends for all trips. ■TIP➔ Keep an eye out for dolphins, which sometimes swim alongside the ferries.

GOLF CARTS   Golf carts constitute the island's main form of transportation for sightseeing in the area, but they can't be used on the streets in town. You can rent them along Avalon's Crescent Avenue and Pebbly Beach Road for about $40 per hour with a $30 deposit, payable via cash or traveler's checks only.

HELICOPTER   Island Express helicopters depart hourly from San Pedro and Long
TRAVEL   Beach (8 am–dusk). The trip takes about 15 minutes and costs $86 one-way, $164 round-trip (plus tax). Reservations a week in advance are recommended.

TIMING

Although Catalina can be seen in a day, several inviting hotels make it worth extending your stay for one or more nights. A short itinerary might include breakfast along the boardwalk, a tour of the interior, a snorkeling excursion at Casino Point, and a romantic waterfront dinner in Avalon.

After late October, rooms are much easier to find on shorter notice, rates drop dramatically, and many hotels offer packages that include transportation from the mainland and/or sightseeing tours. If you'd rather stay at a charming freestanding cottage or home, contact a local real estate office such as Catalina Island Vacation Rentals.

TOURS

Santa Catalina Island Company runs the following Discovery Tours: a summer-only coastal cruise to Seal Rocks; the *Flying Fish* boat trip (summer evenings only); a comprehensive inland motor tour (which includes an Arabian horse performance); a tour of Skyline Drive; a Casino tour; a scenic tour of Avalon; a glass-bottom-boat tour, an undersea tour on a semisubmersible vessel; and a tour of the Botanical Garden. Reservations are highly recommended for the inland tours. Tours cost $16 to $99. There are ticket booths on the Green Pleasure Pier, at the Casino, in the plaza, and at the boat landing. Catalina Adventure Tours, which has booths at the boat landing and on the pier, arranges similar excursions at comparable prices.

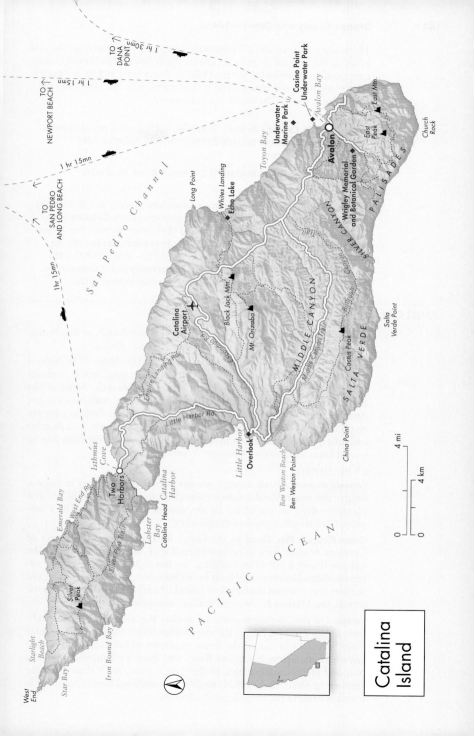

The Santa Catalina Island Conservancy organizes custom ecotours and hikes of the interior. Naturalist guides drive open Jeeps through some gorgeously untrammeled parts of island. Tours start at $98 per person for a three-hour trip (three-person minimum); you can also book half- and full-day tours. The tours run year-round.

ESSENTIALS

Ferry Contacts Catalina Express ☎ *800/481–3470* ⊕ *www.catalinaexpress. com.* **Catalina Passenger Service** ☎ *949/673–5245, 800/830–7744* ⊕ *www.catalinainfo.com.*

Golf Cart Rentals Island Rentals ✉ *125 Pebbly Beach Rd., Avalon* ☎ *310/510–1456.*

Visitor and Tour Information Catalina Adventure Tours ✉ *Box 92766, Long Beach* ☎ *877/510–2888* ⊕ *www.catalinaadventuretours.com.* **Catalina Island Chamber of Commerce & Visitors' Bureau** ✉ *#1 Green Pleasure Pier, Avalon* ✉ *Box 217* ☎ *310/510–1520* ⊕ *www.catalinachamber.com.* **Santa Catalina Island Company** ✉ *Box 737, Long Beach* ☎ *310/510–2800, 800/626–1496* ⊕ *www.scico.com.* **Santa Catalina Island Conservancy** ✉ *125 Claressa Ave., Avalon* ✉ *Box 2739* ☎ *310/510-2595* ⊕ *www.catalinaconservancy.org.*

AVALON

A 1- to 2-hr ferry ride from Long Beach, Newport Beach, or San Pedro; a 15-min helicopter ride from Long Beach or San Pedro.

Avalon, Catalina's only real town, extends from the shore of its natural harbor to the surrounding hillsides. Its resident population is about 3,500 but it swells with tourists on summer weekends. Most of the city's activity, however, is centered on the pedestrian mall on Crescent Avenue, and most sights are easily reached on foot. Private cars are restricted and rental cars aren't allowed, but taxis, trams, and shuttles can take you anywhere you need to go. Bicycles and golf carts can be rented from shops along Crescent Avenue.

EXPLORING

Crescent Avenue. A walk along Crescent Avenue is a nice way to begin a tour of the town. Vivid art deco tiles adorn the avenue's fountains and planters—fired on the island by the now-defunct Catalina Tile Company, the tiles are a coveted commodity.

Green Pleasure Pier. Head to the Green Pleasure Pier, at the center of Crescent Avenue, for a good vantage point of Avalon. At the top of the hill you'll spot a big white building, the Inn at Mt. Ada, now a top-of-the-line B&B but originally built by William Wrigley Jr. for his wife. On the pier you can find the Catalina Island Chamber of Commerce, snack stands, the Harbor Patrol, and scads of squawking seagulls.

★ **Casino.** On the northwest point of Avalon Bay (looking to your right from Green Pleasure Pier) is the majestic landmark Casino. This circular white structure is one of the finest examples of art deco architecture anywhere. Its Spanish-inspired floors and murals gleam with brilliant blue and green Catalina tiles. In this case, *casino,* the Italian word for "gathering place," has nothing to do with gambling. Rather, Casino life revolves around the magnificent ballroom.

Santa Catalina Island Company leads tours of the Casino, lasting about 55 minutes, for $16. You can also visit the **Catalina Island Museum,** in the lower level of the Casino, which investigates 7,000 years of island history; or stop at the **Casino Art Gallery** to see works by local artists. First-run movies are screened nightly at the **Avalon Theatre,** noteworthy for its classic 1929 theater pipe organ. The same big-band dances that made the Casino famous in the 1930s and '40s still take place several times a year. The New Year's Eve dance is hugely popular and sells out well in advance. ⊠ *1 Casino Way* ☎ *310/510–2414 museum, 310/510–0179 Avalon Theatre* ⊕ *www.catalinamuseum.com* ✉ *Museum $5* ⊙ *Call for hours.*

Casino Point Underwater Park. In front of the Casino are the crystal clear waters of the Casino Point Underwater Park, a marine preserve protected from watercraft where moray eels, bat rays, spiny lobsters, halibut, and other sea animals cruise around kelp forests and along the sandy bottom. It's a terrific site for scuba diving, with some shallow areas suitable for snorkeling. Scuba and snorkeling equipment can be rented on and near the pier. The shallow waters of **Lover's Cove,** east of the boat landing, are also good for snorkeling.

Wrigley Memorial and Botanic Garden. Two miles south of the bay via Avalon Canyon Road is Wrigley Memorial and Botanic Garden. Here you can find plants native to Southern California, including several that grow only on Catalina Island: Catalina ironwood, wild tomato, and rare Catalina mahogany. The Wrigley family commissioned the garden as well as the monument, which has a grand staircase and a Spanish mausoleum inlaid with colorful Catalina tile. (The mausoleum was never used by the Wrigleys, who are buried in Los Angeles.) Taxi service from Avalon is available, or you can take a tour bus from the downtown Tour Plaza or ferry landing. ⊠ *Avalon Canyon Rd.* ☎ *310/510–2897* ✉ *$5* ⊙ *Daily 8–5.*

WHERE TO EAT

$$$ ✕ **Catalina Country Club.** The beautifully restored California Mission-
STEAK style structure, which was built in 1921 as a spring-training clubhouse for the Chicago Cubs, is now a restaurant with dark wood, white linen, and an air of formality that's unusual on this casual island. This is the place on the island for a special occasion. The menu emphasizes organic and sustainable ingredients; offerings might include scallops in vanilla beurre blanc, filet mignon, and local sand dabs meunière. The adjacent bar, which connects to the old Cubs locker room and is filled with memorabilia, is great for an after-dinner drink. ⊠ *1 Country Club Dr.* ☎ *310/510–7404* ⌨ *Reservations essential.*

¢ ✕ **Eric's on the Pier.** This little snack bar has been an Avalon family–run
AMERICAN institution since the 1920s. A favorite of Fodor's readers, it's a good place to people-watch while munching a breakfast burrito, hot dog, or signature buffalo burger. Most of the action (and seating) is outside, but you can also sit down at a table inside and dine on a bowl of homemade clam chowder in a baked bread bowl or an order of fish-and-chips. ⊠ *Green Pier No. 2* ☎ *310/510–0894* ⊙ *Closed Thurs. No dinner Nov.–May.*

WHERE TO STAY

For expanded reviews, visit Fodors.com.

¢ ⊡ **Hotel Villa Portofino.** Steps from the beach and the Pleasure Pier, this hotel has a European flair and creates an intimate feel with brick courtyards and walkways. **Pros:** romantic; close to beach; incredible sundeck. **Cons:** though quiet in general, ground floor rooms can be noisy; some rooms are on small side; no elevator. ⊠ *111 Crescent Ave.* ☎ *310/510–0555, 800/346–2326* ⊕ *www.hotelvillaportofino.com* ⇆ *35 rooms* ⟳ *In-room: Wi-Fi. In-hotel: restaurant* ¶⃝ *Breakfast.*

$$$$
Fodor's Choice
★

⊡ **Inn on Mt. Ada.** If you stay in the mansion where Wrigley Jr. once lived, you'll enjoy all the comforts of a millionaire's home—at a millionaire's prices. **Pros:** timeless charm; shuttle from heliport and dock; first-class service. **Cons:** smallish rooms and bathrooms; pricey. ⊠ *398 Wrigley Rd.* ☎ *310/510–2030, 800/608–7669* ⊕ *www.innonmtada.com* ⇆ *6 rooms* ⟳ *In-room: no a/c, Wi-Fi. In-hotel: restaurant, some age restrictions* ¶⃝ *Some meals.*

SPORTS AND THE OUTDOORS

BICYCLING To bike beyond the paved roads of Avalon, you must buy an annual permit from the Catalina Conservancy. Individual passes start at $35; family passes cost $125. You may not ride on hiking paths.

Bike rentals are widely available in Avalon starting at $5 per hour and $12 per day.

Brown's Bikes. Look for rentals on Crescent Avenue and Pebbly Beach Road such as Brown's Bikes. ⊠ *107 Pebbly Beach Rd., next to Island Rentals* ☎ *310/510–0986* 🖷 *310/510–0747* ⊕ *www.catalinabiking.com.*

HIKING **Santa Catalina Island Conservancy.** Permits from the Santa Catalina Island Conservancy are required for hiking into Catalina Island's interior. ■**TIP**➔ **If you plan to backpack overnight, you'll need a camping reservation. The interior is dry and desertlike; bring plenty of water and sunblock.** The permits are free and can be picked up at the main house of the conservancy or at the airport. You don't need a permit for shorter hikes, such as the one from Avalon to the Botanical Garden. The conservancy has maps of the island's east-end hikes, such as Hermit's Gulch Trail. It's possible to hike between Avalon and Two Harbors, starting at the Hogsback Gate, above Avalon, though the 28-mi journey has an elevation gain of 3,000 feet and is not for the weak. ■**TIP**➔ **For a pleasant 4-mi hike out of Avalon, take Avalon Canyon Road to Wrigley Gardens and follow the trail to Lone Pine. At the top, you'll have an amazing view of the Palisades cliffs and, beyond them, the sea.** ⊠ *125 Claressa Ave.* ⊠ *Box 2739* ☎ *310/510–2595* ⊕ *www.catalinaconservancy.org.*

Los Angeles

WORD OF MOUTH

"One great thing about my trip to L.A. was all the free guided tours I was able to take (El Pueblo de Los Angeles, Walt Disney Concert Hall, Central Library). There are so many great places to visit without spending a dime. While museum admission can add up, most museums offer free admission on certain days or hours."

—yk

WELCOME TO
LOS ANGELES

TOP REASONS TO GO

★ **Hollywood magic:** A massive chunk of the world's entertainment is developed, written, filmed, edited, distributed, and sold here; you'll hear people discussing "The Industry" wherever you go.

★ **The beach:** Getting some sand on the floor of your car is practically a requirement here, and the beach is an integral part of the SoCal lifestyle.

★ **Chic shopping:** From Beverly Hills' Rodeo Drive and Downtown's Fashion District to the funky boutiques of Los Feliz, Silver Lake, and Echo Park, L.A. is a shopper's paradise.

★ **Trendy restaurants:** Celebrity is big business here, so it's no accident that the concept of the celebrity chef is a key part of the city's dining scene.

★ **People-watching:** Celeb-spotting in Beverly Hills, trying to get past the velvet rope at hip clubs, hanging out on the Venice Boardwalk . . . there's always something (or someone) interesting to see.

1 Downtown Los Angeles. Downtown L.A. shows off spectacular modern architecture with the swooping Walt Disney Concert Hall and the stark Cathedral of Our Lady of the Angels. The Music Center and the Museum of Contemporary Art anchor a world-class arts scene, while Olvera Street, Chinatown, and Little Tokyo reflect the city's history and diversity.

2 Hollywood and the Studios. Glitzy and tarnished, good and bad—Hollywood is just like the entertainment business itself. The Walk of Fame, Grauman's Chinese Theatre, Paramount Pictures studio, and the Hollywood Bowl keep the neighborhood's romantic past alive. Universal Studios Hollywood, Warner Bros., and NBC Television Studios are in the Valley.

3 The Westside and Beverly Hills. Go for the glamour, the restaurants, and the scene. Rodeo Drive is particularly good for a look at wretched or ravishing excess. But don't forget the Westside's cultural attractions—especially the dazzling Getty Center. West Hollywood's an area for urban indulgences—shopping, restaurants, nightspots—rather than sightseeing. Its main arteries are the Sunset

Strip (Sunset Boulevard), and Melrose Avenue, lined with shops ranging from punk to postmodern.

4 Santa Monica, Venice, and Malibu. These desirable beach communities move from ultrarich, ultracasual Malibu to bohemian/ seedy Venice, with liberal, Mediterranean-style Santa Monica in between.

5 Pasadena Area. Its own separate city, Pasadena is a quiet area with outstanding Arts and Crafts homes, good dining, and a pair of exceptional museums.

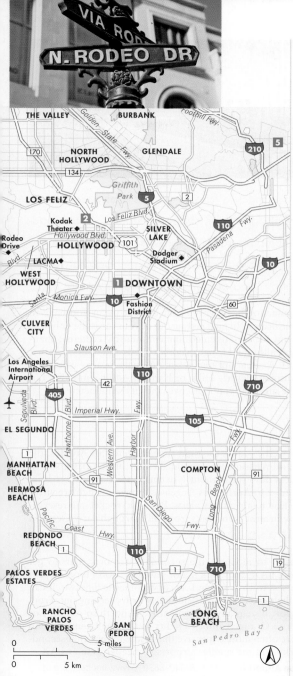

GETTING ORIENTED

Looking at a map of sprawling Los Angeles, first-time visitors are sometimes overwhelmed. Where to begin? What to see first? And what about all those freeways? Here's some advice: relax. Begin by setting your priorities—movie and television buffs should first head to Hollywood, Universal Studios, and a taping of a television show. Beach lovers and nature types might start out in Santa Monica or Venice or Malibu, or spend an afternoon in Griffith Park, one of the largest city parks in the country. Culture vultures should make a beeline for the twin Gettys (the center in Brentwood and the villa near Malibu), the Los Angeles County Museum of Art (LACMA), or the Norton Simon Museum. And urban explorers might begin with Downtown Los Angeles.

Updated by
Cindy Arora,
Tanvi Chheda,
Arlene
Dawson, Lea
Lion, Elline
Lipkin, Susan
MacCallum-
Whitcomb,
Laura Randall

Los Angeles is as much a fantasy as it is a physical city. A mecca for face-lifts, film noir, shopping starlets, beach bodies, and mind-numbing traffic, it sprawls across 467 square mi; add in the surrounding five-county metropolitan area, and you've got an area of more than 34,000 square mi.

Contrary to popular myth, however, that doesn't mean you have to spend all your time in a car. In fact, getting out of your car is the only way to really get to know the various entertainment-industry-centered, financial, beachfront, wealthy, and fringe neighborhoods and mini-cities that make up the vast L.A. area. But remember, no single locale—whether it be Malibu, Downtown, Beverly Hills, or Burbank—fully embodies Los Angeles. It's in the mix that you'll discover the city's character.

PLANNING

WHEN TO GO

Almost any time of the year is the right time to go to Los Angeles; the climate is mild and pleasant year-round. Winter brings crisp, sunny, unusually smogless days from about November to May (expect brief rains from December to April). Los Angeles summers, which are virtually rainless, can lead to air-quality alerts. Prices skyrocket and reservations are a must when tourism peaks from July through early October.

GETTING HERE AND AROUND

AIR TRAVEL

It's generally easier to navigate the secondary airports than to get through sprawling LAX, the city's major gateway. Bob Hope Airport in Burbank is closest to Downtown L.A., and domestic flights to it can be cheaper than flights to LAX—it's definitely worth checking out. From Long Beach Airport it's equally convenient to go north to central Los Angeles or south to Orange County. Flights to Orange County's John Wayne Airport are often more expensive than those to the other secondary airports. Parking at the smaller airports is cheaper than at LAX.

Airports Bob Hope Airport (*BUR*). ☏ *818/840–8830* ⊕ *www.bobhopeairport. com.* **John Wayne/Orange County Airport** (*SNA*). ☏ *949/252–5006*

⊕ www.ocair.com. **Long Beach Airport** (*LGB*). ☎ 562/570–2600 ⊕ www.lgb.org. **Los Angeles International Airport** (*LAX*). ☎ 310/646–5252 ⊕ www.lawa.org or www.airport-la.com. **Ontario International Airport** (*ONT*). ☎ 909/937–2700 ⊕ www.lawa.org.

Shuttles Prime Time ☎ 800/733–8267 ⊕ www.primetimeshuttle.com. **SuperShuttle** ☎ 323/775–6600, 310/782–6600, 800/258–3826 ⊕ www.supershuttle.com. **Xpress Shuttle** ☎ 800/427–7483 ⊕ www.execucarexpress.com.

BUS TRAVEL

Inadequate public-transportation systems have been an L.A. problem for decades. That said, many local trips can be made, with time and patience, by bus. In certain cases, it may be your best option; for example, visiting the Getty Center, going to Universal Studios and/or the adjacent CityWalk, or venturing into Downtown. The Metropolitan Transit Authority DASH (Downtown Area Short Hop) minibuses cover six different circular routes in Hollywood, Mid-Wilshire, and the Downtown area. The buses stop every two blocks or so. The Santa Monica Municipal Bus Line, also known as the Big Blue Bus, is a pleasant and inexpensive way to move around the Westside, where the MTA lines leave off. There's also an express bus to and from Downtown L.A., and a shuttle bus, the Tide Shuttle, which runs between Main Street and the Third Street Promenade and stops at hotels along the way. Culver CityBus Lines run six routes through Culver City.

Bus Information Commute Smart ⊕ www.commutesmart.info. **Culver City-Bus Lines** ☎ 310/253–6500 ⊕ www.culvercity.org. **DASH** ☎ 213/626–4455, 310/808–2273 ⊕ www.ladottransit.com/dash. **Metropolitan Transit Authority (MTA)** ☎ 213/626–4455 ⊕ www.mta.net. **Santa Monica Municipal Bus Line** ☎ 310/451–5444 ⊕ www.bigbluebus.com.

CAR TRAVEL

Most freeways are known by a name and a number; for example, the San Diego Freeway is I–405, the Hollywood Freeway is U.S. 101, the Ventura Freeway is a different stretch of U.S. 101, the Santa Monica Freeway is I–10, and the Harbor Freeway is I–110. It helps, too, to know which direction you're traveling; say, west toward Santa Monica or east toward Downtown Los Angeles. Distance in miles doesn't mean much, depending on the time of day you're traveling: the short 10-mi distance between the San Fernando Valley and Downtown Los Angeles might take an hour to travel during rush hour but only 20 minutes at other times.

Be aware that a number of major streets have similar-sounding names (Beverly Drive and Beverly Boulevard, or numbered streets north to south Downtown and east to west in Hollywood, West Hollywood, and Beverly Hills) or exactly the same name (San Vicente Boulevard in West L.A., Brentwood, Santa Monica, and West Hollywood). Also, some smaller streets seem to exist intermittently for miles, so unless you have good directions, you should use major streets rather than try for an alternative that is actually blocked by a dead end or detours, like the side streets off Sunset Boulevard. Try to get clear directions and stick to them.

If you get discombobulated while on the freeway, remember the rule of thumb: even-numbered freeways run east and west, odd-numbered freeways run north and south.

Information California Highway Patrol ☎ *800/427–7623 for road conditions.* **City of Los Angeles** ⊕ *www.sigalert.com.*

Emergency Services Freeway Service Patrol ☎ *213/922–2957 general information, 323/982–4900 for breakdowns.*

METRO RAIL TRAVEL

Metro Rail covers a limited area of L.A.'s vast expanse, but what there is, is helpful and frequent. The underground Red Line runs from Union Station Downtown through Mid-Wilshire, Hollywood, and Universal City on its way to North Hollywood, stopping at the most popular tourist destinations along the way. The light commuter rail Green Line stretches from Redondo Beach to Norwalk, while the partially underground Blue Line goes from Downtown to the South Bay (Long Beach/San Pedro). The Green and Blue lines are not often used by visitors, though the Green is gaining popularity as an alternative, albeit time-consuming, way to reach LAX. The monorail-like Gold Line begins at Union Station and heads northeast to Pasadena and Sierra Madre. The Orange Line, a 14-mi bus corridor, connects the North Hollywood subway station with the western San Fernando Valley.

The Web site is the best way to get info on Metro Rail.

Metro Rail Information Metropolitan Transit Authority (MTA) ☎ *800/266–6883, 213/626–4455* ⊕ *www.mta.net.*

TAXI AND LIMOUSINE TRAVEL

Don't even try to hail a cab on the street in Los Angeles. Instead, phone one of the many taxi companies. The metered rate is $2.45 per mile, plus a $2.65 per-fare charge. Taxi rides from LAX have an additional $2.50 surcharge. Be aware that distances between sights in L.A. are vast, so cab fares add up quickly. On the other end of the price spectrum, limousines come equipped with everything from a full bar and telephone to a hot tub. If you open any L.A.–area yellow pages, the number of limo companies will astound you. Most charge by the hour, with a three-hour minimum.

Limo Companies ABC Limousine & Sedan Service ☎ *818/980–6000, 888/753–7500.* **American Executive** ☎ *800/927–2020.* **Black & White Transportation Services** ☎ *800/924–1624.* **Chauffeur's Unlimited** ☎ *888/546–6019* ⊕ *www.chaufusa.com.* **Dav El Chauffeured Transportation Network** ☎ *800/922–0343* ⊕ *www.davel.com.* **First Class Limousine Service by Norman Lewis** ☎ *800/400–9771* ⊕ *www.first-classlimo.com.* **ITS** ☎ *800/487–4255.*

Taxi Companies Beverly Hills Cab Co. ☎ *800/273–6611.* **Checker Cab** ☎ *800/300–5007.* **Independent Cab Co.** ☎ *800/521–8294* ⊕ *www.taxi4u.com.* **United Independent Taxi** ☎ *800/411–0303, 800/822–8294.* **Yellow Cab/LA Taxi Co-Op** ☎ *800/200–1085, 800/200–0011.*

TRAIN TRAVEL

Union Station in Downtown Los Angeles is one of the great American railroad stations. The interior is well kept and includes comfortable seating, a restaurant, and snack bars. As the city's rail hub, it's the place to catch an Amtrak train. Among Amtrak's Southern California routes are 13 daily trips to San Diego and seven to Santa Barbara. Amtrak's luxury *Coast Starlight* travels along the spectacular coastline from Seattle to Los Angeles in just a day and a half (though it's often a little late). The *Sunset Limited* goes to Los Angeles from Florida (via New Orleans and Texas), and the *Southwest Chief* from Chicago.

Information Amtrak ☎ *800/872–7245* ⊕ *www.amtrak.com.*
Union Station ⊠ *800 N. Alameda St.* ☎ *213/683–6979.*

VISITOR INFORMATION

Contacts Beverly Hills Conference and Visitors Bureau ☎ *310/248–1000,* *800/345–2210* ⊕ *beverlyhillschamber.com, beverlyhillsbehere.com.* **California Office of Tourism** ☎ *916/444–4429, 800/862–2543* ⊕ *visitcalifornia.com.* **Hollywood Chamber of Commerce Info Center** ☎ *323/469–8311* ⊕ *www.hollywoodchamber.net.* **L.A. Inc./The Convention and Visitors Bureau** ☎ *213/624–7300, 800/228–2452* ⊕ *discoverlosangeles.com.* **Pasadena Convention and Visitors Bureau** ☎ *626/795–9311* ⊕ *www.pasadenacal.com.* **Redondo Beach Visitors Bureau** ☎ *310/376-6911, 800/282–0333* ⊕ *www. visitredondo.com.* **Santa Monica Convention & Visitors Bureau** ☎ *310/319– 6263, 800/544–5319* ⊕ *www.santamonica.com.* **West Hollywood Convention and Visitors Bureau** ☎ *310/289–2525, 800/368–6020* ⊕ *www.visitwesthollywood.com.*

EXPLORING LOS ANGELES

Star-struck . . . excessive . . . smoggy . . . superficial. . . . There's a modicum of truth to each of the adjectives regularly applied to L.A. But Angelenos—and most objective visitors—dismiss their prevalence as signs of envy from people who hail from places less blessed with fun and sun. Pop culture, for instance, *does* permeate life in LaLaLand: A massive economy employing millions of Southern Californians is built around it.

However, this city also boasts high-brow appeal, having amassed an impressive array of world-class museums and arts venues. Moreover, it has burgeoning neighborhoods that bear little resemblance to those featured on *The Hills* or *Entourage.* America's second-largest city has more depth than paparazzi shutters can ever capture.

DOWNTOWN LOS ANGELES

Once the lively heart of Los Angeles, Downtown has been a glitz-free businessman's domain of high-rises for the past few decades. But if there's one thing Angelinos love, it's a makeover, and now city planners have put the wheels in motion for a dramatic revitalization. Glance in every direction and you'll find construction crews building luxury lofts and retail space in hopes of attracting new high-class residents.

TOP ATTRACTIONS

Fodor'sChoice
★
Cathedral of Our Lady of the Angels. A half block away from the giant rose-shaped steel grandeur of Frank Gehry's curvaceous Disney Concert Hall sits Cathedral of Our Lady of the Angels. Not only is it a spiritual draw but an architectural attraction. The exterior is all strict soaring angles and the building is as heavy, solid, and hunkering as the Gehry building is feminine and ethereal.

Controversy surrounded Spanish architect José Rafael Moneo's unconventional, costly, austere design for the seat of the Archdiocese of Los Angeles. But judging from the swarms of visitors and the standing-room-only holiday masses, the church has carved out a niche for itself in Downtown's daily life.

Opened in 2002, the ocher-concrete cathedral looms up by the Hollywood Freeway. The plaza in front is relatively austere, glaringly bright on sunny days; a children's play garden with bronze animals helps relieve the stark space.

Imposing bronze entry doors, designed by local artist Robert Graham, are decorated with multicultural icons and New World images of the Virgin Mary. The canyonlike interior of the church is spare, polished, and airy. By day, sunlight illuminates the sanctuary through translucent curtain walls of thin Spanish alabaster, a departure from the usual stained glass.

Artist John Nava used residents from his hometown of Ojai, California, as models for some of the 135 figures in the tapestries that line the nave walls. Make sure to go underground to wander the bright, mazelike white-marble corridors of the mausoleum.

Free guided tours start at the entrance fountain at 1 on weekdays. Check for free concerts inside of Cathedral on Wednesdays at noon. There's plenty of underground visitor parking; the vehicle entrance is on Hill Street. ■TIP→ The café in the plaza has become one of Downtown's favorite lunch spots. You can pick up a fresh, reasonably priced meal to eat at one of the outdoor tables. ⊠ *555 W. Temple St., Downtown* ☎ *213/680–5200* ⊕ *www.olacathedral.org* ✆ *Free, parking $3 every 20 min, $18 maximum* ⊗ *Weekdays 6:00–6, Sat. 9–6, Sun. 7–6.*

★
The Geffen Contemporary. Frank Gehry transformed what was a 40,000-square-foot former police warehouse in Little Tokyo into this top-notch museum, originally built as a temporary exhibit hall while the **Museum of Contemporary Art (MOCA)** was under construction at California Plaza. Thanks to its popular reception, it remains one of two satellite museums of MOCA (the other is outside the Pacific Design Center in West Hollywood) and houses a sampling of its permanent collection. In addition, it puts on one or two special exhibits yearly. Call before you visit because the museum sometimes closes for installations. ⊠ *152 N. Central Ave., Downtown* ☎ *213/626–6222* ⊕ *www.moca-la.org* ✆ *$10, free with MOCA admission on same day and on Thurs. evenings.* ⊗ *Mon. 11–5, Thurs. 11–8, Fri. 11–5, weekends 11–6.*

Fodor'sChoice
★
The Museum of Contemporary Art (MOCA). The MOCA's permanent collection of American and European art from 1940 to the present divides itself between three spaces: this linear red-sandstone building at California Plaza, the **Geffen Contemporary,** in nearby Little Tokyo, and the

satellite gallery at West Hollywood's **Pacific Design Center.** Likewise, its exhibitions are split between the established and the cutting edge.

Heavy hitters such as Mark Rothko, Franz Kline, Susan Rothenberg, Diane Arbus, and Robert Frank are part of the permanent collection that's rotated into the museum exhibits at different times, while at least 20 theme shows are featured annually.

It's a good idea to check the schedule in advance, since some shows sell out, especially on weekends. The museum occasionally closes for exhibit installation. ⊠ *250 S. Grand Ave., Downtown* ☎ *213/626–6222* ⊕ *www.moca.org* ⊠ *Grand Ave. and Geffen Contemporary $10, free Thurs. 5–8; Pacific Design Center free* ⊙ *Mon. and Fri. 11–5, Thurs. 11–8, weekends 11–6; Pacific Design Center closed on Monday, Tues.– Fri. 11–5, weekends 11–6.*

4

☺ **Olvera Street.** This busy pedestrian block tantalizes with piñatas, mari-
★ achis, and fragrant Mexican food. As the major draw of the oldest section of the city, known as **El Pueblo de Los Angeles,** Olvera Street has come to represent the rich Mexican heritage of L.A. It had a close shave with disintegration in the early 20th century, until the socialite Christine Sterling walked through in 1926. Jolted by the historic area's decay, Sterling fought to preserve key buildings and led the transformation of the street into a Mexican-American marketplace. Today this character remains; vendors sell puppets, leather goods, sandals, serapes (woolen shawls) and handicrafts from stalls that line the center of the narrow street. On weekends, the restaurants are packed as musicians play in the central plaza. The weekends that fall around two Mexican holidays, Cinco de Mayo (May 5) and Independence Day (September 16), also draw huge crowds. ■ TIP➡ To see Olvera Street at its quietest, visit late on a weekday afternoon, when long shadows heighten the romantic feeling of the passageway. For information, stop by the **Olvera Street Visitors Center** (⊠ *622 N. Main St., Downtown* ☎ *213/628–1274* ⊕ *www. olvera-street.com*), in the Sepulveda House, a Victorian built in 1887 as a hotel and boardinghouse. The center is open weekdays and weekends 9–4. Free hour-long walking tours leave here at 10, 11, and noon Tuesday–Saturday.

★ **Union Station.** Once the key entry point into Los Angeles prior to LAX, Union Station is worth a visit even if you don't plan to go anywhere but merely want to wallow in the ambience of one of the country's last great rail stations.

Evoking an era when travel and style went hand in hand, Union Station will transport you to another destination, and another time. Built in 1939 and designed by City Hall architects John and Donald Parkinson, it combines Spanish colonial revival and art deco styles that have retained their classic warmth and quality.

The waiting hall's commanding scale and enormous chandeliers have provided the setting for countless films, TV shows, and music videos. The indoor restaurant, **Traxx,** offers a glamorous vintage setting for lunch and dinner. ⊠ *800 N. Alameda St., Downtown.*

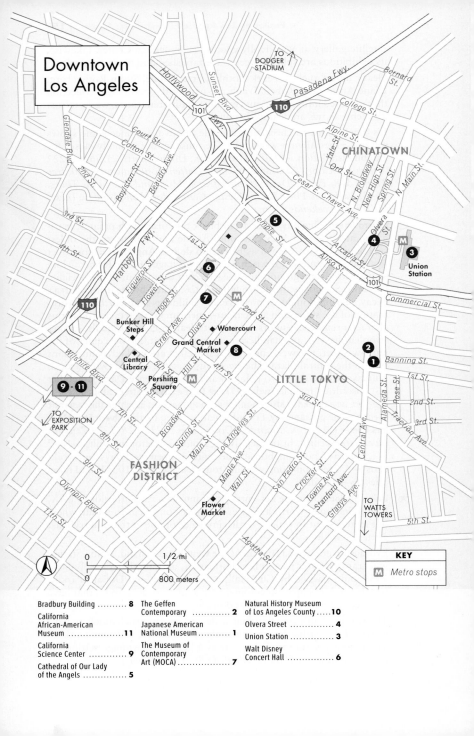

Downtown Los Angeles

CHINATOWN

TO DODGER STADIUM

Union Station

LITTLE TOKYO

Bunker Hill Steps

Central Library

Watercourt

Grand Central Market

Pershing Square

TO EXPOSITION PARK

9 · 11

FASHION DISTRICT

Flower Market

TO WATTS TOWERS

0   1/2 mi
0   800 meters

KEY

Ⓜ *Metro stops*

Fodor's Choice
★

Walt Disney Concert Hall. L.A.'s crown jewel, designed by Frank Gehry, opened in 2003 and instantly became a stunning icon of the city. The gorgeous stainless-steel-clad exterior soars upward, seeming to defy the laws of engineering.

Inside, there's a billowing ceiling of Douglas fir, and an enormous pine-clad organ centerpiece said to have been inspired by a box of McDonald's french fries. The carpet, named "Lily," is a wild collage of petals inspired by Lillian Disney's love of flowers, as is the "Rose for Lily" fountain—made entirely of bits of Delftware, Mrs. Disney's favorite collectible—in the tranquil outdoor public garden.

Docent-led and self-guided audio tours of the Hall are available free to the public for parties of 14 and less, but note that entry to the performance space is subject to rehearsal schedules. Your chances are better in summer when the Philharmonic moves to the Hollywood Bowl.

Additional children's performances, lectures, and experimental works are held in surrounding smaller theater spaces: the indoor BP Hall, two outdoor mini amphitheaters, and CalArts's intimate 266-seat REDCAT Theatre.

The Hall is part of the 11-acre **Music Center** campus, which has served as L.A.'s major performing arts venue since its opening in 1964, and was where the Academy Awards was held until it moved to the Kodak Theatre. It's reminiscent of New York's Lincoln Center because the buildings that house the Los Angeles Philharmonic, the Los Angeles Opera, the Center Theater Group, and the Los Angeles Master Chorale all surround a large courtyard. Glorya Kaufman Presents Dance at the Music Center is another program that features the best of dance, from global to traditional ballet. At intermission, patrons spill into the plaza to drink wine and enjoy the lighted "dancing" fountain or occasional art exhibits.

The largest of the center's four theaters is the **Dorothy Chandler Pavilion,** named after the philanthropic wife of former *Los Angeles Times* publisher Norman Chandler. The **Ahmanson,** at the north end, is a flexible venue for major musicals and plays. In between these two sits the round **Mark Taper Forum,** an intimate 700-seat theater.

Activity isn't limited to merely ticketed events; free tours of the entire Music Center campus are available by volunteer docents who provide a wealth of architectural and behind-the-scenes information while escorting you through elaborate, art-punctuated VIP areas. ⊠ *135 N. Grand Ave., at 1st St., Downtown* ☎ *213/972–7211, 213/972–3688 for tour information* ⊕ *www.musiccenter.org.*

WORTH NOTING

★ **Bradbury Building.** Stunning wrought-iron railing, blond-wood and brick interior, ornate moldings, pink marble staircases, Victorian-style sky-lighted atrium that rises almost 50 feet, and a birdcage elevator: it's easy to see why the Bradbury leaves visitors awestruck.

Designed in 1893 by a novice architect who drew his inspiration from a science-fiction story and a conversation with his dead brother via a Ouija board, the office building was originally the site of turn-of-the-20th-century sweatshops, but now houses a variety of businesses that try to keep normal working conditions despite the barrage of daily tourist visits and filmmakers. *Blade Runner, Chinatown,* and *Wolf* were filmed here.

For that reason, visits (and photo-taking) are limited to the lobby and the first-floor landing. The building is open daily 9–5 for a peek, as long as you don't wander beyond visitor-approved areas. ⊠ *304 S. Broadway, southeast corner Broadway and 3rd St., Downtown* ☎ *213/626–1893.*

California African-American Museum. Works by 20th-century African-American artists and contemporary art of the African Diasporas are the backbone of this museum's permanent collection. Its exhibits document the African-American experience from Emancipation and Reconstruction through the 20th century, especially as expressed by artists in California and elsewhere in the West. Special musical as well as educational and cultural events are offered the first Sunday of every month. ⊠ *600 Exposition Park, Exposition Park* ☎ *213/744–7432* ⊕ *www.caamuseum.org* ☐ *Free, parking $8* ⊘ *Tues.–Sat. 10–5, Sun. 11–5.*

⟳ **California Science Center.** You're bound to see excited kids running up to the dozens of interactive exhibits here that illustrate the relevance of science to everyday life, from bacteria to airplanes. Clustered in different "Worlds," this center provides opportunities to examine such topics as structures and communications, where you can be an architect and design your own building and learn how to make it earthquake-proof, to "Life" itself where Tess, the 50-foot animatronic star of the exhibit "Body Works," dramatically demonstrates how the body's organs work together. Air and Space Exhibits show what it takes to go to outer space with Gemini 11, a real capsule flown into space by Pete Conrad and Dick Gordon in September 1966. An IMAX theater shows large-format releases. ⊠ *700 State Dr., Exposition Park* ☎ *213/744–7400, 323/724–3623* ⊕ *www.casciencectr.org* ☐ *Free, except for IMAX, prices vary; parking $8* ⊘ *Daily 10–5.*

Japanese American National Museum. What was it like to grow up on a sugar plantation in Hawaii? How difficult was life for Japanese-Americans interned in concentration camps during World War II? These questions are addressed by changing exhibits at this museum in Little Tokyo. Insightful volunteer docents are on hand to share their own stories and experiences. The museum occupies an 85,000-square-foot adjacent pavilion as well as its original site in a renovated 1925 Buddhist temple. ⊠ *369 E. 1st St., at Central Ave., next to Geffen Contemporary, Downtown* ☎ *213/625–0414* ⊕ *www.janm.org* ☐ *$9, free Thurs. 5–8 and 3rd Thurs. of month* ⊘ *Tues., Wed., and Fri.–Sun. 11–5; Thursday 12–8.*

⟳ **Natural History Museum of Los Angeles County.** The completed renovation of the museum's 1913 Beaux Arts building sets the stage for new visitor experiences leading up to the centennial in 2013.

In summer 2011 the new Dinosaur Hall will open, featuring more than 300 fossils, 20 full-body specimens, manual and digital interactivity, and large-format video, as well as a T. rex series that includes adult, juvenile, and baby specimens. An exhibit focusing on the natural and cultural history of Southern California dating from prehistoric times to modern-day Hollywood will open in 2012.

The museum has the same quaint feel of many natural history museums, with enclosed dioramas of animals in their natural habitats. But it mixes

Frank Gehry's Walt Disney Concert Hall is the crown jewel of the Music Center, if not all of Downtown Los Angeles.

it up with interactive displays such as the Butterfly Pavilion in a separate small building in front of the museum; The Discovery Center, where kids can touch real animal pelts; the Insect Zoo; and their Dino Lab, where you can watch actual paleontologists work on dinosaur fossils.

In addition, there are also exhibits typifying various cultural groups, including pre-Columbian artifacts and a display of crafts from the South Pacific as well as marine-life exhibits. ⊠ *900 Exposition Blvd., Exposition Park* ☎ *213/763–3466* ⊕ *www.nhm.org* ✉ *$9, free 1st Tues. of month* ⊙ *Weekdays 9:30–5, weekends 10–5.*

HOLLYWOOD AND THE STUDIOS

The Tinseltown mythology of Los Angeles was born in Hollywood. Daytime attractions can be found on foot around the home of the Academy Awards at the Kodak Theatre, part of the Hollywood & Highland entertainment complex. The adjacent Grauman's Chinese Theatre delivers silver screen magic with its cinematic facade and ornate interiors from a bygone era. Walk the renowned Hollywood Walk of Stars to find your favorite celebrities' hand- and footprints. In summer, visit the crown jewel of Hollywood, the Hollywood Bowl, which features shows by the Los Angeles Philharmonic.

The San Fernando Valley gets a bad rap. There are even some Angelenos who swear, with a sneer, that they will never set foot in "the Valley." But despite all the snickering, it's where the majority of studios that have made Los Angeles famous are located.

TOP ATTRACTIONS

★ **Grauman's Chinese Theatre.** A place that inspires the phrase "only in Hollywood," these stylized Chinese pagodas and temples have become a shrine to stardom. Although you have to buy a movie ticket to appreciate the interior trappings, the courtyard is open to the public. The main theater itself is worth visiting, if only to see a film in the same seats as hundreds of celebrities who have attended big premieres here. You could also opt for a tour for $12.50 that takes you around the theaters and the VIP lounge. And then, of course, outside in front are the oh-so-famous cement hand- and footprints. This tradition is said to have begun at the theater's opening in 1927, with the premiere of Cecil B. DeMille's *King of Kings,* when actress Norma Talmadge just happened to step into wet cement. Now more than 160 celebrities have contributed imprints for posterity, including some oddball specimens, such as ones of Whoopi Goldberg's dreadlocks. ⊠ *6925 Hollywood Blvd., Hollywood* ☎ *323/464–8111, 323/463–9576 for tours* ⊕ *www.manntheatres.com.*

Fodor'sChoice **Griffith Observatory.** High on a hillside overlooking the city, the Griffith
★ Observatory is one of the most celebrated icons of Los Angeles. And now, its interior is as impressive as its exterior after a massive expansion and cosmic makeover. Highlights of the building include the Foucault's pendulum hanging in the main lobby, the planet exhibitions on the lower level, and the playful wall display of galaxy-themed jewelry along the twisty indoor ramp.

In true L.A. style, the Leonard Nimoy Event Horizon Theater presents guest speakers and shows on current space-related topics and discoveries. The planetarium now features a new dome, laser digital projection system, theatrical lighting, and a stellar sound system. Shows are $7.

For a fantastic view, come at sunset to watch the sky turn fiery shades of red with the city's skyline silhouetted. ⊠ *2800 E. Observatory Rd., Griffith Park* ☎ *213/473–0800* ⊕ *www.griffithobservatory.org* ☉ *Tues.– Fri. noon–10, weekends 10–10.*

Fodor'sChoice **Hollywood Museum.** Lovers of Hollywood's glamorous past will be sing-
★ ing "Hooray for Hollywood" when they stop by this gem of cinema history. It's inside the Max Factor Building, purchased in 1928. Factor's famous makeup was made on the top floors, and on the ground floor was a salon. After its renovation, this art deco landmark now holds more than 10,000 bits of film memorabilia.

The extensive exhibits inside include those dedicated to Marilyn Monroe and Bob Hope and to costumes and set props from such films as *Moulin Rouge, The Silence of the Lambs,* and *Planet of the Apes.* There's an impressive gallery of photos showing movie stars frolicking at such venues as the Brown Derby, Ciro's, the Trocadero, and the Mocambo.

Hallway walls are covered with the stunning autograph collection of ultimate fan Joe Ackerman; aspiring filmmakers will want to check out an exhibit of early film equipment. The museum's showpiece, however, is the Max Factor exhibit, where separate dressing rooms are dedicated to Factor's "color harmony": creating distinct looks for "brownettes" (Factor's term), redheads, and of course, bombshell blondes. You can practically smell the peroxide of Marilyn Monroe

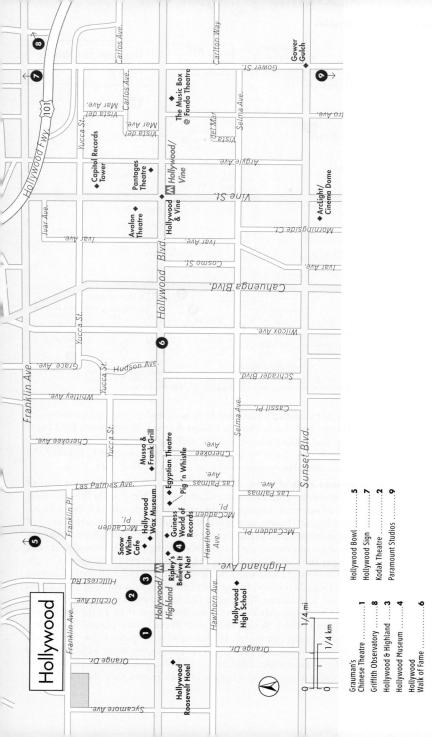

Hollywood

Carlos Ave.
Carlos Ave.
Carlton Way

Gower Gulch

Gower St.

The Music Box @ Fonda Theatre

Vista del Mar Ave.
Vista del Mar Ave.
Selma Ave.

tro Ave.

Capitol Records Tower

Pantages Theatre

Hollywood/ Vine

Argyle Ave.
Vista del Mar

Hollywood Fwy.

101

Yucca St.

Ivar Ave.

Avalon Theatre

Hollywood & Vine

Vine St.

Arclight/ Cinema Dome

Morningside Ct.

Ivar Ave.
Ivar Ave.

Cosmo St.

Hollywood Blvd.

Cahuenga Blvd

Wilcox Ave.

Franklin Ave.

Grace Ave.

Yucca St.

Hudson Ave.

Schrader Blvd.

Whitley Ave.

Yucca St.

Cassil Pl.

Selma Ave.

Cherokee Ave.

Yucca St.

Musso & Frank Grill

Egyptian Theatre
Pig 'n Whistle

Cherokee Ave.

Sunset Blvd.

Las Palmas Ave.

Hollywood Wax Museum

Guiness World of Records

Las Palmas Ave.

Las Palmas Ave.

Franklin Pl.

Snow White Cafe

Ripley's Believe It Or Not

McCadden Pl.

Hawthorn Ave.

McCadden Pl.

Highland Ave.

Hillcrest Rd.

Hollywood/ Highland

Hollywood High School

Orchid Ave.

Hawthorn Ave.

Franklin Ave.

Hollywood Roosevelt Hotel

Orange Dr.

Sycamore Ave.

1/4 mi
1/4 km

0
0

4

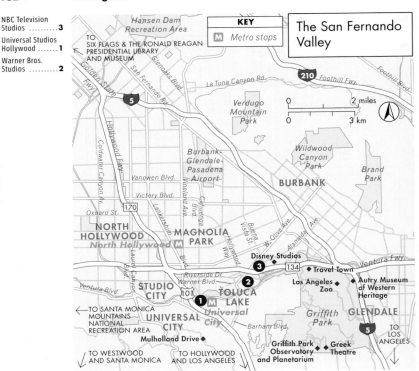

getting her trademark platinum look here, and see makeup cases owned by Lucille Ball, Lana Turner, Ginger Rogers, Bette Davis, Rita Hayworth, and others who made the makeup as popular as the starlets who wore it. ⊠ *1660 N. Highland Ave., Hollywood* ☏ *323/464–7776* ⊕ *www.thehollywoodmuseum.com* ⊒ *$15* ◷ *Wed.–Sun. 10–5.*

★ **Hollywood Walk of Fame.** Along Hollywood Boulevard runs a trail of affirmations for entertainment-industry overachievers. On this mile-long stretch of sidewalk, inspired by the concrete handprints in front of Grauman's Chinese Theatre, names are embossed in brass, each at the center of a pink star embedded in dark-gray terrazzo. They're not all screen deities; many stars commemorate people who worked in a technical field. The first eight stars were unveiled in 1960 at the northwest corner of Highland Avenue and Hollywood Boulevard: Olive Borden, Ronald Colman, Louise Fazenda, Preston Foster, Burt Lancaster, Edward Sedgwick, Ernest Torrence, and Joanne Woodward (some of these names have stood the test of time better than others). Since then, more than 1,600 others have been immortalized, though that honor doesn't come cheap—upon selection by a special committee, the personality in question (or more likely his or her movie studio or record company) pays about $15,000 for the privilege. Stars are identified by one of five icons: a motion-picture camera, a radio microphone, a television set, a record, or a theatrical mask.

Contact the **Hollywood Chamber of Commerce** (✉ *7018 Hollywood Blvd.* ☎ *323/469–8311* ⊕ *www.hollywoodchamber.net*) for celebrity-star locations and information on future star installations.

WORTH NOTING

Hollywood & Highland. Bringing some glitz, foot traffic and commerce back to Hollywood, the hotel-retail-entertainment complex here has become a huge tourist magnet. The design pays tribute to the city's film legacy with a grand staircase leading up to a pair of white stucco 33-foot-high elephants, a nod to the 1916 movie *Intolerance*. ■ **TIP→ Pause at the entrance arch, Babylon Court, which frames the "Hollywood" sign in the hills above for a picture-perfect view.**

There are plenty of clothing stores and eateries, and you may find yourself ducking into these for a respite from the crowds and street artists. In the summer and during Christmas vacation—when the complex is at its busiest—special music programs and free entertainment keep strollers entertained.

A Metro Red Line station provides easy access to and from other parts of the city, and there's plenty of underground parking accessible from Highland Avenue. ✉ *Hollywood Blvd. and Highland Ave., Hollywood* ☎ *323/467–6412 visitor center* ⊕ *www.hollywoodandhighland.com* 🅿 *Parking $2 with validation* ☉ *Mon.–Sat. 10–10, Sun. 10–7.*

Hollywood Bowl. Classic Hollywood doesn't get better than this. Summer-evening concerts have been a tradition since 1922 at this amphitheater cradled in the Hollywood Hills. The Bowl is the summer home of the Los Angeles Philharmonic, but the musical fare also includes pop and jazz. A new much larger shell arrived in 2004, improving the acoustics and allowing the occasional dance and theater performance on stage with the orchestra. Evoking the 1929 shell structure, the new shell ripples out in a series of concentric rings. The 17,000-plus seating capacity ranges from boxes (where alfresco preconcert meals are catered) to concrete bleachers in the rear. Most of the box seats are reserved for season ticket holders, but the ideally located "super seats," with comfortable armrests and great sight lines, are your best bet. Dollar tickets are available for some weeknight classical and jazz performances. Come early to picnic on the grounds.

Before the concert, or during the day, visit the **Hollywood Bowl Museum** for a time-capsule version of the Bowl's history. The microphone used during Frank Sinatra's 1943 performance is just one of the pieces of rare memorabilia on display. Throughout the gallery, drawers open to reveal vintage programs or letters written by fans tracing their fondest memories of going to the Bowl. Listen with headphones to recordings of such great Bowl performers as Amelita Galli-Curci, Ella Fitzgerald, and Paul McCartney. Videos give you a tantalizing look at performances by everyone from the Beatles to Esa-Pekka Salonen. Be sure to pick up a map and take the "Bowl Walk" to explore the parklike grounds of this beautiful setting. During the summer, the store stays open until showtime. ☎ *323/850–2058* ☉ *Tues.–Fri. 10–5, Sat. by appointment* ✉ *2301 N. Highland Ave., Hollywood* ☎ *323/850–2000* ⊕ *www.hollywoodbowl.com* 🅿 *Museum free* ☉ *Grounds daily dawn–dusk, call or check online for performance schedule.*

VISITING THE STUDIOS

If you've never been to L.A.—or if you have, and are coming back with your kids—it's hard to resist the allure of being where the magic happens among the cameras, props, and backlots of Tinseltown's studios.

(above) Go to Universal Studios for a big-bang theme park experience of moviemaking. (lower right) Warner Bros. Studios. (upper right) Paramount Pictures.

Nearly 70% of all L.A.'s entertainment productions happen in the Valley. And to really get behind the scenes, studio tours are the best way for mere mortals to get close to where celebs and the industry's crème-de-la-crème work.

Most tours last several hours, and allow you to see where hit television shows are filmed, spot actors on the lot, and visit movie soundstages—some directors even permit visitors on the set while shooting.

Specific sights change daily, so if there's something in particular you're dying to see, it's best to call ahead and ask.

IT'S ALL ABOUT LOCATION

Many L.A. first-timers make the incorrect assumption that because Hollywood is where all the action takes place, it's also where the stars work.

The only studio that's still located in Hollywood is Paramount; Warner Bros., Universal Studios Hollywood, and NBC Television Studios are north of Hollywood, in Universal City and Burbank.

PARAMOUNT PICTURES

BEST FOR

Paramount offers an intimate—eight to 10 people at a time—two-hour tour of its 63-acre lot. It's probably the most authentic studio tour you can take, giving you a real sense of the film industry's history. Paramount is the only studio left in Hollywood—all the others are in Burbank, Universal City, or Culver City.

TOURING BASICS

Guests primarily visit sets and soundstages that are not in use—though directors occasionally allow visitors during production, so there's a decent chance of seeing a celebrity. Other stops include the New York back-lot and the studio's iconic Bronson Gate.

WHAT'S BEEN FILMED HERE

Chinatown, The Godfather, The Untouchables, Breakfast at Tiffany's, Austin Powers, Cloverfield, Titanic, Star Trek, and the most recent installment of Indiana Jones are just a few of the notable films shot here.

TIPS FOR TOURING

For an inexpensive lunch costing as little as $10, try The Café, the studio's commissary, a buffet where you can grab everything from sandwiches to pizza to Mexican food.

GETTING HERE

From Melrose Avenue, enter on Windsor Boulevard at the main gate. Parking is just north of the gate on the left, and there's additional parking at the lot on the southwest corner of Windsor and Melrose.

VISITOR INFORMATION

Kids must be 12 or older to tour the studio. ✉ *5555 Melrose Ave., Hollywood* ☎ *323/956–1777* 🌐 *www.paramount. com* 🎟 *Tours weekdays by reservation only, $35.*

WARNER BROS. STUDIOS

BEST FOR

If you're looking for an authentic behind-the-scenes look at how films and TV shows are made, head to this major studio center, one of the world's busiest. There aren't many bells and whistles here, but you'll get a much better idea of production work than you will at Universal Studios.

TOURING BASICS

On the VIP Tour, which lasts almost 90 minutes, you'll see the studio from inside an electric cart with 11 others. The specifics of what you'll actually see changes daily, but after viewing a short film on WB movies and shows, you'll be taken by tram to visit sets like the often-recycled Anytown U.S.A.,

Sometimes you can get lucky and meet your favorite stars at Universal Studios.

as well as soundstages and back-lot locations for popular films and shows. The studio's museum has a floor dedicated to *Casablanca* and 85 years of WB history; another belongs exclusively to *Harry Potter*. The tour ends here, and you can explore it at your leisure.

The Deluxe Tour is a five-hour affair that takes you onto working production sets and includes lunch at the commissary (great stargazing ops).

WHAT'S BEEN FILMED HERE
Without A Trace, *The Mentalist*, *Friends*, the original *Ocean's Eleven*, *Casablanca*, and *Rebel Without a Cause*.

TIPS FOR TOURING
Showing up about 20 minutes before the scheduled time of your tour is recommended. VIP Tours leave continuously throughout the day; the Deluxe Tour leaves daily at 10:20 am.

GETTING HERE
The studio's Web site (⊕ *www2.warner bros.com/vipstudiotour*) provides good directions from all parts of the city, including Downtown (take 101 north).

VISITOR INFORMATION
✉ *3400 W. Riverside Dr., Burbank* ☎ *818 /972–8687* ⊕ *www.wbsf.com* 🎞 *VIP Tour is $48 per person; the Deluxe Tour is $225 per person* ☉ *Weekdays 8:30– 4:30. Children under 8 are not admitted. Advance booking is recommended. Parking is $7 at Gate 6.*

UNIVERSAL STUDIOS HOLLYWOOD

BEST FOR
This studio is more a theme park with lots of roller coasters and thrill rides than a backstage pass, though its studio tour does provide a good firsthand look at familiar TV shows and major movie sets.

TOURING BASICS
The tour lasts about an hour and you'll sit on a tram with nearly 100 other people. You'll pass back-lots, dressing rooms, and production offices.

There's also a VIP Tour where you can explore a historic, working movie studio's back-lot and score a closer view of sets, costumes, and props. It's a full-day outing that includes a two-hour studio tour, lunch, valet parking, and front-of-the-line privileges for the theme park's thrill rides.

WHAT'S BEEN FILMED HERE

See the airplane wreckage from *War of the Worlds*, the *Desperate Housewives'* Wisteria Lane, *King Kong* miniatures, *Psycho*'s infamous Bates Motel, and the animatronic Great White Shark from *Jaws*.

TIPS FOR TOURING

You may be tempted to get the $109 pass that takes you to the front of the line. Try to resist this splurge. Once inside, you'll find that the lines, if any, move quickly. Pass on the premium and spend it on a decent lunch outside the park.

GETTING HERE

The park is located in Universal City. From Hollywood, take the 101 Hollywood Freeway north to Universal Studios Boulevard.

VISITOR INFORMATION

✉ *100 Universal City Plaza, Universal City* ☏ *818/622–3801* ⊕ *www.universalstudioshollywood.com* 🎫 *Ticket prices for the studio tour are included in park admission ($74); $239 VIP tour, parking is $15; $10 after 3 pm. Preferred parking is available for $20* ☽ *Contact park for seasonal hrs.*

bands rehearsing, view setups for jokes, check out rehearsals, see sets under construction, and visit the prop warehouse and the studios where shows are taped.

WHAT'S FILMED HERE

The Tonight Show with Jay Leno, Days of Our Lives, The Ellen DeGeneres Show, and *Access Hollywood.*

TIPS FOR TOURING

If you decide to take a last minute studio tour, definitely call ahead; low ticket prices and advance purchase means tickets tend to sell out quickly the day of.

GETTING HERE

The studio is located in Burbank. The best way to get here from Downtown or the Hollywood area is to take the Hollywood Freeway 101 North to Barham Boulevard, which forks off onto West Olive Avenue. Make a right on West Alameda Avenue and then a right on Bob Hope Drive. The studio is on the right.

VISITOR INFORMATION

✉ *3000 W. Alameda Ave., Burbank* ☏ *818/840–3537* ⊕ *www.nbc.com* 🎫 *Tours $8.50. There's no minimum age requirement for children; those under 4 are free.*

NBC TELEVISION STUDIOS

BEST FOR

In contrast to other studio tours, you get to walk on the set rather than being confined to a tram. It's the only TV studio that offers a behind-the-scenes look at production.

TOURING BASICS

The guided 70-minute tour—a rare opportunity to see the inside of a TV studio—emphasizes the history of the station from its roots in radio. You'll visit an old broadcast booth, listen to

Jurassic Park—the Ride at Universal Studios.

4

★ **Hollywood Sign.** With letters 50 feet tall, Hollywood's trademark sign can be spotted from miles away. The sign, which originally read "Hollywoodland," was erected on Mt. Lee in the Hollywood Hills in 1923 to promote a real-estate development.

In 1949 the "land" portion of the sign was taken down. By 1973, the sign had earned landmark status, but since the letters were made of wood, its longevity came into question. A makeover project was launched and the letters were auctioned off (rocker Alice Cooper bought the "o", singing cowboy Gene Autry sponsored an "l") to make way for a new sign made of sheet metal.

Inevitably, the sign has drawn pranksters who have altered it over the years, albeit temporarily, to spell out "Yollyweed" (in the 1970s, to commemorate lenient marijuana laws), "go navy" (before a Rose Bowl game), and "Perotwood" (during the 1992 presidential election). A fence and surveillance equipment have since been installed to deter intruders. Use caution if driving up to the sign on residential streets since many cars speed around the blind corners. ⊕ *www.hollywoodsign.org.*

★ **Kodak Theatre.** Taking a half-hour tour of the theater that hosts the Academy Awards isn't cheap, but it's a worthwhile expense for movie buffs who just can't get enough insider information.

Tour guides share plenty of behind-the-scenes tidbits about Oscar ceremonies as they take you through the theater. You'll get to step into the VIP George Eastman Lounge, where celebrities mingle on the big night, and get a bird's-eye view from the balcony seating.

The interior design was inspired by European opera houses, but underneath all the trimmings, the space has one of the finest technical systems in the world.

If you aren't one of the lucky few with a ticket to the Oscars, get a glimpse of the inside by attending a musical or concert performance. ✉ *6801 Hollywood Blvd., Hollywood* ☎ *323/308–6300* ⊕ *www. kodaktheatre.com* 🎟 *Free; tours $15* ⊙ *Daily 10:30–4.*

BEVELERY HILLS AND THE WESTSIDE

If you only have a day to see L.A., see Beverly Hills. Love it or hate it, it delivers on a dramatic, cinematic scale of wealth and excess. West Hollywood is not a place to see things (like museums or movie studios) as much as it is a place to do things—like go to a nightclub, eat at a world-famous restaurant, or attend an art gallery opening.

The three-block stretch of Wilshire Boulevard known as Museum Row, east of Fairfax Avenue, racks up five intriguing museums and a prehistoric tar pit to boot. Only a few blocks away are the historic Farmers Market and The Grove shopping mall, a great place to people-watch over breakfast. Wilshire Boulevard itself is something of a cultural monument—it begins its grand 16-mi sweep to the sea in Downtown Los Angeles.

For some privileged Los Angelenos, the city begins west of La Cienega Boulevard, where keeping up with the Joneses becomes an epic pursuit. Chic, attractive neighborhoods with coveted postal codes—Bel-Air,

A mural depicting Hollywood legends (John Wayne, Elvis Presley, and Marilyn Monroe are pictured here) adorns a wall of West Hollywood's Stella Adler Academy on Highland Avenue.

Brentwood, Westwood, West Los Angeles, and Pacific Palisades—are home to power couples pushing power kids in power strollers. Still, the Westside is rich in culture—and not just entertainment-industry culture. It's home to UCLA, the monumental Getty Center, and the engrossing Museum of Tolerance.

TOP ATTRACTIONS

Fodor's Choice ★ **Farmers Market and The Grove.** The saying "Meet me at 3rd and Fairfax" became a standard line for generations of Angelenos who ate, shopped, and spotted the stars who drifted over from the studios for a breath of unpretentious air.

Starting back in 1934 when two entrepreneurs convinced oil magnate E.B. Gilmore to open a vacant field for a bare-bones market, this spot became a humble shop for farmers selling produce out of their trucks. From this seat-of-the-pants situation grew a European-style open-air market and local institution at the corner of 3rd Street and Fairfax Avenue.

Now the market includes 110 stalls and more than 30 restaurants, plus the landmark 1941 Clock Tower. The Grove celebrated its 10th anniversary in 2012, and the outdoor mall, with its pseudo-European facade, cobblestones, marble mosaics, and pavilions has never been more popular or packed, especially on weekends.

Los Angeles history gets a nod with the electric steel-wheeled Red Car trolley, which shuttles two blocks through the Farmers Market and The Grove. If you hate crowds, try visiting The Grove before noon for the most comfortable shopping experience. By afternoon, it bustles with shoppers and teens hitting the movie theaters and chain stores such as Banana Republic, Crate & Barrel, Barnes & Noble, and J. Crew. Fashionistas find a haven at the Barney's Co-Op store.

The parking structure on the east side for The Grove handles the cars by monitoring the number of spaces available as you go up each level. The first hour of parking is free, as is the second with a validated ticket. Surface parking for the Farmers Market is two hours free with validation. ⊠ *Farmers Market, 6333 W. 3rd St.; The Grove, 189 The Grove Dr., Fairfax District* ☎ *323/933–9211 Farmers Market, 323/900–8080 The Grove* ⊕ *www.farmersmarketla.com* ⊗ *Farmers Market weekdays 9–9, Sat. 9–8, Sun. 10–7; The Grove Mon.–Thurs. 10–9, Fri. and Sat. 10–10, Sun. 11–8. Some vendors, bars, and restaurants are open earlier and stay open later.*

ⓒ
Fodor'sChoice
★

The Getty Center. With its curving walls and isolated hilltop perch, the Getty Center resembles a pristine fortified city of its own. You may have been lured up by the beautiful views of L.A. (on a clear day stretching all the way to the Pacific Ocean), but the architecture, uncommon gardens, and fascinating art collections will be more than enough to capture and hold your attention. When the sun is out, the complex's rough-cut travertine marble skin seems to soak up the light. You'll need to do some advance planning, since parking reservations are sometimes required during vacation periods, but the experience is well worth the effort.

J. Paul Getty, the billionaire oil magnate and art collector, began collecting Greek and Roman antiquities and French decorative arts in the 1930s. He opened the J. Paul Getty Museum at his Malibu estate in 1954, and in the 1970s, he built a re-creation of an ancient Roman village to house his initial collection. When Getty died in 1976, the museum received an endowment of $700 million that grew to a reported $4.2 billion. The Malibu villa, reopened in 2006, is devoted to the antiquities. The Getty Center, designed by Richard Meier, opened in 1998 and pulled together the rest of the collections, along with the museum's affiliated research, conservation, and philanthropic institutes.

Getting to the center involves a bit of anticipatory lead-up. At the base of the hill, a pavilion disguises the underground parking structure. From there you either walk or take a smooth, computer-driven tram up the steep slope, checking out the Bel Air estates across the humming 405 freeway. The five pavilions that house the museum surround a central courtyard and are bridged by walkways. From the courtyard, plazas, and walkways, you can survey the city from the San Gabriel Mountains to the ocean.

In a ravine separating the museum and the Getty Research Institute, conceptual artist Robert Irwin created the playful Central Garden in stark contrast to Meier's mathematical architectural geometry. The garden's design is what Hollywood feuds are made of: Meier couldn't control Irwin's vision, and the two men sniped at each other during construction, with Irwin stirring the pot with every loose twist his garden path took. The result is a refreshing garden walk whose focal point is an azalea maze (some insist the Mickey Mouse shape is on purpose) in a reflecting pool.

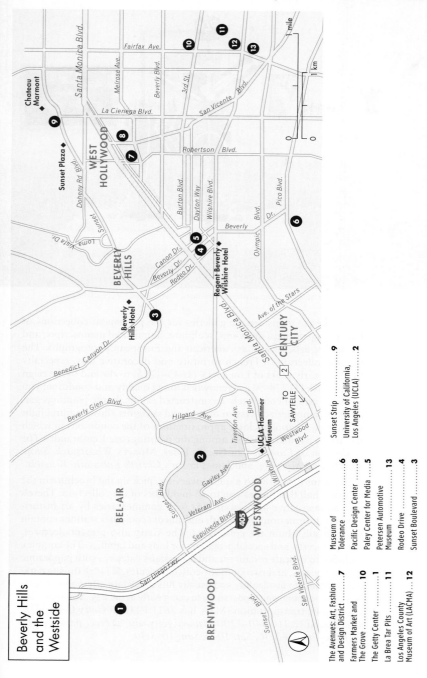

Beverly Hills
and the
Westside

The collection at the Los Angeles County Museum of Art includes more than 100,000 objects, dating from ancient times to the present.

Inside the pavilions are the galleries for the permanent collections of European paintings, drawings, sculpture, illuminated manuscripts, and decorative arts, as well as American and European photographs. The Getty's collection of French furniture and decorative arts, especially from the early years of Louis XIV (1643–1715) to the end of the reign of Louis XVI (1774–92), is renowned for its quality and condition; you can see a pair of completely reconstructed salons. In the paintings galleries, a computerized system of louvered skylights allows natural light to filter in, creating a closer approximation of the conditions in which the artists painted. Notable among the paintings are Rembrandt's *The Abduction of Europa*, Van Gogh's *Irises*, Monet's *Wheatstack, Snow Effects*, and *Morning*, and James Ensor's *Christ's Entry into Brussels*.

If you want to start with a quick overview, pick up the brochure in the entrance hall that guides you to 15 highlights of the collection. There's also an instructive audio tour ($5) with commentaries by art historians. Art information rooms with multimedia computer stations contain more details about the collections. The Getty also presents lectures, films, concerts, and special programs for kids and families. The complex includes an upscale restaurant and downstairs cafeteria with panoramic window views, and two outdoor coffee bar cafés. ■ TIP→ On-site parking is subject to availability and usually fills up by late afternoon on holidays and summer weekends, so try to come early in the day. You may also take public transportation (MTA Bus 761). ⊠ *1200 Getty Center Dr., Brentwood* ☎ *310/440–7300* ⊕ *www.getty.edu* ✉ *Free, parking $15* ⊙ *Tues.–Fri. 10–5:30, Sat. 10–9, Sun. 10–5:30.*

🌑 ★ **La Brea Tar Pits.** Do your children have dinos on the brain? Show them where dinosaurs come from by taking them to the stickiest park in town. About 40,000 years ago, deposits of oil rose to the earth's surface, collected in shallow pools, and coagulated into asphalt. In the early 20th century, geologists discovered that all that goo contained the largest collection of Pleistocene, or Ice Age, fossils ever found at one location: more than 600 species of birds, mammals, plants, reptiles, and insects. Roughly 100 tons of fossil bones have been removed in excavations over the last seven decades, making this one of the world's most famous fossil sites. You can see most of the pits through chain-link fences. (They can be a little smelly, but your kids are sure to love it.) Pit 91 and Project 23 are ongoing excavation projects; tours are available, and you can volunteer to help with the excavations in summer. There are several pits scattered around Hancock Park and the surrounding neighborhood; construction in the area has often had to accommodate them, and in nearby streets and along sidewalks, little bits of tar occasionally ooze up, unstoppable. The nearby **Page Museum at the La Brea Tar Pits** displays fossils from the tar pits and has a "Fishbowl Lab," which is a glass-walled laboratory that allows visitors a rare look behind-the-scenes of the museum where paleontologists and volunteers work on specimens. ✉ *5801 Wilshire Blvd., Hancock Park, Miracle Mile* ☎ *323/934–7243* ⊕ *www.tarpits.org* 🎟 *$7, Children under 5 free, free on 1st Tues. of each month.*

Fodor's Choice ★ **Los Angeles County Museum of Art (LACMA).** Withouth a doubt, LACMA is the focal point of the museum district that runs along Wilshire Boulevard. Chris Burden's *Urban Light* sculpture, composed of more than two hundred restored cast-iron antique street lamps, elegantly illuminate building's front.

Inside, vistors will find one of the country's most comprehensive collections of more than 100,000 objects dating from ancient times to the present. Since opening in 1965, the museum has grown into a campus of several different buildings interconnected via walkways, stretching across a 20-acre campus.

Works from the museum's rotating permanent collection include Latin American artists such as Diego Rivera and Frida Kahlo, prominent Southern California artists, collections of Islamic and European art, paintings by Henri Matisse and René Magritte, as well as works by Paul Klee and Wassily Kandinsky. There's also a solid collection of art representing the ancient civilizations of Egypt, the Near East, Greece, and Rome, plus a vast costume and textiles collection dating back to the 16th century.

As part of an ambitious 10-year face-lift plan that is becoming a work of art on its own, entitled "Transformation: The LACMA Campaign," the museum is adding buildings, exhibition galleries, and redesigning public spaces and gardens.

In early 2008, the impressive Broad Contemporary Art Museum (BCAM) opened. With three vast floors, BCAM's integrates contemporary art into LACMA's collection, exploring the interplay of current times with that of the past. Then in 2010, the Lynda and Stewart Resnick Exhibition

Pavilion was added, a stunning, light-filled space designed by Renzo Piano.

LACMA other buildings include the Ahmanson Building, which contains African, Middle Eastern, South and Southeast Asian collections, as well as the Gore Rifkind Gallery for German Expressionism; the Art of the Americas building; the Pavilion for Japanese Art, featuring scrolls, screens, drawings, paintings, textiles, and decorative arts from Japan; the Bing Center, a research library, resource center, and film theater; and the Boone's Children's Gallery, located inside the Korean art galleries in the Hammer Building, where kids can take advantage of activities such as storytime and learning how to brush paint.

The museum organizes special exhibitions and hosts major traveling shows. In 2012, the extraordinarily popular "Pacific Standard Time: Art in L.A. 1945–1980" involved more than sixty other cultural institutions in Southern California, and "California Design 1930–1965: Living in a Modern Way" is the first major study of California mid-century modern design.

■TIP→ Temporary exhibits sometimes require tickets purchased in advance, so check the calendar ahead of time. ⊠ *5905 Wilshire Blvd., Miracle Mile* 🖀 *323/857–6000* ⊕ *www.lacma.org* 🖼 *$15* ⊙ *Mon., Tues., and Thurs. noon–8, Fri. noon–9, weekends 11–8.*

☺ **Museum of Tolerance.** Using interactive technology, this important museum (part of the Simon Wiesenthal Center) challenges visitors to confront bigotry and racism. One of the most affecting sections covers the Holocaust, with film footage of deportation scenes and simulated sets of concentration camps. Each visitor is issued a "passport" bearing the name of a child whose life was dramatically changed by the German Nazi rule and by World War II; as you go through the exhibit, you learn the fate of that child. Anne Frank artifacts are part of the museum's permanent collection as is Wiesenthal's Vienna office, set exactly as the famous "Nazi hunter" had it while performing his research that brought more than 1,000 war criminals to justice. Interactive exhibits include the "Millennium Machine," which engages visitors in finding solutions to human rights abuses around the world; Globalhate.com, which examines hate on the Internet by exposing problematic sites via touch-screen computer terminals; and the "Point of View Diner," a re-creation of a 1950s diner, red booths and all, that "serves" a menu of controversial topics on video jukeboxes. Renovations brought a new youth action floor and revamped 300-seat theater space. To ensure a visit to this popular museum, make reservations in advance (especially for Friday, Sunday, and holidays) and plan to spend at least three hours there. Testimony from Holocaust survivors is offered at specified times. Museum entry stops at least two hours before the actual closing time. Although every exhibit may not be appropriate for children, school tours regularly visit the museum. ⊠ *9786 W. Pico Blvd., just south of Beverly Hills* 🖀 *310/553–8403* ⊕ *www.museumoftolerance.com* 🖼 *$15* ⊙ *Weekdays 10–5, Sun. 11–5, early close at 3 pm Fri. Nov.–Mar.*

☺ **Petersen Automotive Museum.** You don't have to be a gearhead to appreciate this building full of antique and unusual cars. The Petersen is likely to be one of the coolest museums in town with its take on some of the most unusual creations on wheels and rotating exhibits of the icons who drove them. Lifelike dioramas and street scenes spread through the ground floor help to establish a local context for the history of the automobile. The second floor may include displays of Hollywood-celebrity and movie cars, "muscle" cars (like a 1969 Dodge Daytona 440 Magnum), alternative-powered cars, motorcycles, and a showcase of the Ferrari. You can also learn about the origins of our modern-day car-insurance system, as well as the history of L.A.'s formidable free-way network. A children's interactive Discovery Center illustrates the mechanics of the automobile and fun child-inspired creations; there is also a gift shop. ✉ *6060 Wilshire Blvd., Miracle Mile* ☎ *323/930–2277* ⊕ *www.petersen.org* ⊠ *$10* ☉ *Tues.–Sun. 10–6.*

★ **Sunset Boulevard.** One of the most fabled avenues in the world, Sunset Boulevard began humbly enough in the 18th century as a route from El Pueblo de Los Angeles (today's Downtown L.A.) to the ranches in the west and then to the Pacific Ocean. Now as it winds its way across the L.A. basin to the ocean, it cuts through gritty urban neighborhoods and what used to be the working center of Hollywood's movie industry. In West Hollywood, it becomes the sexy and seductive Sunset Strip, then slips quietly into the tony environs of Beverly Hills and Bel Air, twisting and winding past gated estates. Continuing on past UCLA in Westwood, through Brentwood and Pacific Palisades, Sunset finally descends to the beach, the edge of the continent, and the setting sun.

★ **Sunset Strip.** For 60 years the Hollywood's night owls have headed for the 1¾-mi stretch of Sunset Boulevard between Crescent Heights Boulevard on the east and Doheny Drive on the west, known as the Sunset Strip. In the 1930s and '40s, stars such as Tyrone Power, Errol Flynn, Norma Shearer, and Rita Hayworth came for wild evenings of dancing and drinking at nightclubs like Trocadero, Ciro's, and Mocambo. By the '60s and '70s, the Strip had become the center of rock and roll for acts like Johnny Rivers, the Byrds, and the Doors. The '80s punk riot gave way to hair metal lead by Mötley Crüe and Guns N' Roses on the stages of the Whisky A Go-Go (✉ *8901 Sunset Blvd.* ☎ *310/652–4202* ⊕ *www.whis-kyagogo.com*) and The Roxy (✉ *9009 Sunset Blvd.* ☎ *310/276–2222* ⊕ *www.theroxyonsunset.com*). Nowadays it's the Viper Room (✉ *8852 Sunset Blvd.* ☎ *310/358–1880* ⊕ *www.viperroom.com*), the House of Blues (✉ *8430 Sunset Blvd.* ☎ *323/848–5100* ⊕ *www.hob.com*), and the Key Club (✉ *9039 Sunset Blvd.* ☎ *310/274–5800* ⊕ *www.keyclub.com*), where you'll find on-the-cusp actors, rock stars, club-hopping regulars, and out-of-towners all mingling over drinks and live music. Parking and traffic around the Strip can be tough on weekends; expect to pay around $10–$25 to park, which can take a bite out of your partying budget, but the time and money may be worth it if you plan to make the rounds—most clubs are within walking distance of each other.

WORTH NOTING

The Avenues: Art, Fashion and Design District. Established in 1996, the area defined by Melrose Avenue and Robertson and Beverly boulevards is The Avenues: Art, Fashion & Design District. More than 300 busi-nesses including art galleries, antique shops, contemporary furniture and interior design stores, high-end boutiques, and about 40 restaurants are clustered here. Note that some showrooms are reserved for design professionals and require trade credentials, and not open to the public. ☎ *310/289–2534* ⊕ *avenueswh.com.*

Pacific Design Center. World-renowned architect Cesar Pelli's original vision for the Pacific Design Center was three buildings that together housed a trifecta of designer showrooms, office buildings, parking and more—a virtual multi-building shrine to design. These architecturally intriguing buildings were built years apart: the building sheathed in blue glass (known as the Blue Whale) opened in 1975, the green building opened in 1988, and as of 2012 the final "Red" building is scheduled to open completing Pelli's grand vision all of these many years later. All together the 1.2-million-square-foot vast complex covers over 14 acres, houses over 130 design showrooms as well as 2,200 interior product lines, making this the largest interior design complex in the western United States. You'll also find restaurants such as Red Seven by Wolfgang Puck, the Silverscreen movie theater, an outpost of the Museum of Contemporary Art as well as a myriad of special events. Focused on the professional trade, some showrooms are only to professionals such as credentialed decorators but many other showrooms are open to the public. The PDC also has a Designer Service to help non-professionals shop and get access to certain designers and showrooms.

MOCA Gallery. The Downtown Museum of Contemporary Art has a small satellite MOCA Gallery here that shows works from current artists and designers and hosts exhibit-related talks. ⊠ *8687 Melrose Ave., West Hollywood* ☎ *310/657–0800* ⊕ *www.pacificdesigncenter. com* ☉ *Weekdays 9–5.*

Paley Center for Media. Formerly the Museum of Television and Radio, this institution changed its name in 2007 with a look toward a future that encompasses all media in the ever-evolving world of entertainment and information. Reruns are taken to a curated level in this sleek stone-and-glass building, designed by Getty architect Richard Meier. A sister to the New York location, the Paley Center carries a duplicate of its collection: more than 100,000 programs spanning eight decades. Search for your favorite commercials and television shows on easy-to-use computers. A radio program listening room provides cozy seats supplied with headphones playing snippets of a variety of programming from a toast to Dean Martin to an interview with John Lennon. Frequent seminars with movers 'n' shakers from the film, television, and radio worlds are big draws, as well as screenings of documentaries and short films. Free parking is available in the lot off Santa Monica Boulevard. ⊠ *465 N. Beverly Dr., Beverly Hills* ☎ *310/786–1000* ⊕ *www.paleycenter.org* ☉ *Wed.–Sun. noon–5.*

Rodeo Drive. The ultimate shopping indulgence—Rodeo Drive is one of Southern California's bona fide tourist attractions. The art of window-shopping is prime among the retail elite: Tiffany & Co., Gucci, Jimmy Choo, Valentino, Harry Winston, Prada—you get the picture. Several nearby restaurants have patios where you can sip a drink while watching career shoppers in their size 2 threads saunter by with shopping bags stuffed with superfluous delights. At the southern end of Rodeo Drive (at Wilshire Boulevard), **Via Rodeo,** a curvy cobblestone street designed

to resemble a European shopping area, makes the perfect backdrop to strike a pose for that glamour shot. The holidays bring a special magic to Rodeo and the surrounding streets with twinkling lights, swinging music, and colorful banners. ⊠ *Beverly Hills.*

University of California, Los Angeles (UCLA). With spectacular buildings such as a Romanesque library, the parklike UCLA campus makes for a fine stroll through one of California's most prestigious universities. In the heart of the north campus, the **Franklin Murphy Sculpture Garden** contains more than 70 works of artists such as Henry Moore and Gaston Lachaise. The **Mildred Mathias Botanic Garden,** which contains some 5,000 species of plants from all over the world in a 7-acre outdoor garden, is in the southeast section of the campus and is accessible from Tiverton Avenue. West of the main-campus bookstore, the **Morgan Center Hall of Fame** displays the sports memorabilia and trophies of the university's athletic departments. ☎ *310/825–8764* for reservations, which are required several days to two weeks in advance. The campus has cafés, plus bookstores selling UCLA Bruins paraphernalia. The main-entrance gate is on Westwood Boulevard. Campus parking costs $10.

Fowler Museum at UCLA. Many visitors head straight to the Fowler Museum at UCLA, which presents exhibits on the world's diverse cultures and visual arts, especially those of Africa, Asia, the Pacific, and Native and Latin America. Museum admission is free; use parking lot 4 off Sunset Boulevard ($10). The Fowler Museum is open Wednesday–Sunday noon–5, Thursday until 8 pm. ☎ *310/825–4361* ⊕ *www.fowler.ucla.edu* ⊠ *Bordered by Le Conte, Hilgard, and Gayley Aves. and Sunset Blvd., Westwood* ⊕ *www.ucla.edu.*

SANTA MONICA, VENICE, AND MALIBU

Hugging the Santa Monica Bay in an arch, the desirable communities of Malibu, Santa Monica, and Venice move from the ultrarich, ultracasual Malibu to the bohemian/seedy Venice. What they have in common, however, is cleaner air, mild temperatures, horrific traffic, and an emphasis on the beach-focused lifestyle that many people consider the hallmark of Southern California.

TOP ATTRACTIONS

Fodor'sChoice **Getty Villa Malibu.** Feeding off the cultures of ancient Rome, Greece, and
★   Etruria, the remodeled Getty Villa opened in 2006 with much fanfare—and some controversy concerning the acquisition and rightful ownership of some of the Italian artifacts on display. The antiquities are astounding, but on a first visit even they take a backseat to their environment. This megamansion sits on some of the most valuable coastal property in the world. Modeled after an Italian country home, the Villa dei Papiri in Herculaneum, the Getty Villa includes beautifully manicured gardens, reflecting pools, and statuary. The largest and most lovely garden, the Outer Peristyle, gives you glorious views over a rectangular reflecting pool and geometric hedges to the Pacific. The new structures blend thoughtfully into the rolling terrain and significantly improve the public spaces, such as the new outdoor amphitheater, gift store, café, and entry arcade. Talks

and educational programs are offered at an indoor theater. ■**TIP→** An advance timed-entry ticket is required for admission. Tickets are free and may be ordered from the Web site or by phone. ✉ *17985 Pacific Coast Hwy., Pacific Palisades* ☎ *310/440–7300* ⊕ *www.getty.edu* ✉ *Free, tickets required. Parking $15, cash only* ⊙ *Wed.–Mon. 10–5.*

Third Street Promenade. Stretch your legs along this pedestrians-only three-block stretch of 3rd Street, just a whiff away from the Pacific, lined with jacaranda trees, ivy-topiary dinosaur fountains, strings of lights, and branches of nearly every major U.S. retail chain. Outdoor cafés, street vendors, movie theaters, and a rich nightlife make this a main gathering spot for locals, visitors, as well as street musicians and performance artists. Plan a night just to take it all in or take an afternoon for a long people-watching stroll. There's plenty of parking in city structures on the streets flanking the promenade.

Santa Monica Place reopened in 2010 at the south end of the promenade as a sleek outdoor mall and foodie haven. Its three stories are home to Bloomingdale's, Burberry, Coach, and other upscale retailers. Don't miss the ocean views from the rooftop food court. ✉ *Third Street, between Colorado and Wilshire Blvds., Santa Monica* ⊕ *www. thirdstreetpromenade.com.*

★ **Venice Beach Oceanfront Walk.** The surf and sand of Venice are fine, but the main attraction here is the boardwalk scene, which is a cosmos all its own. Go on weekend afternoons for the best people-watching experience. There are also swimming, fishing, surfing, basketball (it's the site of some of L.A.'s most hotly contested pickup games), racquetball, handball, and shuffleboard. You can rent a bike or some in-line skates and hit the Strand bike path. ⊠ *1800 Ocean Front Walk, west of Pacific Ave., Venice* 🖀 *310/305–9503* ☞ *Parking, restrooms, food concessions, showers, playground.*

WORTH NOTING

Malibu Lagoon State Beach. Bird-watchers, take note: in this 5-acre marshy area you can spot egrets, blue herons, avocets, and gulls. (You need to stay on the boardwalks so as not to disturb their habitats.) The path leads out to a rocky stretch of beach and makes for a pleasant stroll. You're also likely to spot a variety of marine life. Look for the signs to help identify these sometimes exotic-looking creatures. The lagoon is open 24 hours and is particularly enjoyable in the early morning and at sunset. The parking lot has limited hours but street-side parking is usually available at off-peak times. ⊠ *23200 Pacific Coast Hwy., Malibu.*

☾ **Santa Monica Pier.** Souvenir shops, a psychic adviser, carnival games, arcades, eateries, an outdoor trapeze school, and **Pacific Park** are all part the festive atmosphere of this truncated pier at the foot of Colorado Boulevard below Palisades Park. The pier's indoor trademark 46-horse Looff Carousel, built in 1922, has appeared in several films, including *The Sting.* Free concerts are held on the pier in summer. ⊠ *Colorado Ave. and the ocean, Santa Monica* 🖀 *310/458–8900* ⊕ *www.santamonicapier. org* 🖃 *$3-$5* ⊗ *Hours vary by season; check Web site before visiting.*

PASADENA AREA

Although seemingly absorbed into the general Los Angeles sprawl, Pasadena is a separate and distinct city. Noted for its Tournament of Roses, seen around the world each New Year's Day, the city brims with noteworthy spots, from its gorgeous Craftsman homes to its exceptional museums, particularly the Norton Simon and the Huntington Library, Art Collections, and Botanical Gardens. Where else can you see a Chaucer manuscript and rare cacti in one place?

TOP ATTRACTIONS

Fodor'sChoice **Huntington Library, Art Collections, and Botanical Gardens.** If you have
★ time for only one stop in the Pasadena area, it should be the Huntington, built in the early 1900s as the home of railroad tycoon Henry E. Huntington. You can truly forget you're in a city here wandering the ground's 150 acres, just over the Pasadena line in San Marino.

Henry and his wife, Arabella (who was his aunt by marriage), voraciously collected rare books and manuscripts, botanical specimens, and 18th-century British art. The institution they established became one of the most extraordinary cultural complexes in the world. ■TIP➔ Ongoing gallery renovations occasionally require some works from the permanent collection to be shifted to other buildings for display.

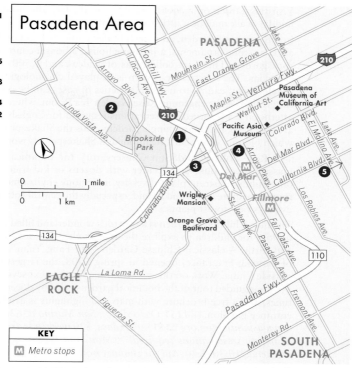

Pasadena Area

KEY

Ⓜ *Metro stops*

Among the highlights are John Constable's intimate *View on the Stour near Dedham* and the monumental *Sarah Siddons as the Tragic Muse,* by Joshua Reynolds. In the Virginia Steele Scott Gallery of American Art, which reopened in May 2009 after extensive renovations, you can see paintings by Mary Cassatt, Frederic Remington, and more.

The library contains more than 700,000 books and 4 million manuscripts, including such treasures as a Gutenberg Bible, the Ellesmere manuscript of Chaucer's *Canterbury Tales,* George Washington's genealogy in his own handwriting, scores of works by William Blake, and a world-class collection of early editions of Shakespeare. You'll find some of these items in the Library Hall with more than 200 important works on display. In 2006 the library acquired more than 60,000 rare books and reference volumes from the Cambridge, Massachusetts–based Bundy Library, making the Huntington the source of one of the biggest history of science collections in the world.

Although the art collections are increasingly impressive here, don't resist being lured outside into the stunning Botanical Gardens. From the main buildings, lawns and towering trees stretch out toward specialty areas. The 10-acre Desert Garden, for instance, has one of the world's largest groups of mature cacti and other succulents, arranged by continent.

Visit this garden on a cool morning or in the late afternoon, or a hot midday walk may be a little too authentic.

In the Japanese Garden, an arched bridge curves over a pond; the area also has stone ornaments, a Japanese house, a bonsai court, and a Zen rock garden. There are collections of azaleas and 1,500 varieties of camellias. The 3-acre rose garden is displayed chronologically, so the development leading to modern varieties of roses can be observed; on the grounds is the charming Rose Garden Tea Room, where traditional afternoon tea is served. (Reservations required for English tea.) There are also herb, palm, and jungle gardens, plus the Shakespeare Garden, which blooms with plants mentioned in Shakespeare's works.

The Rose Hills Foundation Conservatory for Botanical Science, a massive greenhouse–style center with dozens of kid-friendly, hands-on exhibits illustrate plant diversity in various environments. (These rooms are quite warm and humid, especially the central rotunda, which displays rain-forest plants.)

The Bing Children's Garden is a tiny tot's wonderland filled with opportunities for children to explore the ancient elements of water, fire, air, and earth. A classical Chinese Garden "Liu Fang Yuan" (or Garden of Flowing Fragrance) opened in spring 2008, the largest of its kind outside China. Work on this will continue for the next several years. A 1¼-hour guided tour of the botanical gardens is led by docents at posted times, and a free brochure with map and highlights is available in the entrance pavilion. ⊠ *1151 Oxford Rd., San Marino* 🕾 *626/405–2100* ⊕ *www.huntington.org* 🖾 *$15 weekdays, $20 weekends, free 1st Thurs. of month (reservations required)* ☉ *Mon. and Wed.–Fri. noon–4:30, weekends 10:30–4:30; call for summer hours.*

Fodor'sChoice   **Norton Simon Museum.** Long familiar to television viewers of the New
★   Year's Day Rose Parade, this low-profile brown building is more than just a background for the passing floats. It's one of the finest small museums anywhere, with an excellent collection that spans more than 2,000 years of Western and Asian art. It all began in the 1950s when Norton Simon (Hunt-Wesson Foods, McCalls Corporation, and Canada Dry) started collecting the works of Degas, Renoir, Gauguin, and Cézanne. His collection grew to include old masters, impressionists, and modern works from Europe and Indian and Southeast Asian art. After he retired, Simon reorganized the failing Pasadena Art Institute and continued to assemble one of the world's finest collections.

Today the Norton Simon Museum is richest in works by Rembrandt, Goya, Picasso, and, most of all, Degas: this is one of the only two U.S. institutions to hold the complete set of the artist's model bronzes (the other is New York's Metropolitan Museum of Art). Renaissance, baroque, and rococo masterpieces include Raphael's profoundly spiritual *Madonna with Child with Book* (1503), Rembrandt's *Portrait of a Bearded Man in a Wide-Brimmed Hat* (1633), and a magical Tiepolo ceiling, *The Triumph of Virtue and Nobility Over Ignorance* (1740–50). The museum's collections of Impressionist (Van Gogh, Matisse, Cézanne, Monet, Renoir) and Cubist (Braque, Gris) works are extensive. Several Rodin sculptures are placed throughout the museum. Head down to the bottom floor to see rotating exhibits and phenomenal Southeast Asian and Indian sculptures and artifacts, where graceful pieces like a Ban Chiang blackware vessel date to well before 1000 BC. Don't miss a living artwork outdoors: the garden, conceived by noted southern California landscape designer Nancy Goslee Power. The tranquil pond was inspired by Monet's gardens at Giverny. ⊠ *411 W. Colorado Blvd., Pasadena* ☎ *626/449–6840* ⊕ *www.nortonsimon.org* ⊠ *$8, free 1st Fri. of month 6–9 pm* ☉ *Wed., Thurs., and Sat.–Mon. noon–6, Fri. noon–9.*

WORTH NOTING

★ **Gamble House.** Built by Charles and Henry Greene in 1908, this is a spectacular example of American Arts and Crafts bungalow architecture. The term *bungalow* can be misleading, since the Gamble House is a huge three-story home. To wealthy Easterners such as the Gambles (as in Procter & Gamble), this type of vacation home seemed informal compared with their mansions back home. What makes admirers swoon is the incredible amount of handcraftsmanship, including a teak staircase and cabinetry, Greene and Greene–designed furniture, and an Emil Lange glass door. The dark exterior has broad eaves, with sleeping porches on the second floor. An hour-long, docent-led tour of the Gamble's interior will draw your eye to the exquisite details. If you want to see more Greene and Greene homes, buy a self-guided tour map of the neighborhood in the bookstore. ⊠ *4 Westmoreland Pl., Pasadena* ☎ *626/793–3334* ⊕ *www.gamblehouse.org* ⊠ *$10* ☉ *Thurs.–Sun. noon–3; tickets go on sale Thurs.–Sat. at 10, Sun. at 11:30. 1-hr tour every 15-20 min.*

★ **Old Town Pasadena.** Once the victim of decay, the area was revitalized in the 1990s as a blend of restored 19th-century brick buildings with a contemporary overlay. A phalanx of chain stores has muscled in, but there are still some homegrown shops and plenty of tempting cafés and restaurants. In the evening and on weekends, streets are packed with people, and Old Town crackles with energy. The 12-block historic district is anchored along Colorado Boulevard between Pasadena Avenue and Arroyo Parkway.

Rose Bowl. With an enormous rose, the city of Pasadena's logo, adorned on its exterior, it's hard to miss this 100,000-seat stadium, host of many Super Bowls and home to the UCLA Bruins. Set in Brookside Park at the wide bottom of an arroyo, the facility is closed except during games and special events such as the monthly Rose Bowl Flea Market, which is considered the granddaddy of West Coast flea markets. If you want the best selection of items, show up early. People start arriving here at the crack of dawn, but note you will also pay a higher entry fee for having first dibs on the selection. The best bargaining takes place at the end of the day when vendors would rather settle for a few less dollars then have to lug their goods home. ⊠ *1001 Rose Bowl Dr. at Rosemont Ave., Pasadena* ☎ *626/577–3100* ⊕ *www.rosebowlstadium.com for flea market, www. rgcshows.com for shows* ⊠ *$8 from 9 am on, $10 for 8–9 am entrance, $15 for 7–8 am entrance* ☉ *Flea market 2nd Sun. of month 9–3.*

4

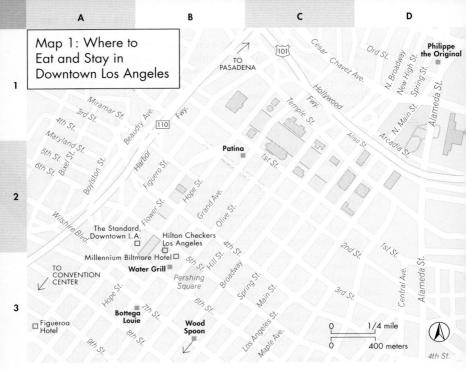

Map 1: Where to Eat and Stay in Downtown Los Angeles

WHERE TO EAT

Dining out in Los Angeles tends to be a casual affair, and even at some of the most expensive restaurants you're likely to see customers in jeans (although this is not necessarily considered in good taste). Despite its veneer of decadence, L.A. is not a particularly late-night city for eating. (The reenergized Hollywood dining scene is emerging as a notable exception.) The peak dinner times are from 7 to 9, and most restaurants won't take reservations after 10 pm. Generally speaking, restaurants are closed either Sunday or Monday; a few are shuttered both days. Most places—even the upscale spots—are open for lunch on weekdays, when Hollywood megadeals are conceived.

Use the coordinate (⊕ 1:A1) at the end of each listing to locate a site on the corresponding map.

WHAT IT COSTS					
	¢	$	$$	$$$	$$$$
Restaurants	under $10	$10–$17	$18–$24	$25–$35	over $35

Prices are for a main course at dinner, excluding 9.75% tax.

DOWNTOWN WITH LOS FELIZ

DOWNTOWN

$$ ✗**Bottega Louie.** This former Brooks Brothers suit store was reincarnated
ITALIAN into a lively Italian restaurant and gourmet market in 2008 and quickly
Fodor's Choice crowned Downtown's new culinary darling. Vast open space, stark
★ white walls and long windows that stretch from floor to ceiling give it
a grand and majestic appeal. An army of stylish servers weaves in-and-
out of the crowds carrying bowls of pasta, trays of bubbly prosecco,
and thin-crust pizzas. Pick and choose from a bevy of salads, pastas,
pizzas. and entrées that range from wild Italian sea bass to a *bistecca
arrabiata* (seared steak with long peppers and tomatoes). Or simply
order from its small-plates menu with favorites: asparagus with fried
egg, jambon Serrano, heirloom carrots, tomato bruschetta, and fried
calamari. Don't let the crowd of people waiting for a table deter you,
order a cocktail from the bar, peruse the gourmet market, and nibble
on a brightly colored macaroon. ✉ *700 S. Grand Ave., Downtown*
☎ *213/802–1470* ⌘ *Reservations not accepted* ✛ *1:B3.*

$$$ ✗**Patina.** In a bold move, chef-owner Joachim Splichal moved his
FRENCH flagship restaurant from Hollywood to Downtown's striking Frank
Gehry–designed Walt Disney Concert Hall. His gamble paid off—the
contemporary space, surrounded by a rippled "curtain" of rich wal-
nut, is an elegant, dramatic stage for the acclaimed restaurant's contemporary French cuisine. Specialties include copious amounts of foie
gras, butter-poached lobster, and medallions of venison served with
lady apples. Finish with a hard-to-match cheese tray (orchestrated by a
genuine *maître fromager*) and an apple tatin with a crisp Granny Smith
apple sorbet served as its companion. ✉ *Walt Disney Concert Hall, 141
S. Grand Ave., Downtown* ☎ *213/972–3331* ⊕ *www.patinagroup.com*
⌘ *Reservations essential* ☾ *Closed Mon. Lunch Tues.–Sun.* ✛ *1:B2.*

¢ ✗**Philippe the Original.** L.A.'s oldest restaurant (1908), Philippe claims
AMERICAN the French dip sandwich originated here. You can get one made with
☺ beef, pork, ham, lamb, or turkey on a freshly baked roll; the house hot
Fodor's Choice mustard is as famous as the sandwiches. Its reputation is earned by
★ maintaining traditions, from sawdust on the floor to long communal
tables where customers debate the Dodgers or local politics. The home
cooking—orders are taken at the counter where some of the moth-
erly servers have managed their long lines for decades—includes huge
breakfasts, chili, pickled eggs, and an enormous pie selection. The best
bargain: a cup of java for 10¢ including tax. ✉ *1001 N. Alameda St.,
Downtown* ☎ *213/628–3781* ⊕ *www.philippes.com* ⌘ *Reservations
not accepted* ▭ *No credit cards* ✛ *1:D1.*

$$$ ✗**Water Grill.** There's a bustling, enticing rhythm here as platters of glisten-
SEAFOOD ing shellfish get whisked from the oyster bar to the cozy candlelit booths.
Start with a roasted beet salad with lavender cured feta or the Tahitian
albacore served with chili sauce, ruby-red grapefruit and mint leaves. For
entrées, explore the king salmon with a poached egg and polenta, the
sturgeon with a beet risotto and the big eyed tuna elegantly paired with
a dried cranberry quinoa. A sesaonlly driven and sophisticated menu that
brings all the seafood greats together in one amazing menu. Excellent
desserts and a fine wine list round out this top-notch dining experience.

BEST BETS FOR LOS ANGELES DINING

With thousands of restaurants to choose from, how will you decide where to eat? Fodor's writers and editors have selected their favorite restaurants by price and cuisine in the Best Bets lists *below. You can also search by neighborhood—just peruse the following pages to find specific details about a restaurant in the full reviews later in the chapter.*

Fodor'sChoice★

Angelini Osteria, $$$, p. 193
A.O.C. $$$, p. 194
The Apple Pan, $, p. 195
Bouchon Bistro, $$$, p. 191
Bottega Louie, $$, p. 185
Cube Café and Marketplace, $$, p. 188
Little Dom's, $$, p. 187
Mélisse, $$$, p. 197
Philippe the Original, ¢, p. 185
Pizzeria Mozza, $$, p. 189
Providence, $$$$, p. 191
Spago Beverly Hills, $$$, p. 192
Urasawa, $$$$, p. 193
Yuca's Hut, $, p. 187

By Price

¢

Pink's Hot Dogs, p. 189
Philippe the Original, p. 185
Zankou Chicken, p. 191

$

The Apple Pan, p. 195
Artisan Cheese Gallery, p. 191
Father's Office, p. 197
La Serenata Gourmet, p. 196
Little Flower Candy Company, p. 198
Porto's Bakery, p. 187
Wood Spoon, p. 187
Yuca's Hut, p. 187

$$

Bombay Café, p. 196
Bottega Louie, p. 185
Cube Café and Marketplace, p. 188
Gjelina, p. 197
Little Dom's, p. 187
Pizzeria Mozza, p. 189
Tanzore, p. 193

$$$

Angelini Osteria, p. 193
Animal, p. 188
A.O.C., p. 194
Bouchon Bistro, p. 191
Campanile, p. 194
Cobras & Matadors, p. 195
Enoteca Drago, p. 192
Oliverio, p. 192
Osteria Mozza, p. 188
Spago Beverly Hills, p. 192
Water Grill, p. 185

$$$$

Gordon Ramsay at The London, p. 195
Providence, p. 191
Urasawa, p. 193

By Cuisine

CHINESE

Mandarette, $, p. 195

FRENCH

Mélisse, $$$, p. 197

INDIAN

Bombay Café, $$, p. 196
Tanzore, $$, p. 193

ITALIAN

Angelini Osteria, $$$, p. 193
Cube Café and Marketplace, $$, p. 188
Osteria Mozza, $$$, p. 188
Pizzeria Mozza, $$, p. 189
Valentino, $$$, p. 197

JAPANESE

Urasawa, $$$$, p. 193

MEDITERRANEAN

A.O.C., $$$, p. 194
Campanile, $$$, p. 194

MEXICAN

La Serenata Gourmet, $, p. 196
Yuca's Hut, $$, p. 187

SEAFOOD

Providence, $$$$, p. 191
Water Grill, $$$, p. 185

SPANISH

Cobras & Matadors, $$$, p. 195

544 S. Grand Ave., Downtown 213/891–0900 www.watergrill.com Reservations essential No lunch weekends 1:B3.

$ BRAZILIAN **Wood Spoon.** There's no sign for this cozy bistro in Downtown's Fashion District, just a big wood spoon that locals have come to know as the beacon for great Brazilian food. Loved by students from the fashion institute, Brazilian expats, and concertgoers heading to the Orpheum Theatre for a show, this place is an affordable gem in a high-priced dining area. Order from the small plate's selection, such as *coxinha* (a Brazilian street snack made with chicken), calabreza sausage with potatoes, and the hearts of palm frittata. The house favorite is a Brazilian chicken potpie or pork burger served with yam fries. *107 W. 9th St., Downtown 213/629–1765 www.woodspoonla.com Reservations essential Closed Sun. 1:B3.*

LOS FELIZ

$$ ITALIAN Fodor's Choice ★ **Little Dom's.** With a $15 Monday night supper, a vintage bar with a barkeep who mixes up seasonally inspired retro cocktails and an attached Italian deli where one can pick up a pork cheek sub, it's not surprising why Little Dom's is a neighborhood favorite. Cozy and inviting with big leather booths one can sink into for the night, the menu blends classic Italian fare with a modern sensibility, with dishes like the baked ricotta and wild boar soppressatta, classic pappardelle with homemade sausage, whitefish picatta, and a New York strip steak with fennel béarnaise. This is a terrific spot for weekend brunch; grab a shot of rich hot chocolate and take a seat on the sidewalk patio. *2128 Hillhurst Ave., Los Feliz 323/661–0055 www.littledoms.com Reservations essential Breakfast and lunch served to 3 pm daily 2:F1.*

$ MEXICAN Fodor's Choice ★ **Yuca's Hut.** Blink and you can miss this place, whose reputation far exceeds its size (it may be the tiniest place to have ever won a James Beard award). It's known for carne asada, carnitas, and *cochinita pibil* (Yucatán-style roasted pork) tacos, burritos, and banana leaf-wrapped tamales. This is a fast-food restaurant in the finest tradition—independent, family-owned, and sticking to what it does best. The liquor store next door sells lots of Coronas to Hut customers soaking up the sun on the makeshift parking-lot patio. There's no chance of satisfying a late-night craving, though; it closes at 6 pm. *2056 N. Hillhurst Ave., Los Feliz 323/662–1214 Reservations not accepted No credit cards Closed Sun. 2:F1.*

HOLLYWOOD AND THE STUDIOS

BURBANK

$ CAFÉ **Porto's Bakery.** Waiting in line at Porto's is as much a part of the experience as is indulging in a roasted pork sandwich and chocolate-dipped croissant. Locals love this neighborhood bakery and café that has been an L.A. staple for 35 years. This is its second location just minutes away from the studios and makes for a great spot to take a stroll and peruse the consignment shops run by former movie stylists. The crowded café bustles with an ambitious lunch crowd, but counter service is quick and efficient. Go for one of its tasty Cuban sandwiches like the media noche or the potato sandwich (potato stuffed with ground beef), or order the house specialty: chorizo pie. Skipping dessert here would just be wrong. Your sweet tooth will thank you later. ⊠ *3614 W. Magnolia Blvd., Burbank* ☎ *818/846–9100* ⊗ *Mon.–Sat., 6:30 am–7:30 pm, Sun. 6:30 am–5:30 pm* ✛ *2:E1.*

HOLLYWOOD

$$$
AMERICAN

✕ **Animal.** When foodies in Los Angeles need a culinary thrill, they come to this minimalist restaurant in the Fairfax District, which is light on the flash but heavy on serious food. The James Beard award–winning restaurant is owned by Jon Shook and Vinny Dotolo, two young chefs who shot to fame with a stint on *Iron Chef* and later with their own Food Network show, *Two Dudes Catering*. With a closing time of 2 am, the small restaurant is an L.A. anomaly. That assessment is also true for the restaurant's diverse clientele, which ranges from neighborhood dwellers to young Hollywood celebrities to food snobs in search of their new favorite dish. The daily menu consists of small plates and entrées that make it easy to explore many items, like barbecue pork belly sandwiches, *poutine* with oxtail gravy, foie gras *loco moco* (a hamburger topped with foie gras, quail egg, and Spam), and fried quail served with maple *au jus*. For dessert, the house specialty is a multilayered bacon-chocolate crunch bar. ⊠ *435 N. Fairfax Ave., Hollywood* ☎ *323/782–9225* ⊕ *www.animalrestaurant.com* ⊗ *No lunch* ✛ *2:C2.*

$$
ITALIAN
Fodor'sChoice
★

✕ **Cube Café & Marketplace.** Cheese, charcuterie, and pasta lovers take heed: this dark and cozy Italian restaurant will ruin you for all the others. With more than 85 varieties of cheese, an enviable salami selection, pasta made in-house, and a passionate and earnest staff, this former pasta company turned upscale café and gourmet market is one of L.A.'s more affordable culinary gems. Take a seat at the cheese bar and order the *Sleepless in Salumi* plate or the *When in Rome* and pair it with a glass of Italian wine. For dinner, order the antipasti of braised octopus, and then move onto the seasonally driven pasta dishes, like the wild boar gnocchi, veal ravioli, or pumpkin-stuffed pasta. ⊠ *615 N. La Brea Blvd., Hollywood* ☎ *323/939–1148* ⊗ *Mon.–Sat. 11 am–10:30 pm. Closed Sun.* ✛ *2:D3.*

$$
AMERICAN

✕ **Musso & Frank Grill.** Liver and onions, lamb chops, goulash, shrimp Louis salad, dry gin martinis, gruff waiters—you'll find all the old favorites here in Hollywood's oldest restaurant. A film-industry hangout since it opened in 1919, Musso & Frank still attracts the working studio set to its maroon faux-leather booths, along with tourists and locals nostalgic for Hollywood's golden era. Great breakfasts are served all day, but the kitchen's famous "flannel cakes" (pancakes) are served only until 3 pm. ⊠ *6667 Hollywood Blvd., Hollywood* ☎ *323/467–7788* ⊗ *Closed Sun. and Mon.* ✛ *2:D1.*

$$$
ITALIAN

✕ **Osteria Mozza.** Born from the immensely popular collaboration between celebrated bread maker Nancy Silverton (founder of L.A.'s La Brea Bakery and Campanile) and Iron Chef Mario Batali, Osteria Mozza features candlelit, linen-clad tables surrounding a central marble-topped mozzarella bar, ideal for solo diners. From that bar come several presentations of velvety *burrata* cheese and perfectly dressed salads, while the kitchen turns out an oversize *raviolo* oozing ricotta and egg in brown butter sauce, blissful sweetbreads piccata and grilled

Cube Café & Marketplace.

whole *orata* (Mediterranean sea bream), capped off with Italian cheeses and delicious rosemary–olive oil cakes. If you can't score a reservation here, treat yourself to the partners' pizzeria next door. ⊠ *6602 Melrose Ave., Hollywood* ☎ *323/297–0100* ⊕ *www.mozza-la.com* ⌒ *Reservations essential* ⊘ *No lunch* ✛ *2:D2.*

¢   ✕ **Pink's Hot Dogs.** Orson Welles ate 18 of these hot dogs in one sitting, AMERICAN   and you, too, will be tempted to order more than one. The chili dogs are ☺   the main draw, but the menu has expanded to include a Martha Stewart Dog (a 10-inch frank topped with mustard, relish, onions, tomatoes, sauerkraut, bacon, and sour cream). Since 1939, Angelenos and tourists alike have been lining up to plunk down some modest change for one of the greatest guilty pleasures in L.A. Pink's is open until 3 am on weekends. ⊠ *709 N. La Brea Ave., Hollywood* ☎ *323/931–4223* ⊕ *www.pinkshollywood.com* ⌒ *Reservations not accepted* ⊟ *No credit cards* ✛ *2:D2.*

$$ ✕ **Pizzeria Mozza.** The other, more casual half of Batali and Silverton's ITALIAN   partnership (the first being Osteria Mozza), this casual venue gives **Fodor's**Choice   newfound eminence to the humble "pizza joint." With traditional ★   Mediterranean items like white anchovies, lardo, squash blossoms, and Gorgonzola, Mozza's pies—thin-crusted delights with golden, blistered edges—are much more Campania than California, and virtually every one is a winner. Antipasti include simple salads, roasted bone marrow, and platters of *salumi*. All sing with vibrant flavors thanks to superb market-fresh ingredients, and daily specials may include favorites like lasagna. Like the menu, the wine list is both interesting and affordable. ⊠ *641 N. Highland Ave., Hollywood* ☎ *323/297–0101* ⌒ *Reservations essential* ✛ *2:D2.*

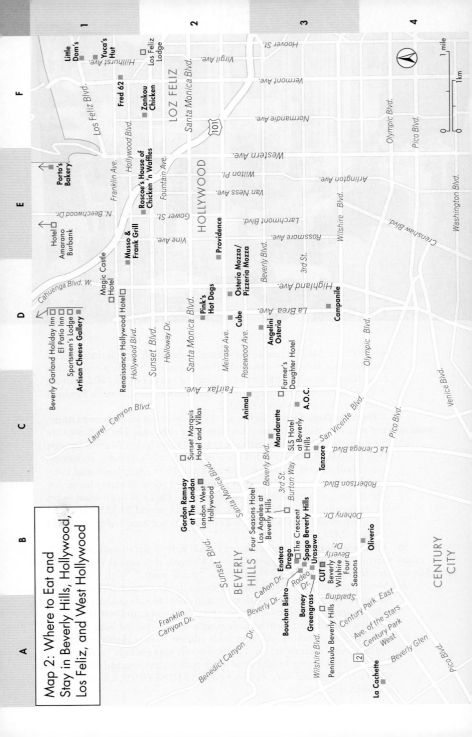

Map 2: Where to Eat and
Stay in Beverly Hills, Hollywood,
Los Feliz, and West Hollywood

$$$$ ✕**Providence.** Chef-owner Michael Cimarusti has elevated Providence
SEAFOOD to the ranks of America's finest seafood restaurants. The elegant dining
Fodor's Choice room, outfitted with subtle nautical accents, is smoothly overseen by co-
★ owner–general manager Donato Poto. Obsessed with quality and fresh-
ness, the meticulous chef maintains a network of specialty purveyors,
some of whom tip him off to their catch before it even hits the dock.
This exquisite seafood then gets the Cimarusti treatment of French technique, traditional American themes, and Asian accents, often presented
in elaborate tasting menus. Pastry chef Adrian Vasquez's exquisite desserts are not to be missed; consider a three- to eight-course dessert tasting menu. ⊠ *5955 Melrose Ave., Hollywood* ☎ *323/460–4170* ⊙ *No
lunch Mon.–Thurs. and weekends* ✢ *2:D2.*

¢ ✕**Zankou Chicken.** Forget the Colonel. Zankou's aromatic, Armenian-
MIDDLE EASTERN style rotisserie chicken with perfectly crisp, golden skin is one of L.A.'s
☺ truly great budget meals. It's served with pita bread, veggies, hummus,
and unforgettable garlic sauce. If this doesn't do it for you, try the
kebabs, falafel, or sensational *shawarma* (spit-roasted lamb or chicken)
plates. ⊠ *5065 W. Sunset Blvd., Hollywood* ☎ *323/665–7845* ⊕ *www.
zankouchicken.com* ⟤ *Reservations not accepted* ✢ *2:F2.*

STUDIO CITY

$ ✕**Artisan Cheese Gallery.** Taste your way through triple creams, blues,
DELI goat's milk, and stinky cheeses from all over the globe at this charming
☺ locale that offers cheese and charcuterie plates, sandwiches, oversize salads, and hot panini sandwiches. Taste-testing is encouraged, so don't be
shy to ask. Grab a table in small outdoor patio and enjoy the neighborhood scenery; it's a great way to experience the Valley. ⊠ *12023 Ventura
Blvd., Studio City* ☎ *818/762–1221* ⊕ *www.artisancheesegallery.com*
⟤ *Reservations not accepted* ✢ *2:D1.*

BEVERLY HILLS AND THE WESTSIDE

BEVERLY HILLS

$$$ ✕**Bouchon Bistro.** Famed chef Thomas Keller finally made it to Los Ange-
FRENCH les and has set up his French bistro in swanky Beverly Hills. Grand and
Fodor's Choice majestic, but still casual and friendly, there is nothing about a night at
★ Bouchon that doesn't make you feel pampered. With little details that
separate it from the pack, there's filtered Norwegian water served at
every table, a twig-shaped baguette made fresh in the kitchen, and an
expansive wine list celebrating California wines. It's a foodie scene that
welcomes L.A.'s high-profile chefs, celebrities, and locals. Start with
its classic onion soup that arrives with a bubbling lid of cheese or the
salmon rillettes, which are big enough to share. For dinner, there's a tra-
ditional steak and frites, roasted chicken, steamed Maine mussels, and
a delicious grilled *croque madame.* Bouchon Bistro is also known for
its beautiful French pastries. For a sweet bite, order an espresso and the
profiteroles or the Bouchons (bite-size brownies served with homemade
vanilla ice cream). Ask for a tour of the kitchen for a sneak peek inside
the operation. ⊠ *235 N. Canon Dr., Beverly Hills* ☎ *310/271–9910*
⊕ *www.bouchonbistro.com* ⟤ *Reservations essential* ✢ *2:B3.*

A feeling of simple elegance comes through in the food (and décor) at Patina, in Downtown Los Angeles.

$$$
ITALIAN

✕ Enoteca Drago. High-flying Sicilian chef Celestino Drago scores with this sleek but unpretentious version of an *enoteca* (a wine bar serving small snacks). It's an ideal spot for skipping through an Italian wine list—more than 50 wines are available by the glass—and enjoying a menu made up of small plates such as stuffed olives, an assortment of cheeses and *salumi*, ricotta-stuffed zucchini flowers, or *crudo* (Italy's answer to ceviche) from the raw bar. Although the miniature mushroom-filled ravioli bathed in foie gras–truffle sauce is a bit luxurious for an enoteca, it's one of the city's best pasta dishes. Larger portions and pizzas are also available here, but the essence of an enoteca is preserved. ⊠ *410 N. Cañon Dr., Beverly Hills* ☏ *310/786–8236* ⊕ *www.celestinodrago.com* ⌕ *Reservations essential* ✛ *2:B3.*

$$$
ITALIAN

✕ Oliverio. This restaurant in the Avalon Hotel, an eco-friendly property in a renovated 1950s apartment complex, feels straight out of the *Valley of the Dolls* movie. Mid-century design gives vintage appeal that blends in with the restaurant's modern Italian cuisine and Californian sensibility. Fresh food concepts are created by chef Mirko Padernois, who uses seasonal ingredients inspired from the hotel's rooftop garden. Enjoy a starter of fritto misto or a cauliflower soufflé; for dinner try the braised lamb tortelli, beef short ribs, or a risotto Milanese. Reserve a private cabana poolside to eat your dessert underneath the stars while enjoying Southern California's patio lifestyle. ⊠ *9400 W. Olympic Ave., Beverly Hills* ☏ *310/277–5221* ⊕ *www.avalonbeverlyhills.com* ✛ *2:B4.*

$$$
NEW AMERICAN
Fodor's Choice
★

✕ Spago Beverly Hills. The famed flagship restaurant of Wolfgang Puck is justifiably a modern L.A. classic. Spago centers on a buzzing outdoor courtyard shaded by 100-year-old olive trees. From an elegantly appointed table inside, you can glimpse the exhibition kitchen and, on rare occasions, the affable owner greeting his famous friends (these days, compliments to the chef are directed to Lee Hefter). The people-watching here is worth the price of admission, but the clientele is surprisingly inclusive, from the biggest Hollywood stars to Midwestern tourists to foodies more preoccupied with vintages of Burgundy than with faces from the cover of *People*. Foie gras has disappeared, but the daily-changing menu might offer a four-cheese pizza topped with truffles, *côte de boeuf* with Armagnac-peppercorn sauce, Cantonese-style duck, and some traditional Austrian specialties. Acclaimed pastry chef Sherry Yard works magic with everything from an ethereal apricot soufflé to Austrian *kaiserschmarrn* (crème fraîche pancakes with fruit). ⊠ *176 N. Cañon Dr., Beverly Hills* ☎ *310/385–0880* ⊕ *www.wolfgangpuck.com* ⌂ *Reservations essential* ⊘ *No lunch Sun.* ✛ *2:B3.*

$$ ✕ **Tanzore.** The design and menu of a venerable traditional Indian restaurant has been dramatically transformed to create a totally new experi-
INDIAN ence. Now lighter contemporary fare prepared with seasonal California ingredients—like coriander-crusted tuna with avocado raita (a yogurt-based condiment), tandoori sea bass, and wok-fried tofu masala—dominates the menu, while its colorful spaces encompass sleek blond wood surfaces, water features, a showy glass-ensconced wine cellar, and an ultrahip lounge. ⊠ *50 N. La Cienega Blvd., Beverly Hills* ☎ *310/652–3894* ⊕ *www.tanzore.com* ⌂ *Reservations essential* ✛ *2:C3.*

$$$$ ✕ **Urasawa.** Shortly after celebrated sushi chef Masa Takayama packed
JAPANESE his knives for the Big Apple, his soft-spoken protégé Hiroyuki Urasawa
Fodor's Choice settled into the master's former digs. The understated sushi bar has few
★ precious seats, resulting in incredibly personalized service. At a minimum of $350 per person for a strictly *omakase* (chef's choice) meal, Urasawa remains the priciest restaurant in town, but the endless parade of masterfully crafted, exquisitely presented dishes renders few regrets. The maple sushi bar, sanded daily to a satin-like finish, is where most of the action happens. You might be served velvety bluefin toro paired with beluga caviar, slivers of foie gras to self-cook *shabu shabu* style, or egg custard layered with *uni* (sea urchin), glittering with gold leaf. This is also the place to come during fugu season, when the legendary, potentially deadly blowfish is artfully served to adventurous diners. ⊠ *2 Rodeo, 218 N. Rodeo Dr., Beverly Hills* ☎ *310/247–8939* ⌂ *Reservations essential* ⊘ *Closed Monday. No lunch* ✛ *2:B3.*

WEST HOLLYWOOD

$$$ ✕ **Angelini Osteria.** You might not guess it from the modest, rather con-
ITALIAN gested dining room, but this is one of L.A.'s most celebrated Italian
Fodor's Choice restaurants. The key is chef-owner Gino Angelini's thoughtful use of
★ superb ingredients, evident in dishes such as a salad of lobster, apples, and pomegranate; and pumpkin tortelli with butter, sage, and asparagus. An awesome lasagna verde, inspired by Angelini's grandmother, is not to be missed. Whole branzino, crusted in sea salt, and boldly flavored rustic specials (e.g., tender veal kidneys, rich oxtail stew) consistently impress. An intelligent selection of mostly Italian wines complements the menu, and desserts like the open-face chocolate tart with coffee cream and hazelnut gelato are baked fresh daily. ⊠ *7313 Beverly*

CLOSE UP

Local Chains Worth Stopping For

It's said that the drive-in burger joint was invented in L.A., probably to meet the demands of an ever-mobile car culture. Burger aficionados line up at all hours outside **In-N-Out Burger** (⊕ www.in-n-out.com, multiple locations), still a family-owned operation whose terrific made-to-order burgers are revered by Angelenos. Visitors may recognize the chain as the infamous spot where Paris Hilton got nabbed for drunk driving, but locals are more concerned with getting their burger fix off the "secret" menu, with variations like "Animal Style" (mustard-grilled patty with grilled onions and extra spread), a "4 x 4" (four burger patties and four cheese slices, for big eaters) or the bun-less "Protein Style" that comes wrapped in a bibb of lettuce. The company's Web site lists explanations for other popular secret menu items.

Tommy's sells a delightfully sloppy chili burger; the original location (⊠ 2575 Beverly Blvd., Los Angeles ☎ 213/389–9060) is a no-frills

culinary landmark. For rotisserie chicken that will make you forget the Colonel forever, head to **Zankou Chicken** (⊠ 5065 Sunset Blvd., Hollywood ☎ 323/665–7845 ⊕ www.zankouchicken.com), a small chain noted for its golden crispy-skinned birds, potent garlic sauce, and Armenian specialties. Homesick New Yorkers will appreciate **Jerry's Famous Deli** (⊠ 10925 Weyburn Ave., Westwood ☎ 310/208–3354 ⊕ www. jerrysfamousdeli.com), where the massive menu includes all the classic deli favorites. With a lively bar scene, good barbecued ribs, and contemporary takes on old favorites, the more upscale **Houston's** (⊠ 202 Wilshire Blvd., Santa Monica ☎ 310/576–7558 ⊕ www.hillstone.com) is a popular local hangout. And **Señor Fish** (⊠ 422 E. 1st St., Downtown ☎ 213/625–0566 ⊕ www.senor-fish.com) is known for its healthy Mexican seafood specialties, such as scallop burritos and ceviche tostadas.

Blvd., West Hollywood ☎ 323/297–0070 ⊕ www.angelinoosteria.com ⊙ Closed Mon. No lunch weekends ✛ 2:E3.

$$$
MEDITERRANEAN
Fodor'sChoice
★

✕**A.O.C.** Since it opened in 2002, this restaurant and wine bar has revolutionized dining in L.A., pioneering the small-plate format that has now swept the city. The space is dominated by a long, candle-laden bar serving more than 50 wines by the glass. There's also a charcuterie bar, an L.A. rarity. The tapas-like menu is perfectly calibrated for the wine list; you could pick duck confit, warm salt cod tart with orange salad, an indulgent slab of pork rillettes (a sort of pâté), or just plunge into one of the city's best cheese selections. Named for the acronym for Appellation d'Origine Contrôlée, the regulatory system that ensures the quality of local wines and cheeses in France, A.O.C. upholds the standard of excellence. ⊠ 8022 W. 3rd St., West Hollywood ☎ 323/653–6359 ⊕ www.aocwinebar.com ⟁ Reservations essential ⊙ No lunch ✛ 2:D3.

$$$
MEDITERRANEAN

✕**Campanile.** Chef-owner Mark Peel has mastered the mix of robust Mediterranean flavors with homey Americana. The 1926 building (which once housed the offices of Charlie Chaplin) exudes a lovely Renaissance charm and Campanile is one of L.A.'s most acclaimed and beloved restaurants. Appetizers may include fried risotto pancakes or a grapefruit and fennel salad, while pan-seared black cod with white bean–eggplant puree and grilled prime rib with tapenade are likely to appear as entrées. Thursday night, grilled cheese sandwiches are a huge draw, as the beloved five-and-dime classic is morphed into exotic creations. For an ultimate L.A. experience, come for weekend brunch on the enclosed patio. ⊠ *624 S. La Brea Ave., West Hollywood* ☎ *323/938–1447* ⊕ *www.campanilerestaurant.com* ⌒ *Reservations essential* ◷ *No dinner Sun.* ✛ *2:E4.*

$$$
SPANISH

✕ **Cobras & Matadors.** A bustling storefront spot whose cramped tables and long bar channel the aura of a Madrid side street, Cobras & Matadors hits the mark with quality ingredients and value-oriented pricing. Among the numerous appetizers and tapas are favorites like grilled squid salad, crispy green lentils, and charred green asparagus with walnut vinaigrette. Larger plates include the grilled Angus steak, pan-roasted white fish, and homemade paella. There's no wine list here, but no corkage fee either—bring a bottle from your own cellar or buy one from the owner's wine shop next door, where the intriguing inventory leans heavily toward Spanish vino. ⊠ *7615 Beverly Blvd., West Hollywood* ☎ *323/932–6178* ◷ *No lunch* ✛ *2:D3.*

$$$$
FRENCH

✕ **Gordon Ramsay at the London.** The foul-mouthed celebrity chef from Fox's *Hell's Kitchen* demonstrates why he nevertheless ranks among the world's finest chefs at this fine-dining restaurant in a West Hollywood boutique hotel. Two pastel-color dining rooms with city views flank a formidable white marble bar, creating a space that feels trendy yet surprisingly unpretentious. A menu of small plates accommodates both light suppers and indulgent feasts alike. Highlights include crisp pork with figs, flilet mignon and braised short ribs, and a Maine Lobster with coconut froth and mushroom ravioli. To maximize the experience, consider one of the flexible tasting menus ($95 or $110), artfully crafted by Ramsay's local culinary team and orchestrated by a polished, gracious serving staff. ⊠ *The London, 1020 N. San Vicente Blvd., West Hollywood* ☎ *310/358–7788* ⌒ *Reservations essential* ✛ *2:C2.*

$
CHINESE
☺

✕ **Mandarette.** Clad in warm wood and copper finishes, this inviting café began as a casual spin-off of the Mandarin in Beverly Hills, but the casual concept has outlasted its high-end originator. Start with cucumber salad with spicy peanut dressing, scallion pancakes, or curried chicken dumplings before indulging in kung pao scallops or crispy sesame beef. ⊠ *8386 Beverly Blvd., West Hollywood* ☎ *323/655–6115* ⊕ *www.mandarettecafe.com* ✛ *2:C3.*

WEST LOS ANGELES

$
AMERICAN
Fodor's Choice
★

✕ **The Apple Pan.** A burger-insider haunt since 1947, this unassuming joint with a horseshoe-shaped counter—no tables here—turns out one heck of a good burger topped with Tillamook cheddar, plus an excellent hickory burger with barbecue sauce. You can also find great fries and, of course, an apple pie indulgent enough to christen the restaurant (although many regulars argue that the banana cream deserves the honor). Be prepared to wait, but the veteran countermen turn the stools at a quick pace. In the meantime, grab a cup of Sanka and enjoy a little L.A. vintage. ⊠ *10801 W. Pico Blvd., West L.A.* ☎ *310/475–3585* ⌒ *Reservations not accepted* ▭ *No credit cards* ◷ *Closed Mon.* ✛ *3:D2.*

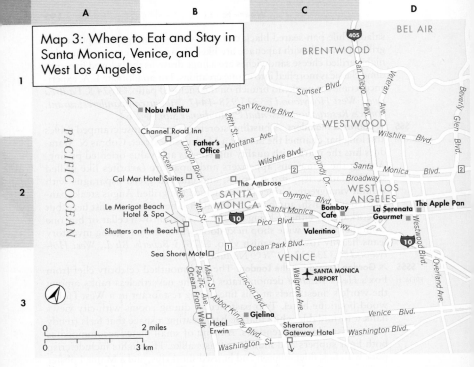

Map 3: Where to Eat and Stay in Santa Monica, Venice, and West Los Angeles

$$ **✕Bombay Café.** Some of the menu items at Bombay Café are strictly
INDIAN authentic, others have been lightened up a bit to suit Southern Califor-
nia sensibilities, and a few are truly innovative (e.g., ginger margarita,
California tandoori salad with lemon-cilantro dressing). Regulars (and
there are many) swear by the chili-laden lamb *frankies* (burritolike
snacks sold by vendors on the beaches of Bombay), *sev puri* (wafers
topped with onions, potatoes, and chutneys), and Sindhi chicken, a
complex poached-then-sautéed recipe with an exotically seasoned
crust. ⊠ *12021 W. Pico Blvd., West L.A.* ☎*310/473–3388* ⊕*www.
bombaycafe-la.com* ✛ *3:C2.*

$ **✕La Serenata Gourmet.** With uncomfortable chairs and crowds from
MEXICAN the nearby Westside Pavilion boosting decibel levels, this branch of
the East L.A. original isn't ideal for leisurely conversation. But the res-
taurant scores big points for its boldly flavored Mexican cuisine. Pork
dishes and moles are delicious, but seafood is the real star—there are
chubby *gorditas* (cornmeal pockets stuffed with shrimp), juicy shrimp
enchiladas in tomatillo sauce, and flavorful grilled fish with cilantro
or garlic sauce. If your experience with Mexican food has been on the
Tex-Mex end of the spectrum, come here to broaden your taste buds'
horizons. ⊠ *10924 W. Pico Blvd., West L.A.* ☎*310/441–9667* ⊕*www.
laserenataonline.com* ✛ *3:D2.*

SANTA MONICA AND VENICE

SANTA MONICA

$ ✕**Father's Office.** With a facade distinguished only by a vintage neon
AMERICAN sign, Father's Office is a congested, gentrified pub famous for handcrafted beers and what is widely regarded as L.A.'s best burger. Topped
with Gruyère and Maytag blue cheeses, arugula, caramelized onions,
and applewood-smoked bacon compote, the "Office Burger" is a guilty
pleasure worth waiting in line for (which is usually required). Other
options include steak frites and Spanish tapas, with side orders of addictive sweet potato fries served in a miniature shopping cart with aïoli—
don't even think of asking for ketchup, because FO enforces a strict
no-substitutions policy. So popular is the Office Burger that chef-owner
Sang Yoon has recently opened a second location in Culver City. Note:
Because Father's Office is a bar, it's strictly 21 and over. ⊠ *1018 Montana Ave., Santa Monica* ☎ *310/393–2337* ⊕ *www.fathersoffice.com*
🍴 *Reservations not accepted* ⊗ *No lunch weekdays* ✛ *3:B2.*

$$$ ✕**Mélisse.** In a city where informality reigns, this is one of L.A.'s more
FRENCH dressy, but not stuffy, restaurants. The dining room is contemporary yet
Fodor's Choice elegant, with well-spaced tables topped with flowers and Limoges china.
★ The garden room loosens up with a stone fountain and a retractable
roof. Chef-owner Josiah Citrin enhances his modern French cooking
with seasonal California produce. Consider seared sweet white corn
ravioli in brown butter–truffle froth, lobster Bolognese, slow cooked
rabbit, or duck confit. The cheese cart is packed with domestic and
European selections. ⊠ *1104 Wilshire Blvd., Santa Monica* ☎ *310/395–
0881* ⊕ *www.melisse.com* 🍴 *Reservations essential* ⊗ *Closed Sun. and
Mon. No lunch* ✛ *3:B2.*

$$$ ✕**Valentino.** Renowned as one of the country's top Italian restaurants,
ITALIAN Valentino has a truly awe-inspiring wine list. With nearly 2,800 labels
consuming 130 pages, backed by a cellar overflowing with nearly
100,000 bottles, this restaurant is nothing short of heaven for serious oenophiles. In the 1970s, suave owner Piero Selvaggio introduced L.A. to his exquisite modern Italian cuisine, and he continues
to impress guests with dishes like a timballo of wild mushrooms with
rich Parmigiano-Reggiano–saffron *fonduta*, squid ink–tinted risotto
with Maine lobster, a memorable osso buco, and sautéed branzino
with lemon emulsion. A welcome addition to this exalted venue is its
more casual wine bar for wine tasting and nibbles like *crudo* and car-
paccio. ⊠ *3115 Pico Blvd., Santa Monica* ☎ *310/829–4313* ⊕ *www.
valentinorestaurantgroup.com* 🍴 *Reservations essential* ⊗ *Closed Sun.
No lunch Sat. and Mon.–Thurs.* ✛ *3:C2.*

VENICE

$$ ✕**Gjelina.** This handsome restaurant comes alive with personality the
AMERICAN minute you walk through its oversize rustic wooden door. There are
long communal tables, hanging light fixtures that soften the room and
make it glow, and an outdoor patio. The menu is smart and seasonal
with small plates, cheese and charcuterie, pastas, and pizza. Begin
with a mushroom, goat cheese and truffle oil pizza, spinach heirloom
salad, mussels with chorizo, or grilled Monterey squid with fingerling

4

potatoes. For the main course, there's the chicken with saffron qui-noa or the Niman Ranch pork chop with mixed mushrooms. Typi-cally crowded and noisy, it is a great spot that dazzles all four senses. ⊠ *1429 Abbot Kinney Blvd., Venice* ☎ *310/450–1429* ⊕ *www.gjelina. com* ⌕ *Reservations essential* ⊙ *Open until midnight daily* ✛ *3:B3.*

PASADENA

$ ✕ **Little Flower Candy Company.** Just off the beaten path of Old Town
CAFÉ   Pasadena sits this quaint café that has charmed the hearts and taste
⊙   buds of locals with its seasonally driven menu of sandwiches, salads, fresh soups, and incredible baked goods. The café is owned by Chris-tine Moore, who made a name for herself in the candy world as a cre-ator of addicting sea salt caramels and oversize sugar marshmallows. She opened shop a few years ago to sell her sweets, but also ended up creating a neighborhood hub for northeast Los Angeles. The café is nestled up against the sloping hills for a small-town feel even though Downtown L.A. is a few miles away. It's a terrific place to grab a cof-fee, a fig pastry, or a light lunch before heading out for an afternoon of shopping. ⊠ *1424 W. Colorado Blvd., Pasadena* ☎ *626/304–4800* ⊕ *www.littleflowercandyco.com* ⊙ *Mon.–Sat. 7–5, Sun. 7–4* ✛ *5:A2.*

WHERE TO STAY

When looking for a hotel, don't write off the pricier establishments immediately. Price categories are determined by "rack rates"—the list price of a hotel room, which is usually discounted. Specials abound, particularly Downtown on the weekends. Many hotels have packages that include breakfast, theater tickets, spa services, or exotic rental cars. Pricing is very competitive, so always check out the hotel Web site in advance for current special offers. When making reservations, particu-larly last-minute ones, check the hotel's Web site for exclusive Internet specials or call the property directly.

For expanded hotel reviews, visit Fodors.com.

Use the coordinate (✛ 1:B2) at the end of each listing to locate a site on the corresponding map.

WHAT IT COSTS				
¢	$	$$	$$$	$$$$
Hotels	under $100	$100–$200	$201–$300	$301–$400	over $400

Prices are for a standard double room in high season, excluding 10% to 15.5% tax.

The Rooftop Bar at The Standard, Downtown L.A., is a swanky place to enjoy a nightcap.

DOWNTOWN WITH LOS FELIZ

DOWNTOWN

$ **Figueroa Hotel.** On the outside, it feels like Spanish colonial; on the inside, this 12-story hotel, built in 1926, is a mix of Mexican, Mediterranean, and Moroccan styles, with earth tones, hand-glazed walls, and wrought-iron beds. **Pros:** a short walk to Nokia Theatre, L.A. Live, Convention Center; well-priced; great poolside bar. **Cons:** somewhat funky room decor; small bathrooms; gentrifying neighborhood. ⊠ *939 S. Figueroa St., Downtown* ☎ *213/627–8971, 800/421–9092* ⊕ *www. figueroahotel.com* ↩ *285 rooms, 6 suites* ⚭ *In-room: a/c, Wi-Fi. In-hotel: restaurant, bar, pool, parking* ✛ *1:A3.*

$$$ **Hilton Checkers Los Angeles.** Opened as the Mayflower Hotel in 1927,
Fodor's Choice Checkers retains much of its original character; its various-size rooms
★ all have charming period details, although they also have contemporary luxuries like pillow-top mattresses, coffeemakers, 24-hour room service, and plasma TVs. **Pros:** historic charm; business-friendly; rooftop pool and spa. **Cons:** no on-street parking; some rooms compact; urban setting. ⊠ *535 S. Grand Ave., Downtown* ☎ *213/624–0000, 800/445–8667* ⊕ *www.hiltoncheckers.com* ↩ *188 rooms, 5 suites* ⚭ *In-room: a/c, Internet, Wi-Fi. In-hotel: restaurant, bar, pool, gym, spa, parking* ✛ *1:B3.*

$$$ **Millennium Biltmore Hotel.** One of Downtown L.A.'s true treasures, the gilded 1923 Beaux Arts masterpiece exudes ambience and history. **Pros:** historic character; famed filming location; club-level rooms have many hospitable extras. **Cons:** pricey valet parking; standard rooms are truly compact. ⊠ *506 S. Grand Ave., Downtown* ☎ *213/624–1011, 866/866–8086* ⊕ *www.thebiltmore.com* ↩ *635 rooms, 48 suites* ⚭ *In-room: a/c,*

BEST BETS FOR LOS ANGELES LODGING

Fodor's offers a selective listing of lodging experiences at every price range. Here, we've compiled our top recommendations by price and experience. The very best properties are designated in the listings with the Fodor's Choice logo.

Peninsula Beverly Hills, p. 204

Shutters on the Beach, p. 206

SLS Hotel at Beverly Hills, p. 204

By Experience

BEST DESIGN

Figueroa Hotel, $, p. 199

The Standard, Downtown L.A., $$, p. 201

BEST SPAS

Four Seasons Hotel, Los Angeles at Beverly Hills, $$$$, p. 204

Renaissance Hollywood Hotel, $$, p. 202

Shutters on the Beach, $$$$, p. 206

GREEN FOCUS

The Ambrose, $$, p. 205

Los Feliz Lodge, $, p. 201

MOST KID-FRIENDLY

Magic Castle Hotel, $, p. 201

Renaissance Hollywood Hotel, $$, p. 202

Shutters on the Beach, $$$$, p. 206

Fodor's Choice ★

Channel Road Inn, $$, p. 205

The Crescent Beverly Hills, $$, p. 202

Farmer's Daughter Hotel, $$, p. 201

Hilton Checkers Los Angeles, $$$, p. 199

Hotel Erwin, $$, p. 206

The Langham Huntington, Pasadena, $$, p. 206

Peninsula Beverly Hills, $$$$, p. 204

Renaissance Hollywood Hotel, $$, p. 202

Shutters on the Beach, $$$$, p. 206

Sunset Marquis Hotel & Villas, $$$, p. 204

By Price

¢

El Patio Inn, p. 202

$

The Beverly Garland Holiday Inn, p. 202

Figueroa Hotel, p. 199

Los Feliz Lodge, p. 201

Magic Castle Hotel, p. 201

Sea Shore Motel, p. 205

Sportsmen's Lodge, p. 202

$$

The Ambrose, p. 205

Cal Mar Hotel Suites, p. 205

Channel Road Inn, p. 205

The Crescent Beverly Hills, p. 202

Farmer's Daughter Hotel, p. 201

Hotel Erwin, p. 206

The Langham Huntington, Pasadena, p. 206

London West Hollywood, p. 204

Renaissance Hollywood Hotel, p. 202

Sheraton Gateway Los Angeles Hotel, p. 205

The Standard, Downtown L.A., p. 201

$$$

Hilton Checkers Los Angeles, p. 199

Hotel Amarano Burbank, p. 201

Millennium Biltmore Hotel, p. 199

Sunset Marquis Hotel & Villas, p. 204

$$$$

Beverly Wilshire, a Four Seasons Hotel, p. 202

Four Seasons Hotel, Los Angeles at Beverly Hills, p. 204

Le Merigot Beach Hotel & Spa, p. 205

Internet, Wi-Fi. In-hotel: restaurant, bar, pool, gym, business center, parking ⊕ 1:B3.

$$ ⊡ **The Standard, Downtown L.A.** Built in 1955 as Standard Oil's company's headquarters, the building was completely revamped under the sharp eye of owner André Balazs. **Pros:** on-site Rudy's barbershop for grooming; 24/7 coffee shop for dining; rooftop pool and lounge for fun. **Cons:** disruptive party scene weekends and holidays; street noise; hipper-than-thou scene in lounge. ⊠ *550 S. Flower St., Downtown* ☎ *213/892–8080* ⊕ *www.standardhotel.com* ↵ *171 rooms, 36 suites* ⟂ *In-room: a/c, Internet, Wi-Fi. In-hotel: restaurant, bar, pool, gym, business center, parking, some pets allowed ⊕ 1:A2.*

LOS FELIZ

$ ⊡ **Los Feliz Lodge.** Checking into this bungalow-style lodge is like crashing at an eco-minded and artsy friend's place: you let yourself into an apartment with fully stocked kitchen, washer and dryer, and a communal patio. **Pros:** homey feel; walking distance to restaurants. **Cons:** no on-site restaurant or pool. ⊠ *1507 N. Hoover St., Los Feliz* ☎ *323/660–4150* ⊕ *www.losfelizlodge.com* ↵ *4 rooms* ⟂ *In-room: a/c, kitchen, Internet, Wi-Fi. In-hotel: laundry facilities ⊕ 2:F2.*

HOLLYWOOD AND THE STUDIOS

BURBANK

$$$ ⊡ **Hotel Amarano Burbank.** Close to Burbank's TV and movie studios, the smartly designed Amarano feels like a Beverly Hills boutique hotel. **Pros:** boutique style in a Valley location; pleasant breakfast room. **Cons:** no pool to cool off during scorching summertime; Pass Avenue street noise. ⊠ *322 N. Pass Ave., Burbank* ☎ *818/842–8887, 888/956–1900* ⊕ *www.hotelamarano.com* ↵ *91 rooms, 10 suites* ⟂ *In-room: a/c, kitchen, Internet, Wi-Fi. In-hotel: restaurant, bar, gym, business center, parking, some pets allowed ⊕ 2:E1.*

HOLLYWOOD

$$
Fodor's Choice
★

⊡ **Farmer's Daughter Hotel.** Tongue-in-cheek country style is the name of the game at this motel: rooms are upholstered in blue gingham with denim bedspreads, and farm tools serve as art. **Pros:** great central city location; across from the cheap eats of the Farmers Market and The Grove's shopping and entertainment mix. **Cons:** pricey restaurant; roadside motel-size rooms; shaded pool; less than stellar service. ⊠ *115 S. Fairfax Ave., Farmers Market* ☎ *323/937–3930, 800/334–1658* ⊕ *www. farmersdaughterhotel.com* ↵ *63 rooms, 2 suites* ⟂ *In-room: a/c, Wi-Fi. In-hotel: restaurant, pool, parking, some pets allowed ⊕ 2:C3.*

$
☾

⊡ **Magic Castle Hotel.** Close to the action (and traffic) of Hollywood, this former apartment building faces busy Franklin Avenue and is a quick walk to the nearby Red Line stop at Hollywood & Highland. **Pros:** remarkably friendly and able staff; free Wi-Fi; good value. **Cons:** traffic-y locale; no elevator; small bathrooms. ⊠ *7025 Franklin Ave., Hollywood* ☎ *323/851–0800, 800/741–4915* ⊕ *www.magiccastlehotel. com* ↵ *7 rooms, 33 suites* ⟂ *In-room: a/c, kitchen, Internet, Wi-Fi. In-hotel: pool, laundry facilities, parking* ⊚*Breakfast ⊕ 2:D1.*

$$ **Renaissance Hollywood Hotel.** Part of the massive Hollywood & High-
☺ land shopping and entertainment complex, this 20-story Renaissance
Fodor's Choice is at the center of Hollywood's action. **Pros:** large rooms with new
★ contemporary-styled furniture; Red Line Metro–station adjacent. **Cons:**
corporate feeling; very touristy. ⊠ *1755 N. Highland Ave., Hollywood*
☎ *323/856–1200, 800/769–4774* ⊕ *www.renaissancehollywood.com*
⇨ *604 rooms, 33 suites* ⚖ *In-room: a/c, Internet, Wi-Fi. In-hotel: res-
taurant, bar, pool, gym, spa, business center, parking* ✛ *2:D1.*

NORTH HOLLYWOOD

$ **The Beverly Garland Holiday Inn.** The Hollywood connection starts in
☺ the lobby where framed photos of hotel namesake actress Beverly Gar-
land decorate the lobby. **Pros:** large pool and play area; unpretentious
and friendly feel; on-site Wi-Fi café. **Cons:** small bathrooms; touristy;
$14 self-parking lot charge. ⊠ *4222 Vineland Ave., North Hollywood*
☎ *818/980–8000, 800/238–3759* ⊕ *www.beverlygarland.com* ⇨ *238
rooms, 17 suites* ⚖ *In-room: a/c, Internet, Wi-Fi. In-hotel: restaurant,
bar, pool, tennis court, gym, laundry facilities, parking* ✛ *2:D1.*

STUDIO CITY

¢   **El Patio Inn.** Behind a classic hacienda-style adobe and neon-lighted
facade, El Patio Inn is a throwback to 1960s-era roadside motels. **Pros:**
close to Universal Studios and a Metro line stop; Ventura Boulevard
has an endless supply of restaurants; low rates. **Cons:** no pool; service
matches the low rates; zero amenities. ⊠ *11466 Ventura Blvd., Studio
City* ☎ *818/508–5828* ⊕ *www.elpatioinn.com* ⇨ *16 rooms* ⚖ *In-room:
a/c, Internet. In-hotel: parking, some pets allowed* ✛ *2:D1.*

$ **Sportsmen's Lodge.** The sprawling five-story hotel is under new owner-
☺ ship and management, and the lobby, bar, and popular coffee shop now
have a contemporary look. **Pros:** close to Ventura Boulevard's plentiful
restaurants; free shuttle and discounted tickets to Universal Hollywood;
garden-view rooms are quietest. **Cons:** $11 daily self-parking fee. ⊠ *12825
Ventura Blvd., Studio City* ☎ *818/769–4700, 800/821–8511* ⊕ *www.
slhotel.com* ⇨ *177 rooms, 13 suites* ⚖ *In-room: a/c, Internet, Wi-Fi. In-
hotel: restaurant, bar, pool, gym, laundry facilities, parking* ✛ *2:D1.*

BEVERLY HILLS AND THE WESTSIDE

BEVERLY HILLS

$$$$ **Beverly Wilshire, a Four Seasons Hotel.** Built in 1928, the Italian Renais-
sance–style Wilshire wing of this fabled hotel is replete with elegant
details: crystal chandeliers, oak paneling, walnut doors, crown mold-
ings, and marble. **Pros:** chic location; top-notch service; and refined
vibe. **Cons:** small lobby; valet parking backs up at peak times; expensive
dining choices. ⊠ *9500 Wilshire Blvd., Beverly Hills* ☎ *310/275–5200,
800/427–4354* ⊕ *www.fourseasons.com/beverlywilshire* ⇨ *258 rooms,
137 suites* ⚖ *In-room: a/c, Internet, Wi-Fi. In-hotel: restaurant, bar,
pool, gym, spa, business center, parking, some pets allowed* ✛ *2:B3.*

$$ **The Crescent Beverly Hills.** Built in 1926 as a dorm for silent film actors,
Fodor's Choice the Crescent is now a sleek boutique hotel within the Beverly Hills
★ shopping triangle. **Pros:** the on-site restaurant CBH's tasty cuisine and

Farmer's Daughter Hotel

Renaissance Hollywood Hotel

The Crescent Beverly Hills

Peninsula Beverly Hills

Channel Road Inn

convivial happy hour; the lobby is fashionista central. **Cons:** dorm-size rooms; gym an additional fee and only accessed outside hotel via Sports Club/LA; no elevator. ✉ *403 N. Crescent Dr., Beverly Hills* ☎ *310/247–0505* ⊕ *www.crescentbh.com* ⇆ *35 rooms* ⚴ *In-room: a/c, Wi-Fi. In-hotel: restaurant, bar, parking* ✛ *2:B3.*

$$$$ ⬛ **Four Seasons Hotel, Los Angeles at Beverly Hills.** High hedges and patio gardens make this hotel a secluded retreat that even the hum of traffic can't permeate. **Pros:** expert concierge; deferential service; celebrity magnet. **Cons:** Hollywood scene in bar and restaurant means rarefied prices. ✉ *300 S. Doheny Dr., Beverly Hills* ☎ *310/273–2222, 800/332–3442* ⊕ *www.fourseasons.com/losangeles* ⇆ *185 rooms, 100 suites* ⚴ *In-room: a/c, kitchen, Internet, Wi-Fi. In-hotel: restaurant, bar, pool, gym, spa, business center, parking, some pets allowed* ✛ *2:B3.*

$$$$ ⬛ **Peninsula Beverly Hills.** This French Rivera–style palace is a favorite
Fodor's Choice of Hollywood boldface names, but all kinds of visitors consistently
★ describe their stay as near perfect—though expensive. **Pros:** central, walkable Beverly Hills location; stunning flowers; one of the best concierges in the city. **Cons:** serious bucks required to stay here. ✉ *9882 S. Santa Monica Blvd., Beverly Hills* ☎ *310/551–2888, 800/462–7899* ⊕ *www.beverlyhills.peninsula.com* ⇆ *142 rooms, 36 suites, 16 villas* ⚴ *In-room: a/c, Internet, Wi-Fi. In-hotel: restaurant, bar, pool, gym, spa, business center, parking, some pets allowed* ✛ *2:A3.*

$$$$ ⬛ **SLS Hotel at Beverly Hills.** Imagine dropping into Alice in Wonderland's rabbit hole: this is the colorful, textured, and tchotchke-filled lobby of the SLS from design maestro Philippe Starck. **Pros:** a vibrant newcomer with lofty ambitions; excellent design and cuisine. **Cons:** standard rooms are compact but you pay for the scene; pricey hotel dining. ✉ *465 S. La Cienega Blvd., Beverly Hills* ☎ *310/247–0400* ⊕ *www.slshotels.com* ⇆ *236 rooms, 61 suites* ⚴ *In-room: a/c, Internet, Wi-Fi. In-hotel: restaurant, bar, pool, gym, spa, business center, parking, some pets allowed* ✛ *2:C3.*

WEST HOLLYWOOD

$$ ⬛ **The London West Hollywood.** Just off the Sunset Strip, cosmopolitan and chic in design, the London WeHo is a remake of 1984-built Bel Age. **Pros:** perfectly designed interiors; hillside and city views in generous-size suites all with balconies and steps from the Strip. **Cons:** too refined for kids to be comfortable; lower floors have mundane views. ✉ *1020 N. San Vicente Blvd., West Hollywood* ☎ *310/854–1111, 866/282–4560* ⊕ *www.thelondonwesthollywood.com* ⇆ *200 suites* ⚴ *In-room: a/c, Internet, Wi-Fi. In-hotel: restaurant, bar, pool, gym, business center, parking, some pets allowed* ✛ *2:B2.*

$$$ ⬛ **Sunset Marquis Hotel & Villas.** If you're in town to cut your new hit
Fodor's Choice single, you'll appreciate the two on-site recording studios here. **Pros:**
★ superior service; discreet setting just off the Strip; clublike atmosphere; free passes to Equinox nearby. **Cons:** standard suites are somewhat small. ✉ *1200 N. Alta Loma Rd., West Hollywood* ☎ *310/657–1333, 800/858–9758* ⊕ *www.sunsetmarquis.com* ⇆ *102 suites, 52 villas* ⚴ *In-room: a/c, kitchen, Internet, Wi-Fi. In-hotel: restaurant, bar, pool, gym, spa, business center, parking, some pets allowed* ✛ *2:C2.*

SANTA MONICA, VENICE, AND LAX

LOS ANGELES INTERNATIONAL AIRPORT

$$ ⚐ **Sheraton Gateway Los Angeles Hotel.** LAX's coolest-looking hotel is so swank that guests have been known to ask to buy the black-and-white photos hanging behind the front desk. **Pros:** weekend rates significantly lower; free LAX shuttle. **Cons:** convenient to airport but not much else. ⊠ *6101 W. Century Blvd., Los Angeles International Airport* ☎ *310/642–1111, 800/325–3535* ⊕ *www.sheratonlosangeles.com* ⛱ *714 rooms, 88 suites* ♿ *In-room: a/c, Internet, Wi-Fi. In-hotel: restaurant, bar, pool, gym, business center, parking, some pets allowed* ✛ *3:C3.*

SANTA MONICA

$$ ⚐ **The Ambrose.** An air of tranquillity pervades the four-story Ambrose, which blends right into its mostly residential Santa Monica neighborhood. **Pros:** L.A.'s most eco-conscious hotel with nontoxic housekeeping products and recycling bins in each room. **Cons:** quiet, residential area of Santa Monica; no restaurant on-site. ⊠ *1255 20th St., Santa Monica* ☎ *310/315–1555, 877/262–7673* ⊕ *www.ambrosehotel.com* ⛱ *77 rooms* ♿ *In-room: a/c, Internet, Wi-Fi. In-hotel: gym, business center, parking* ✛ *3:B2.*

$$ ⚐ **Cal Mar Hotel Suites.** On a residential street one block from the Third Street Promenade and within a short walk to the beach, this low-profile, two-story, all-suites hotel is a comparative bargain. **Pros:** lower off-season rates; full kitchens; low-key vibe. **Cons:** street noise; no a/c but ocean breeze is present. ⊠ *220 California Ave., Santa Monica* ☎ *310/395–5555, 800/776–6007* ⊕ *www.calmarhotel.com* ⛱ *36 suites* ♿ *In-room: no a/c, Wi-Fi. In-hotel: pool, laundry facilities, parking* ✛ *3:B2.*

$$ ⚐ **Channel Road Inn.** A quaint surprise in Southern California, the Channel Road Inn is every bit the country retreat B&B lovers adore, with four-poster beds with fluffy duvets and a cozy living room with fireplace. **Pros:** quiet residential neighborhood close to beach; free Wi-Fi and evening wine and hors d'oeuvres. **Cons:** no pool. ⊠ *219 W. Channel Rd., Santa Monica* ☎ *310/459–1920* ⊕ *www.channelroadinn.com* ⛱ *15 rooms* ♿ *In-room: a/c, Internet, Wi-Fi. In-hotel: business center, parking* ⍾ *Breakfast* ✛ *3:B2.*

Fodor'sChoice
★

$$$$ ⚐ **Le Merigot Beach Hotel & Spa.** Steps from Santa Monica's expansive beach, Le Merigot caters largely to a corporate clientele. **Pros:** steps from the beach and pier; welcoming to international travelers; walk to Third Street Promenade. **Cons:** small shaded pool. ⊠ *1740 Ocean Ave., Santa Monica* ☎ *310/395–9700, 800/539–7899* ⊕ *www.lemerigothotel.com* ⛱ *160 rooms, 15 suites* ♿ *In-room: a/c, Internet, Wi-Fi. In-hotel: restaurant, bar, pool, gym, spa, beach, business center, parking, some pets allowed* ✛ *3:B2.*

$ ⚐ **Sea Shore Motel.** On Santa Monica's busy Main Street, the Sea Shore is a throwback to Route 66 and to '60s-style, family-run roadside motels. **Pros:** close to beach and great restaurants; free Wi-Fi and parking. **Cons:** street noise; motel-style decor and beds. ⊠ *2637 Main St., Santa Monica* ☎ *310/392–2787* ⊕ *www.seashoremotel.com* ⛱ *19 rooms, 5 suites* ♿ *In-room: a/c, kitchen, Internet, Wi-Fi. In-hotel: restaurant, laundry facilities, business center, parking, some pets allowed* ✛ *3:B3.*

4

$$$$ 🏨 **Shutters on the Beach.** Set right on the sand, this gray-shingle inn
☾ has become synonymous with in-town escapism. **Pros:** romantic; dis-
Fodor'sChoice creet; residential vibe. **Cons:** service not as good as it should be. ✉ *1*
★ *Pico Blvd., Santa Monica* 🕾 *310/458–0030, 800/334–9000* ⊕ *www.*
shuttersonthebeach.com ⤸ *186 rooms, 12 suites* ⅙ *In-room: a/c, Inter-*
net, Wi-Fi. In-hotel: restaurant, bar, pool, gym, spa, beach, business
center, parking ⊕ *3:B2.*

VENICE

$$ 🏨 **Hotel Erwin.** Formerly a Best Western, this now bona fide boutique hotel
Fodor'sChoice just off the Venice Beach boardwalk had a major face-lift in 2009. **Pros:**
★ great location, great food; close to Santa Monica without hefty prices.
Cons: some rooms face a noisy alley; no pool. ✉ *1697 Pacific Ave., Venice*
🕾 *310/452–1111, 800/786–7789* ⊕ *www.hotelerwin.com* ⤸ *119 rooms*
⅙ *In-room: a/c, kitchen, Internet, Wi-Fi. In-hotel: restaurant, bar, gym,*
beach, business center, parking, some pets allowed ⊕ *3:B3.*

PASADENA

$$ 🏨 **The Langham Huntington, Pasadena.** An azalea-filled Japanese garden
☾ and the unusual Picture Bridge, with murals celebrating California's
Fodor'sChoice history, are just two of this grande dame's picturesque attributes. **Pros:**
★ great for romantic escape; excellent restaurant; top-notch spa. **Cons:**
set in a suburban neighborhood far from local shopping and dining. ✉ *1401 S. Oak Knoll Ave., Pasadena* 🕾 *626/568–3900* ⊕ *www.*
pasadena.langhamhotels.com ⤸ *342 rooms, 38 suites* ⅙ *In-room: a/c,*
Internet, Wi-Fi. In-hotel: restaurant, bar, pool, tennis court, gym, spa,
business center, parking, some pets allowed ⊕ *3:D2.*

NIGHTLIFE AND THE ARTS

Hollywood and West Hollywood, where hip and happening nightspots
liberally dot Sunset and Hollywood boulevards, are the epicenter of
L.A. nightlife. The city is one of the best places in the world for seeing soon-to-be-famous rockers as well as top jazz, blues, and classical
performers. Movie theaters are naturally well represented here, but
the worlds of dance, theater, and opera have flourished in the past few
years as well.

For a thorough listing of local events, ⊕ *www.la.com* and *Los Angeles Magazine* are both good sources. The Calendar section of the *Los
Angeles Times* (⊕ *www.calendarlive.com*) also lists a wide survey of Los
Angeles arts events, especially on Thursday and Sunday, as do the more
alternative publications, *LA Weekly* and *Citybeat Los Angeles* (both
free, and issued every Thursday). Call ahead to confirm that what you
want to see is ongoing.

THE ARTS

CONCERT HALLS

Fodor's Choice ★ **Walt Disney Concert Hall.** Built in 2003 as a grand addition to L.A.'s Music Center, the 2,265-seat architectural wonder is now the home of the Los Angeles Master Chorale as well as the Los Angeles Philharmonic, under the direction of passionate, new Music Director Gustavo Dudamel, an international celebrity conductor in his own right. The theater, a sculptural monument of gleaming, curved steel designed by master architect Frank Gehry, is part of a complex that includes a public park, gardens, and shops as well as two outdoor amphitheaters for children's and preconcert events. ■ TIP➜ In the main hall, the audience completely surrounds the stage, so it's worth checking the seating chart when buying tickets to gauge your view of the performers. ✉ *111 S. Grand Ave., Downtown* ☎ *323/850–2000.*

★ **Dorothy Chandler Pavilion.** One of the Music Center's most cherished and impressive music halls, the 3,200-seat landmark remains an elegant space to see performances with its plush red seats and giant gold curtain. It presents an array of music programs and L.A. Opera's classics from September through June. Music director Plácido Domingo encourages fresh work (in 2006, for instance, he ushered in *Grendel,* a new opera staged by the hypercreative director Julie Taymor) as much as old favorites (the 2010 season marked the world renown production of Wagner's *Der Ring des Nibelungen* or *Ring Cycle* that ran in conjunction with *Ring Festival L.A.*—a celebration of the arts and L.A. style). There's also a steady flow of touring ballet and modern ballet companies. ✉ *135 N. Grand Ave., Downtown* ☎ *213/972–7211.*

Greek Theatre. In the beautiful tree-enclosed setting of Griffith Park, this open-air auditorium in Los Feliz is in the company of stunning Hollywood Hills homes and the nearby Griffith Observatory shining atop the hill. The Greek has hosted some of the biggest names in entertainment across all genres. Go for the laid-back California experience and the unique opportunity to experience your favorite performers in the warm western air with a view of the sparkling lights of the city flats splayed at your feet. After the concert go for a later-night snack or cocktail in the hipster neighborhood hotspots nearby. Open from May through November. ✉ *2700 N. Vermont Ave., Los Feliz* ☎ *323/665–5857.*

★ **Hollywood Bowl.** Ever since it opened in 1920, in a park surrounded by mountains, trees, and gardens, the Hollywood Bowl has been one of the world's largest and most atmospheric outdoor amphitheaters. Its season runs from May through September; the L.A. Philharmonic spends its summers here. There are performances daily except Monday (and some Sundays); the program ranges from jazz to pop to classical. Concertgoers usually arrive early and bring picnic suppers (picnic tables are available). Additionally, a moderately priced outdoor grill and a more upscale restaurant are among the dining options operated by the Patina Group. ■ TIP➜ Be sure to bring a sweater—it gets chilly here in the evening. You might also bring or rent a cushion to apply to the wood seats. Avoid the hassle of parking by taking one of the Park-and-Ride buses, which leave from various locations around town; call the Bowl for information. ✉ *2301 Highland Ave., Hollywood* ☎ *323/850–2000* ⊕ *www.hollywoodbowl.com.*

Kodak Theatre. This jewel in the crown of Hollywood & Highland was created as the permanent host of the Academy Awards, and the lavish 3,500-seat theater is also used for music concerts and ballets. Awe-inspiring Cirque Du Soleil is scheduled to come to the Kodak in summer 2011. Seeing a show at the Kodak is worthwhile just to witness the gorgeous, crimson-and-gold interior, with its box seating and glittering chandeliers. ✉ *6801 Hollywood Blvd., Hollywood* ☎ *323/308–6363* ⊕ *www.kodaktheatre.com.*

Shrine Auditorium. Former home of the Oscars, the 6,300-seat Arabic-inspired space was built in 1926 as Al Malaikah Temple. Touring companies from all over the world perform here as well as do assorted gospel and choral groups, and other musical acts. High-profile awards shows, including SAG and NAACP Image Awards are still televised on-site. ✉ *665 W. Jefferson Blvd., Downtown* ☎ *213/748–5116.*

Gibson Amphitheater. Adjacent to Universal Studios, this 6,250-seat space hosts more than 100 performances a year, including star-studded benefit concerts and all-star shindigs for local radio station KROQ 106.7. ✉ *100 Universal City Plaza, Universal City* ☎ *818/622–4440.*

FILM

The American Cinemathèque Independent Film Series. Screen classics are shown here, plus recent independent films, sometimes with question-and-answer sessions with the filmmakers. The main venue is the Lloyd E. Rigler Theater, within the 1922 Egyptian Theater, which combines an exterior of pharaoh sculptures and columns with a modern, high-tech design inside.

Aero Theater. The Cinemathèque also screens movies at the 1940 Aero Theater. ✉ *1328 Montana Ave., Santa Monica* ☎ *323/466–3456* ✉ *6712 Hollywood Blvd., Hollywood* ☎ *323/466–3456* ⊕ *americancinematheque.com.*

★ **The Silent Movie Theatre.** A treasure of pretalkies and nonsilent films (the artier the better) are screened here. Live musical accompaniment and shorts precede some films. Each show is made to seem like an event in itself, and it's just about the only theater of its kind. The schedule—which also offers occasional DJ and live-music performances—varies, but you can be sure to catch silent screenings every Wednesday. ✉ *611 N. Fairfax Ave., Fairfax District* ☎ *323/655–2510* ⊕ *www.cinefamily.org.*

THEATER

LA Stage Alliance. LA Stage Alliance also gives information on what's playing in Los Angeles, albeit with capsules that are either noncommittal or overly enthusiastic. Its LAStageTIX service allows you to buy tickets online the day of the performance at roughly half price. ⊕ *www.lastagealliance.com.*

The musical comedy *Minsky's* had its world premier at the Ahmanson Theater in 2009.

Geffen Playhouse. Jason Robards and Nick Nolte got their starts here. This acoustically superior, 498-seat theater offers new plays in summer—primarily musicals and comedies and many of the productions are on their way to or from Broadway. ✉ *10886 Le Conte Ave., Westwood* ☎ *310/208–5454* ⊕ *www.geffenplayhouse.com.*

★ **The Music Center.** Three theaters are part of this big Downtown complex.

Ahmanson Theatre. The 2,140-seat Ahmanson Theatre presents both classics and new plays. ☎ *213/628–2772* ⊕ *www.centertheatregroup.org.*

Dorothy Chandler Pavilion. The 3,200-seat Dorothy Chandler Pavilions shows a smattering of plays between the more prevalent musical performances.

Mark Taper Forum. The 760-seat Mark Taper Forum presents new works that often go on to Broadway, such as Rajiv Joseph's *Bengal Tiger at the Baghdad Zoo.* ☎ *213/628–2772* ⊕ *www.centertheatregroup.org* ✉ *135 N. Grand Ave., Downtown* ☎ *213/972–7211* ⊕ *www.musiccenter.org.*

Pantages Theatre. The home of the Academy Awards telecast from 1949 to 1959, this is a massive (2,600-seat) and splendid example of high-style Hollywood art deco, presenting large-scale Broadway musicals such as *The Lion King* and *Wicked.* ✉ *6233 Hollywood Blvd., Hollywood* ☎ *323/468–1770* ⊕ *www.broadwayla.org.*

Ricardo Montalbán Theatre. There's an intimate feeling here despite its 1,038-seat capacity. Plays, concerts, seminars, and workshops with an emphasis on Latin culture are all presented. ✉ *1615 N. Vine St., Hollywood* ☎ *323/463–0089* ⊕ *www.themontalban.com.*

NIGHTLIFE

Although the ultimate in velvet-roped vampiness and glamour used to be the Sunset Strip, in the past couple of years the glitz has definitely shifted to Hollywood Boulevard and its surrounding streets. The lines are as long as the skirts are short outside the Hollywood club du jour (which changes so fast, it's often hard to keep track). But the Strip still has plenty going for it, with comedy clubs, hard-rock spots, and restaurants. West Hollywood's Santa Monica Boulevard bustles with gay and lesbian bars and clubs. For less conspicuous—and congested— alternatives, check out the events in Downtown L.A.'s performance spaces and galleries. Silver Lake and Echo Park are best for boho bars and live music clubs.

Note that parking, especially after 7 pm, is at a premium in Hollywood. In fact, it's restricted on virtually every side street along the "hot zone" of West Hollywood (Sunset Boulevard from Fairfax to Doheny). Posted signs indicate the restrictions, but these are naturally harder to notice at night. Paying $5 to $20 for valet or lot parking is often the easiest way to go.

BARS

HOLLYWOOD

★ **Beauty Bar.** This bar cum salon offers manicures and makeovers along with the perfect martinis, but the hotties who flock to this retro spot (the little sister of the Beauty Bars in NYC and San Fran) don't really need the cosmetic care—this is where the edgy beautiful people hang. ⊠ *1638 N. Cahuenga Blvd., Hollywood* ☎ *323/464–7676* ⊕ *www.thebeautybar.com.*

★ **Three Clubs.** This casually hip club is in a strip mall, beneath a sign that simply reads "cocktails." The DJs segue through the many faces and phases of rock-and-roll and dance music. With dark-wood paneling, lamp-lighted tables, and even some sofas, you could be in a giant basement rec room from decades past—no fancy dress required, but fashionable looks suggested. ⊠ *1123 Vine St., Hollywood* ☎ *323/462–6441* ⊕ *www.threeclubs.com.*

★ **Yamashiro.** A lovely L.A. tradition is to meet at here for cocktails at sunset. In the elegant restaurant, waitresses glide by in kimonos, and entrées can zoom up to $39; on the terrace, a spectacular hilltop view spreads out before you. ■ **TIP➔** Mandatory valet parking is $7.50. ⊠ *1999 N. Sycamore Ave., Hollywood* ☎ *323/466–5125* ⊕ *www.yamashiroresraurant.com.*

WEST HOLLYWOOD

★ **Bar Marmont.** As at so many other nightspots in this neck of the woods, the popularity and clientele of this hotel bar bulged—and changed— after word got out it was a favorite of celebrities. Lately, it's gotten a second wind thanks to a strong DJ selection and luscious cocktails. The bar is next to the inimitable hotel Chateau Marmont, which bold-face names continue to haunt. ⊠ *8171 Sunset Blvd., West Hollywood* ☎ *323/650–0575* ⊕ *www.chateaumarmont.com.*

★ **Rainbow Bar & Grill.** In the heart of the Strip and next door to the legend-ary Roxy, the Rainbow is a landmark in its own right as *the* drinking spot of the '80s hair-metal scene—and it still attracts a music-industry crowd. ⊠ *9015 Sunset Blvd., West Hollywood* ☎ *310/278–4232* ⊕ *www.rainbowbarandgrill.com.*

★ **The Standard.** A classic Hollywood makeover—formerly a nursing home, this spot in the happening part of Sunset Strip got converted into a smart, brash-looking hotel, the Standard, for the young, hip, and connected. (Check out the live model in the lobby's terrarium.) The hotel and especially the bar here is popular with those in the biz. ⊠ *8300 Sunset Blvd., West Hollywood* ☎ *323/650–9090* ⊕ *www.standardhotels.com.*

ECHO PARK AND SILVER LAKE

★ **Cha Cha Lounge.** Seattle's coolest rock bar, now aims to repeat its success with this colorful, red-lighted space. Think part tiki hut, part tacky Tijuana party palace. The tabletops pay homage to the lounge's former performers; they've got portraits of Latin drag queens. ⊠ *2375 Glendale Blvd., Silver Lake* ☎ *323/660–7595* ⊕ *www.chachalounge.com.*

★ **The Echo.** This Echo Park mainstay sprang from the people behind the Silver Lake rock joint Spaceland. Most evenings this dark and divey space's tiny dance floor and well-worn booths attract artsy local bands and their followers, but things rev up when DJs spin reggae, rock, and funk. ⊠ *1154 Glendale Blvd.*

★ **Tiki-Ti.** The tiny Hawaiian-theme room is one of the most charming drinking huts in the city. You can spend hours just looking at the Polynesian artifacts strewn all about the place, but be careful—time flies in this tiny tropical bar, and the colorful drinks can be so potent that you may have to stay marooned for a while. ⊠ *4427 Sunset Blvd., Silver Lake* ☎ *323/669–9381* ⊕ *www.tiki-ti.com.*

DOWNTOWN

Fodor's Choice **Downtown L.A. Standard.** This futuristic hotel has a groovy lounge with
★ pink sofas and DJs, as well as an all-white restaurant that looks like something out of *2001: A Space Odyssey*. But it's the rooftop bar, with an amazing view of the city's illuminated skyscrapers, a heated swimming pool, and private, podlike water-bed tents, that's worth waiting in line to get into. And wait you probably will, especially on weekends and in summer. Friday and Saturday $20 cover charge after 7 pm. ⊠ *550 S. Flower St., Downtown* ☎ *213/892–8080* ⊕ *www.standardhotels.com.*

COMEDY

Comedy Store. A nightly premiere comedy showcase, this comedy venue has been going strong for more than two decades, with three stages (with covers ranging from free to $20) to supply the yuks. Famous comedians occasionally make unannounced appearances. ⊠ *8433 Sunset Blvd., West Hollywood* ☎ *323/650-6268* ⊕ *www.thecomedystore.com.*

★ **Groundling Theatre.** More than a quarter century old, this renowned theater company has been a breeding ground for *Saturday Night Live* performers; alumni include Lisa Kudrow and *Curb Your Enthusiasm*'s Cheryl Hines. The primarily sketch and improv comedy shows run Wednesday–Sunday, costing $14–$18. ⊠ *7307 Melrose Ave., Hollywood* ☎ *323/934–4747* ⊕ *www.groundlings.com.*

Improv. Richard Pryor got his start here, a renowned establishment showcasing stand-up comedy. Reservations are recommended. Cover is $15–$20, and there's a two-drink minimum. ⊠ *8162 Melrose Ave., West Hollywood* ☎ *323/651–2583* ⊕ *www.improv.com.*

Laugh Factory. Look for top stand-ups—and frequent celeb residents, like Bob Saget, or unannounced drop-ins, like Chris Rock. The club has shows on Sunday through Thursday nights at 8 pm and 10 pm, plus an additional show on Friday and Saturday at midnight; the cover is $20–$30. ⊠ *8001 Sunset Blvd., West Hollywood* ☎ *323/656–1336* ⊕ *www.laughfactory.com.*

Upright Citizens Brigade. New York's UCB marched in with a mix of sketch comedy and wild improvisations skewering pop culture. Members of the L.A. Brigade include VH1 commentator Paul Scheer and *Mad TV*'s Andrew Daly. ⊠ *5919 Franklin Ave., Hollywood* ☎ *323/908–8702* ⊕ *www.ucbtheatre.com.*

★   **Boardner's.** This bar has a multidecade history (in the '20s it was a speakeasy), but with the adjoining ballroom, which was added a couple of years ago, it's now a state-of-the-art dance club. DJs may be spinning electronica, funk, or something else depending on the night—at the popular Saturday Goth event "Bar Sinister," patrons must wear black or risk not getting in. The cover here hovers around $5–$10. ⊠ *1652 N. Cherokee Ave., Hollywood* ☎ *323/462–9621* ⊕ *www.boardners.com.*

★   **The Ruby.** This three-room dance venue is popular for young indie-rock and retro-loving twentysomethings. You might find anything from doomy Goth and industrial ("Perversion") to '80s retro ("Beat It") to '60s–'70s Brit pop and soul ("Bang") to trance and techno. ⊠ *7070 Hollywood Blvd., Hollywood* ☎ *323/467–7070.*

GAY AND LESBIAN CLUBS

Some of the most popular gay and lesbian "clubs" are weekly theme nights at various venues, so read the preceding list of clubs, *LA Weekly* listings, and gay publications such as *Odyssey* in addition to the following recommendations.

★   **Here.** Nowhere is more gregarious than here (no pun intended), where there are hot DJs and an even hotter clientele. Some weekly highlights include "Truck Stop" on Friday, "Neon" on Saturday, and "Stripper Circus" Wednesday. ⊠ *696 N. Robertson Blvd., West Hollywood* ☎ *310/360–8455* ⊕ *www.herelounge.com.*

The Palms. A long-running gay-gal fave, this club continues to thrive thanks to great DJs spinning dance tunes as well as karaoke and comedy shows. There are also an outdoor patio, pool tables, and an occasional live performance. ⊠ *8572 Santa Monica Blvd., West Hollywood* ☎ *310/652–1595* ⊕ *www.thepalmsbar.com.*

Rage. This spot is a longtime favorite of the "gym boy" set, with DJs following a different musical theme every night of the week (alternative rock, house, dance remixes, etc.). The cover ranges from free to $10. ⊠ *8911 Santa Monica Blvd., West Hollywood* ☎ *310/652–7055.*

ROCK AND OTHER LIVE MUSIC

In addition to the venues listed below, many smaller bars book live music, if less frequently or with less publicity.

Avalon. The landmark formerly known as the Palace is now the Avalon. The multilevel art deco building opposite Capitol Records has a fabulous sound system, four bars, and a balcony. Big-name rock and pop concerts hit the stage during the week, but on weekends the place becomes a dance club, with the most popular night the DJ-dominated Avaland on Saturday. Upstairs, but with a separate entrance, you can find celeb hub **Bardot,** a glamorous tribute to Old Hollywood where celebs and their entourages are frequent visitors. ✉ *1735 N. Vine St., Hollywood* ☎ *323/462–8900* ⊕ *www.avalonhollywood.com.*

Key Club. This flashy, multitier rock club offers four bars presenting current artists of all genres (some on national tours, others local aspirants). After the concerts, there's often dancing with DJs spinning techno and house. ✉ *9039 Sunset Blvd., West Hollywood* ☎ *310/274–5800* ⊕ *www.keyclub.com.*

Largo. Musician-producer Jon Brion (Fiona Apple, Aimee Mann, and others) shows off his ability to play virtually any instrument and any song in the rock lexicon—and beyond—as host of a popular evening of music some Fridays at Largo. Other nights, low-key rock and singer-songwriter fare is offered at this cozy venue. And when comedy comes in, about one night a week, it's usually one of the best comedy nights in town, with folks like Sarah Silverman. ✉ *366 N. La Cienega Blvd., Hollywood* ☎ *310/855–0350* ⊕ *www.largo-la.com.*

McCabe's Guitar Shop. This famous guitar shop is rootsy-retro-central, where all things earnest and (preferably) acoustic are welcome—chiefly folk, blues, bluegrass, and rock. It *is* a guitar shop (so no liquor license), with a room full of folding chairs for concert-style presentations. Shows on weekends only. Make reservations well in advance. ✉ *3101 Pico Blvd., Santa Monica* ☎ *310/828–4497, 310/828–4497 for concert information* ⊕ *www.mccabes.com.*

The Roxy. A Sunset Strip fixture for decades, this live music club hosts local and touring rock, alternative, blues, and rockabilly bands. Not the comfiest club around, but it's the site of many memorable shows. ✉ *9009 Sunset Blvd., West Hollywood* ☎ *310/278–9457* ⊕ *www.theroxyonsunset.com.*

Silver Lake Lounge. Neighborhoody and relaxed, this lounge draws a mixed collegiate and boho crowd. The club is very unmainstream "cool," the booking policy an adventurous mix of local and touring alt-rockers. Bands play three to five nights a week; covers vary but are low. ✉ *2906 Sunset Blvd., Silver Lake* ☎ *323/663–9636.*

★ **Spaceland.** The hottest bands of tomorrow, surprises from yesteryear, and unclassifiable bands of today perform at this low-key Silver Lake venue, which has a bar, jukebox, and pool table. Monday is always free, with monthlong gigs by the indie fave du jour. Spaceland has a nice selection of beers and a hip but relaxed interior. ✉ *1717 Silver Lake Blvd., Silver Lake* ☎ *323/661–4380* ⊕ *www.clubspaceland.com.*

The Troubadour. One of the best and most comfortable clubs in town, this live music Mecca has weathered the test of time since its '60s debut as a folk club. After surviving the '80s heavy-metal scene, this all-ages, wood-panel venue has caught a second (third? fourth?) wind

Rocking out at the Roxy.

by booking hot alternative rock acts. There's valet parking, but if you don't mind walking up Doheny a block or three, there's usually ample street parking (check the signs carefully). ⊠ *9081 Santa Monica Blvd., West Hollywood* ☎ *310/276–6168* ⊕ *www.troubador.com.*

Viper Room. Actor Johnny Depp sold his share of the infamous rock venue in 2004, but the place continues to rock with a motley live music lineup, if a less stellar crowd. ⊠ *8852 W. Sunset Blvd., West Hollywood* ☎ *310/358–1881* ⊕ *www.viperroom.com.*

Whisky-A-Go-Go. The Whisky, as locals call it, is the most famous rock-and-roll club on the Strip, where back in the '60s, Johnny Rivers cut hit singles and the Doors, Love, and the Byrds cut their musical eyeteeth. It's still going strong, with up-and-coming alternative, hard rock, and punk bands, though mostly of the unknown variety. ⊠ *8901 Sunset Blvd., West Hollywood* ☎ *310/652–4202* ⊕ *www.whiskyagogo.com.*

SPORTS AND THE OUTDOORS

BEACHES

Los Angeles County beaches (and state beaches operated by the county) have lifeguards on duty year-round, with expanded forces during the summer. Public parking is usually available, though fees can range anywhere from $8–$20; in some areas, it's possible to find free street and highway parking. Both restrooms and beach access have been brought up to the standards of the Americans with Disabilities Act. Generally, the northernmost beaches are best for surfing, hiking, and fishing, and the wider and sandier southern beaches are better for tanning and relaxing. ■TIP➔ Almost all are great for swimming, but beware: pollution in Santa Monica Bay sometimes approaches dangerous levels, particularly after storms.

The following beaches are listed in north–south order:

Leo Carrillo State Park. On the very edge of Ventura County, this narrow beach is better for exploring than for sunning or swimming (watch that strong undertow!). On your own or with a ranger, venture down at low tide to examine the tide pools among the rocks. Sequit Point, a promontory dividing the northwest and southeast halves of the beach, creates secret coves, sea tunnels, and boulders on which you can perch and fish. Generally, anglers stick to the northwest end of the beach; experienced surfers brave the rocks to the southeast. Campgrounds are set back from the beach; call ahead to reserve campsites. ✉ *35000 Pacific Coast Highway, Malibu* ☎ *818/880–0363, 800/444–7275 for camping reservations* ⚓ *Parking, lifeguard (year-round, except only as needed in winter), restroom, showers, fire pits.*

Fodor's Choice
★

Robert H. Meyer Memorial State Beach. Part of Malibu's most beautiful coastal area, this beach is made up of three minibeaches: El Pescador, La Piedra, and El Matador—all with the same spectacular view. Scramble down the steps to the rocky coves where nude sunbathers sometimes gather—although in recent years, police have been cracking down. "El Mat" has a series of caves, Piedra some nifty rock formations, and Pescador a secluded feel; but they're all picturesque and fairly private. ■TIP➔ One warning: watch the incoming tide and don't get trapped between those otherwise scenic boulders. ✉ *32350, 32700, and 32900 PCH, Malibu* ☎ *818/880–0363* ⚓ *Parking, 1 roving lifeguard unit, restrooms.*

Zuma Beach Park. Zuma, 2 mi of white sand usually littered with tanning teenagers, has it all: from fishing and diving to swings for the kids to volleyball courts. Beachgoers looking for quiet or privacy should head elsewhere. Stay alert in the water: the surf is rough and inconsistent. ✉ *30000 Pacific Coast Highway, Malibu* ☎ *310/305–9503* ⚓ *Parking, lifeguard (year-round, except only as needed in winter), restrooms, food concessions.*

Malibu Surfrider Beach. Steady 3- to 5-foot waves make this beach, just west of Malibu Pier, a surfing paradise. Water runoff from Malibu Canyon forms a natural lagoon that's a sanctuary for 250 species of birds. Unfortunately, the lagoon is often polluted and algae filled. If you're leery of going into the water, you can bird-watch, play volleyball, or take a walk on one of the nature trails, which are perfect for romantic sunset strolls. ✉ *23050 Pacific Coast Highway, Malibu* ☎ *818/880-0363* ⚓ *Parking, lifeguard (year-round), restrooms, picnic tables.*

Will Rogers State Beach. This clean, sandy, 3-mi beach, with a dozen volleyball nets, gymnastics equipment, and playground equipment for kids, is an all-around favorite. The surf is gentle, perfect for swimmers and beginning surfers. However, it's best to avoid the place after a storm, when untreated water flows from storm drains into the sea. ✉ *17700 PCH, 2 mi* *north of Santa Monica Pier, Pacific Palisades* ☎ *310/305–9503* ⚑ *Parking, lifeguard (year-round, except only as needed in winter), restrooms.*

★ **Santa Monica State Beach.** It's the first beach you'll hit after the Santa Monica Freeway (I–10) runs into the PCH, and it's one of L.A.'s best known. Wide and sandy, Santa Monica is *the* place for sunning and socializing: be prepared for a mob scene on summer weekends, when parking becomes an expensive ordeal. Swimming is fine (with the usual poststorm pollution caveat); for surfing, go elsewhere. For a memorable view, climb up the stairway over the PCH to Palisades Park, at the top of the bluffs. Summer-evening concerts are often held here. ✉ *1642 Promenade, PCH at California Incline, Santa Monica* ☎ *310/305–9503* ⚑ *Parking, lifeguard (year-round), restrooms, showers.*

★ **Redondo Beach.** The Redondo Beach Pier marks the starting point of this wide, sandy, busy beach along a heavily developed shoreline community. Restaurants and shops flourish along the pier, excursion boats and privately owned crafts depart from launching ramps, and a reef formed by a sunken ship creates prime fishing and snorkeling conditions. If you're adventurous, you might try to kayak out to the buoys and hobnob with pelicans and sea lions. A series of free rock and jazz concerts takes place at the pier every summer. ✉ *Torrance Blvd. at Catalina Ave., Redondo Beach* ☎ *310/372–2166* ⚑ *Parking, lifeguard (year-round), restrooms, food concessions, showers.*

GOLF

Rancho Park Golf Course. The City Parks and Recreation Department lists seven public 18-hole courses in Los Angeles, and L.A. County runs some good ones, too. Rancho Park Golf Course is one of the most heavily played links in the country. It's a beautifully designed course, but the towering pines present an obstacle for those who slice or hook. There's a two-level driving range, a 9-hole pitch "n' putt, a snack bar, and a pro shop where you can rent clubs. ✉ *10460 W. Pico Blvd., West L.A.* ☎ *310/838–7373.*

Los Verdes Golf Course. If you want a scenic course, the county-run, par-71 Los Verdes Golf Course has fierce scenery. You get a cliff-top view of the ocean—time it right and you can watch the sun set behind Catalina Island. ✉ *7000 W. Los Verdes Dr., Rancho Palos Verdes* ☎ *310/377–7370.*

Griffith Park. Griffith Park has two splendid 18-hole courses along with two challenging 9-hole courses. **Harding Municipal Golf Course** and **Wilson Municipal Golf Course** (✉ *4900 Griffith Park Dr., Los Feliz* ☎ *323/663–2555*) are about 1½ mi inside the park entrance, at Riverside Drive and Los Feliz Boulevard. Bridle paths surround the outer fairways, and the San Gabriel Mountains make a scenic background.

Roosevelt Municipal Golf Course. The 9-hole Roosevelt Municipal Golf Course can be reached through the park's Vermont Avenue entrance. ✉ *2650 N. Vermont Ave., Los Feliz* ☎ *323/665–2011.*

Surf City

Nothing captures the laid-back cool of California quite like surfing. Those wanting to sample the surf here should keep a few things in mind before getting wet. First, surfers can be notoriously territorial. Beginners should avoid Palos Verdes and Third Point, at the north end of Malibu Lagoon State Beach, where veterans rule the waves. Once in the water, be as polite and mellow as possible. Give other surfers plenty of space—do *not* cut them off—and avoid swimmers. Beware of rocks and undertows. Surfing calls for caution: that huge piece of flying fiberglass beneath you could kill someone. If you're not a strong swimmer, think twice before jumping in; fighting the surf to where the waves break is a strenuous proposi-

tion. The best and safest way to learn is by taking a lesson.

When you hit the surfing hot spots, surf shops with rentals will be in long supply. Competition keeps prices comparable; most rent long and short boards and miniboards (kid-size surfboards) from $20 per day and wet suits from $10 per day (some give discounts for additional days).

Learners should never surf in a busy area; look for somewhere less crowded where you'll catch more waves anyway. Good beaches for beginners are Malibu Lagoon State Beach and Huntington City Beach north of the pier, but you should always check conditions, which change throughout the day, before heading into the water.

SHOPPING

AROUND BEVERLY HILLS

Rodeo Drive. New York City has Fifth Avenue, but L.A. has famed Rodeo Drive. The triangle, between Santa Monica and Wilshire boulevards and Beverly Drive, is one of the city's biggest tourist attractions and is lined with shops featuring the biggest names in fashion.

You can see well-coifed, well-heeled ladies toting multiple packages to their Mercedes and paparazzi staking out street corners. Although the dress code in L.A. is considerably laid-back, with residents wearing flip-flops year-round, you might find them to be jewel-encrusted on Rodeo.

Steep price tags on designer labels make it a "just looking" experience for many residents and tourists alike, but salespeople are used to the ogling and window shopping. In recent years, more midrange shops have opened up on the strip and surrounding blocks. Keep in mind that some stores are by appointment only.

★ **Beverly Center.** This is one of the more traditional malls you can find in L.A., with eight levels of stores, including Macy's, Bloomingdale's, and the newer addition: luxury retailer Henri Bendel. Fashion is the biggest draw and there's a little something from everyone, from D&G to H&M, and many shops in the midrange, including Banana Republic, Club Monaco, and Coach. Look for accessories at Aldo, inexpensive accessories and fun fashion at Forever 21 and there's even a destination for the racecar obsessed at the Ferrari Store.

For a terrific view of the city, head to the top-floor terrace and rooftop food court. Next door is Loehmann's, which offers a huge selection of discounted designer wear. ⊠ *8500 Beverly Blvd., bounded by Beverly, La Cienega, and San Vicente Blvds. and 3rd St., between Beverly Hills and West Hollywood* ☎ *310/854–0071.*

DOWNTOWN

The Jewelry District. This area resembles a slice of Manhattan, with the crowded sidewalks, diverse aromas, and haggling bargain hunters. Expect to save 50% to 70% off retail for everything from wedding bands to sparkling belt buckles. The more upscale stores are along Hill Street between 6th and 7th streets. There's a parking structure next door on Broadway. ⊠ *Between Olive St. and Broadway from 5th to 8th St., Downtown* ⊕ *www.lajd.net.*

Fodor'sChoice   **Olvera Street.** Historic buildings line this redbrick walkway overhung
★   with grape vines. At dozens of clapboard stalls you can browse south-of-the-border goods—leather sandals, bright woven blankets, devotional candles, and the like—as well as cheap toys and tchotchkes. With the musicians and cafés providing background noise, the area is constantly lively. ⊠ *Between Cesar Chavez Ave. and Arcadia St., Downtown.*

HOLLYWOOD

Local shops may be a mixed bag, but at least you can read the stars below your feet as you browse along Hollywood Boulevard. Lingerie and movie memorabilia stores predominate here, but there are numerous options in the retail-hotel-dining-entertainment complex Hollywood & Highland. Hollywood impersonators (Michael Jackson, Marilyn Monroe, and, er, Chewbacca) join break-dancers and other street entertainers in keeping tourists entertained on Hollywood Boulevard's sidewalks near the Kodak Theater, home to the Oscars. Along La Brea Avenue, you'll find plenty of trendy, quirky, and hip merchandise, from records to furniture and clothing.

★   **Hollywood & Highland.** Bringing some glitz, foot traffic and commerce back to Hollywood, the hotel-retail-entertainment complex here has become a huge tourist magnet. The design pays tribute to the city's film legacy with a grand staircase leading up to a pair of white stucco 33-foot-high elephants, a nod to the 1916 movie *Intolerance.* (Something tells us that the reference is lost on most visitors.) ■ TIP→ Pause at the entrance arch, Babylon Court, which frames the "Hollywood" sign in the hills above for a picture-perfect view.

There are plenty of clothing stores and eateries, and you may find yourself ducking into these for a respite from the crowds and street artists. In the summer and during Christmas vacation—when the complex is at its busiest—special music programs and free entertainment keep strollers entertained.

The Santa Monica Pier is packed with fun diversions and hosts free concerts in summer.

A Metro Red Line station provides easy access to and from other parts of the city, and there's plenty of underground parking accessible from Highland Avenue. ⊠ *Hollywood Blvd. and Highland Ave., Hollywood* 🕾 *323/467–6412 visitor center* ⊕ *www.hollywoodandhighland.com* 🎫 *Parking $2 with validation* ☉ *Mon.–Sat. 10–10, Sun. 10–7.*

LOS FELIZ, SILVER LAKE, AND ECHO PARK

There's a hipster rock-and-roll vibe to this area, which has grown in recent years to add just the slightest shine to its edge. Come for home-grown, funky galleries, vintage shops, and local designers' boutiques. Shopping areas are concentrated along Vermont Avenue and Hollywood Boulevard in Los Feliz; Sunset Boulevard in both Silver Lake (known as Sunset Junction) and Echo Park; and Echo Park Avenue in Echo Park. ■TIP→ Keep in mind that things are spread out enough to necessitate a couple of short car trips, and many shops in these neighborhoods don't open until noon but stay open later, so grab dinner or drinks at one of the area's über-cool spots after shopping.

WEST HOLLYWOOD AND MELROSE AVENUE

West Hollywood is prime shopping real estate. And as they say with real estate, it's all about location, location, location. Depending on the street address, West Hollywood has everything from upscale art, design, and antiques stores to ladies-who-lunch clothing boutiques to megamusic stores and specialty book vendors. Melrose Avenue, for instance, is part bohemian-punk shopping district (from North Highland to Sweetzer) and part upscale art and design mecca (upper Melrose Avenue and Melrose Place). Discerning locals and celebs haunt the posh boutiques around Sunset Plaza (Sunset Boulevard at Sunset Plaza Drive), on Robertson Boulevard (between Beverly Boulevard and 3rd Street), and along upper Melrose Avenue.

The huge, blue Pacific Design Center, on Melrose at San Vicente Boulevard, is the focal point for this neighborhood's art- and interior design–related stores, including many on nearby Beverly Boulevard. The Beverly–La Brea neighborhood also claims a number of trendy clothing stores. Perched between Beverly Hills and West Hollywood, 3rd Street (between La Cienega and Fairfax) is a magnet for small, friendly designer boutiques. Finally, the Fairfax District, along Fairfax below Melrose, encompasses the flamboyant, historic Farmers Market, at Fairfax Avenue and 3rd Street; the adjacent shopping extravaganza, The Grove; and some excellent galleries around Museum Row at Fairfax Avenue and Wilshire Boulevard.

SANTA MONICA AND VENICE

The breezy beachside communities of Santa Monica and Venice are ideal for leisurely shopping. Scads of tourists (and some locals) gravitate to the Third Street Promenade, a popular pedestrians-only strolling–shopping area that is within walking range of the beach and historic Santa Monica Pier. A number of modern furnishings stores are nearby on 4th and 5th streets. Main Street between Pico Boulevard and Rose Avenue offers upscale chain stores, cafés, and some original shops, while Montana Avenue is a great source for distinctive clothing boutiques and child-friendly shopping, especially between 7th and 17th streets. ■ TIP→ Parking in Santa Monica is next to impossible on Wednesday, when some streets are blocked off for the farmers' market, but there are several parking structures with free parking for an hour or two. In Venice, Abbot Kinney Boulevard is abuzz with mid-century furniture stores, art galleries and boutiques, and cafés.

★ **Third Street Promenade.** Whimsical dinosaur-shaped, ivy-covered fountains, and buskers of every stripe set the scene along this pedestrians-only shopping stretch. Stores are mainly the chain variety (Restoration Hardware, Urban Outfitters, Apple), but there are also Quiksilver and Rip Curl outposts for cool surf attire. Movie theaters, bookstores, pubs, and restaurants ensure that virtually every need is covered. ⊠ *3rd St. between Broadway and Wilshire Blvd.*

The Central Coast

FROM VENTURA TO BIG SUR

WORD OF MOUTH

"I was blown away by the immense outdoor pool at the Hearst Castle. It is huge, and yet incredibly serene in its surroundings. The Castle is situated on top of the hills in the San Simeon area and allows for massive views of nearly 360 degrees around."

—photo by L Vantreight, Fodors.com member

WELCOME TO THE CENTRAL COAST

TOP REASONS TO GO

★ **Incredible nature:** Much of the Central Coast looks as wild and wonderful as it did centuries ago; the area is home to Channel Islands National Park, two national marine sanctuaries, state parks and beaches, and the vast and rugged Los Padres National Forest.

★ **Edible bounty:** Land and sea provide enough fresh regional foods to satisfy even the savviest of foodies—grapes, strawberries, seafood, olive oil . . . the list goes on and on. Get your fill at countless farmers' markets, wineries, and restaurants.

★ **Outdoor activities:** Kick back and revel in the casual California lifestyle. Surf, golf, kayak, hike, play tennis—or just hang out and enjoy the gorgeous scenery.

★ **Small-town charm, big-city culture:** Small, friendly, uncrowded towns offer an amazing array of cultural amenities. With all the art and history museums, theater, music, and festivals, you might start thinking you're in L.A. or San Francisco.

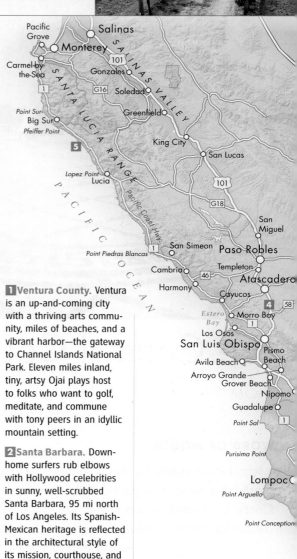

1 Ventura County. Ventura is an up-and-coming city with a thriving arts community, miles of beaches, and a vibrant harbor—the gateway to Channel Islands National Park. Eleven miles inland, tiny, artsy Ojai plays host to folks who want to golf, meditate, and commune with tony peers in an idyllic mountain setting.

2 Santa Barbara. Down-home surfers rub elbows with Hollywood celebrities in sunny, well-scrubbed Santa Barbara, 95 mi north of Los Angeles. Its Spanish-Mexican heritage is reflected in the architectural style of its mission, courthouse, and many homes and public buildings.

3 **Santa Barbara County.** Wineries, ranches, and small villages dominate the quintessentially Californian landscape here.

4 **San Luis Obispo County.** Friendly college town San Luis Obispo serves as hub of a burgeoning wine region that stretches nearly 100 mi from Pismo Beach north to Paso Robles; the 230-plus wineries here have earned reputations for high-quality vintages that rival those of northern California.

5 **The Big Sur Coastline.** Rugged cliffs meet the Pacific for more than 60 mi—one of the most scenic and dramatic drives in the world.

6 **Channel Islands National Park.** Home to 145 species of plants and animals found nowhere else on Earth, this relatively undiscovered gem of a park encompasses five islands and a mile of surrounding ocean.

GETTING ORIENTED

The Central Coast region begins about 60 mi north of Los Angeles, near the seaside city of Ventura. From there the coastline stretches north about 200 mi, winding through the small cities of Santa Barbara and San Luis Obispo, then north through the small towns of Morro Bay and Cambria to Carmel. The drive through this region, especially the section of Highway 1 from San Simeon to Big Sur, is one of the most scenic in the state.

5

HIGHWAY 1: SANTA MONICA TO BIG SUR

Hearst Castle

THE PLAN

Distance: approx. 335 mi

Time: 3-5 days

Good Overnight Options:
Malibu, Santa Barbara, Pismo Beach, San Luis Obispo, Cambria, Carmel

For more information on the sights and attractions along this portion of Highway 1, please see Los Angeles and Central Coast chapters

SANTA MONICA TO MALIBU (approx. 26 mi)

Highway 1 begins in Dana point, but it seems more appropriate to begin a PCH adventure in **Santa Monica.** Be sure to experience the beach culture, then balance the tacky pleasures of Santa Monica's amusement pier with a stylish dinner in a neighborhood restaurant.

MALIBU TO SANTA BARBARA (approx. 70 mi)

The PCH follows the curve of Santa Monica Bay all the way to **Malibu** and **Point Mugu,**

Santa Monica

near **Oxnard.** Chances are you'll experience *déjà vu* driving this 27-mile stretch: mountains on one side, ocean on the other, opulent homes perched on hillsides; you've seen this piece of coast countless times on TV and film. Be sure to walk out on the **Malibu Pier** for a great photo opp, then check out **Surfrider Beach,** with three famous points where perfect waves ignited a worldwide surfing rage in the 1960s.

After Malibu you'll drive through miles of protected, largely unpopulated coastline. Ride a wave at **Zuma Beach,** scout for offshore whales at **Point Dume State Preserve,** or hike the trails at **Point Mugu State Park.** After skirting Point Mugu, Highway 1 merges with U.S. 101 for about 70 mi before reaching **Santa Barbara.** A mini-tour of the city includes a real Mexican lunch at **La Super-Rica,** a visit to the magnificent Spanish **Mission Santa Barbara,** and a walk down hopping **State Street to Stearns Wharf.**

SANTA BARBARA TO SAN SIMEON (approx. 147 mi)

North of Santa Barbara, Highway 1 morphs into the Cabrillo Highway, separating

Santa Barbara

from and then rejoining U.S. 101. The route winds through rolling vineyards and rangeland to **San Luis Obispo,** where any legit road trip includes a photo stop at the quirky **Madonna Inn.** Be sure to also climb the humungous dunes at **Guadalupe-Nipomo Dunes Preserve.**

In downtown San Luis Obispo, the **Mission San Luis Obispo de Tolosa** stands by a tree-shaded creek edged with shops and cafés. Highway 1 continues to **Morro Bay** and up the coast. About 15 mi north of Morro Bay, you'll reach the town of **Harmony** (population 18), a tiny burg with artists' studios, a wedding chapel, shops, and a winery. The road continues through **Cambria** to solitary **Hearst San Simeon State Historical Monument**—the art-filled pleasure palace at **San Simeon.** Just four miles north of the castle, elephant seals grunt and cavort at the

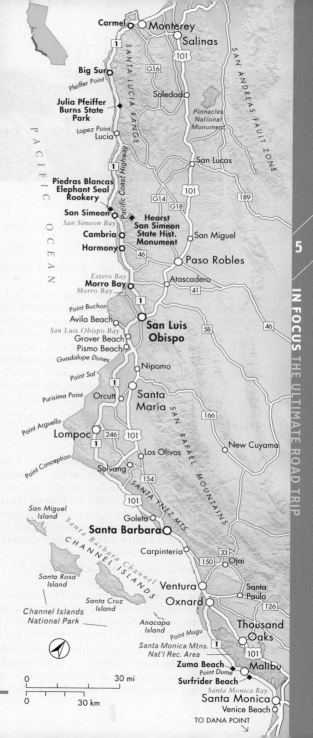

Big Sur

TOP 5 PLACES TO LINGER

- Point Dume State Preserve
- Santa Barbara
- Hearst San Simeon State Historical Monument
- Big Sur/Julia Pfeiffer Burns State Park
- Carmel

Piedras Blancas Elephant Seal Rookery, just off the side of the road.

SAN SIMEON TO CARMEL (approx. 92 mi) Heading north, you'll drive through **Big Sur,** a place of ancient forests and rugged shoreline stretching 90 mi from San Simeon to **Carmel.** Much of Big Sur lies within several state parks and the 165,000-acre **Ventana Wilderness,** itself part of the **Los Padres National Forest.** This famously scenic stretch of the coastal drive, which twists up and down bluffs above the ocean, can last hours. Take your time.

At **Julia Pfeiffer Burns State Park** one easy but rewarding hike leads to an iconic waterfall off a beach-front cliff. When you reach lovely **Carmel,** stroll around the picture-perfect town's mission, galleries, and shops.

Updated by Cheryl Crabtree

Balmy weather, glorious beaches, crystal clear air, and serene landscapes have lured people to the Central Coast since prehistoric times. It's an ideal place to relax, slow down, and appreciate the good things in life.

Along the Pacific coast, the scenic variety is stunning—everything from dramatic cliffs and grass-tufted bluffs to wildlife estuaries and miles of dunes. Offshore, a pristine national park and a vast marine sanctuary protect the wild, wonderful underwater resources of this incredible corner of the planet. But not all of the Central Coast's top attractions are natural: the small cities of Ventura, Santa Barbara, and San Luis Obispo are filled with sparkling examples of Spanish-Mediterranean architecture, bustling shopping districts, and first-rate restaurants showcasing regional foods and wines.

PLANNING

WHEN TO GO

The Central Coast climate is usually mild throughout the year. If you like to sunbathe and swim in warmer (though still nippy) ocean waters, July and August are the best months to visit. Be aware that this is also high season. Fog often rolls in all along the coastal areas in early summer; you'll need a jacket, especially after sunset, close to the shore. The rains usually come from December through March. From April to early June and in the early fall the weather is almost as fine as in high season, and the pace is less hectic.

GETTING HERE AND AROUND

BY AIR

Alaska Air, American, Frontier, Horizon Air, United, and US Airways fly to Santa Barbara Municipal Airport, 12 mi from downtown. United Express and US Airways provide service to San Luis Obispo County Regional Airport, 3 mi from downtown San Luis Obispo.

Santa Barbara Airbus shuttles travelers between Santa Barbara and Los Angeles for $48 one-way and $90 round-trip (slight discount with 24-hour notice, larger discount for groups of six or more). The Santa Barbara Metropolitan Transit District Bus 11 ($1.75) runs every 30 minutes from the airport to the downtown transit center. A taxi between the airport and the hotel district runs $20 to $28.

Airport Contacts San Luis Obispo County Regional Airport
✉ 903–5 Airport Dr., San Luis Obispo ☏ 805/781–5205 ⊕ www.sloairport.com. **Santa Barbara Airport** ✉ 500 Fowler Rd., Santa Barbara ☏ 805/683–4011, 800/423–1618 ⊕ www.flysba.com.

Airport Transfer Contacts Santa Barbara Airbus ☏ 805/964–7759, 800/423–1618 ⊕ www.santabarbaraairbus.com. **Santa Barbara Metropolitan Transit District** ☏ 805/963–3366 ⊕ www.sbmtd.gov.

BY BUS

Greyhound provides service from San Francisco and Los Angeles to San Luis Obispo, Ventura, and Santa Barbara. From Monterey and Carmel, Monterey-Salinas Transit operates buses to Big Sur between May and mid-October. From San Luis Obispo, Central Coast Transit runs buses around Santa Maria and out to the coast. Santa Barbara Metropolitan Transit District provides local service. The Downtown/State Street and Waterfront shuttles cover their respective sections of Santa Barbara during the day. Gold Coast Transit buses serve the entire Ventura County region.

Bus Contacts Central Coast Transit ☏ 805/781–4472 ⊕ www.slorta.org. **Gold Coast Transit** ☏ 805/487–4222 for Oxnard and Port Hueneme, 805/643–3158 for Ojai and Ventura ⊕ www.goldcoasttransit.org. **Greyhound** ☏ 800/231–2222 ⊕ www.greyhound.com. **Monterey-Salinas Transit** ☏ 888/678–2871 ⊕ www.mst.org. **San Luis Obispo Transit** ☏ 805/781–4472 ⊕ www.slorta.org. **Santa Barbara Metropolitan Transit District** ☏ 805/963–3366 ⊕ www.sbmtd.gov.

BY CAR

Driving is the easiest way to experience the Central Coast. A car gives you the flexibility to stop at scenic vista points along Highway 1, take detours through Wine Country, and drive to rural lakes and mountains. Traveling north through Ventura County to San Luis Obispo (note that from just south of Ventura up to San Luis Obispo, U.S. 101 and Highway 1 are the same road), you can take in the rolling hills, peaceful valleys, and rugged mountains that stretch for miles along the shore.

Highway 1 and U.S. 101 run north–south and more or less parallel along the Central Coast, with Highway 1 hugging the coast and U.S. 101 running inland. The most dramatic section of the Central Coast is the 70 mi between Big Sur and San Simeon. Don't expect to make good time along here: The road is narrow and twisting with a single lane in each direction, making it difficult to pass the many lumbering RVs. In fog or rain the drive can be downright nerve-racking; in wet seasons mudslides can close portions of the road. Once you start south from Carmel, there is no route east from Highway 1 until Highway 46 heads inland from Cambria to connect with U.S. 101. At Morro Bay, Highway 1 turns inland for 13 mi and connects with U.S. 101 at San Luis Obispo. From here south to Pismo Beach the two highways run concurrently. South of Pismo Beach to Las Cruces the roads separate, then run together all the way to Oxnard. Along any stretch where they are separate, U.S. 101 is the quicker route.

U.S. 101 and Highway 1 will get you to the Central Coast from Los Angeles and San Francisco. If you are coming from the east, you can take Highway 46 west from I–5 in the Central Valley (near Bakersfield) to U.S. 101 at Paso Robles, where it continues to the coast, intersecting Highway 1 a few miles south of Cambria. Highway 33 heads south from I–5 at Bakersfield to Ojai. About 60 mi north of Ojai, Highway 166 leaves Highway 33, traveling due west through the Sierra Madre to Santa Maria at U.S. 101 and continuing west to Highway 1 at Guadalupe. South of Carpinteria, Highway 150 winds from Highway 1/U.S. 101 through sparsely populated hills to Ojai. From Highway 1/U.S. 101 at Ventura, Highway 33 leads to Ojai and the Los Padres National Forest. South of Ventura, Highway 126 runs east from Highway 1/U.S. 101 to I–5.

Contacts Caltrans ☎ *800/427–7623* ⊕ *www.dot.ca.gov.*

BY TRAIN

The Amtrak *Coast Starlight*, which runs between Los Angeles and Seattle via Oakland, stops in Paso Robles, San Luis Obispo, Santa Barbara, and Oxnard. Amtrak runs several *Pacific Surfliner* trains daily between San Luis Obispo, Santa Barbara, Los Angeles, and San Diego. Metrolink Regional Rail Service trains connect Ventura and Oxnard with Los Angeles and points between.

Train Contacts Amtrak ☎ *800/872–7245, 805/963–1015 in Santa Barbara, 805/541–0505 in San Luis Obispo* ⊕ *www.amtrakcalifornia.com.* **Metrolink** ☎ *800/371–5465* ⊕ *www.metrolinktrains.com.*

TOUR OPTIONS

Cloud Climbers Jeep and Wine Tours offers four types of daily tours: wine-tasting, mountain, sunset, and a discovery tour for families. These trips to the Santa Barbara/Santa Ynez mountains and Wine Country are conducted in open-air, six-passenger jeeps. Fares range from $89 to $129 per adult. The company also offers a four-hour All Around Ojai Tour for $99 per adult and arranges biking, horseback riding, and trap-shooting tours and Paso Robles wine tours by appointment. Wine Edventures operates customized Santa Barbara County tours and narrated North County wine-country tours in 25-passenger minicoaches. Fares for the wine tours are $110 per person. The Grapeline Wine Country Shuttle leads daily wine and vineyard picnic tours with flexible itineraries in San Luis Obispo County and Santa Barbara County Wine Country; they stop at many area hotels and can provide private custom tours with advance reservations. Fares range from $88 to $115, depending on pickup location and tour choice.

Spencer's Limousine & Tours offers customized tours of the city of Santa Barbara and Wine Country via sedan, limousine, van, or minibus. A five-hour basic tour with at least four participants costs about $90 per person. Sultan's Limousine Service has a fleet of super stretches; each can take up to eight passengers on Paso Robles and Edna Valley–Arroyo Grande wine tours and tours of the San Luis Obispo County coast. Hiring a limo for a four-hour Wine Country tour typically costs $400 to $450 with tip. Sustainable Vine Wine Tours' biodiesel-powered vans can take you on a day of eco-friendly wine touring in the Santa Ynez Valley. Trips include door-to-door transportation from your location in the Santa Barbara or Santa Ynez Valley area, tastings at green-minded wineries, and a gourmet organic picnic lunch.

Tour Contacts Cloud Climbers Jeep and Wine Tours ☎ 805/646–3200 ⊕ www.ccjeeps.com. **The Grapeline Wine Country Shuttle** ☎ 888/894–6379 ⊕ www.gogrape.com. **Spencer's Limousine & Tours** ☎ 805/884–9700 ⊕ www.spencerslimo.com. **Sultan's Limousine Service** ☎ 805/466–3167 North SLO County, 805/544–8320 South SLO County, 805/771–0161 coastal SLO County cities ⊕ www.sultanslimo.com. **Sustainable Vine Wine Tours** ☎ 805/698–3911 ⊕ www.sustainablevine.com. **Wine Edventures** ✉ 3463 State St. #228, Santa Barbara ☎ 805/965–9463 ⊕ www.welovewines.com.

VISITOR INFORMATION

Contacts San Luis Obispo County Visitors and Conference Bureau ✉ 811 El Capitan Way, #200, San Luis Obispo ☎ 805/541–8000 ⊕ www.sanluisobispocounty.com. **Santa Barbara Conference and Visitors Bureau** ✉ 1601 Anacapa St., Santa Barbara ☎ 805/966–9222 ⊕ www.santabarbaraca.com.

RESTAURANTS

The cuisine in Ventura and Santa Barbara is every bit as eclectic as it is in California's bigger cities; fresh seafood is a standout. The region from Solvang to Big Sur is far enough off the Interstate to ensure that nearly every restaurant or café has its own personality—from chic to down-home and funky. A foodie renaissance has overtaken the entire region from Ventura to Paso Robles, spawning dozens of new restaurants touting locavore cuisine made with fresh organic produce and meats.

Dining attire on the Central Coast is generally casual, though slightly dressy casual wear is the custom at pricier restaurants.

HOTELS

There are plenty of lodging options throughout the Central Coast—but expect to pay top dollar for any rooms along the shore, especially in summer. Moderately priced hotels and motels do exist—most just a short drive inland from their higher-price counterparts. Make your reservations as early as possible and take advantage of midweek specials to get the best rates. It's common for hotels to require minimum stays on holidays and some weekends, especially in summer, and to double their rates during festivals and other events.

WHAT IT COSTS				
¢	$	$$	$$$	$$$$
Restaurants	under $10	$10–$15	$16–$22	$23–$30	over $30
Hotels	under $90	$90–$120	$121–$175	$176–$250	over $250

Restaurant prices are for a main course at dinner, excluding sales tax of 7.25%–7.75% (depending on location). Hotel prices are for two people in a standard double room in high season, excluding service charges and 9%–10% tax.

VENTURA COUNTY

Ventura County was first settled by the Chumash Indians. Spanish missionaries were the first Europeans to arrive, followed by Americans and other Europeans, who established bustling towns, transportation networks, and highly productive farms. Since the 1920s, though, agriculture has been steadily replaced as the area's main industry—first by the oil business, and more recently, by tourism.

VENTURA

60 mi north of Los Angeles on U.S. 101.

Like Los Angeles, the city of Ventura enjoys gorgeous weather and sun-kissed beaches—but without the smog and congestion. The city is filled with classic California buildings, farmers' and fish markets, art galleries, and shops. The miles of beautiful beaches attract both athletes—bodysurfers and boogie boarders, runners and bikers—and those who'd rather doze beneath a rented umbrella all day. Ventura Harbor is home to the Channel Islands National Park Visitor Center and myriad fishing boats, restaurants, and water-activity centers where you can rent boats and take harbor cruises. Foodies can get their fix here, too; dozens of upscale cafés and wine and tapas bars have opened in recent years. Ventura is also a magnet for arts and antiques buffs who come to browse the dozens of galleries and shops in the downtown area.

GETTING HERE AND AROUND

Amtrak trains stop near the Ventura County Fairgrounds, a short walk from downtown. Metrolink trains travel from Los Angeles to southern Ventura. U.S. 101 is the main artery through town from north or south. For a scenic coastal route, drive along Highway 1 north along the coast from Santa Monica through Malibu. The road merges with U.S. 101 in Oxnard, just south of Ventura. To reach historic downtown Ventura, exit southbound U.S. 101 at Ventura Avenue or northbound U.S. 101 at California Street. Gold Coast Transit buses provide service throughout the city.

ESSENTIALS

Visitor Information Ventura Visitors and Convention Bureau ✉ *101 S. California St.* ☎ *805/648–2075, 800/483–6214* ⊕ *www.ventura-usa.com.*

EXPLORING

Visitor Center. You can pick up culinary, shopping, and other guides downtown at the visitor center run by the Ventura Visitors and Convention Bureau. ✉ *101 S. California St.* ☎ *805/648–2075, 800/483–6214* ⊕ *www.ventura-usa.com.*

Ventura Oceanfront. Four miles of gorgeous coastline stretch from the county fairgrounds at the northern border of the city of San Buenaventura, through San Buenaventura State Beach, down to Ventura Harbor in the south. The main attraction here is the San Buenaventura City Pier, a historic landmark built in 1872 and restored in 1993. Surfers rip the waves just north of the pier, and sunbathers relax on white-sand beaches on either side. The mile-long promenade and the Omer Rains Bike Trail north of the pier attract scores of joggers, surrey cyclers, and bikers throughout the year. ⊠ *California St., at ocean's edge.*

⟲ **Lake Casitas Recreation Area.** Lunker largemouth bass, rainbow trout, crappie, redears, and channel catfish live in the waters at Lake Casitas Recreation Area, an impoundment of the Ventura River. The lake is one of the country's best bass-fishing areas, and anglers come from all over the United States to test their luck. The park, nestled below the Santa Ynez Mountains' Laguna Ridge, is also a beautiful spot for pitching a tent or having a picnic. The Casitas Water Adventure, which has two water playgrounds and a lazy river for tubing and floating, is a great place to take kids in summer ($12 for an all-day pass; $6 from 5 to 7 pm). The park is 13 miles northwest of Ventura. ⊠ *11311 Santa Ana Rd., off Hwy. 33* ☎ *805/649–2233, 805/649–1122 campground reservations* ⊕ *www.lakecasitas.info* ⌫ *$10–$15 per vehicle, $10 per boat* ⊙ *Daily.*

Mission San Buenaventura. The ninth of the 21 California missions, Mission San Buenaventura was established in 1782 but burned to the ground in the 1790s. It was rebuilt and rededicated in 1809. A self-guided tour takes you through a small museum, a quiet courtyard, and a chapel with 250-year-old paintings. ⊠ *211 E. Main St.* ☎ *805/643–4318* ⊕ *www. sanbuenaventuramission.org* ⌫ *$2* ⊙ *Weekdays 10–5, Sat. 9–5, Sun. 10–4.*

WHERE TO EAT

$$$
AMERICAN
✕ **Brooks.** Innovative chef Andy Brooks and his wife Jayme—whose grandfather co-owned the famous Chi Chi supper club in Palm Springs in the 1960s—serve some of the town's finest meals in a slick, contemporary downtown dining room. The ever-changing menu centers on seasonal, mostly local, organic ingredients and features a nightly five-course tasting menu, which might include limoncello steamed mussels, cornmeal fried shrimp, or free-range chicken breast with sautéed collard greens and goat cheese-potato puree. Ask for the romaine salad dressed in the legendary Chi Chi creamy garlic dressing. Live music and hip martinis and margaritas attract a loyal following after 9 pm on weekends. ⊠ *545 E. Thompson Blvd.* ☎ *805/652–7070* ⊕ *www. restaurantbrooks.com* ⊙ *Closed Mon. No lunch.*

$$
SEAFOOD
✕ **Brophy Bros.** The Ventura outpost of this wildly popular Santa Barbara restaurant provides the same fresh seafood-oriented meals in a spacious second-story setting overlooking the harbor. Feast on everything from fish and chips and crab cakes to chowder and delectable fish—often straight from the boats moored below. ⊠ *1559 Spinnaker Dr., in Ventura Harbor Village* ☎ *805/639–0865* ⊕ *www.brophybros. com* ⌫ *Reservations not accepted.*

TRAFFIC TIMING

The southbound freeway from Santa Barbara to Ventura and L.A. slows from 4 pm to 6 or 7 pm; the reverse is true heading from Ventura to Santa Barbara in the early morning hours. Traffic in the greater Los Angeles region can clog the roads as early as 2 pm. Traveling south, it's best to depart Santa Barbara before 1 pm, or after 6 pm. Heading north, you probably won't encounter many traffic problems until you reach the Salinas/San Jose corridor.

5

¢   ✗ **Busy Bee Cafe.** A local favorite for decades, this classic 1950s diner has
AMERICAN   a jukebox on every table and serves hearty burgers and American comfort food (think meat loaf and mashed potatoes, pot roast, and Cobb
salad). For breakfast, tuck into a huge omelet; for a snack or dessert,
be sure to order a shake or hot fudge sundae from the soda fountain.
⊠ *478 E. Main St.* ☎ *805/643–4864* ⊕ *www.busybeecafe.biz.*

$ ✗ **Christy's.** You can get breakfast all day—don't miss the breakfast bur-
AMERICAN   rito—at this cozy, nautical-theme locals' hangout in the harbor, across
the water from the Channel Islands. It also serves burgers, sandwiches,
and soup. ⊠ *1559 Spinnaker Dr.* ☎ *805/642–3116.*

$$ ✗ **Jonathan's at Peirano's.** The main dining room here has a gazebo where
MEDITERRANEAN   you can eat surrounded by plants and local art. The menu has dishes
from Spain, Portugal, France, Italy, Greece, and Morocco. Standouts are
the various paellas, the *penne checca* pasta, and the ahi tuna encrusted
with pepper and pistachios. The owners also run an evening tapas bar
next door, which serves exotic martinis. ⊠ *204 E. Main St.* ☎ *805/648–
4853* ⊕ *www.jonathansatpeiranos.com.*

WHERE TO STAY

For expanded hotel reviews, visit Fodors.com.

$$ 🏨 **Crowne Plaza Ventura Beach.** An enviable SoCal location is the main
draw of this full-service, 12-story hotel: on the beach, next to an historic
pier, within easy walking distance of downtown restaurants and nightlife, and steps from the Amtrak train station. Pros: right on the beach,
walk to downtown and main attractions, steps from waterfront activities. Cons: trains whiz by early morning, waterfront area crowded in
summer, most rooms on the small side ⊠ *450 E. Harbor Blvd., Ventura*
☎ *800/842–0800* ⊕ *cpventura.com* ⟐ *254 rooms, 4 suites* △ *In-room:*
a/c, Wi-Fi. In-hotel: restaurant, bar, pool, gym, beach, water sports,
laundry facilities, business center, parking, some pets allowed.

$$ 🏨 **Four Points by Sheraton Ventura Harbor.** The spacious, contemporary
rooms here are still gleaming from a total renovation that was com-
pleted in 2009. **Pros:** close to island transportation; mostly quiet; short
drive or bus ride to historic downtown Ventura. **Cons:** not in the heart
of downtown; noisy seagulls sometimes congregate nearby. ⊠ *1050*
Schooner Dr. ☎ *805/658–1212* ⊕ *www.fourpoints.com/ventura* ⟐ *102*
rooms, 4 suites △ *In-room: a/c, Internet, Wi-Fi. In-hotel: restaurant,*
bar, pool, gym, business center, some pets allowed.

$$ 🏨 **Holiday Inn Express Ventura Harbor.** A favorite among Channel Islands
visitors, this quiet, comfortable, lodge-inspired property sits right at the
Ventura Harbor entrance. **Pros:** quiet at night; easy access to harbor
restaurants and activities; on shuttle bus route to city attractions. **Cons:**
busy area on weekends; five-minute drive to downtown sights. ⊠ *1080*
Navigator Dr. ☎ *805/856–9533, 800/315–2621* ⊕ *www.hiexpress.com*
⟐ *68 rooms, 23 suites* △ *In-room: no a/c, kitchen, Internet. In-hotel:*
pool, gym, business center, some pets allowed ⦿| *Breakfast.*

$$$ 🏨 **Pierpont Inn.** Back in 1910, Josephine Pierpont-Ginn built the original
Pierpont Inn on a hill overlooking Ventura Beach. **Pros:** near the beach;
lush gardens; Tempur-Pedic mattresses and pillows. **Cons:** near the free-
way and train tracks; difficult to walk downtown from here. ⊠ *550*

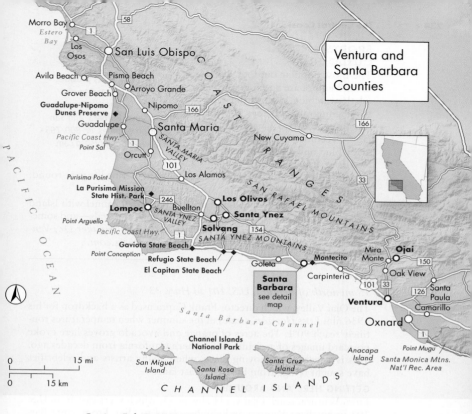

Ventura and
Santa Barbara
Counties

Sanjon Rd. ☎ *805/643–6144* ⊕ *www.pierpontinn.com* ⬋ *65 rooms, 9 suites, 2 cottages* ⌂ *In-room: no a/c, Wi-Fi. In-hotel: restaurant, bar, pool, tennis court, gym, spa, business center* ¶○¶ *Breakfast.*

$$$ ▧ **Ventura Beach Marriott.** Spacious, contemporary rooms, a peaceful location just steps from San Buenaventura State Beach, and easy access to historic downtown Ventura's arts and culture district make the Marriott a popular choice for travelers who want to explore Ventura. **Pros:** walk to beach and biking/jogging trails; a block from historic pier; great value for location. **Cons:** close to highway; near busy intersection. ✉ *2055 E. Harbor Blvd.* ☎ *805/643–6000, 888/236–2427* ⊕ *www. marriottventurabeach.com* ⬋ *272 rooms, 12 suites* ⌂ *In-room: a/c, Internet, Wi-Fi. In-hotel: restaurant, bar, pool, gym, laundry facilities, business center, parking, some pets allowed* ¶○¶ *Breakfast.*

SPORTS AND THE OUTDOORS

The most popular outdoor activities in Ventura are beach-going and whale-watching. California gray whales migrate offshore through the Santa Barbara Channel from late December through March; giant blue and humpback whales feed here from mid-June through September. In fact, the channel is teeming with marine life year-round, so tours include more than just whale sightings.

Island Packers. A cruise through the Santa Barbara Channel with Island Packers will give you the chance to spot dolphins and seals—and sometimes even whales—throughout the year. ✉ *1691 Spinnaker Dr., Ventura Harbor* ☎ *805/642–1393* ⊕ *www.islandpackers.com.*

OJAI

15 mi north of Ventura, U.S. 101 to Hwy. 33.

The Ojai Valley, which director Frank Capra used as a backdrop for his 1936 film *Lost Horizon*, sizzles in the summer when temperatures routinely reach 90°F. The acres of orange and avocado groves here evoke postcard images of agricultural Southern California from decades ago. This is a lush, slow-moving place, where many artists and celebrities have sought refuge from life in the fast lane.

GETTING HERE AND AROUND

From Ventura, reach Ojai via Highway 33, which veers east from U.S. 101 in northern Ventura and climbs inland to Ojai. From Santa Barbara, exit U.S. 101 at Highway 150 in Carpinteria, then travel inland 20 mi to Ojai (it's a twisty, two-lane country road, not recommended at night or during poor weather). You can also access Ojai from Highway 126, which runs between U.S. 101 and inland Highway 5. Exit at Santa Paula and follow Highway 150 16 mi north to Ojai. Get around Ojai Valley on the Ojai Valley Trolley.

ESSENTIALS

Visitor Information Ojai Visitors Bureau ☎ *888/652–4669* ⊕ *www.ojaivisitors.com.*

EXPLORING

Ojai Valley Trolley. The town can be easily explored on foot; you can also hop on the Ojai Valley Trolley, which follows two routes around Ojai and neighboring Miramonte between 7:15 and 5:15 on weekdays, 9 and 5 on weekends. If you tell the driver you're a visitor, you'll get an informal guided tour. ⊕ *www.ojaitrolley.com* 🚃 *50¢.*

Ojai Visitors Bureau. Maps and tourist information are available at the Ojai Visitors Bureau at the Ojai Chamber of Commerce. ✉ *201 S. Signal St.* ☎ *888/652–4669* ⊕ *www.ojaichamber.org* ⊗ *Weekdays 9–4.*

Ojai Avenue. The work of local artists is displayed in the Spanish-style shopping arcade along Ojai Avenue (Highway 150). Organic and specialty growers sell their produce on Sunday 9–1 at the farmers' market behind the arcade.

Ojai Center for the Arts. The Ojai Center for the Arts exhibits artwork and presents theater, dance, and other performances. ⊠ *113 S. Montgomery St.* ☎ *805/646–0117* ⊕ *www.ojaiartcenter.org.*

Ojai Valley Museum. The Ojai Valley Museum has exhibits on the valley's history and many Native American artifacts. ⊠ *130 W. Ojai Ave.* ☎ *805/640–1390* ⊕ *www.ojaivalleymuseum.org* ☜ *$4.*

Ojai Valley Trail. The 18-mi Ojai Valley Trail is open to pedestrians, bikers, joggers, equestrians, and nonmotorized vehicles. You can access it anywhere along its route. ⊠ *Parallel to Hwy. 33 from Soule Park in Ojai to ocean in Ventura* ☎ *888/652–4669* ⊕ *www.ojaivisitors.com.*

WHERE TO EAT

$$
MEDITERRANEAN

✕ **Azu.** Delectable tapas, a full bar, slick furnishings, and piped jazz music lure diners to this popular, artsy Mediterranean bistro. You can also order soups, salads, and bistro fare such as tagine, roasted chicken, and paella. Save room for the homemade gelato. ⊠ *457 E. Ojai Ave.* ☎ *805/640–7987* ⊕ *www.azuojai.com* ⊗ *No lunch Sun. and Mon.*

$
ITALIAN

✕ **Boccali's.** Edging a ranch, citrus groves, and a seasonal garden that provides much of the produce for menu items, family-run Boccali's has attracted droves of loyal fans to its modest but cheery restaurant since 1986. In the warmer months, you can dine alfresco in the oak-shaded patio and lawn area and sometimes listen to live music. Best known for their hand-rolled pizzas and homestyle pastas (don't miss the eggplant lasagna), Boccali's also serves a seasonal strawberry shortcake that some patrons drive many miles to savor every year. ⊠ *3277 Ojai Ave., about 2 mi east of downtown* ☎ *805/646–6116* ⊕ *www.boccalis.com* ☐ *No credit cards* ⊗ *No lunch Mon. and Tues.*

$$$
AMERICAN
★

✕ **The Ranch House.** This elegant yet laid-back eatery—said to be the best in town—has been around for decades. Main dishes such as rack of lamb in an oyster-and-mushroom cream sauce, and grilled diver scallops with curried sweet-corn sauce are not to be missed. The verdant patio is a wonderful place to have Sunday brunch. ⊠ *500 S. Lomita Ave.* ☎ *805/646–2360* ⊕ *www.theranchhouse.com* ⊗ *Closed Mon. No lunch.*

$$$
CONTINENTAL

✕ **Suzanne's Cuisine.** Peppered filet mignon, linguine with steamed clams, and pan-roasted salmon with a roasted mango sauce are among the offerings at this European-style restaurant. Game, seafood, and vegetarian dishes dominate the dinner menu, and salads and soups star at lunchtime. All the breads and desserts are made on the premises. ⊠ *502 W. Ojai Ave.* ☎ *805/640–1961* ⊕ *www.suzannescuisine.com* ⊗ *Closed Tues.*

WHERE TO STAY

For expanded hotel reviews, visit Fodors.com.

$

⌂ **The Blue Iguana Inn & Suites.** Artists run this Southwestern-style hotel, and their work (which is for sale) decorates the rooms. **Pros:** colorful art everywhere; secluded property; breakfast delivered to each room. **Cons:** 2 mi from the heart of Ojai; sits on the main highway to Ventura; small. ⊠ *11794 N. Ventura Ave., Hwy. 33* ☎ *805/646–5277* ⊕ *www.blueiguanainn.com* ⟲ *4 rooms, 7 suites, 8 cottages* ⌂ *In-room: a/c, kitchen, Wi-Fi. In-hotel: pool, some pets allowed* ⋈ *Breakfast.*

$$$ 🏨 **Oaks at Ojai.** Rejuvenation is the name of the game at this comfortable spa resort. **Pros:** great place to get fit; peaceful retreat; healthy meals. **Cons:** rooms are basic; sits on the main highway through town. ⊠ *122 E. Ojai Ave.* ☎ *805/646–5573, 800/753–6257* ⊕ *www.oaksspa.com* ⇔ *44 rooms, 2 suites* 占 *In-room: a/c, Wi-Fi. In-hotel: restaurant, pool, gym, spa, laundry facilities, business center* ⊙ *All meals* ☞ *2-night minimum stay.*

$$$$ 🏨 **Ojai Valley Inn & Spa.** This outdoorsy, golf-oriented resort and spa ★ is set on beautifully landscaped grounds, with hillside views in nearly all directions. **Pros:** gorgeous grounds; exceptional outdoor activities; romantic yet kid-friendly. **Cons:** expensive; staff isn't always attentive. ⊠ *905 Country Club Rd.* ☎ *805/646–1111, 888/697–8780* ⊕ *www. ojairesort.com* ⇔ *231 rooms, 77 suites* 占 *In-room: a/c, Internet, Wi-Fi. In-hotel: restaurant, bar, golf course, pool, tennis court, spa, children's programs, some pets allowed.*

$$$ 🏨 **Su Nido Inn.** Just a short walk from downtown Ojai sights and restaurants, this posh Mission revival–style inn is nested in a quiet neighborhood a few blocks from Libbey Park. **Pros:** walking distance from downtown; homey feel. **Cons:** no pool; can get hot during summer. ⊠ *301 N. Montgomery St.* ☎ *805/646–7080, 866/646–7080* ⊕ *www. sunidoinn.com* ⇔ *3 rooms, 9 suites* 占 *In-room: a/c, kitchen, Internet, Wi-Fi. In-hotel: bar, business center.*

SANTA BARBARA

27 mi northwest of Ventura and 29 mi west of Ojai on U.S. 101.

Santa Barbara has long been an oasis for Los Angelenos seeking respite from hectic big-city life. The attractions begin at the ocean and end in the foothills of the Santa Ynez Mountains. A few miles up the coast—but still very much a part of Santa Barbara—is the exclusive residential district of Hope Ranch. Santa Barbara is on a jog in the coastline, so the ocean is actually to the south, instead of the west; for this reason, directions can be confusing. "Up" the coast toward San Francisco is west, "down" toward Los Angeles is east, and the mountains are north.

GETTING HERE AND AROUND

A car is handy but not essential if you're planning to stay in town. The beaches and downtown are easily explored by bicycle or on foot. You can also hop aboard one of the electric shuttles that cruise the downtown and waterfront every 8 to 15 minutes (25¢ each way) and connect with local buses such as Line 22, which goes to major visitor sights (⊕ *www.sbmtd.gov*).

Santa Barbara Trolley Co. A motorized San Francisco–style cable car operated by Santa Barbara Trolley Co. makes 90-minute runs from 10 to 4 past major hotels, shopping areas, and attractions. Get off whenever you like, and pick up another trolley when you're ready to move on (they come every hour). Try to get a seat on the newest vehicle in the fleet, a biodiesel trolley with all seats on the top deck. Trolleys depart from and return to Stearns Wharf. The fare is $19 for the day. ☎ *805/965–0353* ⊕ *www.sbtrolley.com*.

Santa Barbara Car Free. Visit Santa Barbara Car Free for bike route and walking-tour maps and car-free vacation packages with substantial lodging discounts. ⊕ *www.santabarbaracarfree.org.*

ESSENTIALS

Visitor Information Santa Barbara Conference and Visitors Bureau ✉ *1601 Anacapa St.* ☎ *805/966–9222* ⊕ *www.santabarbaraca.com.* **Santa Barbara Chamber of Commerce Visitor Information Center** ✉ *1 Garden St., at Cabrillo Blvd.* ☎ *805/965–3021, 805/568–1811* ⊕ *www.sbchamber.org.*

EXPLORING

Santa Barbara's waterfront is beautiful, with palm-studded promenades and plenty of sand. In the few miles between the beaches and the hills are downtown, the old mission, and the botanic gardens.

Andree Clark Bird Refuge. This peaceful lagoon and its gardens sit north of East Beach. Bike trails and footpaths, punctuated by signs identifying native and migratory birds, skirt the lagoon. ✉ *1400 E. Cabrillo Blvd.* ✉ *Free.*

5

☾ **Carriage and Western Art Museum.** The country's largest collection of old horse-drawn vehicles—painstakingly restored—is exhibited here. Everything from polished hearses to police buggies to old stagecoaches and circus vehicles is on display. In August the Old Spanish Days Fiesta borrows many of the vehicles for a jaunt about town. This is one of the city's true hidden gems, a wonderful place to help history come alive—especially for children. Docents lead tours the third Sunday of every month from 1 to 4 pm. ✉ *129 Castillo St.* ☎ *805/962–2353* ⊕ *www. carriagemuseum.org* ✉ *Free* ☾ *Weekdays 9–3.*

★ **El Presidio State Historic Park.** Founded in 1782, El Presidio was one of four military strongholds established by the Spanish along the coast of California. The park encompasses much of the original site in the heart of downtown. El Cuartel, the adobe guardhouse, is the oldest building in Santa Barbara and the second oldest in California. ✉ *123 E. Canon Perdido St.* ☎ *805/965–0093* ⊕ *www.sbthp.org* ✉ *$5* ☾ *Daily 10:30–4:30.*

Karpeles Manuscript Library. Ancient political tracts and old Disney cartoons are among the holdings at this facility, which also houses one of the world's largest privately owned collections of rare manuscripts. Fifty display cases contain a sampling of the archive's million-plus documents. ✉ *21 W. Anapamu St.* ☎ *805/962–5322* ⊕ *www.karpeles.com* ✉ *Free* ☾ *Daily 10–4.*

Fodor's Choice
★ **Mission Santa Barbara.** Widely referred to as the "Queen of Missions," this is one of the most beautiful and frequently photographed buildings in coastal California. Dating to 1786, the architecture evolved from adobe-brick buildings with thatch roofs to more permanent edifices as the mission's population burgeoned. An earthquake in 1812 destroyed the third church built on the site. Its replacement, the present structure, is still a functioning Catholic church. Mission Santa Barbara has a splendid Spanish/Mexican colonial art collection, as well as Chumash sculptures and the only Native American–made altar and tabernacle left in the California missions. Docents lead 90-minute tours ($8 adult) Thursday and Friday at 11 and Saturday at 10:30; these include a stroll

Continued on page 244

ON A MISSION

Their soul may belong to Spain, their heart to the New World, but the historic missions of California, with their lovely churches, beckon the traveler on a soulful journey back to the very founding of the American West.

by Cheryl Crabtree and Robert I.C. Fisher

California history changed forever in the 18th century when Spanish explorers founded a series of missions along the Pacific coast. Believing they were following God's will, they wanted to spread the gospel and convert as many natives as possible. The process produced a collision between the Hispanic and California Indian cultures, resulting in one of the most striking legacies of Old California: the Spanish mission churches. Rising like mirages in the middle of desert plains and rolling hills, these saintly sites transport you back to the days of the Spanish colonial period.

GOD AND MAN IN CALIFORNIA

The Alta California territory came under pressure around 1750 when Spain feared foreign advances into the territory explorer Juan Rodríguez Cabrillo had claimed for the Spanish crown back in 1542. But how could Spain create a visible and viable presence halfway around the world? They decided to build on the model that had already worked well in Spain's Mexico colony. The plan involved establishing a series of missions, to be operated by the Catholic Church and protected by four of Spain's *presidios* (military outposts). The native Indians— after quick conversion to Christianity—would provide the labor force necessary to build mission towns.

FATHER OF THE MISSIONS

Father Junípero Serra is an icon of the Spanish colonial period. At the behest of the Spanish government, the diminutive padre—then well into his fifties, and despite a chronic leg infection— started out on foot from Baja California to search for suitable mission sites, with a goal of reaching Monterey. In 1769 he helped establish Alta California's first mission in San Diego and continued his travels until his death, in 1784, by which time he had founded eight more missions.

The system ended about a decade after the Mexican government took control of Alta California in the early 1820s and began to secularize the missions. The church lost horses and cattle, as well as vast tracts of land, which the Mexican government in turn granted to private individuals. They also lost laborers, as the Indians were for the most part free to find work and a life beyond the missions. In 1848, the Americans assumed control of the territory, and California became part of the United States. Today, these missions stand as extraordinary monuments to their colorful past.

Altarpiece at Mission San Gabriel Arcángel

MISSION ACCOMPLISHED

California's Mission Trail is the best way to follow in the fathers' footsteps. Here, below, are its 21 settlements, north to south.

Amazingly, all 21 Spanish missions in California are still standing—some in their pristine historic state, others with modifications made over the centuries. Many are found on or near the "King's Road"—El Camino Real—which linked these mission outposts. At the height of the mission system the trail was approximately 600 miles long, eventually extending from San Diego to Sonoma. Today the road is commemorated on portions of routes 101 and 82 in the form of roadside bell markers erected by CalTrans every one to two miles between Orange County and San Francisco.

San Francisco Solano, Sonoma (1823; this was the final California mission constructed.)

San Rafael, San Rafael (1817)

San Francisco de Asís (aka Mission Dolores), San Francisco (1776). Situated in the heart of San Francisco,

Mission Santa Clara de Asís

these mission grounds and nearby Arroyo de los Dolores (Creek of Sorrows) are home to the oldest intact building in the city.

Santa Clara de Asís, Santa Clara (1777). On the campus of Santa Clara University, this beautifully restored mission contains original paintings, statues, a bell, and hundreds of artifacts, as well as a spectacular rose garden.

San José, Fremont (1797)

Santa Cruz, Santa Cruz (1791)

San Juan Bautista, San Juan Bautista (1797). Immortalized in Hitchcock's *Vertigo*, this remarkably preserved pueblo contains the largest church of all the California missions, as well as 18th- and 19th-century buildings and a sprawling plaza.

San Carlos Borromeo del Río Carmelo, Carmel (1770). Carmel Mission was head-

quarters for the California mission system under Father Serra and the Father Presidents who succeeded him; the on-site museum includes Serra's tiny sleeping quarters (where he died in 1784).

Nuestra Señora de la Soledad, Soledad (1791)

San Antonio de Padua, Jolon (1771)

San Miguel Arcángel, San Miguel (1797). San Miguel boasts the only intact original interior work of art in any of the missions, painted in 1821 by Native American converts under the direction of Spanish artist Esteban Muras.

Painting from 1818, San Juan Bautista.

Mission Santa Inés

San Luis Obispo de Tolosa, San Luis Obispo (1772). Bear meat from grizzlies captured here saved the Spaniards from starving, which helped convince Father Serra to establish a mission.

La Purísima Concepción, Lompoc (1787). La Purísima is the nation's most completely restored mission complex. It is now a living-history museum with a church and nearly forty craft and residence rooms.

Santa Inés, Solvang (1804). Home to one of the most significant pieces of liturgical art created by a California mission Indian.

Santa Bárbara, Santa Barbara (1786). The "Queen of the Missions" has twin bell towers, gorgeous gardens with heirloom plant varietals, a massive collection of rare artworks and artifacts, and lovely stonework.

San Buenaventura, Ventura (1782). This was the last mission founded by Father Serra; it is still an active parish in the Archdiocese of Los Angeles.

Mission San Fernando Rey de España

San Fernando Rey de España, Mission Hills (1797)

San Gabriel Arcángel, San Gabriel (1771)

San Luis Rey de Francia, Oceanside (1798)

San Juan Capistrano, San Juan Capistrano (1776). This mission is famed for its Saint Joseph's Day (March 19) celebration of the return of swallows in the springtime. The mission's adobe walls enclose acres of lush gardens and historic buildings.

San Diego de Alcalá, San Diego (1769). This was the first California missions constructed, although the original was destroyed in 1775.

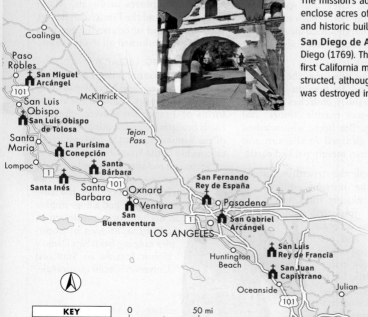

KEY

✝ Mission

0   50 mi

0   50 km

Coalinga
Paso Robles
✝ San Miguel Arcángel
101
San Luis Obispo
✝ San Luis Obispo de Tolosa
McKittrick
Santa Maria
✝ La Purísima Conepción
Tejon Pass
Lompoc
✝ Santa Bárbara
Santa Inés   Santa Barbara
101
Oxnard
Ventura
✝ San Buenaventura
San Fernando Rey de España
Pasadena
LOS ANGELES
1
✝ San Gabriel Arcángel
Huntington Beach
✝ San Luis Rey de Francia
✝ San Juan Capistrano
Oceanside
Julian
101
SAN DIEGO
✝ San Diego de Alcalá

MEXICO

5

IN FOCUS ON A MISSION

SPANISH MISSION STYLE

(left) Mission San Luis Rey de Francia; (right) Mission San Antonio de Padua

The Spanish mission churches derive much of their strength and enduring power from their extraordinary admixture of styles. They are spectacular examples of the combination of races and cultures that bloomed along Father Serra's road through Alta California.

SPIRIT OF THE PLACE

In building the missions, the Franciscan padres had to rely on available resources. Spanish churches back in Europe boasted marble floors and gilded statues. But here, whitewashed adobe walls gleamed in the sun and floors were often merely packed earth.

However simple the structures, the art within the mission confines continued to glorify the Church. The padres imported much finery to decorate the churches and perform the mass—silver, silk and lovely paintings to teach the life of Christ to the Indians and soldiers and settlers. Serra himself com-

missioned fine artists in Mexico to produce custom works using the best materials and according to exact specifications. Sculptures of angels, Mary, Joseph, Jesus and the Franciscan heroes and saints—and of course the Stations of the Cross—adorned all the missions.

AN ENDURING LEGACY

Mission architecture reflects a gorgeous blend of European and New World influences. While naves followed the simple forms of Franciscan Gothic, cloisters (with beautiful arcades) adopted aspects of the Romanesque style, and ornamental touches of the Spanish Renaissance—including red-tiled roofs and wrought -iron grilles—added even more elegance. In the 20th century, the Mission Revival Style had a huge impact on architecture and design in California, as seen in examples ranging from San Diego's Union Station to Stanford University's main quadrangle.

Father Junípero Serra statue at Mission San Gabriel

FOR WHOM THE BELLS TOLLED

Perhaps the most famous architectural motif of the Spanish Mission churches was the belltower. These took the form of either a campanile—a single tower called a campanario—or, more spectacularly, of an open-work espedaña, a perforated adobe wall housing a series of bells (notable examples of this form are at San Miguel Arcángel and San Diego de Alcalá). Bells were essential to maintaining the routines of daily life at the missions.

MISSION LIFE

Morning bells summoned residents to chapel for services; noontime bells introduced the main meal, while the evening bells sounded the alert to gather around 5 pm for mass and dinner. Many of the natives were happy with their new faith, and even enjoyed putting in numerous hours a week working as farmers, soapmakers, weavers, and masons.

Others, however, were less willing to abandon their traditional culture, but were coerced to abide by the new Spanish laws and mission rules. Natives were sometimes mistreated by the friars, who used a system of punishments to enforce submission to their teachings.

NATIVE TRAGEDY

In the end, mission life proved extremely destructive to the Native Californian population. European diseases and contaminated water caused the death of nearly a third, with some tribes—notably the Chumash—being virtually decimated. One friar was quoted as noting that the Indians "live well free but as soon as we reduce them to a Christian and community life . . . they fatten, sicken, and die."

Though so many native Indians died during the mission era, small numbers did survive. After the Mexican government secularized the missions in 1833, a majority of the native population was reduced to poverty. Some stayed at the missions, while others went to live in the pueblos, ranchos, and countryside—a tragic end for those whose labor was largely responsible for the magnificent mission churches we see today.

FOR MORE INFORMATION

California Missions Foundation

✉ 26555 Carmel Rancho Blvd., Ste. 7 Carmel, CA 93923

☎ 831/622-7500

⊕ www.california missionsfoundation.org

Top and bottom, Mission San Gabriel Arcángel.

5

IN FOCUS ON A MISSION

through to the adjacent La Huerta Project—a re-creation of the Spanish-era gardens with native and heirloom plants. ✉ *2201 Laguna St.* ☎ *805/682–4149, 805/682–4713* ⊕ *www.santabarbaramission.org* 🎫 *$5* ⊙ *Daily 9–4:30.*

Montecito. Since the late 1800s the tree-studded hills and valleys of this town have attracted the rich and famous (Hollywood icons, business tycoons, dot-commers who divested before the crash, and old-money families who installed themselves here years ago). Shady roads wind through the community, which consists mostly of gated estates. Swank boutiques line Coast Village Road, where well-heeled residents such as Oprah Winfrey sometimes browse for truffle oil, picture frames, and designer sweats. Residents also hang out in the Upper Village, a chic shopping area with restaurants and cafés at the intersection of San Ysidro and East Valley roads. Montecito is about 3 mi east of Santa Barbara.

SANTA BARBARA STYLE

Why does downtown Santa Barbara look so scrubbed and uniform? After a 1925 earthquake, which demolished many buildings, the city seized a golden opportunity to create a Spanish-Mediterranean look. It established an architectural board of review, which, along with city commissions, created strict architectural codes for the downtown district: red tile roofs, earth-tone facades, arches, wrought-iron embellishments, and height restrictions (about four stories).

Lotusland. The 37-acre Montecito estate called Lotusland once belonged to Polish opera singer Ganna Walska. Many of the exotic trees and other subtropical flora were planted in 1882 by horticulturist R. Kinton Stevens. On the two-hour guided tour (the only option for visiting unless you're a member), you'll see an outdoor theater, a topiary garden, a huge collection of rare cycads (an unusual plant genus that has been around since the time of the dinosaurs), and a lotus pond. Tours are conducted mid-February through mid-November, Wednesday through Saturday at 10 and 1:30. Reservations are required. Child-friendly family tours are available for groups with children under the age of 10; contact Lotusland for scheduling. ✉ *695 Ashley Rd.* ☎ *805/969–9990* ⊕ *www.lotusland.org* 🎫 *$35*

Outdoors Santa Barbara Visitor Center. The small office provides maps and other information about Channel Islands National Park, Channel Islands National Marine Sanctuary, and the Santa Barbara Maritime Museum, which occupies the same building in the harbor. ✉ *113 Harbor Way* ☎ *805/884–1475* ⊕ *outdoorsb.noaa.gov* 🎫 *Free* ⊙ *Daily 11–5.*

Santa Barbara Botanic Garden. Scenic trails meander through the garden's 78 acres of native plants. The Mission Dam, built in 1806, stands just beyond the redwood grove and above the restored aqueduct that once carried water to Mission Santa Barbara. More than a thousand plant species thrive in various themed sections of the garden, including mountains, deserts, meadows, redwoods, and Channel Islands. ✉ *1212 Mission Canyon Rd.* ☎ *805/682–4726* ⊕ *www.sbbg.org* 🎫 *$8* ⊙ *Mar.–Oct., daily 9–6; Nov.–Feb., daily 9–5. Guided tours weekdays at 2, weekends at 11 and 2.*

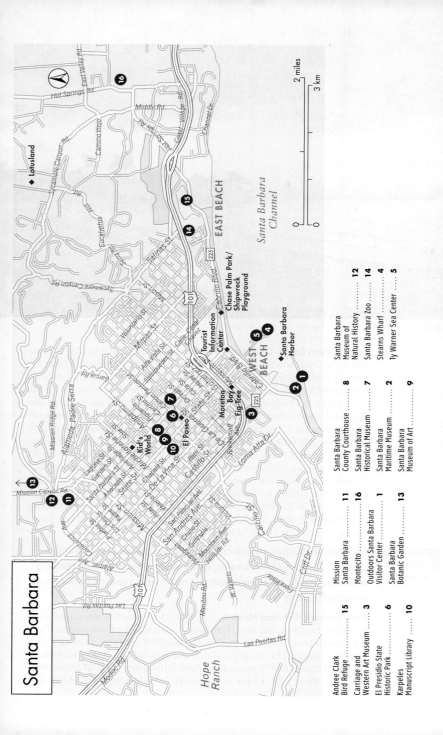

Santa Barbara

Andree Clark
Bird Refuge **15**

Carriage and
Western Art Museum **3**

El Presidio State
Historic Park **6**

Karpeles
Manuscript Library **10**

Mission
Santa Barbara **11**

Montecito **16**

Outdoors Santa Barbara
Visitor Center **1**

Santa Barbara
Botanic Garden **13**

Santa Barbara
County Courthouse **8**

Santa Barbara
Historical Museum **7**

Santa Barbara
Maritime Museum **2**

Santa Barbara
Museum of Art **9**

Santa Barbara Museum of
Natural History **12**

Santa Barbara Zoo **14**

Stearns Wharf **4**

Ty Warner Sea Center **5**

◆ Lotusland

Hot Springs Rd.

Middle Rd.

EAST BEACH

Santa Barbara Channel

Chase Palm Park/
Shipwreck
Playground

Tourist
Information
Center

WEST
BEACH

◆ Santa Barbara
Harbor

Moreton Bay
Fig Tree

El Paseo

Kid's
World

Mission Canyon Rd.

Hope Ranch

Las Positas Rd.

2 miles

3 km

Santa Barbara's downtown is attractive, but be sure also to visit its beautiful—and uncrowded—beaches.

★ **Santa Barbara County Courthouse.** Hand-painted tiles and a spiral staircase infuse the courthouse with the grandeur of a Moorish palace. This magnificent building was completed in 1929, part of a rebuilding process after a 1925 earthquake destroyed many downtown structures. At the time, Santa Barbara was also in the midst of a cultural awakening, and the trend was toward an architectural style appropriate to the area's climate and history. The result is the harmonious Mediterranean–Spanish look of much of the downtown area, especially the municipal buildings. An elevator rises to an arched observation area in the courthouse tower that provides a panoramic view of the city. The murals in the ceremonial chambers on the courthouse's second floor were painted by an artist who did backdrops for some of Cecil B. DeMille's films. ⊠ *1100 block of Anacapa St.* ☎ *805/962–6464* ⊕ *www.santabarbaracourthouse.org* ☉ *Weekdays 8–4:45, weekends 10–4:30. Free guided tours Mon., Tues., Weds., and Fri. at 10:30, daily at 2.*

QUICK BITES **Kids' World.** Children and adults can enjoy themselves at Kids' World, a public playground with a complex, castle-shape maze of fanciful climbing structures, slides, and tunnels built by Santa Barbara parents. ⊠ *Garden St. at Micheltorena St.*

Santa Barbara Historical Museum. The historical society's museum exhibits decorative and fine arts, furniture, costumes, and documents from the town's past. Adjacent to it is the Gledhill Library, a collection of books, photographs, maps, and manuscripts. ⊠ *136 E. De La Guerra St.* ☎ *805/966–1601* ⊕ *www.santabarbaramuseum.com* ☎ *Museum by donation; library $2–$5 per hr for research* ☉ *Museum Tues.–Sat. 10–5,*

Sun. noon–5, guided tours Sat. at 2; library Tues.–Fri. 10–4, 1st Sat. of month 10–1.

☺ **Santa Barbara Maritime Museum.** California's seafaring history is the focus at this museum. High-tech, hands-on exhibits, such as a sportfishing activity that lets you catch a "big one" and a local surfing history retrospective make this a fun stop for families. ☒ *113 Harbor Way* ☎ *805/962–8404* ⊕ *www. sbmm.org* ☜ *$7* ☽ *June–Aug., Thurs.–Tues. 10–6; Sept.–May, Thurs.–Tues. 10–5.*

Santa Barbara Museum of Art. The highlights of this museum's permanent collection include ancient sculpture, Asian art, impressionist paintings, contemporary Latin American art, and American works in several media. ☒ *1130 State St.* ☎ *805/963–4364* ⊕ *www.sbma.net* ☜ *$9, free on Sun.* ☽ *Tues.–Sun. 11–5. Free guided tours Tues.–Sun. at noon and 1.*

☺ **Santa Barbara Museum of Natural History.** The gigantic skeleton of a blue whale greets you at the entrance of this complex. The major draws include the planetarium, space lab, and a gem and mineral display. A room of dioramas illustrates Chumash Indian history and culture. Startlingly alive-looking stuffed specimens, complete with nests and eggs, roost in the bird diversity room. Many exhibits have interactive components. Outdoors you can stroll on nature trails that wind through the serene oak-studded grounds. Admission is free on the third Sunday of each month. Ask about the Nature Pass, which includes discounted unlimited two-day admission to both the Museum of Natural History and the Ty Warner Sea Center on Stearns Wharf. ☒ *2559 Puesta del Sol Rd.* ☎ *805/682–4711* ⊕ *www.sbnature.org* ☜ *$10* ☽ *Daily 10–5.*

☺ **Santa Barbara Zoo.** The grounds of this smallish zoo are so gorgeous people book their weddings here long in advance. The palm-studded lawns on a hilltop overlooking the beach are perfect spots for family picnics. The natural settings of the zoo shelter elephants, gorillas, exotic birds like the rare California condor, and big cats such as the rare snow leopard, a thick-furred, high-altitude dweller from Asia. For small children, there's a scenic railroad and barnyard petting zoo. ☒ *500 Niños Dr.* ☎ *805/962–5339 main line, 805/962–6310 information* ⊕ *www. santabarbarazoo.org* ☜ *Zoo $12, parking $5* ☽ *Daily 10–5.*

QUICK BITES

Chase Palm Park and Shipwreck Playground. The antique carousel, large playground with a nautical theme, picnic areas, and snack bar make the scenic waterfront Chase Palm Park and Shipwreck Playground a favorite destination for kids and parents. ☒ *Cabrillo Blvd., between Garden St. and Calle Cesar Chavez.*

LAND SHARK!

Land and Sea Tours. Land and Sea Tours takes visitors on narrated, 90-minute land-and-sea adventures in an amphibious 49-passenger vehicle, nicknamed the Land Shark. Tours begin with a drive through the city and continue with a plunge into the harbor for a cruise along the coast. ☒ *State St. at Stearns Wharf* ☎ *805/683–7600* ⊕ *www. out2seesb.com* ☜ *$25* ☽ *Tours May–Oct., daily noon, 2, and 4; Nov.–Apr., daily noon and 2.*

5

Stearns Wharf. Built in 1872, historic Stearns Wharf is Santa Barbara's most visited landmark. Expansive views of the mountains, cityscape, and harbor unfold from every vantage point on the three-block-long pier. Although it's a nice walk from the Cabrillo Boulevard parking areas, you can also park on the pier and then wander through the shops or stop for a meal at one of the wharf's restaurants. ⊠ *Cabrillo Blvd., at foot of State St.* ☎ *805/897–2683 info line, 805/564–5531 harbormaster* ⊕ *www.stearnswharf.org.*

Ty Warner Sea Center. A branch of the Santa Barbara Museum of Natural History, the Sea Center specializes in Santa Barbara Channel marine life and conservation. In 2005 it reopened in a new $6.5 million facility bearing the name of Ty Warner, Beanie Baby mogul and local resident, whose hefty donation helped the center complete the final stages of construction. The new Sea Center is small compared to aquariums in Monterey and Long Beach, but it's a fascinating, hands-on marine science laboratory that lets you participate in experiments, projects, and exhibits, including touch tanks. Haul up and analyze water samples, learn to identify marine mammals, and check out amazing creatures in the tide-pool lab and animal nursery. The two-story glass walls open to stunning ocean, mountain, and city views. Ask about the Nature Pass, which includes discounted unlimited two-day admission to both the Sea Center and the Museum of Natural History. ⊠ *211 Stearns Wharf* ☎ *805/962–2526* ⊕ *www.sbnature.org* ⊠ *$8* ⊙ *Daily 10–5.*

Urban Wine Trail. Nearly a dozen winery tasting rooms are sprinkled around the downtown area; most are within walking/biking distance of the beach and lower State Street shopping/restaurant district. ⊠ *Santa Barbara* ⊕ *urbanwinetrailsb.com.*

WHERE TO EAT

$$
JAPANESE

✕ **Arigato Sushi.** You might have to wait 45 minutes for a table at this trendy, two-story restaurant and sushi bar—locals line up early for the hip, casual atmosphere and wildly creative combination rolls. Fans of authentic Japanese food sometimes disagree about the quality of the seafood, but all dishes are fresh and artfully presented. The menu includes traditional dishes as well as innovative creations such as sushi pizza on seaweed and Hawaiian sashimi salad. ⊠ *1225 State St.* ☎ *805/965–6074* ⊕ *www. arigatosantabarbara.com* ⌫ *Reservations not accepted* ⊙ *No lunch.*

$$
SEAFOOD

✕ **Brophy Bros.** The outdoor tables at this casual harborside restaurant have perfect views of the marina and mountains. The staff serves enormous, exceptionally fresh fish dishes—don't miss the seafood salad and chowder—and provides you with a pager if there's a long wait for a table. You can stroll along the waterfront until the beep lets you know your table's ready. This place is hugely popular, so it can be crowded and loud, especially on weekend evenings. ⊠ *119 Harbor Way* ☎ *805/966–4418* ⊕ *www.brophybros.com.*

$$$
AMERICAN

✕ **Elements.** Different sections within this chic, contemporary restaurant and bar reflect nature's elements: an outdoor porch overlooking the sunken gardens at the Santa Barbara Courthouse across the street (air); the gold-tone main dining room (earth); an intimate corner with sofas for romantic dining (fire); and an often lively, ocean-hue area where professionals unwind over specialty martinis after work at the slick granite bar. The seasonal world-fusion menu, designed around organic and sustainable foods, might include a grilled ahi tuna wrap with wasabi mayonnaise at lunch, or lemongrass and panko-crusted sea bass with curry-coconut sauce and gingered basmati rice for dinner. ✉ *129 E. Anapamu St.* ☎ *805/884–9218* ⊕ *www.elementsrestaurantandbar.com* ☾ *Closed Mondays.*

> **BEST VIEWS**
>
> Drive along Alameda Padre Serra, a hillside road that begins near the mission and continues to Montecito, to feast your eyes on spectacular views of the city and the Santa Barbara Channel.

$ ⨉ **Flavor of India.** Feast on authentic northern Indian dishes like tandoori chicken, saag paneer, lamb biryani, and a host of curries at this cozy local favorite in a residential Upper State neighborhood. Best bets include the combination dinners served in a traditional Indian tray and the all-you-can-eat lunch buffet ($9). ✉ *3026 State St., Santa Barbara* ☎ *805/682–6561* ⊕ *www.flavorofindiasb.com* ☾ *Closed Sundays.*

INDIAN

$$$ ⨉ **The Hungry Cat.** The hip Santa Barbara sibling of a famed Hollywood eatery, run by chefs David Lentz and his wife Suzanne Goin, dishes up savory seafood in a small but lively nook in the downtown arts district. Feast on sea urchin, addictive peel-and-eat shrimp, and creative cocktails made from farmers' market fruits and veggies. A busy nightspot on weekends, the Cat also awakens for a popular brunch on Sunday. Night or day, come early or be prepared for a wait. ✉ *1134 Chapala St.* ☎ *805/884–4701* ⊕ *www.thehungrycat.com* ☾ *Closed Mon. Sept.–April.*

SEAFOOD

¢   ⨉ **La Super-Rica.** Praised by Julia Child, this food stand with a patio on the east side of town serves some of the spiciest and most authentic Mexican dishes between Los Angeles and San Francisco. Fans drive for miles to fill up on the soft tacos served with yummy spicy or mild sauces and legendary beans. Three daily specials are offered each day. Portions are on the small side; order several dishes and share. ✉ *622 N. Milpas St., at Alphonse St.* ☎ *805/963–4940* ▭ *No credit cards* ☾ *Closed Wed.*

MEXICAN
★

$$$ ⨉ **Olio e Limone.** Sophisticated Italian cuisine (with an emphasis on Sicily) is served at this restaurant near the Arlington Center for the Performing Arts. The juicy veal chop is a popular dish, but surprises abound here; be sure to try unusual dishes such as ribbon pasta with quail and sausage in a mushroom ragout, duck ravioli, or swordfish with Sicilian ratatouille. Tables are placed a bit close together, so this may not be the best spot for intimate conversations. For casual artisanal Italian fare, head next door to the Olio pizzeria/enoteca/bar. ✉ *17 W. Victoria St.* ☎ *805/899–2699* ⊕ *www.olioelimone.com* ☾ *No lunch Sun.*

ITALIAN

$$$ ⨉ **Palace Grill.** Mardi Gras energy, team-style service, lively music, and great food have made the Palace a Santa Barbara icon. Acclaimed for its Cajun and Creole dishes such as blackened redfish and jambalaya with dirty rice, the Palace also serves Caribbean fare, including a delicious coconut-shrimp dish. If you're spice-phobic, you can choose pasta, soft-shell crab, or filet mignon. Be prepared to wait as long as 45 minutes

SOUTHERN

5

for a table on Friday and Saturday night (when reservations are taken for a 5:30 seating only), though the live entertainment and free appetizers, sent out front when the line is long, will whet your appetite for the feast to come. ⊠ 8 E. Cota St. ☎ 805/963–5000 ⊕ www.palacegrill.com.

$$$
ECLECTIC
✕ **Roy.** Owner-chef Leroy Gandy serves a $25 fixed-price dinner (some selections are $20, some $30)—a real bargain—that includes a small salad, fresh soup, homemade organic bread, and a selection from a rotating list of contemporary American main courses. If you're lucky, the entrée choices might include grilled local fish with a mandarin beurre blanc, or bacon-wrapped filet mignon. You can also choose from an à la carte menu of inexpensive appetizers and entrées, plus local wines. Half a block from State Street in the heart of downtown, Roy is a favorite spot for late-night dining (it's open until midnight and has a full bar). ⊠ 7 W. Carrillo St. ☎ 805/966–5636 ⊕ www.restaurantroy.com ⊗ No lunch.

$$$$
AMERICAN
★
✕ **The Stonehouse.** Part of the San Ysidro Ranch resort, this elegantly rustic restaurant is housed in a century-old granite farmhouse. Executive chef James West harvests herbs and veggies from the on-site garden, then adds them to an array of top-quality local ingredients to create outstanding regional cuisine. The menu changes constantly but typically includes favorites such as crab cake with persimmon relish appetizer and local spiny lobster with mascarpone risotto. Dine on the radiant-heated oceanview deck with stone fireplace, next to a fountain under a canopy of loquat trees, or in the romantic, candlelit dining room overlooking a creek. The Plow & Angel pub, downstairs, offers more casual bistro fare. ⊠ 900 San Ysidro La., Montecito ☎ 805/565–1700 ⊕ www.sanysidroranch.com ⌂ Reservations essential ⊗ No lunch Mon.–Sat.

$$$
AMERICAN
✕ **Wine Cask.** When the Wine Cask closed suddenly in February 2009, the community mourned. So did Doug Margerum, whose family had operated the venerable restaurant, tucked in a romantic courtyard in historic El Paseo, from 1982 to 2007, before selling to an out-of-towner. He teamed up with local restaurateur Mitchel Sjerven to resurrect the Wine Cask, which reopened at year's end. The "new" Wine Cask serves bistro-style meals in a casual, comfortable and classy dining room, with a gold-wood interior and a massive fireplace. The seasonal menu revolves around farmers' market ingredients (just a few blocks away twice a week) and pairs with Santa Barbara's most extensive wine list, thanks to Doug's main business as an established winemaker and the wine shop/tasting room, focused on local and specialty handcrafted vintages, just steps away (open daily, noon to 6). The more casual bar-café across the courtyard serves pizzas, salads, small plates, wines, and cocktails from lunch through late evening. ⊠ 813 Anacapa St. ☎ 805/966–9463 ⊕ www.winecask.com ⌂ Reservations essential ⊗ Closed Sundays. No lunch Sat.

WHERE TO STAY

For expanded hotel reviews, visit Fodors.com.

$$$$
▦ **Canary Hotel.** The only full-service hotel in the heart of downtown, the Canary blends the feel of a casual beach getaway with tony urban sophistication. **Pros:** easy stroll to museums, shopping, dining; friendly, attentive service; adjacent fitness center. **Cons:** across from

main bus transit center; some rooms feel cramped. ⊠ *31 W. Carrillo St.* ☎ *805/884–0300, 877/468–3515* ⊕ *www.canarysantabarbara.com* ⮑ *77 rooms, 20 suites* ⚘ *In-room: a/c, Internet, Wi-Fi. In-hotel: restaurant, bar, pool, business center, parking, some pets allowed.*

$$$$ ☐ **Four Seasons Resort The Biltmore Santa Barbara.** Surrounded by lush, per-
★ fectly manicured gardens and across from the beach, Santa Barbara's grande dame has long been a favorite for quiet, California-style luxury. **Pros:** first-class resort; historic Santa Barbara character; personal service; steps from the beach. **Cons:** back rooms are close to train tracks; expensive. ⊠ *1260 Channel Dr.* ☎ *805/969–2261, 800/332–3442* ⊕ *www. fourseasons.com/santabarbara* ⮑ *181 rooms, 26 suites* ⚘ *In-room: a/c, Internet, Wi-Fi. In-hotel: restaurant, bar, pool, tennis court, gym, spa, beach, children's programs, business center, parking, some pets allowed.*

$$$ ☐ **Hyatt Santa Barbara.** A complex of three separate buildings on three landscaped acres, plus a neighboring inn and apartment units, the Mar Monte (managed by Hyatt) provides a wide range of value-laden lodging options in a prime location—right across from East Beach and the Cabrillo Pavilion Bathhouse. **Pros:** steps from the beach; many room types and rates; walk to the zoo and waterfront shuttle. **Cons:** motelish vibe; busy area in summer. ⊠ *1111 E. Cabrillo Blvd.* ☎ *805/963–0744, 800/643–1994* ⊕ *www.santabarbara.hyatt.com* ⮑ *218 rooms, 5 apartments* ⚘ *In-room: a/c, kitchen, Internet, Wi-Fi. In-hotel: restaurant, bar, pool, gym, spa, business center, parking, some pets allowed.*

$$$$ ☐ **Inn of the Spanish Garden.** A half block from the Presidio in the heart of downtown, this elegant Spanish-Mediterranean retreat celebrates Santa Barbara style, from tile floors, wrought-iron balconies, and exotic plants, to original art by famed local plein-air artists. **Pros:** walking distance from downtown; classic Spanish-Mediterranean style; caring staff. **Cons:** far from the beach; not much here for kids. ⊠ *915 Garden St.* ☎ *805/564–4700, 866/564–4700* ⊕ *www.spanishgardeninn.com* ⮑ *23 rooms* ⚘ *In-room: a/c, Internet, Wi-Fi. In-hotel: bar, pool, gym, parking* ⏀*Breakfast.*

$ ☐ **Motel 6 Santa Barbara Beach.** A half block from East Beach amid fancier hotels sits this basic but comfortable motel, which was the first Motel 6 in existence. **Pros:** less than a minute's walk from the zoo and beach; friendly staff; clean and comfortable. **Cons:** no frills; motel-style rooms; no breakfast. ⊠ *443 Corona Del Mar Dr.* ☎ *805/564–1392, 800/466–8356* ⊕ *www.motel6.com* ⮑ *51 rooms* ⚘ *In-room: a/c, Wi-Fi. In-hotel: pool, some pets allowed.*

$ ☐ **Presidio Motel.** Young globetrotting couple Chris Sewell and Kenny Osehan transformed the Presidio, a formerly funky motel, into a simple yet stylish oasis. Two artists individually decorated each room with custom vinyl stickers; all rooms include flat-panel, widescreen TVs, complimentary WiFi, and use of bicycles to tool around town. Situated in the Arts District near the Arlington Theater, this is a good choice for those who want (relatively) affordable lodging within walking distance of downtown attractions; the electric Downtown/Waterfront Shuttle stops just a few blocks away. **Pros:** great downtown location; friendly staff; hip, artsy vibe. **Cons:** smallish rooms; basic baths; thin walls. ⊠ *1620 State St., Santa Barbara* ☎ *805/963–1355* ⊕ *www.thepresidiomotel. com* ⮑ *16 rooms* ⚘ *In-room: Wi-Fi* ⏀*Breakfast.*

$$$$ **San Ysidro Ranch.** At this romantic hideaway on an historic property in
★ the Montecito foothills—where John and Jackie Kennedy spent their
honeymoon and Oprah sends her out-of-town guests—guest cottages
are scattered among groves of orange trees and flower beds. All have
down comforters and fireplaces, most have private outdoor spas, and
one has its own pool. Seventeen miles of hiking trails crisscross 500
acres of open space surrounding the property. The Stonehouse restau-
rant ($$$$; see above) and Plow & Angel Bistro ($$$) are Santa Barbara
institutions. **Pros:** ultimate privacy; surrounded by nature; celebrity
hangout; pet-friendly. **Cons:** very expensive; too remote for some. ⊠ *900
San Ysidro La., Montecito* ☏ *805/565–1700, 800/368–6788* ⊕ *www.
sanysidroranch.com* ⤳ *23 rooms, 4 suites, 14 cottages* ⚏ *In-room: a/c,
Internet, Wi-Fi. In-hotel: restaurant, bar, pool, gym, some pets allowed*
⚲ *2-day minimum stay on weekends, 3 days on holiday weekends.*

$$$$ ⛺ **Simpson House Inn.** If you're a fan of traditional B&Bs, this prop-
★ erty, with its beautifully appointed Victorian main house and acre of
lush gardens, is for you. **Pros:** impeccable landscaping; walking dis-
tance from everything downtown; ranked among the nation's top
B&Bs. **Cons:** some rooms in the main building are small; two-night
minimum stay on weekends. ⊠ *121 E. Arrellaga St.* ☏ *805/963–7067,
800/676–1280* ⊕ *www.simpsonhouseinn.com* ⤳ *11 rooms, 4 cottages*
⚏ *In-room: a/c, Wi-Fi* ⎰*Breakfast.*

NIGHTLIFE AND THE ARTS

Most major hotels present entertainment nightly during the summer
season and on weekends all year. Much of the town's bar, club, and
live-music scene centers on lower State Street (between the 300 and 800
blocks). The thriving arts district, with theaters, restaurants, and cafés,
starts around the 900 block of State Street and continues north to the
Arlington Center for the Performing Arts, in the 1300 block. Santa Bar-
bara supports a professional symphony and a chamber orchestra. The
proximity to the University of California at Santa Barbara assures an
endless stream of visiting artists and performers. To see what's scheduled
around town, pick up a copy of the free weekly *Santa Barbara Indepen-
dent* newspaper or visit their Web site ⊕ *www.independent.com.*

NIGHTLIFE

Blue Agave. Rich leather couches, a crackling fire in chilly weather, a
cigar balcony, and pool tables draw a fancy Gen-X crowd to Blue Agave
for good food and designer martinis. ⊠ *20 E. Cota St.* ☏ *805/899–4694.*

Dargan's. All types of people hang out at Dargan's, a lively pub with four
pool tables, a great selection of draft beer and Irish whiskeys, and a full
menu of traditional Irish dishes. ⊠ *18 E. Ortega St.* ☏ *805/568–0702.*

James Joyce. The James Joyce, which sometimes plays host to folk and
rock performers, is a good place to have a few beers and while away
an evening. ⊠ *513 State St.* ☏ *805/962–2688.*

Joe's Cafe. Joe's Cafe, where steins of beer accompany hearty bar
food, is a fun, if occasionally rowdy, collegiate scene. ⊠ *536 State St.*
☏ *805/966–4638.*

Lucky's. A slick sports bar attached to an upscale steak house owned by the maker of Lucky Brand Dungarees, Lucky's attracts a flock of hip, fashionably dressed patrons hoping to see and be seen. ⊠ *1279 Coast Village Rd., Montecito* ☎ *805/565–7540.*

Milk & Honey. Swank Milk & Honey lures trendy crowds with artfully prepared tapas, coconut-mango mojitos, and exotic cocktails—despite high prices and a reputation for inattentive service. ⊠ *30 W. Anapamu St.* ☎ *805/275–4232.*

SOhO. SOhO—a hip restaurant, bar, and music club—schedules an eclectic mix of live music groups, from jazz to blues to rock, every night of the week. ⊠ *1221 State St.* ☎ *805/962–7776.*

THE ARTS

Arlington Center for the Performing Arts. Arlington Center for the Performing Arts, a Moorish-style auditorium, hosts major events during the two-week Santa Barbara International Film Festival every winter and presents touring performers and films throughout the year. ⊠ *1317 State St.* ☎ *805/963–4408.*

Center Stage Theatre. Center Stage Theatre presents plays, music, dance, and readings. ⊠ *700 block of State St., 2nd fl. of Paseo Nuevo* ☎ *805/ 963–0408.*

Ensemble Theatre Company. Ensemble Theatre Company stages plays by authors ranging from Tennessee Williams and Henrik Ibsen to rising contemporary dramatists. ⊠ *914 Santa Barbara St.* ☎ *805/965–5400.*

Granada. Originally opened in 1924, the landmark Granada theater reopened to great fanfare in 2008 following a $50 million restoration and modernization. ⊠ *1214 State St.* ☎ *805/899–3000 general info, 805/899–2222 box office.*

Lobero Theatre. The Lobero Theatre, a state landmark, hosts community theater groups and touring professionals. ⊠ *33 E. Canon Perdido St.* ☎ *805/963–0761.*

Music Academy of the West. In Montecito, the Music Academy of the West showcases orchestral, chamber, and operatic works every summer. ⊠ *1070 Fairway Rd.* ☎ *805/969–4726, 805/969–8787 box office.*

SPORTS AND THE OUTDOORS

BEACHES Santa Barbara's beaches don't have the big surf of the shoreline farther south, but they also don't have the crowds. You can usually find a solitary spot to swim or sunbathe. In June and July, fog often hugs the coast until about noon.

East Beach. The wide swath of sand at the east end of Cabrillo Boulevard on the harbor front is a great spot for people-watching. East Beach has sand volleyball courts, summertime lifeguard and sports competitions, and arts-and-crafts shows on Sunday and holidays. You can use showers, a weight room, and lockers (bring your own towel) and rent umbrellas and boogie boards at the Cabrillo Bathhouse. Next door, there's an elaborate jungle-gym play area for kids. ⊠ *1118 Cabrillo Blvd.* ☎ *805/897–2680.*

Arroyo Burro County Beach. The usually gentle surf at Arroyo Burro County Beach makes it ideal for families with young children. ⊠ *Cliff Dr., at Las Positas Rd.*

BICYCLING **Cabrillo Bike Lane.** The level, two-lane, 3-mi Cabrillo Bike Lane passes the Santa Barbara Zoo, the Andree Clark Bird Refuge, beaches, and the harbor. There are restaurants along the way, and you can stop for a picnic along the palm-lined path looking out on the Pacific.

Wheel Fun Rentals. Wheel Fun Rentals has bikes, quadricycles, and skates; a second outlet around the block rents small electric cars and scooters. ⊠ *23 E. Cabrillo Blvd.* ☎ *805/966–2282.*

> ### BIRTHPLACE OF THE ENVIRONMENTAL MOVEMENT
>
> In 1969, 200,000 gallons of crude oil spilled into the Santa Barbara Channel, causing an immediate outcry from residents, particularly in the UCSB community. The day after the spill, Get Oil Out (GOO) was established; the group helped lead the successful fight for legislation to limit and regulate offshore drilling in California. The Santa Barbara spill also spawned Earth Day, which is still celebrated in communities across the nation today.

BOATS AND CHARTERS **Santa Barbara Sailing Center.** Santa Barbara Sailing Center offers sailing instruction, rents and charters sailboats, and organizes dinner and sunset champagne cruises, island excursions, and whale-watching trips. ⊠ *Santa Barbara Harbor launching ramp* ☎ *805/962–2826, 800/350–9090.*

☾ **Santa Barbara Water Taxi.** Children beg to ride *L'il Toot*, a cheery yellow water taxi that cruises from the harbor to Stearns Wharf and back again. ⊠ *Santa Barbara Harbor and Stearns Wharf, Santa Barbara* ☎ *805/896–6900* ⊕ *sbwatertaxi.com* ⊠ *$4 one-way* ☉ *Departures every half hour from 12 to 6 in summer, 12 to sunset in winter.*

SEA Landing. SEA Landing operates surface and deep-sea fishing charters year-round. ⊠ *Cabrillo Blvd., at Bath St., and breakwater in Santa Barbara Harbor* ☎ *805/965–3564.*

Condor Express. From SEA Landing, the *Condor Express*, a 75-foot high-speed catamaran, whisks up to 149 passengers toward the Channel Islands on dinner cruises, whale-watching excursions, and pelagic-bird trips. ☎ *805/882–0088, 888/779–4253.*

Truth Aquatics. Truth Aquatics departs from SEA Landing in the Santa Barbara Harbor to ferry passengers on excursions to the National Marine Sanctuary and Channel Islands National Park. Their three dive boats also take scuba divers on single-day and multiday trips. ☎ *805/962–1127.*

GOLF **Sandpiper Golf Club.** Like Pebble Beach, the 18-hole, par-72 Sandpiper Golf Club sits on the ocean bluffs and combines stunning views with a challenging game. Greens fees are $139–$159; a cart (optional) is $16. ⊠ *7925 Hollister Ave., 14 mi north of downtown on Hwy. 101* ☎ *805/968–1541.*

Santa Barbara Golf Club. Santa Barbara Golf Club has an 18-hole, par-70 course. The greens fees are $40–$50; a cart (optional) costs $30 per cart or $15 per person. ⊠ *Las Positas Rd. and McCaw Ave.* ☎ *805/687–7087.*

TENNIS Many hotels in Santa Barbara have courts.

City of Santa Barbara Parks and Recreation Department. The City of Santa Barbara Parks and Recreation Department operates public courts with lighted play until 9 pm weekdays. You can purchase day permits ($7) at the courts, or call the department. ☎ *805/564–5473.*

Municipal Tennis Center. The 12 hard courts at the Municipal Tennis Center include an enclosed stadium court and three lighted courts open daily. ✉ *1414 Park Pl., near Salinas St. and U.S. 101.*

Pershing Park. Pershing Park has eight lighted courts available for public play after 5 pm weekdays and all day on weekends and Santa Barbara City College holidays. ✉ *100 Castillo St., near Cabrillo Blvd.*

SHOPPING

SHOPPING
AREAS

State Street. State Street, roughly between Cabrillo Boulevard and Sola Street, is the commercial hub of Santa Barbara and a shopper's paradise. Chic malls, quirky storefronts, antiques emporia, elegant boutiques, and funky thrift shops abound here. You can do your shopping on foot or by a battery-powered trolley (25¢) that runs between the waterfront and the 1300 block.

Paseo Nuevo. Paseo Nuevo, an open-air mall anchored by chains such as Nordstrom and Macy's, also contains a few local institutions such as the Contemporary Arts Forum and Center Stage Theater. ✉ *700 and 800 blocks of State St.*

El Paseo. Shops, art galleries, and studios share the courtyard and gardens of El Paseo, a historic arcade. ✉ *Canon Perdido St., between State and Anacapa Sts.*

Brinkerhoff Avenue. Antiques and gift shops are clustered in restored Victorian buildings on Brinkerhoff Avenue. ✉ *2 blocks west of State St., at West Cota St.*

Summerland. Serious antiques hunters can head a few miles south of Santa Barbara to the beach town of Summerland, which is full of shops and markets.

CLOTHING

Channel Islands Surfboards. Channel Islands Surfboards stocks the latest in California beachwear, sandals, and accessories. ✉ *36 Anacapa St.* ☎ *805/966–7213.*

Diani. This upscale, European-style women's boutique across from the Arlington Theater dresses clients in designer clothing from around the world. A sibling shoe shop is just a few doors away. ✉ *1324 State St., Santa Barbara* ☎ *877/342–6474* ⊕ *www.dianiboutique.com.*

Wendy Foster. Wendy Foster is a casual-chic clothing store for women. ✉ *833 State St.* ☎ *805/966–2276.*

Santa Barbara Outfitters. Santa Barbara Outfitters carries stylish, functional clothing, shoes, and accessories for active folks: kayakers, climbers, cyclists, runners, and hikers. A connected PrAna store focuses on yoga classes, gear, and attire. ✉ *1200 State St.* ☎ *805/564–1007.*

Surf 'N Wear's Beach House. Surf 'N Wear's Beach House carries surf clothing, gear, and collectibles; it's also the home of Santa Barbara Surf

Shop and the exclusive local dealer of Surfboards by Yater. ⊠ *10 State St.* ☎ *805/963–1281.*

Territory Ahead. Territory Ahead, a high-quality outdoorsy catalog company, sells fashionably rugged clothing for men and women. ⊠ *Main store, 515 State St.* ☎ *805/962–5558.*

EN
ROUTE

If you choose to drive north via U.S. 101 without detouring to the Solvang/Santa Ynez area, you will drive right past some good beaches. In succession from east to west, **El Capitan, Gaviota, and Refugio state beaches** all have campsites, picnic tables, and fire rings.

SANTA BARBARA COUNTY

Residents refer to the glorious 30-mi stretch of coastline from Carpinteria to Gaviota as the South Coast. The Santa Ynez Mountains divide the county geographically; U.S. 101 passes through a mountain tunnel leading inland. Northern Santa Barbara County used to be known for its sprawling ranches and strawberry and broccoli fields. Today its 100-plus wineries and 22,000 acres of vineyards dominate the landscape from the Santa Ynez Valley in the south to Santa Maria in the north.

The hit film *Sideways* was filmed almost entirely in the North County Wine Country; when the movie won Golden Globe and Oscar awards in 2005, it sparked national and international interest in visits to the region.

ESSENTIALS
Visitor Information Santa Barbara County Vintners' Association ☎ *805/688–0881* ⊕ *www.sbcountywines.com.*

The Santa Barbara Conference & Visitors Bureau. The Santa Barbara Conference & Visitors Bureau created a detailed map highlighting film location spots. Maps can be downloaded from visitor bureau Web sites: ⊕ *www.santaynezvalleyvisit.com* or *www.santabarbaraca.com.* ☎ *805/966–9222* ⊕ *www.santabarbaraca.com.*

SANTA YNEZ

31 mi north of Goleta via Hwy. 154.

Founded in 1882, the tiny town of Santa Ynez still has many of its original frontier buildings. You can walk through the three-block downtown area in just a few minutes, shop for antiques, and hang around the old-time saloon. At some of the eponymous valley's best restaurants, you just might bump into one of the many celebrities who own nearby ranches.

GETTING HERE AND AROUND
If you're coming from Santa Barbara, two-lane Highway 154 over San Marcos Pass is the shortest and most scenic route to Santa Ynez. You can also drive along U.S. 101 north 43 mi to Buellton, then 7 mi east through Solvang to Santa Ynez. Santa Ynez Valley Transit shuttle buses connect Santa Ynez with Solvang and other north county towns.

ESSENTIALS
Visitor Information Santa Ynez Valley Visitors Association ☎ *805/686–0053, 800/742–2843* ⊕ *www.santaynezvalleyvisit.com.*

EXPLORING

Chumash Casino Resort. Just south of Santa Ynez on the Chumash Indian Reservation lies the sprawling, Las Vegas–style Chumash Casino Resort. The casino has 2,000 slot machines, and the property includes three restaurants, a spa, and an upscale hotel ($$$–$$$$). ⊠ *3400 E. Hwy. 246* ☎ *800/248–6274.*

WHERE TO EAT AND STAY

$$

ITALIAN

★

✕ **Trattoria Grappolo.** Authentic Italian fare, an open kitchen, and festive, family-style seating make this trattoria equally popular with celebrities from Hollywood and ranchers from the Santa Ynez Valley. Italian favorites on the extensive menu range from thin-crust pizza to homemade ravioli, risottos, and seafood linguine to grilled lamb chops in red-wine sauce. The noise level tends to rise in the evening, so this isn't the best spot for a romantic getaway. ⊠ *3687-C Sagunto St.* ☎ *805/688–6899* ⊕ *www.trattoriagrappolo.com* ⊗ *No lunch Mon.*

$$$$

⊡ **Santa Ynez Inn.** This posh two-story Victorian inn in downtown Santa Ynez was built from scratch in 2002. **Pros:** near several restaurants; unusual antiques; spacious rooms. **Cons:** high price for location; not in a historic building. ⊠ *3627 Sagunto St.* ☎ *805/688–5588, 800/643–5774* ⊕ *www.santaynezinn.com* ⊶ *20 rooms, 3 suites* ⊘ *In-room: a/c, Internet, Wi-Fi. In-hotel: gym* ⏏ *Breakfast.*

LOS OLIVOS

4 mi north of Santa Ynez on Hwy. 154.

This pretty village in the Santa Ynez Valley was once on Spanish-built El Camino Real (Royal Highway) and later a stop on major stagecoach and rail routes. It's so sleepy today, though, that the movie *Return to Mayberry* was filmed here. Tasting rooms, art galleries, antiques stores, and country markets line Grand Avenue and intersecting streets for several blocks.

GETTING HERE AND AROUND

From U.S. 101 north or south, exit at Highway 154 and drive east about 8 mi. From Santa Barbara, travel 30 mi northwest on Highway 154. Santa Ynez Valley Transit provides shuttle bus service between Los Olivos, Ballard, Solvang, and other towns.

EXPLORING

Carhartt Vineyard Tasting Room. Inside the intimate, 99-square-foot Carhartt Vineyard Tasting Room, you're likely to meet owners and winemakers Mike and Brooke Carhartt, who pour samples of their small-lot, handcrafted vintages most days. ⊠ *2990-A Grand Ave.* ☎ *805/693–5100* ⊕ *www.carharttvineyard.com.*

Daniel Gehrs Tasting Room. Historic Heather Cottage, originally an early-1900s doctor's office, houses the Daniel Gehrs Tasting Room. Here you can sample Gehrs's various varietals, produced in limited small-lot quantities. ⊠ *2939 Grand Ave.* ☎ *805/693–9686* ⊕ *www.danielgehrswines.com.*

Firestone Vineyard. Firestone Vineyard has been around since 1972. It has daily tours, grassy picnic areas, and hiking trails in the hills overlooking the valley; the views are fantastic. ⊠ *5000 Zaca Station Rd.* ☎ *805/688–3940* ⊕ *www.firestonewine.com.*

WHERE TO EAT AND STAY

$$$$ ✕**Brothers Restaurant at Mattei's Tavern.** In the stagecoach days, Mat-
AMERICAN tei's Tavern provided wayfarers with hearty meals and warm beds.
Fodor'sChoice Chef-owners and brothers Matt and Jeff Nichols renovated the 1886
★ building, and while retaining the original character, transformed it into
one of the best restaurants in the valley. The casual, unpretentious dining rooms with their red-velvet wallpaper and historic photos reflect
the rich history of the tavern. The menu changes every few weeks but
often includes house favorites such as spicy fried calamari, prime rib,
and salmon, and the locally famous jalapeño corn bread. There's also
a full bar and an array of vintages from the custom-built cedar wine
cellar. ⊠ *2350 Railway Ave.* ☎ *805/688–4820* ⊕ *www.matteistavern.
com* ⌣ *Reservations essential* ☉ *No lunch.*

$$ ✕**Los Olivos Cafe.** Site of the scene in *Sideways* where the four main
AMERICAN characters dine together and share a few bottles of wine, this down-to-
earth restaurant not only provided the setting but served the actors real
food from their existing menu during filming. Part wine store and part
social hub for locals, the café focuses on wine-friendly fish, pasta, and
meat dishes made from local bounty, plus salads, pizzas, and burgers.
Don't miss the homemade muffuletta and olive tapenade spreads. Other
house favorites include an artisanal cheese plate, baked Brie with honey-
roasted hazelnuts, and braised pot roast with whipped potatoes. ⊠ *2879
Grand Ave.* ☎ *805/688–7265, 888/946–3748* ⊕ *www.losolivoscafe.com.*

$$$ ⊡ **The Ballard Inn & Restaurant.** Set among orchards and vineyards in
the tiny town of Ballard, 2 mi south of Los Olivos, this inn makes an
elegant wine-country escape. **Pros:** exceptional food; attentive staff;
secluded. **Cons:** some baths could use updating; several miles from Los
Olivos and Santa Ynez. ⊠ *2436 Baseline Ave., Ballard* ☎ *805/688–
7770, 800/638–2466* ⊕ *www.ballardinn.com* ⌥ *15 rooms* ⌂ *In-room:
a/c, no TV, Wi-Fi. In-hotel: restaurant* ⏀*Breakfast.*

$$$$ ⊡ **Fess Parker's Wine Country Inn and Spa.** This luxury inn includes an
elegant, tree-shaded French country–style main building and an equally
attractive annex across the street with a pool, hot tub, and day spa. **Pros:**
convenient wine touring base; walking distance from restaurants and
galleries; well-appointed rooms. **Cons:** pricey; staff attention is inconsistent. ⊠ *2860 Grand Ave.* ☎ *805/688–7788, 800/446–2455* ⊕ *www.
fessparker.com* ⌥ *20 rooms, 1 suite* ⌂ *In-room: a/c, Internet. In-hotel:
restaurant, bar, pool, gym, spa, some pets allowed* ⏀*Breakfast.*

SOLVANG

↻ *5 mi south of Los Olivos on Alamo Pintado Rd., Hwy. 246, 3 mi east
of U.S. 101.*

You'll know you've reached the town of Solvang when the architecture
suddenly changes to half-timber buildings and windmills. This town
was settled in 1911 by a group of Danish educators (the flatlands and
rolling green hills reminded them of home), and even today, more than
two-thirds of the residents are of Danish descent. Although it's attracted
tourists for decades, in recent years it has become more sophisticated,
with galleries, upscale restaurants, and wine-tasting rooms. Most shops

5

are locally owned; the city has an ordinance prohibiting chain stores. A good way to get your bearings is to park your car in one of the many free public lots and stroll around town. Stop in at the visitor center at 2nd Street and Copenhagen Drive for maps and helpful advice on what to see and do. Don't forget to stock up on Danish pastries from the town's excellent bakeries before you leave.

GETTING HERE AND AROUND

Highway 246 West (Mission Drive) traverses the town—access the road from U.S. 101 and Buellton from the west, and Highway 154 from the east. Alamo Pintado Road connects Solvang with Ballard and Los Olivos to the north. Santa Ynez Valley Transit shuttle buses run between Solvang and other nearby towns.

ESSENTIALS

Visitor Information Solvang Conference & Visitors Bureau ⊠ *1639 Copenhagen Dr.* ☎ *805/688–6144, 800/468–6765* ⊕ *www.solvangusa.com.*

EXPLORING

Alma Rosa Winery. Just outside Solvang is the Alma Rosa Winery. Owners Richard and Thekla Sanford helped put Santa Barbara County on the international wine map with a 1989 Pinot Noir. Recently the Sanfords started a new winery, Alma Rosa, with wines made from grapes grown on their 100-plus-acre certified organic vineyards in the Santa Rita Hills. You can taste the current releases at one of the most environmentally sensitive tasting rooms and picnic areas in the valley. All their vineyards are certified organic, and the Pinot Noirs and Chardonnays are exceptional. ⊠ *7250 Santa Rosa Rd.* ☎ *805/688–9090* ⊕ *www. almarosawinery.com.*

Mission Santa Inés. Often called the Hidden Gem of the missions, Mission Santa Inés has an impressive collection of paintings, statuary, vestments, and Chumash and Spanish artifacts in a serene bluff-top setting. Take a self-guided tour through the museum, sanctuary, and tranquil gardens. ⊠ *1760 Mission Dr.* ☎ *805/688–4815* ⊕ *www.missionsantaines. org* ⊠ *$5* ⊙ *Daily 9–4:30.*

Rideau Vineyard. Housed in an 1884 adobe, the Rideau Vineyard tasting room provides simultaneous blasts from the area's ranching past and from its hand-harvested, Rhône-varietal wine-making present. ⊠ *1562 Alamo Pintado Rd.* ☎ *805/688–0717* ⊕ *www.rideauvineyard.com.*

WHERE TO EAT AND STAY

$$$ ✕ **The Hitching Post II.** You'll find everything from grilled artichokes to
AMERICAN ostrich at this casual eatery just outside of Solvang, but most people come for what is said to be the best Santa Maria–style barbecue in the state. The oak used in the barbecue imparts a wonderful smoky taste. Be sure to try a glass of owner-chef-winemaker Frank Ostini's signature Highliner Pinot Noir, a star in the 2004 film *Sideways.* ⊠ *406 E. Hwy. 246* ☎ *805/688–0676* ⊕ *www.hitchingpost2.com* ⊙ *No lunch.*

$$$ ✕ **Root 246.** The name of this chic outpost at Hotel Corque is a play
AMERICAN on the main route through the Santa Ynez Valley (Highway 246). Chef
★ Bradley Ogden and his team tap local purveyors and shop for organic foods at farmers' markets before deciding on the day's menu. Depending

on the season, you might feast on local squid with sweet baby prawns, prime rib eye steak grilled over an oak fire and served with root vegetable gratin, or rhubarb and polenta upside-down cake. The attentive wait staff can recommend pairings from the restaurant's 1,800-bottle selection of regional wines. The gorgeous design incorporates wood, stone, tempered glass, and leather elements in several distinct areas, including a slick 47-seat dining room (but jeans and casual wine-touring attire are welcome), a more casual bar with sofas and chairs, and a hip lounge. ⌧ *420 Alisal Rd.* ☎ *805/686–8681* ⊕ *www.root-246.com* ☯ *No lunch. Closed Mondays and Tuesdays.*

$$$$ 🏨 **Alisal Guest Ranch and Resort.** Since 1946 this 10,000-acre ranch has been
★ popular with celebrities and plain folk alike. **Pros:** Old West atmosphere; tons of activities; ultraprivate. **Cons:** isolated; cut off from the high-tech world; some units are aging. ⌧ *1054 Alisal Rd.* ☎ *805/688–6411, 800/425–4725* ⊕ *www.alisal.com* 🛏 *36 rooms, 37 suites* ⌂ *In-room: no a/c, no TV, Wi-Fi. In-hotel: restaurant, bar, golf course, pool, tennis court, gym, spa, children's programs, business center* ⑪ *Some meals.*

$$$ 🏨 **Hotel Corque.** Sleek, stunning Hotel Corque—the largest hotel in the
★ Santa Ynez Valley—provides a full slate of upscale amenities on the edge of town. **Pros:** all front desk staff are trained concierges; short walk to shops, tasting rooms and restaurants; smoke-free property. **Cons:** no kitchenettes or laundry facilities; not low-budget. ⌧ *400 Alisal Rd.* ☎ *805/688–8000, 800/624–5572* ⊕ *www.hotelcorque.com* 🛏 *122 rooms, 10 suites* ⌂ *In-room: a/c, Wi-Fi. In-hotel: restaurant, bar, pool, business center.*

$$ 🏨 **Solvang Gardens Inn.** Lush gardens with fountains and waterfalls, friendly staff, and cheery English-country-theme rooms with antiques make for a peaceful retreat just a few blocks—but worlds away—from Solvang's main tourist area. **Pros:** homey; family-friendly; colorful gardens. **Cons:** some rooms are tiny; some need upgrades. ⌧ *293 Alisal Rd.* ☎ *805/688–4404, 888/688–4404* ⊕ *www.solvanggardens.com* 🛏 *16 rooms, 8 suites* ⌂ *In-room: a/c, kitchen, Wi-Fi. In-hotel: spa, business center* ⑪ *Breakfast.*

LOMPOC

20 mi west of Solvang on Hwy. 246.

Known as the flower-seed capital of the world, Lompoc is blanketed with vast fields of brightly colored flowers that bloom from May through August.

GETTING HERE AND AROUND

Driving is the easiest way to get to Lompoc. From Santa Barbara, follow U.S. 101 north to Highway 1 exit off Gaviota Pass, or Highway 246 west at Buellton. The City of Lompoc Transit (COLT) buses travel throughout the city and surrounding neighborhoods; COLT's Wine Country Express buses run between Lompoc, Buellton, and Solvang weekdays. COLT also provides limited service to and from downtown Santa Barbara.

EXPLORING

Lompoc Valley Flower Festival. For five days around the last weekend of June, the Lompoc Valley Flower Festival brings a parade, carnival, and crafts show to town. ☎ *805/735–8511* ⊕ *www.flowerfestival.org.*

☺ **La Purisima Mission State Historic Park.** At La Purisima Mission State Historic Park you can see Mission La Purisima Concepción, the most fully restored mission in the state. Founded in 1787, it stands in a stark and still remote location and powerfully evokes the lives of California's Spanish settlers. Docents lead tours every afternoon, and displays illustrate the secular and religious activities that were part of mission life. From March through October the mission holds special events, including crafts demonstrations by costumed docents. ✉ *2295 Purisima Rd., off Hwy. 246* ☎ *805/733–3713* ⊕ *www.lapurisimamission.org* ☞ *$6 per vehicle* ☉ *Daily 9–5; tour daily at 1.*

SAN LUIS OBISPO COUNTY

San Luis Obispo County's pristine landscapes and abundant wildlife areas, especially those around Morro Bay and Montaña de Oro State Park, have long attracted nature lovers. In the south, Pismo Beach and other coastal towns have great sand and surf; inland, a booming wine region stretches from the Edna and Arroyo Grande valleys in the south to Paso Robles in the north. With historical attractions, a photogenic downtown, and busy shops and restaurants, the college town of San Luis Obispo is at the heart of the county.

ESSENTIALS

Visitor Information San Luis Obispo County Visitors and Conference Bureau ✉ *811 El Capitan Way, Suite 200, San Luis Obispo* ☎ *805/541–8000* ⊕ *www.sanluisobispocounty.com.*

PISMO BEACH

U.S. 101/Hwy. 1, about 40 mi north of Lompoc.

About 20 mi of sandy shoreline—nicknamed the Bakersfield Riviera for the throngs of vacationers who come here from the Central Valley—begins at the town of Pismo Beach. The southern end of town runs along sand dunes, some of which are open to cars and off-road vehicles; sheltered by the dunes, a grove of eucalyptus trees attracts thousands of migrating monarch butterflies November through February. A long, broad beach fronts the center of town, where a municipal pier extends into the sea at the foot of shop-lined Pomeroy Street. To the north, hotels and homes perch atop chalky oceanfront cliffs.

Fewer than 10,000 people live in this quintessential surfer haven, but Pismo Beach has a slew of hotels and restaurants with great views of the Pacific Ocean. Still, rooms can sometimes be hard to come by. Each Father's Day weekend the Pismo Beach Classic, one of the West Coast's largest classic-car and street-rod shows, overruns the town. A Dixieland jazz festival in February also draws crowds.

GETTING HERE AND AROUND

Pismo Beach straddles both sides of U.S. 101. If you're traveling from Santa Barbara and have time for a scenic drive, exit the 101 in Santa Maria and take Highway 166 8 mi west to Guadalupe and follow Highway 1 north 16 mi to Pismo Beach. South County Area Transit (SCAT) buses run throughout the city and connect with nearby towns and the city of San Luis Obispo. In summer, the free Avila Trolley extends service to Pismo Beach.

> ## VOLCANOES?
>
> Those funny looking, sawed-off peaks along the drive from Pismo Beach to Morro Bay are the Seven Sisters—a series of ancient volcanic plugs. Morro Rock, the northern-most sibling and a state historic monument, is the most famous and photographed of the clan.

EN ROUTE

Guadalupe-Nipomo Dunes Preserve. The spectacular Guadalupe-Nipomo Dunes Preserve stretches 18 mi along the coast south of Pismo Beach. It's the largest and most ecologically diverse dune system in the state, and a habitat for more than 200 species of birds as well as sea otters, black bears, bobcats, coyotes, and deer. The 1,500-foot Mussel Rock is the highest beach dune in the western states. As many as 20 movies have been filmed here, including Cecil B. DeMille's 1923 silent *The Ten Commandments*. The main entrances to the dunes are at Oso Flaco Lake (about 13 mi south of Pismo Beach on U.S. 101/Highway 1, then 3 mi west on Oso Flaco Road) and at the far west end of Highway 166 (Main Street) in Guadalupe. Parking at Oso Flaco Lake is $5 per vehicle.

Dunes Center. At the Dunes Center, you can get nature information and view an exhibit about *The Ten Commandments* movie set, which weather and archaeologists are slowly unearthing near Guadalupe Beach. ⊠ *1055 Guadalupe St., 1 mi north of Hwy. 166* ☎ *805/343–2455* ⊕ *www.dunescenter.org* ⊗ *April-September Wed.–Sun. 10–4, Oct.-March Thurs.-Sun. 10–4.*

WHERE TO EAT

$$
SEAFOOD
✕ **Cracked Crab.** This traditional New England–style crab shack imports fresh seafood daily from Australia, Alaska, and the East Coast. Fish is line-caught, much of the produce is organic, and everything is made from scratch. For a real treat, don a bib and chow through a bucket of steamed shellfish with Cajun sausage, potatoes, and corn on the cob, all dumped right onto your table. The menu changes daily. ⊠ *751 Price St.* ☎ *805/773–2722* ⊕ *www.crackedcrab.com* ⌲ *Reservations not accepted.*

$$
ITALIAN
✕ **Giuseppe's Cucina Italiana.** The classic flavors of southern Italy are highlighted at this lively, warm downtown spot. Most recipes originate from Bari, a seaport on the Adriatic; the menu includes breads and pizzas baked in the wood-burning oven, hearty dishes such as osso buco and lamb, and homemade pastas. The wait for a table can be long at peak dinner hours, but sometimes an accordion player gets the crowd singing. Next door, their bakery sells take-out selections. ⊠ *891 Price St.* ☎ *805/773–2870* ⊕ *www.giuseppesrestaurant.com* ⌲ *Reservations not accepted* ⊗ *No lunch weekends.*

5

San Luis Obispo
County and Big Sur

PACIFIC OCEAN

0   15 mi
0   15 km

¢   ✕ **Splash Café.** Folks line up all the way down the block for clam chow-
SEAFOOD   der served in a sourdough bread bowl at this wildly popular seafood
stand. You can also order beach food such as fresh steamed clams,
burgers, and fried calamari at the counter (no table service)—and many
items on the menu are $8 or less. The grimy, cramped, but cheery
hole-in-a-wall, a favorite with locals and savvy visitors, is open daily
for lunch and dinner (plus a rock-bottom basic breakfast starting at 8
am), but closes early on weekday evenings during low season. ⊠ *197
Pomeroy St.* ☏ *805/773–4653* ⊕ *www.splashcafe.com.*

WHERE TO STAY
For expanded hotel reviews, visit Fodors.com.

$$$ ⊡ **The Cliffs Resort.** Perched dramatically on an oceanfront cliff, this full-
service resort is surrounded by lawns and palm trees; the pool, with a
cascading fountain, overlooks the sea. ⊠ *2757 Shell Beach Rd., Pismo
Beach* ☏ *805/773–5000, 800/342–4295* ⊕ *www.cliffsresort.com* ⤺ *160
rooms* ⌂ *In-room: a/c, safe, Wi-Fi. In-hotel: restaurant, bar, pool, spa,
beach, parking, some pets allowed.*

$$$$ ⊡ **Dolphin Bay.** Perched on grass-covered bluffs overlooking Shell Beach,
this luxury resort looks and feels like an exclusive community of villas.
Pros: lavish apartment units; as upscale as you can get; killer views;
walking distance from the beach. **Cons:** hefty price tag; upper-crust vibe.

✉ *2727 Shell Beach Rd.* ☎ *805/773–4300, 800/516–0112 reservations, 805/773–8900 restaurant* ⊕ *www.thedolphinbay.com* 🛏 *62 suites* ♿ *In-room: no a/c, kitchen, Internet, Wi-Fi. In-hotel: restaurant, bar, pool, gym, spa, beach, children's programs, laundry facilities, business center, parking, some pets allowed.*

$$$$ ⚞ **Pismo Lighthouse Suites.** Each of the well-appointed two-room, two-bath suites at this oceanfront resort has a private balcony or patio. **Pros:** lots of space for families and groups; nice pool area. **Cons:** not easy to walk to main attractions; some units are next to busy road. ✉ *2411 Price St.* ☎ *805/773–2411, 800/245–2411* ⊕ *www.pismolighthousesuites. com* 🛏 *70 suites* ♿ *In-room: no a/c, Internet, Wi-Fi. In-hotel: pool, gym, spa, laundry facilities* ⏍ *Breakfast.*

$$$ ⚞ **Sea Venture Resort.** The bright, homey rooms at this hotel all have fireplaces and featherbeds; most have balconies with private hot tubs, and some have beautiful ocean views. **Pros:** on the beach; excellent food; romantic rooms. **Cons:** touristy area; some rooms and facilities are beginning to age; dark hallways. ✉ *100 Ocean View Ave.* ☎ *805/773–4994, 800/760–0664* ⊕ *www.seaventure.com* 🛏 *50 rooms* ♿ *In-room: no a/c, Internet, Wi-Fi. In-hotel: restaurant, spa, beach, business center, parking* ⏍ *Breakfast.*

$ ⚞ **Shell Beach Inn.** Just 2½ blocks from the beach, this basic but cozy motor court is a great bargain for the area. **Pros:** walking distance from the beach; clean rooms; friendly and dependable service. **Cons:** sits on a busy road; small rooms; tiny pool. ✉ *653 Shell Beach Rd.* ☎ *805/773–4373, 800/549–4727* ⊕ *www.shellbeachinn.com* 🛏 *10 rooms* ♿ *In-room: no a/c, Wi-Fi. In-hotel: pool, some pets allowed.*

AVILA BEACH

🕐 *4 mi north of Pismo Beach on U.S. 101/Hwy. 1.*

Because the village of Avila Beach and the sandy, cove-front shoreline for which it's named face south into the Pacific Ocean, they get more sun and less fog than any other stretch of coast in the area. It can be bright and warm here while just beyond the surrounding hills communities shiver under the marine layer. With its fortuitous climate and protected waters, Avila's public beach draws plenty of sunbathers and families; weekends are very busy. Demolished in 1998 to clean up extensive oil seepage from a Unocal tank farm, downtown Avila Beach has sprung back to life. The seaside promenade has been fully restored and shops and hotels have quickly popped up; with mixed results the town has tried to re-create its former offbeat character. For real local color, head to the far end of the cove and watch the commercial fishing boats offload their catch on the old Port San Luis wharf. A few seafood shacks and fish markets do business on the pier while sea lions congregate below. On Fridays from mid-April through mid-September, a fish and farmers' market livens up the beach area with music, fresh local produce and seafood, and children's activities.

GETTING HERE AND AROUND

Exit U.S. 101 at Avila Beach Drive and head 3 mi west to reach the beach. The free Avila Shuttle operates weekends year-round, plus Friday afternoon/evenings from April to September. The minibuses connect Avila Beach and Port San Luis to Shell Beach, with multiple stops along the way. Service extends to Pismo Beach in summer.

WHERE TO EAT AND STAY

$$$$ **Avila La Fonda.** Modeled after a village in early California's Mexican period, Avila La Fonda surrounds guests with rich jewel tones, fountains, and upscale comfort. **Pros:** one-of-a-kind theme and artwork; flexible room combinations; a block from the beach. **Cons:** pricey; most rooms don't have an ocean view. ⊠ *101 San Miguel St.* ☎ *805/595–1700* ⊕ *www.avilalafondahotel.com* ⏎ *28 rooms, 1 suite* ⟁ *In-room: a/c, kitchen, Internet, Wi-Fi. In-hotel: laundry facilities, business center, some pets allowed.*

$$ **Sycamore Mineral Springs Resort.** This wellness resort's hot mineral springs bubble up into private outdoor tubs on an oak-and-sycamore-forest hillside. **Pros:** great place to rejuvenate; nice hiking; incredible spa services. **Cons:** rooms vary in quality; 2½ mi from the beach. ⊠ *1215 Avila Beach Dr., San Luis Obispo* ☎ *805/595–7302, 800/234–5831* ⊕ *www.sycamoresprings. com* ⏎ *26 rooms, 50 suites* ⟁ *In-room: a/c, kitchen, Internet, Wi-Fi. In-hotel: restaurant, bar, pool, spa, business center, parking.*

SAN LUIS OBISPO

8 mi north of Avila Beach on U.S. 101/Hwy. 1.

About halfway between San Francisco and Los Angeles, San Luis Obispo—nicknamed SLO—spreads out below gentle hills and rocky extinct volcanoes. Its main appeal lies in its architecturally diverse and commercially lively downtown, especially several blocks of Higuera Street. The pedestrian-friendly district bustles with shoppers, restaurant goers, and students from California Polytechnic State University, known as Cal Poly. On Thursday from 6 pm to 9 pm a farmers' market fills Higuera Street with local produce, entertainment, and food stalls. SLO is less a vacation destination than a pleasant stopover along Highway 1; it's a nice place to stay while touring the Wine Country south of town.

GETTING HERE AND AROUND

U.S. 101/Highway 1 traverses the city for several miles. From the north, Highway 1 jogs inland from the coast and merges with the interstate when it reaches the city of San Luis Obispo. SLO City Transit buses operate daily; Regional Transit Authority (SLORTA) buses connect with towns throughout the north county. The Downtown Trolley lumbers through the city's hub on Thursdays, Fridays, and Saturdays.

ESSENTIALS

Visitor Information San Luis Obispo Chamber of Commerce ⊠ *1039 Chorro St.* ☎ *805/781–2777* ⊕ *www.visitslo.com.* **San Luis Obispo Vintners Association** ☎ *805/541–5868* ⊕ *www.slowine.com.***San Luis Obispo City Visitor Information.** Visit the City of San Luis Obispo's Web site for details on nearly 40 lodging options, a current events calendar, and other visitor information. ⊠ *San Luis Obispo* ⊕ *www.sanluisobispovacations.com.*

DID YOU KNOW?

You can unwind in a private tub fed by hot mineral springs at Avila Beach's Sycamore Mineral Springs Resort.

EXPLORING

★ **Mission San Luis Obispo de Tolosa.** Special events often take place on sun-dappled Mission Plaza in front of Mission San Luis Obispo de Tolosa, established in 1772. Its small museum exhibits artifacts of the Chumash Indians and early Spanish settlers, and docents sometimes lead tours of the church and grounds. ⊠ *751 Palm St.* ☎ *805/543–6850* ⊕ *www. missionsanluisobispo.org* ✑ *$3 suggested donation* ☉ *Apr.–late-Oct., daily 9–5; late Oct.–Mar., daily 9–4.*

☝ **San Luis Obispo Children's Museum.** The delightful San Luis Obispo Children's Museum has 21 indoor and outdoor activities that present a kid-friendly version of the city of San Luis Obispo. Visitors enter through an "imagination-powered" elevator, which transports them to a series of underground caverns beneath the city, while simulated lava and steam sputters from an active volcano. Kids can pick rubber fruit at a farmers' market, clamber up a clockworks tower, race to fight a fire on a fire engine, and learn about solar energy from a 15-foot sunflower. The museum attracts mostly kids under eight; older children may become bored quickly. ⊠ *1010 Nipomo St.* ☎ *805/545–5874* ⊕ *www.slocm.org* ✑ *$8* ☉ *Apr.–Sept., Tues.–Fri. 10–4, Sat. 10–5, Sun. and select Mon. holidays 11–5; Oct.–Mar., Tues.–Fri. 10–3, Sat. 10–5, Sun. and select Mon. holidays 1–5.*

☝ **History Center of San Luis Obispo County.** Across the street from the old Spanish mission, the History Center of San Luis Obispo County presents rotating exhibits on various aspects of county history—such as Native American life, California ranchos, and the impact of railroads. A separate children's room has theme activities where kids can earn prizes. Visit the center's Web site to download a self-guided historic walking tour of downtown San Luis Obispo. ⊠ *696 Monterey St.* ☎ *805/543–0638* ⊕ *historycenterslo.org* ✑ *Free* ☉ *Wed.–Sun. 10–4.*

Edna Valley/Arroyo Grande Valley Wine Country. San Luis Obispo is the commercial center of Edna Valley/Arroyo Grande Valley Wine Country, whose appellations stretch east–west from San Luis Obispo toward the coast and toward Lake Lopez in the inland mountains. Many of the 20 or so wineries line Highway 227 and connecting roads. The region is best known for Chardonnay and Pinot Noir, although many wineries experiment with other varietals and blends. Wine-touring maps are readily available around town; note that many wineries charge a small tasting fee and most tasting rooms close at 5.

Edna Valley Vineyard. For sweeping views of the Edna Valley while you sample estate-grown Chardonnay, go to the modern tasting bar at Edna Valley Vineyard. ⊠ *2585 Biddle Ranch Rd.* ☎ *805/544–5855* ⊕ *www. ednavalleyvineyard.com.*

Baileyana Winery. A refurbished 1909 schoolhouse serves as tasting room for Baileyana Winery, which produces concentrated Chardonnays, Pinot Noirs, and Syrahs. Its sister winery, Tangent, creates alternative white wines and shares the tasting room. ⊠ *5828 Orcutt Rd.* ☎ *805/269–8200* ⊕ *www.baileyana.com.*

Claiborne & Churchill. An eco-friendly winery built from straw bales, Claiborne & Churchill makes small lots of exceptional Alsatian-style wines such as dry Riesling and Gewürztraminer, plus Pinot Noir and Chardonnay. ✉ *2649 Carpenter Canyon Rd.* ☎ *805/544–4066* ⊕ *www.claibornechurchill.com.*

Old Edna. While touring Edna Valley Wine Country, be sure to stop at Old Edna, a peaceful, 2-acre site that once was the town of Edna. Browse for local art, taste wines, pick up sandwiches at the gourmet deli, and stroll along Old Edna Lane. ✉ *Hwy. 227, at Price Canyon Rd.* ☎ *805/544–8062* ⊕ *www. oldedna.com.*

DEEP ROOTS

Way back in the 1700s, the Spanish padres who accompanied Father Junípero Serra planted grapevines from Mexico along California's Central Coast, and began using European wine-making techniques to turn the grapes into delectable vintages.

WHERE TO EAT

$$ ✕ **Big Sky Café.** A popular gathering spot three meals a day, this quintessentially Californian, family-friendly (and sometimes noisy) café turns local and organically grown ingredients into global dishes. Brazilian churasco chicken breast, Thai catfish, New Mexican *pozole* (hominy stew): just pick your continent. Vegetarians have lots to choose from. ✉ *1121 Broad St.* ☎ *805/545–5401* ⊕ *www.bigskycafe.com* ⚐ *Reservations not accepted.*

$$ ✕ **Buona Tavola.** Homemade pasta with river shrimp in a creamy tomato
ITALIAN sauce and porcini-mushroom risotto are among the northern Italian
★ dishes served at this casual spot. Daily fresh fish and salad specials and an impressive wine list attract a steady stream of regulars. In good weather you can dine on the flower-filled patio. The Paso Robles branch is equally enjoyable. ✉ *1037 Monterey St.* ☎ *805/545–8000* ⊕ *www. btslo.com* ⊗ *No lunch weekends.*

¢ ✕ **Mo's Smokehouse BBQ.** Barbecue joints abound on the Central Coast,
SOUTHERN but this one excels. A variety of Southern-style sauces seasons tender hickory-smoked ribs and shredded meat sandwiches; sides such as baked beans, coleslaw, homemade potato chips, and garlic bread extend the pleasure. ✉ *1005 Monterey St.* ☎ *805/544–6193* ⊕ *www. smokinmosbbq.com.*

$ ✕ **Novo Restaurant & Lounge.** In the colorful dining room or on the large creek-side deck, this animated downtown eatery will take you on a culinary world tour. The salads, small plates, and entrées come from nearly every continent. The wine and beer list also covers the globe (you can sample various international wines paired with tapas Sunday evenings)— and includes local favorites. Many of the decadent desserts are baked at the restaurant's sister property in Cambria, the French Corner Bakery. ✉ *726 Higuera St.* ☎ *805/543–3986* ⊕ *www.novorestaurant.com.*

WHERE TO STAY

For expanded hotel reviews, visit Fodors.com.

$$$ ⛄ **Apple Farm.** Decorated to the hilt with floral bedspreads and watercolors by local artists, this Victorian country-style hotel is one of the most popular places to stay in San Luis Obispo. **Pros:** flowers everywhere; convenient to Cal Poly and Highway 101; creek-side setting. **Cons:** hordes

of tourists stop here during the day; too floral for some people's tastes. ✉ *2015 Monterey St.* ☎ *800/255–2040* ⊕ *www.applefarm.com* ⇆ *104 rooms* ☐ *In-room: a/c, Internet, Wi-Fi. In-hotel: restaurant, pool, spa.*

$$ ⛉ **Garden Street Inn.** From this fully restored 1887 Italianate Queen Anne, the only lodging in downtown SLO, you can walk to many restaurants and attractions. **Pros:** classic B&B; walking distance from everywhere downtown; nice wine-and-cheese reception. **Cons:** city noise filters through some rooms; not a great place for families. ✉ *1212 Garden St.* ☎ *805/545–9802, 800/488–2045* ⊕ *www.gardenstreetinn.com* ⇆ *9 rooms, 4 suites* ☐ *In-room: no a/c, no TV, Wi-Fi* |◎| *Breakfast.*

$$$ ⛉ **Madonna Inn.** From its rococo bathrooms to its pink-on-pink frou-frou steak house, the Madonna Inn is fabulous or tacky, depending on your taste. **Pros:** fun one-of-a-kind experience. **Cons:** rooms vary widely; must appreciate kitsch. ✉ *100 Madonna Rd.* ☎ *805/543–3000, 800/543–9666* ⊕ *www.madonnainn.com* ⇆ *106 rooms, 4 suites* ☐ *In-hotel: restaurant, bar, pool, gym, spa.*

$$ ⛉ **Petit Soleil.** A cobblestone courtyard, country-French custom furnishings, and Gallic music piped through the halls evoke a Provençal mood at this cheery inn on upper Monterey Street's motel row. **Pros:** French details throughout; scrumptious breakfasts; cozy rooms. **Cons:** sits on a busy avenue; cramped parking. ✉ *1473 Monterey St.* ☎ *805/549–0321, 800/676–1588* ⊕ *www.psslo.com* ⇆ *15 rooms, 1 suite* ☐ *In-room: no a/c, Internet, Wi-Fi* |◎| *Breakfast.*

NIGHTLIFE AND THE ARTS

NIGHTLIFE

The club scene in this college town is centered on Higuera Street off Monterey Street.

Frog and Peach. The Frog and Peach is a decent spot to nurse an English beer and listen to live music. ✉ *728 Higuera St.* ☎ *805/595–3764.*

Koberl at Blue. A trendy urban crowd hangs out at the slick bar at Koberl at Blue, an upscale Wine Country restaurant with late-night dining, exotic martinis, and a huge list of local and imported beer and wine. ✉ *998 Monterey St.* ☎ *805/783–1135.*

Linnaea's Cafe. Linnaea's Cafe, a mellow java joint, sometimes holds poetry readings, as well as blues, jazz, and folk music performances. ✉ *1110 Garden St.* ☎ *805/541–5888.*

MoTav. Chicago-style MoTav draws crowds with good pub food and live entertainment in a turn-of-the-20th-century setting (complete with antique U.S. flags and a wall-mounted moose head). ✉ *725 Higuera St.* ☎ *805/541–8733.*

THE ARTS

Performing Arts Center. The Performing Arts Center at Cal Poly hosts live theater, dance, and music performances by artists from around the world. ✉ *1 Grand Ave.* ☎ *805/756–7222, 805/756–2787 box office, 888/233–2787 toll-free* ⊕ *www.pacslo.org.*

Festival Mozaic. Festival Mozaic celebrates five centuries of classical music and takes place in late July and early August. ☎ *805/781–3008* ⊕ *www. festivalmozaic.com.*

San Luis Obispo Museum of Art. San Luis Obispo Museum of Art displays and sells a mix of traditional work and cutting-edge arts and crafts by Central Coast, national, and international artists. The museum's permanent collection conserves an artistic legacy on the Central Coast. ✉ *1010 Broad St., at Mission Plaza* ☎ *805/543–8562* ⊕ *www.sloma. org* ⊙ *Open 11–4. Closed Tues. early Sept.–late June.*

SPORTS AND THE OUTDOORS

Parks and Recreation Department. Hilly greenbelts with vast amounts of open space and extensive hiking trails surround the city of San Luis Obispo. For information on trailheads, call the city Parks and Recreation Department or visit its Web site to download a trail map. ☎ *805/781–7300* ⊕ *www.slocity.org/parksandrecreation.*

EN
ROUTE

5

Montaña de Oro State Park. Instead of continuing north on Highway 1 from San Luis Obispo to Morro Bay, consider taking Los Osos Valley Road (off Madonna Road, south of downtown) past farms and ranches to dramatic Montaña de Oro State Park. The park has miles of nature trails along rocky shoreline, wild beaches, and hills overlooking some of California's most spectacular scenery. Check out the tide pools, watch the waves roll into the bluffs, and picnic in the eucalyptus groves. ✉ *7 mi south of Los Osos on Pecho Rd.* ☎ *805/528–0513, 805/772–7434* ⊕ *www.parks.ca.gov.*

MORRO BAY

14 mi north of San Luis Obispo on Hwy. 1.

Commercial fishermen slog around Morro Bay in galoshes, and beat-up fishing boats bob in the bay's protected waters.

GETTING HERE AND AROUND

From U.S. 101 south or north, exit at Highway 1 in San Luis Obispo and head west. Scenic Highway 1 passes through the eastern edge of town. From Atascadero, two-lane Highway 41 West treks over the mountains to east Morro Bay. RTA Route 12 buses operate year-round between Morro Bay, San Luis Obispo, Cayucos, Cambria, San Simeon, Hearst Castle. The Morro Bay Shuttle picks up riders throughout the town Friday–Monday in summer ($1.25).

ESSENTIALS

Visitor Information Morro Bay Visitors Center. Stop at the Morro Bay Visitors Center and Chamber of Commerce to pick up maps and get information from friendly staffers. ✉ 845 Embarcadero Rd., Morro Bay ☎ 805/772–4467, 800/231–0592 ⊕ www.morrobay.org ⊙ Weekdays 9-5, Sat. 10-4, Sun. 10-2.

EXPLORING

Morro Rock. At the mouth of Morro Bay, which is both a state and national estuary, stands 576-foot-high Morro Rock, one of nine such small volcanic peaks, or morros, in the area. A short walk leads to a breakwater, with the harbor on one side and the crashing waves of the Pacific on the other. You may not climb the rock, where endangered falcons and other birds nest. Sea lions and otters often play in the water at the foot of the peak. ✉ *Northern end of Embarcadero.*

Embarcadero. The center of the action on land is the Embarcadero, where vacationers pour in and out of souvenir shops and seafood restaurants and stroll or bike along the scenic half-mile Harborwalk to Morro Rock. From here, you can get out on the bay in a kayak or tour boat. ⊠ *On waterfront from Beach St. to Tidelands Park.*

☾ **Morro Bay State Park Museum of Natural History.** South of downtown ★ Morro Bay, interactive exhibits at the spiffy Morro Bay State Park Museum of Natural History teach kids and adults about the natural environment and how to preserve it—both in the Morro Bay estuary and on the rest of the planet. ⊠ *State Park Rd.* ☎ *805/772–2694* ⊕ *www.ccnha.org* ⊠ *$3* ☉ *Daily 10–5.*

WHERE TO EAT

$ ✕ **Taco Temple.** The devout stand in line at this family-run diner that
SOUTHWESTERN serves some of the freshest food around. Seafood anchors a menu of
★ dishes—salmon burritos, superb fish tacos with mango salsa—hailing from somewhere between California and Mexico. Desserts get rave reviews, too. Make an effort to find this gem tucked away in the corner of a supermarket parking lot north of downtown—it's on the frontage road parallel to Highway 1, just north of the Highway 41 junction. ⊠ *2680 Main St., at Elena* ☎ *805/772–4965* ⌿ *Reservations not accepted* ☐ *No credit cards* ☉ *Closed Tues.*

$$$ ✕ **Windows on the Water.** From giant picture windows at this second-
SEAFOOD floor spot, watch the sun set over the water. Fresh fish and other dishes based on local ingredients emerge from the wood-fired oven in the open kitchen; a variety of oysters on the half shell beckon from the raw bar. About 20 of the wines on the extensive, mostly California list are poured by the glass. ⊠ *699 Embarcadero* ☎ *805/772–0677* ⊕ *www. windowsmb.com* ☉ *No lunch.*

WHERE TO STAY

For expanded hotel reviews, visit Fodors.com.

$$$ ⊡ **Anderson Inn.** The innkeepers' friendly personal service and an oceanfront setting lure a steady stream of loyal patrons to this new inn on the Embarcadero, built from scratch in 2009. **Pros:** walk to restaurants and sights; well-appointed rooms; attentive service. **Cons:** waterfront area gets crowded on weekends and in summer; not low-budget. ⊠ *897 Embarcadero, Morro Bay* ☎ *805/772–3434* ⊕ *www. andersoninnmorrobay.com* ⇆ *8 rooms* ⌂ *In-room: a/c, safe, Wi-Fi.*

$$$ ⊡ **Cass House.** The original 1867 home of shipping pioneer Captain James Cass is now a luxurious B&B boasting colorful rose gardens in the heart of Cayucos, a tiny oceanfront enclave about 4 miles north of Morro Bay just west of Highway 1. **Pros:** historic property; some ocean views; excellent meals. **Cons:** not near Morro Bay nightlife or tourist attractions; not designed for families. ⊠ *222 N. Ocean Ave., Cayucos* ☎ *805/995–3669* ⊕ *www.casshouseinn.com* ⇆ *5 rooms* ⌂ *In-room: no a/c, Wi-Fi. In-hotel: restaurant* ⦿ *Breakfast.*

SPORTS AND THE OUTDOORS

Kayak Horizons. Kayak Horizons rents kayaks and gives lessons and guided tours. ⊠ *551 Embarcadero* ☎ *805/772–6444* ⊕ *www. kayakhorizons.com.*

Lost Isle Adventures. Captain Alan Rackov's Tiki-Boat cruises into the bay and out to Morro Rock every hour starting at 11 am daily. ⊠ *At Giovanni's Fish Market on the Embarcadero, 1001 Front St., Morro Bay* ☎ *805/440–8170* ⊕ *lostisleadventures.com.*

Sub-Sea Tours. Sub-Sea Tours operates glass-bottom boat and catamaran cruises, and has kayak and canoe rentals and summer whale-watching cruises. ⊠ *699 Embarcadero* ☎ *805/772–9463* ⊕ *subseatours.com.*

Virg's Landing. Virg's Landing conducts deep-sea fishing and whale-watching trips. ⊠ *1215 Embarcadero* ☎ *805/772–1222* ⊕ *www.virgs.com.*

PASO ROBLES

30 mi north of San Luis Obispo on U.S. 101; 25 mi northwest of Morro Bay via Hwy. 41 and U.S. 101.

In the 1860s tourists began flocking to this dusty ranching outpost to "take the cure" in a luxurious bathhouse fed by underground mineral hot springs. An Old West town, complete with opera house, emerged; grand Victorian homes went up, followed in the 20th century by Craftsman bungalows. A 2003 earthquake demolished or weakened several beloved downtown buildings, but historically faithful reconstruction has proceeded rapidly.

Today the wine industry booms and mile upon mile of vineyards envelop Paso Robles; golfers play the four local courses and spandex-clad bicyclists race along the winding back roads. A mix of down-home and upmarket restaurants, bars, antiques stores, and little shops fills the streets around oak-shaded City Park, where special events of all kinds—custom car shows, an olive festival, Friday night summer concerts—take place on many weekends. Still, Paso (as the locals call it) more or less remains cowboy country: each year in late July and early August, the city throws the two-week California Mid-State Fair, complete with livestock auctions, carnival rides, and corn dogs.

GETTING HERE AND AROUND

U.S. 101 runs through the city of Paso Robles. Highway 46 West links Paso Robles to Highway 1/Cambria on the coast. Highway 46 East connects Paso Robles with Highway 5 and the San Joaquin Valley. The Paso Express public transit system extends throughout the city.

ESSENTIALS

Visitor Information Paso Robles Wine Country Alliance ⊠ *744 Oak St.* ☎ *805/239–8463* ⊕ *www.pasowine.com.* **Paso Robles Chamber of Commerce** ⊠ *1225 Park St.* ☎ *888/988–7276* ⊕ *www.travelpaso.com.*

EXPLORING

Harris Stage Lines. Former pro rodeo riders and horse trainers Tom and Debby Harris offer stagecoach rides (learn to hitch the team of horses beforehand), riding/driving lessons, and an array of Old West-themed events at their Old West ranch on the north side of town. ⊠ *5995 North River Rd., Paso Robles* ☎ *805/237–1860* ⊕ *www.harrisstagelines.com.*

Paso Robles Pioneer Museum. Take a look back at California's rural heritage at the Paso Robles Pioneer Museum. Displays of historical ranching paraphernalia, horse-drawn vehicles, hot springs artifacts, and photos evoke the town's old days; a one-room schoolhouse is part of the complex. ✉ *2010 Riverside Ave.* ☎ *805/239–4556* ⊕ *www. pasoroblespioneermuseum.org* 🎫 *Free* ⊙ *Thurs.–Sun. 1–4.*

River Oaks Hot Springs & Spa. The lakeside River Oaks Hot Springs & Spa, on 240 hilly acres near the intersection of U.S. 101 and Highway 46E, is a great place to relax before and after wine tasting or festival-going. Soak in a private indoor or outdoor hot tub fed by natural mineral springs, or indulge in a massage or facial. ✉ *800 Clubhouse Dr.* ☎ *805/238–4600* ⊕ *www.riveroakshotsprings.com* 🎫 *Hot tubs $13 to $24 per person per hr* ⊙ *Tues.–Sun. 9–9.*

Paso Robles Wine Country. In Paso Robles Wine Country, nearly 200 wineries and more than 26,000 vineyard acres pepper the wooded hills west of U.S. 101 and blanket the flatter, more open land on the east side. The region's brutally hot summer days and cool nights yield stellar grapes that make noteworthy wines, particularly robust reds such as Cabernet Sauvignon, Merlot, Zinfandel, and Rhône varietals such as Syrah. An abundance of exquisite whites also comes out of Paso, including Chardonnay and Rhône varietals such as Viognier. Small-town friendliness prevails at most wineries, especially smaller ones, which tend to treat visitors like neighbors. Pick up a regional wine-touring map at lodgings, wineries, and attractions around town. Most tasting rooms close at 5 pm; many charge a small fee.

Paso Robles Wine Festival. Most of the local wineries pour at the Paso Robles Wine Festival, held mid-May in City Park. The outdoor tasting—the largest such California event—includes live bands and diverse food vendors. Winery open houses and winemaker dinners round out the weekend. ✉ *Spring St., between 10th and 12th Sts., City Park* ☎ *805/239–8463, 800/549–9463* ⊕ *www.pasowine.com* 🎫 *$55 basic admission, designated driver/child $15.*

Paso Wine Centre. Choose among 48 local wines available for tasting via enomatic dispensers at Paso Wine Centre, a spacious, contemporary space with comfy sofas and handhewn oak tables just off the town square. More than 200 wines are available for purchase. ✉ *1240 Park St., Paso Robles* ☎ *805/239–9156* ⊕ *www.pasorobleswinecenter.com.*

Justin Vineyards & Winery. Small but swank Justin Vineyards & Winery makes Bordeaux-style blends at the western end of Paso Robles Wine Country. This reader favorite offers winery, vineyard, and barrel-tasting tours ($15 to $100). In the tasting room there's a deli bar; a tiny high-end restaurant is also part of the complex. ✉ *11680 Chimney Rock Rd.* ☎ *805/238–6932, 800/726–0049* ⊕ *www.justinwine.com.*

Tablas Creek Vineyard. Tucked in the far-west hills of Paso Robles, Tablas Creek Vineyard makes some of the area's finest wine by blending organically grown, hand-harvested Rhône varietals such as Syrah, Grenache, Roussanne, and Viognier. Tours include a chance to graft your own grapevine; call to reserve space. ✉ *9339 Adelaida Rd.* ☎ *805/237–1231* ⊕ *www.tablascreek.com.*

★ **Pasolivo.** While touring the idyllic west side of Paso Robles, take a break from wine by stopping at Pasolivo. Find out how they make their Tuscan-style Pasolivo olive oils on a high-tech Italian press, and taste the widely acclaimed results. ✉ *8530 Vineyard Dr.* ☎ *805/227–0186* ⊕ *www.pasolivo.com.*

Wild Horse Winery & Vineyards. In southeastern Paso Robles Wine Country, Wild Horse Winery & Vineyards was a pioneer Central Coast producer. You can try delicious, well-priced Pinot Noir, Chardonnay, and Merlot in their simple tasting room. ✉ *1437 Wild Horse Winery Ct., Templeton* ☎ *805/434–2541* ⊕ *www.wildhorsewinery.com.*

Firestone Walker Fine Ales. As they say around Paso Robles, it takes a lot of beer to make good wine, and to meet that need the locals turn to Firestone Walker Fine Ales. In the brewery's taproom, sample medal-winning craft beers such as Double Barrel Ale. They close at 7 pm. ✉ *1400 Ramada Dr.* ☎ *805/238–2556* ⊕ *www.firestonebeer.com.*

LAID-BACK WINE COUNTRY

Hundreds of vineyards and wineries dot the hillsides from Paso Robles to San Luis Obispo, through the scenic Edna Valley and south to northern Santa Barbara County. The wineries offer much of the variety of northern California's Napa and Sonoma valleys—without the glitz and crowds. Since the early 1980s the region has developed an international reputation for high-quality wines, most notably Pinot Noir, Chardonnay, and Zinfandel. Wineries here tend to be small, but most have tasting rooms (some have tours), and you'll often meet the winemakers themselves.

Eberle Winery. Even if you don't drink wine, stop at Eberle Winery for a fascinating tour of the huge wine caves beneath the east-side Paso Robles vineyard. Gary Eberle, one of Paso wine's founding fathers, is obsessed with Cabernet Sauvignon. ✉ *Hwy. 46E, 3½ mi east of U.S. 101* ☎ *805/238–9607* ⊕ *www.eberlewinery.com.*

WHERE TO EAT

$$$
AMERICAN

✕ **Artisan.** Innovative renditions of traditional American comfort foods, a well-chosen list of regional wines, a stylish full bar, and a sophisticated urban vibe lure winemakers, locals, and tourists to this small, family-run American bistro in an art deco building near the town square. Chris Kobayashi (Chef Koby, recently nominated for a James Beard award) uses local, organic, wild-caught ingredients to whip up regional favorites, which might include red abalone with fried green tomatoes and pancetta, scallops with laughing bird prawns, mussels, clams, Spanish chorizo, and saffron, or flatiron steak with shallots, fries, and Cabernet butter. Try to nab a booth facing the open kitchen, and save room for the restaurant's famed homestyle desserts: brownies, peach crumbles, crème brûlée, and the like. ✉ *1401 Park St.* ☎ *805/237–8084* ⊕ *www.artisanpasorobles.com.*

$$$
FRENCH
★

✕ **Bistro Laurent.** Owner-chef Laurent Grangien has created a handsome, welcoming French bistro in an 1890s brick building across from City Park. He focuses on traditional dishes such as osso buco, cassoulet, rack of lamb, goat-cheese tart, and onion soup, but always offers a few updated dishes as daily specials. Wines, sourced from the adjacent wine shop, come from around the world. ✉ *1202 Pine St.* ☎ *805/226–8191* ⊕ *www.bistrolaurent.com* ☽ *Closed Sun. and Mon.*

$$$
AMERICAN

✕ **McPhee's Grill.** The grain silos across the street and the floral oilcloths on the tables belie the sophisticated cuisine at this casual chophouse. In an 1860s building in the tiny cow town of Templeton (just south of Paso Robles), the restaurant serves creative, contemporary versions of traditional Western fare—such as oak-grilled filet mignon and cedar-planked salmon. House-label wines, made especially for McPhee's, are quite good. ⊠ *416 S. Main St., Templeton* ☎ *805/434–3204* ⊕ *www.mcphees.com.*

$
FRENCH

✕ **Panolivo Family Bistro.** Scrumptious French bistro fare draws a loyal crowd of locals to this cheery downtown café, just a block north of the town square. For breakfast, try a fresh pastry or quiche, or build your own omelet. Lunch and dinner choices include traditional French dishes like snails baked in garlic-butter sauce or cassoulet as well as sandwiches, salads, and fresh pastas—including the house-made beef cannelloni. ⊠ *1344 Park St.* ☎ *805/239–3366.*

$$
AMERICAN
CASUAL

✕ **Thomas Hill Organics.** In a casual bistro off a tiny alley, Joe and Debbie Thomas serve delectable locavore cuisine made from regional ingredients; much of the produce comes from their own ten-acre organic farm down the road. The menu changes weekly, depending on what's in-season and available, and includes a good selection of Central Coast wines. There's also a wine bar stocked with local vintages. A festive group of locals gathers every Monday evening for a family-style, multi-course feast ($25) with live music. Ask for a table in the outdoor courtyard on fair-weather days. ⊠ *1305 Park St., Templeton* ☎ *805/226–5888* ⊕ *thomashillorganics.com* ⊗ *Closed Tuesdays.*

$$$
SOUTHWESTERN

✕ **Villa Creek.** With a firm nod to the rancho and mission cuisine of California's early Spanish settlers, chef Tom Fundero conjures distinctly modern magic with local and sustainable ingredients. The seasonal menu has included butternut-squash enchiladas and braised lamb shank with saffron risotto and classic beef bourgignon with parsnip and cauliflower purée, but you might also find duck breast with sweet-potato latkes. Central Coast wines dominate the list, with a smattering of Spanish and French selections. All brick and bare wood, the dining room can get loud when winemakers start passing their bottles from table to table, but it's always festive. For lighter appetites or wallets, the bar serves smaller plates—not to mention a killer margarita. ⊠ *1144 Pine St.* ☎ *805/238–3000* ⊕ *www.villacreek.com* ⊗ *No lunch.*

WHERE TO STAY
For expanded hotel reviews, visit Fodors.com.

¢
Fodor's Choice
★

⊞ **Adelaide Inn.** Family-owned and -managed, this clean, friendly oasis with meticulous landscaping offers spacious rooms and everything you need: coffeemaker, iron, hair dryer, and peace and quiet. **Pros:** great bargain; attractive pool area; ideal for families. **Cons:** not a romantic retreat; near a busy intersection and freeway. ⊠ *1215 Ysabel Ave.* ☎ *805/238–2770, 800/549–7276* ⊕ *www.adelaideinn.com* ⇌ *109 rooms* ⌂ *In-room: a/c, Internet, Wi-Fi. In-hotel: pool, gym, laundry facilities* ⦿I *Breakfast.*

$$$$

⊞ **Hotel Cheval.** Equestrian themes surface throughout this intimate, sophisticated, European-style inn just a half-block from the main square and a short walk to some of Paso's best restaurants. **Pros:** walking distance from downtown restaurants; European-style facilities; personal service. **Cons:** views aren't great; no pool or hot tub. ✉ *1021 Pine St.* ☏ *805/226–9995, 866/522–6999* ⊕ *www.hotelcheval.com* ⤥ *16 rooms* ♨ *In-room: a/c, Internet, Wi-Fi. In-hotel: bar* ❑ *Breakfast.*

$$$ ⌧ **La Bellasera Hotel & Suites.** The swankest full-service hotel for miles around, the La Bellasera, completed in 2008, caters to those looking for luxurious high-tech amenities and close proximity to major Central Coast roadways. **Pros:** new property; tons of amenities. **Cons:** far from town square; located at major intersection. ✉ *206 Alexa Court* ☏ *805/238–2834, 866/782–9669* ⊕ *www.labellasera.com* ⤥ *35 rooms, 25 suites* ♨ *In-room: a/c, kitchen, Wi-Fi. In-hotel: restaurant, bar, pool, gym, spa, laundry facilities, business center, parking.*

$$ ⌧ **Paso Robles Inn.** On the site of a luxurious old spa hotel by the same name, the inn is built around a lush, shady garden with a pool. **Pros:** private spring-fed hot tubs; historic property; across from park and town square. **Cons:** fronts a busy street; rooms vary in size and quality. ✉ *1103 Spring St.* ☏ *805/238–2660, 800/676–1713* ⊕ *www. pasoroblesinn.com* ⤥ *92 rooms, 6 suites* ♨ *In-room: a/c, Internet, Wi-Fi. In-hotel: restaurant, bar, pool.*

CAMBRIA

28 mi west of Paso Robles on Hwy. 46; 20 mi north of Morro Bay on Hwy. 1.

Cambria, set on piney hills above the sea, was settled by Welsh miners in the 1890s. In the 1970s, the gorgeous, isolated setting attracted artists and other independent types; the town now caters to tourists, but it still bears the unmistakable imprint of its bohemian past. Both of Cambria's downtowns, the original East Village and the newer West Village, are packed with art and crafts galleries, antiques shops, cafés, restaurants, and B&Bs. Late-Victorian homes stand along side streets, and the hills are filled with redwood-and-glass residences.

GETTING HERE AND AROUND
Highway 1 leads to Cambria from north and south. From U.S. 101 at Paso Robles, Highway 246 West curves through mountains to Cambria and the coast. RTA Route 12 buses ferry passengers between San Luis Obispo and Hearst Castle, stopping in Cambria along the way.

ESSENTIALS
Visitor Information Cambria Chamber of Commerce ☏ *805/927–3624* ⊕ *www.cambriachamber.org.*

EXPLORING
Moonstone Beach Drive. Lined with low-key motels, Moonstone Beach Drive runs along a bluff above the ocean. The boardwalk that winds along the beach side of the drive makes a great walk.

Leffingwell's Landing. Leffingwell's Landing, a state picnic ground, is a good place for examining tidal pools and watching otters as they frolic in the surf. ✉ *North end of Moonstone Beach Dr.* ☏ *805/927–2070.*

Nit Wit Ridge. Arthur Beal (aka Captain Nit Wit, Der Tinkerpaw) spent 51 years building Nit Wit Ridge, a home with terraced rock gardens. For building materials, he used all kinds of collected junk: beer cans, rocks, abalone shells, car parts, TV antennas—you name it. The site, above Cambria's West Village, is a State Historic Landmark. You can drive by and peek in; better yet, call ahead for a guided tour of the house and grounds. ⊠ *881 Hillcrest Dr.* ☎ *805/927–2690* 🖃 *$10* ☽ *Daily by appointment.*

WHERE TO EAT

$$$
AMERICAN

✕ **Black Cat Bistro.** Jazz wafts through the several small rooms of this intimate East Village bistro where stylish cushions line the banquettes. Start with an order of the fried olives stuffed with Gorgonzola, accompanied by a glass from the eclectic list of local and imported wines. The daily-changing menu is centered on sustainable ingredients and might include roasted rack of elk rubbed in cocoa or breast of pheasant stuffed with caramelized apples. ⊠ *1602 Main St.* ☎ *805/927–1600* ⊕ *www.blackcatbistro.com* ⚖ *Reservations essential* ☽ *Closed Tues. and Wed. No lunch.*

¢
CAFÉ

✕ **French Corner Bakery.** Place your order at the counter and then sit outside to watch the passing East Village scene (if the fog has rolled in, take a seat in the tiny deli). The rich aroma of coffee and fresh breakfast pastries makes mouths water in the morning; for lunch, try a quiche with flaky crust or a sandwich on house-baked bread. ⊠ *2214 Main St.* ☎ *805/927–8227* ⚖ *Reservations not accepted* ☽ *No dinner.*

$$
ECLECTIC

✕ **Robin's.** A truly multiethnic and vegetarian-friendly dining experience awaits you at this East Village cottage filled with country antiques. At dinner, choose from lobster enchiladas, pork osso buco, Thai green chicken curry, and more. Lunchtime's extensive salad and sandwich menu embraces burgers and tofu alike. Unless it's raining, ask for a table on the secluded (and heated) garden patio. ⊠ *4095 Burton Dr.* ☎ *805/927–5007* ⊕ *www.robinsrestaurant.com.*

$$$
SEAFOOD

✕ **The Sea Chest.** By far the best seafood place in town—readers give it a big thumbs-up—this Moonstone Beach restaurant fills soon after it opens at 5:30. Those in the know grab seats at the oyster bar, where they can take in spectacular sunsets while watching the chefs broil fresh halibut and steam garlicky clams. If you can't get there early, play some cribbage or checkers while you wait for a table. ⊠ *6216 Moonstone Beach Dr.* ☎ *805/927–4514* ⊕ *www.seachestrestaurant.com* ⚖ *Reservations not accepted* ▭ *No credit cards* ☽ *Closed Tues. mid-Sept.–May. No lunch.*

WHERE TO STAY

For expanded hotel reviews, visit Fodors.com.

¢

▦ **Bluebird Inn.** This sweet motel in Cambria's East Village sits amid beautiful gardens along Santa Rosa Creek. **Pros:** excellent value; well-kept gardens; friendly staff. **Cons:** few frills; basic rooms; on Cambria's main drag. ⊠ *1880 Main St.* ☎ *805/927–4634, 800/552–5434* ⊕ *www. bluebirdmotel.com* ⇆ *37 rooms* ⚃ *In-room: a/c, Wi-Fi.*

$$

▦ **Cambria Pines Lodge.** With lots of recreational facilities and a range of accommodations—from basic state park–style cabins to motel-style standard rooms to large fireplace suites—this 25-acre retreat up the hill from the East Village is a good choice for families. **Pros:** short walk from downtown; verdant gardens; spacious grounds. **Cons:** front desk service and housekeeping not always top-quality; some units could use an update. ✉ *2905 Burton Dr.* ☎ *805/927–4200, 800/966–6490* ⊕ *www. cambriapineslodge.com* ⤏ *72 rooms, 18 cabins, 62 suites* ⚿ *In-room: a/c, Internet, Wi-Fi. In-hotel: restaurant, bar, pool, spa, business center, some pets allowed* ✦⃝ *Breakfast.*

$$ ⚏ **Moonstone Landing.** Friendly staff, lots of amenities, and reasonable
★ rates make this up-to-date motel a top pick with readers who like to stay right on Moonstone Beach. **Pros:** sleek furnishings; across from the beach; cheery lounge. **Cons:** narrow property; some rooms overlook a parking lot. ✉ *6240 Moonstone Beach Dr.* ☎ *805/927–0012, 800/830–4540* ⊕ *www.moonstonelanding.com* ⤏ *29 rooms* ⚿ *In-room: no a/c, Wi-Fi* ✦⃝ *Breakfast.*

SAN SIMEON

Hwy. 1, 9 mi north of Cambria and 65 mi south of Big Sur.

Whalers founded San Simeon in the 1850s but had virtually abandoned the town by the time Senator George Hearst reestablished it 20 years later. Hearst bought up most of the surrounding ranch land, built a 1,000-foot wharf, and turned San Simeon into a bustling port. His son, William Randolph Hearst, further developed the area during the construction of Hearst Castle. Today the town, 4 mi south of the entrance to Hearst San Simeon State Historical Monument, is basically a strip of gift shops and mediocre motels along Highway 1.

GETTING HERE AND AROUND

Highway 1 is the only way to reach San Simeon. From northern California, follow Highway 1 from Big Sur south to San Simeon. From U.S. 101 north or south, exit at Highway 1 in San Luis Obispo and follow it northwest 42 mi to San Simeon. Alternative rural routes to reach Highway 1 from the 101 include Highway 41 West (Atascadero to Morro Bay) and Highway 46 West (Paso Robles to Cambria).

EXPLORING

★ **Hearst Castle.** Hearst Castle, officially known as "Hearst San Simeon State Historical Monument," sits in solitary splendor atop La Cuesta Encantada (the Enchanted Hill). Its buildings and gardens spread over 127 acres that were the heart of newspaper magnate William Randolph Hearst's 250,000-acre ranch. Hearst devoted nearly 30 years and about $10 million to building this elaborate estate. He commissioned renowned architect Julia Morgan—who also designed buildings at the University of California at Berkeley—but he was very much involved with the final product, a hodgepodge of Italian, Spanish, Moorish, and French styles. The 115-room main building and three huge "cottages" are connected by terraces and staircases and surrounded by pools, gardens, and statuary. In its heyday the castle was a playground for Hearst and his guests, many of them Hollywood celebrities. Construction began in 1919 and was never officially completed. Work was halted in 1947 when Hearst had to leave San Simeon because of failing health. The Hearst family presented the property to the State of California in 1958.

Access to the castle is through the large visitor center at the foot of the hill, which contains a collection of Hearst memorabilia and a giant-screen theater that shows a 40-minute film giving a sanitized version of Hearst's life and of the castle's construction. Buses from the visitor center zigzag up the hillside to the neoclassical extravaganza, where guides conduct three different daytime tours of various parts of the main house and grounds. All three tours include movie tickets and take you to the indoor and outdoor pools. Tours last about two hours, including the bus ride up the hill, about 40 minutes with a guide, and time to stroll the grounds on your own.

The Grand Rooms Tour provides a good overview of the highlights; the others focus on the upstairs suites, cottages, and kitchens. In spring and fall, docents in period costume portray Hearst's guests and staff for an evening tour, which begins at sunset.(The Web site has specific dates.) All tours include a ½-mi walk and between 150 and 400 stairs. Reservations for the tours, which can be made up to eight weeks in advance, are necessary. ⊠ *San Simeon State Park, 750 Hearst Castle Rd.* ☎ *800/444–4445* ⊕ *www.hearstcastle.com* ✉ *Daytime tours $25,* ☉ *Tours daily 8:20–3:20, later in summer; additional tours take place most Fri. and Sat. evenings Mar.–May and Sept.–Dec.*

Old San Simeon. Turn west from Highway 1 across from the Hearst Castle entrance to see Old San Simeon, an 1850s whaling village that morphed into an outpost for Hearst employees. There's a historic one-room schoolhouse and Spanish-style buildings; don't miss Sebastian's General Store in an 1852 building. Now a state historic landmark, Sebastian's houses a café with excellent sandwiches and salads, a store, and a wine tasting room. ⊠ *West of Highway 1, across from Hearst Castle entrance, San Simeon.*

☾ **Piedras Blancas Elephant Seal Rookery.** A large and growing colony (at last count 15,000 members) of elephant seals gathers every year at Piedras Blancas Elephant Seal Rookery, on the beaches near Piedras Blancas Lighthouse. The huge males with their pendulous, trunklike noses typically start appearing on shore in late November, and the females begin to arrive in December to give birth—most babies are born in the last two weeks of January. The newborn pups spend about four weeks nursing before their mothers head out to sea, leaving them on their own; the "weaners" leave the rookery when they are about 3½ months old. The seals return in the spring and summer months to molt or rest, but not en masse as in winter. You can watch them from a boardwalk along the bluffs just a few feet above the beach; do not attempt to approach them, as they are wild animals. Docents are often on hand to give background information and statistics. The rookery is just south of Piedras Blancas Lighthouse (4½ mi north of Hearst San Simeon State Historical Monument); the nonprofit Friends of the Elephant Seal runs a small visitor center and gift shop at their San Simeon office. ⊠ *Friends of the Elephant Seal, 250 San Simeon Ave., Suite 3* ☎ *805/924–1628* ⊕ *www.elephantseal.org.*

WHERE TO STAY

For expanded hotel reviews, visit Fodors.com.

$$ **Best Western Cavalier Oceanfront Resort.** Reasonable rates, an oceanfront location, evening bonfires, and well-equipped rooms—some with wood-burning fireplaces and private patios—make this motel one of the best choices in San Simeon. **Pros:** on the bluffs; fantastic views; close to Hearst Castle; bluff bonfires. **Cons:** room amenities and sizes vary; pools are small and sometimes crowded. ⊠ *9415 Hearst Dr.* ☎ *805/927–4688, 800/826–8168* ⊕ *www.cavalierresort.com* ⇨ *90 rooms* ♿ *In-room: a/c, Internet, Wi-Fi. In-hotel: restaurant, pool, gym, laundry facilities, business center, some pets allowed.*

$$ **The Morgan San Simeon.** On the ocean side of Highway 1, near San Simeon restaurants and shops, the Morgan offers a range of motel-style rooming options while paying tribute to famed Hearst Castle architect Julia Morgan. **Pros:** fascinating artwork; easy access to Hearst Castle and Highway 1; some ocean views. **Cons:** not right on beach; no fitness room or laundry facilities. ⊠ *9135 Hearst Dr.* ☎ *805/927–3878, 800/451–9900* ⊕ *www.hotel-morgan.com* ⇨ *54 rooms, 1 suite* ♿ *In-room: Wi-Fi. In-hotel: bar, pool, spa* ¶◎ *Breakfast.*

BIG SUR COASTLINE

Long a retreat of artists and writers, Big Sur is a place of ancient forests and rugged shoreline, stretching 90 mi from San Simeon to Carmel. Residents have protected it from overdevelopment, and much of the region lies within several state parks and the more than 165,000-acre Ventana Wilderness, itself part of the Los Padres National Forest.

ESSENTIALS

Visitor Information Big Sur Chamber of Commerce ☎ *831/667–2100* ⊕ *www.bigsurcalifornia.org.*

SOUTHERN BIG SUR

Hwy. 1 from San Simeon to Julia Pfeiffer Burns State Park.

This especially rugged stretch of oceanfront is a rocky world of mountains, cliffs, and beaches.

GETTING HERE AND AROUND

Highway 1 is the only major access route from north or south. From the south, access Highway 1 from U.S. 101 in San Luis Obispo. From the north, take rural routes Highway 46 West (Paso Robles to Cambria) or Highway 41 West (Atascadero to Morro Bay). Nacimiento-Fergusson Road snakes through mountains and forest from U.S. 101 at Jolon about 25 mi to Highway 1 at Kirk Creek, about 4 mi south of Lucia; this curvy, at times precipitous road is a motorcyclist favorite, not recommended for the faint of heart or during inclement weather.

EXPLORING

Fodor's Choice ★ **Highway 1.** One of California's most spectacular drives, Highway 1 snakes up the coast north of San Simeon. Numerous pullouts along the way offer tremendous views and photo ops. On some of the beaches,

huge elephant seals lounge nonchalantly, seemingly oblivious to the attention of rubberneckers—but keep your distance.

CalTrans. In rainy seasons, portions of Highway 1 north and south of Big Sur are sometimes shut down by mudslides. Contact CalTrans for road conditions. ☎ 800/427–7623 ⊕ www.dot.ca.gov

Jade Cove. In Los Padres National Forest just north of the town of Gorda is Jade Cove, a well-known jade-hunting spot. Rock hunting is allowed on the beach, but you may not remove anything from the walls of the cliffs. ⊠ Hwy. 1, 34 mi north of San Simeon.

Julia Pfeiffer Burns State Park. Julia Pfeiffer Burns State Park provides some fine hiking, from an easy ½-mi stroll with marvelous coastal views to a strenuous 6-mi trek through the redwoods. The big attraction here, an 80-foot waterfall that drops into the ocean, gets crowded in summer; still, it's an astounding place to sit and contemplate nature. Migrating whales, as well as harbor seals and sea lions, can sometimes be spotted not far from shore. ⊠ Hwy. 1, 53 mi north of San Simeon, 15 mi north of Lucia ☎ 831/667–2315 ⊕ www.parks.ca.gov ⌨ $10 ☉ Daily sunrise–sunset.

WHERE TO STAY
For expanded hotel reviews, visit Fodors.com.

$$ 🏨 **Ragged Point Inn.** At this cliff-top resort—the only inn and restaurant for miles around—glass walls in most rooms open to awesome, unobstructed ocean views. **Pros:** on the cliffs; great food; idyllic views. **Cons:** busy road stop during the day; often booked for weekend weddings. ⊠ 19019 Hwy. 1, 20 mi north of San Simeon, Ragged Point ☎ 805/927–4502, 805/927–5708 restaurant ⊕ raggedpointinn.com ⌨ 30 rooms ⟐ In-room: no a/c, kitchen. In-hotel: restaurant, laundry facilities.

$$ 🏨 **Treebones Resort.** Perched on a hilltop, surrounded by national forest and stunning, unobstructed ocean views, this yurt resort opened in 2004. **Pros:** 360-degree views; spacious pool area; comfortable beds. **Cons:** steep paths; no private bathrooms; more than a mile from the nearest store; not a good place for families with children under six. ⊠ 71895 Hwy. 1, Willow Creek Rd., 32 mi north of San Simeon, 1 mi north of Gorda ☎ 805/927–2390, 877/424–4787 ⊕ www.treebonesresort.com ⌨ 16 yurts, 5 campsites, 1 human nest w/campsite ⟐ In-room: no a/c. In-hotel: restaurant, pool, spa, laundry facilities, business center, some pets allowed ⏐◯⏐ Breakfast.

CENTRAL BIG SUR

Hwy. 1, from Partington Cove to Bixby Bridge.

The countercultural spirit of Big Sur—which instead of a conventional town is a loose string of coast-hugging properties along Highway 1—is alive and well today. Its few residents include the very wealthy, the enthusiastically outdoorsy, and the thoroughly evolved: since the 1960s the Esalen Institute, a center for alternative education and East–West philosophical study, has attracted seekers of higher consciousness and devotees of the property's hot springs. Today, posh and rustic resorts hidden among the redwoods cater to visitors drawn from near and far by the extraordinary scenery and serene isolation.

GETTING HERE AND AROUND

From the north, follow Highway 1 south from Carmel. From the south, access scenic Highway 1 from U.S. 101 at San Luis Obispo. Alternate connections from U.S. 101 north or south are rural roads Highway 46 West (Paso Robles to Cambria) and Highway 41 West (Atascadero to Morro Bay). MST Line 22 Big Sur travels between Monterey, Carmel, and Big Sur on weekends (daily in summer).

EXPLORING

Pfeiffer Beach. Through a hole in one of the gigantic boulders at secluded Pfeiffer Beach, you can watch the waves break first on the sea side and then on the beach side. Keep a sharp eye out for the unsigned, ungated road to the beach: it branches west of Highway 1 between the post office and Pfeiffer Big Sur State Park. The 2-mile, one-lane road descends sharply. ⊠ *Off Hwy. 1, 1 mi south of Pfeiffer Big Sur State Park* ⊑ *$10 per vehicle per day.*

Pfeiffer Big Sur State Park. Among the many hiking trails at Pfeiffer Big Sur State Park ($10 per vehicle for day use) a short route through a redwood-filled valley leads to a waterfall. You can double back or continue on the more difficult trail along the valley wall for views over miles of treetops to the sea. Stop in at the Big Sur Station visitor center, off Highway 1, less than ½ mi south of the park entrance, for information about the entire area; it's open 8–4:30. ⊠ *47225 Hwy. 1* ☎ *831/667–2315* ⊕ *www.parks.ca.gov* ⊑ *$10 per vehicle* ⊙ *Daily dawn–dusk.*

★ **Point Sur State Historic Park.** Point Sur State Historic Park is the site of an 1889 lighthouse that still stands watch from atop a large volcanic rock. Four lighthouse keepers lived here with their families until 1974, when the light station became automated. Their homes and working spaces are open to the public only on 2½- to 3-hour ranger-led tours. Considerable walking, including up two stairways, is involved. Strollers are not allowed. ⊠ *Hwy. 1, 7 mi north of Pfeiffer Big Sur State Park* ☎ *831/625–4419* ⊕ *www.pointsur.org* ⊑ *$10* ⊙ *Tours generally Nov.–Mar., weekends at 10, Wed. at 1; Apr.–Oct., Sat. and Wed. at 10 and 2, Sun. at 10; call to confirm.*

Bixby Creek Bridge. The graceful arc of Bixby Creek Bridge is a photographer's dream. Built in 1932, it spans a deep canyon, more than 100 feet wide at the bottom. From the parking area on the north side you can admire the view or walk across the 550-foot span. ⊠ *Hwy. 1, 6 mi north of Point Sur State Historic Park, 13 mi south of Carmel.*

WHERE TO EAT

$$
ECLECTIC
✕ **Big Sur Roadhouse.** At this colorful, casual bistro, feast on innovative, well-executed California Latin–fusion fare. Crispy striped bass atop a pillow of carrot-coconut puree, tangy-smoky barbecue chicken breast beneath a julienne of jicama and cilantro: the zesty, balanced flavors wake up your mouth. Emphasizing new-world vintages, the wine list is gently priced. The chocolate-caramel layer cake may bring tears to your eyes. ⊠ *Hwy. 1, 1 mi north of Pfeiffer Big Sur State Park* ☎ *831/667–2264* ⊕ *www.bigsurroadhouse.com* ⊙ *Closed Tues. No lunch.*

$$$
AMERICAN

✕ **Deetjen's Big Sur Inn.** The candlelighted, creaky-floor restaurant in the main house at the historic inn of the same name is a Big Sur institution. It serves spicy seafood paella, steak, and rack of lamb for dinner and wonderfully flavorful eggs Benedict for breakfast. The chef procures much of the fish, meats, and produce from purveyors who practice sustainable farming and fishing practices. ✉ *Hwy. 1, 3½ mi south of Pfeiffer Big Sur State Park* ☎ *831/667–2377* ⊕ *www.deetjens. com* ☽ *No lunch.*

$$$
AMERICAN

✕ **Nepenthe.** It may be that no other restaurant between San Francisco and Los Angeles has a better coastal view; no wonder Orson Welles and Rita Hayworth once owned the place. The food and drink are overpriced but good; there are burgers, sandwiches, and salads for lunch, and fresh fish and hormone-free steaks for dinner. For the real show, settle on the terraced deck in the late afternoon, order a glass from the extensive wine list, and watch the sun slip into the Pacific Ocean. The less expensive, outdoor Café Kevah serves brunch and lunch. ✉ *Hwy. 1, 2½ mi south of Big Sur Station* ☎ *831/667–2345* ⊕ *www.nepenthebigsur.com.*

$$$$
AMERICAN

✕ **The Restaurant at Ventana.** Closed for remodeling for more than a year after a kitchen fire, the Restaurant at Ventana (formerly Cielo) rose from the ashes in stunning fashion in fall 2009. Redwood, copper, and cedar elements pay tribute to the historic natural setting, while gleaming new fixtures and dining accoutrements place the restaurant firmly in the 21st century. Chef Trueman Jones' seasonal menu showcases fine California cuisine, from rabbit loin and California white sea bass to artichokes and abalone, and a full slate of regional and international wines. Much of the produce comes from the restaurant's organic vegetable garden. The restaurant is also open for lunch—ask for a table on the outdoor terrace, where ocean views unfold on clear, sunny days. ✉ *Hwy. 1, 1½ mi south of Pfeiffer Big Sur State Park* ☎ *831/667–2242* ⊕ *www.ventanainn.com* ⟡ *Reservations essential.*

$$$$
AMERICAN

✕ **Sierra Mar.** Ocean-view dining doesn't get much better than this. Perched at cliff's edge 1,200 feet above the Pacific at the ultra-chic Post Ranch Inn, Sierra Mar serves cutting-edge American food made from mostly organic, seasonal ingredients, including a stellar four-course prix-fixe menu. The restaurant's wine list is one of the most extensive in the nation. ✉ *Hwy. 1, 1½ mi south of Pfeiffer Big Sur State Park* ☎ *831/667–2800* ⟡ *Reservations essential.*

WHERE TO STAY

$$$

🛏 **Big Sur Lodge.** The modern motel-style cottages in Pfeiffer Big Sur State Park sit in a meadow surrounded by trees and flowering shrubbery. Renovated in 2005, with Mission-style furnishings and vaulted ceilings, some rooms have fireplaces and some have kitchens; all have a deck or patio. The larger, multi-bedded rooms and suites are a good choice for families. **Pros:** near trailheads; good camping alternative. **Cons:** basic rooms; walk to main lodge. ✉ *47225 Hwy. 1 (Pfeiffer Big Sur State Park)* ☎ *831/667–3100, 800/424–4787* ⊕ *www.bigsurlodge.com* ⤳ *61 rooms* ⟐ *In-room: kitchen, no TV. In-hotel: restaurant, bar, pool.*

¢

🛏 **Deetjen's Big Sur Inn.** This historic 1930s Norwegian-style property is endearingly rustic and charming, especially if you're willing to go with a camplike flow. **Pros:** surrounded by Big Sur history; tons of character; wooded grounds. **Cons:** rustic; thin walls; some rooms don't have private baths. ☒ *Hwy. 1, 3½ mi south of Pfeiffer Big Sur State Park* ☎ *831/667–2377* ⊕ *www.deetjens.com* ↩ *20 rooms, 15 with bath* ⅋ *In-room: no a/c, no TV. In-hotel: restaurant.*

$$$$
Fodor's Choice
★
🛏 **Post Ranch Inn.** This luxurious retreat, designed exclusively for adult getaways, has remarkably environmentally conscious architecture. **Pros:** world-class resort; spectacular views; gorgeous property with hiking trails. **Cons:** expensive; austere design; not a good choice if you're scared of heights. ☒ *Hwy. 1, 1½ mi south of Pfeiffer Big Sur State Park* ☒ *Hwy. 1, Box 219* ☎ *831/667–2200, 888/524–4787* ⊕ *www. postranchinn.com* ↩ *39 units* ⅋ *In-room: a/c, Internet, Wi-Fi. In-hotel: restaurant, bar, pool, gym, spa, business center* ¶◯¶ *Breakfast.*

$$$$
Fodor's Choice
★
🛏 **Ventana Inn & Spa.** Hundreds of celebrities, from Oprah Winfrey to Sir Anthony Hopkins, have escaped to Ventana, a romantic resort on 243 tranquil acres 1,200 feet above the Pacific. **Pros:** nature trails everywhere; great food; secluded. **Cons:** simple breakfast; no ocean view from rooms. ☒ *Hwy. 1, almost 1 mi south of Pfeiffer Big Sur State Park* ☎ *831/667–2331, 800/628–6500* ⊕ *www.ventanainn.com* ↩ *25 rooms, 31 suites* ⅋ *In-room: a/c, Internet, Wi-Fi. In-hotel: restaurant, bar, pool, gym, spa* ¶◯¶ *Breakfast.*

Channel Islands National Park

WORD OF MOUTH

"We were just [in the Channel Islands] and it was beautiful. The water is crystal clear turquoise, and the caves are gorgeous."

—Sandals

WELCOME TO CHANNEL ISLANDS NATIONAL PARK

TOP REASONS TO GO

★ **Rare flora and fauna:** The Channel Islands are home to 145 species of terrestrial plants and animals found nowhere else on Earth.

★ **Time travel:** With no cars, phones, or services, these undeveloped islands provide a glimpse of what California was like hundreds of years ago, away from hectic modern life.

★ **Underwater adventures:** The incredibly healthy channel waters rank among the top 10 diving destinations on the planet—but you can also visit the kelp forest virtually via an underwater video program.

★ **Marvelous marine mammals:** More than 30 species of seals, sea lions, whales, and other marine mammals ply the park's waters at various times of year.

★ **Sea-cave kayaking:** Paddle around otherwise inaccessible portions of the park's 175 mi of gorgeous coastline—including one of the world's largest sea caves.

1 Anacapa. Tiny Anacapa is a 5-mi stretch of three islets, with towering cliffs, caves, natural bridges, and rich kelp forests.

2 San Miguel. Isolated, windswept San Miguel, the park's westernmost island, has an ancient caliche forest and hundreds of archaeological sites chronicling the Chumash Indian's 11,000-year history on the island. More than 30,000 pinnipeds (seals and sea lions) hang out on the island's beaches during certain times of year.

3 Santa Barbara. Nearly 6 mi of scenic trails crisscross this tiny island, known for its excellent wildlife viewing and native plants. It's a favorite destination for diving, snorkeling, and kayaking.

Goleta
Goleta Point
Montecito
Santa Barbara
Carpinteria
154
150
33
101

SANTA YNEZ MOUNTAINS

Ventura
Visitor Center
El Rio
126
101

Oxnard
1

Point Mugu

C h a n n e l

Painted Cave
Scorpion Ranch
San Pedro Point
Summit Peak 936 ft
Prisoners Harbor
4
Mount Diablo 2,450 ft
Main Ranch
Central Valley
Morse Point
Santa Cruz Island
Smugglers Cove
Anacapa Passage
1
Light Station & Museum
Anacapa Island

0 ——— 10 mi
0 ——— 10 km

Santa Barbara island is approximately 52 miles southeast of Santa Cruz Island
Santa Barbara Island Light
3 ◆ *Santa Barbara Island*

6

GETTING ORIENTED

Channel Islands National Park includes five of the eight Channel Islands and the nautical mile of ocean that surrounds them. The islands range in size from 1-square-mi Santa Barbara to 96-square-mi Santa Cruz. Together they form a magnificent nature preserve with 145 endemic or unique species of plants and animals. Half the park lies underwater, and the 5 mi of surrounding channel waters are teeming with life, including dolphins, whales, seals, sea lions, and seabirds.

4 Santa Cruz. The park's largest island offers some of the best hikes and kayaking opportunities, one of the world's largest and deepest sea caves, and more species of flora and fauna than any other park island.

5 Santa Rosa. Campers love to stay on Santa Rosa, with its myriad hiking opportunities, stunning white-sand beaches, and rare grove of Torrey pines. It's also the only island accessible by plane.

Updated by
Sura Wood
and Cheryl
Crabtree

On crystal-clear days the craggy peaks of Channel Islands are easy to see from the mainland, jutting from the Pacific in such sharp detail it seems you could reach out and touch them. The islands really aren't that far away—a high-speed boat will whisk you to the closest ones in less than an hour— yet very few people ever visit them. Those fearless, adventurous types who do will experience one of the most splendid land-and-sea wilderness areas on the planet.

PLANNING

WHEN TO GO

Channel Islands National Park records about 620,000 visitors each year, but many never venture beyond the visitor center. The busiest times are holidays and summer weekends. If you're going then, make your transportation and accommodation arrangements far in advance.

The warm, dry summer months are the best time to go camping. Humpback and blue whales arrive to feed from late June through early fall. The rains usually come from December through March—but this is also the best time to spot gray whales and to get discounts at area hotels. In the late spring, thousands of migratory birds descend on the islands to hatch their young, and wildflowers carpet the slopes. The water temperature is nearly always cool, so bring a wet suit if you plan to spend much time in the ocean, even in the summer. Fog, high winds, and rough seas can happen any time of the year.

GETTING HERE AND AROUND

The visitor center for Channel Islands National Park is on California's mainland, in the town of Ventura, off U.S. 101. From the harbors at Ventura, Santa Barbara, and Oxnard you can board a boat to one of the islands. You also can catch a flight to some of the islands from the Camarillo Airport, near Oxnard, and the Santa Barbara Airport.

If you have your own boat, you can land at any of the islands, but each island has certain closed and restricted areas, so boaters should contact the park ranger on each island for instructions. Private vehicles are not permitted on the islands. Pets are also not allowed in the park.

Several private companies provide transportation by boat or plane to and from the mainland to one of more of the Channel Islands.

To reach the Ventura harbor, exit U.S. 101 in Ventura at Seaward Boulevard or Victoria Avenue and follow the signs to Ventura Harbor/Spinnaker Drive. In Santa Barbara, exit U.S. 101 at Castillo Street and head south to Cabrillo Boulevard, then turn right for the harbor entrance. To access Channel Islands Harbor in Oxnard, exit U.S. 101 at Victoria Avenue and head south approximately 7 mi to Channel Islands Boulevard. Amtrak makes stops in Santa Barbara, Ventura, and Oxnard; from the Amtrak station, just take a taxi or waterfront shuttle bus to the harbor.

FLORA AND FAUNA

The Channel Islands are home to species found nowhere else on Earth: mammals such as the island fox and the island deer mouse, birds like the island scrub jay, and plants such as the Santa Barbara Island Liveforever are on the endangered species list. Thousands of western gulls hatch each summer on Anacapa, then fly off to the mainland where they spend about four years learning all their bad habits. Then they return to the island to roost and have chicks of their own. It all adds up to a living laboratory not unlike the one naturalist Charles Darwin discovered off the coast of South America 200 years ago, which is why the Channel Islands are often called the North American Galapagos.

6

PARK ESSENTIALS

ADMISSION FEES AND PERMITS

There is no fee to enter Channel Islands National Park, but unless you have your own boat, you will pay $32 or more per person for a ride with a boat operator. The cost of taking a boat to the park varies depending on which operator you choose. Also, there is a $15 per day fee for staying in one of the islands' campgrounds.

ADMISSION HOURS

The islands are open every day of the year. Channel Islands Visitor Center in Ventura is closed on Thanksgiving and Christmas.

PARK CONTACT INFORMATION

Channel Islands Visitor Center ✉ *1901 Spinnaker Dr., Ventura, CA* ☎ *805/658–5730* ⊕ *www.nps.gov/chis.*

SAFETY

In the event of an emergency, contact a park ranger on patrol or call the park dispatch at ☎ *805/658–5700* (during business hours) or *911.* Boaters can use marine radio channel 16.

TRANSPORTATION OPTIONS

Channel Islands Aviation (✉ *305 Durley Ave., Camarillo* ☎ *805/987–1301* ⊕ *www.flycia.com* ✈ *$179 per person, $326 per person if camping*) provides day excursions, surf fishing, and camper transportation year-round, flying from Camarillo Airport, about 10 mi east of Oxnard, to an airstrip on Santa Rosa. The operator will also pick up groups of six or more at Santa Barbara Airport, but no camper transportation is available from Santa Barbara.

Sailing on two high-speed catamarans from Ventura or Oxnard, **Island Packers** (✉ *3600 S. Harbor Blvd., Oxnard* ☎ *805/642–1393* ✉ *1691 Spinnaker Dr., Ventura* ☎ *805/642–1393* ⊕ *www.islandpackers.com* 💺 *$56-$78–*) goes to Santa Cruz Island daily most of the year, weather permitting. The boats also go to Anacapa several days a week, and to the other islands three or four times a month, most frequently May through October.

Truth Aquatics (✉ *301 W. Cabrillo Blvd., Santa Barbara* ☎ *805/962–1127* ⊕ *www.truthaquatics.com* 💺 *$140 for scuba day trips, average of $170 per day for all-inclusive trips*) departs from Santa Barbara for scuba trips and multiday excursions (where travelers sleep aboard ship) to the islands.

EXPLORING

THE ISLANDS

★ **Anacapa Island.** Although most people think of it as an island, Anacapa is actually comprised of three narrow islets. The tips of these volcanic formations nearly touch but are inaccessible from one another except by boat. All three islets have towering cliffs, isolated sea caves, and natural bridges; Arch Rock, on East Anacapa, is one of the best-known symbols of Channel Islands National Park. Wildlife viewing is the reason most people come to East Anacapa—particularly in summer when seagull chicks are newly hatched and sea lions and seals lounge on the beaches. Trips to Middle Anacapa Island require a ranger escort.

San Miguel Island. The westernmost of the Channel Islands, San Miguel is frequently battered by storms sweeping across the North Pacific. The 15-square-mi island's wild, windswept landscape is lush with vegetation. Point Bennett, at the western tip, offers one of the world's most spectacular wildlife displays when more than 30,000 pinnipeds hit its beach. Explorer Juan Rodríguez Cabrillo was the first European to visit this island; he claimed it for Spain in 1542. Legend holds that Cabrillo died on one of the Channel Islands—no one knows where he's buried, but there's a memorial to him on a bluff above Cuyler Harbor.

Santa Barbara Island. At about 1 square mi, this is the smallest of the Channel Islands and nearly 35 mi south of the others. Triangular in shape, Santa Barbara's steep cliffs—which offer a perfect nesting spot for the Xantus's murrelet, a rare seabird—are topped by twin peaks. In spring, you can enjoy a brilliant display of yellow coreopsis. Learn about the wildlife on and around the islands at the island's small museum (⊙ *Daily 10–5).*

★ **Santa Cruz Island.** Five miles west of Anacapa, at 96-square-mi this is the largest of the Channel Islands. The National Park Service manages the easternmost 24% of the island; the rest is owned by the Nature Conservancy, which requires a permit to land. When your boat drops you off on the 70 mi of craggy coastline, you see two rugged mountain ranges with peaks soaring to 2,500 feet and deep canyons traversed by streams. This landscape is the habitat of a remarkable variety of flora and fauna—more than 600 types of plants, 140 kinds of land birds, 11 mammal species, five varieties of reptiles, and three amphibian species live here. Bird-watchers may want to look for the endemic island scrub jay, which is found nowhere else in the world. The largest and deepest sea cave in the world, **Painted Cave,** lies along the northwest coast of Santa Cruz. Named for the colorful lichen and algae that cover its walls, Painted Cave is nearly ¼ mi long and 100 feet wide. In spring a waterfall cascades over the entrance. Kayakers may encounter seals or sea lions cruising alongside their boats inside the cave. The Channel Islands hold some of the richest archeological resources in North America; all artifacts are protected within the park. Remnants of a dozen Chumash villages can be seen on the island. The largest of these villages, at the eastern end of the island, occupied the area now called **Scorpion Ranch.** The Chumash mined extensive chert deposits on the island for tools to produce shell-bead money, which they traded with people on the mainland. Visitors can also explore remnants of the early-1900s ranching era in the restored historic adobe and outbuildings.

Santa Rosa Island. Set between Santa Cruz and San Miguel, this is the second largest of the Channel Islands and has a relatively low profile, broken by a central mountain range rising to 1,589 feet. The coastal areas range from broad sandy beaches to sheer cliffs. The island is home to about 500 species of plants, including the rare Torrey pine. Three unusual mammals—the endemic island fox, spotted skunk, and deer mouse—are among those that make their home here. They hardly compare to the mammoths that once roamed the island; a nearly complete skeleton of a 6-foot-tall pygmy mammoth was unearthed here in 1994.

The island was once home to the **Vail & Vickers Ranch,** where sheep and cattle were raised from 1901 to 1998. You can catch a glimpse of what the operation was like when you walk from the landing dock to the campground; the route passes by the historic ranch buildings, barns, equipment, and the wooden pier where cattle were brought onto the island. (Note that these buildings are not accessible to the public.)

VISITOR CENTERS

Channel Islands National Park Robert J. Lagomarsino Visitor Center. The park's main visitor center has a museum, a bookstore, a three-story observation tower with telescopes, and exhibits about the islands. Rangers lead various free public programs describing park resources on weekends and holidays at 11 and 3; they can also give you a detailed map and trip-planning packet if you're interested in visiting the actual islands. ⊠ *1901 Spinnaker Dr., Ventura* ☎ *805/658–5730* ⊕ *www.nps. gov/chis* ☉ *Daily 8:30–5.*

6

Camping on the Channel Islands

Camping is the best way to experience the natural beauty and isolation of Channel Islands National Park. Campsites are primitive, with no water (except on Santa Rosa and Santa Cruz) or electricity. And campfires are not allowed on the islands, though you may use enclosed camp stoves. Campers must arrange transportation to the islands before reserving a campsite (and yes, park personnel do check).

You can get specifics on each campground and reserve a campsite ($15–$25 per night) by contacting the **National Park Service Reservation System** (☎ *877/444–6777* ⊕ *www.recreation.gov*) up to six months in advance.

SPORTS AND THE OUTDOORS

DIVING

Some of the best snorkeling and diving in the world can be found in the cool waters surrounding the Channel Islands. The best time to scuba dive is in the summer and fall, when the water is often clear up to a 100-foot depth.

HIKING

The terrain on most of the islands ranges from flat to moderately hilly. There are no services (and no public phones; cell-phone reception is dicey) on the islands—you need to bring all your own food, water, and supplies. To hike on San Miguel, call ☎ *805/658–5711* to be matched up to a ranger, who must accompany you there.

KAYAKING

The most remote parts of the Channel Islands are accessible only by a sea kayak. Some of the best kayaking in the park can be found on Anacapa, Santa Barbara, and the eastern tip of Santa Cruz. It's too far to kayak from the mainland out to the islands, but outfitters have tours that take you to the islands. ⚠ Channel waters can be unpredictable and challenging. Don't venture out alone unless you are an experienced kayaker; guided trips are highly recommended.

WHALE-WATCHING

About a third of the world's cetacean species (27 to be exact) can be seen in the Santa Barbara Channel. In July and August, humpback and blue whales feed off the north shore of Santa Rosa. From late December through March, up to 10,000 gray whales pass through the Santa Barbara Channel on their way from Alaska to Mexico and back again, and on a whale-watching trip during this time frame, you should see one or more of them. Other types of whales, but fewer in number, swim the channel June through August.

The Monterey Bay Area

FROM CARMEL TO SANTA CRUZ

WORD OF MOUTH

"To be able to see, up close, the wonders of the ocean, is an amazing experience at the wonderful Monterey Bay Aquarium."
—photo by mellifluous, Fodors.com member

WELCOME TO THE MONTEREY BAY AREA

TOP REASONS TO GO

★ **Marine life:** Monterey Bay is home to the world's third-largest marine sanctuary, home to whales, otters, and other underwater creatures.

★ **Getaway central:** For more than a century, urbanites have come to the Monterey Bay area to unwind, relax, and have fun. It's a great place to browse unique shops and galleries, ride a giant roller coaster, or play a round of golf on a world-class course.

★ **Nature preserves:** More than the sea is protected here—the region boasts nearly 30 state parks, beaches, and preserves, fantastic places for walking, jogging, hiking, and biking.

★ **Wine and dine:** The area's rich agricultural bounty translates to abundant fresh produce, great wines, and fabulous dining. It's no wonder more than 300 culinary events take place here every year.

★ **Small-town vibes:** Even the cities here are friendly, walkable places where you'll feel like a local.

1 Carmel and Pacific Grove. Exclusive Carmel-by-the-Sea and Carmel Valley Village burst with historic charm, fine dining, and unusual boutiques that cater to celebrity residents and well-heeled visitors. Nearby 17-Mile Drive—quite possibly the prettiest stretch of road you'll ever travel—runs between Carmel-by-the-Sea and Victorian-studded Pacific Grove, home to thousands of migrating monarch butterflies between October and February.

2 Monterey. A former Spanish military outpost, Monterey's well-preserved historic district is a hands-on history lesson. Cannery Row, the former center of Monterey's once-thriving sardine industry, has been reborn as a tourist attraction with shops, restaurants, hotels, and the Monterey Bay Aquarium.

3 Around the Bay. Much of California's lettuce, berries, artichokes, and Brussels sprouts come from Salinas and Watsonville. Salinas is also home of the National Steinbeck Center, and Moss Landing and Watsonville encompass pristine wildlife wetlands. Aptos, Capitola, and Soquel are former lumber towns that became popular seaside resorts more than a century ago. Today they're filled with antiques shops, restaurants, and wine-tasting rooms; you'll also find some of the bay's best beaches along the shore here.

4 Santa Cruz. Santa Cruz shows its colors along an old-time beach boardwalk and municipal wharf. A University of California campus imbues the town with arts and culture and a liberal mind-set.

GETTING ORIENTED

North of Big Sur the coastline softens into lower bluffs, windswept dunes, pristine estuaries, and long, sandy beaches, bordering one of the world's most amazing marine environments—the Monterey Bay. On the Monterey Peninsula, at the southern end of the bay, are Carmel-by-the-Sea, Pacific Grove, and Monterey; Santa Cruz sits at the northern tip of the crescent. In between, Highway 1 cruises along the coastline, passing windswept beaches piled high with sand dunes. Along the route are wetlands, artichoke and strawberry fields, and workaday towns such as Castroville and Watsonville.

7

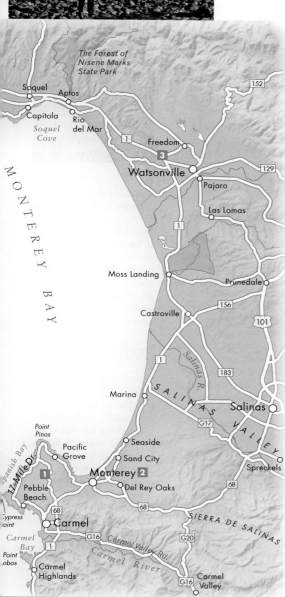

The Forest of Nisene Marks State Park

152

Soquel
Aptos
Capitola
Rio del Mar
Soquel Cove
Freedom
3
Watsonville
Pajaro
129
Las Lomas
1
M O N T E R E Y   B A Y
Moss Landing
Prunedale
Castroville
156
101
Salinas R.
183
Marina
S A L I N A S   V A L L E Y
Salinas
G17
Point Pinos
Pacific Grove
Seaside
Sand City
Spreckels
Spanish Bay
1
Monterey 2
Del Rey Oaks
68
17-Mile Dr.
Pebble Beach
68
68
Cypress Point
Carmel
S I E R R A   D E   S A L I N A S
Carmel Bay
G16
Carmel Valley Rd.
G20
Point Lobos
1
Carmel River
Carmel Highlands
G16
Carmel Valley

HIGHWAY 1: CARMEL TO SAN FRANCISCO

San Francisco

THE PLAN

Distance: approx. 123 mi

Time: 2-4 days

Good Overnight Options: Carmel, Monterey, Santa Cruz, Half Moon Bay, San Francisco

For more information on the sights and attractions along this portion of Highway 1, please see the Monterey Bay chapter.

CARMEL TO MONTEREY (approx. 4 mi)

Between **Carmel** and **Monterey,** the Highway 1 cuts across the base of the Monterey Peninsula. Pony up the toll and take a brief detour to follow famous **17-Mile Drive,** which traverses a surf-pounded landscape of cypress trees, sea lions, gargantuan estates, and the world famous **Pebble Beach Golf Links.** Take your time here as well, and be sure to allow lots of time for pulling off to enjoy the gorgeous views.

If you have the time, spend a day checking out the sights in **Monterey,** especially the kelp forests and bat rays of the **Monterey Bay Aquarium** and the adobes and artifacts of **Monterey State Historic Park.**

MONTEREY TO SANTA CRUZ (approx. 42 mi)

From Monterey the highway rounds the gentle curve of Monterey Bay, passing through sand dunes and artichoke fields on its way to **Moss Landing** and the **Elkhorn Slough National Estuarine Marine Preserve.** Kayak or walk through the protected wetlands here, or board a pontoon safari boat—don't forget your binoculars. The historic seaside villages of **Aptos, Capitola,** and **Soquel,** just off the highway near the bay's midpoint, are ideal stopovers for beachcombing, antiquing, and hiking through redwoods. In boho **Santa Cruz,** just 7 mi north, walk along the **wharf,** ride the historic roller coaster on the **boardwalk,** and perch on the cliffs to watch surfers peel through tubes at **Steamer Lane.**

SANTA CRUZ TO SAN FRANCISCO (approx. 77 mi)

Highway 1 hugs the ocean's edge once again as it departs Santa Cruz and runs

Davenport cliffs, Devenport

northward past a string of secluded beaches and small towns. Stop and stretch your legs in the tiny, artsy town of **Davenport,** where you can wander through several galleries and enjoy sumptuous views from the bluffs. At **Año Nuevo State Reserve,** walk down to the dunes to view gargantuan elephant

FRIGID WATERS

If you're planning to jump in the ocean in Northern California, wear a wetsuit or prepare to shiver. Even in summer, the water temperatures warm up to just barely tolerable. The fog tends to burn off earlier in the day at relatively sheltered beaches near Monterey Bay's midpoint, near Aptos, Capitola and Santa Cruz. These beaches also tend to attract softer waves than those on the bay's outer edges.

Half Moon Bay

TOP 5 PLACES TO LINGER

- 17 Mile Drive
- Monterey
- Santa Cruz
- Año Nuevo State Reserve
- Half Moon Bay

seals lounging on shore, then break for a meal or snack in **Pescadero** or **Half Moon Bay.**

From Half Moon Bay to **Daly City,** the road includes a number of shoulderless twists and turns that demand slower speeds and nerves of steel. Signs of urban development soon appear: mansions holding fast to Pacific cliffs and then, as the road veers slightly inland to merge with Skyline Boulevard, boxlike houses sprawling across **Daly City** and **South San Francisco.**

Updated
by Cheryl
Crabtree

Natural beauty is at the heart of this region's enormous appeal—you sense it everywhere, whether you're exploring one of Monterey Bay's attractive coast-side towns, relaxing at a luxurious resort, or touring the coast on the lookout for marine life.

It's been this way for a long time: an abiding current of plenty runs through the region's history. Military buffs see it in centuries' worth of battles for control of the rich territory. John Steinbeck saw it in the success of a community built on the elbow grease of farm laborers in the Salinas Valley and fishermen along Cannery Row. Biologists see it in the ocean's potential as a more sustainable source of food.

Downtown Carmel-by-the-Sea and Monterey are walks through history. The bay itself is protected by the Monterey Bay National Marine Sanctuary, the nation's largest undersea canyon—bigger and deeper than the Grand Canyon. And of course, the backdrop of natural beauty is still everywhere to be seen.

PLANNING

WHEN TO GO

Summer is peak season; mild weather brings in big crowds. In this coastal region, a cool breeze generally blows and fog often rolls in from offshore; you will frequently need a sweater or windbreaker. Off-season, from November through April, fewer people visit and the mood is mellower. Rainfall is heaviest in January and February, but autumn through spring days are crystal clear more often than in summer.

GETTING HERE AND AROUND

BY AIR

Monterey Peninsula Airport is 3 mi east of downtown Monterey (take Olmstead Road off Highway 68). It's served by Allegiant Air, American Eagle, United/United Express, and US Airways. Taxi service to downtown runs about $15 to $17; to Carmel the fare is $23 to $32. To and from San Jose International Airport and San Francisco International

Airport, Monterey Airbus starts at $35 and the Early Bird Airport Shuttle runs $75 to $190.

Airport Contacts Monterey Peninsula Airport ✉ *200 Fred Kane Dr., Monterey* ☎ *831/648–7000* ⊕ *www.montereyairport.com.*

Central Coast Cab Company ☎ *831/626–3333.* **Monterey Airbus** ☎ *831/373–7777* ⊕ *www.montereyairbus.com.* **Early Bird Airport Shuttle** ☎ *831/462–3933* ⊕ *www.earlybirdairportshuttle.com.*

Taxi Contacts Yellow Checker Cabs ☎ *831/646–1234.*

BY BUS

Greyhound serves Santa Cruz and Salinas from San Francisco and San Jose three or four times daily. The trips take about 3 and 4½ hours, respectively. Monterey-Salinas Transit provides frequent service between the peninsula's towns and many major sightseeing spots and shopping areas. Fares are $1, $2, or $3, depending on the line. Commuter lines, e.g., between Monterey and San Jose, cost $10. A day pass costs $6 to $12, depending on how many zones you'll be traveling through. Monterey-Salinas Transit also runs the MST Trolley, which links major attractions on the Monterey waterfront. The free shuttle operates late May through early September, daily from 10 to 7; from July 5 through early September service is extended weekends and holidays from 10 to 8.

Bus Contacts Greyhound ☎ *800/231–2222* ⊕ *www.greyhound.com.* **Monterey-Salinas Transit** ☎ *888/678–2871* ⊕ *www.mst.org.*

BY CAR

Highway 1 runs south–north along the coast, linking the towns of Carmel-by-the-Sea, Monterey, and Santa Cruz; some sections have only two lanes. The freeway, U.S. 101, lies to the east, roughly parallel to Highway 1. The two roads are connected by Highway 68 from Pacific Grove to Salinas; Highway 156 from Castroville to Prunedale; Highway 152 from Watsonville to Gilroy; and Highway 17 from Santa Cruz to San Jose. Highway 17 crosses the redwood-filled Santa Cruz Mountains. ■TIP→ Traffic near Santa Cruz can crawl to a standstill during commuter hours.

The drive south from San Francisco to Monterey can be made comfortably in three hours or less. The most scenic way is to follow Highway 1 down the coast past flower, pumpkin, and artichoke fields and small seaside communities. Unless you drive on sunny weekends when locals are heading for the beach, the two-lane coast highway may take no longer than the freeway. A sometimes-faster route is I–280 south from San Francisco to Highway 17, north of San Jose. A third option is to follow U.S. 101 south through San Jose to Prunedale and then take Highway 156 west to Highway 1 south into Monterey.

From Los Angeles the drive to Monterey can be made in five to six hours by heading north on U.S. 101 to Salinas and then west on Highway 68. The spectacular but slow alternative is to take U.S. 101 to San Luis Obispo and then follow the hairpin turns of Highway 1 up the coast. Allow about three extra hours if you take this route.

BY TRAIN

Amtrak's *Coast Starlight* runs between Los Angeles, Oakland, and Seattle. From the train station in Salinas, connecting Amtrak Thruway buses serve Monterey and Carmel-by-the-Sea; from San Jose, connecting buses serve Santa Cruz.

Train Contacts Amtrak ☎ 800/872–7245 ⊕ www.amtrakcalifornia.com. **Salinas Amtrak Station** ⊠ 30 Railroad Ave., Salinas ☎ 800/872–7245.

TOUR OPTIONS

California Parlor Car Tours operates motor-coach tours from San Francisco that include one or two days in Monterey and Carmel. Ag Venture Tours runs wine-tasting, sightseeing, and agricultural tours in the Monterey, Salinas, Carmel Valley, and Santa Cruz areas.

Tour Contacts Ag Venture Tours ☎ 831/761–8463 ⊕ www.agventuretours. com. **California Parlor Car Tours** ☎ 415/474–7500, 800/227–4250 ⊕ www.calpartours.com.

VISITOR INFORMATION

Contacts Monterey County Convention & Visitors Bureau ☎ 877/666–8373 ⊕ www.seemonterey.com. **Monterey County Vintners and Growers Association** ☎ 831/375–9400 ⊕ www.montereywines.org. **Pajaro Valley Chamber of Commerce & Agriculture** ⊠ 449 Union St., Watsonville ☎ 831/724–3900 ⊕ www.pajarovalleychamber.com. **Salinas Valley Chamber of Commerce** ⊠ 119 E. Alisal St., Salinas ☎ 831/751–7725 ⊕ www.salinaschamber.com. **San Lorenzo Valley Chamber of Commerce** ⊠ Box 1510, Felton ☎ 831/222–2120 ⊕ www.slvchamber.org. **Santa Cruz County Conference and Visitors Council** ⊠ 303 Water St., Santa Cruz ☎ 831/425–1234, 800/833–3494 ⊕ www.santacruz. org. **Santa Cruz Mountain Winegrowers Association** ⊠ 7605-A Old Dominion Ct., Aptos ☎ 831/685–8463 ⊕ www.scmwa.com.

RESTAURANTS

Between San Francisco and Los Angeles, some of the finest dining to be found is around Monterey Bay. The surrounding waters are full of fish, wild game roams the foothills, and the inland valleys are some of the most fertile in the country—local chefs draw on this bounty for their fresh, truly California cuisine. Except at beachside stands and inexpensive eateries, where anything goes, casual but neat dress is the norm. Only a few places require formal attire.

HOTELS

Monterey-area accommodations range from no-frills motels to luxurious hotels. Pacific Grove, amply endowed with ornate Victorian houses, has quietly turned itself into the region's B&B capital; Carmel also has charming inns in residential areas. Truly lavish resorts, with everything from featherbeds to heated floors, cluster in exclusive Pebble Beach and pastoral Carmel Valley.

High season runs April through October. Rates in winter, especially at the larger hotels, may drop by 50% or more, and B&Bs often offer midweek specials in the off-season. However, special events throughout the year can fill lodgings far in advance. Whatever the month, even the simplest of the area's lodgings are expensive, and many properties require a two-night stay on weekends. ⚠ Many of the fancier accommodations are not suitable for children, so if you're traveling with kids, be sure to ask before you book.

Bed and Breakfast Inns of Santa Cruz County. Bed and Breakfast Inns of Santa Cruz County, an association of innkeepers, can help you find a bed-and-breakfast. ⊕ *www.santacruzbnb.com.*

WHAT IT COSTS					
	¢	$	$$	$$$	$$$$
Restaurants	under $10	$10–$15	$16–$22	$23–$30	over $30
Hotels	under $90	$90–$120	$121–$175	$176–$250	over $250

Restaurant prices are for a main course at dinner, excluding sales tax of 8.25%–9.5% (depending on location). Hotel prices are for two people in a standard double room in high season, excluding service charges and 10%–10.5% tax.

CARMEL AND PACIFIC GROVE

CARMEL-BY-THE-SEA

26 mi north of Big Sur on Hwy. 1.

Although the community has grown quickly through the years and its population quadruples with tourists on weekends and in summer, Carmel-by-the-Sea, commonly referred to as Carmel, retains its identity as a quaint village. Self-consciously charming, the town is populated by many celebrities, major and minor, and has more than its share of quirky ordinances. For instance, women wearing high heels do not have the right to pursue legal action if they trip and fall on the cobblestone streets, and drivers who hit a tree and leave the scene are charged with hit-and-run.

Buildings still have no street numbers (street names are written on discreet white posts) and consequently no mail delivery (if you really want to see the locals, go to the post office). Artists started this community, and their legacy is evident in the numerous galleries. Wandering the side streets off Ocean Avenue, where you can poke into hidden courtyards and stop at cafés for tea and crumpets, is a pleasure.

GETTING HERE AND AROUND

From north or south follow Highway 1 to Carmel. To access Highway 1 from U.S. 101 take Highway 156 West from Prunedale, about 10 mi north of Salinas, or Highway 68 from Salinas. Head west at Ocean Avenue to reach the main village hub. In summer the MST Carmel-by-the-Sea Trolley loops around town to the beach and mission every 30 minutes or so.

ESSENTIALS

Visitor Information Carmel Chamber of Commerce ✉ *San Carlos, between 5th and 6th* ☎ *831/624–2522, 800/550–4333* ⊕ *www.carmelcalifornia.org.*

Carmel Walks. For insight into Carmel's colorful history and culture, join a guided two-hour Carmel Walks tour through hidden courtyards, gardens, and pathways around town. Tours ($25) depart from the Pine Inn courtyard on

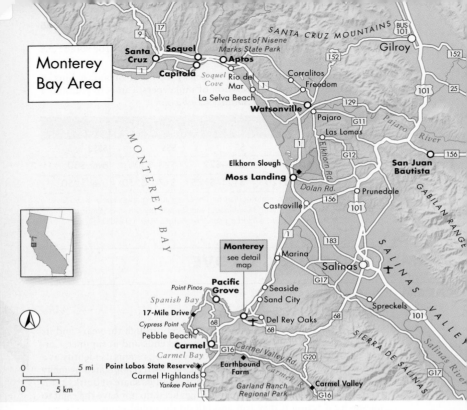

Monterey Bay Area

Santa Cruz · Soquel · Aptos · Capitola · Rio del Mar · La Selva Beach · Watsonville · Pajaro · Las Lomas · Moss Landing · Elkhorn Slough · Castroville · Prunedale · San Juan Bautista · Marina · Seaside · Sand City · Salinas · Spreckels · Pacific Grove · Point Pinos · Spanish Bay · 17-Mile Drive · Cypress Point · Pebble Beach · Del Rey Oaks · Carmel · Carmel Bay · Point Lobos State Reserve · Carmel Highlands · Yankee Point · Earthbound Farm · Carmel Valley · Garland Ranch Regional Park

Santa Cruz Mountains · The Forest of Nisene Marks State Park · Corralitos · Freedom · Gilroy · Pajaro River · Elkhorn Rd. · Dolan Rd. · Carmel Valley Rd. · Gabilan Range · Salinas Valley · Sierra de Salinas · Salinas River · Monterey Bay

0 — 5 mi
0 — 5 km

Lincoln near Ocean Avenue Tues.–Fri. at 10 and Sat. at 10 and 2; call to reserve a spot. ⊠ *Lincoln St. at 6th Ave.* 🕾 *831/642–2700* ⊕ *www.carmelwalks.com.*

EXPLORING

Ocean Avenue. Downtown Carmel's chief lure is shopping, especially along its main street, Ocean Avenue, between Junipero Avenue and Camino Real; the architecture here is a mishmash of ersatz Tudor, Mediterranean, and other styles.

Carmel Plaza. Carmel Plaza, in the east end of the village proper, holds more than 50 shops and restaurants. ⊠ *Ocean and Junipero Aves.* 🕾 *831/624–1385* ⊕ *www.carmelplaza.com.*

★ **Carmel Mission.** Long before it became a shopping and browsing destination, Carmel was an important religious center during the establishment of Spanish California. That heritage is preserved in the Mission San Carlos Borroméo del Rio Carmelo, more commonly known as the Carmel Mission. Founded in 1771, it served as headquarters for the mission system in California under Father Junípero Serra. Adjoining the stone church is a tranquil garden planted with California poppies. Museum rooms at the mission include an early kitchen, Serra's spartan sleeping quarters, and the first college library in California. ⊠ *3080 Rio Rd., at Lasuen Dr.* 🕾 *831/624–3600* ⊕ *www.carmelmission.org* 🖾 *$6.50* ⊘ *Mon.–Sat. 9:30–5, Sun. 10:30–5.*

Tor House. Scattered throughout the pines in Carmel-by-the-Sea are houses and cottages originally built for the writers, artists, and photographers who discovered the area decades ago. Among the most impressive dwellings is Tor House, a stone cottage built in 1919 by poet Robinson Jeffers on a craggy knoll overlooking the sea. Portraits, books, and unusual art objects fill the low-ceiling rooms. The highlight of the small estate is Hawk Tower, a

detached edifice set with stones from the Carmel coastline—as well as one from the Great Wall of China. The docents who lead tours (six people maximum) are well informed about the poet's work and life. Advance reservations for tours via e-mail at 🖃 *thf@torhouse.org* are recommended. ✉ *26304 Ocean View Ave.* ☎ *831/624–1813* ⊕ *www.torhouse.org* 🖃 *$10* 🕙 *Tours on hr Fri. and Sat. 10–3* ☞ *No children under 12.*

Carmel Beach. Carmel-by-the-Sea's greatest attraction is its rugged coastline, with pine and cypress forests and countless inlets. Carmel Beach, an easy walk from downtown shops, has sparkling white sands and magnificent sunsets. ■TIP→ Dogs are allowed to romp off-leash here. ✉ *End of Ocean Ave.*

Carmel River State Beach. This sugar-white beach, stretching 106 acres along Carmel Bay, is adjacent to a bird sanctuary, where you might spot pelicans, kingfishers, hawks, and sandpipers. ✉ *Off Scenic Rd. south of Carmel Beach* ☎ *831/624–4909, 831/649–2836* ⊕ *www.parks.ca.gov* 🖃 *Free* 🕙 *Daily 8 am–½ hr after sunset.*

★ **Point Lobos State Reserve.** A 350-acre headland harboring a wealth of marine life, this reserve lies a few miles south of Carmel. The best way to explore here is to walk along one of the many trails. The Cypress Grove Trail leads through a forest of Monterey cypress (one of only two natural groves remaining), which clings to the rocks above an emerald-green cove. Sea Lion Point Trail is a good place to view sea lions. From those and other trails you may also spot otters, harbor seals, and (in winter and spring) migrating whales. An additional 750 acres of the reserve is an undersea marine park open to qualified scuba divers. ■TIP→ Arrive early (or in late afternoon) to avoid crowds; the parking lots fill up. No pets are allowed. ✉ *Hwy. 1* ☎ *831/624–4909, 831/624–8413 for scuba-diving reservations* ⊕ *www.pointlobos.org* 🖃 *$10 per vehicle* 🕙 *Daily 8 am–½ hr after sunset.*

WHERE TO EAT

$$$

FRENCH BISTRO

★

✗ **André's Bouchée.** The food here presents an innovative bistro-style take on local ingredients. A Monterey Bay sea scallop reduction adorns pan-seared veal tenderloin; grilled rib-eye steaks are topped with a shallot–Cabernet Sauvignon sauce. With its copper wine bar, the dining room feels more urban than most of Carmel; perhaps that's why this is the "cool" place in town to dine. The stellar wine list sources the selection at adjoining Andre's Wine Merchant. ⊠ *Mission St., between Ocean and 7th Aves.* ☎ *831/626–7880* ⊕ *www.andresbouchee.com* ⌂ *Reservations essential* ☾ *No lunch Mon. and Tues.*

$$$ ✕ **Anton and Michel.** Carefully prepared European cuisine is the draw at
CONTINENTAL this airy restaurant. The rack of lamb is carved at the table, the grilled Halloumi cheese and tomatoes are meticulously stacked and served with basil and kalamata olive tapenade, and the desserts are set aflame before your eyes. In summer, you (and your dog!) can have lunch served in the courtyard; inside, the dining room looks onto a lighted fountain. ⊠ *Mission St. and 7th Ave.* ☎ *831/624–2406* ⊕ *www.antonandmichel. com* ⌂ *Reservations essential.*

$$$$ ✕ **Casanova.** Built in a former home, this cozy restaurant inspires Euro-
★ pean-style celebration and romance—chairs are painted in all colors,
MEDITERRANEAN accordions hang from the walls, and tiny party lights dance along the low ceilings. All entrées include antipasti and your choice of appetizers, which all but insist that you sit back and enjoy a long meal. The food consists of delectable seasonal dishes from southern France and northern Italy. Private dining and a special menu are offered at Van Gogh's Table, a special table imported from France's Auberge Ravoux, the artist's final residence. ⊠ *5th Ave., between San Carlos and Mission Sts.* ☎ *831/625–0501* ⊕ *www.casanovarestaurant.com* ⌂ *Reservations essential.*

$ ✕ **The Cottage Restaurant.** For the best breakfast in Carmel, look no fur-
AMERICAN ther: The menu here offers six different preparations of eggs Benedict, and all kinds of sweet and savory crepes. This family-friendly spot serves sandwiches, pizzas, and homemade soups at lunch and simple entreés at dinner, but the best meals appear on the breakfast menu (good thing it's served all day). ⊠ *Lincoln St., between Ocean and 7th Aves.* ☎ *831/625–6260* ⊕ *www.cottagerestaurant.com* ☾ *No dinner Sun.–Wed.*

$$$ ✕ **Flying Fish Grill.** Simple in appearance yet bold with its flavors, this Jap-
SEAFOOD anese–California seafood restaurant is one of Carmel's most inventive eateries. Among the best entrées is the almond-crusted sea bass served with Chinese cabbage and rock shrimp stir-fry. The warm, wood-lined dining room is broken up into very private booths. For the entrance, go down the steps near the gates to Carmel Plaza. ⊠ *Mission St., between Ocean and 7th Aves.* ☎ *831/625–1962* ☾ *No lunch.*

$ ✕ **Jack London's.** If anyone's awake after dinner in Carmel, he's at Jack
AMERICAN London's. This publike local hangout is the only Carmel restaurant to serve food until midnight (Sunday through Thursday until 11). The menu includes everything from nachos to steaks. ⊠ *Su Vecino Court on Dolores St., between 5th and 6th Aves.* ☎ *831/624–2336* ⊕ *jacklondons.com.*

$ ✕ **Katy's Place.** Locals flock to Katy's cozy, country-style eatery to fill
AMERICAN up on hearty eggs Benedict dishes. (There are 16 types to choose from, each made with three fresh eggs.) The huge breakfast menu also includes omelets, pancakes, and eight types of Belgian waffles. An assortment of salads, sandwiches, and burgers is available at lunch—try the grilled calamari burger with melted Monterey Jack cheese. ⊠ *Mission St., between 5th and 6th Aves.* ☎ *831/624–0199* ⊕ *www.katysplacecarmel. com* ▭ *No credit cards* ☾ *No dinner.*

Point Lobos Reserve State Park is home to one of the only two natural stands of Monterey Cypress in the world.

$$$ ✕**L'Escargot.** Chef-owner Kericos Loutas personally sees to each plate of
FRENCH food served at this romantic and mercifully unpretentious French restaurant (which also has a full bar). Take his recommendation and order the duck confit in puff pastry or the bone-in steak in truffle butter; or, if you can't decide, choose the three-course prix-fixe dinner. Service is warm and attentive. ⊠ *Mission St., between 4th and 5th Aves.* ☎ *831/620–1942* ⊕ *www.escargot-carmel.com* ⌂ *Reservations essential* ⊘ *No lunch.*

$ ✕**Tuck Box.** This bright little restaurant is in a cottage right out of a
AMERICAN fairy tale, complete with a stone fireplace that's lighted on rainy days. Handmade scones are the house specialty, and are good for breakfast or afternoon tea. ⊠ *Dolores St., between Ocean and 7th Aves.* ☎ *831/624–6365* ⊕ *www.tuckbox.com* ⌂ *Reservations not accepted* ⊟ *No credit cards* ⊘ *No dinner.*

WHERE TO STAY
For expanded reviews, visit Fodors.com.

$$$$ 🏨 **Cypress Inn.** The decorating style here is luxurious but refreshingly simple. **Pros:** luxury without snobbery; popular lounge; traditional British-style afternoon tea. **Cons:** not for the pet-phobic. ⊠ *Lincoln St. and 7th Ave., Box Y* ☎ *831/624–3871, 800/443–7443* ⊕ *www.cypress-inn. com* ⇆ *39 rooms, 5 suites* ⌂ *In-room: a/c, Wi-Fi. In-hotel: restaurant, bar, some pets allowed* ❙⊙❙ *Breakfast.*

$$$$ 🏨 **Highlands Inn, A Hyatt Hotel.** High on a hill overlooking the Pacific,
★ this place has superb views. **Pros:** killer views; romantic getaway; great food. **Cons:** thin walls; must drive to Carmel. ⊠ *120 Highlands Dr.* ☎ *831/620–1234, 800/233–1234* ⊕ *highlandsinn.hyatt.com* ⇆ *46*

rooms, 2 suites ⚅ In-room: no a/c, kitchen, Internet, Wi-Fi. In-hotel: restaurant, bar, pool, gym, laundry facilities, business center.

$$$$
Fodor's Choice
★
L'Auberge Carmel. Stepping through the doors of this elegant inn is like being transported to a little European village. **Pros:** in town but off the main drag; four blocks from the beach. **Cons:** touristy area; not a good choice for families. ⊠ Monte Verde, at 7th Ave. 📞 831/624–8578 ⊕ www.laubergecarmel.com 🛏 20 rooms ⚅ In-room: a/c, Wi-Fi. In-hotel: restaurant, bar 🍴 Breakfast.

$$
Mission Ranch. The property at Mission Ranch is gorgeous and includes a sprawling sheep pasture, bird-filled wetlands, and a sweeping view of the ocean. **Pros:** farm setting; pastoral views; great for tennis buffs. **Cons:** busy parking lot; must drive to the heart of town. ⊠ 26270 Dolores St. 📞 831/624–6436, 800/538–8221, 831/625-9040 restaurant ⊕ www.missionranchcarmel.com 🛏 31 rooms ⚅ In-room: no a/c. In-hotel: restaurant, bar, tennis court, gym, business center 🍴 Breakfast.

$$
Sea View Inn. In a residential area a few hundred feet from the beach, this restored 1905 home has a double parlor with two fireplaces, Oriental rugs, canopy beds, and a spacious front porch. **Pros:** quiet; private; close to the beach. **Cons:** small building; uphill trek to the heart of town. ⊠ Camino Real, between 11th and 12th Aves. 📞 831/624–8778 ⊕ www.seaviewinncarmel.com 🛏 8 rooms, 6 with private bath ⚅ In-room: no a/c, no TV, Wi-Fi 🍴 Breakfast.

$$$$
Tickle Pink Inn. Atop a towering cliff, this inn has views of the Big Sur coastline, which you can contemplate from your private balcony. **Pros:** close to great hiking; intimate; dramatic views. **Cons:** close to a big hotel; lots of traffic during the day. ⊠ 155 Highland Dr. 📞 831/624–1244, 800/635–4774 ⊕ www.ticklepink.com 🛏 23 rooms, 10 suites, 1 cottage ⚅ In-room: no a/c, Wi-Fi. In-hotel: business center 🍴 Breakfast.

$$$$
★
Tradewinds Carmel. Its sleek decor inspired by the South Seas, this converted motel encircles a courtyard with waterfalls, a meditation garden, and a fire pit. **Pros:** serene; within walking distance of restaurants; friendly service. **Cons:** no pool; long walk to the beach. ⊠ Mission St., at 3rd Ave. 📞 831/624–2776 ⊕ www.tradewindscarmel.com 🛏 26 rooms, 2 suites ⚅ In-room: no a/c, safe, Wi-Fi. In-hotel: spa, some pets allowed 🍴 Breakfast.

SHOPPING

ART GALLERIES   **Carmel Art Association.** Carmel Art Association exhibits the original paintings and sculptures of local artists. ⊠ Dolores St., between 5th and 6th Aves. 📞 831/624–6176 ⊕ www.carmelart.org.

Galerie Plein Aire. Galerie Plein Aire showcases oil paintings by a group of local artists. ⊠ Dolores St., between 5th and 6th Aves. 📞 831/625–5686 ⊕ www.galeriepleinaire.com.

Weston Gallery. Run by the family of the late Edward Weston, Weston Gallery is hands down the best photography gallery around, with contemporary color photography complemented by classic black-and-whites. ⊠ 6th Ave., between Dolores and Lincoln Sts. 📞 831/624–4453 ⊕ www.westongallery.com.

SPECIALTY
SHOPS

Bittner. Bittner has a fine selection of collectible and vintage pens from around the world. ⊠ *Ocean Ave., between Mission and San Carlos Sts.* ☎ *831/626–8828, 888/248–8637 toll free* ⊕ *www.bittner.com.*

Intima. Intima is the place to find European lingerie that ranges from lacy to racy. ⊠ *Mission St., between Ocean and 7th Aves.* ☎ *831/625–0599.*

Jan de Luz. Jan de Luz monograms and embroiders fine linens (including bathrobes) while you wait. ⊠ *Dolores St., between Ocean and 7th Aves.* ☎ *831/622–7621* ⊕ *www.jandeluz.com.*

Madrigal. Madrigal carries sportswear, sweaters, and accessories for women. ⊠ *Carmel Plaza and Mission St.* ☎ *831/624–3477.*

CARMEL VALLEY

10 mi east of Carmel, Hwy. 1 to Carmel Valley Rd.

Carmel Valley Road, which heads inland from Highway 1 south of Carmel-by-the-Sea, is the main thoroughfare through this valley, a secluded enclave of horse ranchers and other well-heeled residents who prefer the area's sunny climate to the fog and wind on the coast. Once thick with dairy farms, the valley has recently proved itself as a venerable wine appellation. Tiny Carmel Valley Village, about 13 mi southeast of Carmel-by-the-Sea via Carmel Valley Road, has several crafts shops and art galleries, as well as tasting rooms for numerous local wineries.

GETTING HERE AND AROUND

From U.S. 101 north or south, exit at Highway 68 and head west toward the coast. Scenic, two-lane Laureles Grade winds over the mountains to Carmel Valley Road, just a few miles north of Carmel Valley Village. You can also continue on Highway 68 to Monterey, then head south on Highway 1 to Carmel and turn east on Carmel Valley Road.

EXPLORING

Bernardus Tasting Room. At Bernardus Tasting Room, you can sample many of the wines—including older vintages and reserves—from the nearby Bernardus Winery and Vineyard. ⊠ *5 W. Carmel Valley Rd.* ☎ *831/298–8021, 800/223–2533* ⊕ *www.bernardus.com* ☉ *Daily 11–5.*

Earthbound Farm. Pick up fresh veggies, ready-to-eat meals, gourmet groceries, flowers, and gifts at 32-acre Earthbound Farm, the world's largest grower of organic produce. You can also take a romp in the kid's garden, cut your own herbs, and stroll through the chamomile aromatherapy labyrinth. On Saturday from April through December the farm offers special events, from bug walks to garlic-braiding workshops. ⊠ *7250 Carmel Valley Rd.* ☎ *831/625–6219* ⊕ *www.ebfarm.com* ☑ *Free* ☉ *Mon.–Sat. 8–6:30, Sun. 9–6.*

Garland Ranch Regional Park. Garland Ranch Regional Park has hiking trails across nearly 4,500 acres of property that includes meadows, forested hillsides, and creeks. ⊠ *Carmel Valley Rd., 9 mi east of Carmel-by-the-Sea* ☎ *831/659–4488.*

Château Julien. The extensive Château Julien winery, recognized internationally for its Chardonnays and Merlots, gives weekday tours at 10:30 and 2:30 and weekends at 12:30 and 2:30, all by appointment. The

7

tasting room is open daily. ✉ *8940 Carmel Valley Rd.* ☎ *831/624–2600* ⊕ *www.chateaujulien.com* ⊗ *Weekdays 8–5, weekends 11–5.*

WHERE TO EAT

$$
STEAKHOUSE

✕**Café Rustica.** Italian-inspired country cooking is the focus at this lively roadhouse. Specialties include roasted meats, pastas, and thin-crust pizzas from the wood-fired oven. Because of the tile floors, it can get quite noisy inside; opt for a table outside if you want a quieter meal. ✉ *10 Delfino Pl.* ☎ *831/659–4444* ⊕ *www.caferusticacarmel.com* ⌕ *Reservations essential* ⊗ *Closed Mon.*

$
AMERICAN

✕**Wagon Wheel Coffee Shop.** This local hangout decorated with wagon wheels, cowboy hats, and lassos serves up terrific hearty breakfasts, including oatmeal and banana pancakes, eggs Benedict, and biscuits and gravy. The lunch menu includes a dozen different burgers and other sandwiches. ✉ *Valley Hill Center, Carmel Valley Rd., next to Quail Lodge* ☎ *831/624–8878* ▭ *No credit cards* ⊗ *No dinner.*

$$$
AMERICAN

✕**Will's Fargo.** On the main street of Carmel Valley Village since the 1920s, this restaurant calls itself a "dressed-up saloon." Steer horns and gilt-frame paintings adorn the walls of the Victorian-style dining room; you can also eat on the patios. The menu is mainly seafood and steaks, including a 20-ounce porterhouse. ✉ *16 E. Carmel Valley Rd.* ☎ *831/659–2774* ⊕ *www.bernardus.com* ⊗ *No lunch. Closed Tues. and Wed.*

WHERE TO STAY

For expanded hotel reviews, visit Fodors.com.

$$$$
Fodor's Choice
★

⌂ **Bernardus Lodge.** Even before you check in at this luxury spa resort, the valet hands you a glass of Sauvignon Blanc. **Pros:** exceptional personal service; outstanding food and wine. **Cons:** some guests can seem snooty; pricey. ✉ *415 Carmel Valley Rd.* ☎ *831/658–3400, 888/648–9463* ⊕ *www.bernardus.com* ⇌ *56 rooms, 1 suite* ⌂ *In-room: a/c, Internet, Wi-Fi. In-hotel: restaurant, bar, pool, tennis court, gym, spa, business center.*

$$$$

⌂ **Carmel Valley Ranch Resort & Spa.** Hotel scion John Pritzker bought this 500-acre all-suites resort in 2009 and committed more than $30 million to transform the property into an upscale experiential getaway nonpareil. **Pros:** stunning natural setting; tons of activities; state-of-the-art amenities. **Cons:** must drive several miles to shops and nightlife; pricey. ✉ *1 Old Ranch Rd.* ☎ *831/626–2510* ☎ *855/687–7262* ⊕ *www.carmelvalleyranch.com* ⇌ *139 suites* ⌂ *In-room: a/c, Wi-Fi. In-hotel: restaurant, bar, golf course, pool, tennis court, gym, spa, children's programs, some pets allowed.*

WINE TOURING WITH THE MST

Why risk driving while wine tasting when you can hop aboard the Carmel Valley Grapevine Express? This Monterey-Salinas Transit bus travels between downtown Monterey and Carmel Valley Village, with stops near wineries, restaurants, and shopping centers. Buses depart daily every hour from 11 to 6. At $6 for a ride-all-day pass, it's an incredible bargain. For more information, call ☎ *888/678–2871* or visit ⊕ *www.mst.org.*

$$$$ ☺ **Stonepine Estate Resort.** Set on 330 pastoral acres, this former estate
Fodor's Choice   of the Crocker banking family has been converted to a luxurious inn.
★   **Pros:** supremely exclusive. **Cons:** difficult to get a reservation; far from
the coast. ⊠ *150 E. Carmel Valley Rd.* ☎ *831/659–2245* ⊕ *www.
stonepineestate.com* ⤳ *3 rooms, 9 suites, 3 cottages* ⚘ *In-room: no
a/c, safe, kitchen, Wi-Fi. In-hotel: restaurant, golf course, pool, tennis
court, gym, some pets allowed.*

GOLF

Rancho Cañada Golf Club. Rancho Cañada Golf Club is a public course
with 36 holes, some of them overlooking the Carmel River. Fees range
from $40 to $70, plus $19 per rider for cart rental, depending on
course and tee time. ⊠ *4860 Carmel Valley Rd., 1 mi east of Hwy. 1*
☎ *831/624–0111.*

17-MILE DRIVE

Fodor's Choice   *Off North San Antonio Rd. in Carmel-by-the-Sea or off Sunset Dr. in*
★   *Pacific Grove.*

Primordial nature resides in quiet harmony with palatial late-20th-cen-
tury estates along 17-Mile Drive, which winds through an 8,400-acre
microcosm of the Monterey coastal landscape. Dotting the drive are
rare Monterey cypress, trees so gnarled and twisted that Robert Louis
Stevenson described them as "ghosts fleeing before the wind." Some
sightseers balk at the $9.50-per-car fee collected at the gates—this is
one of only two private toll roads west of the Mississippi—but most
find the drive well worth the price. An alternative is to grab a bike.
■ TIP→ Cyclists tour for free. Visitors who dine at a Pebble Beach restaurant
receive a fee refund if they show a receipt at the exit gate.

GETTING HERE AND AROUND

If you drive south from Monterey on Highway 1, exit at 17-Mile-Drive/
Sunset Drive in Pacific Grove to find the northern entrance gate. Coming from Carmel, exit at Ocean Avenue and follow the road almost to
the beach; turn right on N. San Antonio Road to the Carmel Gate. You
can also enter through the Highway 1 Gate at Scenic Drive/Sunridge
Road. MST buses provide regular service in and around Pebble Beach.

EXPLORING

Pebble Beach Golf Links. You can take in views of the impeccable greens
at Pebble Beach Golf Links over a drink or lunch at the Lodge at Pebble
Beach. The ocean plays a major role in the 18th hole of the famed
links. Each February the course is the main site of the AT&T Pebble
Beach Pro-Am (formerly the Bing Crosby Pro-Am), where show business celebrities and golf pros team up for one of the nation's most
glamorous tournaments. ⊠ *17-Mile Dr., near Lodge at Pebble Beach*
☎ *800/654–9300* ⊕ *www.pebblebeach.com.*

Crocker Marble Palace. Many of the stately homes along 17-Mile Drive
reflect the classic Monterey or Spanish Mission style typical of the
region. A standout is the Crocker Marble Palace, about a mile south
of the Lone Cypress (⇨ *below*). It's a private waterfront estate inspired
by a Byzantine castle, easily identifiable by its dozens of marble arches.

7

Lone Cypress. The most-photographed tree along 17-Mile Drive is the weather-sculpted Lone Cypress, which grows out of a precipitous out-cropping above the waves about 1½ mi up the road from Pebble Beach Golf Links. You can stop for a view of the Lone Cypress at a parking area, but you can't walk out to the tree.

Seal Rock. Sea creatures and birds—as well as some very friendly ground squirrels—make use of Seal Rock, the largest of a group of islands about 2 mi north of Lone Cypress.

Bird Rock. Bird Rock, the largest of several islands at the southern end of the Monterey Peninsula Country Club's golf course, teems with harbor seals, sea lions, cormorants, and pelicans.

WHERE TO STAY

For expanded hotel reviews, visit Fodors.com.

$$$$ ★ 🏨 **Casa Palmero.** This exclusive spa resort evokes a stately Mediterranean villa. **Pros:** ultimate in pampering; more private than sister resorts; right on the golf course. **Cons:** pricey; may be *too* posh for some. ✉ *1518 Cypress Dr.* ☎ *831/622–6650, 800/654–9300* ⊕ *www.pebblebeach.com* 🛏 *21 rooms, 3 suites* ⚱ *In-room: a/c, Wi-Fi. In-hotel: bar, golf course, pool, spa.*

$$$$ 🏨 **Inn at Spanish Bay.** This resort sprawls across a breathtaking stretch of shoreline, and has lush, 600-square-foot rooms. **Pros:** attentive service; tons of amenities; spectacular views. **Cons:** huge hotel; four miles from other Pebble Beach Resort facilities. ✉ *2700 17-Mile Dr.* ☎ *831/647–7500, 800/654–9300* ⊕ *www.pebblebeach.com* 🛏 *252 rooms, 17 suites* ⚱ *In-room: no a/c, Internet, Wi-Fi. In-hotel: restaurant, bar, golf course, pool, tennis court, gym, beach, business center.*

$$$$ ★ 🏨 **Lodge at Pebble Beach.** All rooms have fireplaces and many have won-derful ocean views at this circa 1919 resort. **Pros:** world-class golf; bor-ders the ocean and fairways; fabulous facilities. **Cons:** some rooms are on the small side; very pricey. ✉ *1700 17-Mile Dr.* ☎ *831/624–3811, 800/654–9300* ⊕ *www.pebblebeach.com* 🛏 *142 rooms, 19 suites* ⚱ *In-room: no a/c, Internet, Wi-Fi. In-hotel: restaurant, bar, golf course, pool, tennis court, gym, spa, beach, business center, some pets allowed.*

GOLF

Links at Spanish Bay. The Links at Spanish Bay, which hugs a choice stretch of shoreline, is designed in the rugged manner of a traditional Scottish course, with sand dunes and coastal marshes interspersed among the greens. The greens fee is $260, plus $35 per person for cart rental (cart is included for resort guests); nonguests can reserve tee times up to two months in advance. ✉ *17-Mile Dr., north end* ☎ *831/624–3811, 831/624–6611, 800/654–9300.*

Pebble Beach Golf Links. Pebble Beach Golf Links attracts golfers from around the world, despite a greens fee of $495, plus $35 per person for an optional cart (complimentary cart for guests of the Pebble Beach and Spanish Bay resorts). Tee times are available to guests who book a mini-mum two-night stay. Nonguests can reserve a tee time only one day in advance on a space-available basis (up to a year for groups); resort guests can reserve up to 18 months in advance. ✉ *17-Mile Dr., near Lodge at Pebble Beach* ☎ *831/624–3811, 831/624–6611, 800/654–9300.*

Peter Hay. Peter Hay, a 9-hole, par-3 course, charges $30 per person, no reservations necessary. ⊠ *17-Mile Dr.* ☎ *831/622–8723.*

Poppy Hills. Poppy Hills, a splendid 18-hole course designed in 1986 by Robert Trent Jones Jr., has a greens fee of $200; an optional cart costs $36. Individuals may reserve up to one month in advance, groups up to a year. ⊠ *3200 Lopez Rd., at 17-Mile Dr.* ☎ *831/625–2035* ⊕ *www. poppyhillsgolf.com.*

Spyglass Hill. Spyglass Hill is among the most challenging Pebble Beach courses. With the first five holes bordering on the Pacific and the other 13 reaching deep into the Del Monte Forest, the views offer some consolation. The greens fee is $360, and an optional cart costs $35 (the cart is complimentary for resort guests). Reservations are essential and may be made up to one month in advance (18 months for guests). ⊠ *Stevenson Dr. and Spyglass Hill Rd.* ☎ *831/624–3811, 831/624–6611, 800/654–9300.*

PACIFIC GROVE

3 mi north of Carmel-by-the-Sea on Hwy. 68.

This picturesque town, which began as a summer retreat for church groups more than a century ago, recalls its prim and proper Victorian heritage in its host of tiny board-and-batten cottages and stately mansions. However, long before the church groups flocked here the area received thousands of annual pilgrims—in the form of bright orange-and-black monarch butterflies. They still come, migrating south from Canada and the Pacific Northwest to take residence in pine and eucalyptus groves from October through March. In Butterfly Town USA, as Pacific Grove is known, the sight of a mass of butterflies hanging from the branches like a long, fluttering veil is unforgettable.

A prime way to enjoy Pacific Grove is to walk or bicycle the 3 mi of city-owned shoreline along Ocean View Boulevard, a cliff-top area landscaped with native plants and dotted with benches meant for sitting and gazing at the sea. You can spot many types of birds here, including colonies of web-foot cormorants crowding the massive rocks rising out of the surf.

GETTING HERE AND AROUND
Reach Pacific Grove via Highway 68 off Highway 1, just south of Monterey. From Cannery Row in Monterey, head north until the road merges with Ocean Boulevard and follow it along the coast. MST buses travel within Pacific Grove and surrounding towns.

EXPLORING
Ⓒ **Monarch Grove Sanctuary.** The Monarch Grove Sanctuary is a fairly reliable spot for viewing the butterflies between October and February. ⊠ *1073 Lighthouse Ave., at Ridge Rd.* ⊕ *www.pgmuseum.org.*

Pacific Grove Museum of Natural History. Contact the Pacific Grove Museum of Natural History for the latest information about the butterfly population. If you're in Pacific Grove when the monarch butterflies aren't, you can view the well-crafted butterfly tree exhibit at the museum. ⊠ *165 Forest Ave.* ☎ *831/648–5716* ⊕ *www.pgmuseum.org* ☜ *$3 suggested donation* ☉ *Tues.–Sun. 10–5.*

Pryor House. Among the Victorians of note is the Pryor House, a massive, shingled, private residence with a leaded- and beveled-glass doorway. ✉ *429 Ocean View Blvd.*

Green Gables. Green Gables, a romantic Swiss Gothic–style mansion with peaked gables and stained-glass windows, is a B&B. ✉ *5th St. and Ocean View Blvd.* ☎ *800/722–1774* ⊕ *www.greengablesinnpg.com.*

🔄 **Lovers Point Park.** The view of the coast is gorgeous from Lovers Point Park, on Ocean View Boulevard midway along the waterfront. The park's sheltered beach has a children's pool and picnic area, and the main lawn has a sandy volleyball court and snack bar. ☎ *831/648–5730.*

🔄 **Point Pinos Lighthouse.** At the 1855-vintage Point Pinos Lighthouse, the oldest continuously operating lighthouse on the West Coast, you can learn about the lighting and foghorn operations and wander through a small museum containing U.S. Coast Guard memorabilia. ✉ *Lighthouse Ave., off Asilomar Blvd.* ☎ *831/648–3176* ⊕ *www.pgmuseum.org* 🗂 *$2* ⏱ *Thurs.–Mon. 1–4.*

Asilomar State Beach. Asilomar State Beach, a beautiful coastal area, is on Sunset Drive between Point Pinos and the Del Monte Forest in Pacific Grove. The 100 acres of dunes, tidal pools, and pocket-size beaches form one of the region's richest areas for marine life—including surfers, who migrate here most winter mornings. ☎ *831/646–6440* ⊕ *www. parks.ca.gov.*

WHERE TO EAT

$$$
MEDITERRANEAN

✕ **Fandango.** The menu here is mostly Mediterranean and southern French, with such dishes as calves' liver and onions and paella served in a skillet. The decor follows suit: stone walls and country furniture give the restaurant the earthy feel of a European farmhouse. This is where locals come when they want to have a big dinner with friends, drink wine, have fun, and generally feel at home. ✉ *223 17th St.* ☎ *831/372–3456* ⊕ *www.fandangorestaurant.com.*

$$
SEAFOOD

✕ **Fishwife.** Fresh fish with a Latin accent makes this a favorite of locals for lunch or a casual dinner. Standards are the sea garden salads topped with your choice of fish and the fried seafood plates with fresh veggies. Large appetites appreciate the fisherman's bowls, which feature fresh fish served with rice, black beans, spicy cabbage, salsa, vegetables, and crispy tortilla strips. ✉ *1996½ Sunset Dr., at Asilomar Blvd.* ☎ *831/375–7107* ⊕ *www.fishwife.com.*

$$
ITALIAN

✕ **Joe Rombi's.** Pastas, fish, steaks, and chops are the specialties at this modern trattoria, which is the best in town for Italian food. The look is spare and clean, with colorful antique wine posters decorating the white walls. Next door, Joe Rombi's La Piccola Casa serves lunch and early dinner Wednesday through Sunday. ✉ *208 17th St.* ☎ *831/373–2416* ⊕ *www.joerombi.com* ⏱ *Closed Mon. and Tues. No lunch.*

$$$
NEW AMERICAN
★

✕ **Passionfish.** South American artwork and artifacts decorate the room, and Latin and Asian flavors infuse the dishes at Passionfish. Chef Ted Walter—lauded for his commitment to using eco-friendly, sustainable ingredients—shops at local farmers' markets several times a week to find the best produce, fish, and meat available, then pairs it with creative sauces. The ever-changing menu might include crispy squid with spicy orange-cilantro vinaigrette. ✉ *701 Lighthouse Ave.* ☏ *831/655–3311* ⊕ *www.passionfish.net* ☽ *No lunch.*

$ ✕ **Peppers Mexicali Cafe.** A local favorite, this cheerful white-walled
MEXICAN   storefront serves traditional dishes from Mexico and Latin America, with an emphasis on fresh seafood. Excellent red and green salsas are made throughout the day, and there's a large selection of beers, along with fresh lime margaritas. ✉ *170 Forest Ave.* ☏ *831/373–6892* ⊕ *www. peppersmexicalicafe.com* ☽ *Closed Tues. No lunch Sun.*

$$ ✕ **Red House Café.** When it's nice out, sun pours through the big windows
AMERICAN   of this cozy restaurant and across tables on the porch; when fog rolls in, the fireplace is lit. The American menu changes with the seasons, but typically includes grilled lamb fillets atop mashed potatoes for dinner and a huge Dungeness crab cake over salad for lunch. Breakfast on weekends is a local favorite. ✉ *662 Lighthouse Ave.* ☏ *831/643–1060* ⊕ *www.redhousecafe.com* ☽ *Closed Mon.*

$$ ✕ **Taste Café and Bistro.** A favorite of locals, Taste serves hearty European-
AMERICAN   inspired food in a casual, airy room with high ceilings and an open kitchen. Meats, such as grilled marinated rabbit, roasted half chicken, and filet mignon, are the focus. ✉ *1199 Forest Ave.* ☏ *831/655–0324* ⊕ *www.tastecafebistro.com* ☽ *Closed Mon.*

WHERE TO STAY

For expanded reviews, go to Fodors.com.

$$$ 🛏 **Green Gables Inn.** Stained-glass windows and ornate interior details
★   compete with spectacular ocean views at this Queen Anne–style mansion, built by a businessman for his mistress in 1888. **Pros:** exceptional views; impeccable attention to historic detail. **Cons:** some rooms are small; thin walls. ✉ *301 Ocean View Blvd.* ☏ *831/375–2095, 800/722–1774* ⊕ *www.greengablesinnpg.com* ⤳ *10 rooms, 3 with bath; 1 suite* ⚑ *In-room: no a/c, Wi-Fi. In-hotel: business center* ⦿⊙ *Breakfast.*

$$ 🛏 **The Inn at 213 Seventeen Mile Drive.** Set in a residential area just past town, this carefully restored 1920s Craftsman-style home and cottage are surrounded by gardens and redwood, cypress, and eucalyptus trees. **Pros:** killer gourmet breakfast; historic charm; verdant gardens. **Cons:** far from restaurants and shops; few extra amenities. ✉ *213 17-Mile Dr., at Lighthouse Dr.* ☏ *831/642–9514, 800/526–5666* ⊕ *www.innat17.com* ⤳ *14 rooms* ⚑ *In-room: no a/c, Wi-Fi. In-hotel: some pets allowed* ⦿⊙ *Breakfast.*

$$ 🛏 **Lighthouse Lodge and Resort.** Near the tip of the peninsula, this complex straddles Lighthouse Avenue—the lodge is on one side, the all-suites Lighthouse Resort facility on the other. **Pros:** near lighthouse and 17-Mile Drive; friendly reception; many room options. **Cons:** next to a cemetery; lodge rooms are basic. ✉ *1150 and 1249 Lighthouse Ave.* ☏ *831/655–2111, 800/858–1249* ⊕ *www.lhls.com* ⤳ *64 rooms, 31 suites* ⚑ *In-room: no a/c, Wi-Fi. In-hotel: pool, spa, some pets allowed* ⦿⊙ *Breakfast.*

$$$ 🛏 **Martine Inn.** The glassed-in parlor and many guest rooms at this 1899 Mediterranean-style villa have stunning ocean views. **Pros:** romantic; fancy breakfast; ocean views. **Cons:** not child-friendly; sits on a busy thoroughfare. ✉ *255 Ocean View Blvd.* ☏ *831/373–3388, 800/852–5588* ⊕ *www.martineinn.com* ⤳ *24 rooms* ⚑ *In-room: no a/c, Internet, Wi-Fi. In-hotel: business center* ⦿⊙ *Breakfast.*

MONTEREY

2 mi southeast of Pacific Grove via Lighthouse Ave.; 2 mi north of Carmel-by-the-Sea via Hwy. 1.

Early in the 20th century Carmel Martin, the first mayor of the city of Monterey, saw a bright future for his town: "Monterey Bay is the one place where people can live without being disturbed by manufacturing and big factories. I am certain that the day is coming when this will be the most desirable place in the whole state of California." It seems that Mayor Martin was not far off the mark.

GETTING HERE AND AROUND

From San Jose or San Francisco, take U.S. 101 south to Highway 156 West at Prunedale. Head west about 8 mi to Highway 1 and follow it about 15 mi south. From San Luis Obispo, take U.S. 101 north to Salinas and drive west on Highway 68 about 20 mi to reach Monterey. In summer the MST Monterey Trolley travels from downtown Monterey along Cannery Row to the Aquarium and back.

ESSENTIALS

Visitor Information Monterey County Convention & Visitors Bureau ☎ *877/666–8373* ⊕ *www.seemonterey.com.*

EXPLORING

7

A Taste of Monterey. Without driving the back roads, you can taste the wines of more than 90 area vintners while taking in fantastic bay views. Purchase a few bottles and pick up a map and guide to the county's wineries and vineyards. ⊠ *700 Cannery Row, Suite KK* ☎ *831/646–5446, 888/646–5446* ⊕ *www.tastemonterey.com* 🍷 *Wine tastings $10–$20* ☉ *Daily 11–6.*

California's First Theatre. This adobe began its life in 1846 as a saloon and lodging house for sailors. Four years later stage curtains were fashioned from army blankets, and some U.S. officers staged plays to the light of whale oil lamps. As of this writing, the building is not open but you can stroll in the garden. ⊠ *Monterey State Historic Park, Scott and Pacific Sts.* ☎ *831/649–7118* ⊕ *www.parks.ca.gov/mshp* 🍷 *Free* ☉ *Call for hrs.*

Cannery Row. When John Steinbeck published the novel *Cannery Row* in 1945, he immortalized a place of rough-edged working people. The waterfront street, edging a mile of gorgeous coastline, once was crowded with sardine canneries processing, at their peak, nearly 200,000 tons of the smelly silver fish a year. During the mid-1940s, however, the sardines disappeared from the bay, causing the canneries to close. Through the years the old tin-roof canneries have been converted into restaurants, art galleries, and malls with shops selling T-shirts, fudge, and plastic sea otters. Recent tourist development along the row has been more tasteful, however, and includes several stylish inns and hotels, wine tasting rooms, and upscale specialty shops. ⊠ *Cannery Row, between Reeside and David Aves.* ⊕ *www.canneryrow.com.*

Casa Soberanes. A classic low-ceiling adobe structure built in 1842, this was once a Custom House guard's residence. Exhibits at the house survey life

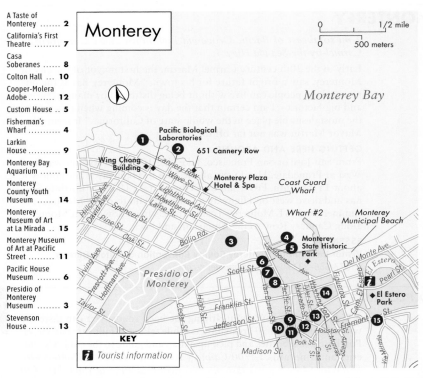

in Monterey from the era of Mexican rule to the present. The building is currently closed, but feel free to stop at the peaceful rear garden, which has a lovely rose-covered arbor and sitting benches. ⊠ *Monterey State Historic Park, 336 Pacific St.* ☎ *831/649–7118* ⊕ *www.parks.ca.gov/mshp* ≋ *Free.*

Colton Hall. A convention of delegates met in 1849 to draft the first state constitution at California's equivalent of Independence Hall. The stone building, which has served as a school, a courthouse, and the county seat, is a city-run museum furnished as it was during the constitutional convention. The extensive grounds outside the hall surround the Old Monterey Jail. ⊠ *500 block of Pacific St., between Madison and Jefferson Sts.* ☎ *831/646–5648* ⊕ *www.monterey.org/museum/coltonhall. html* ≋ *Free* ⊙ *Daily 10–4.*

Cooper-Molera Adobe. The restored 2-acre complex includes a house dating from the 1820s, a visitor center, a bookstore, and a large garden enclosed by a high adobe wall. The mostly Victorian-era antiques and memorabilia that fill the house provide a glimpse into the life of a prosperous early sea merchant's family. If the house is closed, you can still visit the Cooper Museum visitor center and pick up walking tour maps and walk around the grounds. ⊠ *Monterey State Historic Park, Polk and Munras Sts.* ☎ *831/649–7118, 831/649–7111* ⊕ *www.parks. ca.gov/mshp* ≋ *$5* ⊙ *Weekends. Call for hrs.*

Custom House. This adobe structure, built by the Mexican government in 1827—now California's oldest standing public building—was the first stop for sea traders whose goods were subject to duties. At the beginning of the Mexican-American War, in 1846, Commodore John Sloat raised the American flag over the building and claimed California for the United States. The house's lower floor displays cargo from a 19th-century trading ship. While the house is currently closed, you can still visit the cactus gardens and stroll around the plaza. ✉ *Monterey State Historic Park, 1 Custom House Plaza, across from Fisherman's Wharf* ☎ *831/649–7118* ⊕ *www.parks.ca.gov/mshp* ✉ *Free* ☉ *Weekends 10–4.*

> ### JOHN STEINBECK'S CANNERY ROW
>
> *"Cannery Row in Monterey in California is a poem, a stink, a grating noise, a quality of light, a tone, a habit, a nostalgia, a dream. Cannery Row is the gathered and scattered, tin and iron and rust and splintered wood, chipped pavement and weedy lots and junk heaps, sardine canneries of corrugated iron, honky tonks, restaurants and whore houses, and little crowded groceries, and laboratories and flophouses."*
> —John Steinbeck, Cannery Row

Fisherman's Wharf. The mournful barking of sea lions provides a steady soundtrack all along Monterey's waterfront, but the best way to actually view the whiskered marine mammals is to walk along one of the two piers across from Custom House Plaza. Fisherman's Wharf is lined with souvenir shops, seafood restaurants, and whale-watching tour boats. It's undeniably touristy, but still a lively and entertaining place. Up the harbor to the right is Wharf No. 2, a working municipal pier where you can see fishing boats unloading their catches to one side, and fishermen casting their lines into the water on the other. The pier has a couple of low-key restaurants, from whose seats lucky customers may spot otters and harbor seals. ✉ *At end of Calle Principal* ☎ *831/649–6544* ⊕ *www.montereywharf.com.*

Larkin House. A veranda encircles the second floor of this architecturally significant two-story adobe built in 1835, whose design bears witness to the Mexican and New England influences on the Monterey style. The rooms are furnished with period antiques, many of them brought from New Hampshire by the building's namesake, Thomas O. Larkin, an early California statesman. The building is closed weekdays, but you can stroll the historic gardens and peek in the windows. ✉ *Monterey State Historic Park, 464 Calle Principal, between Jefferson and Pacific Sts.* ☎ *831/649–7118* ⊕ *www.parks.ca.gov/mshp* ✉ *$5* ☉ *Weekends; call for hrs.*

Monterey Bay Aquarium. The minute you hand over your ticket at this extraordinary aquarium you're surrounded by sea creatures; right at the entrance, you can see dozens of them swimming in a three-story-tall, sunlit kelp forest tank. The beauty of the exhibits here is that they are all designed to give a sense of what it's like to be in the water with the animals—sardines swim around your head in a circular tank, and jellyfish drift in and out of view in dramatically lighted spaces that suggest the ocean depths. A petting pool gives you a hands-on experience with bat rays, and the million-gallon Open Seas tank shows the vast variety

Fodor'sChoice
★

7

of creatures (from sharks to placid-looking turtles) that live in the eastern Pacific. A Splash Zone with 45 interactive bilingual exhibits opened in 2008: here, kids (and kids-at-heart) can commune with sea dragons, potbellied seahorses, and other fascinating creatures. The only drawback to the experience is that it must be shared with the throngs of people that crowd the place daily; most think it's worth it. To avoid the crowds, arrive as soon as the aquarium opens or visit after 2 pm, when field trip groups depart and youngsters head home for their naps. Weekend evenings in summer, the aquarium stays open later and is usually less crowded during the extended hours. ■ TIP→ Reserve a lunch table at the aquarium's restaurant, perched on ocean's edge. Otters and other sea creatures often frolic just outside the floor-to-ceiling windows. ⊠ *886 Cannery Row* ☎ *800/555–3656 info, 800/756–3737 for advance tickets* ⊕ *www.montereybayaquarium. org* ✉ *$30* ⊙ *Late May–June and early Sept., daily 9:30–6; July and Aug., weekdays 9:30–6, weekends 9:30–8; early Sept.–late May, daily 10–5.*

Ⓒ **Monterey County Youth Museum (MY Museum).** Monterey Bay comes to life from a child's perspective in this fun-filled, interactive indoor exploration center that opened in the heart of the historic district in late 2008. The seven exhibit galleries showcase the science and nature of the Big Sur coast, theater arts, Pebble Beach golf, and beaches. There's also a live performance theater, a creation station, a hospital emergency room, and an agriculture corner where kids follow artichokes, strawberries, and other fruits and veggies on their evolution from sprout to harvest to farmers' markets. ⊠ *425 Washington St.* ☎ *831/649–6444* ⊕ *www.mymuseum. org* ✉ *$7* ⊙ *Mon., Tues., and Thurs.–Sat. 10–5, Sun. noon–5.*

Monterey Museum of Art at La Mirada. Asian and European antiques fill this 19th-century adobe house. A newer 10,000-square-foot gallery space, designed by Charles Moore, houses Asian and California regional art. Outdoors are magnificent rose and rhododendron gardens. A single fee covers admission to the La Mirada and Pacific Street facilities of the Monterey Museum of Art. ⊠ *720 Via Mirada, at Fremont St.* ☎ *831/372–3689* ⊕ *www.montereyart.org* ✉ *$5* ⊙ *Wed.–Sat. 11–5, Sun. 1–4.*

Ⓒ **Dennis the Menace Playground.** El Estero Park's Dennis the Menace Playground is an imaginative play area designed by the late Hank Ketcham, the well-known cartoonist. The equipment is on a grand scale and made for daredevils; there's a roller slide, a clanking suspension bridge, and a real Southern Pacific steam locomotive. You can rent a rowboat or a paddleboat for cruising around U-shaped Lake El Estero, populated with an assortment of ducks, mud hens, and geese. The park is open 10 to dusk and closed Tuesday September–May. ⊠ *Pearl St. and Camino El Estero* ☎ *831/646–3866.*

Monterey Museum of Art at Pacific Street. Photographs by Ansel Adams and Edward Weston, as well as works by other artists who have spent time on the peninsula, are on display here. There's also a colorful collection of international folk art; the pieces range from Kentucky hearth brooms to Tibetan prayer wheels. A single fee covers admission to the Pacific Street and La Mirada facilities of the Monterey Museum of Art. ⊠ *559 Pacific St., across from Colton Hall* ☎ *831/372–5477* ⊕ *www. montereyart.org* ✉ *$5* ⊙ *Wed.–Sat. 11–5, Sun. 1–4.*

Trained "seals" that perform in circuses are actually California sea lions, intelligent, social animals that live (and sleep) close together in groups.

Monterey State Historic Park. You can glimpse Monterey's early history in the well-preserved adobe buildings scattered along several city blocks. Far from being a hermetic period museum, the park facilities are an integral part of the day-to-day business life of the town—within some of the buildings are a store, a theater, and government offices. At some of the historic houses, the gardens (open daily 10 to 5 in summer, 10 to 4 rest of the year) are worthy sights themselves. ■ TIP→ **At this writing, many buildings are closed and tours on hiatus due to state park budget cuts. Visit the Web site for up-to-date information.** ⊠ *20 Custom House Plaza* 🖼 *831/649–7118* ⊕ *www.parks.ca.gov/mshp* ⊠ *Free* ⊙ *Call for hrs.*

Pacific House Museum. Once a hotel and saloon, this visitor center and museum now commemorates early-California life with gold-rush relics and photographs of old Monterey. The upper floor displays Native American artifacts, including gorgeous baskets and pottery. ⊠ *Monterey State Historic Park, 10 Custom House Plaza* 🖼 *831/649–7118* ⊕ *www. parks.ca.gov/mshp* ⊠ *Free* ⊙ *Open weekends 10–4.*

Presidio of Monterey Museum. This spot has been significant for centuries as a town, a fort, and the site of several battles, including the skirmish in which the pirate Hipoleto Bruchard conquered the Spanish garrison that stood here. Its first incarnation was as a Native American village for the Rumsien tribe; then it became known as the landing site for explorer Sebastián Vizcaíno in 1602, and father of the California missions, Father Serra, in 1770. The indoor museum tells the stories; the outdoor sites are marked with plaques. ⊠ *Corporal Ewing Rd., Presidio of Monterey* 🖼 *831/646–3456* ⊕ *www.monterey.org/museum/pom/* ⊠ *Free* ⊙ *Mon. 10–1, Thurs.–Sat. 10–4, Sun. 1–4.*

Stevenson House. This house was named in honor of author Robert Louis Stevenson, who boarded here briefly in a tiny upstairs room. Items from his family's estate furnish Stevenson's room; period-decorated chambers elsewhere in the house include a gallery of the author's memorabilia and a children's nursery stocked with Victorian toys and games. ⊠ *Monterey State Historic Park, 530 Houston St.* ☎ *831/649–7118* ⊕ *www.parks.ca.gov/mshp* ⊡ *Free* ☉ *Open Sat. 1–4.*

> **MONTEREY: FORMER CAPITAL OF CALIFORNIA**
>
> In 1602 Spanish explorer Sebastián Vizcaíno stepped ashore on a remote California peninsula. He named it after the viceroy of New Spain—Count de Monte Rey. Soon the Spanish built a military outpost, and the site was the capital of California until the state came under American rule.

WHERE TO EAT

¢
AMERICAN

✕ **Café Lumiere.** Attached to the lobby of Monterey's art-house cinema, this café shows work by local artists. Eat a light breakfast or lunch, drink coffee, or choose a pot of tea from the extensive selection. The menu includes baked goods, cakes, sandwiches, granola, and other breakfast items. Most patrons bring their laptops for the free Wi-Fi, and most tables are shared. Close to downtown bars, it's open until 10 pm. ⊠ *365 Calle Principal* ☎ *831/920–2451* ⊕ *www.montereylumiere.com.*

$$
SEAFOOD

✕ **Monterey's Fish House.** Casual yet stylish, and removed from the hubbub of the wharf, this always-packed seafood restaurant attracts locals and frequent visitors to the city. If the dining room is full, you can wait at the bar and savor deliciously plump oysters on the half shell. The bartenders and waitstaff will gladly advise you on the perfect wine to go with your poached, blackened, or oak-grilled seafood. ⊠ *2114 Del Monte Ave.* ☎ *831/373–4647* ☉ *No lunch weekends.*

$$$
AMERICAN
Fodor'sChoice
★

✕ **Montrio Bistro.** This quirky, converted firehouse, with its rawhide walls and iron indoor trellises, has a wonderfully sophisticated menu. Chef Tony Baker uses organic produce and meats and sustainably sourced seafood to create imaginative dishes that reflect local agriculture, such as artichokes stuffed with fire-roasted Brie, and grilled lamb tenderloin with rosemary, garlic sauce, and broccolini. Likewise, the wine list draws primarily on California, and many come from the Monterey area. ⊠ *414 Calle Principal* ☎ *831/648–8880* ⊕ *www.montrio.com* ⚏ *Reservations essential* ☉ *No lunch.*

$
AMERICAN

✕ **Old Monterey Café.** Breakfast here gets constant local raves. Its fame rests on familiar favorites in many incarnations: a dozen kinds of omelets, and pancakes from blueberry to cinnamon-raisin-pecan. The lunch and dinner menus have good soups, salads, and sandwiches, and this is a great place to relax with an afternoon cappuccino. ⊠ *489 Alvarado St.* ☎ *831/646–1021* ⊕ *www.cafemonterey.com* ⚏ *Reservations not accepted.*

$$
AMERICAN

✕ **Tarpy's Roadhouse.** Fun, dressed-up American favorites—a little something for everyone—are served in this renovated early-1900s stone farmhouse several miles outside town. The kitchen cranks out everything from Cajun-spiced prawns to meat loaf with Marsala-mushroom gravy to grilled ribs

The Underwater Kingdom

Although Monterey's coastal landscapes are stunning, their beauty is more than equaled by the wonders that lie offshore. The huge Monterey Bay National Marine Sanctuary—which stretches 276 mi, from north of San Francisco almost all the way down to Santa Barbara—teems with abundant life, and has topography as diverse as that aboveground.

The preserve's 5,322 square mi include vast submarine canyons, which reach down 10,663 feet at their deepest point. They also encompass dense forests of giant kelp—a kind of seaweed that can grow more than a hundred feet from its roots on the ocean floor. These kelp forests are especially robust off Monterey.

The sanctuary was established in 1992 to protect the habitat of the many species that thrive in the bay. Some animals can be seen quite easily from land. In summer and winter you might glimpse the offshore spray of gray whales as they migrate between their summer feeding grounds in Alaska and their breeding grounds in Baja. Clouds of marine birds—including white-faced ibis, three types of albatross, and more than 15 types of gull—skim above the waves, or roost in the rock islands along 17-Mile Drive. Sea otters dart and gambol in the calmer waters of the bay; and of course, you can watch the sea lions—and hear their round-the-clock barking—on the wharves in Santa Cruz and Monterey.

The sanctuary supports many other creatures, however, that remain unseen by most on-land visitors. Some of these are enormous, such as the giant blue whales that arrive to feed on plankton in summer; others, like the more than 22 species of red algae in these waters, are microscopic. So whether you choose to visit the Monterey Bay Aquarium, take a whale-watch trip, or look out to sea with your binoculars, remember you're seeing just a small part of a vibrant underwater kingdom.

7

and steaks. Eat indoors by a fireplace or outdoors in the courtyard. ⊠ *2999 Monterey–Salinas Hwy., Hwy. 68* ☎ *831/647–1444* ⊕ *www.tarpys.com.*

WHERE TO STAY

For expanded reviews, go to Fodors.com.

$ 🖼 **Best Western Beach Resort Monterey.** With a great waterfront location about 2 mi north of town—with views of the bay and the city skyline—and a surprising array of amenities, this hotel is one of the best values in town. **Pros:** on the beach; great value; family-friendly. **Cons:** several miles from major attractions; big-box mall neighborhood. ⊠ *2600 Sand Dunes Dr.* ☎ *831/394–3321, 800/242–8627* ⊕ *www.montereybeachresort.com* ↪ *196 rooms* ⌂ *In-room: a/c, Wi-Fi. In-hotel: restaurant, bar, pool, gym, beach, business center, parking, some pets allowed.*

$$$$ 🖼 **InterContinental The Clement Monterey.** Spectacular bay views, assiduous
ᏟᏋ service, a slew of upscale amenities, and a superb waterfront location next to the aquarium propelled this full-service luxury hotel to immediate stardom when it opened in 2008. **Pros:** a block from the aquarium; fantastic

views from some rooms; great for families. **Cons:** a tad formal; not budget-friendly. ✉ *750 Cannery Row* ☎ *831/375–4500, 866/781-2406 toll free* ⊕ *www.ictheclementmonterey. com* 🛏 *192 rooms, 16 suites* ⟨⟩ *In-room: a/c, Internet, Wi-Fi. In-hotel: restaurant, bar, pool, gym, spa, children's programs, business center, some pets allowed.*

$$
★
Monterey Bay Lodge. Location (on the edge of Monterey's El Estero Park) and superior amenities give this cheerful facility an edge over other motels in town. **Pros:** within walking distance of beach and playground; quiet at night; good family choice. **Cons:** near busy boulevard. ✉ *55 Camino Aguajito* ☎ *831/372–8057, 800/558–1900* ⊕ *www.montereybaylodge.com* 🛏 *43 rooms, 3 suites* ⟨⟩ *In-room: a/c, Internet, Wi-Fi. In-hotel: restaurant, pool, some pets allowed.*

$$$
Monterey Plaza Hotel and Spa. This hotel commands a waterfront location on Cannery Row, where you can see frolicking sea otters from the wide outdoor patio and many room balconies. **Pros:** on the ocean; lots of amenities; attentive service. **Cons:** touristy area; heavy traffic. ✉ *400 Cannery Row* ☎ *831/646–1700, 800/334–3999* ⊕ *www. montereyplazahotel.com* 🛏 *280 rooms, 10 suites* ⟨⟩ *In-room: a/c, Internet, Wi-Fi. In-hotel: restaurant, bar, gym, spa, business center.*

$$$$
Fodor'sChoice
★
Old Monterey Inn. This three-story manor house was the home of Monterey's first mayor, and today it remains a private enclave within walking distance of downtown. **Pros:** gorgeous gardens; refined luxury; serene. **Cons:** must drive to attractions and sights; fills quickly. ✉ *500 Martin St.* ☎ *831/375–8284, 800/350–2344* ⊕ *www.oldmontereyinn. com* 🛏 *6 rooms, 3 suites, 1 cottage* ⟨⟩ *In-room: a/c, Internet, Wi-Fi. In-hotel: spa, business center, some pets allowed* ⊙| *Breakfast.*

$
Quality Inn Monterey. This attractive motel has a friendly, country-inn feeling. **Pros:** indoor pool; bargain rates; cheerful innkeepers. **Cons:** street is busy during the day; some rooms are dark. ✉ *1058 Munras Ave.* ☎ *831/372–3381* ⊕ *www.qualityinnmonterey.com* 🛏 *55 rooms* ⟨⟩ *In-room: a/c, Internet, Wi-Fi. In-hotel: pool* ⊙| *Breakfast.*

$$$
Spindrift Inn. This boutique hotel on Cannery Row has beach access and a rooftop garden that overlooks the water. **Pros:** close to aquarium; steps from the beach; friendly staff. **Cons:** throngs of visitors outside; can be noisy; not good for families. ✉ *652 Cannery Row* ☎ *831/646–8900, 800/841–1879* ⊕ *www.spindriftinn.com* 🛏 *45 rooms* ⟨⟩ *In-room: no a/c, Wi-Fi. In-hotel: business center* ⊙| *Breakfast.*

> **THE FIRST ARTICHOKE QUEEN**
>
> Castroville, a tiny town off Highway 1 between Monterey and Watsonville, produces about 95% of U.S. artichokes. Back in 1948, the town chose its first queen to preside during its Artichoke Festival—a beautiful young woman named Norma Jean Mortenson, who later changed her name to Marilyn Monroe.

THE ARTS

★ **Dixieland Monterey.** Dixieland Monterey, held on the first full weekend of March, presents traditional jazz bands at waterfront venues on the harbor. ☎ 831/675–0298, 888/349–6879 ⊕ www.dixieland-monterey.com.

Monterey Bay Blues Festival. The Monterey Bay Blues Festival draws blues fans to the Monterey Fairgrounds the last weekend in June. ☎ 831/394–2652 ⊕ www.montereyblues.com.

Monterey Jazz Festival. The Monterey Jazz Festival, the world's oldest, attracts jazz and blues greats from around the world to the Monterey Fairgrounds on the third full weekend of September. ☎ 925/275–9255 ticket office, 831/373–3366 ⊕ www.montereyjazzfestival.org.

Bruce Ariss Wharf Theater. The Bruce Ariss Wharf Theater focuses on American musicals past and present. ⊠ One Fisherman's Wharf ☎ 831/ 372–1373.

SPORTS AND THE OUTDOORS

Throughout most of the year, the Monterey Bay area is a haven for those who love tennis, golf, surfing, fishing, biking, hiking, scuba diving, and kayaking. In the rainy winter months, when the waves grow larger, adventurous surfers flock to the water.

Monterey Bay National Marine Sanctuary. The Monterey Bay National Marine Sanctuary, home to mammals, seabirds, fishes, invertebrates, and plants, encompasses a 276-mi shoreline and 5,322 square mi of ocean. Ringed by beaches and campgrounds, it's a place for kayaking, whale-watching, scuba diving, and other water sports. ☎ 831/647–4201 ⊕ montereybay.noaa.gov.

BICYCLING

Bay Bikes. For bicycle and surrey rentals and tours, visit Bay Bikes. ⊠ 585 Cannery Row ☎ 831/655–2453 ⊕ www.baybikes.com.

Adventures by the Sea, Inc. Adventures by the Sea, Inc. offers bike tours and rents surreys and tandem and standard bicycles. ⊠ 299 Cannery Row and 210 Alvarado Mall next to the Portola Plaza Hotel ☎ 831/372–1807, 831/648–7236 ⊕ www.adventuresbythesea.com.

FISHING

Randy's Fishing and Whale Watching Trips. Randy's Fishing and Whale Watching Trips, a small family-run business, has been operating since 1949. ⊠ 66 Fisherman's Wharf ☎ 831/372–7440, 800/251–7440 ⊕ www.randysfishingtrips.com.

SCUBA DIVING

Monterey Bay waters never warm to the temperatures of their Southern California counterparts (the warmest they get is low 60s), but that's one reason why the marine life here is among the world's most diverse.

Aquarius Dive Shop. The staff at Aquarius Dive Shop gives diving lessons and tours, and rents equipment. Their scuba-conditions information line is updated daily. ⊠ 2040 Del Monte Ave. ☎ 831/375–1933, 831/657–1020 diving conditions ⊕ www.aquariusdivers.com.

WALKING

Monterey Bay Coastal Trail. From Custom House Plaza, you can walk along the coast in either direction on the 29-mi-long Monterey Bay Coastal Trail for spectacular views of the sea. It runs all the way from north of Monterey to Pacific Grove, with sections continuing around Pebble Beach. ☎ *831/372–3196* ⊕ *www.mtycounty.com/pgs-parks/bike-path.html.*

WHALE-WATCHING

Thousands of gray whales pass close by the Monterey Coast on their annual migration between the Bering Sea and Baja California. The gigantic creatures are sometimes visible through binoculars from shore, but a whale-watching cruise is the best way to get a close look at these magnificent mammals. The migration south takes place from December through March; January is prime viewing time. The whales migrate north from March through June. In addition, some 2,000 blue whales and 600 humpbacks pass the coast and are easily spotted in late summer and early fall.

★ **Monterey Bay Whale Watch.** Monterey Bay Whale Watch, which operates out of the Monterey Bay Whale Watch Center at Fisherman's Wharf, gives three- to five-hour tours led by marine biologists. ✉ *84 Fisherman's Wharf* ☎ *831/375–4658* ⊕ *www.montereybaywhalewatch.com.*

Monterey Whale Watching. Monterey Whale Watching provides three tours a day on a 150-passenger high-speed cruiser and a large 75-foot boat. ✉ *96 Fisherman's Wharf #1* ☎ *831/372–2203, 800/979–3370* ⊕ *www.montereywhalewatching.com.*

AROUND THE BAY

As Highway 1 follows the curve of the bay between Monterey and Santa Cruz, it passes through a rich agricultural zone. Opening right onto the bay, where the Salinas and Pajaro rivers drain into the Pacific, a broad valley brings together fertile soil, an ideal climate, and a good water supply to create optimum growing conditions for crops such as strawberries, artichokes, Brussels sprouts, and broccoli. Several beautiful beaches line this part of the coast.

MOSS LANDING

17 mi north of Monterey on Hwy. 1.

Moss Landing is not much more than a couple of blocks of cafés and restaurants, art galleries, and studios plus a busy fishing port, but therein lies its charm. It's a fine place to overnight or stop for a meal and get a dose of nature.

GETTING HERE AND AROUND

From Highway 1 north or south, exit at Moss Landing Road on the ocean side. From U.S. 101, take Highway 156 West from Prunedale 8 mi to Castroville and follow Highway 1 about 3 mi to Moss Landing Road. Public transit via MST connects Moss Landing with all Monterey County destinations and the Watsonville Transit Center in southern Santa Cruz County.

ESSENTIALS

Visitor Information Monterey County Convention & Visitors Bureau ✉ *Box 1770, Monterey* ☎ *877/666–8373* ⊕ *www.seemonterey.com.* **Moss Landing Chamber of Commerce** ✉ *8071 Moss Landing Rd., Monterey* ☎ *831/633-4501*

EXPLORING

★ **Elkhorn Slough National Estuarine Research Reserve.** In the Elkhorn Slough National Estuarine Research Reserve, 1,400 acres of tidal flats and salt marshes form a complex environment that supports some 300 species of birds. A walk or a kayak trip along the meandering waterways and wetlands can reveal hawks, white-tailed kites, owls, herons, and egrets. Sea otters, sharks, rays, and many other animals also live or visit here. On weekends guided walks from the visitor center to the heron rookery begin at 10 and 1. Although the reserve lies across the town line in Watsonville, you reach its entrance through Moss Landing. ✉ *1700 Elkhorn Rd., Watsonville* ☎ *831/728–2822* ⊕ *www.elkhornslough.org* ✏ *$2.50* ☉ *Wed.–Sun. 9–5.*

Elkhorn Slough Safari. Aboard a 27-foot pontoon boat operated by Elkhorn Slough Safari, a naturalist leads an up-close look at wetlands denizens. Advance reservations are required for the two-hour tours ($35). ✉ *Moss Landing Harbor* ☎ *831/633–5555* ⊕ *www.elkhornslough.com.*

WHERE TO EAT AND STAY

$ ✕ **Phil's Fish Market & Eatery.** Exquisitely fresh, simply prepared seafood
SEAFOOD (try the cioppino) is on the menu at this warehouselike restaurant on the harbor; all kinds of glistening fish are on offer at the market in the front. ■ TIP➔ **Phil's Snack Shack, a tiny sandwich-and-smoothie joint, serves quicker meals at the north end of town.** ✉ *7600 Sandholdt Rd.* ☎ *831/633–2152* ⊕ *www.philsfishmarket.com.*

$$ ⌕ **Captain's Inn.** Commune with nature and pamper yourself with upscale creature comforts at this green-certified getaway in the heart of town. **Pros:** walk to restaurants and shops; tranquil natural setting; homey atmosphere **Cons:** rooms in historic building don't have water views; far from urban amenities; not appropriate for young children. ✉ *8122 Moss Landing Rd., Moss Landing* ☎ *831/633–5550* ⊕ *www. captainsinn.com* ⇆ *10* ⌂ *In-room: no a/c, Internet, Wi-Fi. In-hotel: spa, parking* ⦿ *Breakfast.*

WATSONVILLE

7 mi north of Moss Landing on Hwy. 1.

If ever a city was built on strawberries, Watsonville is it. Produce has long driven the economy here, and this is where the county fair takes place each September.

GETTING HERE AND AROUND

From Santa Cruz or Monterey, follow Highway 1 to Watsonville. Santa Cruz Metropolitan Transit District buses operate throughout the county; buses run regularly from the Santa Cruz Transit Center to the Watsonville Transit Center. From U.S. 101, take Highway 152 West from Gilroy (a curvy but scenic road over the mountains) or Highway 129 West from just north of San Juan Bautista.

SALINAS AND JOHN STEINBECK'S LEGACY

National Steinbeck Center. Salinas (17 mi east of Monterey), a hardworking city surrounded by vegetable fields, honors the memory and literary legacy of John Steinbeck, its most well-known native, at the modern National Steinbeck Center. Exhibits document the life of the Pulitzer- and Nobel-prize winner and the history of the local communities that inspired Steinbeck novels such as *The Grapes of Wrath.* Highlights include reproductions of the green pickup-camper from *Travels with Charley* and of the bunkroom from *Of Mice and Men;* you can watch actors read from Steinbeck's books on video screens throughout the museum. The museum is the centerpiece of the revival of Old Town Salinas, where handsome turn-of-the-20th-century stone buildings have been renovated and filled with shops and restaurants.

Steinbeck House. Two blocks from the National Steinbeck Center is the author's Victorian birthplace, Steinbeck House. It operates as a lunch spot Tuesday through Saturday and displays some Steinbeck memorabilia. ⊠ *132 Central Ave., Salinas* ☎ *831/424–2735* ⊠ *1 Main St., 17 mi east of Monterey via Hwy. 68, Salinas* ☎ *831/796–3833 administration, 831/775–4721 admission* ⊕ *www.steinbeck.org* 🖾 *$11* ☉ *Daily 10–5.*

EXPLORING

☺ **Agricultural History Project.** One feature of the Santa Cruz County Fairgrounds is the Agricultural History Project, which preserves the history of farming in the Pajaro Valley. In the Codiga Center and Museum you can examine antique tractors and milking machines, peruse an exhibit on the era when Watsonville was the "frozen food capitol of the West," and watch experts restore farm implements and vehicles. ⊠ *2601 E. Lake Ave.* ☎ *831/724–5898* ⊕ *www.aghistoryproject.org* 🖾 *$2 suggested donation* ☉ *Thurs.–Sun. noon–4.*

☺ **Watsonville Fly-in & Air Show.** Every Labor Day weekend, aerial performers execute elaborate aerobatics at the Watsonville Fly-in & Air Show. More than 300 classic, experimental, and military aircraft are on display; concerts and other events fill three days. ⊠ *Watsonville Municipal Airport, 100 Aviation Way* ☎ *831/763–5600* ⊕ *www.watsonvilleflyin.org* 🖾 *$15.*

APTOS

7 mi north of Watsonville on Hwy. 1.

Backed by a redwood forest and facing the sea, downtown Aptos—known as Aptos Village—is a place of wooden walkways and false-fronted shops. Antiques dealers cluster along Trout Gulch Road, off Soquel Drive east of Highway 1.

GETTING HERE AND AROUND

Use Highway 1 to reach Aptos from Santa Cruz or Monterey. Exit at State Park Drive to reach the main shopping hub and Aptos Village. You can also exit at Freedom Boulevard or Rio del Mar. Soquel Drive is the main artery through town.

SAN JUAN BAUTISTA

About as close to early-19th-century California as you can get, San Juan Bautista (15 mi east of Watsonville on Highway 156) has been protected from development since 1933, when much of it became a state park. Small antiques shops and restaurants occupy the Old West and art deco buildings that line 3rd Street.

The wide green plaza of San Juan Bautista State Historic Park is ringed by 18th- and 19th-century buildings, many of them open to the public. The cemetery of the long, low, colonnaded mission church contains the unmarked graves of more than 4,300 Native American converts. Nearby is an adobe home furnished with Spanish-colonial antiques, a hotel frozen in the 1860s, a blacksmith shop, a stable, a pioneer cabin, and a jailhouse.

The first Saturday of each month, costumed volunteers engage in quilting bees, tortilla making, and other frontier activities. ⊕ *www.san-juan-bautista.ca.us.*

ESSENTIALS

Visitor Information Aptos Chamber of Commerce ⊠ *7605-A Old Dominion Ct.* ☎ *831/688–1467* ⊕ *www.aptoschamber.com.*

EXPLORING

Seacliff State Beach. Sandstone bluffs tower above Seacliff State Beach, a favorite of locals. You can fish off the pier, which leads out to a sunken World War I tanker ship built of concrete. ⊠ *201 State Park Dr.* ☎ *831/685–6442* ⊕ *www.parks.ca.gov* ⊠ *$10 per vehicle.*

WHERE TO EAT AND STAY

$$$

MEDITERRANEAN

★

✕ **Bittersweet Bistro.** A large old tavern with cathedral ceilings houses this popular bistro, where chef-owner Thomas Vinolus draws culinary inspiration from the Mediterranean. The menu changes seasonally, but regular highlights include pan-seared Monterey Bay petrale sole, seafood *puttanesca* (pasta with a spicy sauce of garlic, tomatoes, anchovies, and olives), and fire-roasted pork tenderloin. The decadent chocolate desserts are not to be missed. You can order many of the entrées in small or regular portions. Lunch is available to go from the express counter. ⊠ *787 Rio Del Mar Blvd.* ☎ *831/662–9799* ⊕ *www.bittersweetbistro.com.*

$$$

☆ **Best Western Seacliff Inn.** A favorite lair of families and business travelers, this 6-acre Best Western near Seacliff State Beach is more resort than hotel. **Pros:** walking distance from the beach; family-friendly; includes hot breakfast buffet. **Cons:** close to the freeway; occasional nighttime bar noise. ⊠ *7500 Old Dominion Ct.* ☎ *831/688–7300, 800/367–2003* ⊕ *www.seacliffinn.com* ☞ *139 rooms, 10 suites* � *In-room: a/c, Internet, Wi-Fi. In-hotel: restaurant, bar, pool, gym, laundry facilities* ☒ *Breakfast.*

$$$

☆ **Flora Vista.** Multicolor fields of flowers, strawberries, and veggies unfold in every direction at this luxury neo-Georgian inn set on two serene acres in a rural community just south of Aptos; Sand Dollar Beach is just a short walk away. **Pros:** super-private; near the beach; flowers everywhere. **Cons:** no restaurants or nightlife within walking distance; not a good place for kids. ⊠ *1258 San Andreas Rd., La Selva*

Beach ☎ 831/724–8663, 877/753–5672 ⊕ www.floravistainn.com ⌗ 5 rooms ⌂ In-room: no a/c, Wi-Fi. In-hotel: tennis court ⎡◯⎤ Breakfast.

$$$$ ⌗ **Seascape Beach Resort.** On a bluff overlooking Monterey Bay, Seascape
☺   is a full-fledged resort that makes it easy to unwind. **Pros:** time-share-style apartments; access to miles of beachfront; superb views. **Cons:** far from city life; most bathrooms are small. ⊠ 1 Seascape Resort Dr. ☎ 831/688–6800, 800/929–7727 ⊕ www.seascaperesort.com ⌗ 285 suites ⌂ In-room: no a/c, kitchen, Wi-Fi. In-hotel: restaurant, bar, pool, gym, spa, beach, children's programs, laundry facilities, business center.

CAPITOLA AND SOQUEL

4 mi northwest of Aptos on Hwy. 1.

On the National Register of Historic places as California's first seaside resort town, the village of Capitola has been in a holiday mood since the late 1800s. Its walkable downtown is jam-packed with casual eateries, surf shops, and ice-cream parlors. Inland, across Highway 1, antiques shops line Soquel Drive in the town of Soquel. Wineries dot the Santa Cruz Mountains beyond.

GETTING HERE AND AROUND

From Santa Cruz or Monterey, follow Highway 1 to the Capitola/Soquel (Bay Avenue) exit about 7 mi south of Santa Cruz and head toward the ocean to reach Capitola. Turn east and you'll find the heart of Soquel Village. On summer weekends, park for free in the lot behind the Crossroads Center just a block west of the freeway and hop aboard the free Capitola Shuttle to the village.

ESSENTIALS

Visitor Information Capitola-Soquel Chamber of Commerce ⊠ 716-G Capitola Ave. ☎ 831/475–6522, 800/474-6522 ⊕ www.capitolachamber.com.

EXPLORING

New Brighton State Beach. New Brighton State Beach, once the site of a Chinese fishing village, is now a popular surfing and camping spot. Its Pacific Migrations Visitor Center traces the history of the Chinese and other peoples who settled around Monterey Bay, as well as the migratory patterns of the area's wildlife, such as monarch butterflies and gray whales. ■ TIP➔ **New Brighton Beach connects with Seacliff Beach, and at low tide you can walk or run along this scenic stretch of sand for nearly 16 mi south (you might have to wade through a few creeks). The 1½-mi stroll from New Brighton to Seacliff's cement ship is a local favorite.** ⊠ 1500 State Park Dr. ☎ 831/464–6330 ⊕ www.parks.ca.gov ⌗ $10 per vehicle.

WHERE TO EAT AND STAY

¢   ✕ **Carpo's.** Locals line up in droves at Carpo's counter, hankering for
SEAFOOD   mouthwatering, casual family meals. The menu leans heavily toward
☺   seafood, but also includes burgers, salads, and steaks. Favorites include the fishermen's baskets of fresh battered snapper, calamari and prawns, seafood kabobs, and homemade olallieberry pie. Nearly everything here costs less than $10. Go early to beat the crowds, or be prepared to wait for a table. ⊠ 2400 Porter St. ☎ 831/476–6260 ⊕ www.carposrestaurant.com.

¢
CAFÉ
☺

✕ **Gayle's Bakery & Rosticceria.** Whether you're in the mood for an orange-olallieberry muffin, a wild rice and chicken salad, or tri-tip on garlic toast, this bakery-cum-deli's varied menu is likely to satisfy. Munch your chocolate macaroon on the shady patio or dig into the daily blue-plate dinner—there's a junior blue plate for the kids—amid the whirl inside. ✉ *504 Bay Ave.* ☎ *831/462–1200* ⊕ *www.gaylesbakery.com.*

$$
AMERICAN

✕ **Michael's on Main.** Classic comfort food with a creative gourmet twist, reasonable prices, and attentive service draw a lively crowd of locals to this upscale-but-casual creekside eatery. Chef Michael Clark's commitment to locally sustainable fisheries and farmers has earned him community accolades and infuses dishes with the inimitable taste that comes from using fresh local ingredients. The menu changes seasonally, but you can always count on finding such home-style dishes as pork osso bucco in red wine tomato citrus sauce as well as unusual entrées like pistachio-crusted salmon with mint vinaigrette. For a quiet conversation spot, ask for a table on the romantic patio overlooking the creek. The busy bar area hosts live music Wednesday through Saturday. ✉ *2591 Main St.* ☎ *831/479–9777* ⊕ *www.michaelsonmain.net* ⊗ *Closed Mon.*

$$$
CONTINENTAL

✕ **Shadowbrook.** To get to this romantic spot overlooking Soquel Creek, you can take a cable car or walk the stairs down a steep, fern-lined bank beside a running waterfall. Dining room options include the rooftop Redwood Room, the wood-paneled Wine Cellar, and the airy, glass-enclosed Garden Room. Prime rib and grilled seafood are the stars of the simple menu. A cheaper menu of light entrées is available in the lounge. ✉ *1750 Wharf Rd.* ☎ *831/475–1511, 800/975–1511* ⊕ *www. shadowbrook-capitola.com* ⊗ *No lunch.*

$$$$

▦ **Inn at Depot Hill.** This inventively designed B&B in a former rail depot sees itself as a link to the era of luxury train travel. **Pros:** short walk to beach and village; historic charm; excellent service. **Cons:** fills quickly; hot tub conversation on the patio may irk second-floor guests. ✉ *250 Monterey Ave.* ☎ *831/462–3376, 800/572–2632* ⊕ *www.innatdepothill. com* ➭ *12 rooms* ☖ *In-room: no a/c, Wi-Fi* ⭕ *Breakfast.*

CALIFORNIA'S OLDEST RESORT TOWN

As far as anyone knows for certain, Capitola is the oldest seaside resort town on the Pacific Coast. In 1856 a pioneer acquired Soquel Landing, the picturesque lagoon and beach where Soquel Creek empties into the bay, and built a wharf. Another man opened a campground along the shore, and his daughter named it Capitola after a heroine in a novel series. After the train came to town in the 1870s, thousands of vacationers began arriving to bask in the sun on the glorious beach.

7

SANTA CRUZ

5 mi west of Capitola on Hwy. 1; 48 mi north of Monterey on Hwy. 1.

The big city on this stretch of the California coast, Santa Cruz (pop. 57,500) is less manicured than Carmel or Monterey. Long known for its surfing and its amusement-filled beach boardwalk, the town is a mix of grand Victorian-era homes and rinky-dink motels. The opening of the University of California campus in the 1960s swung the town sharply to the left, and the counterculture more or less lives on here. At the same time, the revitalized downtown and an insane real-estate market reflect the city's proximity to Silicon Valley and to a growing wine country in the surrounding mountains.

GETTING HERE AND AROUND

From San Francisco Bay Area, take Highway 17 South over the mountains to Santa Cruz, where it merges with Highway 1. Use Highway 1 to get around the area and to access all Monterey Bay coastal destinations. The main Santa Cruz Transit Center is in the heart of downtown, a short walk from the Wharf and Boardwalk; from here, connect with public transit throughout the Monterey Bay and San Francisco Bay areas.

ESSENTIALS

Visitor Information Santa Cruz County Conference and Visitors Council ⊠ *303 Water St.* ☎ *831/425–1234, 800/833–3494* ⊕ *www.santacruzcounty.travel.*

EXPLORING

☼ **Santa Cruz Beach Boardwalk.** Santa Cruz has been a seaside resort since the mid-19th century. Along one end of the broad, south-facing beach, the Santa Cruz Beach Boardwalk has entertained holidaymakers for almost as long—it celebrated its 100th anniversary in 2007. Its Looff carousel and classic wooden Giant Dipper roller coaster, both dating from the early 1900s, are surrounded by high-tech thrill rides and easygoing kiddie rides with ocean views. Video and arcade games, a mini-golf course, and a laser-tag arena pack one gigantic building, which is open daily even if the rides aren't running. You have to pay to play, but you can wander the entire boardwalk for free while sampling delicacies such as corn dogs and garlic fries. ⊠ *Along Beach St.* ☎ *831/423–5590, 831/426–7433* ⊕ *www.beachboardwalk.com* ◨ *$30 day pass for unlimited rides, or pay per ride* ☉ *Apr.–early Sept., daily; early Sept.–late May, weekends, weather permitting; call for hrs.*

☼ **Santa Cruz Municipal Wharf.** Jutting half a mile into the ocean near one end of the Santa Cruz Beach Boardwalk, the Santa Cruz Municipal Wharf is topped with seafood restaurants; souvenir shops; and outfitters offering bay cruises, fishing trips, and boat rentals. A salty sound track drifts up from under the wharf, where barking sea lions lounge in heaps on crossbeams. ⊠ *Beach St., at Pacific Ave.* ☎ *831/420–6025* ⊕ *www.santacruzwharf.com.*

West Cliff Drive. West Cliff Drive winds along the top of an oceanfront bluff from the municipal wharf to Natural Bridges State Beach. It's a spectacular drive, but it's much more fun to walk, blade, or bike the paved path that parallels the road. Groups of surfers bob and swoosh in Monterey Bay at several points near the foot of the bluff, especially at a break known as Steamer Lane. Named for a surfer who died here in 1965, nearby Mark Abbott Memorial Lighthouse stands at Point Santa Cruz, the cliff's major promontory. From here you can watch pinnipeds hang out, sunbathe, and frolic on Seal Rock.

★ **Santa Cruz Surfing Museum.** The Santa Cruz Surfing Museum, inside the Mark Abbott Memorial Lighthouse, traces local surfing history back to the early 20th century. Historical photographs show old-time surfers, and a display of boards includes rarities such as a heavy redwood plank predating the fiberglass era and the remains of a modern board chomped by a great white shark. Surfer-docents are on-site to talk about the old days. ⊠ *701 W. Cliff Dr.* ☎ *831/420–6289* ⊕ *www. santacruzsurfingmuseum.org* ✉ *$2 suggested donation* ⊙ *Sept.–June, Thurs.–Mon. noon–4; July and Aug., Weds.–Mon. 10–5.*

⟳ **Natural Bridges State Beach.** At the end of West Cliff Drive lies Natural Bridges State Beach, a stretch of soft sand edged with tide pools and sea-sculpted rock bridges. ■ **TIP→** From October to early March a colony of monarch butterflies roosts in a eucalyptus grove. ⊠ *2531 W. Cliff Dr.* ☎ *831/423–4609* ⊕ *www.parks.ca.gov* ✉ *Beach free, parking $10* ⊙ *Daily 8 am–sunset. Visitor center Oct.–Feb., daily 10–4; Mar.–Sept., weekends 10–4.*

⟳ **Seymour Marine Discovery Center.** Seymour Marine Discovery Center, part of Long Marine Laboratory at UCSC's Institute of Marine Sciences, looks more like a research facility than a slick aquarium. Interactive exhibits demonstrate how scientists study the ocean, and the aquarium displays creatures of particular interest to marine biologists. The 87-foot blue whale skeleton is one of the world's largest. Tours (sign up when you arrive) take place at 11, 1, 2, and 3. ⊠ *100 Shaffer Rd., off Delaware St. west of Natural Bridges State Beach* ☎ *831/459–3800* ⊕ *seymourcenter.ucsc.edu* ✉ *$6* ⊙ *Tues.–Sat. 10–5, Sun. noon–5.*

Wilder Ranch State Park. In the Cultural Preserve of Wilder Ranch State Park you can visit the homes, barns, workshops, and bunkhouse of a 19th-century dairy farm. Nature has reclaimed most of the ranch land, and native plants and wildlife have returned to the 7,000 acres of forest, grassland, canyons, estuaries, and beaches. Hike, bike, or ride horseback on miles of ocean-view trails. ⊠ *Hwy. 1, 1 mi north of Santa Cruz* ☎ *831/426–0505 Interpretive Center, 831/423–9703 trail information* ⊕ *www.parks.ca.gov* ✉ *Parking $10* ⊙ *Daily 8 am–sunset.*

Pacific Avenue. When you've had your fill of the city's beaches and waters, take a stroll in downtown Santa Cruz, especially on Pacific Avenue between Laurel and Water streets. Vintage boutiques and mountain sports stores, sushi bars and Mexican restaurants, day spas, and nightclubs keep the main drag and the surrounding streets hopping mid-morning until late evening.

Santa Cruz Mission State Historic Park. On the northern fringes of downtown, Santa Cruz Mission State Historic Park preserves the site of California's 12th Spanish mission, built in the 1790s and destroyed by an earthquake in 1857. A museum in a restored 1791 adobe and a half-scale replica of the mission church are part of the complex. ⊠ *144 School St.* ☎ *831/425–5849* ⊕ *www.parks. ca.gov* ⊠ *Free* ☉ *Thurs.–Sat. 10–4.*

Mystery Spot. Hokey tourist trap or genuine scientific enigma? Since 1940, curious throngs baffled by the Mystery Spot have made it one of the most visited attractions in Santa Cruz. The laws of gravity and physics don't appear to apply in this tiny patch of redwood forest, where balls roll uphill and people stand on a slant. Advance online tickets ($6) are recommended for weekend and holiday visits. ⊠ *465 Mystery Spot Rd.* ☎ *831/423–8897* ⊕ *www.mysteryspot.com* ⊠ *$5 on site, $6 in advance, parking $5* ☉ *Late May–early Sept., daily 10–7; early Sept.–late May, weekdays 10–4, weekends 10–5.*

> ### HAWAIIAN ROYALTY SURFS THE BAY
>
> In 1885 relatives of Hawaiian Queen Kapiolani reputedly visited Santa Cruz and surfed near the mouth of the San Lorenzo River. Nearly 20 years later, legendary Hawaiian surfer Duke Kahanamoku also surfed the Santa Cruz swells.

University of California at Santa Cruz. The modern 2,000-acre campus of the University of California at Santa Cruz nestles in the forested hills above town. Its sylvan setting, sweeping ocean vistas, and redwood architecture make the university worth a visit. Campus tours, offered several times daily (reserve in advance), offer a glimpse of college life and campus highlights. They run about an hour and 45 minutes and combine moderate walking with shuttle transport.

UCSC Arboretum. Half a mile beyond the main campus entrance, the UCSC Arboretum is a stellar collection of gardens arranged by geography. A walking path leads through areas dedicated to the plants of California, Australia, New Zealand, and South Africa. ⊠ *1156 High St.* ☎ *831/427–2998* ⊕ *arboretum.ucsc.edu* ⊠ *$5* ☉ *Daily 9–5, guided tours by appointment* ⊠ *Main entrance at Bay and High Sts.* ☎ *831/459–0111* ⊕ *www.ucsc.edu.*

OFF THE BEATEN PATH

Santa Cruz Mountains. Highway 9 heads northeast from Santa Cruz into hills densely timbered with massive coastal redwoods. The road winds through the lush San Lorenzo Valley, past hamlets consisting of a few cafés, antiques shops, and old-style tourist cabins. Here, residents of the hunting-and-fishing persuasion coexist with hardcore flower-power survivors and wannabes. Along Highway 9 and its side roads are about a dozen **wineries**, most notably Bonny Doon Vineyard, Organic Wineworks, and David Bruce Winery. ■ TIP→ The Santa Cruz Mountains Winegrowers Association (⊕ www.scmwa.com) distributes a wine-touring map at many lodgings and attractions around Santa Cruz.

Felton. On your way into Felton, stop at the tiny, brick-red Bigfoot Discovery Museum, then take a walk in Henry Cowell Redwoods State Park. Off Graham Hill Road in town are a covered bridge and Roaring Camp Railroads, where you can take a vintage train to Bear Mountain year-round or down the San Lorenzo Gorge to Santa Cruz Main Beach in summer. ⊠ *Hwy. 9, 7 mi north of Santa Cruz* ☎ *831/222–2120* ⊕ *www.slvchamber.org.*

Ben Lomond. Ben Lomond has the rough-hewn Henfling's Tavern, which presents a broad spectrum of live American and international music, and the kitschy chalet-style Tyrolean Inn, a Bavarian restaurant (no lunch) offering German beer and music. ⊠ *Hwy. 9, 3 mi north of Felton* ☎ *831/222–2120* ⊕ *www.slvchamber.org.*

Boulder Creek. In Boulder Creek, buildings from the 1880s–1920s line the main street; pick up the walking-tour pamphlet, available at many local businesses, to learn more. ⊠ *Hwy. 9, 2 mi north of Brookdale* ☎ *831/222–2120* ⊕ *www.slvchamber.org.*

Big Basin Redwoods State Park. Boulder Creek is the gateway to Big Basin Redwoods State Park. In California's oldest state park (established in 1902), more than 80 mi of hiking trails thread through redwood groves and past waterfalls. ⊠ *Hwy. 236, Big Basin Way, 9 mi northwest of Boulder Creek, Boulder Creek* ☎ *831/338–8860* ⊕ *www.parks.ca.gov*

WHERE TO EAT

$
SEAFOOD
★

✕ **Crow's Nest.** A local favorite since 1969, this classic California beachside eatery sits right on the water in Santa Cruz Harbor. Vintage surfboards and local surf photography line the walls in the main dining room; nearly every table overlooks the sand and surf. Seafood and steaks, served with local veggies, dominate the menu; favorite appetizers include the chilled shrimp-stuffed artichoke and crispy tempura prawns, served with rice pilaf. No need to pile high on your first trip to the endless salad bar—you can return as often as you like. For sweeping ocean views and more casual fare (think fish tacos and burgers), head upstairs to the Breakwater Bar & Grill. Live entertainment several days a week makes for a dynamic atmosphere year-round. ⊠ *2218 E. Cliff Dr.* ☎ *831/476–4560* ⊕ *www.crowsnest-santacruz.com.*

$$
ITALIAN

✕ **Gabriella Café.** The work of local artists hangs on the walls of this petite, romantic café in a tile-roof cottage. Featuring organic produce from area farms, the seasonal Italian menu has offered wild mushroom risotto, grilled quail with quince mostarda, and roasted beet salad with arugula, goat cheese and pistachios. ⊠ *910 Cedar St.* ☎ *831/457–1677* ⊕ *www.gabriellacafe.com.*

$$$
ITALIAN

✕ **La Posta.** Locals and tourists alike cram into La Posta's cozy, modern-rustic dining room, lured by authentic Italian fare made with fresh local produce. Near everything is house-made, from pizzas and breads baked in the brick oven to pasta and vanilla bean gelato (eggs come from a chicken coop out back). The seasonal menu changes often, but always includes flavorful dishes with a Santa Cruz flair, like fried artichokes, ravioli filled with crab, chicken with Brussels sprouts, or sautéed fish, caught sustainably from local waters. Come Sunday for a lively, family-style, fixed-price dinner—four courses for just $30. ⊠ *538 Seabright Ave.* ☎ *831/457–2782* ⊕ *www.lapostarestaurant.com* ☉ *Closed Mon. No lunch.*

$$$
CONTINENTAL
★

✕ **Oswald.** Sophisticated yet unpretentious European-inspired California cooking is the order of the day at this intimate and stylish bistro. The menu changes seasonally, but might include such items as perfectly prepared sherry-steamed mussels or sautéed duck breast. Sit at the slick marble bar and order a creative concoction like bourbon mixed with

7

local apple and lemon juices or gin with cucumber and ginger beer, or choose from a range of wines and spirits. ⊠ *121 Soquel Ave., at Front St.* ☎ *831/423–7427* ⊕ *www.oswaldrestaurant.com* ☉ *Closed Mon. No lunch weekends.*

$ — AMERICAN ╳ **Seabright Brewery.** Great burgers, big salads, and stellar microbrews make this a favorite hangout in the youthful Seabright neighborhood east of downtown. Sit outside on the large patio or inside at a comfortable, spacious booth; both are popular with families. ⊠ *519 Seabright Ave.* ☎ *831/426–2739* ⊕ *www.seabrightbrewery.com.*

$$ — MEDITERRANEAN ╳ **Soif.** Wine reigns at this sleek bistro and wine shop that takes its name from the French word for thirst. The lengthy list includes selections from near and far, dozens of which you can order by the taste or glass. Infused with the tastes of the Mediterranean, small plates and mains are served at the copper-top bar, the big communal table, and private tables. A jazz combo or solo pianist plays some evenings. ⊠ *105 Walnut Ave.* ☎ *831/423–2020* ⊕ *www.soifwine.com* ☉ *No lunch.*

¢ — AMERICAN ╳ **Zachary's.** This noisy café filled with students and families defines the funky essence of Santa Cruz. It also dishes up great breakfasts: stay simple with sourdough pancakes, or go for Mike's Mess—eggs scrambled with bacon, mushrooms, and home fries, then topped with sour cream, melted cheese, and fresh tomatoes. ■TIP→ **If you arrive after 9 am, expect a long wait for a table; lunch is a shade calmer, but closing time is 2:30 pm.** ⊠ *819 Pacific Ave.* ☎ *831/427–0646* ⌣ *Reservations not accepted* ☉ *Closed Mon. No dinner.*

WHERE TO STAY

For expanded reviews, go to Fodors.com.

$$$ ▦ **Babbling Brook Inn.** Though it's smack in the middle of Santa Cruz, this B&B has lush gardens, a running stream, and tall trees that make you feel as if you're in a secluded wood. **Pros:** close to UCSC; walking distance from downtown shops; woodsy feel. **Cons:** near a high school; some rooms are close to a busy street. ⊠ *1025 Laurel St.* ☎ *831/427–2437, 800/866–1131* ⊕ *www.babblingbrookinn.com* ⌣ *13 rooms* ⌂ *In-room: no a/c, Wi-Fi* ¦○¦ *Breakfast.*

$$$ ▦ **Chaminade Resort & Spa.** A full-on renovation of the entire property, completed in 2009, sharpened this hilltop resort's look, enhanced its amenities, and qualified it for regional green certification. **Pros:** far from city life; spectacular property; ideal spot for romance and rejuvenation. **Cons:** must drive to attractions and sights; near major hospital. ⊠ *1 Chaminade La.* ☎ *800/283–6569 reservations, 831/475–5600* ⊕ *www.chaminade.com* ⌣ *112 rooms, 44 suites* ⌂ *In-room: a/c, Internet, Wi-Fi. In-hotel: restaurant, bar, pool, tennis court, gym, spa, business center, some pets allowed.*

¢ ▦ **Harbor Inn.** Family-run, friendly, and funky, this basic but sparkling-clean lodge offers exceptional value just a few blocks from Santa Cruz Harbor and Twin Lakes Beach. **Pros:** affordable; free Wi-Fi; park your car and walk to the beach. **Cons:** not fancy; not near downtown. ⊠ *645 7th Ave.* ☎ *831/479–9731* ⊕ *www.harborinn.info* ⌣ *17 rooms, 2 suites* ⌂ *In-room: no a/c, Wi-Fi. In-hotel: some pets allowed.*

$$$ **Pacific Blue Inn.** Green themes reign in this three-story, eco-friendly B&B, built from scratch in 2009 on a sliver of prime property on the outer edge of Pacific Avenue, downtown Santa Cruz's main drag. **Pros:** free bicycles; five-minute walk to boardwalk and wharf; right in downtown. **Cons:** tiny property; not suitable for children. ⊠ *636 Pacific Ave.* ☎ *831/600–8880* ⊕ *www.pacificblueinn.com* ➷ *9 rooms* ♿ *In-room: Wi-Fi. In-hotel: some pets allowed* †⃝| *Breakfast.*

$$$ **Pleasure Point Inn.** Tucked in a residential neighborhood at the east end of town, this modern Mediterranean-style B&B sits right across the street from the ocean and a popular surfing beach (where surfing lessons are available). **Pros:** fantastic views; ideal for checking the swells; quirky neighborhood. **Cons:** few rooms; several miles from major attractions. ⊠ *2–3665 E. Cliff Dr.* ☎ *831/475–4657* ⊕ *www.pleasurepointinn.com* ➷ *4 rooms* ♿ *In-room: no a/c, Wi-Fi. In-hotel: beach* †⃝| *Breakfast.*

$$$$ **Santa Cruz Dream Inn.** Just a short stroll from the boardwalk and ★ wharf, this full-service luxury hotel is the only lodging in Santa Cruz directly on the beach. **Pros:** directly on the beach; easy parking; walk to boardwalk and downtown. **Cons:** expensive; area gets congested on busy weekends. ⊠ *175 W. Cliff Dr.* ☎ *831/426–4330, 866/774–7735 reservations* 🖷 *831/427–2025* ⊕ *www.dreaminnsantacruz.com* ➷ *149 rooms, 16 suites* ♿ *In-room: a/c, Wi-Fi. In-hotel: restaurant, bar, pool, beach, business center, parking.*

$$$ **West Cliff Inn.** Perched on the bluffs across from Cowell Beach, this ★ posh nautical-theme inn commands sweeping views of the boardwalk and Monterey Bay. **Pros:** killer views; walking distance from the beach; close to downtown. **Cons:** boardwalk noise; street traffic. ⊠ *174 West Cliff Dr.* ☎ *800/979–0910 toll free, 831/457-2200* ⊕ *www.westcliffinn. com* ➷ *7 rooms, 2 suites, 1 cottage* ♿ *In-room: a/c, Wi-Fi. In-hotel: business center, some pets allowed* †⃝| *Breakfast.*

NIGHTLIFE AND THE ARTS

NIGHTLIFE

★ **Catalyst.** Dance with the crowds at the Catalyst, a huge, grimy downtown club that has regularly featured big names, from Neil Young to the Red Hot Chili Peppers. ⊠ *1011 Pacific Ave.* ☎ *831/423–1338* ⊕ *www. catalystclub.com.*

Kuumbwa Jazz Center. Renowned in the international jazz community, and drawing performers such as Herbie Hancock, Pat Metheny, and Charlie Hunter, the nonprofit Kuumbwa Jazz Center bops with live music most nights; the café serves meals an hour before most shows. ⊠ *320–2 Cedar St.* ☎ *831/427–2227* ⊕ *www.kuumbwajazz.org.*

Moe's Alley. Blues, salsa, reggae, funk: you name it, Moe's Alley has it all, six nights a week. ⊠ *1535 Commercial Way* ☎ *831/479–1854* ⊕ *www.moesalley.com.*

THE ARTS

Cabrillo Festival of Contemporary Music. Each August, the Cabrillo Festival of Contemporary Music brings some of the world's finest artists to the Santa Cruz Civic Auditorium to play groundbreaking symphonic music, including major world premieres. ☎ *831/426–6966, 831/420–5260 box office* ⊕ *www.cabrillomusic.org.*

Santa Cruz Baroque Festival. Using period and reproduction instruments, the Santa Cruz Baroque Festival presents a wide range of classical music at various venues throughout the year. As the name suggests, the focus is on 17th- and 18th-century composers such as Bach and Handel. ☎ *831/457–9693* ⊕ *www.scbaroque.org.*

Shakespeare Santa Cruz. Shakespeare Santa Cruz stages a six-week Shakespeare festival in July and August that may also include the occasional modern dramatic performance. Most performances are outdoors under the redwoods. A holiday program takes place in December. ✉ *SSC/ UCSC Theater Arts Center, 1156 High St.* ☎ *831/459–2121, 831/459– 2159 tickets* ⊕ *www.shakespearesantacruz.org.*

SPORTS AND THE OUTDOORS

BICYCLING

Another Bike Shop. Mountain bikers should head to Another Bike Shop for tips on the best trails around and a look at cutting-edge gear made and tested locally. ✉ *2361 Mission St.* ☎ *831/427–2232* ⊕ *www. anotherbikeshop.com.*

Bicycle Shop Santa Cruz. Park the car and rent a beach cruiser at Bicycle Shop Santa Cruz. ✉ *1325 Mission St.* ☎ *831/454–0909* ⊕ *www. thebicycleshopsantacruz.com.*

BOATS AND CHARTERS

Chardonnay Sailing Charters. Chardonnay Sailing Charters cruises Monterey Bay year-round on a variety of trips, such as whale-watching, astronomy, and winemaker sails. The 70-foot *Chardonnay II* leaves from the yacht harbor in Santa Cruz. Food and drink are served on many of their cruises. Reservations are essential. ☎ *831/423–1213* ⊕ *www.chardonnay.com.*

Stagnaro Sport Fishing. Stagnaro Sport Fishing operates salmon, albacore, and rock-cod fishing expeditions; the fees ($50 to $75) include bait. The company also runs whale-watching, dolphin, and sealife cruises ($45) year-round. ✉ *June–Aug., Santa Cruz Municipal Wharf; Sept.–May, Santa Cruz West Harbor* ☎ *831/427–2334* ⊕ *www.stagnaros.com.*

GOLF

Pasatiempo Golf Club. Designed by famed golf architect Dr. Alister MacKenzie in 1929, semiprivate Pasatiempo Golf Club, set amid undulating hills just above the city, often ranks among the nation's top championship courses in annual polls. Golfers rave about the spectacular views and challenging terrain. The greens fee is $220; an electric cart is $30 per player. ✉ *20 Clubhouse Rd.* ☎ *831/459–9155* ⊕ *www.pasatiempo.com.*

KAYAKING

Kayak Connection. In March, April, and May paddle out in the bay to mingle with gray whales and their calves on their northward journey to Alaska with Kayak Connection. Kayak Connection also guides other

O'Neill: A Santa Cruz Icon

O'Neill wet suits and beachwear weren't exactly born in Santa Cruz, but as far as most of the world is concerned, the O'Neill brand is synonymous with Santa Cruz and surfing legend.

The O'Neill wet suit story began in 1952, when Jack O'Neill and his brother Robert opened their first Surf Shop in a garage across from San Francisco's Ocean Beach. While shaping balsa surfboards and selling accessories, the O'Neills experimented with solutions to a common surfer problem: frigid waters. Tired of being forced back to shore, blue-lipped and shivering, after just 20 or 30 minutes riding the waves, they played with various materials and eventually designed a neoprene vest.

In 1959 Jack moved his Surf Shop 90 mi south to Cowell Beach in Santa Cruz. It quickly became a popular surf hangout, and O'Neill's new wet suits began to sell like hotcakes. In the early 1960s the company opened a warehouse for manufacturing on a larger scale. Santa Cruz soon became a major surf city, attracting wave-riders to prime breaks at Steamer Lane, Pleasure Point, and The Hook. In 1965 O'Neill pioneered the first wet-suit boots, and in 1971 Jack's son invented the surf leash. By 1980, O'Neill stood at the top of the world wet-suit market.

O'Neill operates two flagship stores, one downtown and one close to Jack O'Neill's home on Pleasure Point. Check out the latest versions, along with casual beachwear and surfing gear. You can also pop into a smaller outlet on the Santa Cruz Wharf.

O'Neill Surf Shop ⊠ *110 Cooper St.* ☎ *831/469–4377* ⊕ *www.oneill.com.*

7

---

tours around Monterey Bay, including Natural Bridges State Beach, Capitola, and Elkhorn Slough. ⊠ *413 Lake Ave. #3, Santa Cruz Harbor* ☎ *831/479–1121* ⊕ *www.kayakconnection.com.*

Venture Quest Kayaking. Explore hidden coves and kelp forests with Venture Quest Kayaking. The company's guided nature tours depart from Santa Cruz Wharf or Harbor, depending on the season. A two-hour kayak nature tour and introductory lesson costs $55. A three-hour kayak rental is $30 and includes wet suit and gear. Venture Quest also arranges tours at other Monterey Bay destinations, including Capitola and Elkhorn Slough. ⊠ *#2 Santa Cruz Wharf* ☎ *831/427–2267, 831/425–8445* ⊕ *www.kayaksantacruz.com.*

SURFING

Pleasure Point. Surfers gather for spectacular waves and sunsets at Pleasure Point. ⊠ *E. Cliff and Pleasure Point Drs.*

Steamer Lane. Steamer Lane, near the lighthouse on West Cliff Drive, has a decent break. The area plays host to several competitions in summer.

Club-Ed Surf School and Camps. Find out what all the fun is about at Club-Ed Surf School and Camps. Your first private or group lesson ($85 and up) includes all equipment. ⊠ *Cowell Beach, at Santa Cruz Dream Inn* ☎ *831/464–0177* ⊕ *www.club-ed.com.*

Paradise Surf Shop. The most welcoming place in town to buy or rent surf gear is Paradise Surf Shop. The shop is owned and run by women who aim to help everyone feel comfortable on the water. ✉ *3961 Portola Dr.* ☎ *831/462–3880* ⊕ *www.paradisesurf.com.*

Cowell's Beach Surf Shop. Cowell's Beach Surf Shop sells bikinis, rents surfboards and wet suits, and offers lessons. ✉ *30 Front St.* ☎ *831/427–2355* ⊕ *www.cowellssurfshop.com.*

The Inland Empire

EAST OF LOS ANGELES TO THE SAN JACINTO MOUNTAINS

WORD OF MOUTH

"Callaway [and] Hart are some of my favorite wineries in Temecula, for the grounds, the restaurants, the special events and the wines. If you like sweet bubbles, Wilson Creek's Almond Champagne is lovely."

— fairygemgirl

WELCOME TO THE INLAND EMPIRE

TOP REASONS TO GO

★ **Wine Country:** The Temecula Valley is a mélange of rolling hills, faint ocean breezes, beautiful and funky wineries, lovely lodging options, and gourmet restaurants.

★ **The Mission Inn:** One of the most unique hotels in America, Riverside's rambling, eclectic Mission Inn feels like an urban Hearst Castle.

★ **Apple country:** Oak Glen is one of Southern California's largest apple-growing regions. Attend an old-fashioned hoedown, take a wagon ride, and sample Mile High apple pies and homemade ciders.

★ **Soothing spas:** The lushly landscaped grounds, bubbling hot springs, and playful mud baths of Glen Ivy are ideal spots to unwind, while Kelly's Spa at the historic Mission Inn provides a Tuscan-style retreat.

★ **Alpine escapes:** Breathe in the clean mountain air or cozy up in a rustic cabin at one of the Inland Empire's great mountain hideaways: Lake Arrowhead, Big Bear, and Idyllwild.

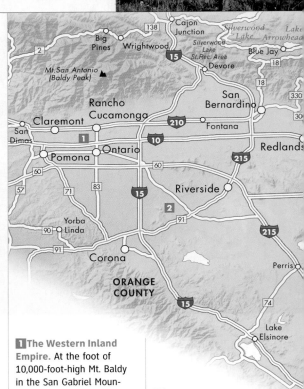

1 The Western Inland Empire. At the foot of 10,000-foot-high Mt. Baldy in the San Gabriel Mountains, the tree-lined communities of Pomona and Claremont are known for their prestigious colleges: California State Polytechnic University–Pomona and the seven-school Claremont college complex. Pomona is urban and industrial, but Claremont is a classic tree-shaded, lively, sophisticated college town that more resembles trendy sections of Los Angeles than the laid back Inland Empire.

2 Riverside Area. In the late 1700s, Mexican settlers called this now-suburban region Valle de Paraiso. Citrus-growing here began in 1873, when homesteader Eliza Tibbets planted two navel-orange trees in her yard. The area's biggest draws are the majestic Mission Inn, with its fine restaurants and unique history and architecture, and Glen Ivy Hot Springs in nearby Corona.

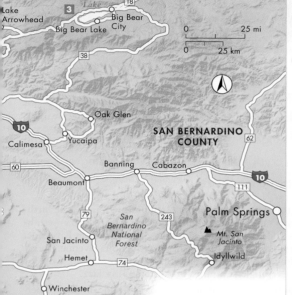

GETTING ORIENTED

Several major freeways provide access to the Inland Empire from the L.A. and San Diego areas. Ontario, Corona, and Temecula line up along I–15, and I–215; and Highway 91 leads from L.A. to Corona, Riverside and San Bernardino. The area's popularity as a bedroom community for Los Angeles has created some nasty freeway congestion on Highway 60, I–10, and I–15, so try to avoid driving during rush hour, usually 6 to 8 am and 4 to 7 pm.

8

3 San Bernardino Mountains. Lake Arrowhead and always-sunny Big Bear are the recreational centers of this area. Though the two are geographically close, they're distinct in appeal—smaller, but similar to Lake Tahoe, say visitors. Lake Arrowhead, with its cool mountain air, trail-threaded woods, and brilliant lake, draws a summertime crowd—a well-heeled one, if the prices in its shops and restaurants are any indication. Big Bear's ski and snowboarding slopes, cross-country trails, and cheerful lodges come alive in winter. Even if you're not interested in the resorts themselves, the Rim of the World Scenic Byway (Highway 18), which connects the two at an elevation up to 8,000 feet, is a magnificent drive; on a clear day, you'll feel like you can see forever.

4 The Southern Inland Empire. Life is quieter in the southern portion of the Inland Empire than it is to the north. In this corner of Riverside County, towns such as Idyllwild and Temecula are oases of the good life for locals and visitors alike.

Updated by
Bobbi Zane

The Inland Empire, an area often overlooked by visitors because of its tangled freeways and suburban sprawl, has its charms. No more than a couple of hours' drive from metropolitan Los Angeles, you can ski a 7,000-foot mountain overlooking a crystal blue lake or go wine tasting at a vineyard cooled by ocean breezes.

At the heart of this desert and mountain region is Riverside, the birthplace of California's multimillion-dollar navel-orange industry—established in 1875—and home of the University of California at Riverside. The tree that started it all still flourishes on Magnolia Avenue. Today the streets of downtown buzz with people on their way to shop for antiques, eat in exciting restaurants, and listen to live jazz.

The scene is completely different northeast of Riverside, in the San Bernardino Mountains. There Big Bear Lake and Lake Arrowhead are set like bowls surrounded by wooded mountain peaks. To the south, in the San Jacinto Mountains just west of Palm Springs, Idyllwild is a popular year-round getaway with romantic cottages, an impressive collection of art galleries, and cozy restaurants. In the southernmost reaches of the Inland Empire, on the way from Riverside to San Diego, is what is known as the Southern California Wine Country around Temecula, a hip and trendy destination for oenophiles. This is also prime territory for hot-air ballooning, golfing, fine dining, and—of course—vineyard tours and wine tasting.

PLANNING

WHEN TO GO

The climate varies greatly depending on what part of the Inland Empire you're visiting. Summer temperatures in the mountains and in Temecula, 20 mi from the coast, usually hover around 80°F, though it's not uncommon for Riverside to reach temperatures over 100°F. From September to March this area is subject to increasingly high Santa Ana winds, sometimes strong enough to overturn trucks on the freeway. In winter, temperatures in the mountains and in Temecula usually range from 30°F to 55°F, and in the Riverside area 40°F to 60°F. Most of the ski areas open when the first natural snow falls (usually in November) and close in mid-March.

GETTING HERE AND AROUND

AIR TRAVEL

Aero Mexico, Alaska, American, Continental, Delta, Southwest, United, US Airways, and Great Lakes Airlines serve LA/Ontario International Airport.

Airport Contacts LA/Ontario International Airport ⊠ *Airport Dr., Archibald Ave. exit off I–10, 2900 Airport Dr., Ontario* ☎ *909/937–2700* ⊕ *www.lawa.org.*

BUS TRAVEL

Greyhound serves Riverside, San Bernardino, and Temecula. Most stations are open daily during business hours; some are open 24 hours.

The Foothill Transit Bus Line serves Pomona, Claremont, and Montclair, with stops at Cal Poly and the Fairplex. Riverside Transit Authority (RTA) serves Riverside and some outlying communities, as does OmniTrans.

Bus Contacts Foothill Transit ☎ *800/743–3463* ⊕ *www.foothilltransit.org.* **Omnitrans** ☎ *800/966–6428* ⊕ *www.omnitrans.org.* **Riverside Transit Authority** ☎ *800/800–7821* ⊕ *www.rrta.com.*

CAR TRAVEL

Avoid Highway 91 if possible; it's almost always backed up from Corona through Orange County.

Car Contact CalTrans Information Service 24-hour road info ☎ *800/427–7623* ⊕ *www.dot.ca.gov/hq/roadinfo.*

TRAIN TRAVEL

■TIP➔ Many locals use the Metrolink to get around, which is clean and quick, and generally a much nicer way to travel than by bus.

Metrolink has several Inland Empire stations on its Inter-County, San Bernardino, and Riverside rail lines. The Riverside Line connects downtown Riverside, Pedley, East Ontario, and downtown Pomona with City of Industry, Montebello/City of Commerce, and Union Station in Los Angeles. The Inland Empire Orange County Line connects San Bernardino, downtown Riverside, Riverside La Sierra, and West Corona with San Juan Capistrano and other Orange County destinations. Metrolink's busiest train, the San Bernardino Line, connects Pomona, Claremont, Montclair, and San Bernardino with the San Gabriel Valley and downtown Los Angeles. Bus service extends the reach of train service, to spots including L.A./Ontario Airport, the Claremont colleges, and the Fairplex at Pomona. You can buy tickets and passes at the ticket vending machine at each station, or by telephone. 511 Travel Information Service is a phone and web-based service where you can get real-time traffic information and trip planning help. A recorded message announces Metrolink schedules 24 hours a day.

Train Contact Metrolink ☎ *800/371–5465* ⊕ *www.metrolinktrains.com.*

HEALTH AND SAFETY

In an emergency dial 911.

Emergency Services Big Bear Lake Sheriff ☎ 909/866–0100. **Parkview Community Hospital** ✉ 3865 Jackson St., Riverside ☎ 951/688–2211 ⊕ www.pchmc.org. **Rancho Springs Medical Center** ✉ 25500 Medical Center Dr., Murietta ☎ 951/696–6000 ⊕ www.swhealthcaresystem.com.**Riverside Community Hospital** ✉ 4445 Magnolia Ave., Riverside ☎ 951/788–3000 ⊕ www.rchc.org. **St. Bernardine Medical Center** ✉ 2101 N. Waterman Ave., San Bernardino ☎ 909/883–8711 ⊕ www.stbernardinemedicalcenter.org.

RESTAURANTS

Inland Empire residents no longer have to travel to L.A. or Orange County for a good meal. Downtown Riverside is home to a few ambitious restaurants, along with the chains you can find in most areas. The college towns of Claremont and Redlands focus on creative contemporary, ethnic, and traditional selections. Excellent innovative cuisine has become an art in Temecula, especially at the wineries, many of which showcase their products alongside fine dining. Your options are limited in the smaller mountain communities; typically each town supports a single upscale restaurant, along with fast-food outlets, steak-and-potatoes family spots, and perhaps an Italian or Mexican eatery. Universally, dining out is casual.

HOTELS

In the San Bernardino mountains, many accommodations are bed-and-breakfasts or rustic cabins, though Lake Arrowhead and Big Bear offer more luxurious resort lodging. Rates for Big Bear lodgings fluctuate widely, depending on the season. When winter snow brings droves of Angelenos to the mountains for skiing, expect to pay sky-high prices for any kind of room. Most establishments require a two-night stay on weekends. In Riverside, you might enjoy a stay at the landmark Mission Inn, a rambling Spanish-style hotel with elaborate courtyards, fountains, and a mixture of ornate Mission revival–, Spanish baroque–, Renaissance revival–, and Asian-architecture styles. In the Wine Country, lodgings can be found at wineries, golf resorts, and chain hotels.

WHAT IT COSTS				
¢	$	$$	$$$	$$$$
Restaurants	under $10	$10–$15	$16–$22	$23–$30	over $30
Hotels	under $90	$90–$120	$121–$175	$176–$250	over $250

Restaurant prices are for a main course at dinner, excluding sales tax of 7.75%. Hotel prices are for two people in a standard double room in high season, excluding service charges and 7.75% tax.

THE WESTERN INLAND EMPIRE

Straddling the line between Los Angeles and San Bernardino counties, the western section of the Inland Empire is home to some of California's oldest vineyards and original citrus orchards. Now a busy suburban community and site of the LA Ontario International Airport, it holds the closest ski slopes to metro LA, Fairplex, where the LA County Fair is held each year, and Claremont, home to a collection of high ranking colleges.

POMONA

23 mi north of Anaheim on Hwy. 57; 27 mi east of Pasadena on I–210.

The green hills of Pomona, dotted with horses and houses, are perhaps best known as the site of the Los Angeles County Fair and of California State Polytechnic University–Pomona. Named for the Roman goddess of fruit, the city has a rich citrus-growing heritage.

GETTING HERE AND AROUND

Interstate 10 bisects the Western Inland Empire west to east. Points of interest lie at the base of the San Gabriel Mountains, north of the freeway. You can reach this area by public transportation, but you'll need a car to get around unless you plan to spend all your time in the Village. Shuttle service is available to the LA metro area. Some areas are quite walkable, especially the Claremont colleges where you can stroll through parks from one school building to another.

ESSENTIALS

Visitor Information Pomona Chamber of Commerce ⊠ *101 W. Mission Blvd., #222* ☎ *909/622–1256* ⊕ *www.pomonachamber.org* ☱ *No credit cards.*

EXPLORING

Arabian Horse Shows. The classic Arabian Horse Shows, started by Kellogg in 1926, are still a tradition on the CSU–Pomona campus. More than 85 of the purebreds still call Kellogg's ranch home, and the university offers exhibitions of the equines in English and Western tack every first Sunday at 2 pm from October through May; tours of the stables and pony rides are available after the show. ⊠ *3801 W. Temple Ave.* ☎ *909/869–2224* ☲ *$4.*

California Polytechnic University at Pomona. California Polytechnic University at Pomona occupies 1,438 acres of the Kellogg Ranch, originally the winter home of cereal magnate W.K. Kellogg. The university specializes in teaching agriculture, and you can find lush grounds here: rose gardens, avocado groves, lots of farm animals, and a working Arabian Horse Ranch. You can sample the best that California agriculture has to offer at the Farm Store (⊠ *4102 University Dr. S.* ☎ *909/869–4906,* open daily 10–6), where you can find locally grown seasonal fruit and vegetables, campus-grown pork and beef, cheeses and other deli items, gift baskets, and plants grown in the university nursery. ⊠ *3801 W. Temple* ☎ *909/869–7659* ⊕ *www.csupomona.edu.*

Fairplex. Site of the Los Angeles County Fair (largest county fair in North America), the Fairplex exposition center has a 9,500-seat grandstand, an outdoor exhibit area, and nine exhibit buildings. The venue is the site of open-air markets, antiques shows, swap meets, roadster shows, historical train and model train exhibits, numerous horse shows, dog shows, a track for Thoroughbred racing during the fair, and the annual International Wine and Spirits competition.

Wally Parks NHRA Motorsports Museum. Fairplex houses the Wally Parks NHRA Motorsports Museum, dedicated to the history of American motor sports with exhibits of vintage racing vehicles. The museum holds a collection of tricked-out drag racing cars. ☎ *909/622–2133* ✉ *$8* ⊘ *Wed.–Sun. 10–5* ✉ *1101 W. McKinley Ave.* ☎ *909/623–3111* ⊕ *www. fairplex.com* ⊘ *Call for current show listings and admission prices.*

WHERE TO EAT AND STAY

$$$
AMERICAN
✕ **Pomona Valley Mining Company.** Perched on a hilltop near an old mining site, this rustic steak-and-seafood restaurant provides a great view of the city at night. The decor reflects the local mining heritage—authentic gold-rush pieces and 1800s memorabilia hang on the walls, and old lanterns are the centerpiece of each table. The food is well prepared, with a special nod to steak and prime rib, and be sure to try the Pickin's Combo, an hors d'oeuvre and more comprised of coconut beer shrimp, calamari and Buffalo wings. Service is friendly. During May book early—this is a favorite spot on prom nights. ✉ *1777 Gillette Rd.* ☎ *909/623–3515* ⊕ *www.pomonavalleyminingco.com* ⊘ *No lunch.*

$
▥ **Sheraton Suites Fairplex.** County-fair murals and whimsical carousel animals welcome you to this all-suites hotel at the entrance to Pomona's Fairplex. **Pros:** adjacent to Fairplex; clean rooms; comfortable beds; signature dog beds. **Cons:** parts of the hotel feel dated; not close to many restaurants. ✉ *601 W. McKinley Ave.* ☎ *888/627–8074* ⊕ *www. sheraton.com* ⇌ *247 suites* ⧉ *In-room: a/c, Internet, Wi-Fi. In-hotel: restaurant, bar, pool, gym, parking, some pets allowed.*

CLAREMONT

4 mi north of Pomona along Gary Ave., then 2 mi east on Foothill Blvd.

The seven Claremont colleges are among the most prestigious in the nation. The campuses are all laid out cheek-by-jowl; as you wander from one leafy street to the next, you won't be able to tell where one college ends and the next begins.

Claremont was originally the home of the Sunkist citrus growers cooperative movement. Today, Claremont Village, home to descendants of those early farmers, is bright and lively. The business district village, with streets named for prestigious eastern colleges (think Yale, Harvard, Princeton), is walkable and appealing with a collection of boutiques, fancy food emporiums, cafés, and lounges. The downtown district is a beautiful place to visit, with Victorian, Craftsman, and Spanish-colonial buildings.

GETTING HERE AND AROUND

If you're driving, exit I-10 at Indian Hill Bouelvard, and drive north to Claremont. Parking can be difficult, although there are metered spots. Overnight parking is prohibited within the village; however there is a parking structure adjacent to the College Heights Packing House Fairplex is also north of the freeway; exit Garey and drive toward the mountains.

ESSENTIALS
Visitor Information **Claremont Chamber of Commerce**
✉ *205 Yale Ave.* ☎ *909/624–1681* ⊕ *www.claremontchamber.org.*

EXPLORING

Claremont Heritage. College walking tours, a downtown tour, and historic home tours are conducted throughout the year by Claremont Heritage. On the first Saturday of each month the organization gives guided walking tours ($5) of the village. ✉ *840 N. Indian Hill Blvd.* ☎ *909/621–0848* ⊕ *www.claremontheritage.org* ✍ *$8.*

Pomona College Museum of Art. Pomona College Museum of Art, a small museum on the campus of Pomona College, holds a significant collection of contemporary art, works by old masters, and examples of Native American arts and artifacts. Highlights include the first mural painted by Mexican artist Jose Clemente Orozco in North America, a collection of first-edition etchings by Goya dating back to the 18th century, and the Kress collection of 15th- and 16th-century Italian panel paintings. ✉ *330 N. College Way* ☎ *909/621–8283* ⊕ *www.pomona.edu/museum* ✍ *Free* ◷ *Tues.–Fri. noon–5, weekends 1–5; closed between exhibits.*

QUICK BITES

Bert & Rocky's Cream Company. This independent ice cream store is known for its innovative and simply sinful concoctions. Hot items are vanilla ice cream, the Elvis special with bananas and peanut butter, Tuscany marble, chocolate raspberry swirl ice cream, and cheesecake ice cream. ✉ *242 Yale Ave.* ☎ *909/625–1852* ◷ *daily from 11 a.m.*

★ **Rancho Santa Ana Botanic Garden.** Founded in 1927 by Susanna Bixby Bryant, a wealthy landowner and conservationist, Rancho Santa Ana Botanic Garden is a living museum and research center dedicated to the conservation of more than 2,800 native-California plant species. You can meander here for hours enjoying the shade of an oak tree canopy or take a guided tour of the grounds. Meandering trails on 86 acres of ponds and greenery guide visitors past such specimens as California wild lilacs (ceanothus), big berry manzanita, and four-needled piñon. Countless birds also make their homes here. Dedicated to preservation of endangered native plants, the garden holds a large botanical research facility. ✉ *1500 N. College Ave.* ☎ *909/625–8767* ⊕ *www.rsabg.org* ✍ *$8* ◷ *Daily 8–5.*

WHERE TO EAT

$$
ITALIAN
✗ **La Parolaccia.** This busy lunch or dinner spot has locals lining up on the weekends to get a table. Bustling waiters zip through a series of small rooms serving up fresh and beautifully seasoned items from an extensive Italian menu. Popular items include spaghetti with fresh salmon and eggplant, rigatoni with Italian sausage and sherry cream sauce, and risotto with seafood, white wine, and tomato sauce. Topping the desert list is bread pudding made with ciabatta bread and crème anglaise. ✉ *201 N. Indian Hill Blvd., Claremont* ☎ *909/624–1516* ⊕ *www.LaParolacciaUSA.com.*

8

$$$ ✕ **Tutti Mangia Italian Grill.** College students have their parents take them
ITALIAN   to Tutti Mangia when they're in town visiting. Filling a corner store-
front, the dining room with tables well spaced feels warm and cozy.
The menu offers lots of choices including herb-crusted Atlantic salmon,
grilled thick-cut pork chops, and veal shank. The Sunday night prime
rib special comes with soup or salad. ✉ *102 Harvard Ave.* ☎ *909/625–
4669* ⊘ *No lunch Sun.*

$$ ✕ **Walter's Restaurant.** With a menu that roams the globe from France to
ECLECTIC   Italy to Afghanistan, Walter's is where locals gather to dine, sip wine,
and chat. You can eat outside on the sidewalk, on the lively patio, or
in a cozy setting inside. Wherever you sit, Nangy (the owner) will stroll
by to make sure you're happy with your meal. He'll urge you to try the
puffy Afghan fries with hot sauce, tabouli salad, or lamb stew. Breakfast
features a long list of omelets, sausage and eggs, or burritos. Lunch and
dinner offer salads, soups, pastas, kabobs, and vegetarian items. ✉ *308
N. Yale Ave., Claremont* ☎ *909/624-4914.*

WHERE TO STAY
For expanded hotel reviews, visit Fodors.com.

$$ ⊡ **Casa 425.** This boutique inn, perched on a corner opposite the College
Fodor's Choice   Heights Lemon Packing House entertainment/shopping complex, is the
★   most attractive lodging choice in Claremont Village. *425 W. First St., Clare-
mont* ☎ *866/450-0425* ⊕ *www.foursisters.com* ⤳ *28* ⌂ *In-room: a/c, safe,
Wi-Fi. In-hotel: restaurant, gym, laundry facilities, parking* ⦿ *Breakfast.*

NIGHTLIFE
Being a college town, Claremont has lots of bars and cafés, some of
which showcase bands.

Flappers Comedy Club. A typical comedy club where the acts are mainly
stand-up performers, Flappers is a branch of a larger club in Burbank.
You can get a bite to eat here, but no alcohol. ✉ *532 W. First St., Cla-
remont* ☎ *818/845-9721* ⊕ *www.flapperscomedy.com.*

SPORTS AND THE OUTDOORS
SKIING   **Mt. Baldy Ski Resort.** The 10,064-foot mountain's real name is Mt. San
Antonio, but Mt. Baldy Ski Resort—the oldest ski area in Southern
California—takes its name from the treeless slopes. It's known for its
steep triple-diamond runs. ■TIP→ **You can also rent snow tubes and
boards here.** The Mt. Baldy base lies at 6,500 feet, and four chairlifts
ascend to 8,600 feet. There are 26 runs; the longest is 2,100 vertical
feet. Whenever abundant fresh snow falls, there's a danger of avalanche
in out-of-bounds areas. Backcountry skiing is available via shuttle in
the spring, and there's a kiddie school on weekends for children ages
five to 12. Winter or summer, you can take a scenic chairlift ride ($20)
to the Top of the Notch restaurant, and hiking and mountain-biking
trails. ✉ *From E. Foothill Blvd., about ½ mi north on N. Claremont
Blvd., then 3 mi north on Monte Vista Ave. and 7 mi east on Mount
Baldy Rd.* ☎ *909/981–3344* ⊕ *www.mtbaldy.com* ▦ *Full day $54–$64,
half day $44* ⊘ *Snow season Nov.–Apr., weekdays 8–4:30, weekends
7:30–4:30; summer season May–Oct., weekends 9–4:30.*

ONTARIO

Junction of I–10 and I–15, 6 mi east of Pomona.

Ontario has a rich agricultural and industrial heritage. The valley's warm climate once supported vineyards that produced Mediterranean-grape varietals such as Grenache, Mourvèdre, and Zinfandel. Today almost all of the vineyards have been replaced by housing tracts and shopping malls. But the LA/Ontario International Airport is here, so you may well find yourself passing through Ontario.

GETTING HERE AND AROUND

Ontario fills a space between I–10 to the north and State Highway 60 (Pomona Freeway) to the south. Exits from both freeways lead to the airport, a large regional facility that is owned by LAX. Metrolink connects the LA area to the airport and other destinations. Driving is the best way to get around the area.

ESSENTIALS

Visitor Information Ontario Convention & Visitors Bureau ⊠ *2000 E. Convention Center Way* ☎ *909/937–3000* ⊕ *www.ontariocvb.com.*

EXPLORING

Graber Olive House. Ontario's oldest existing business, Graber Olive House, opened in 1894 when, at the urging of family and friends, C.C. Graber bottled his meaty, tree-ripened olives and started selling them; they are still sold throughout the United States. Stop by the gourmet shop for a jar, then have a picnic on the shaded grounds. Free tours are conducted year-round; in fall you can watch workers grade, cure, and can the olives. ⊠ *315 E. 4th St.* ☎ *800/996–5483* ⊕ *www.graberolives. com* ⊠ *Free* ☉ *Daily 9–5:30.*

WHERE TO STAY

For expanded hotel reviews, visit Fodors.com.

$$ ⬚ **DoubleTree by Hilton Ontario Airport.** A beautifully landscaped courtyard
☁ greets you at this exceptional chain, the only full-service hotel in Ontario.
★ **Pros:** clean, large rooms; multilingual staff; complimentary shuttle to airport and Ontario Mills Mall; offers government rates. **Cons:** some airport and freeway noise; Internet $12 per day; some rooms feel dated. ⊠ *222 N. Vineyard Ave.* ☎ *909/937–0900, 800/222–8733* ⊕ *www.doubletree. com* ⊠ *482 rooms* ⅏ *In-room: a/c, Internet, Wi-Fi. In-hotel: restaurant, bar, pool, gym, parking, some pets allowed* ❘⊚❘ *Breakfast.*

SHOPPING

☁ **Ontario Mills Mall.** The gargantuan Ontario Mills Mall is California's largest, packing in more than 200 outlet stores including Nordstrom Rack and Sax Fifth Avenue Off 5th, Carleton Day Spa, a 30-screen movie theater, and the Improv Comedy Club and Dinner Theater. Also in the mall are two entertainment complexes: Dave & Buster's pool hall–restaurant–arcade, and GameWorks video-game center. Dining options include the kid-friendly jungle-theme Rainforest Cafe (complete with audio-animatronic elephants and simulated thunderstorms), the Cheesecake Factory, and a 1,000-seat food court. ⊠ *1 Mills Circle, 4th St. and I–15* ☎ *909/484–8300* ⊕ *www.ontariomills.com* ☉ *Mon.–Sat. 10–9, Sun. 11–8.*

8

RANCHO CUCAMONGA

5 mi north of Ontario on I–15.

Once a thriving wine-making area with more than 50,000 acres of wine grapes, Rancho Cucamonga—the oldest wine district in California—lost most of its pastoral charm after real-estate developers bought up the land for a megamall and affordable housing. Most of it is now a squeaky-clean planned community, but the wine-making tradition still thrives at the Joseph Filippi Winery.

GETTING HERE AND AROUND

Historic Route 66 (Foothill Boulevard) cuts across Rancho Cucamonga east to west. The best way to reach this community is via I-10.

EXPLORING

Joseph Filippi Winery. J.P. and Gino Filippi continue the family tradition that was started in 1922 at the Joseph Filippi Winery. They produce handcrafted wines from Cabernet, Sangiovese, and Zinfandel grapes, among other varieties. You can taste up to five wines for $5, and take the free, guided tour that's given at 1 pm, Wednesday through Sunday. The winery holds a small museum chronicling the history of wine making in the Cucamonga area. ⊠ *12467 Base Line Rd.* ☎ *909/899–5755* ⊕ *www.josephfilippiwinery.com* ▢ *Free* ☉ *Mon. 12–5, Tues.–Thurs. 11–6., Fri. and Sat. 11–7, Sun. 12–6.*

♺ ★ **Victoria Gardens.** Classy Victoria Gardens feels a lot like downtown Disneyland with its vintage signs, antique lampposts, and colorful California-theme murals along its 12 city blocks. At this family-oriented shopping, dining, and entertainment complex, such stores as Banana Republic, Abercrombie & Fitch, Williams-Sonoma, and Pottery Barn are flanked by a Macy's and a 12-screen AMC movie theater. After you're finished shopping, grab an ice cream at the Ben & Jerry's shop and linger in the 1920s-style Town Square, a relaxing little park with fountains, grass, and an old-fashioned trolley ($2 per ride). Restaurants such as the Cheesecake Factory, Lucille's Smokehouse Bar-B-Que, P.F. Chang's China Bistro, and the Yard House often have lines out the door. The Victoria Gardens Cultural Center has a library and a 540-seat performing-arts center. ⊠ *12505 N. Mainstreet* ☎ *909/463–2829 general information, 909/477–2775 Cultural Center* ⊕ *www.victoriagardensie. com* ▢ *Free* ☉ *Mon.–Thurs. 10–9, Fri. and Sat. 10–10, Sun. 11–7.*

WHERE TO EAT

$$$$
AMERICAN
★
✕ **The Sycamore Inn.** Flickering gas lamps and a glowing fireplace greet you at this rustic inn. Built in 1921, the restaurant stands on the site of a pre-statehood stagecoach stop on historic Route 66; it's one of the oldest buildings in town. The inn specializes in USDA prime steak—portion sizes range from 8 to 22 ounces—but the menu also offers sushi-quality *ahi*, surf and turf, and Colorado rack of lamb. The wine list is impressive; by the glass, you can choose from more than 40 vintages from the Central Coast, Napa Valley, and such nearby wineries as Joseph Filippi and Temecula. ⊠ *8318 Foothill Blvd.* ☎ *909/982–1104* ⊕ *www. thesycamoreinn.com* ⌲ *Reservations essential* ☉ *No lunch.*

It's OK to get a little dirty at Glen Ivy Hot Springs, which offers a wide variety of treatments at its famous spa—including the red clay pool at Club Mud.

RIVERSIDE AREA

Historic Riverside lies at the heart of the Inland Empire. Major highways linking it to other regional destinations spoke out from this city to the north, south, and east.

CORONA

13 mi south of Ontario on I–15.

Corona's Temescal Canyon is named for the dome-shaped mud saunas that the Luiseño Indians built around the artesian hot springs in the early 19th century. Starting in 1860, weary Overland Stage Company passengers stopped to relax in the soothing mineral springs. In 1890 Mr. and Mrs. W.G. Steers turned the springs into a resort whose popularity has yet to fade.

GETTING HERE AND AROUND

Primarily a bedroom community, Corona lies at the intersection I-15 and State Highway 91. An abundance of roadside malls make it a convenient stop for food or gas.

EXPLORING

Fodor's Choice
★

Glen Ivy Hot Springs. Presidents Herbert Hoover and Ronald Reagan are among the thousands of guests who have soaked their toes at the very relaxing and beautiful Glen Ivy Hot Springs. Colorful bougainvillea and birds-of-paradise surround the secluded canyon day spa, which offers a full range of facials, manicures, pedicures, body wraps, and massages;

CLOSE UP

Navel-oranges in California: Good as Gold

In 1873 a woman named Eliza Tibbets changed the course of California history when she planted two Brazilian navel-orange trees in her Riverside garden.

The trees (which were called Washington Navels in honor of America's first president) flourished in the area's warm climate and rich soil—and before long, Tibbett's garden was producing the sweetest seedless oranges anyone had ever tasted. After winning awards at several major exhibitions, Tibbets realized she could make a profit from her trees. She sold buds to the increasing droves of citrus farmers flocking to the Inland Empire, and by

1882, almost 250,000 citrus trees had been planted in Riverside alone. California's citrus industry had been born.

Today, Riverside still celebrates its citrus-growing heritage. The downtown Marketplace district contains several restored packing houses, and the Riverside Metropolitan Museum is home to a permanent exhibit of historic tools and machinery once used in the industry. The University of California at Riverside still remains at the forefront of citrus research; its Citrus Variety Collection includes specimens of 1,000 different fruit trees from around the world.

some treatments are performed in underground granite spa chambers known collectively as the Grotto, highly recommended by readers. The Under the Oaks treatment center holds a cluster of eight open-air massage rooms surrounded by waterfalls and ancient oak trees. Don't bring your best bikini if you plan to dive into the red clay (brought in daily from a local mine) of Club Mud. Admission gives you use of the property all day. Reserve in advance for treatments that run from $89 to $155 for 50 to 80 minutes. ⊠ 25000 Glen Ivy Rd. ☎ 888/453–6489 ⊕ www.glenivy.com ⊠ Mon.–Thurs. $39, Fri.–Sun. $52 ⊙ Apr.–Oct., daily 9:30–6; Nov.–Mar., daily 9:30–5.

☾ **Tom's Farms.** Opened as a produce stand along I–15 in 1974, Tom's Farms has grown to include a popular hamburger stand, furniture showroom, and sweet shop. You can still buy produce here, but the big draw is various attractions (most $) for the kiddies on weekends: tractor driving, Tom's mining company, a petting zoo, a children's train, a pony ride, free magic shows, face painting, and an old-style carousel. Of interest for adults is the wine-and-cheese shop, which has more than 600 varieties of wine, including many from nearby Temecula Valley; wine tasting ($1 for three samples) takes place daily 11 to 6. ⊠ 23900 Temescal Canyon Rd. ☎ 951/277–4103 ⊕ www.tomsfarms.com ⊠ Free ⊙ Daily 8–8.

RIVERSIDE

14 mi north of Corona on Rte. 91; 34 mi from Anaheim on Rte. 91.

By 1882 Riverside was home to more than half of California's citrus groves, making it the state's wealthiest city per capita in 1895. The prosperity produced a downtown area of opulent architecture, which is well preserved today. Main Street's pedestrian strip is lined with antiques and gift stores, art galleries, salons, and the UCR/California Museum of Photography.

GETTING HERE AND AROUND

Downtown Riverside lies north of State Highway 91 at the University Avenue exit. The hub holding the Mission Inn, museums, shops and restaurants is at the corner of Orange and Mission Inn Ave. Park here and walk.

ESSENTIALS

Visitor Information Riverside Convention and Visitors Bureau ✉ *3750 University Ave., #175* ☎ *888/748–7733, 951/222–4700* ⊕ *www.exploreriverside. com* ⊙ *Mon.–Fri. 8–5.*

EXPLORING

Fodor'sChoice ★ **Mission Inn Museum.** The crown jewel of Riverside is the Mission Inn, a remarkable Spanish-revival hotel whose elaborate turrets, clock tower, mission bells, and flying buttresses rise above downtown. The best way to see it is by taking a docent-led tour of the hotel offered by the Mission Inn Foundation, which also operates an expansive museum with diplays depicting the illustratious history of the building. The inn was designed in 1902 by Arthur B. Benton and Myron Hunt; the team took its cues from the Spanish missions in San Gabriel and Carmel. You can climb to the top of the Rotunda Wing's five-story spiral stairway, or linger awhile in the Courtyard of the Birds, where a tinkling fountain and shady trees invite meditation. You can also peek inside the St. Francis Chapel, where celebrities such as Bette Davis, Humphrey Bogart, and Richard and Pat Nixon tied the knot before the Mexican cedar altar. The Presidential Lounge, a dark, wood-panel bar, has been patronized by eight U.S. presidents. ✉ *3696 Mission Inn Ave.* ☎ *951/788–9556,* ⊕ *www.missioninnmuseum.com* ✉ *Free* ⊙ *Daily 9:30–4.*

Riverside Art Museum. The Riverside Art Museum, designed by Hearst Castle architect Julia Morgan, houses a fine collection of paintings by Southern California landscape artists, including William Keith, Robert Wood, and Ralph Love. Major temporary exhibitions are mounted year-round. ✉ *3425 Mission Inn Ave.* ☎ *951/684–7111* ⊕ *www. riversideartmuseum.org* ✉ *$5* ⊙ *Mon.–Sat. 10–4.*

★ **UCR/California Museum of Photography.** The photography musuem anchors a burgeoning arts district in downtown Riverside. It holds some of the largest and most comprehensive photographic device and image collections in the West, including thousands of Eastman Kodak Brownie and Zeiss Ikon cameras, stereographic prints, and negatives. In the Collection Department, on view by appointment Tuesday–Saturday 12–5, you can see works by Will Connell, Ansel Adams, Harry Pidgeon, and Olindo Ceccarini. ✉ *3824 Main St.* ☎ *951/827–4787* ⊕ *www.cmp. ucr.edu* ✉ *$3* ⊙ *Tues.–Sat. 12–5.*

WHERE TO EAT AND STAY

$$$ ✕ **Mario's Place.** The clientele is as beautiful as the food at this intimate Fodor'sChoice jazz and supper club just across the street from the Mission Inn. The ★ northern Italian cuisine is first-rate, as are the bands that perform Friday and Saturday at 10 pm. Try the pear-and-Gorgonzola wood-fired pizza,

followed by the star anise panna cotta for dessert. ✉ *3646 Mission Inn Ave.* ☎ *951/684–7755* ⊕ *www.mariosplace.com* ⬧ *Reservations essential* ⊘ *Closed Sun. No lunch Fri.*

¢   ✗ **Simple Simon's.** Expect to wait in line at this little sandwich shop on the pedestrian-only shopping strip outside the Mission Inn. Traditional salads, soups, and sandwiches on house-baked breads are served; standout specialties include the chicken-apple sausage sandwich and the roast lamb sandwich topped with grilled eggplant, red peppers, and tomato-fennel-olive sauce. ✉ *3636 Main St.* ☎ *951/369–6030* ⬧ *Reservations not accepted* ⊘ *Closed Sun. No dinner.*

$$$ ⌂ **Mission Inn and Spa.** The Mission Inn, one of the most historic hotels
ℭ   in California, grew from a modest adobe lodge in 1876 to the grand
Fodor's Choice   Spanish-revival hotel it is today with grand archways, flying but-
★   tresses, secluded gardens, and two inspirational chapels. **Pros:** fascinating historical site; luxurious rooms; great restaurants; family-friendly. **Cons:** train noise can be deafening at night. ✉ *3649 Mission Inn Ave.* ☎ *951/784–0300, 800/843–7755* ⊕ *www.missioninn.com* ⬧ *239 rooms, 28 suites* ⬧ *In-room: a/c, Internet, Wi-Fi. In-hotel: restaurant, bar, pool, gym, spa, laundry facilities.*

NIGHTLIFE

NIGHTLIFE   **Cafe Sevilla.** A combination restaurant/nightclub, Cafe Sevilla has a huge tapas menu that includes the traditional small plates and entrée size portions as well. The selection includes Rioja lamb empanadas, *pisto la mancha* (vegetable stew), and paella Valencia. There's live music for dancing nearly every night. Dance lessons are offered Wednesday nights. On weekend nights, the restaurant plays host to a Latin-Euro Top 40 dance club. There is a cover charge of $10-$20. ✉ *3252 Mission Inn Ave.* ☎ *951/778-0611* ⊕ *www.cafesevilla.com.*

REDLANDS

15 mi northeast of Riverside via I–215 north and I–10 east.

Redlands lies at the center of what once was the largest navel-orange-producing region in the world. Orange groves are still plentiful throughout the area. Populated in the late 1800s by wealthy citrus farmers, the town holds a colorful collection of Victorian homes.

GETTING HERE AND AROUND

Redlands straddles I-10 north and south of the freeway at its intersection with State Highway 30 (one of the main roads into the San Bernardino Mountains). You can check out the exhibits at the San Bernardo County Museum and the Lincoln Memorial Shrine, just off the freeway before you reach the town known for its elegant Victorian houses.

ESSENTIALS

Visitor Information Redlands Chamber of Commerce ✉ *1 E. Redlands Blvd.* ☎ *909/793-2546* ⊕ *www.redlandschamber.org.*

EXPLORING

Asistencia Mission de San Gabriel. After the Franciscan Fathers of Mission San Gabriel built it in 1830, the Asistencia Mission de San Gabriel functioned as a mission only for a few years. In 1834 it became part of a

Spanish-colonial rancho; later the mission served as a school and a factory and was finally purchased by the county, which restored it in 1937. The landscaped courtyard contains an old Spanish mission bell; one building holds a small museum. ✉ *26930 Barton Rd.* ☎ *909/793–5402* ⊕ *www.sbcounty.gov/museum* ⌦ *$2* ⊙ *Tues.–Sat. 10–3.*

Kimberly Crest House and Gardens. In 1897 Cornelia A. Hill built Kimberly Crest House and Gardens to mimic the châteaus of France's Loire Valley. Surrounded by orange groves, lily ponds, and terraced Italian gardens, the mansion has a French-revival parlor, a mahogany staircase, a glass mosaic fireplace, and a bubbling fountain in the form of Venus rising from the sea. In 1905 the property was purchased by Alfred and Helen Kimberly, founders of the Kimberly-Clark Paper Company. Their daughter, Mary, lived in the house until 1979. Almost all of the home's 22 rooms are in original condition. ✉ *1325 Prospect Dr.* ☎ *909/792–2111* ⊕ *www.kimberlycrest.org* ⌦ *$10* ⊙ *Sept.–July, Thurs.–Sun. 1–3:30.*

Lincoln Memorial Shrine. The Lincoln Memorial Shrine houses the largest collection of Abraham Lincoln artifacts on the West Coast. You can view a marble bust of Lincoln by sculptor George Grey Barnard, along with more than a dozen letters and rare pamphlets. The gift shop sells many books, toys, and reproductions pertaining to the Civil War. ✉ *125 W. Vine St.* ☎ *909/798–7636, 909/798–7632* ⊕ *www.lincolnshrine.org* ⌦ *Free* ⊙ *Tues.–Sun. 1–5.*

ᗏ **San Bernardino County Museum.** To learn more about Southern California's shaky history, head to the San Bernardino County Museum, where you can watch a working seismometer or check out a display about the San Andreas Fault. Specializing in the natural and regional history of Southern California, the museum is big on birds, eggs, dinosaurs, and mammals. Afterward, go for a light lunch at the Garden Café, open Tuesday through Sunday 11 to 2. ✉ *2024 Orange Tree La.* ☎ *909/307–2669* ⊕ *www.sbcounty.gov/museum/* ⌦ *$8* ⊙ *Tues.–Sun., holiday Mon. 9–5.*

WHERE TO EAT

$$$ ✕ **Joe Greensleeves.** Housed in the 19th-century brick Board of Trade build-
ITALIAN ing, this classic restaurant is homey and inviting. Locals consider one of the best in the region. Wood-grilled steaks, chicken, and fish take up most of the menu, which leans toward Italian. There's a long list of pastas and risottos that includes lobster ravioli, chocolate fettuccini with chopped zucchini in Parmesan cheese sauce, and risotto with asparagus and saffron. Leave your cell phone at home; they are not permitted in the dining room. ✉ *220 N. Orange St.* ☎ *909/792-6969* ⊕ *www.joegreensleevesrestaurant. com* ⌲ *Reservations essential* ⊙ *No lunch weekends.*

OAK GLEN

★ *17 mi east of Redlands via I–10 and Live Oak Canyon Rd.*

More than 60 varieties of apples are grown in Oak Glen. This rustic village, tucked in the foothills above Yucaipa, is home to acres of farms, produce stands, country shops, and homey cafés. The town really comes alive during the fall harvest (September through December), which is celebrated with piglet races, live entertainment, and other events. Most farms also grow berries and stone fruit, which is available during the summer months. You'll find most of the apple farms along Oak Glen Road. Many of the ranches host school groups during the week, when they present historical and educational programs.

BEFORE YOU GO PICKING

Be sure to call before visiting the farms, most of which are family run. Note that unpasteurized cider—sold at some farms—should not be consumed by children, the elderly, or those with weakened immune systems.

GETTING HERE AND AROUND

Oak Glen is tucked into a mountainside about halfway up the San Berndardinos. Exit I-10 at Yucaipa Boulevard, heading east to the intersection with Oak Glen Road. You'll find most of the shops, cafés, and apple orchards strung out along the highway and into the forested hillsides.

ESSENTIALS

Visitor Information Oak Glen Apple Growers Association ✉ *39610 Oak Glen Rd., Yucaipa* ☎ *909/797–6833* ⊕ *www.oakglen.net.*

EXPLORING

Los Rios Rancho. This farm, with 50 acres of apple trees, has a fantastic country store where you can stock up on jams, cookbooks, syrups, and candied apples. Head into the bakery for a hot tri-tip sandwich before going outside to the picnic grounds for lunch. During the fall, you can pick your own apples and pumpkins, take a hayride, or enjoy live bluegrass music. On the grounds of Los Rios Rancho, the **Wildlands Conservancy** is home to 400 acres of preserved nature trails open weekends from 8:30 to 4:30. Guided night walks are offered on the third Saturday of each month, April through December. ✉ *39611 S. Oak Glen Rd.* ☎ *909/797–1005* ⊕ *www.losriosrancho.com* ☼ *Oct.–Nov., daily 9–5; Dec.–Sept., Wed.–Sun. 10–5.*

Mom's Country Orchards. Oak Glen's informal information center is at Mom's Country Orchards, where you can belly up to the bar and learn about the nuances of apple tasting, or warm up with a hot cider heated on an antique stove. Organic produce, local honey, apple butter, and salsa are also specialties here. ✉ *38695 Oak Glen Rd.* ☎ *909/797–4249* ⊕ *www.momscountryorchards.com.*

☺ **Riley's Farm.** Employees dress in period costumes at Riley's Farm, one of the most interactive and kid-friendly ranches in apple country. The farm hosts school groups from September to June. Individuals can join the groups with advance reservations. You can hop on a hayride, take part in a barn dance, pick your own apples, press some cider, or throw a tomahawk while enjoying living-history performances throughout the orchard. The farm is also home to Colonial Chesterfield, a replica New England–style estate where costumed 18th-century reenactors offer lessons in cider pressing, candle dipping, and colonial games and etiquette. The four-hour living history Revolutionary War Adventures are especially popular. Afterward, head into the Public House for a bite of colonial specialties. The warm apple pies—made from the farm's fresh-cut apples—are unforgettable. ⊠ *12261 S. Oak Glen Rd.* ☎ *909/797–7534* ⊕ *www.rileysfarm.com* 🍽 *Free to visit the ranch, $14 for school tour, various fees for activities* ☉ *Mon.-Sat. 9-4.*

WHERE TO EAT

$ ✕ **Law's Oak Glen Coffee Shop.** Since 1953, this old-fashioned coffee shop
AMERICAN has been serving up hot coffee, hearty breakfasts, and famous apple pies to hungry and grateful customers. Service has been known to be slow, so if you're in a hurry, look elsewhere. ⊠ *38392 Oak Glen Rd.* ☎ *909/797–1642* ☉ *Hours vary by season. Call ahead.*

SAN BERNARDINO MOUNTAINS

One of three transverse mountain ranges that lie in the Inland Empire, the San Bernardino range holds the tallest peak in Southern California, Mount San Gorgonio. It's frequently snow-capped in winter, providing the only challenging ski slopes in SoCal. In summer the forested hillsides and lakes provide a cool retreat from the city for many locals.

LAKE ARROWHEAD

37 mi northeast of Riverside via I–215 north, to I–10 east, to Hwy. 30 north, join Hwy. 330 north, to Running Springs, turn left on Hwy. 18 west.

Lake Arrowhead Village is an alpine community with lodgings, shops, outlet stores, and eateries that descend the hill to the lake. Outside the village, access to the lake and its beaches is limited to area residents and their guests.

GETTING HERE AND AROUND

The drive to Lake Arrowhead can be one of the most beautiful in Southern California as State Highway 18, called the Rim of the World, travels a mountainside ledge at 5,000-foot elevation revealing a fabulous city view. At the Lake Arrowhead turnoff, you descend into a wooded bowl surrounding the lake. The village is walkable, but hilly. Scenic Highway 173 winding along the east side of the lake offers scenic blue water views through the forest. (In winter, check for chain control on this route.)

ESSENTIALS

Visitor Information Lake Arrowhead Communities Chamber of Commerce and Visitor Center ⊠ *28200 Hwy. 189, Bldg. R 215, P.O. Box 219, Lake Arrowhead* ☎ *909/337–3715* ⊕ *www.lakearrowhead.net.*

EXPLORING

LeRoy Sports. You can take a 50-minute cruise on the *Arrowhead Queen,* operated daily by LeRoy Sports from the waterfront marina in Lake Arrowhead Village. Tickets are available on a first-come, first-served basis and cost $16. Departure times vary, call for reservations. ☎ *909/336–6992.*

8

WHERE TO EAT AND STAY

$ ✕ **Belgian Waffle Works.** This dockside eatery, just steps from the *Arrow-*
AMERICAN *head Queen*, is quaint and homey, with country decor and beautiful
views of the lake. Don't miss their namesake waffles, crisp on the outside and moist on the inside, topped with fresh berries and cream. Lunch
is also delicious, with choices that include basic burgers, tuna melts,
chili, meat loaf, chicken, and salads. The restaurant gets crowded during lunch on the weekend, so get there early to snag a table with a view.
✉ *28200 Hwy. 189, Bldg. E 140, Lake Arrowhead* ☎ *909/337–5222*
⚐ *Reservations not accepted* ⊘ *No dinner.*

$$$$ ✕ **Casual Elegance.** Just a few miles outside Arrowhead Village, this inti-
AMERICAN mate 1939 house has been charming locals and guests for more than
15 years. Owner-chef Kathleen Kirk's specialties include rack of lamb
prepared with herb crust, crusted filet mignon with Stilton, and steak au
poivre. Featured menu items change weekly. Dine by the fireplace for a
particularly cozy experience. ✉ *26848 Hwy. 189, Blue Jay* ☎ *909/337–*
8932 ⚐ *Reservations essential* ⊘ *Closed Mon. and Tues. No lunch.*

$$ ⛺ **Lake Arrowhead Resort and Spa.** This lakeside lodge is warm and
★   comfy with fireplaces everywhere. **Pros:** beautiful lake views; deli-
cious on-site dining. **Cons:** some rooms have thin walls; resort ame-
nity fee. ✉ *27984 Hwy. 189* ☎ *909/336–1511, 800/800–6792* ⊕ *www.*
lakearrowheadresort.com ⇥ *162 rooms, 11 suites* ⚒ *In-room: a/c,*
Wi-Fi. In-hotel: restaurant, bar, pool, gym, spa, beach, parking, some
pets allowed.

SPORTS AND THE OUTDOORS

McKenzie Waterski School. Waterskiing and wakeboarding lessons are
available on Lake Arrowhead in summer at McKenzie Waterski School,
Memorial Day through Labor Day. 📷 *909/337–3814.*

BIG BEAR LAKE

24 mi east of Lake Arrowhead on Hwy. 18 (Rim of the World Highway).

When Angelinos say they're going to the mountains, they usually mean
Big Bear, where a collection of Alpine-style villages surrounds a 7-mi-
long lake. The south shore of the lake is busy with ski slopes, animal
parks, a gorgeous B&B, water sports, lodging, and restaurants. You'll
find quiet country walks, biking trails, and splendid alpine scenery
along the north shore.

GETTING HERE AND AROUND

Driving is the best way to get to and explore the Big Bear area. But
there are alternatives. The Mountain Area Regional Transit Authority
provides bus service to and in San Bernardino Mountain communities
and connects with public transit in San Bernardino. There's a small
general aviation airport at Big Bear City.

ESSENTIALS

Visitor Information Big Bear Lake Resort Association ✉ *630 Bartlett Rd.*
☎ *909/866–7000, 800/424–4232* ⊕ *www.bigbearinfo.com.*

EXPLORING

☾ **Alpine Slide at Magic Mountain.** Take a ride down a twisting bobsled course in winter, or beat the summer heat on a dual waterslide at Alpine Slide at Magic Mountain. The facility also has an 18-hole miniature golf course, and go carts. ✉ *800 Wildrose La.* ☎ *909/866–4626* ⊕ *www. alpineslidebigbear.com* ✍ *$4 single rides, $18 5-ride pass* ☉ *Daily 10–4.*

☾ **Big Bear Discovery Center.** Operated by the forest service, this nature
Fodor'sChoice center is the place to sign up for a canoe ride through Grout Bay.
★ Naturalist-led Discovery Tours include visits to the Baldwin Lake Ecological Reserve or Holcomb Valley, where a small gold rush took place more than a century ago. You can also participate in a winter bird count. The center also has rotating flora and fauna exhibits and a nature-oriented gift shop. Center staff can provide camping, hiking, and lake information. ✉ *North Shore Dr., Hwy. 38, between Fawnskin and Stanfield Cutoff, 40971 North Shore Dr.* ☎ *909/866–3437* ⊕ *www. bigbeardiscoverycenter.com* ✍ *Free* ☉ *Thurs.-Mon. 8:30–4:30.*

Big Bear Marina. From April through Labor Day, the paddle wheeler *Big Bear Queen* departs daily at 12, 2, and 4 from Big Bear Marina for 90-minute tours of the lake; the cost is $18 per person. The marina also has fishing boats, jet skis, kayaks, and canoes for rent. ✉ *500 Paine Rd.* ☎ *909/866–3218* ⊕ *www.bigbearmarina.com/queen.html.*

☾ **Moonridge Animal Park.** Moonridge Animal Park, a rescue and reha-bilitation center, specializes in animals native to the San Bernardino Mountains. Among its residents are black and (nonnative) grizzly bears, bald eagles, coyote, beavers, mountain lions, grey wolves, and bobcats. You can catch an educational presentation at noon and feeding tour at 3 daily except Wednesday. At this writing, the facility was planning to move in 2013, so call ahead before visiting. ✉ *43285 Goldmine Dr.* ☎ *909/584–1171* ⊕ *www.moonridgezoo.org* ✍ *$9* ☉ *June–Sept., daily 10–5; Sept.–June, weekdays 10–4, weekends 10–5.*

☾ **Time Bandit Pirate Ship.** Featured in the Terry Gilliam 1981 movie of the same name, this ship, a small-scale replica of a 17th century English galleon, cruises Big Bear Lake daily in the warm season (roughly from April 1 to October 31) from Holloway Marina. A sightseeing excur-sion with the crew dressed up like pirates, the cruise is popular with kids and adults. There's a bar, but no dining on the ship. ✉ *Holloway Marina, 398 Edgemoor Rd.* ☎ *909/866-5706* ⊕ *www.bigbearboating. com* ✍ *$19* ☉ *Tours daily at 2 in warm weather; call for schedule.*

WHERE TO EAT

$$$$ ✕ **Evergreen International.** This rustic-style steak house—with sweeping
STEAKHOUSE views of Big Bear Lake—is a good place to go for fine dining. In winter you can stay warm in the comfortable dining room, which has dark panel-ing and exposed beams; in summer head out to the deck to enjoy a glass of wine while you watch the sun set. Lunch and dinner choices include grilled chicken topped with passion fruit sauce, pepper-crusted ahi tuna, or prime rib with king crab legs. ✉ *40771 Big Bear Blvd.* ☎ *909/878–5588.*

$$ ✕ **Madlon's.** The menu at this cozy gingerbread-style cottage includes
AMERICAN sophisticated dishes such as lamb chops with port wine reduction, cream of jalapeño soup, and filet mignon with Drambuie sauce. It's a

8

small place, so reservations are essential on weekends. ✉ *829 W. Big Bear Blvd., Big Bear City* ☎ *909/585–3762* ⚄ *Reservations essential* ⊙ *Closed Tues.*

WHERE TO STAY
For expanded reviews, visit Fodors.com.

$$$ ⊞ **Apples Bed & Breakfast Inn.** Despite its location on a busy road to the
★ ski lifts, the Apples Inn feels remote and peaceful, thanks to the surrounding pine trees. **Pros:** large rooms; clean; free snacks and movies; delicious big breakfast. **Cons:** some traffic noise; sometimes feels very busy. ✉ *42430 Moonridge Rd.* ☎ *909/866–0903* ⊕ *www.applesbigbear. com* ⇨ *19 rooms* ⚬ *In-room: no a/c, Wi-Fi* ⊩ *Breakfast.*

$$$ ⊞ **Gold Mountain Manor.** This restored log mansion, originally built in
★ 1928, has a wide veranda under wooden eaves and Adirondack-style furnishings. **Pros:** gracious hosts; snow shoes and kayaks available; walk to hiking trails. **Cons:** somewhat thin walls; 10-minute drive to the village; one room has detached bathroom. ✉ *1117 Anita Ave., Big Bear City* ☎ *909/585–6997, 800/509–2604* ⊕ *www.goldmountainmanor. com* ⇨ *4 rooms, 3 suites* ⚬ *In-room: no a/c, no TV, Wi-Fi* ⊩ *Breakfast.*

$$$ ⊞ **Northwoods Resort.** A giant log cabin with the amenities of a resort, Northwoods has a lobby that resembles a 1930s hunting lodge: canoes, antlers, fishing poles, and a grand stone fireplace all decorate the walls. **Pros:** pool heated in winter; ski packages available. **Cons:** parts of the hotel are showing their age; rooms can be noisy at night; rates fluctuate depending on whether there is snow. ✉ *40650 Village Dr.* ☎ *909/866– 3121, 800/866–3121* ⊕ *www.northwoodsresort.com* ⇨ *140 rooms, 7 suites* ⚬ *In-room: a/c, Wi-Fi. In-hotel: restaurant, bar, pool, gym, parking.*

$$ ⊞ **Robinhood Resort.** Across the street from the Pine Knot Marina, this family-oriented motel has rooms with fireplaces and some with whirlpool tubs or kitchenettes. **Pros:** short walk from the marina; near shops and restaurants; good on-site restaurant. **Cons:** no a/c in some rooms; parts of motel are showing their age. ✉ *40797 Lakeview Dr.* ☎ *909/866– 4643, 800/990–9956* ⊕ *www.robinhoodresort.info* ⇨ *60 rooms, 10 condos* ⚬ *In-room: a/c, kitchen, Wi-Fi. In-hotel: restaurant, bar.*

SPORTS AND THE OUTDOORS
Baldwin Lake Stables. If you're adventurous you can explore the forested mountain on horseback. Baldwin Lake Stables offers two- to four-hour guided trail rides for two or more guests daily year round. Prices vary by season and length of tour, starting at $35 per person. ✉ *46475 Pioneertown Rd.* ☎ *909/585–6482* ⊕ *www.baldwinlakestables.com.*

Pine Knot Landing Marina. Pine Knot Landing, a full-service marina, also rents fishing boats, pontoon boats, and kayaks and sells bait, ice, and snacks. ✉ *439 Pine Knot Blvd.* ☎ *909/866–6463.*

SKIING **Big Bear Mountain Resorts.** Big Bear Mountain Resorts, consisting of two distinct resorts, is Southern California's largest winter resort and one of the few that will challenge skilled skiers. The megaresort offers 430 skiable acres, 55 runs, and 23 chairlifts, including four high-speed quads. Bear Mountain has a youthful vibe, beginner slopes and training, and The Scene, where you can get a cold beer or warm drink. Snow Summit holds challenging runs and is open for night skiing. On busy winter weekends and holidays it's best to reserve tickets before heading to either mountain. You can rent high-performance skis or boards at Bear.

The resorts are open in summer for mountain biking, hiking, golf, and some special events. The Bear Mountain's Scenic Sky Chair takes you to the mountain's 8,400-foot peak, where you can lunch at View Haus (¢), a casual outdoor restaurant with breathtaking views of the lake and San Gorgonio mountain. Fare includes barbecued-chicken sandwiches, hot dogs, and burgers, along with cold beer and wine. ⊠ *Big Bear, 43101 Goldmine Dr., off Moonridge Rd.* ☎ *909/866–5766* ⊕ *www.bigbearmountainresorts.com* ⊇ *$56–$69.*

THE SOUTHERN INLAND EMPIRE

The southern end of the Inland Empire is devoted to the good life. Mile-high Idyllwild atop Mount San Jacinto holds a renowned arts academy, charming restaurants, and galleries. It's also a good place to hike, mountain climb, and test high-altitude biking skills. Temecula, lying at the base of the mountain, is a popular wine region where you'll find vineyards, tasting rooms, fine dining, and cozy lodgings.

IDYLLWILD

44 mi east of Riverside via State Hwy. 60 and I–10 to State Hwy. 243.

Set in a valley halfway up Mount San Jacinto, Idyllwild has been a serene forested getaway for San Diegans and Angelinos for nearly a century. The town's simple, quiet lifestyle attracts artists and performers as well as outdoor types who enjoy hiking, biking, and rock climbing.

GETTING HERE AND AROUND

There are two routes to Idyllwild from interstates; both are slow and winding, but they reward you with some great mountain views. From I–15 just south of Lake Elsinore, your can take State Highway 74 to the top of the mountain. Scenic State Highway 243 takes off from Banning on I–10. Once you get to Idyllwild, you'll discover that you can walk nearly everywhere in the village. You'll need to drive to trailheads, fishing holes, and rock climbing locations.

ESSENTIALS

Visitor Information Idyllwild Chamber of Commerce ⊠ *54325 N. Circle Dr., Box 304* ☎ *951/659–3259, 888/659–3259* ⊕ *www.idyllwildchamber.com.*

EXPLORING

☺ **Idyllwild Nature Center.** At the Idyllwild Nature Center, you can learn about the area's Native American history, try your hand at astronomy, and listen to traditional storytellers. Outside there are 3 mi of hiking trails, plus biking and equestrian trails and picnic areas. Native plant lectures and wildflower walks are offered every Memorial Day weekend during the center's Wildflower Show. The park is pet-friendly. ⊠ *25225 Hwy. 243* ☎ *951/659–3850* ⊕ *www.rivcoparks.org* ⊇ *$2* ☾ *9–4:30, closed Mon.*

8

WHERE TO EAT

$$$
FRENCH
★

✕ **Restaurant Gastrognome.** Elegant and dimly lighted, with wood paneling, lace curtains, and an oft-glowing fireplace, "The Gnome" is where locals go for a romantic dinner with great food, a full bar, and nice ambience. The overall feel is French, but the menu goes beyond Gallic by offering such entrées as Calamari almandine, sausage pasta, and lobster tacos. The French onion soup is a standout appetizer; the roast duck with orange sauce and Southwest-style grilled pork are excellent entrées. The crème brûlée makes for a sweet finale. For lighter dinner fare, check out the bar menu. ⊠ *54381 Ridgeview Dr.* ☎ *951/659–5055* ⊕ *www.gastrognome.com.*

THE ARTS

Jazz in the Pines. In August, Idyllwild is host of the two-day Jazz in the Pines festival, drawing smooth-jazz greats such as David Benoit. ⊕ *www.idyllwildjazz.com.*

Idyllwild Arts Academy. The Idyllwild Arts Academy is a summer camp offering more than 60 workshops in dance, music, Native American arts, theater, visual arts, and writing. There are free summer concerts and theater productions featuring students and professional performers. ☎ *951/659–2171* ⊕ *www.idyllwildarts.org.*

SPORTS AND THE OUTDOORS

FISHING
Lake Fulmor. Lake Fulmor is stocked with rainbow trout, largemouth bass, catfish, and bluegill. To fish here you'll need a California fishing license and a National Forest Adventure Pass ($5 per vehicle per day). ⊠ *Hwy. 243, 10 mi north of Idyllwild* ☎ *951/659–2117.*

Idyllwild Ranger Station. National Forest Service Adventure Passes, needed for fishing and some hiking trails, are available at the Idyllwild Ranger Station. ⊠ *Pine Crest Ave., off Hwy. 243* ☎ *951/659–2117.*

HIKING
Humber Park. Hike the 2.6-mi Ernie Maxwell Scenic Trail at Humber Park. Along the way you'll have views of Little Tahquitz Creek, Marion Mountain, and Suicide Rock. A permit is not required to hike this trail. ⊠ *At top of Fern Valley Rd.* ☎ *951/659–2117.*

Pacific Crest Trail. The Pacific Crest Trail is accessible at Highway 74, 1 mi east of Highway 371; or via the Fuller Ridge Trail at Black Mountain Road, 15 mi north of Idyllwild. Permits ($5 per day) are required for camping and day hikes in San Jacinto Wilderness. They are available through the Idyllwild Ranger Station (⊠ *Pine Crest Ave., off Hwy. 243* ☎ *951/659–2117).*

EN ROUTE

Winchester Cheese Company. If you're headed for Temecula via Route 74 east from Idyllwild, make a detour to Winchester Cheese Company for a taste of Jules Wesselink's famous goudas, made from the raw milk of his Holstein cows. Take a tour, or sample one of four varieties, including a spicy jalapeño, in the tasting room. If you want to see the cheese-making process, call first. ⊠ *32605 Holland Rd., Winchester* ☎ *951/926–4239* ⊕ *www.winchestercheese.com* ✉ *Free* ⊙ *Weekdays 10–5, weekends 10–4.*

TEMECULA

Fodor's Choice *43 mi south of Riverside on I–15; 60 mi north of San Diego on I–15;*
★ *90 mi southeast of Los Angeles via I–10 and I–15.*

Temecula, with its rolling green vineyards, comfy country inns, and first-rate restaurants, is a fine alternative to Napa Valley if you can't make it up to Northern California. Now billing itself the "Southern California Wine Country," the region is home to more than 36 wineries, several of which offer fine dining, luxury lodging, and spas in addition to appealing boutiques, charming picnic areas, and, of course, award-winning vintages.

The name Temecula comes from a Luiseño Indian word meaning "where the sun shines through the mist"—ideal conditions for growing wine grapes. Intense afternoon sun and cool nighttime temperatures, complemented by ocean breezes that flow through the Rainbow and Santa Margarita gaps in the coastal range, help grapevines flourish in the area's granite soil. Best known for Chardonnay, Temecula Valley winemakers are moving in new directions, producing Viognier, Syrah, old vine Zinfandel, and Pinot Gris varietals. Most wineries charge a small fee ($5 to $15) for a tasting that includes several wines. Most of the wineries are strung out along Rancho California Road, east of I–15; a few newer ones lie along the eastern portion of De Portola Road. For a map of the area's wineries, visit ⊕ *www.temeculawines.org.*

GETTING HERE AND AROUND

I-15 cuts right through Temecula. The wineries lie on the east side of the freeway along Rancho California Road. Old West Temecula lies along the west side of the freeway along Front St. Most visitors drive from one winery to the next, but options include limousine and bus tours.

ESSENTIALS

Visitor Information Temecula Valley Convention and Visitors Bureau
✉ *28690 Mercedes St., Ste. A* ☎ *951/491–6085, 888/363–2852* ⊕ *www. temeculacvb.com.*

EXPLORING

Old Town Temecula. Temecula is more than just vineyards and tasting rooms. For a bit of old-fashioned fun, head to Old Town Temecula, a turn-of-the-20th-century-style cluster of storefronts and boardwalks that holds more than 640 antiques stores, boutiques, and art galleries. ✉ *Front St., between Rancho California Rd. and Hwy. 79* ☎ *888/363–2852.*

☺ **Temecula Children's Museum.** If you have the kids along, check out the Pennypickle's Workshop, the fictional 7,500-square-foot home of Professor Phineas T. Pennypickle, PhD. This elaborately decorated children's museum is filled with secret passageways, machines, wacky contraptions, and time-travel inventions, making it an imaginative way to spend the afternoon. ✉ *42081 Main St.* ☎ *951/308–6376* ⊕ *www.pennypickles.org* ⌑ *$4.50* ⊙ *Tues.–Sat. 10–5, Sun. 12:30–5.*

WINERIES

Baily Vineyard & Winery. Baily Vineyard & Winery is known for its hearty red wines that produce well in the Temecula climate. They include Sangiovese and a French-style Meritage. The restaurant here, Carol's,

WINERY TOURS

Grapeline Wine Country Shuttle. If you plan to visit several wineries (and taste a lot of wine), catch the Grapeline Wine Country Shuttle, which operates daily with pickup at Temecula and San Diego hotels. The Vineyard Picnic Tour at $98 ($118 Saturday) includes transportation, a winemaking demonstration, free tastings at four wineries, and a gourmet picnic lunch catered by Creekside Grill at Wilson Creek Winery. ⊠ *43500 Ridge Park Dr., #204, Temecula* 🕾 *951/693–5755, 888/894–6379* ⊕ *www.gogrape.com* 🖃 *$52 transportation only, $72 Sat.*

Sterling Rose Limo. Many limousine services offer wine-tasting tours, including Sterling Rose Limo, which offers packages that include four to five tasting tickets and a gourmet picnic lunch or winery restaurant lunch. Passenger rates start at $95 per person. 🕾 *800/649–6463* ⊕ *www.sterlingroselimo.com.*

Destination Temecula. Destination Temecula runs daily tours of wine country, with pickups at San Diego hotels and Old Town Temecula. Plan on a full day for these tours as they include stops at three wineries, a chance to explore Old Town, and picnic lunch. Rates run from $89 starting in Temecula and $97 round-trip from San Diego. ⊠ *28475 Old Town Front St.* 🕾 *877/305–0501* ⊕ *www.destem.com.*

is locally popular for lunch and dinner. In the tasting room, browse the gourmet gift shop before sampling the Cabernet, Merlot, and Cabernet Franc. ⊠ *33440 La Serena Way* 🕾 *951/676–9463* ⊕ *www.baily.com* 🖃 *Winery free, tastings $10 for five wines* ☉ *Sun.–Fri. 11–5, Sat. 10–5.*

Briar Rose Winery. Briar Rose Winery is run out of an English cottage that is a replica of one of Snow White's cottages. It was built by Beldon Fields, one of the artisans who worked on Fantasyland. The lush grounds include a rose garden, rustic stone walls, and an olive tree; the small, casual tasting room has copper walls and a river rock fireplace. Try the 2008 Estate Zinfandel, which is aged in American oak for 14 months. ⊠ *41720 Calle Cabrillo Rd.* 🕾 *951/308–1098* ⊕ *www. briarrosewinery.com* 🖃 *Winery free, tastings $10–$15* ⌖ *Reservations essential* ☉ *By appointment.*

Callaway Coastal Vineyards. Established in 1969, Callaway Coastal Vineyards is well-known for Chardonnays and Merlots by winemaker Craig Larson. Complimentary tours are offered weekdays at 11, 1, and 3 and on weekends from 11 to 4 on the hour. The Meritage Restaurant, perched on a hill overlooking the vineyards, is open for prix-fixe lunch ($$) daily and dinner ($$) Friday and Saturday. ⊠ *32720 Rancho California Rd.* 🕾 *951/676–4001* ⊕ *www.callawaywinery.com* 🖃 *Free; $10 tastings* ☉ *Daily 10–5.*

Falkner Winerys. Falkner Winery's big Western-style barn with its wraparound deck overlooking the vineyards is a great spot to enjoy Temecula's cool breezes. Falkner has garnered great word of mouth, especially for their red Tuscan Amante. Winemaker Steve Hagata is also known for his Viognier, Chardonnay, and Riesling. The winery's

8

Pinnacle Restaurant is open for lunch daily. Tours are given at 11 am and 2 pm on weekends. Coupons are on the Web site. ⊠ *40620 Calle Contento Rd.* ☎ *951/676–8231* ⊕ *www.falknerwinery.com* ⊠ *Winery free, tours $10, tastings $10–$15* ⊗ *Daily 10–5.*

Fodor'sChoice
★

Hart Family Winery. With Mediterranean varietals grown on 11 acres of vineyards in Temecula, Hart Family Winery is known for producing some of the best red wines in Temecula Valley. Joe Hart, one of the area's pioneer winemakers, creates small lots of big, hearty Zinfandels, Cabernet Sauvignon, and Sangiovese, and the winery's purple tasting room is decked out with ribbons, medals, and awards. ⊠ *41300 Avenida Biona* ☎ *951/676–6300* ⊕ *www.thehartfamilywinery. com* ⊠ *Winery free, tastings $10* ⊗ *Daily 9–4:30.*

Keyways Vineyard & Winery. Don't be surprised to come upon a barbecue or equestrian event at Keyways Vineyard & Winery, which has an Old West feel. Terri Pebley Delhamer—the only woman winery owner in the Temecula Valley—has created an appealing tasting room decorated with antiques and a roaring fireplace, where you can listen to music while sampling tasty reds such as the Garnacha or Territage. ⊠ *37338 De Portola Rd.* ☎ *951/302–7888* ⊕ *www.keywayswine.com* ⊠ *Winery free, tastings $10* ⊗ *Mon.-Thurs. 11-5:30, Fri.-Sun. 11-6.*

Leonesse Cellars. Leonesse Cellars is a casual farmhouse-style winery with a stone turret overlooking 20 acres of Cabernet Sauvignon grapes. The winery offers a selection of hosted private tours (reservations required) that include rides through the vineyards, tasting seven or eight varietals, wine and cheese pairings, and a bit of chocolate with dessert wines. ⊠ *38311 DePortola Rd.* ☎ *951/302–7601* ⊕ *www.leonessecellars.com* ⊠ *Winery free, tours $14* ⊗ *Daily 11–5.*

Miramonte Winery. Perched on a hilltop, Miramonte Winery may be Temecula's hippest, thanks to the vision of owner Cane Vanderhoof, whose wines have earned 36 medals in recent years. Listen to Spanish-guitar recordings while sampling the Opulente Meritage, a supple Sauvignon Blanc, or the sultry Syrah. On Friday and Saturday nights from 7 to 10, the winery turns into a hot spot with signature wines ($6 to $10) and beer,

---

UP, UP, AND AWAY

California Dreamin' Balloon & Biplane Rides. If you're in the mood to swoop or float above Temecula's green vineyards and country estates, sign up for a trip with California Dreamin' Balloon & Biplane Rides. Balloon trips depart from La Vindemia Vineyards at 5:30 am; the $138 per person fee includes Champagne, coffee, a pastry breakfast, and a souvenir photo. ☎ *800/373-3359* ⊕ *www.californiadreamin.com.*

Balloon and Wine Festival. Temecula Balloon and Wine Festival at Lake Skinner each June is three days of partying, wine tasting, live entertainment, vendors, and glorious early morning balloon ascensions. Camping is popular; there are 400 sites at the lake, plus RV sites nearby. Admission is $20 per day per person or $50 for the three-day event, extra for wine and food tastings. ⊠ *37701 Warren Rd.* ☎ *951/676-6713* ⊕ *www.tvbwf.com.*

live music, and dancing that spills out into the vineyards. ⊠ *33410 Rancho California Rd.* ☎ *951/506–5500* ⊕ *www.miramontewinery.com* ⊠ *Winery free, tastings $10* ⊙ *Tastings Sun.–Thurs. 11–6, Fri. and Sat. 11–10.*

Mount Palomar Winery. Opened in 1969, Mount Palomar Winery was one of the original wineries in Temecula Valley, and the first to introduce Sangiovese grapes to Temecula. (The varietal has proven perfectly suited to the region's soil and climate.) The winery's tasting room is in a Spanish colonial–style building, an excellent setting for sampling red Meritage, white Cortese, and a Cream Sherry that is to die for. Tours are available on weekends. Shorty's Bistro is open for lunch daily and for dinner Friday through Sunday. The Bistro also presents live entertainment Friday evenings. ⊠ *33820 Rancho California Rd.* ☎ *951/676–5047* ⊕ *www.mountpalomar.com* ⊠ *Winery free, tastings $10, $12 Sat. and Sun.* ⊙ *Mon.–Thurs. 10:30–6, Fri.–Sun. 10:30–7.*

★ **Ponte Family Estates.** Lush gardens and 350 acres of vineyards welcome you onto Ponte Family Estates, a rustic winery that fills a beautiful new barn. In the open-beam tasting room, you can sample six different varietals, including Cabernet, Syrah (recommended by readers), Viognier, and Chardonnay. One area is devoted to an eye-popping marketplace selling artisan ceramics, specialty foods, and wine-country gift baskets. The winery's outdoor Restaurant at Ponte serves wood-fired pizza and sustainable fare at lunch. ⊠ *35053 Rancho California Rd.* ☎ *951/694–8855* ⊕ *www.pontewinery.com* ⊠ *Winery free; tastings $12 Mon.–Fri., $20 Sat. and Sun.* ⊙ *Daily 10–5.*

Fodor's Choice ★ **Thornton Winery.** A rambling French Mediterranean–style stone building houses Thornton Winery, a producer best known for its sparkling wine, although recent vintages reflect Rhone/Mediterranean styles. You can taste winemaker David Vergari's brut reserve and Cuvée Rouge at a table in the lounge, or along with some food at Café Champagne. Readers rave about the Syrah. On the weekend, take a free tour of the grounds and the wine cave. Summer Champagne jazz concerts featuring performers such as George Benson, Herb Alpert, and David Beniot (admission is $55–$95), and elaborate winemaker dinners ($120–$170) make this a fun place to spend an afternoon or evening. ⊠ *32575 Rancho California Rd.* ☎ *951/699–0099* ⊕ *www.thorntonwine.com* ⊠ *Winery free, tastings $10–$17* ⊙ *Daily 10–5, winery tours weekends only.*

Wilson Creek Winery & Vineyard. A small stream winds through flower gardens and vineyards at peaceful, parklike Wilson Creek Winery & Vineyard. In the huge tasting room you can find a little bit of heaven in the "Decadencia" chocolate port and the almond Oh-My-Gosh sparkling wine, much loved by Fodor's readers. They do well with more conventional wines; try their Mourvèrde, Petite Syrah dessert wine, or Muscat Canelli. The Creekside Grill Restaurant serves sandwiches, salads, and entrées such as gluten-free vegetable potpie and Mexican white sea bass. The restaurant will deliver your lunch to the spot you select for a picnic on the expansive property. ⊠ *35960 Rancho California Rd.* ☎ *951/699–9463* ⊕ *www.wilsoncreekwinery.com* ⊠ *Winery*

There's no more relaxing way to enjoy Temecula's wine country than by taking a peaceful hot-air balloon ride over the vineyards.

free, tastings $10 weekdays, $12 weekends ⊘ Daily 10–5, restaurant daily 11–5.

WHERE TO EAT AND STAY

$$$
AMERICAN
✕ **Baily's Fine Dining and Front Street Bar & Grill.** These are two restaurants owned by the Baily family that also owns the Baily Winery. Fine dining (dinner only) is upstairs and casual dining is street side at the Front Street Bar & Grill, which also offers entertainment. Locals rave about chef Neftali Torres's well-executed cuisine, which changes weekly according to his creative whims. The menu may include chicken schnitzel drizzled in lemon-caper-wine sauce or salmon Wellington. The wine list includes more than 100 bottles, most from Temecula Valley. ✉ *28699 Front St.* ☎ *951/676–9567* ⊕ *www.oldtowndining.com* ⊘ *No lunch at Baily's Fine Dining.*

$$$$
ECLECTIC
Fodor'sChoice
★
✕ **Café Champagne.** The spacious patio, with its bubbling fountain, flowering trellises, and views of Thornton Winery's vineyards, is the perfect place to lunch on a sunny day. Inside, the dining room is decked out in French-country style, and the open kitchen turns out such dishes as braised boneless beef short ribs and seafood cioppino. The eclectic menu is complemented by a reasonably priced wine list featuring Italian, French, and California wines—including, of course, Thornton sparklers. ✉ *32575 Rancho California Rd.* ☎ *951/699–0088* ⊕ *www.thorntonwine.com/cafe.html* ⌕ *Reservations essential.*

$$
▨ **Temecula Creek Inn.** If you want the relaxation of the wine country and the challenge of hitting the links on a championship golf course, this is the place for you. **Pros:** beautiful grounds; great restaurant; clean and comfortable rooms. **Cons:** resort is a bit isolated from Old Town and

wineries. ⊠ *44501 Rainbow Canyon Rd.* ☏ *951/694–1000, 800/962–7335* ⊕ *www.temeculacreekinn.com* ⇌ *130 rooms, 1 guesthouse* ⌂ *In-room: a/c, Internet, Wi-Fi. In-hotel: restaurant, bar, golf course, pool, tennis court, gym, parking.*

NIGHTLIFE

Pechanga Resort and Casino. Risk-takers can do a bit of gambling at the Pechanga Resort and Casino, where there are also several entertainment venues. The Pechanga Showroom Theater regularly presents stars such as Paul Simon, Daniel Tosh, and Miranda Lambert. Established and up and coming comedians perform at the intimate Comedy Club Friday and Saturday nights, plus ESPN and Showtime championship boxing matches draw thousands of fans. ⊠ *45000 Pala Rd.* ☏ *877/711–2946.*

SHOPPING

Temecula Olive Oil Company. While you're shopping in Old Town, stop by the Temecula Olive Oil Company tasting room for a sample of its extra-virgin olive oils, bath products, and Mission, Ascalano, and Italian olives. ⊠ *28653 Old Town Front St., Suite H* ☏ *951/693–0607* ⊕ *www.temeculaoliveoil.com* ⊙ *Daily 9:30–6.*

SPORTS AND THE OUTDOORS

GOLF   Temecula has seven championship golf courses cooled by the valley's ocean breezes.

Redhawk Golf Club. Redhawk Golf Club has an 18-hole championship course designed by Ron Fream. ⊠ *45100 Redhawk Pkwy.* ☏ *951/302–3850* ⊕ *www.redhawkgolfcourse.com.*

Temeku Golf Club. The public is welcome on the Robinson-designed 18-hole championship course at Temeku Golf Club. It's a challenging course with tiered greens and lots of blind spots. ⊠ *41487 Temeku Dr.* ☏ *951/694–9998* ⊕ *www.temekuhills.com.*

8

Palm Springs

AND THE DESERT RESORTS

WORD OF MOUTH

"I wasn't sure that there was going to be enough [in Palm Springs]
to fill up a week. Boy was I wrong! Between swimming, hiking,
poolside lounging, shopping and a couple day trips to Joshua
Tree National Park and the top of Mt. San Jacinto via the aerial
tramway, we could have filled up two weeks."

—Sam_A

WELCOME TO PALM SPRINGS

TOP REASONS TO GO

★ **Fun in the sun:** The Palm Springs area has 350 days of sun each year, and the weather's usually perfect for playing one of the area's more than 100 golf courses.

★ **Spa under the stars:** Many resorts and small hotels now offer after-dark spa services, including outdoor soaks and treatments you can savor while sipping wine under the clear, starry sky.

★ **Personal pampering:** The resorts here have it all: beautifully appointed rooms packed with amenities, professional staffs, sublime spas, and delicious dining options.

★ **Devine desert scenery:** You'll probably spend a lot of your time here taking in the gorgeous 360-degree natural panorama, a flat desert floor surrounded by 10,000-foot mountains rising into a brilliant blue sky.

★ **The Hollywood connection:** The Palm Springs area has more celebrity ties than any other resort community. So keep your eyes open for your favorite star.

1 The Desert Resorts. Around the desert resorts, privacy is the watchword. Celebrities flock to the desert from Los Angeles, and many communities are walled and guarded. Still, you might spot Hollywood stars, sports personalities, politicians, and other high-profile types in restaurants, out on the town, at the weekly Villagefest, or on a golf course. For the most part, the desert's social, sports, shopping, and entertainment scenes center on Palm Springs, Palm Desert, and (increasingly) La Quinta.

2 Along Twentynine Palms Highway. The towns of Yucca Valley, Joshua Tree, and Twentynine Palms punctuate Twentynine Palms Highway (Highway 62)—the northern highway from the desert resorts to Joshua Tree National Park (⇨ *see Chapter 10*)—and provide visitor information, lodging, and other services to park visitors.

3 Anza-Borrego Desert. If you're looking for a break from the action, you'll find sublime solitude in this 600,000-acre desert landscape.

4 Joshua Tree National Park. This is desert scenery at its best and most abundant. Tiptoe through fields of wildflowers in spring, scramble on and around giant boulders, and check out the park's bizarre namesake trees (⇨ *see Chapter 10*).

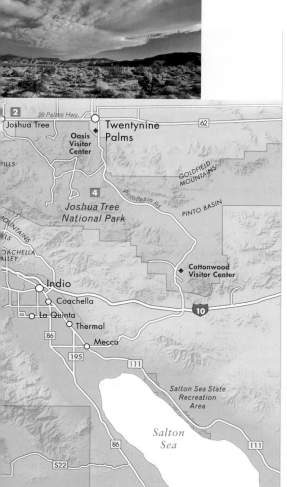

GETTING ORIENTED

The Palm Springs resort area lies within the Colorado Desert, on the western edge of the Coachella Valley. The area holds seven cities that are strung out along Highway 111, with Palm Springs at the northwestern end of this strip and Indio at the southeastern end. North of Palm Springs, between Interstate 10 and Highway 62, is Desert Hot Springs. Northeast of Palm Springs, the towns of the Morongo Valley lie along Twentynine Palms Highway (Highway 62), which leads to Joshua Tree National Park *⇒ see Chapter 10).* Head south on Highway 86 from Indio to reach Anza-Borrego State Park and the Salton Sea. All of the area's attractions are easy day trips from Palm Springs.

9

Updated by
Bobbi Zane

Many millions of years ago, the Southern Desert was the bottom of a vast sea. By 10 million years ago, the waters had receded and the climate was hospitable to prehistoric mastodons, zebras, and camels. The first human inhabitants of record were the Agua Caliente, part of the Cahuilla people, who settled in and around the Coachella Valley about 1,000 years ago.

Lake Cahuilla dried up about 300 years ago, but by then the Agua Caliente had discovered the area's hot springs and were making use of their healing properties during winter visits to the desert. The springs became a tourist attraction in 1871, when the tribe built a bathhouse (on a site near the current Spa Resort Casino in Palm Springs) to serve passengers on a pioneer stage highway. The Agua Caliente still own about 32,000 acres of desert, 6,700 of which lie within the city limits of Palm Springs.

In the last half of the 19th century, farmers established a date-growing industry at the southern end of the Coachella Valley. By 1900 word had spread about the health benefits of the area's dry climate, inspiring the gentry of the northern United States to winter under the warm desert sun. Growth hit the Coachella Valley in the 1970s, when developers began to construct the fabulous golf courses, country clubs, and residential communities that would draw celebrities, tycoons, and politicians. Communities sprang up south and east of what is now Palm Springs, creating a sprawl of tract houses and strip malls and forcing nature lovers to push farther south into the sparsely settled Anza-Borrego Desert.

PLANNING

WHEN TO GO

Desert weather is best between January and April, the height of the visitor season. The fall months are nearly as lovely, but less crowded and less expensive (although autumn draws a lot of conventions and business travelers). In summer, an increasingly popular time for European visitors, daytime temperatures may rise above 110°F (though evenings cool to the mid-70s); some attractions and restaurants close or reduce their hours during this time.

GETTING HERE AND AROUND

AIR TRAVEL

Palm Springs International Airport is the major airport serving California's desert communities. Alaska, Allegiant, American, Delta, Horizon, Sun Country (seasonal), United, US Airways, and WestJet all fly to Palm Springs year-round. A Valley Cabousine has taxis serving the Palm Springs airport.

Airport Information Palm Springs International Airport ☎ 760/323-8299 ⊕ www.palmspringsairport.com.

Airport Transfers A Valley Cabousine ☎ 760/318-3800.

BUS TRAVEL

Greyhound provides service to the Palm Springs depot. SunBus, operated by the SunLine Transit Agency, serves the entire Coachella Valley, from Desert Hot Springs to Mecca.

Bus Contacts Greyhound ☎ 800/231–2222 ⊕ www.greyhound.com.
SunLine Transit ☎ 800/347–8628 ⊕ www.sunline.org.

CAR TRAVEL

The desert resort communities occupy a 20-mi stretch between I–10, to the east, and Palm Canyon Drive (Highway 111), to the west. The area is about a two-hour drive east of Los Angeles and a three-hour drive northeast of San Diego. It can take twice as long to make the trip from Los Angeles to the desert on winter and spring weekends because of heavy traffic. From Los Angeles take the San Bernardino Freeway (I–10) east to Highway 111. From San Diego I–15 heading north connects with the Pomona Freeway (Highway 60), leading to the San Bernardino Freeway (I–10) east.

To reach Borrego Springs from Los Angeles, take I–10 east past the desert resorts area to Highway 86 south, and follow it to the Borrego Salton Seaway (Highway S22). Drive east on S22 to Borrego Springs. You can reach the Borrego area from San Diego via I–8 to Highway 79 through Cuyamaca State Park. This will take you to Highway 78 in Julian, which you follow east to Yaqui Pass Road (S3) into Borrego Springs.

TAXI TRAVEL

A Valley Cabousine serves Palm Desert and goes to the Palm Springs airport. Mirage Taxi serves the Coachella Valley and the Los Angeles and Ontario International airports. Fares in the Coachella Valley run about $2.96 per mi and up to $410 (discount for cash) one-way to LAX.

Taxi Contacts Yellow Cab ☎ 760/340–5845.

TRAIN TRAVEL

The Amtrak *Sunset Limited,* which runs between Florida and Los Angeles, stops in Palm Springs.

Train Contact Amtrak ☎ *800/872–7245* ⊕ *www.amtrakcalifornia.com.*

HEALTH AND SAFETY

Never travel alone in the desert. Let someone know your trip route, destination, and estimated time and date of return. Before setting out, make sure your vehicle is in good condition. Carry a jack, tools, and towrope or chain. Fill up your tank whenever you see a gas pump. Stay on main roads, and watch out for horses and range cattle.

Drink at least a gallon of water a day (three gallons if you're hiking or otherwise exerting yourself). Dress in layered clothing and wear comfortable, sturdy shoes and a hat. Keep snacks, sunscreen, and a first-aid kit on hand. If you suddenly have a headache or feel dizzy or nauseous, you could be suffering from dehydration. Get out of the sun immediately and drink plenty of water. Dampen your clothing to lower your body temperature.

Do not enter mine tunnels or shafts. Avoid canyons during rainstorms. Never place your hands or feet where you can't see them. Rattlesnakes, scorpions, and black widow spiders may be hiding there.

Emergency Services Borrego Medical Center ✉ *4343 Yaqui Pass Rd., Borrego Springs* ☎ *760/767–5051.* **Desert Regional Medical Center** ✉ *1150 N. Indian Canyon Dr., Palm Springs* ☎ *760/323–6511.*

TOUR OPTIONS

Desert Adventures takes to the wilds with two- to four-hour red Jeep tours ($79 to $159) on private land along the canyons and palm oases above the San Andreas earthquake fault. Their other public tours include Indian Cultural Adventure, Pioneer Adventure, and Joshua Tree National Park (⇨ *see Chapter 10*). Groups are small and guides are knowledgeable. Departures are from Palm Springs and La Quinta; hotel pickups are available. Elite Land Tours gives two- to five-hour luxurious treks via Hummer and helicopter led by knowledgeable guides who take you to the San Andreas Fault, Joshua Tree National Park (⇨ *see Chapter 10*), Indian Canyons, Old Indian Pueblo in Desert Hot Springs, and the Salton Sea. Tours include hotel pickup, lunch, snacks, and beverages. The company also offers VIP tours to Los Angeles and San Diego including a one-night stay.

The city of Palm Desert offers four self-guided tours of its 150-piece Art in Public Places collection. Each tour is walkable or drivable: The El Paseo tour features sculptures installed along the grassy median strip that runs the length of the street; the Fred Waring Corridor Tour includes sculptures of bighorn sheep, komodo dragons, and mountain lions along the street named for the bandleader; the City Tour encompasses several large pieces of art ringing the Desert Willow Golf Resort; and the Civic Center Park walk includes a massive water feature and plantings of 68 varieties of roses. Maps are available at the Palm Desert Visitor Center and online.

The Desert Resorts

Palm Springs holds one of the largest collections of homes and public buildings designed by the famed Desert Moderne architects of the 1950s, Albert Frey, Richard Neutra, and William F. Cody. You can see many of these beauties on tours assembled by the city of Palm Desert. The Palm Springs Visitor Center also offers copies of *Palm Springs: Brief History and Architectural Guide.*

Tour Contacts Desert Adventures ✉ *74-794 Lennon Pl., Suite A, Palm Desert* ☎ *760/340–2345* ⊕ *www.red-jeep.com.* **Desert Safari Guides** ☎ *760/861–6292* ⊕ *www.palmspringshiking.com.* **Elite Land Tours** ✉ *540 S. Vella Rd., Palm Springs* ☎ *760/318–1200* ⊕ *www.elitelandtours.com.* **Palm Desert Visitor Center** ✉ *73-470 El Paseo, Suite 7-F, Palm Desert* ☎ *760/568–1441* ⊕ *www.palm-desert.org.* **Palm Springs Tours** ✉ *Palm Springs* ☎ *800/409-3174.*

RESTAURANTS

Dining in the desert is casual and low-key. Expect to find many good, but not stellar, dining experiences. Fare, once limited to Italian and a smattering of French choices, now includes fresh seafood, contemporary Californian, Asian, vegetarian, and steaks; you can find Mexican food everywhere. Restaurants that remain open in July and August frequently discount deeply; others close in July and August or offer limited service.

The green revolution is proudly on display in many parts of the Palm Springs area.

HOTELS

In general you can find the widest choice of lodgings in Palm Springs, ranging from tiny B&Bs and chain motels to business and resort hotels. All-inclusive resorts dominate in down-valley communities. You can stay in the desert for as little as $80 or spend more than $1,000 a night. Rates vary widely by season. Hotel/resort prices are frequently 50% less in summer and fall than in winter and early spring. January through May prices soar, and lodgings book up far in advance. Most resort hotels charge a resort fee that is not included in the room rate; be sure to ask about extra fees when you book.

Small boutique hotels and bed-and-breakfasts have historic character and offer good value; discounts are sometimes given for extended stays. Casino hotels can also offer good deals on lodging. Take care when considering budget lodgings; other than reliable chains, they may not be up to par.

WHAT IT COSTS					
	¢	$	$$	$$$	$$$$
Restaurants	under $10	$10–$15	$16–$22	$23–$30	over $30
Hotels	under $90	$90–$120	$121–$175	$176–$250	over $250

Restaurant prices are for a main course at dinner, excluding sales tax of 8.75 %. Hotel prices are for a standard double room in high season, excluding service charges, resort fees, and 9%–13.5% tax. Most hotels add a resort fee of $15 to $35 per day for parking, newspaper, spa and fitness center admission, in-room Wi-Fi, and other incidentals. Some charge up to $50 per day for pets (in addition to a security deposit).

NIGHTLIFE

Desert nightlife is casual. It's concentrated and abundant in Palm Springs, where there are many straight and gay bars and clubs. The Fabulous Palm Springs Follies—a vaudeville-style revue starring retired professional performers—is a must-see. Arts festivals occur on a regular basis, especially in winter and spring. The "Desert Guide" section of *Palm Springs Life* magazine (available at hotels and visitor information centers) has nightlife listings, as does the "Weekender" pullout in the Friday edition of the *Desert Sun* newspaper. The gay scene is covered in the *Bottom Line* and in the *Gay Guide to Palm Springs,* published by the Desert Gay Tourism Guild.

THE DESERT RESORTS

PALM SPRINGS

90 mi southeast of Los Angeles on I–10.

A tourist destination since the late 19th century, Palm Springs had already caught Hollywood's eye by the time of the Great Depression. It was an ideal hideaway: Celebrities could slip into town, play a few sets of tennis, lounge around the pool, attend a party or two, and, unless things got out of hand, remain safely beyond the reach of gossip columnists. But it took a pair of tennis-playing celebrities to put Palm Springs on the map. In the 1930s actors Charlie Farrell and Ralph Bellamy bought 200 acres of land for $30 an acre and opened the Palm Springs Racquet Club, which soon listed Ginger Rogers, Humphrey Bogart, and Clark Gable among its members.

During its slow, steady growth period from the 1930s to 1970s, the Palm Springs area drew some of the world's most famous architects to design homes for the rich and famous. The collected works, inspired by the mountains and desert sands and notable for the use of glass and indoor–outdoor space, became known as Palm Springs Modernism. The city lost some of its luster in the 1970s as the wealthy moved to newer down-valley, golf-oriented communities. But Palm Springs reinvented itself starting in the 1990s, restoring the bright and airy old midcentury modern houses and hotels, and cultivating a welcoming atmosphere for well-heeled gay visitors.

You'll find reminders of the city's glamorous past in its unique architecture and renovated hotels; change and progress are evidenced by trendy restaurants and upscale shops. Formerly exclusive Palm Canyon Drive is now a lively avenue filled with coffeehouses, outdoor cafés, and bars.

■ TIP→ **Tahquitz Canyon Way marks the division between north and south on major streets (e.g., North and South Palm Canyon Drive).**

GETTING HERE AND AROUND

Most visitors arrive in the Palm Springs area by car from the Los Angeles or San Diego areas via I-10, which intersects with Hwy. 111 just north of Palm Springs. Hwy. 111 connects all the desert cities, west to east. I–10 borders the cities northwest to southeast. From I–10 Ramon

Rd. goes to Cathedral City and Palm Springs. Monterey takes you to Rancho Mirage and Palm Desert. You can get to Indian Wells, La Quinta, and Indio via Washington St. The Palm Springs International Airport lies in the heart of the city.

ESSENTIALS

Visitor Information Palm Springs Desert Resorts Convention and Visitors Authority ✉ *70-100 Hwy. 111, Rancho Mirage* ☎ *760/770–9000, 800/967–3767* ⊕ *www.palmspringsusa.com.* **Palm Springs Visitor Information Center** ✉ *2901 N. Palm Canyon Dr., Palm Springs* ☎ *760/778–8418, 800/347–7746* ⊕ *www.palm-springs.org.*

EXPLORING

Indian Canyons. The Indian Canyons are the ancestral home of the Agua Caliente, part of the Cahuilla people. You can see remnants of their ancient life, including rock art, house pits and foundations, irrigation ditches, bedrock mortars, pictographs, and stone houses and shelters built atop high cliff walls. Short, easy walks through the canyons reveal palm oases, waterfalls, and spring wildflowers. Tree-shaded picnic areas are abundant. The attraction includes three canyons open for touring: Palm Canyon, noted for its stand of Washingtonia palms; Murray Canyon, home of Peninsula bighorn sheep and a herd of wild ponies; and Andreas Canyon, where a stand of fan palms contrasts with sharp rock formations. Ranger-led hikes to Palm and Andreas canyons are offered daily for an additional charge. The trading post at the entrance to Palm Canyon has hiking maps and refreshments, as well as Native American art, jewelry, and weavings. ⊠ *38520 S. Palm Canyon Dr., Palm Springs* ☎ *760/323–6018* ⊕ *www.indian-canyons.com* ✉ *$9, ranger hikes $3* ☉ *Oct.–June, daily 8–5; July–Sept., Fri.–Sun. 8–5.*

☾ **Knott's Soak City.** For a break from the desert heat, head to Knott's Soak City. You'll find 1950s-theme ambience complete with Woodies (antique station wagons from the 1950s), 13 waterslides, a huge wave pool, an arcade, and other fun family attractions. The park also contains the full-service Fitness Point Health Club, where you can take exercise classes—including water aerobics and yoga—use the weight room, or swim; day passes are $12. ⊠ *1500 S. Gene Autry Trail, Palm Springs* ☎ *760/327–0499, 760/325–8155 Fitness Point Health Club* ⊕ *www. knotts.com* ✉ *$32, $22 after 3 pm, $12 health club day pass* ☉ *Mid-March–early Sept., daily; early Sept.–Oct., weekends. Opens at 10 am, closing times vary.*

☾ **Palm Springs Aerial Tramway.** A trip on the Palm Springs Aerial Tramway
★ provides a 360-degree view of the desert through the picture windows of rotating tramcars. The 2½-mi ascent through Chino Canyon, the steep-est vertical cable ride in the United States, brings you to an elevation of 8,516 feet in less than 20 minutes. On clear days, which are common, the view stretches 75 mi—from the peak of Mt. San Gorgonio in the north, to the Salton Sea in the southeast. Stepping out into the snow at the summit is a winter treat. At the top, a bit below the summit of Mt. San Jacinto, are several diversions. Mountain Station has an observation deck, two restaurants, a cocktail lounge, apparel and gift shops, picnic facilities, a small wildlife exhibit, and a theater that screens a worth-while 22-minute film on the history of the tramway. Take advantage of free guided and self-guided nature walks through the adjacent Mount San Jacinto State Park and Wilderness, or if there's snow on the ground, rent skis, snowshoes, or snow tubes (inner tubes or similar contraptions for sliding down hills). The tramway generally closes for maintenance in mid-September. ■TIP➔ Ride-and-dine packages are available in late afternoon. The tram is a popular attraction; to avoid a two-hour or longer wait, arrive before the first car leaves in the morning. ⊠ *1 Tramway Rd., Palm Springs* ☎ *760/325–1391, 888/515–8726* ⊕ *www.pstramway.com* ✉ *$23.25, ride-and-dine package $36* ☉ *Tramcars depart at least every 30 mins from 10 am weekdays and 8 am weekends; last car up leaves at 8 pm, last car down leaves Mountain Station at 9:45 pm.*

☾ **Palm Springs Air Museum.** The Palm Springs Air Museum showcases an impressive collection of World War II aircraft, including a B-17 Fly-ing Fortress bomber, a P-51 Mustang, a Lockheed P-38, and a Grum-man TBF Avenger. Cool exhibits include a Grumman Goose into which kids can crawl, model warships, and a Pearl Harbor diorama. Rare historic photos, artifacts, memorabilia, and uniforms are also on dis-play. The museum also sponsors educational programs on Saturdays. Flight demonstrations are scheduled regularly. ⊠ *745 N. Gene Autry Trail, Palm Springs* ☎ *760/778–6262* ⊕ *www.air-museum.org* ✉ *$14* ☉ *Daily 10–5.*

9

LOVE ME TENDER

Elvis's Honeymoon Hideaway—where the King and Priscilla lived during the first year of their marriage—is perched on a hilltop right up against the mountains in Palm Springs. The house, which is opened for tours, is a stunning example of Palm Springs Mid-Century Modern; it's rich in Elvis lore, photos, and furnishings. Docents describe the fabulous parties, celebrities, and some local legends. You can see some home movies of the loving couple, sit on the King's sofa, and strum one of his guitars. The house, built in 1962 by one of Palm Spring's largest developers Robert Alexander, consists of four perfect circles, each set on a different level. At the time, *Look* magazine described it as the "house of tomorrow." (And indeed many features, like the huge kitchen with circular island, are standard in today's homes.) Tours are offered daily by appointment only; they're $25. Call ☎ 760/322–1192 or visit ⊕ *www.elvishoneymoon.com* for reservations.

★ **Palm Springs Art Museum.** The Palm Springs Art Museum and its grounds hold several wide-ranging collections of contemporary and traditional art displayed in bright, open galleries, with daylight streaming through huge skylights. The permanent collection includes a shimmering display of contemporary studio glass, highlighted by works by Dale Chihuly, Ginny Ruffner, and William Morris. You'll also find handcrafted furniture by the late actor George Montgomery, an array of enormous Native American baskets, and works by artists like Allen Houser, Arlo Namingha, and Fritz Scholder; the museum also displays significant works of 20th century sculpture by Henry Moore, Marino Marina, Deborah Butterfield, and Mark Di Suvero. The Annenberg Theater presents plays, concerts, lectures, operas, and other cultural events. ⊠ *101 Museum Dr., Palm Springs* ☎ *760/322–4800* ⊕ *www.psmuseum.org* ⬚ *$12.50, free Thurs. 4–8 during Villagefest* ☉ *10–5 daily, closed Mon.*

Palm Springs Starwalk. A stroll down shop-lined Palm Canyon Drive will take you along the Palm Springs Starwalk, where nearly 200 bronze stars are embedded in the sidewalk (à la Hollywood Walk of Fame). Most of the names, all with a Palm Springs connection, are ones you'll recognize (such as Elvis Presley, Marilyn Monroe, Lauren Bacall, Lucille Ball, and Liberace). Others are local celebrities. ⊠ *Palm Canyon Dr., around Tahquitz Canyon Way, and Tahquitz Canyon Way, between Palm Canyon and Indian Canyon Drs., Palm Springs.*

Tahquitz Canyon. Ranger-led tours of Tahquitz Canyon take you into a secluded canyon on the Agua Caliente Reservation. Within the canyon are a spectacular 60-foot waterfall, rock art, ancient irrigation systems, and native wildlife and plants. Tours are conducted several times daily; participants must be able to navigate 100 steep steps. (You can also take a self-guided tour of the 1.8-mi trail.) A visitor center at the canyon entrance shows a video tour, displays artifacts, and sells maps. ⊠ *500 W. Mesquite Ave., Palm Springs* ☎ *760/416–7044* ⊕ *www.tahquitzcanyon.com* ⬚ *$12.50* ☉ *Oct.– June, daily 7:30–5; July–Sept., Fri.–Sun. 7:30–5.*

Village Green Heritage Center. Three small museums at the Village Green Heritage Center illustrate pioneer life in Palm Springs. The **Agua Caliente Cultural Museum** traces the culture and history of the Cahuilla tribe with several exhibits. The **McCallum Adobe** holds the collection of the Palm Springs Historical Society. **Rudy's General Store Museum** is a re-creation of a 1930s general store. ⊠ *221 S. Palm Canyon Dr., Palm Springs* ☏ *760/327–2156* ✉ *Agua Caliente Cultural Museum free, McCallum Adobe $2, Rudy's General Store 95¢* ⊙ *Call for hrs.*

WHERE TO EAT

$ ✗ **The Blue Pear Texx Mexx.** Offering a nuanced, sophisticated take on
TEX-MEX Tex-Mex, this restaurant is a step above the usual joint. Most menu items sound familiar: enchiladas, tacos, flautas, chile rellenos, and tamales. But each showcases the deft spice hand of chef Russ Olden, who mixes and matches in surprising ways. Try the chipotle macaroni and cheese and you'll get a creamy, slightly hot tender pasta. Or sample the slow-cooked seasoned spare ribs sauced with the chef's own tomato, cider, and molasses barbecued potion. Most items on the menu are available with no meat. The restaurant, part of a complex that includes the Pool House Inn at the base of the Tramway, holds a collection of small rooms all done in black and white, very modern. There's a popular bar that's getting a reputation for good margaritas, inside and outdoor dining, and best of all nearly everything on the menu is less than $10. ⊠ *2249 N. Palm Canyon Dr., Palm Springs* ☏ *760/778-5500.*

$$$ ✗ **Copley's on Palm Canyon.** Chef Manion Copley is cooking up some of
AMERICAN the most innovative cuisine in the desert in a setting that's straight out of Hollywood—a hacienda once owned by Cary Grant. Dine in the clubby house or under the stars in the garden. Start with such appetizers as roasted beet and warm goat cheese salad or one of the Hawaiian ahi tacos. Oh My Lobster Pot Pie is the biggest hit on an entrée menu that also features an elegant rack of lamb crusted with parsley and lavender. And save room for Copley's sweet and savory servings of herb ice cream. Service is pleasant and friendly. ⊠ *621 N. Palm Canyon Dr., Palm Springs* ☏ *760/327–9555* ⊕ *www.copleypalmsprings.com* ⟁ *Reservations essential* ⊙ *Closed Mon. No lunch.*

$$$$ ✗ **The Falls Steak House.** A mile-long martini menu lures a chic, mon-
STEAKHOUSE eyed crowd to this steak house with an inside waterfall tucked into an upstairs corner overlooking the Palm Canyon Drive action. Reserve well in advance for one of the outdoor balcony tables to get the best view. While this eatery specializes in dry aged beef, you can also get seafood and chops; there's a separate vegetarian menu. Steaks and chops are prepared your way with a selection of sides that includes mac and cheese, roasted potatoes, and steamed asparagus with hollandaise sauce. Go early for the nightly happy hour (between 4 and 6:30) when items on the bar menu are half price—or hang around late to catch the action at the Martini Dome bar. ⊠ *155 S. Palm Canyon Dr., Palm Springs* ☏ *760/416–8664* ⊕ *www.thefallsprimesteakhouse.com* ⟁ *Reservations essential* ⊙ *No lunch.*

$$$$ ✗ **Le Vallauris.** Le Vallauris, in the historic Roberson House, is popular
FRENCH with ladies who lunch, all of whom get a hug from the maître d'. The
★ menu changes daily, and each day it's handwritten on a white board. Lunch entrées may include perfectly rare tuna Niçoise salad, or grilled

9

whitefish with Dijon mustard sauce. Dinner might bring a sublime smoked salmon, sautéed calves' liver, roasted quail with orange sauce, or rack of lamb. Service is beyond attentive. The restaurant has a lovely tree-shaded garden. On cool winter evenings, request a table by the fireplace. ✉ *385 W. Tahquitz Canyon Way, Palm Springs* ☏ *760/325–5059* ⊕ *www.levallauris.com* ☇ *Reservations essential* ⊘ *Closed July and Aug.*

$$
ITALIAN

✕ **Matchbox Vintage Pizza Bistro.** The name says pizza, but this bistro offers much more: you'll find interesting salads topped with grilled tuna, and a selection of sandwiches with fillings like chicken with portobello mushrooms or Angus beef with Gorgonzola. The entree list includes fire roasted maple bourbon chicken, New York strip steak, and fish and chips. The pizzas are made just about any way you'd like, including vegetarian. This is the place to go for cocktails and small plates. The bistro has an upstairs location and overlooks the nightly action on Palm Canyon Drive. ✉ *155 S. Palm Canyon Dr., Palm Springs* ☏ *760/778–6000* ⊕ *www.matchboxpalmsprings.com* ⊘ *No lunch.*

$$$
MEDITERRANEAN
★

✕ **Purple Palm.** The hottest tables in Palm Springs are those that surround the pool at the Colony Palms Hotel, where the hip and elite pay homage to Purple Gang mobster Al Wertheimer, who reportedly built the hotel in the mid-1930s. Now it's a casual, convivial place where you can dine alfresco surrounded by a tropical garden. The dinner menu is about evenly divided between large plates such as roasted Jidori chicken, bouillabaisse, or Angus rib eye steak and small plates like fried avocado, mussels and clams, and crab mac and cheese. An impressive wine list roams the globe. The restaurant is open for breakfast and lunch. ▮**TIP**➔ A visit to the ladies room is a must for Paul Newman fans. The loo holds a fabulous black and white image of a very young Newman. ✉ *572 N. Indian Canyon Dr., Palm Springs* ☏ *800/557–2187* ⊕ *www.colonypalmshotel.com* ☇ *Reservations essential.*

$$
NEW AMERICAN

✕ **The Tropicale.** Tucked onto a side-street corner, the Tropicale offers a mid-century–style watering hole with a contemporary vibe. The bar and main dining room hold cozy leather booths while flowers and water features brighten the outdoor area. The menu roams the world with small and large plates, from miso-glazed salmon rice bowl to Kahlua barbecue pork porterhouse with mashed plantains to *carne asada* pizza with salsa and guacamole. ✉ *330 E. Amado Rd., Palm Springs* ☏ *760/866–1952* ⊕ *www.thetropicale.com* ☇ *Reservations essential* ⊘ *No lunch.*

$$ **⨉ Zini Café Med.** One of the best
MEDITERRANEAN people-watching spots in Palm
Springs, this sidewalk café is a
delightful choice before or after see-
ing the Follies. The lunch and din-
ner menus feature a wide selection
of small plates in addition to hearty
items such as pasta, pizza, *pollo
alla diavolo* (macadamia-crusted
chicken breast), and veal scalop-
pini. On a separate tapas menu you
can find some surprises: spicy chick-
peas with Mediterranean chicken
sausage, layered grilled artichoke,
asparagus topped with a fried
egg, or spicy lime drizzled shrimp.
Service is pleasant and personal.
✉ *140 S. Palm Canyon Dr., Palm
Springs* 🕾 *760/325–9464* ⊕ *www.
zinicafemed.com.*

WHERE TO STAY

For expanded hotel reviews, visit Fodors.com.

HOTELS AND RESORTS

$$ 🏨 **Ace Hotel and Swim Club.** Take a trip back to the 1960s at the Ace. **Pros:**
Amigo Room has late-night dining; poolside stargazing deck; scooter
rentals available on site. **Cons:** party atmosphere not for everyone; limited amenities; casual staff and service. ✉ *701 E. Palm Canyon Dr., Palm
Springs* 🕾 *760/325–9900* ⊕ *www.acehotel.com/palmsprings* ⤴ *180
rooms, 8 suites* ⌂ *In-room: a/c, Wi-Fi. In-hotel: restaurant, bar, pool,
gym, spa, laundry facilities, business center, parking, some pets allowed.*

$$ 🏨 **Colony Palms Hotel.** Detroit's Purple Gang mobsters, Hollywood's
starlets and leading men, and Sea Biscuit all cast a long shadow over
the Colony Palms. **Pros:** glam with a swagger; attentive staff; all that
history. **Cons:** high noise level outside; not for families with young
children. ✉ *572 N. Indian Canyon Dr., Palm Springs, Palm Springs*
🕾 *760/969–1800, 800/577–2187* ⊕ *www.colonypalmshotel.com* ⤴ *43
rooms, 3 suites, 8 casitas* ⌂ *In-room: a/c, Internet, Wi-Fi. In-hotel: res-
taurant, bar, pool, gym, spa, parking, some pets allowed.*

$$$ 🏨 **Hyatt Regency Suites Palm Springs.** The best-situated downtown hotel in
Palm Springs, the Hyatt has rooms where you can watch the sun rise
over the city or set behind the mountains from your bedroom's balcony. **Pros:** underground parking; the fireplace in the bar; nightly happy
hour. **Cons:** lots of business travelers; some street noise. ✉ *285 N. Palm
Canyon Dr., Palm Springs* 🕾 *760/322–9000, 800/633–7313* ⊕ *www.
hyattpalmsprings.com* ⤴ *197 suites* ⌂ *In-room: a/c, Wi-Fi. In-hotel: restaurant, bar, pool, gym, spa, business center, parking, some pets allowed.*

$$$$ 🏨 **The Parker Palm Springs.** A cacophony of color and over-the-top con-
★ temporary art assembled by New York designer Jonathan Adler, this
is the hippest hotel in the desert, appealing to a stylish L.A.-based clientele. **Pros:** fun in the sun; celebrity clientele; high jinks at the Palm

9

Springs Yacht Club Spa. **Cons:** pricey drinks and wine; long walks in the hot sun to get anywhere. ⊠ *4200 E. Palm Canyon Dr., Palm Springs* ☎ *760/770–5000, 800/543–4300* ⊕ *www.theparkerpalmsprings.com* ⇱ *131 rooms, 13 suites* ⌂ *In-room: a/c, Wi-Fi. In-hotel: restaurant, bar, pool, tennis court, gym, spa, parking.*

$$ ⊞ **The Pool House.** Dripping with mid-century charm, the Pool House is all white with chrome and glass, original art on the walls, and smooth simple lines. **Pros:** mountain views; friendly staff; close to Tramway. **Cons:** no phones in rooms; can get busy. ⊠ *2249 N. Palm Canyon Dr, Palm Springs* ☎ *760/778–5500* ⇱ *6 rooms* ⌂ *In-room: Wi-Fi. In-hotel: restaurant, bar, pool, parking, some pets allowed.*

$$$$ ⊞ **Riviera Resort & Spa.** Built in 1958 and reopened in 2008 following an extensive renovation, this mid-century hotel is beyond bling. **Pros:** personal beachy fire pits throughout the property; hip vibe; sublime spa. **Cons:** high noise level outdoors; party atmosphere; location at north end of Palm Springs. ⊠ *1600 N. Indian Canyon Dr., Palm Springs* ☎ *760/327–8311* ⊕ *www.psriviera.com* ⇱ *406 rooms, 43 suites* ⌂ *In-room: a/c, Internet, Wi-Fi. In-hotel: restaurant, bar, pool, tennis court, gym, spa, parking, some pets allowed.*

$$$$ ⊞ **Smoke Tree Ranch.** A world apart from Palm Springs' pulsating urban
☺   village, the area's most exclusive resort occupies 400 pristine desert
★   acres, surrounded by mountains and unspoiled vistas. **Pros:** priceless privacy; simple luxury; many recreation choices include horseback riding, lawn bowling, hiking, and jogging. **Cons:** no glitz or glamour; limited entertainment options; family atmosphere not for everyone. ⊠ *1850 Smoke Tree La., Palm Springs* ☎ *760/327–1221, 800/787–3922* ⊕ *www.smoketreeranch.com* ⇱ *49 cottages, includes 18 suites* ⌂ *In-room: a/c, Wi-Fi. In-hotel: restaurant, bar, pool, tennis court, gym, children's programs, laundry facilities, business center, parking, some pets allowed* ⊙ *Closed Apr.–late Oct.*

¢   ⊞ **Vagabond Inn.** Rooms are smallish at this centrally located motel, but they're clean, comfortable, and a good value. Some are decorated in earth tones of brick red and brown, while others sport soft sky colors, and they all surround an appealing free-form swimming pool. Continental breakfast and daily newspaper are included in the price. BJ's Snack Shoppe has sandwiches and deli items. **Pros:** quiet; kids stay free. **Cons:** limited amenities, facilities, and service. ⊠ *1699 S. Palm Canyon Dr., Palm Springs* ☎ *760/325–7211, 800/522–1555* ⊕ *www.vagabondinn.com* ⇱ *117 rooms* ⌂ *In-room: a/c, Internet, Wi-Fi. In-hotel: restaurant, pool, parking, some pets allowed* ⌶⊙| *Breakfast.*

$$ ⊞ **The Viceroy Palm Springs.** Stepping into the Viceroy you're greeted with
★   a bright, sunny white-and-yellow ambience, reminiscent of a sun-filled desert day. **Pros:** poolside cabanas; celebrity clientele. **Cons:** uneven service; popular wedding site. ⊠ *415 S. Belardo Rd., Palm Springs* ☎ *760/320–4117, 800/327–3687* ⊕ *www.viceroypalmsprings.com* ⇱ *67 rooms, 12 villas* ⌂ *In-room: a/c, kitchen, Internet, Wi-Fi. In-hotel: restaurant, bar, pool, gym, spa, business center, parking, some pets allowed.*

CLOSE UP

Palm Springs Modernism

Some of the world's most forward-looking architects designed and constructed buildings around Palm Springs between 1940 and 1970, and modernism, also popular elsewhere in California in the years after World War II, became an ideal fit for desert living, because it minimizes the separation between indoors and outdoors. See-through houses with glass exterior walls are common. Oversize flat roofs provide shade from the sun, and many buildings' sculptural forms reflect nearby landforms. The style is notable for elegant informality, clean lines, and simple landscaping. Emblematic structures in Palm Springs include public buildings, hotels, stores, banks, and private residences.

Most obvious to visitors are three buildings that are part of the Palm Springs Aerial Tramway complex, built in the 1960s. Albert Frey, a Swiss-born architect, designed the soaring A-frame Tramway Gas Station, visually echoing the pointed peaks behind it. Frey also created the glass-walled Valley Station, from which you get your initial view of the Coachella Valley before you board the tram to the Mountain Station, designed by E. Stewart Williams.

Frey, a Palm Springs resident for more than 60 years, also designed the indoor–outdoor City Hall, Fire Station #1, and numerous houses. You

can see his second home, perched atop stilts on the hillside above the Desert Museum; it affords a sweeping view of the Coachella Valley through glass walls. The classy Movie Colony Hotel, one of the first buildings Frey designed in the desert, may seem like a typical 1950s motel with rooms surrounding a swimming pool now, but when it was built in 1935, it was years ahead of its time.

Donald Wexler, who honed his vision with Los Angeles architect Richard Neutra, brought new ideas about the use of materials to the desert, where he teamed up with William Cody on a number of projects, including the terminal at the Palm Springs airport. Many of Wexler's buildings have soaring overhanging roofs, designed to provide shade from the blazing desert sun. Wexler also experimented with steel framing back in 1961, but the metal proved too expensive. Seven of his steel-frame houses can be seen in a neighborhood off Indian Canyon and Frances drives.

The Palm Springs Modern Committee is protecting these period structures, occasionally protesting projected demolition projects. The committee also publishes a map and driving guide to 52 historic buildings, which is available for $5 at the Palm Springs Visitor Information Center or at ⊕ *www.psmodcom.com*.

9

SMALL HOTELS AND BED-AND-BREAKFASTS

$$$ 🖾 **Calla Lily Inn.** One block from Palm Canyon Drive, this tranquil palm-shaded oasis has spacious rooms decorated in a vaguely tropical style. Furnishings are contemporary wicker, and an image of a calla lily adorns every room, which surround the pool. **Pros:** lush tropical gardens; bikes available. **Cons:** small property; rooms are subjected to pool noise. ⊠ *350 S. Belardo Rd., Palm Springs* ☎ *760/323–3654, 888/888–5787* ⊕ *www.callalilypalmsprings.com* ➾ *9 rooms* ⚭ *In-room: a/c, kitchen, Internet, Wi-Fi. In-hotel: pool, parking.*

$$ ⌂ **East Canyon Hotel & Spa.** Serving a primarily gay clientele, this classy resort is the only one in the desert with an in-house, full-service spa exclusively for men. **Pros:** elegant laid-back feel; attentive service; complimentary poolside cocktails. **Cons:** spa is for men only. ⊠ *288 E. Camino Monte Vista, Palm Springs* ☎ *760/320–1928, 877/324–6835* ⊕ *www.eastcanyonps.com* ⤳ *15 rooms, 1 suite* ⌂ *In-room: a/c, Wi-Fi. In-hotel: pool, spa, parking* ⦿ *Breakfast.*

$$ ⌂ **Movie Colony Hotel.** Designed in 1935 by Albert Frey, this intimate hotel evokes mid-century minimalist ambience. **Pros:** architectural icon; happy hour; cruiser bikes. **Cons:** close quarters; off the beaten path; staff not available 24 hours. ⊠ *726 N. Indian Canyon Dr., Palm Springs* ☎ *760/320–6340, 888/953–5700* ⊕ *www.moviecolonyhotel.com* ⤳ *13 rooms, 3 suites* ⌂ *In-room: a/c, Internet, Wi-Fi. In-hotel: bar, pool, parking, some age restrictions* ⦿ *Breakfast.*

$$ ⌂ **Orbit In Hotel.** Step back to 1957 at this hip inn, located on a quiet back street downtown. **Pros:** saltwater pool; in-room spa services; Orbitini cocktail hour. **Cons:** best for couples; style not to everyone's taste; staff not available 24 hours. ⊠ *562 W. Arenas Rd., Palm Springs* ☎ *760/323–3585, 877/996–7248* ⊕ *www.orbitin.com* ⤳ *9 rooms* ⌂ *In-room: a/c, kitchen, Internet, Wi-Fi. In-hotel: pool, business center, parking, some age restrictions* ⦿ *Breakfast.*

$$$$ ⌂ **Willows Historic Palm Springs Inn.** Within walking distance of most village
★   attractions, this luxurious hillside B&B is next door to the Desert Art Museum and a 2-block walk to plenty of dining and shopping options. **Pros:** ultra luxurious; sublime service. **Cons:** closed June through September; pricey ⊠ *412 W. Tahquitz Canyon Way, Palm Springs* ☎ *760/320–0771, 800/966–9597* ⊕ *www.thewillowspalmsprings.com* ⤳ *8 rooms* ⌂ *In-room: a/c, Internet, Wi-Fi. In-hotel: pool, parking* ⦿ *Breakfast.*

NIGHTLIFE AND THE ARTS

NIGHTLIFE   **Ace Hotel and Swim Club.** A variety of events are held here nearly every night, including films, live concerts, DJs with dancing, parties, and seasonal entertainment. Many are free, and quite a few are family-friendly. Check the hotel's Web site for the schedule. ⊠ *701 E. Palm Canyon Dr., Palm Springs* ☎ *760/325–9900* ⊕ *www.acehotel.com.*

Hair of the Dog English Pub. Drawing a young crowd that likes to tip back English ales and ciders, this bar is lively and popular. ⊠ *238 N. Palm Canyon Dr., Palm Springs* ☎ *760/323–9890.*

Village Pub. With live entertainment, DJs, and friendly service, this is a popular bar that caters to a young crowd. ⊠ *266 S. Palm Canyon Dr., Palm Springs* ☎ *760/323–3265.*

Zelda's. A 30-year Palm Springs institution, Zelda's moved south in 2010. But the high-energy DJs, dancing, and drinking is still going strong, and the dance floor is still thumping with Latin, hip hop, and music from the 60s, 70s, and 80s. The club now offers bottle service in the VIP Sky Box. ⊠ *611 S. Palm Canyon Dr., Palm Springs* ☎ *760/325–2375.*

Casino Morongo. About 20 minutes west of Palm Springs, this casino has 2,000 slot machines, video games, the Vibe nightclub, plus Vegas-style shows. ⊠ *Cabazon off-ramp, I–10, 49500 Seminole Dr., Cabazon* ☎ *800/252–4499, 951/849-3080.*

Palm Springs is a golfer's paradise: the area is home to more than 125 courses.

Spa Resort Casino. The full casino experience: this resort holds 1,000 slot machines, blackjack tables, a high-limit room, four restaurants, two bars, and the Cascade Lounge for entertainment. ⊠ *401 E. Amado Rd., Palm Springs* ☎ *888/999–1995.*

GAY AND LESBIAN **Hunter's Video Bar.** Drawing a young crowd, this is a mainstay of the local clubbing scene. ⊠ *302 E. Arenas Rd., Palm Springs* ☎ *760/323–0700.*

Toucans. A friendly place with a tropical jungle in a rain-forest setting, Toucans serves festive drinks and has live entertainment and theme nights. ⊠ *2100 N. Palm Canyon Dr., Palm Springs* ☎ *760/416–7584.*

Dinah Shore Weekend–Palm Springs. In late March, when the world's finest female golfers hit the links for the Annual LPGA Kraft Nabisco Championship in Rancho Mirage, thousands of lesbians converge on Palm Springs for a four-day party popularly known as Dinah Shore Weekend–Palm Springs. ⇨ *Kraft Nabisco Championship in Rancho Mirage.* ☎ *888/923–4624* ⊕ *www.clubskirts.com.*

White Party. Held on Easter weekend, The White Party draws tens of thousands of gay men from around the country to the Palm Springs area for a round of parties and gala events. Promoter Jeffrey Sanker claims it's the biggest gay dance party in America. ⊕ *jeffreysanker.com.*

THE ARTS **Annenberg Theater.** Located at the Palm Springs Art Museum, this theater is the site of Broadway shows, opera, lectures, Sunday-afternoon chamber concerts, and other events. ⊠ *101 Museum Dr., Palm Springs* ☎ *760/325–4490* ⊕ *www.psmuseum.org.*

Palm Springs International Film Festival. In mid-January this film festival brings stars and more than 150 feature films from 25 countries, plus panel discussions, short films, and documentaries, to the Annenberg Theater area hotels, movie theaters, and other venues. ☎ *760/322–2930, 800/898–7256* ⊕ *www.psfilmfest.org.*

Historic Plaza Theatre. The Spanish-style Historic Plaza Theatre opened in 1936 with a glittering premiere of the MGM film *Camille.* In the '40s and '50s, it presented some of Hollywood's biggest stars, including Bob Hope and Bing Crosby. Home of the Fabulous Palm Springs Follies, it is favored by fans of old-time radio even in the off-season.

Fabulous Palm Springs Follies. The Historic Plaza Theatre plays host to this production, the hottest ticket in the desert, which mounts 10 weekly sell-out performances November through May. The vaudeville-style revue, about half of which focuses on mid-century nostalgia, stars extravagantly costumed, retired (but very fit) showgirls, singers, and dancers. Tickets are $50 to $92. ⊠ *Historic Plaza Theater, 128 S. Palm Canyon Dr., Palm Springs* ☎ *760/327–0225* ⊕ *www.palmspringsfollies. com* ⊠ *128 S. Palm Canyon Dr., Palm Springs* ☎ *760/327–0225.*

SPORTS AND THE OUTDOORS

BICYCLING Many hotels and resorts can make bicycles available for guest use.

Big Wheel Tours. Rent cruisers, performance road bikes, and mountain bikes from this agency in Palm Springs. They also offer road tours to La Quinta Loop, Joshua Tree National Park *(⇨ see Chapter 10),* and the San Andreas fault. Off-road tours are available, too. The company doesn't have a retail outlet but will pick up and deliver bikes to your hotel and supply you with area maps. ☎ *760/779–1837* ⊕ *www. bwbtours.com.*

Palm Springs Recreation Division. This organization can provide you with maps of city bike trails. ⊠ *401 S. Pavilion Way, Palm Springs* ☎ *760/323–8272* ⊘ *Weekdays 7:30–6.*

GOLF **Palm Springs Desert Resorts Convention and Visitors Bureau.** Palm Springs is host to more than 100 golf tournaments annually. Check the Web site for event listings. ⊕ *www.palmspringsusa.com.*

Affordable Palm Springs TeeTimes. This service can match golfers with courses and arrange tee times. If you know which course you want to play, you can book tee times online up to 60 days in advance. ⊕ *www. palmspringsteetimes.com.*

Indian Canyons Golf Resort. An 18-hole course designed by Casey O'Callaghan and Amy Alcott, this spot, at the base of the mountains, is operated by the Aqua Caliente tribe. ⊠ *1097 E. Murray Canyon Dr., Palm Springs* ☎ *760/327–6550* ⊕ *www.indiancanyonsgolf.com.*

Tahquitz Creek Palm Springs Golf Resort. Two 18-hole, par-72 courses and a 50-space driving range are on offer at this resort. Greens fees, including cart, run $55 to $89, depending on the course and day of the week. ⊠ *1885 Golf Club Dr., Palm Springs* ☎ *760/328–1005* ⊕ *www. tahquitzgolfresort.com.*

Tommy Jacobs' Bel Air Greens Country Club. You'll find a 9-hole executive course here. The greens fee is $20 ($12 for replay), walking, carts are $12. ⊠ *1001 S. El Cielo Rd., Palm Springs* ☎ *760/322–6062.*

SPAS **Spa Resort Casino.** Taking the waters at this resort is an indulgent pleasure. You can spend a full day enjoying a five-step, wet-and-dry treatment program that includes a mineral bath, steam, sauna, and eucalyptus inhalation. The program allows you to take fitness classes and use the gym and, for an extra charge, add massage or body treatments. During the week, the spa admission rate is $40 for a full day, less for hotel guests or if you combine it with a treatment; on weekends you cannot purchase a day pass without booking a treatment. ✉ *100 N. Indian Canyon Dr., Palm Springs* ☎ *760/778–1772* ⊕ *www.sparesortcasino.com.*

SHOPPING

North Palm Canyon Drive shopping district. The commercial core of Palm Springs, this shopping district covers the full gamut.

Villagefest. Sponsored by the City of Palm Springs, Villagefest fills the drive with street musicians, a farmers' market, and stalls with food, crafts, art, and antiques every Thursday evening. It's a great place for celebrity spotting. ✉ *Palm Canyon Dr., between Tahquitz Canyon Way and Baristo Rd., Palm Springs* ☎ *760/320–3781* ⊕ *www.villagefest.org* ✉ *Between Alejo and Ramon Rds., Palm Springs.*

Uptown Heritage Galleries & Antiques District. Extending north of the main shopping area, this district is a loose-knit collection of consignment and secondhand shops, galleries, and restaurants whose theme is decidedly retro. Many shops and galleries offer mid-century modern furniture and decorator items, and others carry consignment clothing and estate jewelry. ✉ *N. Palm Canyon Dr., between Amado Rd. and Tachevah Dr., Palm Springs* ☎ ⊕ *www.palmcanyondrive.org.*

Desert Hills Premium Outlets. About 20 mi west of Palm Springs at the Cabazon exit of I–10 lies this outlet center with more than 130 brand-name discount fashion shops, including J. Crew, Giorgio Armani, Gucci, and Prada. ✉ *48400 Seminole Rd., Cabazon* ☎ *951/849–6641* ⊕ *www.premiumoutlets.com.*

CATHEDRAL CITY

2 mi southeast of Palm Springs on Hwy. 111.

One of the fastest-growing communities in the desert, Cathedral City is more residential than tourist-oriented. However, the city has a number of good restaurants and entertainment venues with moderate prices.

GETTING HERE AND AROUND

Cathedral City lies due east of the Palm Springs International Airport. Much of the city is suburban/residential community with large and small malls everywhere. Main streets north and south are Landau and Date Palm; west to east are Ramon Rd., Dinah Shore, and Hwy. 111.

EXPLORING

Boomers Palm Springs. At this theme park you can play miniature golf, drive bumper boats, climb a rock wall, drive a go-kart, swing in the batting cages, test your skill in an arcade, and play video games. ✉ *67–700 E. Palm Canyon Dr.* ☎ *760/770–7522* ⊕ *www.boomerspark.com* 🎟 *$6–$8 per activity, $25 day passes* ☉ *Mon.–Thurs. noon–8, Fri. noon–10, Sat. 10–10, Sun. 10–8.*

Pickford Salon. A small museum inside the Mary Pickford Theater, this venue showcases the life of the famed actress. On display is a selection of personal items contributed by family members, including her 1976 Oscar for contributions to the film industry, a gown she wore in the 1927 film *Dorothy Vernon of Haddon Hall,* and dinnerware from Pickfair, Pickford's storied Beverly Hills mansion. One of the two biographical video presentations was produced by Mary herself. ⊠ *36-850 Pickfair St.* ☎ *760/328–7100* ✉ *Free* ☉ *Daily 10:30 am–midnight.*

WHERE TO EAT AND STAY

$$
CAFÉ
✕ **Cello's.** Open since 2010, this restaurant has earned raves from locals and critics. Tucked into a pair of storefronts in a strip mall, the cafe offers an exciting vibe, an updated classical menu, original art, thoughtful service, and an ultra-friendly owner, Bonnie Barley. Modern takes on old favorites include crab Napoleon and smoked trout appetizers, potato risotto, chicken Caprese, a lighter eggplant Parmesan, and voluptuous cioppino full of shellfish and thick marinara sauce. A community table with about eight chairs is the place to sit if you're dining alone or want to meet locals who are out for the evening. ⊠ *35-943 Date Palm Dr., Cathedral City* ☎ *760/328–5353* ✍ *Reservations essential* ☉ *no lunch.*

$$
ITALIAN
✕ **Trilussa.** Locals gather at this San Francisco–style storefront restaurant for delicious food, big drinks, and a friendly welcome. The congenial bar is busy during happy hour, after which diners drift to their nicely spaced tables indoors and out. The long menu changes daily, but staples include homemade pasta, risotto, veal, and fish. All come with an Italian accent. ⊠ *68718 Hwy. 111* ☎ *760/328–2300* ✍ *Reservations essential.*

¢
Quality Inn & Suites Date Palm. This chain motel is about as close as you can get to Rancho Mirage without paying sky-high prices. **Pros:** good value; barbecues for guest use; suites. **Cons:** highway noise; low light levels. ⊠ *69–151 E. Palm Canyon Dr.* ☎ *760/324–5939, 800/892–5085* ⊕ *www.choicehotels.com* ⌨ *69 rooms, 29 suites* ♿ *In-room: a/c, kitchen, Wi-Fi. In-hotel: pool, laundry facilities, parking* �‖ *Breakfast.*

DESERT HOT SPRINGS

9 mi north of Palm Springs on Gene Autry Trail.

Desert Hot Springs' famous hot mineral waters, thought by some to have curative powers, bubble up at temperatures of 90°F to 148°F and flow into the wells of more than 40 hotel spas.

GETTING HERE AND AROUND

Desert Hot Springs lies due north of Palm Springs. Take Gene Autry Trail north to I–10, where the street name changes to Palm. Continue north to Pierson Blvd., the town's center.

WHERE TO STAY

For expanded hotel reviews, visit Fodors.com.

$$$
The Spring. Designed for those who want to detox, lose weight, or take special treatments, this serious spa caters to guests seeking quiet and personal service. **Pros:** Exquisite quiet; personal pampering; multinational clientele. **Cons:** far from everything; dinner not available;

adults only. ⊠ *12699 Reposo Way* ☎ *760/251–6700, 877/200–2110* ⊕ *www.the-spring.com* ↪ *12 rooms* ⚬ *In-room: a/c, kitchen, no TV, Wi-Fi. In-hotel: pool, spa, some age restrictions.*

RANCHO MIRAGE

4 mi southeast of Cathedral City on Hwy. 111.

Much of the scenery in exclusive Rancho Mirage is concealed behind the walls of gated communities and country clubs. The rich and famous live in estates and patronize elegant resorts and expensive restaurants. The city's golf courses host many high-profile tournaments. When the excesses of the luxe life become too much, the area's residents can check themselves into the Betty Ford Center, the famous drug-and-alcohol rehab center.

You can find some of the swankiest resorts in the desert here—plus great golf, and plenty of peace and quiet.

GETTING HERE AND AROUND

Due east of Cathedral City, Rancho Mirage stretches between Ramon Rd. on the north to the hills south of Hwy. 111. West and east it is between Da Vall and Monterey. Major cross streets are Frank Sinatra and Country Club. Most of the shopping and dining spots are on Hwy. 111.

EXPLORING

Children's Discovery Museum of the Desert. With instructive hands-on exhibits, this museum contains a miniature rock-climbing area, a magnetic sculpture wall, make-it-and-take-it-apart projects, a rope maze, and an area for toddlers. Kids can paint a VW Bug, work as chefs in the museum's pizza parlor, and build pies out of arts and crafts supplies. New exhibits, scheduled to open in fall 2011, will include a race track for which kids can assemble their own cars, work on brain teasers, and balance acts. ⊠ *71–701 Gerald Ford Dr.* ☎ *760/321–0602* ⊕ *www. cdmod.org* 🖾 *$8* ⊙ *Jan.–Apr., daily 10–5; May–Dec., Tues.–Sun. 10–5.*

WHERE TO EAT AND STAY

$$
MEXICAN

✕ **Las Casuelas Nuevas.** Hundreds of artifacts from Guadalajara, Mexico, lend festive charm to this casual restaurant, which has an expansive garden patio. Tamales and shellfish dishes are among the specialties. A special tequila menu lists dozens of aged and reserve selections, served by the shot or incorporated into one of the eatery's margaritas. There's live entertainment nightly. ⊠ *70-050 Hwy. 111* ☎ *760/328–8844* ⊕ *www. lascasuelasnuevas.com.*

$

🏨 **Agua Caliente Casino, Resort & Spa.** Done in Las Vegas style, the Agua Caliente casino is in the lobby, but once you get into the spacious, beautifully appointed rooms of the resort, all of the cacophony at the entrance is forgotten. **Pros:** gorgeous; access to high rollers room offered for $25; value priced. **Cons:** casino ambience; not appropriate for kids. ⊠ *32-250 Bob Hope Dr.* ☎ *888/999–1995* ⊕ *www.hotwatercasino.com* ↪ *340 rooms, 26 suites* ⚬ *In-room: a/c, Wi-Fi. In-hotel: restaurant, bar, pool, gym, spa, business center, parking, some pets allowed.*

9

$$$ 🏨 **Rancho Las Palmas Resort & Spa.** The most family-friendly resort in the desert, this venue completed a $35-million renovation that upgraded the entire 240-acre property, freshened rooms and public areas, and added Splashtopia, a huge water play-zone. **Pros:** family-friendly; trails for hiking and jogging; nightly entertainment. **Cons:** second-floor rooms accessed by very steep stairs; golf course surrounds rooms; resort hosts conventions. ⊠ *41-000 Bob Hope Dr.* ☎ *760/568-2727, 866/423-1195* ⊕ *www.rancholaspalmas.com* 🛏 *422 rooms, 22 suites* ⚬ *In-room: a/c, Internet, Wi-Fi. In-hotel: restaurant, bar, golf course, pool, tennis court, gym, spa, children's programs, business center, parking, some pets allowed.*

$$$$ 🏨 **Westin Mission Hills Resort and Spa.** A sprawling resort on 360 acres, the Westin is surrounded by fairways, putting greens, and a collection of time-share accommodations. **Pros:** gorgeous grounds; first-class golf facilities; excellent for families. **Cons:** lots of dogs; rooms are spread out. ⊠ *71333 Dinah Shore Dr.* ☎ *760/328-5955, 800/544-0287* ⊕ *www.westin.com* 🛏 *512 rooms, 40 suites* ⚬ *In-room: a/c, Internet, Wi-Fi. In-hotel: restaurant, bar, golf course, pool, tennis court, gym, spa, children's programs, parking, some pets allowed.*

NIGHTLIFE

Agua Caliente Casino. The elegant and surprisingly quiet Agua Caliente Casino contains 1,400 slot machines, 39 table games, an 18-table poker room, a high-limit room, and a no-smoking area, and six restaurants. The Show, the resort's concert theater, features such headliners as Matchbox Twenty, Martina McBride, Tony Bennett, John Fogerty, Ringo Starr, and Jay Leno, as well as live sporting events. ⊠ *32-250 Bob Hope Dr.* ☎ *760/321-2000.*

SPORTS AND THE OUTDOORS

Kraft Nabisco Championship. The best female golfers in the world compete in this championship held in late March. ⊠ *Mission Hills Country Club* ☎ *760/324-4546* ⊕ *www.kncgolf.com.*

★ **Westin Mission Hills Resort Golf Club.** Of the two golf courses located here, the 18-hole, par-70 Pete Dye course is especially noteworthy. The club is a member of the Troon Golf Institute, and has several teaching facilities, including the Westin Mission Hills Resort Golf Academy and the *Golf Digest* Golf School. Greens fees are $165 during peak season, including a cart; off-season is $85. ⊠ *71-501 Dinah Shore Dr.* ☎ *760/328-3198* ⊕ *www.westinmissionhillsgolf.com.*

SHOPPING

River at Rancho Mirage. A shopping-dining-entertainment complex, the River at Rancho Mirage has a collection of 20 high-end shops. Bang & Olufsen, Borders Books & Music, Cohiba Cigar Lounge, Tulip Hill Winery tasting room, and other shops front a faux river with cascading waterfalls. The complex includes a 12-screen cinema, an outdoor amphitheater, and eight restaurants, including Flemings Prime Steakhouse, Babe's Bar-B-Que and Brewery, and P.F. Chang's. ⊠ *71-800 Hwy. 111* ☎ *760/341-2711.*

PALM DESERT

2 mi southeast of Rancho Mirage on Hwy. 111.

Palm Desert is a thriving retail and business community, with some of the desert's most popular restaurants, private and public golf courses, and premium shopping.

GETTING HERE AND AROUND

Palm Desert stretches from north of I–10 to the hills south of Hwy. 111, where you'll find the Living Desert Zoo. West–east cross streets north to south are Frank Sinatra, Country Club (lined on both sides with gated golf club communities), and Fred Waring. Monterey Ave. marks the western boundary and Washington St. is the eastern limit.

EXPLORING

★ **El Paseo.** West of and parallel to Highway 111, this mile-long Mediterranean-style avenue is lined with fountains and courtyards, French and Italian fashion boutiques, shoe salons, jewelry stores, children's shops, 23 restaurants, and nearly 20 art galleries. The pretty strip is a pleasant place to stroll, window-shop, people-watch, and exercise your credit cards.

Palm Desert Golf Cart Parade. Each October, this parade launches the "season" with a procession of 80 golf carts decked out as floats buzzing up and down El Paseo. ☎ *760/346–6111* ⊕ *www.golfcartparade. com* ✉ *Between Monterey and Portola Aves.* ☎ *877/735–7273* ⊕ *www. elpaseo.com.*

★ **Living Desert.** Come eyeball-to-eyeball with wolves, coyotes, mountain lions, cheetahs, bighorn sheep, golden eagles, warthogs, and owls at the Living Desert. Easy to challenging scenic trails traverse 1,200 acres of desert preserve populated with plants of the Mojave, Colorado, and Sonoran deserts in 11 habitats. But in recent years, the park has expanded its vision include Africa and a collection of stand-alone exhibits. At the 3-acre African WaTuTu village, there's a traditional marketplace as well as camels, leopards, hyenas, and other African animals. Children can pet African domestic animals, including goats and guinea fowl, in a "petting kraal." Gecko Gulch is a children's playground with crawl-through underground tunnels, climb-on snake sculptures, a carousel, and a Discovery Center that holds ancient Pleistocene animal bones. You can walk among butterflies and hummingbirds within a small enclosure. Recently added is a cool model train that travels through many of California's historic towns. Yet another exhibit demonstrates the path of the San Andreas Fault across the Coachella Valley. The park holds a snack shop and gift shop. ■TIP→ A garden center sells native desert flora, much of which is unavailable elsewhere. ✉ *47-900 Portola Ave.* ☎ *760/346–5694* ⊕ *www.livingdesert.org* ✐ *$14.25* ☽ *Mid-June–Aug., daily 8–1:30; Sept.–mid-June, daily 9–5.*

Santa Rosa and San Jacinto Mountains National Monument. Administered by the Bureau of Land Management, this monument protects Peninsula bighorn sheep and other wildlife on 280,000 acres of desert habitat. Stop by the visitor center—staffed by knowledgeable volunteers—for an introduction to the site and information about the natural history

9

of the desert. A landscaped garden displays native plants and frames a sweeping view. Staff can recommend a variety of hiking trails that show off the beauties of the desert. Free guided hikes are offered on Tuesdays and Saturdays. ⊠ *51-500 Hwy. 74* ☎ *760/862–9984* ⊕ *www. ca.blm.gov/palmsprings* 🎫 *Free* ⊙ *Daily 9–4.*

WHERE TO EAT AND STAY

$$$$
FRENCH
✕ **Cuistot.** The creation of chef-owner Bernard Dervieux, Cuistot is a big, bright, airy reproduction of a rustic French farmhouse on El Paseo's west end. Service is both inside and outside on a tree-shaded patio. The restaurant attracts a moneyed clientele, who savor classic Lyonnaise cuisine. Roasted rack of lamb, quail stuffed with sweetbreads, roasted rabbit with Dijon sauce, and made to order soufflés are listed on the menu. If you want a small taste of several items, choose the Cuistot Lunch Box, four small plates on a single platter. ⊠ *72-595 El Paseo* ☎ *760/340–1000* ⊕ *www. cuistotrestaurant.com* 🍴 *Reservations essential* ⊙ *Closed Mon. and July and Aug. No lunch Sun.*

$$$$
SEAFOOD
✕ **Pacifica Seafood.** Sublime seafood, rooftop dining, and reduced-price sunset dinners draw locals to this busy restaurant tucked into a second floor corner of the Gardens of El Paseo. Seafood that shines in such dishes as butter poached Maine lobster tail, grilled Pacific swordfish, and barbecued sugar-spiced salmon arrives daily from San Diego; the menu also includes a small selection of chicken, steaks, and entree salads. Preparations feature sauces such as orange-cumin glaze, Szechuan peppercorn butter, and green curry-coconut. The restaurant bar also boasts a 130-bottle collection of vodka. Servers are pleasant and knowledgeable. ■ TIP→ Arrive between 3 and 5:30 to select from a lower priced sunset menu. ⊠ *73505 El Paseo* ☎ *760/674–8666* ⊕ *www. pacificaseafoodrestaurant.com* 🍴 *Reservations essential.*

$$$
♨
🏨 **Desert Springs J. W. Marriott Resort and Spa.** With a dramatic U-shape design, this sprawling convention-oriented hotel is set on 450 landscaped acres. **Pros:** gondola rides to restaurants; caters to families; lobby bar is a popular watering hole. **Cons:** crowded in season; rooms and facilities are spread out; business traveler vibe. ⊠ *74-855 Country Club Dr.* ☎ *760/341–2211, 800/331–3112* ⊕ *www.desertspringsresort. com* 🛏 *833 rooms, 51 suites* ♿ *In-room: a/c, Internet, Wi-Fi. In-hotel: restaurant, bar, golf course, pool, tennis court, gym, spa, children's programs, parking.*

THE ARTS

McCallum Theatre. The principal cultural venue in the desert, this theater stages a variety of productions fall through spring. *Fiddler on the Roof* has played here; Lorna Luft and Michael Feinstein performed, and the Joffrey Ballet pirouetted across its stage. ⊠ *73-000 Fred Waring Dr.* ☎ *760/340–2787* ⊕ *www.mccallumtheatre.com.*

GREEN PALM DESERT

The City of Palm Desert has a plan to reduce energy consumption by 30% by 2012. The most ambitious plan of its kind in California, it involves incentives to install efficient pool pumps, air-conditioners, refrigeration, and lighting. The city has also banned drive-through restaurants and made golf carts legal on city streets.

SPORTS AND THE OUTDOORS

BALLOONING **Fantasy Balloon Flights.** Operating sunrise excursions over the southern end of the Coachella Valley, Fantasy Balloon offers flights ($185 per person) that run from an hour to an hour and a half, followed by a traditional Champagne toast. ✉ *74-181 Parosella St.* ☎ *760/568–0997* ⊕ *www.fantasyballoonflights.com.*

BICYCLING **Big Wheel Bike Tours.** Palm Desert-based Big Wheel delivers rental mountain, three-speed, and tandem bikes to area hotels. The company also conducts full- and half-day escorted on- and off-road bike tours throughout the area, starting at about $125 per person. ☎ *760/779–1837* ⊕ *www.bwbtours.com.*

GOLF **Desert Willow Golf Resort.** Praised for its environmentally smart design, this golf resort features pesticide-free and water-thrifty turf grasses. The clubhouse holds a display of contemporary art, including an original blown glass chandelier by Dale Chihuly. A public course, managed by the City of Palm Desert, has two challenging 18-hole links plus a golf academy. The greens fee is $150–180, including cart. ✉ *38-500 Portola Ave.* ☎ *760/346–7060* ⊕ *www.desertwillow.com.*

SHOPPING

Gardens on El Paseo. In addition to El Paseo's other shopping treasures, check out Gardens on El Paseo, a shopping center anchored by Saks Fifth Avenue and populated by such mainstream retailers as Brooks Brothers, Williams-Sonoma, Tommy Bahama's Emporium, the Apple Store, and Pacifica Seafood Restaurant. ✉ *El Paseo, at San Pablo Ave.* ☎ *760/862–1990* ⊕ *www.thegardensonelpaseo.com.*

INDIAN WELLS

5 mi east of Palm Desert on Hwy. 111.

For the most part a quiet residential community, Indian Wells is the site of golf and tennis tournaments throughout the year, including the BNP Paribus Open tennis tournament. The city has three hotels that share access to city-owned championship golf and tennis facilities.

GETTING HERE AND AROUND

Indian Wells lies between Palm Desert and La Quinta with most of its hotels, restaurants, and shopping set back from Hwy. 111. Private country clubs and gated residential communities are tucked away on back roads.

WHERE TO STAY

For expanded hotel reviews, visit Fodors.com.

$$$ 🏨 **Hyatt Grand Champions Resort.** On 45 acres, this stark-white resort is one of the grandest in the desert. **Pros:** spacious rooms; excellent business services; butler service in some rooms. **Cons:** big and impersonal; spread out over many acres; noisy public areas. ✉ *44-600 Indian Wells La.* ☎ *760/341–1000, 800/552–4386* ⊕ *www.grandchampions.hyatt. com* ⇥ *454 rooms, 26 suites, 40 villas* ⚭ *In-room: a/c, Wi-Fi. In-hotel: restaurant, bar, golf course, pool, tennis court, gym, spa, children's programs, parking.*

9

$$$ ⚐ **Miramonte Resort & Spa.** A warm
★ bit of Tuscany against a backdrop of
the Santa Rosa Mountains charac-
terizes the smallest, most intimate,
and most opulent of the Indian Wells
hotels. **Pros:** romantic intimacy;
gorgeous gardens; discreet service.
Cons: adult-oriented; limited resort
facilities on-site. ✉ *45-000 Indian
Wells La.* ☎ *760/341–2200* ⊕ *www.
miramonteresort.com* ⤳ *215 rooms*

> **FROM DATES TO DOLLARS**
>
> Originally several communities
> of date farmers, Indian Wells
> residents now have six-figure
> annual incomes per family, making
> this 15-square-mi city one of the
> wealthiest in the country.

⚒ *In-room: a/c, Wi-Fi. In-hotel: restaurant, bar, golf course, pool, tennis
court, gym, spa, parking, some pets allowed.*

$$$ ⚐ **Renaissance Esmeralda Resort and Spa.** The centerpiece of this luxuri-
☾ ous resort is an eight-story atrium lobby, which most rooms open onto.
Pros: balcony views; adjacent to golf-tennis complex; free bicycles available. **Cons:** higher noise level in rooms surrounding pool; somewhat
impersonal ambience. ✉ *44-400 Indian Wells La.* ☎ *760/773–4444,
800/214–5540* ⊕ *www.renaissanceesmeralda.com* ⤳ *538 rooms, 22
suites* ⚒ *In-room: a/c, Internet, Wi-Fi. In-hotel: restaurant, bar, golf
course, pool, tennis court, gym, spa, children's programs, parking.*

SPORTS AND THE OUTDOORS

GOLF **Golf Resort at Indian Wells.** Adjacent to the Hyatt Grand Champions
Resort, the municipal Indian Wells Golf Resort was renovated and
enlarged in 2006 to the 7,050-yard Celebrity Course designed by Clive
Clark and the 7,376-yard Players Course designed by John Fought.
Both courses replaced older, smaller ones; they consistently rank among
the to 25 in California by *Golf Magazine*. The resort recently opened
the IW Club, which holds a restaurant, jazz cafe, and Callaway Performance Center where you can get fitted with quality golf clubs. You can
also seek out lessons at the golf school, or receive private instruction.
Greens fees range from $75 to $180 depending upon season. Since this
is a public facility, it pays to reserve well in advance, up to 60 days.
✉ *44-500 Indian Wells La.* ☎ *760/346–4653.*

TENNIS **BNP Paribas Open.** Drawing 200 of the world's top players, this tournament takes place at Indian Wells Tennis Garden for two weeks in
March. A variety of ticket plans is available, with some packages including stays at the adjoining hotels: Hyatt Grand Champions and Renaissance Esmerelda. ☎ *800/999–1585 for tickets* ⊕ *www.bnpparibasopen.
org* ⌨ *$40 per day.*

LA QUINTA

4 mi south of Indian Wells via Washington St.

The desert became a Hollywood hideout in the 1920s, when La Quinta
Hotel (now La Quinta Resort) opened, introducing the Coachella Valley's first golf course. Old Town La Quinta is a popular attraction, the
complex holds dining spots, shops, and galleries.

GETTING HERE AND AROUND

Most of La Quinta lies south of Hwy. 111. The main drag through town is Washington St., but you'll find miles of shopping malls by driving south on Hwy. 111.

WHERE TO EAT AND STAY

$$$$ ✕ **Arnold Palmer's.** From the photos

AMERICAN   on the walls to the trophy-filled display cases to the putting green for diners awaiting a table, Arnie's image fills this restaurant. It's a big, clubby place where families gather for birthdays and Sunday dinners, and the service is attentive and knowledgeable. Don't eat too many of the addictive house-made potato chips with blue cheese sauce before the main attraction arrives: barbecued pork ribs, filet with béarnaise sauce, certified Angus beef, or seared scallops. And save room for the splendid desserts, which range from Coachella date bread pudding to grasshopper ice-cream sandwiches. Arnie's Pub offers a more limited menu of burgers, fish and chips, and shrimp tacos. Chef Brett Maddock has amassed an impressive collection of wine that he displays in a new wine room where he presides over a Chef's Table occasionally. There's entertainment most nights. ✉ *78-164 Ave. 52* ☎ *760/771–4653* ⊕ *www.arnoldpalmersrestaurant. com* ⚠ *Reservations essential.*

$$$ ✕ **Hog's Breath Inn La Quinta.** Clint Eastwood watches over this replica

AMERICAN   of his Hog's Breath restaurant in Carmel; his presence is felt in the larger-than-life photos that fill the walls of its bright dining room. The menu lists a large selection of American comfort food ranging from Guinness-braised beef ribs to sole stuffed with crab and shrimp to butternut squash ravioli. The signature dish is the Dirty Harry dinner: chopped sirloin with capers, garlic mashed potatoes, red cabbage with horseradish mushroom sauce. ✉ *78-065 Main St.* ☎ *760/564–5556, 866/464–7888.*

$$$$ ☷ **La Quinta Resort and Club.** Opened in 1926 (and now a member of the Waldorf-Astoria Collection), the desert's oldest resort is a lush green oasis set on 45 acres. **Pros:** individual swimming pools; gorgeous gardens; best golf courses in the desert. **Cons:** a party atmosphere sometimes prevails; spotty housekeeping/maintenance. ✉ *49-499 Eisenhower Dr.* ☎ *760/564–4111, 800/598–3828* ⊕ *www.laquintaresort.com* ⤶ *562 rooms, 24 suites, 210 villas* ♿ *In-room: a/c, Internet, Wi-Fi. In-hotel: restaurant, bar, golf course, pool, tennis court, gym, spa, parking, some pets allowed.*

SPORTS AND THE OUTDOORS

★   **PGA West.** A world-class golf destination where Phil Nickelson and Jack Nicklaus play, this venue operates three 18-hole, par-72 championship courses and provides instruction and golf clinics. Greens fees (which

---

THE FIRST CELEBRITY HOTEL

Frank Capra probably started the trend when he booked a casita at the then-new, very remote La Quinta Hotel (now Resort) to write the script for the movie *It Happened One Night.* The movie went on to earn an Academy Award, and Capra continued to book that room whenever he had some writing to do. A long line of Hollywood stars followed Capra's example over the years; the current list includes Oprah Winfrey, Adam Sandler, and Christina Aguilera.

9

include a mandatory cart) range from $50 on weekdays in summer to $235 on weekends in February and March. Bookings are accepted 30 days in advance, but prices are lower when you book close to the date you need. ⊠ *49-499 Eisenhower Dr.* ☎ *760/564–5729 for tee times* ⊕ *www.pgawest.com.*

INDIO

5 mi east of Indian Wells on Hwy. 111.

Indio is the home of the date shake, which is exactly what it sounds like: a delicious, extremely thick milk shake made with dates. The city and surrounding countryside generate 95% of the dates grown and harvested in the United States. If you take a hot-air balloon ride, you will likely drift over the tops of date palm trees.

GETTING HERE AND AROUND

Indio is east of Indian Wells and north of La Quinta. Hwy. 111 runs right through it and I–10 skirts it to the north.

EXPLORING

Coachella Valley History Museum. Displays at this museum, in a former farmhouse, explain how dates are harvested and how the desert is irrigated for date farming. Another part of the complex, the Date History Museum illustrates how the date industry was brought to the desert in the early 1900s. On the grounds you'll find a restored 1909 schoolhouse and displays depicting Native American and pioneer life. ⊠ *82-616 Miles Ave.* ☎ *760/342–6651* ⊕ *www.coachellavalleymuseum.org* 🖃 *$5* ⊙ *Oct.–May, Thurs.–Sat. 10–4, Sun. 1–4.*

National Date Festival and Riverside County Fair. Indio celebrates its raison d'être each February at this festival and county fair. The midmonth festivities include an Arabian Nights pageant, camel and ostrich races, exhibits of local dates, plus monster truck shows, demolition derby, a nightly musical pageant and a rodeo. Admission includes camel rides. ⊠ *Riverside County Fairgrounds, 46-350 Arabia St.* ☎ *800/811–3247* ⊕ *www.datefest.org* 🖃 *$8.*

Shields Date Gardens and Cafe. You can sample, select, and take home some of Shields' large collection of locally grown dates. Ten varieties are available including the giant super sweet medjools. Specialty date products such as date crystals, stuffed dates, and confections are also offered. The shop also operates the Date Garden Cafe, open daily for breakfast and lunch, where you can try an iconic date shake, some date pancakes, or date tamales. ⊠ *80225 Hwy. 111, Indio* ☎ *760/347–0996* ⊕ *www.shieldsdategardens.com* ⊙ *store 9–5, café 8–2.*

WHERE TO EAT AND STAY

$$
ITALIAN
✕ **Ciro's Ristorante and Pizzeria.** Serving pizza and pasta since the 1970s, this popular casual restaurant has a few unusual pies on the menu, including cashew with three cheeses. The decor is classic pizza joint, with checked tablecloths and bentwood chairs. Daily pasta specials vary but might include red- or white-clam sauce or scallops with parsley and red wine. ⊠ *81-963 Hwy. 111* ☎ *760/347–6503* ⊕ *www.cirospasta.com* ⊙ *No lunch Sun.*

$$$ ✕ **Jackalope Ranch.** It's worth the
AMERICAN drive to Indio to sample flavors of
the Old West here, 21st-century
style. Inside a rambling 21,000-ft
building holding a clutch of indoor/
outdoor dining spaces, you may be
seated near an open kitchen, a bar,
fountains, fireplaces, or waterworks
(both inside and out). Jackalope
can be a busy, noisy place; ask for a
quiet corner if that's your pleasure.
The large menu roams the west, fea-
turing grilled and barbecued items
of all sorts, spicy and savory sauces,
flavorful vegetables, and sumptu-
ous desserts. Locals like the place,
especially the bar; but some reviews
complain that the quality of the food doesn't match the setting. ✉ *80400
Hwy. 111, Indio* ☎ *760/342–1999* ⊕ *www.thejackaloperanch.com.*

ROCKIN' AT COACHELLA

The Coachella Valley Music and
Arts Festival, one of the biggest
parties in SoCal, draws hundreds
of thousands of rock music fans
to Indio for three days of live con-
certs and dancing each April. Hun-
dreds of bands show up, including
headliners such as Jack Johnson,
the Raconteurs, Portishead, Roger
Waters, and My Morning Jacket.
Everybody camps at the polo
grounds. Visit ⊕ *www.coachella.
com* for details and tickets.

$$ ▦ **Fantasy Springs Resort Casino.** Operated by the Cabazon Band of
⟳ Mission Indians, this family-oriented resort casino stands out in the
Coachella Valley, affording mountain views from most rooms and the
rooftop wine bar. **Pros:** headliner entertainment; great views from the
rooftop bar; bowling alley. **Cons:** in the middle of nowhere; average staff
service. ✉ *84-245 Indio Springs Pkwy.* ☎ *760/342–5000, 800/827–2946*
⊕ *www.fantasyspringsresort.com* ⇄ *240 rooms, 11 suites* ⚅ *In-room:
a/c, Wi-Fi. In-hotel: restaurant, bar, golf course, pool, gym, parking.*

**EN
ROUTE** **Coachella Valley Preserve.** For a glimpse of how the desert appeared
before development, head northeast from Palm Springs to this preserve. It has a system of sand dunes and several palm oases that were
formed because the San Andreas Fault lines here allow water flowing
underground to rise to the surface. A mile-long walk along Thousand
Palms Oasis reveals pools supporting the tiny endangered desert pupfish and more than 183 bird species. The preserve has a visitor center,
nature and equestrian trails, restrooms, and picnic facilities. Note that
it is exceptionally hot in summer.

Covered Wagon Tours. Covered Wagon Tours can take you on a
two- or four-hour tour of the Coachella Valley Preserve via mule-
drawn covered wagon October through May. Schedule your visit with
or without a cookout and entertainment at the end of the journey.
✉ *East end of Ramon Rd.* ☎ *760/347–2161, 800/367–2161* ⊕ *www.
coveredwagontours.com* ✉ *29200 Thousand Palms Canyon Rd.*
☎ *760/343–2733* ⊕ *www.coachellapreserve.org* ✉ *Free* ☾ *Visitor Center daily 8–4.*

9

ALONG TWENTYNINE PALMS HIGHWAY

Designated a California Scenic Highway, the Twentynine Palms Highway not only connects two of the three entrances to Joshua Tree National Park, it also offers a gorgeous view of the High Desert, especially in winter and spring when you may be driving beneath snow-capped peaks or through a field of wildflowers. Park entrances are located at Joshua Tree and Twentynine Palms. Yucca Valley and Twentynine Palms have lodging, dining options, and other services.

YUCCA VALLEY

30 mi northeast of Palm Springs on Hwy. 62, Twentynine Palms Hwy.

One of the fastest-growing cities in the high desert, Yucca Valley is emerging as a bedroom community for people who work as far away as Ontario, 85 mi to the west. In this sprawling suburb you can shop for necessities, get your car serviced, and chow down at the fast-food outlets.

GETTING HERE AND AROUND

The drive to Yucca Valley and beyond on Hwy. 62/Twentynine Palms Hwy. is a California designated scenic drive. From the west, it starts at the intersection of Hwy. 62, passes through the Painted Hills and drops down into a valley. The first town you come to is Yucca Valley, where there are accommodations along both sides of the highway. Take Pioneertown Rd. north to the Old West outpost.

EXPLORING

Hi-Desert Nature Museum. Containing creatures that make their homes in Joshua Tree National Park *(⇨ see Chapter 10)*, this nature museum has a small live-animal display that includes scorpions, snakes, ground squirrels, and chuckwallas (a type of lizard). You'll also find a collection of rocks, minerals, and fossils from the Paleozoic era, a collection of Native American artifacts, and a children's room. ⊠ *57-116 Twentynine Palms Hwy.* ☎ *760/369-7212* ⊕ *www.highdesertnaturemuseum. org* ⊠ *Free* ☉ *Tues.–Sun. 10–5.*

Pioneertown. In 1946 Roy Rogers, Gene Autry, the Sons of the Pioneers (the music group for whom the town is named), and Russ Hayden built Pioneertown, an 1880s-style Wild West movie set complete with hitching posts, saloon, and an OK Corral. Today 250 people call the place home, even as film crews continue shooting. You can stroll past wooden and adobe storefronts and feel like you're back in the Old West. The owners of Pappy & Harriet's have an outdoor concert venue for about 500 people where they present popular bands and singers. Gunfights are staged April through October, weekends at 2:30. ⊠ *Pioneertown Rd., 4 mi north of Yucca Valley* ⊕ *www.pioneertown.com.*

WHERE TO EAT AND STAY

$$

AMERICAN

✕ **Pappy & Harriet's Pioneertown Palace.** Smack in the middle of a Western-movie-set town is this Western-movie-set saloon where you can have dinner, dance to live country-and-western music, or just relax with a drink at the bar. There's no cover charge for most bands. The food ranges from Tex-Mex to Santa Maria barbecue to steak and burgers—no surprises but plenty of fun. ■TIP➔ Pappy & Harriet's may be in the middle of nowhere, but you'll need reservations for dinner on weekends. ✉ *53688 Pioneertown Rd., Pioneertown* ☎ *760/365–5956* ⊕ *www.pappyandharriets. com* ⚍ *Reservations essential* ⊗ *Closed Tues. and Wed.*

¢ ⌂ **Best Western Yucca Valley Hotel & Suites.** Opened in 2008, this hotel is a welcome addition to the slim pickings near Joshua Tree National Park (⇨ *see Chapter 10)*. **Pros:** convenient to Joshua Tree NP; pleasant lounge. **Cons:** location on busy highway; limited service. ✉ *56525 Twentynine Palms Hwy.* ☎ *760/365–3555* ⊕ *www.bestwestern.com* ⇥ *95 rooms* ⚭ *In-room: a/c, safe, kitchen, Wi-Fi. In-hotel: pool, gym, laundry facilities, business center, parking* ⦙⊙⦙ *Breakfast.*

TWENTYNINE PALMS

24 mi east of Yucca Valley on Hwy. 62, Twentynine Palms Hwy.

The main gateway town to Joshua Tree National Park (⇨ *see Chapter 10)*, Twentynine Palms is also the location of the U.S. Marine Air Ground Task Force Training Center. You can find services, supplies, and limited lodgings in town.

GETTING HERE AND AROUND

If you follow Hwy. 62 east for about 24 mi, you'll reach Twentynine Palms, southern gateway to Joshua Tree National Park. The park fills the hills and mountains to the south and east; the entrance here is by Utah Trail. Most of the businesses here center around Hwy. 62 and Utah Trail.

ESSENTIALS

Visitor Information Twentynine Palms Chamber of Commerce and Visitor Center ✉ 73484 Twentynine Palms Hwy. ☎ 760/367–3445 ⊕ www.visit29.org.

EXPLORING

Oasis of Murals. The history and current life of Twentynine Palms is depicted in this collection of 20 murals painted on the sides of buildings. If you drive around town, you can't miss the murals, but you can also pick up a free map from the Twentynine Palms Chamber of Commerce.

29 Palms Art Gallery. This gallery features work by local painters, sculptors, and jewelry makers who find inspiration in the desert landscape. ✉ *74055 Cottonwood Dr.* ☎ *760/367–7819* ⊕ *www.29palmsartgallery. com* ⊗ *Wed.–Sun. noon–3.*

WHERE TO STAY

For expanded reviews, visit Fodors.com.

\$\$ ⌂ **29 Palms Inn.** The funky 29 Palms is the closest lodging to the entrance to Joshua Tree National Park (⇨ *see Chapter 10)*. **Pros:** gracious hospitality; exceptional bird-watching; popular with artists. **Cons:** rustic accommodations; limited amenities. ✉ *73-950 Inn Ave.* ☎ *760/367–3505* ⊕ *www.29palmsinn.com* ⇥ *18 rooms, 5 suites* ⚭ *In-room: a/c. In-hotel: restaurant, pool, parking, some pets allowed* ⦙⊙⦙ *Breakfast.*

\$\$ ⌂ **Roughley Manor.** To the wealthy pioneer who erected the stone man-
★ sion now occupied by this B&B, expense was no object, which is evident in the 50-foot-long planked maple floor in great room, the intricate carpentry on the walls, and the huge stone fireplaces that warm the house

on the rare cold night. **Pros:** elegant rooms and public spaces; good star-gazing in the gazebo; great horned owls on property. **Cons:** somewhat isolated location; three-story main building doesn't have an elevator. ⊠ *74-744 Joe Davis Rd.* ☎ *760/367–3238* ⊕ *www.roughleymanor.com* ↴ *2 suites, 7 cottages* ⚲ *In-room: a/c, kitchen. In-hotel: pool, some pets allowed* ⊺⊙⧵ *Breakfast.*

ANZA-BORREGO DESERT

Largely uninhabited, the Anza-Borrego Desert is popular with those who love solitude, silence, space, starry nights, light, and sweeping mountain vistas. The desert lies south of the Palm Springs area, stretching along the western shore of the Salton Sea down toward Interstate 8 along the Mexican border. Isolated from the rest of California by mile-high mountains to the north and west, most of this desert falls within the borders of Anza-Borrego Desert State Park, which at more than 600,000 acres is the largest state park in the contiguous United States. This is a place where you can escape the cares of the human world.

For thousands of years Native Americans of the Cahuilla and Kumeyaay people inhabited this area, spending their winters on the warm desert floor and their summers in the mountains. The first Europeans—a party led by Spanish explorer Juan Baptiste de Anza—crossed this desert in 1776. Anza, for whom the desert is named, made the trip through here twice. Roadside signs along highways 86, 78, and S2 mark the route of the Anza expedition, which spent Christmas Eve 1776 in what is now Anza-Borrego Desert State Park. Seventy-five years later thousands of immigrants on their way to the goldfields up north crossed the desert on the Southern Immigrant Trail, remnants of which remain along Highway S2. Permanent settlers arrived early in the 20th century, and by the 1930s the first adobe resort cottage had been built.

BORREGO SPRINGS

59 mi south of Indio via Hwys. 86 and S22.

The permanent population of Borrego Springs, set squarely in the middle of Anza-Borrego Desert State Park, hovers around 2,500. Long a quiet town, it's emerging as a laid-back destination for desert lovers. September through June, when temperatures stay in the 80s and 90s, you can engage in outdoor activities such as hiking, nature study, golf, tennis, horseback riding, and mountain biking. If winter rains cooperate, Borrego Springs puts on some of the best wildflower displays in the low desert. In some years the desert floor is carpeted with color: yellow dandelions and sunflowers, pink primrose, purple sand verbena, and blue wild heliotrope. The bloom generally runs from late February through April. For current information on wildflowers around Borrego Springs, call Anza-Borrego Desert State Park's wildflower hotline (☎ *760/767–4684*).

GETTING HERE AND AROUND

You can reach the Anza Borrego Desert from the Palm Springs area by taking the Hwy. 86 exit from I–10, south of Indio. Hwy. 86, mostly not freeway, passes through Coachella and along the western shore of the Salton Sea. Turn west on Hwy. S22 at Salton City and follow it to Peg Leg Rd., where you turn south until you reach Palm Canyon Dr. Turn west and the road leads to the center of Borrego Springs, Christmas Circle, where most major roads come together. Well-signed roads radiating from the circle will take you to the most popular sites in the park. If you are coming from the San Diego area, you'll need to drive east on I–8 to the Cuyamaca Mountains, exit at Hwy. 79 and enjoy a lovely 23-mile drive through the mountains until you reach Julian; head east on Hwy. 78 and follow well marked signs to Borrego Springs.

ESSENTIALS

Visitor Information Borrego Springs Chamber of Commerce ✉ *786 Palm Canyon Dr.* ☎ *760/767–5555, 800/559–5524* ⊕ *www.borregosprings.org.*

EXPLORING

★ **Anza-Borrego Desert State Park.** One of the richest living natural-history museums in the nation, this state park is a vast, nearly uninhabited wilderness where you can step through a field of wildflowers, cool off in a palm-shaded oasis, count zillions of stars in the black night sky, and listen to coyotes howl at dusk. The landscape, largely undisturbed by humans, reveals a rich natural history. There's evidence of a vast inland sea in the piles of oyster beds near Split Mountain and of the power of natural forces such as earthquakes and flash floods. In addition, recent scientific work has confirmed that the Borrego Badlands, with more than 6,000 meters of exposed fossil-bearing sediments, is likely the richest such deposit in North America, telling the story of 7 million years of climate change, upheaval, and prehistoric animals. They've found evidence of saber-tooth cats, flamingos, zebras, and the largest flying bird in the northern hemisphere beneath the now-parched sand. Today the desert's most treasured inhabitants are the herds of elusive and endangered native bighorn sheep, or *borrego*, for which the park is named. Among the strange desert plants you may observe are the gnarly elephant trees. As these are endangered, rangers don't encourage visitors to seek out the secluded grove at Fish Creek, but there are a few examples at the visitor center garden. After a wet winter you can see a short-lived but stunning display of cacti, succulents, and desert wildflowers in bloom.

The park is unusually accessible to visitors. Admission to the park is free, and few areas are off-limits. Unlike most parks in the country, Anza-Borrego lets you camp anywhere; just follow the trails and pitch a tent wherever you like. There are more than 500 mi of dirt roads, two huge wilderness areas, and 110 mi of riding and hiking trails. Many of the park's sites can be seen from paved roads, but some require driving on dirt roads, for which rangers recommend you use a four-wheel-drive vehicle. When you do leave the pavement, carry the appropriate supplies: a cell phone (which may be unreliable in some areas), a shovel and other tools, flares, blankets, and plenty of water. The canyons are susceptible to flash flooding, so inquire about weather conditions (even on sunny days) before entering.

If you think the desert is just a sandy wasteland, the colorful beauty of the Anza-Borrego Desert will shock you.

Visitors Information Center. To get oriented in Anza-Borrego Desert State Park and obtain information on weather and wildlife conditions, stop by the Visitors Information Center. Designed to keep cool during the desert's blazing hot summers, the center is built underground, beneath a demonstration desert garden. A nature trail here takes you through a garden containing examples of most of the native flora and a little pupfish pond. Displays inside the center illustrate the natural history of the area. Picnic tables are scattered throughout the area, making is a good place to linger and enjoy the view. ■TIP➔ Borrego resorts, restaurants, and the state park have Wi-Fi, but the service is spotty at best. If you need to talk to someone in the area, it's best to find a phone with a landline. ⊠ *200 Palm Canyon Dr., Hwy. S22* ☎ *760/767–5311, 760/767–4684 wildflower hotline* ⊕ *www.parks.ca.gov* ✉ *Free* ☉ *Thurs.–Mon. 9–5.*

Borrego Palm Canyon. At Borrego Palm Canyon, a 1.5-mi trail leads to one of the few native palm groves in North America. There are more than 1,000 native fan palms in the grove, and a stream and waterfall greet you at trail's end. The moderate hike is the most popular in the park. ⊠ *Palm Canyon Dr., Hwy. S22, about 1 mi west of the Visitors Information Center.*

Yaqui Well Nature Trail. A 1.6 mi round trip nature trail, this takes you along a path to a desert water hole where birds and wildlife are abundant. It's also a good place to look for wildflowers in spring. Pick up a self-guided brochure at the trailhead. ⊠ *Hwy. 78, across from Tamarisk Campground.*

Coyote Canyon. With a year-round stream and lush plant life, this canyon is one of the best places to see and photograph spring wildflowers. Portions of the canyon road follow a section of the old Anza Trail. This area is closed between June 15 and September 15 to allow native bighorn sheep undisturbed use of the water. The dirt road that gives access to the canyon may be sandy enough to require a four-wheel-drive vehicle. ⊠ *Off DiGiorgio Rd., 4½ mi north of Borrego Springs.*

Font's Point. The late-afternoon vista of the Borrego badlands from Font's Point is one of the most breathtaking views seen in the desert, especially when the setting sun casts a golden glow in high relief on the eroded mountain slopes. The road from the Font's Point turnoff can be rough enough to make using a four-wheel-drive vehicle advisable; inquire about its condition at the visitor center before starting out. Even if you can't make it out on the paved road, you can see some of the view from the highway. ⊠ *Off Borrego Salton Seaway, Hwy. S22, 13 mi east of Borrego Springs.*

Narrows Earth Trail. East of Tamarisk Grove campground, this trail is a short walk off the road. Along the way you can see evidence of the many geologic processes involved in forming the canyons of the desert, such as a contact zone between two earthquake faults, and sedimentary layers of metamorphic and igneous rock. ⊠ *Off Hwy. 78, 13 mi west of Borrego Springs.*

Split Mountain. Geology students from all over the world visit the Fish Creek area of Anza-Borrego to explore this canyon. The narrow gorge with 600-foot walls was formed by an ancient stream. Fossils in this area indicate that a sea once covered the desert floor. ⊠ *Split Mountain Rd., 9 mi south of Hwy. 78, at Ocotillo Wells.*

Pictograph/Smuggler's Canyon Trail. Traversing a boulder-strewn trail is this easy, mostly flat path. At the end is a collection of rocks covered with muted red and yellow pictographs painted within the last hundred years or so by Native Americans. Walk about ½ mi beyond the pictures to reach Smuggler's Canyon, where an overlook provides views of the Vallecito Valley. The hike is 2 to 3 mi round-trip. ⊠ *Blair Valley, Hwy. S2, 6 mi southeast of Hwy. 78, at Scissors Crossing intersection.*

Carrizo Badlands Overlook. Just a few steps off the paved road, this overlook offers a view of eroded and twisted sedimentary rock that obscures the fossils of the mastodons, saber-tooths, zebras, and camels that roamed this region a million years ago. The route to the overlook through Earthquake Valley and Blair Valley parallels the Southern Emigrant Trail. ⊠ *Off Hwy. S2, 40 mi south of Scissors Crossing, intersection of Hwys. S2 and 78.*

Galleta Meadows. Flowers aren't the only things popping up from the earth in Borrego Springs. At Galleta Meadows camels, llamas, sabretoothed tigers, tortoises, and monumental gomphotherium (a sort of ancient elephant) appear to roam the earth again. These life-size bronze figures are of prehistoric animals whose fossils can be found in the Borrego Badlands. The collection, more than 50 sets of animals, is the project of a wealthy Borrego Springs resident who has installed the works of art on property he owns for the entertainment of locals and

Spa Life, Desert-Style

These days, taking the waters at a spa in Palm Springs is massively different from the experience imagined by the Cahuilla Indians when they first discovered the healing powers of their hot springs more than a century ago.

While you can still savor that tradition at the Spa Hotel, most desert spas offer more: gorgeous environments, luxury, pampering, highly trained estheticians, innovative treatments, and a variety of spa menus. Most venues offer signature treatments employing local materials such as clay, desert dwelling plants, salts, or sugars.

Below are some of the best spa options.

The Viceroy Hotel Estrella Spa earns top honors each year for the indoor/outdoor spa experience it offers with a touch of Old Hollywood ambience. You can enjoy your massage in one of four outdoor treatment rooms, experience a Vichy shower massage, have a facial or pedicure fireside, or enjoy a couple's full-body treatment with lemon crystals in the spa's Ice Haus. Whatever the treatment, you can use the spa's private pool, dine on a spa lunch, even order a drink from the hotel's bar.

It's all about fun at the **Palm Springs Yacht Club in the Parker Hotel,** according to Commodore Stephanie Neely, who invites guests to play video games, use iPod Touches, select a book from the spa's library, or watch the game on TV poolside indoors. You can get a complementary shot of whiskey, vodka, or the Commodore Special while lounging in a poolside tent reminiscent of Somerset Maugham's colonial India. Get massages, body treatments, or a Daily

Excursion (three treatments). Personal trainers can help you with your workout in the gym; go get heated in the sauna or practice a little yoga poolside. When you're ready to crash, wander out to the outdoor café, the Deck, and order a burger and Pimm's.

The Spring, located on a flower-decked hillside in Desert Hot Springs, offers a laid-back alternative to other "more is more" resort spas. It also heads many national lists as a great place to get away from the urban world, and "focus on cleansing, detoxification, and rejuvenation," according to spa director Maria Lease. The setting is simple, as are the rooms. Offering both day spa services and multi-day packages, you can immerse yourself for four to five hours of personal pampering, plus spend time in the Finnish sauna and the mineral pools for which Desert Hot Springs is famous. You can get the most out of a signature treatment such as the European Power Polish that will send you home cleaned, exfoliated, stimulated, and ready for a deep massage. The Spring Day offers three hours of bliss.

Despite all its funkiness, the **Feel Good Spa at the Ace Hotel** takes its services very seriously. Spa Director Lisa Ross spins a lot of magic to help "bring your bod back to the good ol' days of health and balance." Lotions, essential oils, rubs, and scrubs are organic botanicals here; you can even blend your own. The estheticians use a lot of local clay, mud, and sea algae. The Ace offers a variety of choices of where to have your rubdown, but the coolest is inside one of the two yurts set up poolside.

visitors. Maps are available from Borrego Springs Chamber of Commerce. ⊠ *Borrego Springs Rd. from Christmas Circle to Henderson Canyon* ☎ *760/767–5555* ⊕ *www.galletameadows.com* ☞ *Free.*

WHERE TO EAT AND STAY

$$

AMERICAN

✕ **The Arches.** Set right on the edge of the Borrego Springs Golf Course, beneath a canopy of grapefruit trees, this is one of the most pleasant dining options in the area. You'll find abundant options at every meal. Breakfast features standard fare plus breakfast burritos, a variety of pancakes, and biscuits and gravy. Lunches, enjoyed best on the patio, are sandwiches and salads. Dinner selections, offered with wine pairing options, include seafood, steak, and the signature chicken pot pie. Items from the spa menu are available for lunch and dinner. ⊠ *1112 Tilting T Dr.* ☎ *760/767–5700* ⊘ *Summer hrs vary; call ahead.*

$

MEXICAN

✕ **Carmelita's Mexican Grill and Cantina.** A friendly, family-run eatery tucked into a back corner of what is called "The Mall," Carmelita's draws locals and visitors all day whether it's for a hearty breakfast, a cooked-to-order enchilada or burrito, or to tip back a brew at the bar. The menu lists typical combination plates (enchiladas, burritos, tamales, and tacos). Salsas have a bit of zing, and the *masas* (corn dough used to make tortillas and tamales) are tasty and tender. ⊠ *575 Palm Canyon Dr.* ☎ *760/767–5666.*

$$

AMERICAN

✕ **Krazy Coyote/Red Ocotillo.** These two restaurants are operated together by the owners of the Palms at Indian Head. Krazy Coyote is a fine dining spot with white tablecloths where you can get New Zealand rack of lamb or filet mignon for dinner . . . or select a crumbled bacon Benedict, burger, Caesar salad, or fish and chips from the Red Ocotillo breakfast/lunch menu. What you eat is less important than the lovely atmosphere of the place, where poolside dining rules in this 1950s modern setting. If you have a canine with you, Krazy Coyote has a menu "for our four-legged friends" featuring peanut butter dog cookies. ⊠ *2220 Hoberg Rd., Borrego Springs* ☎ *760/767–7400* ⚲ *Reservations essential* ⊘ *Jul.–Aug., Krazy Coyote no breakfast or lunch.*

$$$

★

🏨 **Borrego Valley Inn.** Desert gardens of mesquite, ocotillo, and creosote surround the adobe Southwestern-style buildings here. The spacious rooms with plenty of natural light hold original art, and amenities include lodgepole pine beds with down comforters, walk-in showers with garden views, and double futons facing corner fireplaces. Every room opens onto its own enclosed garden with chaises, chairs, and table. In-room spa services may be arranged. **Pros:** swim under the stars in the clothing-optional pool; exquisite desert gardens. **Cons:** potential street noise in season; not a good choice for families with young children. ⊠ *405 Palm Canyon Dr.* ☎ *760/767–0311, 800/333–5810* ⊕ *www.borregovalleyinn.com* ⇆ *15 rooms, 1 suite* ⚲ *In-room: kitchen, Wi-Fi. In-hotel: pool, parking, some age restrictions* ⑩ *Breakfast.*

SPORTS AND THE OUTDOORS

GOLF

Borrego Springs Resort and Country Club. The 27 holes of golf at this resort and country club are open to the public. Three 9-hole courses, with natural desert landscaping and mature date palms, can be played individually or in any combination. Greens fees are $55 to $65, depending on the course and the day of the week, and include a cart and range balls.

Golf lessons are also offered. ✉ *1112 Tilting T Dr.* ☎ *760/767–5700* ⊕ *www.borregospringsresort.com.*

Roadrunner Club. This club has an 18-hole par 3 golf course. The greens fee is $35, including cart. ✉ *1010 Palm Canyon Dr.* ☎ *760/767–5373* ⊕ *www.roadrunnerclub.com.*

Springs at Borrego. Part of an RV park complex, the Springs at Borrego has one 18-hole course; greens fees are $25 to $50, not including cart fees. ✉ *2255 DiGiorgio Rd.* ☎ *760/767–2004* ⊕ *www.springsatborrego.com.*

HORSEBACK RIDING   **Smoketree Arabian Ranch.** You can select from a variety of equine encounters at this institute and ranch, which gives desert horseback rides on Arabian or quarter horses, pony rides for kids, and a nonriding human-to-horse communication experience similar to horse-whispering. ☎ *760/207–1427* ⊕ *www.smoketreearabianranch.com.*

TENNIS   **Anza Borrego Tennis Center.** A tennis club that's also open for public play, this center holds four hard surface courts, a swimming pool, and clubhouse with snack bar. Daily rates are $5. The facility is closed in summer. ✉ *286 Palm Canyon Dr., Borrego Springs* ☎ *760/767–0577.*

SHOPPING

Anza-Borrego State Park Store. Anza-Borrego Foundation operates this store, where you can find guidebooks and maps, clothing, desert art, and gifts for kids. The knowledgeable staff organizes interesting hikes, naturalist talks, classes, research programs, and nature walks within the park. Or they can help you organize your own visit. Proceeds from sales benefit preservation of the park and its resources. ✉ *587 Palm Canyon Dr., #110, Borrego Springs* ☎ *760/767-4063.*

Borrego Outfitters. There's a little bit of everything in this contemporary general store. Owner Donna Nourse carries high-end outdoor gear from Kelty and Columbia, personal care items from Burt's Bees, footwear from Teva and Acorn, Speedo and Fresh Produce swimsuits, and tabletop and home decor items. You can browse through racks of clothing and piles of hats, all suited to the desert climate. If you're peckish, treat yourself to artisan cheeses and wines. If you shop here in the off-season, you could find some great bargains. ✉ *519 The Mall, Borrego Springs* ☎ *760/767-3502 760 /767-3502.*

SALTON SEA

★   *30 mi southeast of Indio via Hwy. 86S on western shore and via Hwy. 111 on eastern shore; 29 mi east of Borrego Springs via Hwy. S22.*

The Salton Sea, one of the largest inland seas on Earth, is the product of both natural and artificial forces. The sea occupies the Salton Basin, a remnant of prehistoric Lake Cahuilla. Over the centuries the Colorado River flooded the basin and the water drained into the Gulf of California. In 1905 a flood once again filled the Salton Basin, but the exit to the gulf was blocked by sediment. The floodwaters remained in the basin, creating a saline lake 228 feet below sea level, about 35 mi long and 15 mi wide, with a surface area of nearly 380 square mi. The sea, which lies along the Pacific Flyway, supports 400 species of birds. Fishing for tilapia, boating, camping, and bird-watching are popular activities year-round.

GETTING HERE AND AROUND

Salton Sea State Recreation Area includes about 14 mi of coastline on the northeasten shore of the sea, about 30 mi south of India via Hwy. 111. Sonny Bono Salton Sea National Wildlife Refuge fills the southernmost tip of the sea's shore. To reach it from the SRA, continue south about 60 mi to Niland; continue south to Sinclair Rd., and turn west following the road to the Refuge Headquarters.

EXPLORING

Salton Sea State Recreation Area. On the north shore of the sea, this huge recreation area draws thousands each year to its playgrounds, hiking trails, fishing spots, and boat launches. Ranger guided bird walks are offered on Saturdays; you'll see migrating and native birds including Canada geese, pelicans, and shorebirds. The park also offers free kayak tours of the sea on Sundays. The Headquarters Visitor Center contains exhibits and shows a short film on the history of the Salton Sea. Unfortunately, because of budget cuts, this park is slated to close in 2012. Call ahead for updates. ⊠ *100–225 State Park Rd., North Shore* ☎ *760/393–3052* ⊕ *www.seaandesert.org* ⊠ *$5* ☉ *Park daily 8–sunset; visitor center Oct.–Apr., daily 10–sunset May–Sept., open hours vary, call ahead.*

Sonny Bono Salton Sea National Wildlife Refuge. The 2,200-acre wildlife refuge here, on the Pacific Flyway, is a wonderful spot for viewing migratory birds. There's an observation deck where you can watch migrating Canada geese. Along the trails you catch a view of eared grebes, burrowing owls, great blue herons, ospreys, or yellow-footed gulls. ⊠ *906 W. Sinclair Rd., Calipatria* ☎ *760/348–5278* ⊕ *www.fws.gov/saltonsea* ⊠ *Free* ☉ *Oct.–Feb., daily sunrise–sunset visitor center weekdays 7–3; Mar.–Sept., visitor center closed weekends.*

9

Joshua Tree
National Park

WORD OF MOUTH

"We got [to Joshua Tree] in time for a plethora of wildflowers in bloom. It was a spectacular show. Seeing such display of colors and variety of species in bloom was simply breathtaking."

—210

WELCOME TO JOSHUA TREE NATIONAL PARK

TOP REASONS TO GO

★ **Rock climbing:** Joshua Tree is a world-class site with challenges for climbers of just about every skill level.

★ **Peace and quiet:** Savor the solitude of one of the last great wildernesses in America.

★ **Stargazing:** You'll be mesmerized by the Milky Way flowing across the dark night sky. For spectacular natural fireworks, visit in mid-August during the Perseid meteor shower and watch shooting stars streak overhead.

★ **Wildflowers:** In spring, the hillsides explode in a patchwork of yellow, blue, pink, and white.

★ **Sunsets:** Twilight is a special time here, especially during the winter, when the setting sun casts a golden glow on the mountains.

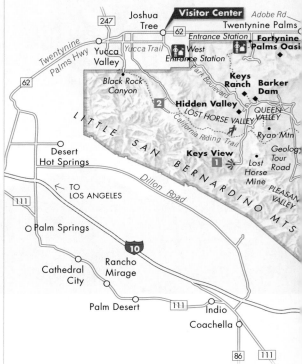

1 Keys View. This is the most dramatic overlook in the park—on clear days you can see Signal Mountain in Mexico.

2 Hidden Valley. Crawl between the big rocks and you'll understand why this boulder-strewn area was once a cattle rustlers' hideout.

3 Cholla Cactus Garden. Come here in the late afternoon, when the spiky stalks of the bigelow (jumping) cholla cactus are backlit against an intense blue sky.

4 Oasis of Mara. Walk the nature trail around this desert oasis, which the first settlers, the Serrano, dubbed "the place of little springs and much grass."

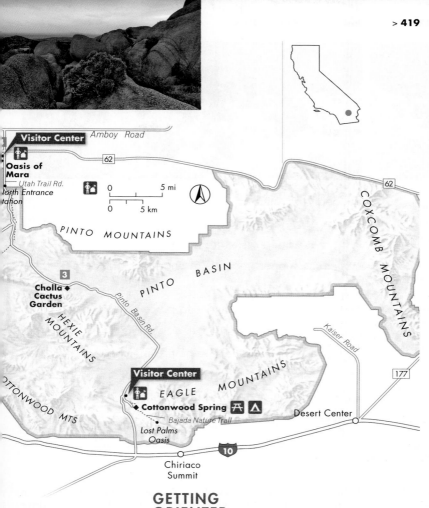

Visitor Center

Oasis of Mara

Amboy Road

62

Utah Trail Rd.

North Entrance Station

0   5 mi

0   5 km

62

PINTO   MOUNTAINS

COXCOMB   MOUNTAINS

PINTO   BASIN

3

Cholla Cactus Garden

Pinto Basin Rd.

PINTO

HEXIE MOUNTAINS

Kaiser Road

177

Visitor Center

EAGLE   MOUNTAINS

Cottonwood Spring

COTTONWOOD MTS

Bajada Nature Trail

Lost Palms Oasis

Desert Center

10

Chiriaco Summit

GETTING ORIENTED

Daggerlike tufts grace the branches of the namesake of Joshua Tree National Park in southeastern California, where the arid Mojave Desert meets the sparsely vegetated Colorado Desert (part of the Sonoran Desert, which lies within California and Northern Mexico).

Passenger cars are fine for paved areas, but you'll need four-wheel drive for many of the rugged backcountry roadways. At the park's most popular sites, parking is limited. Joshua Tree does not have public transportation.

10

Updated by
Sura Wood
and Bobbi
Zane

Ruggedly beautiful desert scenery attracts nearly 2 million visitors each year to Joshua Tree National Park, one of the last great wildernesses in the continental United States. Its mountains support mounds of enormous boulders and jagged rock; natural cactus gardens and lush oases shaded by tall fan palms mark the meeting place of the Mojave (high) and Sonora (low) deserts. Extensive stands of Joshua trees gave the park its name; the plants (members of the Yucca family of shrubs) reminded early white settlers of the biblical Joshua, with their thick, stubby branches representing the prophet raising his arms toward heaven.

PLANNING

GETTING HERE AND AROUND

Joshua Tree National Park is within a short drive of 11 million Southern California residents. Most visitors, in fact, make the two-hour drive from the Los Angeles area. The urban sprawl of Palm Springs (home to the nearest airport) is 45 mi away, but gateway towns Joshua Tree, Yucca Valley, and Twentynine Palms are just north of the park. If you're staying in the Palm Springs area, you can enjoy the highlights of the park in one day, including a stop for a picnic at a scenic spot.

WHEN TO GO

October through May, when the desert is cooler, is when most visitors arrive. Daytime temperatures range from the mid-70s in December and January to mid-90s in October and May. Lows can dip to near freezing in mid-winter. Summers can be torrid, with daytime temperatures reaching 110°F.

FLORA AND FAUNA

Joshua Tree will shatter your notions of the desert as a vast waste-land. Life flourishes here, as flora and fauna have adapted to heat and drought. In most areas you'll be walking among native Joshua trees, ocotillos, and yuccas. One of the best spring desert wildflower displays in Southern California blooms here. You'll see plenty of animals—reptiles such as nocturnal sidewinders, birds like golden eagles or burrowing owls, and mammals like coyotes and bobcats.

PARK ESSENTIALS

ADMISSION FEES AND PERMITS

Park admission is $15 per car, $5 per person on foot. The Joshua Tree Pass, good for one year, is $30. Free permits—available at all visitor centers—are required for rock climbing.

ADMISSION HOURS

The park is open every day, around the clock.

EMERGENCIES

Emergency assistance within Joshua Tree is limited. Emergency-only phones are at Intersection Rock at the entrance to Hidden Valley Campground and Indian Cove Campground; call San Bernardino Dispatch at ☎ *909/383–5651*, or dial 911.

PARK CONTACT INFORMATION

Joshua Tree National Park ⊠ *74485 National Park Dr., Twentynine Palms, CA* ☎ *760/367–5500* ⊕ *www.nps.gov/jotr.*

SCENIC DRIVES

★ **Park Boulevard.** Traversing the most scenic portions of Joshua Tree, this well-paved road connects the north and west entrances in the park's high desert section. Along with some sweeping desert views, you'll see jumbles of splendid boulder formations, stands of Joshua trees, and Hidden Valley and Barker Dam, remnants of the area's wild and woolly past. From the Oasis Visitor Center, drive south. After about 5 mi, the road forks; turn right and head west toward Jumbo Rocks (clearly marked with a road sign).

EXPLORING

HISTORIC SITES

Hidden Valley. This legendary cattle-rustlers hideout is set among big boulders, which kids love to scramble over and around. ⊠ *Park Blvd., 14 mi south of West Entrance.*

★ **Keys Ranch.** This 150-acre ranch that once belonged to William and Frances Keys illustrates one of the area's most successful attempts at home-steading. The couple raised five children under extreme desert conditions. Most of the original buildings, including the house, school, store, and workshop, have been restored to the way it was when William died in 1969. The only way to see the ranch is on one of the 60-minute, ranger-led walking tours, offered weekdays October–May; tour reservations

10

are essential. ✉ *2 mi north of Barker Dam Rd.* ☎ *760/367–5555* 💲 *$5* 🕐 *Oct.–May, tours weekdays and weekends at 10 and 1.*

SCENIC STOPS

Cholla Cactus Garden. This stand of bigelow cholla (sometimes called jumping cholla, since its hooked spines seem to jump at you) is best seen and photographed in late afternoon, when the backlit spiky stalks stand out against a colorful sky. ✉ *Pinto Basin Rd., 20 mi north of Cottonwood Visitor Center.*

Cottonwood Spring. Home to the native Cahuilla people for centuries, this spring provided water for travelers and early prospectors. The area, which supports a large stand of fan palms, is a stop for migrating birds and a winter water source for bighorn sheep. A number of gold mills were located here, and the area still has some remains, including an *arrastra* (gold-mining tool) and concrete pillars. You can access the site via a 1-mi paved trail that begins at sites 13A and 13B of the Cottonwood Campground. ✉ *Cottonwood Visitor Center.*

Fortynine Palms Oasis. A short drive off Highway 62, this site is a bit if a preview of what the park's interior has to offer: stands of fan palms, interesting petroglyphs, and evidence of fires built by early American Indians. Since animals frequent this area, you may spot a coyote, bobcat, or roadrunner. ✉ *End of Canyon Rd., 4 mi west of Twentynine Palms.*

★ **Keys View.** At 5,185 feet, this point affords a sweeping view of the Santa Rosa Mountains and Coachella Valley, the mountains of the San Bernardino National Forest, the Salton Sea, San Andreas Fault, and—on a rare clear day—Signal Mountain in Mexico. Sunrise and sunset are magical times, when the light throws rocks and trees into high relief before bathing the hills in brilliant shades of red, orange, and gold. ✉ *Keys View Rd., 21 mi south of west entrance.*

Lost Palms Oasis. More than 100 fan palms comprise the largest group of the exotic plants in the park. A spring bubbles from between the rocks, but disappears into the sandy, boulder-strewn canyon. As you hike along the 4-mi trail, you might spot bighorn sheep. ✉ *Cottonwood Visitor Center.*

VISITOR CENTERS

Cottonwood Visitor Center. Exhibits in this small center, staffed by rangers and volunteers, illustrate the region's natural history. ✉ *Pinto Basin Rd.* ☎ *No phone* ⊕ *www.nps.gov/jotr* 🕐 *Daily 8–4.*

Joshua Tree Visitor Center. This visitor center, opened in 2006, holds exhibits illustrating park geology, cultural and historic sites, and hiking and rock-climbing activities. There's also a small bookstore. ✉ *6554 Park Blvd., Joshua Tree* ☎ *760/366–1855* ⊕ *www.nps.gov/jotr* 🕐 *Daily 8–5.*

Oasis Visitor Center. Exhibits here illustrate how Joshua Tree was formed, reveal the differences between the two types of desert within the park, and demonstrate how plants and animals eke out an existence in this arid climate. Take the ½-mi nature walk through the nearby Oasis of Mara, which is alive with cottonwood trees, palm trees, and mesquite shrubs. ☒ *74485 National Park Dr., Twentynine Palms* ☏ *760/367– 5500* ⊕ *www.nps.gov/jotr* ☾ *Daily 8–4:30.*

SPORTS AND THE OUTDOORS

HIKING

There are more than 191 mi of hiking trails in Joshua Tree, ranging from quarter-of-a-mile nature trails to 35-mi treks. Some connect with each other, so you can design your own desert maze. Remember that drinking water is hard to come by—you won't find water in the park except at the entrances. Bring along at least a gallon per person for all but the shortest hikes, more if the weather is hot. Before striking out on a hike or apparent nature trail, check out the signage. Roadside signage identifies hiking- and rock-climbing routes.

EASY

Cap Rock. This ½-mi wheelchair-accessible loop—named after a boulder that sits atop a huge rock formation like a cap—winds through fascinating rock formations and has signs that explain the geology of the Mojave Desert. ☒ *Trailhead at junction of Park Blvd. and Keys View Rd.*

MODERATE

Fodor'sChoice
★ **Ryan Mountain Trail.** The payoff for hiking to the top of 5,461-foot Ryan Mountain is one of the best panoramic views of Joshua Tree. From here you can see Mt. San Jacinto, Mt. San Gorgonio, Lost Horse Valley, and the Pinto Basin. You'll need two to three hours to complete the 3-mi round-trip. ☒ *Trailhead at Ryan Mountain parking area, 16 mi southeast of park's west entrance or Sheep Pass, 16 mi southwest of Oasis Visitor Center.*

DIFFICULT

★ **Mastodon Peak Trail.** Some boulder scrambling is required on this 3-mi hike up 3,371-foot Mastodon Peak, but the journey rewards you with stunning views of the Salton Sea. The trail passes through a region where gold was mined from 1919 to 1932, so be on the lookout for open mines. The peak draws its name from a large rock formation that early miners believed looked like the head of a prehistoric behemoth. ☒ *Trailhead at Cottonwood Spring Oasis.*

ROCK CLIMBING

Fodor'sChoice
★ With an abundance of weathered igneous boulder outcroppings, Joshua Tree is one of the nation's top winter climbing destinations and offers a full menu of climbing experiences—from bouldering for beginners in the Wonderland of Rocks to multiple-pitch climbs at Echo Rock and Saddle Rock. The best-known climb in the park is Hidden Valley's Sports Challenge Rock. A map inside the *Joshua Tree Guide* shows locations of selected wilderness and nonwilderness climbs.

10

Camping at Joshua Tree

Camping is the best way to experience the stark beauty of Joshua Tree. You'll also have a rare opportunity to sleep outside in a semi-wilderness setting. The campgrounds, set at elevations from 3,000 to 4,500 feet, have only primitive facilities; few have drinking water. Black Rock and Indian Cove campgrounds, on the northern edge of the park (but not on a road that transits the park) accept reservations up to six months in advance (☎ 877/444–6777 ⊕ www.recreation. gov). Campsites elsewhere are on a first-come, first-served basis. Camping fees are $10 to $25 per site per night. You can pay with your credit card (AE, MC, V) at a visitor center; otherwise it's cash or personal check only at the self-registration stations at the campgrounds.

During fall and spring weekends, plan to arrive early in the day to ensure a site; if you have an organized group, reserve one of the group sites in advance. Temperatures can drop at night year-round—bring a sweater or light jacket. If you plan to camp in late winter or early spring, be prepared for the gusty Santa Ana winds. Backcountry camping is permitted in certain wilderness areas of Joshua Tree. You must sign in at a backcountry register board if you plan to stay overnight. For more information, stop at the visitor centers

or ranger stations. Two of our recommended campgrounds are below.

⚠ **Black Rock Canyon Campground.** Set among juniper bushes, cholla cacti, and other desert shrubs, Black Rock Canyon is one of the prettiest campgrounds in Joshua Tree. South of Yucca Valley, it's the closest campground to most of the desert communities. Located on the California Riding and Hiking Trail, it has facilities for horses and mules. **Pros:** reservations available; good choice for RVs; ranger talks. **Cons:** fills up early; outside the main park. ⊠ *Joshua La., south of Hwy. 62 and Hwy. 247* ☎ *760/367–5500, 877/444–6777 for reservations* ⊕ *www.recreation.gov* ⚠ *100 tent/RV sites* ⚐ *Flush toilets, dump station, drinking water, fire pits, picnic tables, ranger station* ▭ *AE, D, MC, V.*

⚠ **Jumbo Rocks.** Each campsite at this well-regarded campground tucked among giant boulders has a bit of privacy. It's a good home base for visiting many of Joshua Tree's attractions, including Geology Tour Road. Sites are first-come, first-served. **Pros:** good stargazing. **Cons:** crowded in spring; some small sites. ⊠ *Park Blvd., 11 mi from Oasis of Mara* ☎ *760/367–5500* ⊕ *www.nps.gov/jotr* ⚠ *125 tent/ RV sites* ⚐ *Pit toilets, fire pits, picnic tables* ▭ *No credit cards.*

Joshua Tree Rock Climbing School offers several programs, from one-day introductory classes to multiday programs for experienced climbers. The school provides all needed equipment. Beginning classes are limited to six people age 13 or older. ⌂ *Box 3034, Joshua Tree, CA 92252* ☎ *760/366–4745 or 800/890–4745* ⊕ *www.joshuatreerockclimbing. com* ▤ *$135 for beginner class.*

The Mojave Desert

WITH OWENS VALLEY

WORD OF MOUTH

"There is plenty to see in the Mojave National Preserve—including lots of Joshua trees, sand dunes, volcanic rock and flowers if you are there at the right time."

—tomfuller

WELCOME TO THE MOJAVE DESERT

TOP REASONS TO GO

★ **Nostalgia:** Old neon signs, historic motels, and restored Harvey House rail stations abound across this desert landscape. Don't miss some of the classic eateries along the way, including Bagdad Cafe in Newberry Springs, Emma Jean's Holland Burger Cafe in Victorville, and Summit Inn on the Cajon Pass.

★ **Death Valley wonders:** Visit this strange landscape to tour some of the most breathtaking desert terrain in the world. (⇨ Chapter 12, Death Valley National Park.)

★ **Great ghost towns:** California's gold rush brought miners to the Mojave, and each of the towns they left behind has its own unique charms.

★ **Cool down in Sierra country:** Head up Highway 395 toward Bishop to visit the High Sierra, home to majestic Mt. Whitney.

★ **Explore ancient history:** The Mojave Desert is replete with rare petroglyphs, some dating back almost 16,000 years.

1 The Western Mojave. Stretching from the town of Ridgecrest to the base of the San Gabriel Mountains, the western Mojave is a varied landscape of ancient Native American petroglyphs, tufa towers, and hillsides covered in bright orange poppies.

2 The Eastern Mojave. Joshua trees and cacti dot a predominantly flat landscape that is interrupted by dramatic, rock-strewn mountains. It also has more greenery and regular stretches of cool weather. Much of this area is uninhabited, so be cautious when driving the back roads, where towns and services are scarce.

3 Owens Valley. Lying in the shadow of the eastern Sierra Nevada, the Owens Valley stretches along U.S. 395 from the Mono–Inyo county line, in the north, to the town of Olancha, in the south. This stretch of highway is dotted with tiny towns, and its scenery is among the most quietly powerful you will see in the state. If you're traveling between Yosemite National Park and Death Valley National Park or are headed from Lake Tahoe or Mammoth to the desert, U.S. 395 is your corridor.

4 Death Valley National Park. This arid desert landscape is one of the hottest, lowest, and driest places in North America. Here, among the beautiful canyons and wide-open spaces, you'll find some quirky bits of Americana, including the elaborate Scotty's Castle and eclectic Amargosa Opera House. (⇨ *Chapter 12, Death Valley National Park.*)

GETTING ORIENTED

The Mojave Desert, once part of an ancient inland sea, is one of the largest swaths of open land in Southern California. Its boundaries to the south include the San Gabriel and San Bernardino mountain ranges; the areas of Palmdale and Ridgecrest to the west; Death Valley (⇨ *Chapter 12*) to the north; and Needles and Lake Havasu in Arizona and Primm, Nevada, to the east. The area is instantly distinguishable by its wide-open sandy spaces, peppered with creosote bushes, Joshua trees, cacti, and abandoned homesteads. You can access the Mojave via interstates 40 and 15, and highways 14, 95, and 395.

Updated by
Reed Parsell

Dust and desolation, tumbleweeds and rattlesnakes, barren landscapes—these are the bleak images that come to mind when most people hear the word *desert*. But east of the Sierra Nevada, where the land quickly flattens and the rain seldom falls, the desert is anything but a wasteland.

The topography here is extreme; whereas Death Valley (⇨ *Chapter 12, Death Valley National Park*) drops to almost 300 feet below sea level and contains the lowest (and hottest) spot in the Western Hemisphere, the Mojave Desert, which lies to the south, has elevations ranging from 3,000 to 5,000 feet. These remote regions (which are known, respectively, as low desert and high desert) possess a singular beauty found nowhere else in California: there are vast open spaces populated with spiky Joshua trees, undulating sand dunes, faulted mountains, and dramatic rock formations. Owens Valley is where the desert meets the mountains; its 80-mi width separates the depths of Death Valley from Mt. Whitney, the highest mountain in the continental United States.

PLANNING

WHEN TO GO
Spring and fall are the best seasons to tour the desert and Owens Valley. Winters are generally mild, but summers can be cruel. If you're on a budget, keep in mind that room rates drop as the temperatures rise.

GETTING HERE AND AROUND
AIR TRAVEL
Inyokern Airport, near Ridgecrest, is served by United Express from Los Angeles. McCarran International Airport, in Las Vegas, Nevada, served by dozens of major airlines, is about as close as Inyokern Airport to Furnace Creek, in Death Valley National Park (⇨ *Chapter 12*). Needles Airport serves small, private planes, as does Furnace Creek's 3,000-foot airstrip in Death Valley.

11

Contacts Inyokern Airport (⊠ *Inyokern Rd., Hwy. 178, 9 mi west of Ridgecrest, Inyokern* ☎ *760/377–5844* ⊕ *www.inyokernairport.com).*
McCarran International Airport (⊠ *5757 Wayne Newton Blvd., Las Vegas, NV* ☎ *702/261–5733* ⊕ *www.mccarran.com).* **Needles Airport** (⊠ *711 Airport Rd., Needles* ☎ *760/326–5263).*

CAR TRAVEL

Much of the desert can be seen from the comfort of an air-conditioned car. You can approach Death Valley (⇨ *Chapter 12*) from the west or the southeast. Whether you've come south from Bishop or north from Ridgecrest, head east from U.S. 395 on Highway 190 or 178. To enter Death Valley from the southeast, take Highway 127 north from Interstate 15 in Baker and link up with Highway 178, which travels west into the valley and then cuts north toward Highway 190 at Furnace Creek.

The major north–south route through the western Mojave is U.S. 395, which intersects with I–15 between Cajon Pass and Victorville. U.S. 395 travels north into the Owens Valley, passing such dusty little stops as Lone Pine, Independence, Big Pine, and Bishop. Farther west, Highway 14 runs north–south between Inyokern (near Ridgecrest) and Palmdale. Two major east–west routes travel through the Mojave: to the north, I–15 to Las Vegas, Nevada; to the south, I–40 to Needles. At the intersection of the two interstates, in Barstow, I–15 veers south toward Victorville and Los Angeles, and I–40 gives way to Highway 58 west toward Bakersfield.

■ TIP➜ For the latest Mojave traffic and weather, tune in to the Highway Stations (98.1 FM near Barstow, 98.9 FM near Essex, and 99.7 FM near Baker). The stations cover 40,000 square mi of the desert. Traffic can be especially troublesome Friday through Sunday, when scores of harried Angelenos head to Las Vegas for a bit of R&R.

Contact California Highway Patrol 24-hour road info (☎ *800/427–7623* ⊕ *www.dot.ca.gov/cgi-bin/roads.cgi).*

TRAIN TRAVEL

Amtrak makes stops in Victorville, Barstow, and Needles, but the stations are not staffed and do not have phone numbers, so you'll have to purchase your tickets in advance and handle your own baggage. You can travel west to connect with the *Coast Starlight* in Los Angeles or the *Pacific Surfliner* in Fullerton. The *Southwest Chief* stops twice a day at the above cities on its route from Los Angeles to Chicago and back. The Barstow station is served daily by Amtrak California motor coaches that travel among Los Angeles, Bakersfield, and Las Vegas.

Contact Amtrak (☎ *800/872–7245* ⊕ *www.amtrakcalifornia.com).*

HEALTH AND SAFETY

In an emergency dial 911.

Let someone know your trip route, destination, and estimated time of return. Before setting out, make sure your vehicle is in good condition. Carry water, a jack, tools, and towrope or chain. Fill up your tank whenever you see a gas pump. Stay on main roads, and watch out for wild burros, horses, and cattle.

Drink at least a gallon of water a day (three gallons if you're hiking or otherwise exerting yourself). Dress in layered clothing and wear comfortable, sturdy shoes and a hat. Keep snacks, sunscreen, and a first-aid kit on hand. If you have a headache or feel dizzy or nauseous, you could be suffering from dehydration. Get out of the sun immediately and drink plenty of water. Dampen your clothing to lower your body temperature.

Do not enter abandoned mine tunnels or shafts, of which there are hundreds in the Mojave Desert. The structures may be unstable, and there may be hidden dangers such as pockets of bad air. Avoid canyons during rainstorms. Floodwaters can quickly fill up dry riverbeds and cover or wash away roads. Never place your hands or feet where you can't see them. Rattlesnakes, scorpions, and black widow spiders may be hiding there.

Contacts BLM Rangers (🖀 760/255–8700). **Community Hospital** (✉ Barstow 🖀 760/256–1761). **Northern Inyo Hospital** (✉ 150 Pioneer La., Bishop 🖀 760/873–5811). **San Bernardino County Sheriff** (🖀 760/256–1796 in Barstow; 760/733–4448 in Baker).

HOURS

Early morning is the best time to visit sights and avoid crowds, but some museums and visitor centers don't open until 10. If you schedule your town arrivals for late afternoon, you can drop by the visitor centers just before closing hours to line up an itinerary for the next day.

TOUR OPTIONS

The Mojave Group of the Sierra Club regularly organizes field trips to interesting spots, and the San Gorgonio Sierra Club chapter also conducts desert excursions.

Contact Sierra Club (✉ 3345 Wilshire Blvd., Suite 508, Los Angeles 🖀 213/387–4287; 951/684–6203 for San Gorgonio chapter ⊕ www.sierraclub.com).

VISITOR INFORMATION

Contacts Bureau of Land Management (✉ California Desert District Office, 6221 Box Springs Blvd., Riverside 🖀 909/697–5200 ⊕ www.ca.blm.gov). **California Welcome Center** (✉ 2796 Tanger Way, Barstow 🖀 760/253–4782 ⊕ www.visitcwc.com). **Death Valley Chamber of Commerce** (✉ 118 Hwy. 127, Shoshone 🖀 760/852–4524 ⊕ www.deathvalleychamber.com). **San Bernardino County Regional Parks Department** (✉ 777 E. Rialto Ave., San Bernardino 🖀 909/387–2594 ⊕ www.co.san-bernardino.ca.us/parks).

RESTAURANTS

Throughout the desert and the eastern Sierra, dining is a fairly simple affair. Owens Valley is home to many mom-and-pop eateries, as well as a few fast-food chains. The restaurants in Death Valley (⇨ Chapter 12) range from coffee shops to upscale cafés. In the Mojave there are chain establishments in Ridgecrest, Victorville, and Barstow, as well as some ethnic eateries.

HOTELS

Hotel chains and roadside motels make up most of the lodging options in the desert. The tourist season runs through the summer months, from late May through September, when many travelers are heading out of California on Interstate 15. Reservations are never a problem: you're almost always guaranteed a room. But if your plans take you to the most luxurious resort in the entire desert—the Furnace Creek Inn, in Death Valley—be sure to book in advance for the winter season.

WHAT IT COSTS					
	¢	$	$$	$$$	$$$$
Restaurants	under $10	$10–$15	$16–$22	$23–$30	over $30
Hotels	under $90	$90–$120	$121–$175	$176–$250	over $250

Restaurant prices are for a main course at dinner, excluding sales tax of 7.75%. Hotel prices are for two people in a standard double room in high season, excluding service charges and 7.25% tax.

THE WESTERN MOJAVE

This vast area can strikingly beautiful, especially along Highway 395. and especially from January through March, when wildflowers are in bloom and temperatures are manageable.

PALMDALE

60 mi north of Los Angeles on Hwy. 14.

Before calling itself the aerospace capital of the world, the desert town of Palmdale was an agricultural community. Swiss and German descendants, moving west from Nebraska, settled here in 1886. Most residents made their living as farmers, growing alfalfa, pears, and apples. After World War II, with the creation of Edwards Air Force Base and U.S. Air Force Plant 42, the area turned into a center for aerospace and defense, with such big companies as McDonnell Douglas, Rockwell, Northrop, and Lockheed establishing factories here. Until the housing crisis and most recent recession struck, it was one of the fastest-growing cities in Southern California.

GETTING HERE AND AROUND
Metrolink (☎ 800/371–5465 ⊕ *www.metrolinktrains.com*) runs here weekdays from Los Angeles and the San Fernando Valley, and **Antelope Valley Transit Authority** (☎ 661/945–9445 ⊕ *www.avta.com*) buses operate about town. The only practical way to see the town and its nearby attractions, however, is by car. From the Los Angeles basin take Highway 14, from the east arrive via the Pearblossom Highway (Highway 18/138).

EXPLORING
Devil's Punchbowl Natural Area. A mile from the San Andreas Fault, the namesake of this attraction is a natural bowl-shaped depression in the earth, framed by 300-foot rock walls. At the bottom is a stream, which you can reach via a moderately strenuous 1-mi hike. You also can veer off on a short nature trail; at the top an interpretive center has displays of native flora and fauna, including live animals such as snakes, lizards, and birds of prey. ✉ *28000 Devil's Punchbowl Rd., south of Hwy. 138, Pearblossom* ☎ *661/944–2743* ✉ *Free* ☉ *Park daily sunrise–sunset, center daily 8–4.*

St. Andrew's Abbey. This Benedictine monastery stands on 760 acres of lush greenery and natural springs. A big draw here is the property's ceramics studio, established in 1969; St. Andrew's Ceramics sells handmade tile saints, angels, and plaques designed by Father Maur van Doorslaer, a monk from Sint Andries in Bruges, Belgium, whose work is collected across the United States and Canada. Don't miss the abbey's fall festival, where you can sample tasty dishes and enjoy entertainment that includes singing nuns and dancing monks. ⊠ *31101 N. Valyermo Rd., south of Hwy. 138, Valyermo* ☎ *888/454–5411; 661/944–1047 ceramics studio* ⊕ *www.saintsandangels.org* ⊠ *Free* ⊗ *Weekdays 9–12:30 and 1:30–4:30, weekends 9–11:45 and 12:30–4:30.*

Southern California Soaring Academy. Adventure-seekers will enjoy flying over the scenic San Gabriel mountain pines, across the jagged San Andreas Fault, and over the sandy soil of El Mirage Dry Lake at this academy, the only place near Los Angeles that offers sailplane rides (no engines!). You'll be accompanied by an FAA-certified instructor, who will teach you the basics of airspeed control, straight flight, and turns before letting you handle the craft on your own. Flights range from $109 to $199. Advance reservations are required. ⊠ *32810 165th St. E, Llano* ☎ *661/944–1090* ⊕ *www.soaringacademy.org* ⊗ *Fri.–Mon. 9–sunset, Tues.–Thurs. by appointment.*

Brian Ranch Airport. You can take ultralight (very small two-seater planes that can be flown without a pilot's license) lessons at this airport, which offers 15-minute ($40), half-hour ($75), and hour-long ($125) rides across the Mojave. The airport is also known for its annual "World's Smallest Air Show" every Memorial Day weekend, which draws aviation enthusiasts from around the country. ⊠ *34180 Largo Vista Rd., Llano* ☎ *661/261–3216* ⊕ *www.brianranch.com.*

Shambala Preserve. An 80-acre wildlife operation run by famous Hitchcock actress Tippi Hedren, this is probably the closest you'll get to a safari outside Africa. Noon to 3 pm safaris, held twice a month (during one weekend) by advance reservation only, get you as close as a foot away from 70 rescued wildcats. ⊠ *6867 Soledad Canyon, Acton* ☎ *661/268–0380* ⊕ *www.shambala.org* ⊠ *$50 minimum donation.*

WHERE TO STAY
For expanded hotel reviews, visit Fodors.com.

¢ 🔡 **Best Western John Jay Inn & Suites.** Antique furnishings decorate the rooms and suites at this modern hotel. **Pros:** clean; good rates; spacious rooms. **Cons:** no on-site restaurant; rather corporate. ⊠ *600 W. Palmdale Blvd.* ☎ *661/575–9322* ⊕ *www.bestwestern.com* ⤻ *54 rooms, 13 suites* △ *In-room: a/c, Wi-Fi. In-hotel: pool, gym* ⦿*Breakfast.*

¢ 🔺 **Red Rock Canyon State Park.** Open year-round, the park's Ricardo Campground is in the colorful cliff region of the southern El Paso Mountains, where there are lots of hiking trails. Spring and fall fill quickly, so be sure to arrive early to get a spot. The drive-in sites are remote and beautiful, with wonderful views of the cliffs. △ *Pit toilets, drinking water, fire pits, picnic tables* ⤻ *50 sites* ⊠ *Off Hwy. 14, 30 mi southwest of Ridgecrest* ☎ *661/942–0662* ⌦ *Reservations not accepted.*

¢ ⚠ **Mojave Narrows Regional Park.** In one of the few spots where the Mojave River flows aboveground, this park has two lakes surrounded by cottonwoods and cattails. You'll find fishing, rowboat rentals, a bait shop, equestrian paths, and a wheelchair-accessible trail. The campsites cluster by the lake amid grass and trees. ■TIP→ **The park is also home to the annual Huck Finn Jubilee (⊕ www.huckfinn.com), a festive, down-home event with live bluegrass music, trout fishing, cow-chip throwing contests, and Southern grub that draws thousands every Father's Day weekend.** ⚘ *Flush toilets, full hookups, dump station, drinking water, showers, fire pits, grills, picnic tables, electricity, public telephone, play area* ➷ *87 sites, 37 with hookups* ✉ *18000 Yates Rd., Victorville* ☎ *760/245–2226.*

NOT SOUVENIRS
You may spot fossils at some of the archaeological sites in the desert. If you do, leave them where they are; it's against the law to remove them.

¢ ⚠ **Calico Ghost Town Regional Park.** This dusty, flat campground with views of the ghost town provides an authentic Wild West atmosphere. In addition to the campsites, you have six cabins ($28) and bunkhouse accommodations ($5 per person, with a 12-person minimum) to choose from. There's a two-night minimum during Calico Ghost Town festival weekends. ⚘ *Flush toilets, full hookups, partial hookups, dump station, drinking water, showers, fire pits, grills, picnic tables, electricity, public telephone, general store* ➷ *250 sites, 104 with hookups* ✉ *Ghost Town Rd., 3 mi north of I–15, 5 mi east of Barstow* ☎ *760/254–2122 or 800/862–2542* ⊕ *www.calicotown.com.*

HIKING

Hiking trails are abundant throughout the desert and along the eastern base of the Sierra, meandering toward sights that you can't see from the road. Some of the best trails are unmarked; ask locals for directions. Among the prime hiking spots are Death Valley National Park and the John Muir Trail, which starts near Mt. Whitney. Whether you're exploring the high or low desert, wear sunblock, protective clothing, and a hat. Be wary of tarantulas, black widows, scorpions, snakes, and other potentially hazardous creatures.

LANCASTER

8 mi north of Palmdale via Hwy. 14.

Lancaster was founded in 1876, when the Southern Pacific Railroad arrived. Before that it was inhabited by Native American tribes: Kawaiisu, Kitanemuk, Serrano, Tataviam, and Chemehuevi. Descendants of some of these tribes still live in the surrounding mountains. Points of interest around Lancaster are far from the downtown area, some in neighboring communities.

GETTING HERE AND AROUND

As is the case with nearby Palmdale, cars are the only viable way to see the town and scattered nearby sites. From the Los Angeles basin take Highway 14, which proceeds north to Mojave and Highway 58, a link between Bakersfield and Barstow. **Metrolink** (☎ *800/371–5465* ⊕ *www.*

metrolinktrains.com) runs here weekdays from Los Angeles and the San Fernando Valley, and **Antelope Valley Transit Authority** (☎ *661/945–9445* ⊕ *www.avta.com*) buses operate about town.

EXPLORING

★ **Antelope Valley Poppy Reserve.** The California poppy, the state flower, can be spotted just about anywhere in the state, but the densest concentration is in this quiet park. Seven miles of trails (parts of which are paved, but inclines are too steep for wheelchairs) lead you through 1,745 acres of hills carpeted with poppies and other wildflowers. Peak blooming time is usually March through May, though you can hike the grounds year-round. The visitor center has books and information about the reserve and other desert areas. ⊠ *Ave. I, between 110th and 170th Sts. W* ☎ *661/724–1180 or 661/942–0662* ⊕ *www.parks.ca.gov* 🖾 *$8 per vehicle* ☉ *Visitor center mid-Mar.–mid-May, daily 9–5.*

OFF THE BEATEN PATH

Desert Tortoise Natural Area. Between mid-March and mid-June, this natural habitat of the elusive desert tortoise blazes with desert candles, primroses, lupine, and other wildflowers. Get there bright and early to spot the state reptile, while it grazes on fresh flowers and grass shoots. It's also a great spot to see desert kit fox, red-tailed hawks, cactus wrens, and Mojave rattlesnakes. ⊠ *8 mi northeast of California City via Randsburg Mojave Rd.* ☎ *951/683–3872* ⊕ *www.tortoise-tracks. org* 🖾 *Free* ☉ *Daily.*

🐾 **Exotic Feline Breeding Compound & Feline Conservation Center.** About a dozen species of wildcats, from the weasel-size jaguarundi to leopards, tigers, and jaguars, inhabit this small, orderly facility. You can see the cats (behind barrier fences) in the parklike public zoo and research center. Those concerned with animal rights will want to know that the center supplies city zoos with wild cats and does a few rescues. And the on-site museum's taxidermied cats all died of old age. ⊠ *Off Mojave-Tropico Rd., Rosamond* ☎ *661/256–3793* ⊕ *www.cathouse-fcc.org* 🖾 *$5* ☉ *Thurs.–Tues. 10–4.*

Antelope Valley Winery and Buffalo Company. A winery in the middle of the desert? Only in California could you find a place like this. Industry scoffing hasn't stopped Cecil W. McLester, a graduate of UC Davis's renowned wine-making and viticulture program, from crafting a decent batch of wines, including the award-winning AV Burgundy (a house red) and Paloma Blanca (a Riesling-style blend of French Colombard, chenin blanc, and muscat grapes). The winery is also home to the Antelope Valley Buffalo Company, a producer of fine buffalo steaks, patties, and jerky, made from its roaming herd in the Leona Valley. ⊠ *42041 20th St. W* ☎ *661/722–0145* ⊕ *www.avwinery.com* 🖾 *Winery free, wine tasting $6* ☉ *Wed.–Sun. 11–6.*

RED ROCK CANYON STATE PARK

48 mi north of Lancaster via Hwy. 14; 17 mi west of U.S. 395 via Red Rock–Randsburg Rd.

GETTING HERE AND AROUND

The only viable way to get here is by car, taking Highway 14 north from Los Angeles and the Palmdale/Lancaster area or south from Ridgecrest.

Red Rock Canyon State Park. A geological feast for the eyes with its layers of pink, white, red, and brown rock, this remote canyon is also a region of fascinating biological diversity—the ecosystems of the Sierra Nevada, the Mojave Desert, and the Basin Range all converge here. Entering the park from the south on Red Rock–Randsburg Road, you pass through a steep-walled gorge to a wide bowl tinted pink by volcanic ash. Native Americans known as the Old People lived here some 20,000 years ago; later, Mojave Indians roamed the land for centuries. Gold-rush fever hit the region in the mid-1800s, and you can still see remains of mining operations in the park. In the 20th century, Hollywood invaded the canyon, shooting westerns, TV shows, commercials, music videos, and movies such as *Jurassic Park* here. Be sure to check out the Red Cliffs Preserve on Highway 14, across from the entrance to the Red Rock campground. ⊠ *Ranger station: Abbott Dr. off Hwy. 14* ☎ *661/942–0662* ⊕ *www. parks.ca.gov* ⊠ *$6 per vehicle* ☉ *Visitor center Fri.–Sun. 10–4.*

> **LIQUID REFRESHMENT**
>
> After driving through the hot desert, you'll surely appreciate a cold one at **Indian Wells Brewing Company** (⊠ *2565 N. Hwy. 14, Inyokern* ✛ *2 mi west of Hwy. 395* ☎ *760/377–5989* ⊠ *$5 beer tasting* ☉ *Daily 9:30–5*), where master brewer Rick Lovett lovingly crafts his Desert Pale Ale, Eastern Sierra Lager, Mojave Gold, and Sidewinder Missile Ales. If you have the kids along, grab a six-pack of his specialty root beer, black cherry, orange, or cream sodas.

RIDGECREST

28 mi northeast of Red Rock Canyon State Park via Hwy. 14; 77 mi south of Lone Pine via U.S. 395.

A military town that serves the U.S. Naval Weapons Center to its north, Ridgecrest has dozens of stores, restaurants, and hotels. As you head northeast, it's the last city of any significant size (about 25,000 residents) you'll encounter as you head toward Death Valley National Park.

GETTING HERE AND AROUND

Come here by car so you can see regional attractions such as the Trona Pinnacles. Arrive via Highway 395 or, from the Los Angeles area, Highway 14. In town, **City Transit** (☎ *760/499–5040*) caters to locals' needs.

ESSENTIALS

Visitor Information Ridgecrest Area Convention and Visitors Bureau (⊠ *100 W. California Ave., Ridgecrest* ☎ *760/375–8202 or 800/847–4830* ⊕ *www.visitdeserts.com*).

EXPLORING

Maturango Museum. Small but informative exhibits here detail the natural and cultural history of the northern Mojave; there's also a small bookstore and an information desk. Outside you'll find a short but creative nature trail. The museum runs wildflower tours in March and April. ⊠ *100 E. Las Flores Ave.* ☎ *760/375–6900* ⊕ *www.maturango.org* ☜ *$5* ⊗ *Daily 10–5.*

Fodor's Choice ★

Petroglyph Canyons. Guided tours conducted by the Maturango Museum are the only way to see these canyons, among the desert's most amazing spectacles. The two canyons, commonly called Big Petroglyph and Little Petroglyph, are in the Coso Mountain Range on the million-acre U.S. Naval Weapons Center at China Lake. Each of the canyons holds a superlative concentration of ancient rock art, the largest of its kind in the Northern Hemisphere. Thousands of well-preserved images of animals and humans—some more than 16,000 years old—are scratched or pecked into dark basaltic rocks. The tour takes you through 3 mi of sandy washes and boulders, so wear comfortable walking shoes. ■TIP➜ At an elevation of 5,000 feet, weather conditions can be quite extreme, so dress in layers and bring plenty of drinking water (none is available at the site) and snacks. Children under 10 are not allowed on the tour. The military requires you to provide a U.S. passport; no non-U.S. citizens may participate. ⊠ *Tours depart from Maturango Museum* ☎ *760/375–6900* ⊕ *www.maturango.org* ☜ *$40* ⊗ *Museum daily 10–5. Tours Feb.–June and Sept. or Oct.–early Dec.; call for tour times but note reservations must be made via mail.*

☾ **Wild Horse and Burro Corrals.** Rounded up by the Bureau of Land Management on public lands throughout the Southwest, the animals corralled here are available for adoption. You can bring along an apple or carrot to feed the horses, but the burros are usually too wild to approach. Individual and group tours are available. ⊠ *Off Hwy. 178, 3 mi east of Ridgecrest* ☎ *760/384–5765* ⊕ *www.blm.gov* ☜ *Free* ⊗ *Weekdays 7:30–4.*

Trona Pinnacles National Natural Landmark. It's worth the effort (especially for sci-fi buffs, who might recognize the landscape from the film *Star Trek V*) to drive out here from Ridgecrest. These fantastic-looking formations of calcium carbonate, known as tufa, were formed underwater along fault lines in the bed of what is now Searles Dry Lake. The dirt road from Highway 178 is decaying, so proceed slowly. The main parking lot has an outhouse, but that's it for man-made touches other than a few interpretive signs. There's no formal trail; walk wherever you'd like, but beware of sharp, coral-like rocks underfoot. Prime photography

FORMER BOOMTOWNS

The towns of Randsburg, Red Mountain, and Johannesburg make up the **Rand Mining District** (⊠ *U.S. 395, 20 mi south of Ridgecrest*), which first boomed with the discovery of gold in the Rand Mountains in 1895. Rich tungsten ore, used in World War I to make steel alloy, was discovered in 1907, and silver was found in 1919. The boom has gone bust, but the area still has a few residents, a dozen antiques shops, and plenty of character. Johannesburg is overlooked by an archetypal Old West cemetery in the hills above town.

times are in early morning and just before sunset. ✉ *5 mi south of Hwy. 178, 18 mi east of Ridgecrest* ☎ *760/384–5400 Ridgecrest BLM office* ⊕ *www.blm.gov/ca/st/en/fo/ridgecrest/trona.3.html.*

WHERE TO STAY

For expanded hotel reviews, visit Fodors.com.

$ 🏨 **Carriage Inn.** All the rooms at this large hotel are roomy and well kept, but the poolside cabanas are a bit cozier. **Pros:** full complimentary breakfast; nice outdoor pool. **Cons:** old decor; some rooms could use an update. ✉ *901 N. China Lake Blvd.* ☎ *760/446–7910 or 800/772–8527* ⊕ *www.carriageinn.biz* 🛏 *152 rooms, 8 suites, 2 cabanas* ♿ *In-room: a/c, Wi-Fi. In-hotel: 2 restaurants, bar, pool, gym* ◍ *Some meals.*

THE EASTERN MOJAVE

Majestic, wide-open spaces define this region, with the Mojave National Preserve being one of the state's most remote but rewarding destinations.

VICTORVILLE

87 mi south of Ridgecrest on U.S. 395. Turn east onto Bear Valley Rd. and travel 2 mi to town center.

At the southwest corner of the Mojave is the sprawling town of Victorville, a town rich in Route 66 heritage. Victorville was named for Santa Fe Railroad pioneer Jacob Nash Victor, who drove the first locomotive through the Cajon Pass here in 1885. Once home to Native Americans, the town later became a rest stop for Mormons and missionaries. In 1941 George Air Force Base (which now serves as an airport and storage area) brought scores of military families to the area, many of which have stayed on to raise families of their own. February is one of the best times to visit, when the city holds its annual Roy Rogers and Dale Evans Western Film Festival and Adelanto Grand Prix, the largest motorcycle and quad off-road event in the country.

GETTING HERE AND AROUND

Drive here on Interstate 15 from Los Angeles or Las Vegas, or from the north via Highway 395. **Amtrak** (☎ *800/872–7245*) and Greyhound (☎ *760/245–2041*) stop here. **The Victor Valley Transit Authority** (☎ *760/948–3030* ⊕ *www.vvta.org*) runs buses among Adelanto, Apple Valley, Hesperia, Victorville, and San Bernardino County for locals, but it's of little use to visitors.

ESSENTIALS

Visitor Information Victorville Chamber of Commerce (✉ *14174 Green Tree Blvd., Victorville* ☎ *760/245–6506* ⊕ *www.vvchamber.com*).

EXPLORING

California Route 66 Museum. Fans of the Mother Road will love this museum, whose exhibits chronicle the history of America's most famous highway. At the museum you can pick up a book that details a self-guided tour of the old Sagebrush Route from Oro Grande to Helendale. The road passes Route 66 icons such as Potapov's Gas and Service Station (where the words "Bill's Service" are still legible) and the once-rowdy Sagebrush Inn, now a private residence. ✉ *16825 D St., Rte. 66* ☎ *760/951–0436* ⊕ *www.califrt66museum.org* ⧅ *Free* ⊙ *Thurs., Fri., and Mon. 10–4, Sun. 11–3.*

Silverwood Lake State Recreation Area. Situated at the base of the San Bernardino Mountains, this recreation area is 10 mi east of Cajon Pass. One of the desert's most popular boating and fishing areas, 1,000-acre Silverwood Lake also has a beach with a lifeguard. You can fish for trout, largemouth bass, crappie, and catfish; hike and bike the trails; or come in winter to count bald eagles, which nest in the tall Jeffrey pines by the shore. Campgrounds accommodate tents and RVs. At the marina, you can rent pontoon and fishing boats as well as paddleboats, kayaks, and WaveRunners. Campfire programs are offered in summer, and public Wi-Fi is available in the park. ✉ *14651 Cedar Cir., Hesperia* ☎ *760/389–2303* ⊕ *www.parks.ca.gov* ⧅ *$10 per car, $8 per boat* ⊙ *May–Sept., daily 6 am–9 pm; Oct.–Apr., daily 7–7.*

WHERE TO EAT

¢ ✕ **Emma Jean's Holland Burger Cafe.** This circa-1940s diner sits right on

AMERICAN U.S. Historic Route 66 and is favored by locals for its generous portions

★ and old-fashioned home cooking. Try the biscuits and gravy, chicken-fried steak, or the famous Trucker's Sandwich, chock-full of roast beef, bacon, chilies, and cheese; the Brian Burger also elicits consistent praise. ✉ *17143 D St.* ☎ *760/243–9938* ⊙ *Closed Sun. No dinner.*

BARSTOW

32 mi northeast of Victorville on I–15.

In 1886, when a subsidiary of the Atchison, Topeka, and Santa Fe Railway began construction of a depot and hotel here, Barstow was born. Today outlet stores, chain restaurants, and motels define the landscape, though old-time neon signs light up the town's main street.

GETTING HERE AND AROUND

Driving here on Interstate 15 from Los Angeles or Las Vegas is by far your best option, although you can reach Barstow via **Amtrak** (☎ *800/872–7245*) or **Greyhound** (☎ *760/245–2041*). **Barstow Area Transit** (☎ *760/256–0311*) runs buses among Barstow, Hinkley, Lenwood, Grandview, Yermo, Harvard, Daggett, and Newberry Springs.

ESSENTIALS

Visitor Information Barstow Area Chamber of Commerce and Visitors Bureau (✉ *681 N. 1st Ave., Barstow* ☎ *760/256–8617* ⊕ *www.barstowchamber.com*).

Many of the buildings in the popular Calico Ghost Town are authentic.

EXPLORING

Skyline Drive-In Theatre. When the sun sets in the Mojave, check out a bit of surviving Americana at this dusty drive-in, where you can watch the latest Hollywood flicks among the Joshua trees and starry night sky in good old-fashioned stereo FM sound. ✉ *31175 Old Hwy. 58* 🕾 *760/256–3333* 🎟 *$6* 🕘 *Shows Wed.–Sun. at 7:30; closed Mon. and Tues.*

California Welcome Center. See exhibits about desert ecology, wildflowers, and wildlife here, as well as general visitor information for the state of California. ✉ *2796 Tanger Way* 🕾 *760/253–4782* ⊕ *www.visitcwc. com* 🕘 *Daily 9–6.*

★ **Calico Early Man Archaeological Site.** The earliest-known Americans fashioned the artifacts buried in the walls and floors of the pits here. Nearly 12,000 stone tools—used for scraping, cutting, and gouging—have been excavated here. The apparent age of some of these items (said to be as much as 200,000 years old) contradicts the dominant archaeological theory that humans populated North America only 13,000 years ago. Noted archaeologist Louis Leakey was so impressed with the Calico site that he became its director in 1963 and served in that capacity until his death in 1972. His old camp is now a visitor center and museum. The only way into the site is by guided tour (call ahead, as scheduled tours sometimes don't take place). ✉ *Off I–15, Minneola Rd. exit, 15 mi northeast of Barstow* 🕾 *760/254–2248* ⊕ *www.blm.gov/ca/st/en/fo/ barstow/calico.html* 🎟 *$5* 🕘 *Visitor center Wed. 12:30–4:30, Thurs.– Sun. 9–4:30; tours Wed. 1:30 and 3:30, Thurs.–Sun. 9:30, 11:30, 1:30, and 3:30.*

★ **Calico Ghost Town.** Once a wild and wealthy mining town, Calico took off in 1881 when prospectors found a rich deposit of silver in the area, and by 1886 more than $85 million worth of silver, gold, and other precious metals had been harvested from the surrounding hills. Many buildings here are authentic, but the restoration has created a sanitized version of the 1880s. You can stroll the wooden sidewalks of Main Street, browse shops filled with Western goods, roam the tunnels of Maggie's Mine ($1), and take an enjoyable ride on the Calico-Odessa Railroad ($3). Calico is a fun and mildly educational place for families to stretch their legs on the drive between Los Angeles and Las Vegas. Festivals in March, May, October, and November celebrate Calico's Wild West theme. ⊠ *Ghost Town Rd., 3 mi north of I–15, 5 mi east of Barstow* ☎ *760/254–2122* ⊕ *www.calicotown.com* ⊠ *$6* ⊗ *Daily 9–5.*

Desert Discovery Center. Stop by this center to see exhibits of fossils, plants, and local animals. The main attraction here is Old Woman Meteorite, the second-largest such celestial object ever found in the United States. It was discovered in 1976 about 50 mi from Barstow in the Old Woman Mountains. The center also has visitor information for the Mojave Desert. ⊠ *831 Barstow Rd.* ☎ *760/252–6060* ⊕ *www. discoverytrails.org* ⊠ *Free* ⊗ *Tues.–Sat. 11–4.*

Mojave River Valley Museum. Two blocks from the Desert Discovery Center, this complementary museum is crowded with exhibits that include American Indian pottery, mammoth bones, and elephant tracks. Browse the impressive collection (more than 300) of regional books, and outside check out the iron-strap jail and Santa Fe drovers car, one of only two left in the world. ⊠ *270 E. Virginia Way* ☎ *760/256–5452* ⊕ *www. mojaverivervalleymuseum.org* ⊠ *Free* ⊗ *Daily 11–4.*

★ **Rainbow Basin National Natural Landmark.** Many science-fiction movies set on Mars have been filmed at this landmark, 8 mi north of Barstow. Huge slabs of mildly red, orange, white, and green stone tilt at crazy angles like ships about to capsize; hike the washes, and you might see the fossilized remains of mastodons and bear-dogs, which roamed the basin up to 16 million years ago. Owl Canyon Campground is on the east side of Rainbow Basin. After heavy rains in late 2010, four-wheel drive was mandated here, and road improvements were not in the works. ⊠ *Fossil Bed Rd., 3 mi west of Fort Irwin Rd.* ☎ *760/252–6000* ⊕ *www.blm.gov/ca/barstow/basin.html.*

Western American Rail Museum. If you're a railroad buff, then you'll love the Western American Rail Museum. It houses memorabilia from Barstow's early railroad days, as well as interactive and historic displays on railroad history. Check out the old locomotives and cabooses for a truly nostalgic experience. ⊠ *685 N. 1st St.* ☎ *760/256–9276* ⊕ *www. barstowrailmuseum.org* ⊠ *Free* ⊗ *Fri.–Sun. 11–4.*

Fodor's Choice ★ **Goldstone Deep Space Communications Complex.** That satellite dish on your roof is but a speck compared with the radar devices you find at this 53-square-mi complex, where the friendly and enthusiastic staff gives guided tours by appointment. Start out at the Goldstone Museum, which details past and present missions and Deep Space Network history. From there, drive out to see the massive concave antennas, starting with those used for the 1960s

Genesis and Apollo space missions and culminating with the 11-story-tall "listening" device and its always-staffed mission control room used to track spacecraft that have drifted beyond our solar system. ⊠ *35 mi north of Barstow on Ft. Irwin Military Base* ☏ *760/255–8687 or 760/255–8688* ⊕ *deepspace.jpl.nasa. gov/dsn/features/goldstonetours.html* ☏ *Free* ☉ *Guided tours by appointment only.*

WHERE TO EAT AND STAY

¢–$ ✗ **Bagdad Café.** Tourists from all over the world flock to the site where the 1988 film of the same name was shot. Built in the 1940s, this Route 66 eatery serves a home-style menu of burgers, chicken-fried steak, and seafood. The walls are crammed with memorabilia donated by visitors from far and wide, famous and otherwise. ⊠ *46548 National Trails Hwy., Newberry Springs* ☏ *760/257–3101.*

AMERICAN

★

$$$ ✗ **Idle Spurs Steakhouse.** Since the 1950s this roadside ranch has been a Barstow dining staple, and it's still beloved by locals. Covered in cacti outside and Christmas lights inside, it's a colorful, cheerful place with a big wooden bar. The menu features prime cuts of meat, ribs, and lobster, and there's a great microbrew list. ⊠ *690 Hwy. 58* ☏ *760/256–8888* ⊕ *www.idlespurssteakhouse.com* ☉ *No lunch weekends.*

AMERICAN

★

$ ✗ **Slash X Ranch Cafe.** If you have a craving for cold beer, burgers, and chili-cheese fries, look no further than this Wild West-esque watering hole, established in 1954. Named for the cattle ranch that preceded it, the café lures a mix of visitors and locals, who relish its rowdy atmosphere, hearty portions, and friendly service. Shuffleboard tables and horseshoe pits add to the fun, provided it's not too sizzling hot outside. ⊠ *28040 Barstow Rd.* ☏ *760/252–1197* ☉ *Closed weekdays.*

SOUTHERN

¢ ☷ **Ramada Inn.** Though this large property is slightly more expensive than others lining Main Street, it also has more amenities (which is why it tends to attract business travelers). **Pros:** clean; large rooms. **Cons:** dreary location in terms of chain restaurants and the like; occasional nighttime train noise. ⊠ *1511 E. Main St.* ☏ *760/256–5673* ⊕ *www. ramada.com* ⤺ *148 rooms* ⚭ *In-room: Wi-Fi. In-hotel: restaurant, pool, some pets allowed* ☕ *Breakfast.*

AFTON CANYON

Because of its colorful, steep walls, **Afton Canyon** (⊠ *Off Afton Canyon Rd., 36 mi northeast of Barstow via I-15*) is often called the Grand Canyon of the Mojave. It was carved over thousands of years by the rushing waters of the Mojave River, which makes one of its few aboveground appearances here. The dirt road that leads to the canyon is ungraded in spots, so you are best off driving it in an all-terrain vehicle.

BAKER

63 mi northeast of Barstow on I–15; 84 mi south of Death Valley Junction via Hwy. 127.

The small town of Baker is Death Valley's gateway to the western Mojave. There are several gas stations and restaurants (many of them fast-food outlets), a few motels, and a general store (that for many years has claimed to sell the most winning Lotto tickets in California).

GETTING HERE AND AROUND

Baker sits at the intersection of I–15 and Highway 127. The only practical way to get here is by car.

EXPLORING

You can't help but notice Baker's 134-foot-tall **thermometer** (⊠ *72157 Baker Blvd.*), whose world-record height in feet pays homage to the record-high U.S. temperature: 134°F, recorded in Death Valley on July 10, 1913.

PRIMM, NV

52 mi northeast of Baker, via I–15; 118 mi east of Death Valley, via Hwy. 160 and I–15; 114 mi north of Barstow, via I–15.

Amid the rugged beauty of the Mojave's landscapes, this three-casino cluster is a small-scale substitute for those who are overwhelmed by Las Vegas—or who simply cannot wait to get there. The resorts here are tucked on the Nevada side where Interstate 15 crosses the border.

GETTING HERE AND AROUND

If for some reason you want to make this rather than Las Vegas your gambling base, you can catch shuttles here from McCarran International Airport. Otherwise, pull off I–15 in your car. It's not a stretch to park at one casino and walk among the three.

EXPLORING

Though there are some family-friendly activities in Primm (such as shopping at the mall, hitting the waterslide at Whiskey Pete's, or the amusement park at Buffalo Bill's), guests under 21 are not allowed on the casino floors, and children under 13 may not be left unattended. Each of the casinos has a video arcade, which may provide some solace for the teenage set.

WHERE TO STAY

For expanded hotel reviews, visit Fodors.com.

¢ ⊞ **Buffalo Bill's Resort and Casino.** Decorated in the style of a Western frontier town, this hotel is the biggest and most popular in Primm. **Pros:** swimming pool and large amusement park; on-site restaurants and shops; comparatively exciting atmosphere. **Cons:** roller coaster noise at night; basic rooms seem a little worn. ⊠ *31700 Las Vegas Blvd. S* ☎ *702/386–7867 or 800/386–7867* ⊕ *www.primmvalleyresorts.com* ⋑ *1,193 rooms, 49 suites* ⌂ *In-room: a/c, kitchen (some). In-hotel: restaurants, bars, pool.*

SPORTS AND THE OUTDOORS

All hotel guests have privileges at the **Primm Valley Golf Club** (☎ *888/847–2757*), which has two 18-hole courses designed by Tom Fazio that rank among the top 100 in the nation. Two putting greens and a pro shop complete the club, which is 4 mi south of Primm Valley Resort.

MOJAVE NATIONAL PRESERVE

Between I–15 and I–40, roughly east of Baker and Ludlow to the California/Nevada border.

The 1.4 million acres of the Mojave National Preserve hold a surprising abundance of plant and animal life—especially considering their elevation (nearly 8,000 feet in some areas). There are traces of human history here as well, including abandoned army posts and vestiges of mining and ranching towns. The town of Cima still has a small functioning store.

GETTING HERE AND AROUND

The only way to see the preserve, unless you have time to hike or bicycle through, is by car. The fully paved Kelbaker Road bisects the park north–south; Essex Road gets you to Hole-in-the-Wall with pavement, but is graveled beyond.

EXPLORING

★ **Hole-in-the-Wall.** Created millions of years ago by volcanic activity, Hole-in-the-Wall formed when gases were trapped between layers of deposited ash, rock, and lava; the gas bubbles left holes in the solidified material. The area was named by Bob Hollimon, a member of the Butch Cassidy gang, because it reminded him of his former hideout in Wyoming. And here, rather unexpectedly, you will encounter one of California's most distinctive hiking experiences. Proceeding clockwise from a small visitor center, you walk gently down and around a craggy hill, past cacti and fading petroglyphs to Banshee Canyon, whose pockmarked walls resemble Swiss cheese. From there you head back out of the canyon, supporting yourself with widely spaced iron rings (some of which wiggle precariously from their rock moorings) as you ascend a 200-foot incline that deposits you back near the visitor center. It's a mildly dangerous adventure, but wholly entertaining. The entire hike should take no more than 90 minutes. Keep your eyes open for native lizards such as the chuckwalla. ✉ *Black Canyon Rd., 9 mi north of Mitchell Caverns* ☎ *760/928–2572* ⊕ *www.nps.gov/moja* ☾ *Fri.–Sun. 9–4.*

★ **Kelso Dunes.** As you enter the preserve from the south, you'll pass miles of open scrub brush, Joshua trees, and beautiful red-black cinder cones before encountering the Kelso Dunes. These golden, fine-sand slopes cover 70 square mi, reaching heights of 600 feet. You can reach them via a ½-mi walk from the main parking area, but be prepared for a serious workout. When you reach the top of a dune, kick a little bit of sand down the lee side and listen to the sand "sing." North of the dunes, in the town of Kelso, is the Mission revival–style **Kelso Depot Information Center,** flanked by five palm trees. The striking building, which dates to 1923, was extensively renovated in 2005 and contains several rooms of desert- and train-themed exhibits. The Depot's restaurant, The Beanery, has an early- to mid-20th-century diner look that will have you reaching for your camera. ✉ *Kelbaker Rd., 90 mi east of I–15 and 14 mi north of I–40* ☎ *760/928–2572 or 760/252–6100* ⊕ *www.nps.gov/moja*

○ ★ **Providence Mountains State Recreation Area.** The National Park Service administers most of the Mojave preserve, but Providence Mountains State Recreation Area is under the jurisdiction of the California Department of Parks. The visitor center has views of mountain peaks, dunes, buttes, crags, and desert valleys. At **Mitchell Caverns** (▱ $6) you have a rare opportunity to see all three types of cave formations—dripstone, flowstone, and erratics—in one place. Tours, the only way to see the caverns, are given daily at 1:30. Reservations must be made by mail and at least three weeks in advance; call first to check availability. Note: The caverns were closed for much of 2011 due to state budget cuts, and their reopening was planned but not assured by October 2011. ✉ *Essex Rd., 16 mi north of I–40* ☎ *760/928–2586* ⊕ *www.parks.ca.gov* ⊙ *Visitor center May–Sept., weekends 9–4.*

NEEDLES

I–40, 150 mi east of Barstow.

On Route 66 and the Colorado River, Needles is a decent base for exploring many desert attractions, including Mojave National Preserve. Founded in 1883, the town of Needles, named for the jagged mountain peaks that overlook the city, served as a stop along the Santa Fe Railroad. One of its crown jewels was the elegant El Garces Harvey House Train Depot, a lovely façade that is sadly in need of massive renovations. Today, Needles is a remote and dusty getaway for California residents who want to enjoy the Colorado River a little closer to home.

GETTING HERE AND AROUND

Greyhound and Amtrak both pass through town once or twice a day. Most everyone arrives here by private automobile, either via Interstate 40 (east-west) or Highway 95 (north-south).

ESSENTIALS

Visitor Information Needles Chamber of Commerce (✉ *100 G St., Needles* ☎ *760/326–2050* ⊕ *www.needleschamber.com*).

EXPLORING

El Garces Harvey House Train Depot. Stop and gawk at the lovely but crumbling 1908 train depot, one of the many restaurant–boarding-houses built by the Fred Harvey company, and imagine how magnificent it would look in the unlikely event it were restored. There's a shady city park out front that has inviting benches. ✉ *900 Front St.* ☎ *760/326–5678.*

○ Fodor'sChoice ★ **Havasu National Wildlife Refuge.** In 1941, after the construction of Parker Dam, President Franklin D. Roosevelt set aside Havasu National Wildlife Refuge, a 24-mi stretch of land along the Colorado River between Needles and Lake Havasu City. Best seen by boat, this beautiful waterway is punctuated with isolated coves, sandy beaches, and Topock Marsh, a favorite nesting site of herons, egrets, and other waterbirds. You can see wonderful petroglyphs on the rocky red canyon cliffs of Topock Gorge. The park has 11 access points, including boat launches at Catfish Paradise, Five Mile Landing, and Pintail Slough. There's camping below Castle Rock. ✉ *Off I–40, 13 mi southeast of Needles* ☎ *760/326–3853* ⊕ *www.fws.gov/southwest/refuges/arizona/havasu.*

Moabi Regional Park. Moabi Regional Park, on the banks of the Colorado River, is a good place for swimming, boating, picnicking, horseback riding, and fishing. Bass, bluegill, and trout are plentiful in the river. There are 600 campsites with full amenities, including RV hookups, laundry and showers, and grills. ⊠ *Park Moabi Rd., off I-40, 11 mi southeast of Needles* ☎ *760/326–3831* ⌑ *Day use $10, camping $15–$40.*

WHERE TO EAT AND STAY

$
PIZZA

✕ **River City Pizza.** It's slim pickins in Needles when it comes to finding good grub, but this little pizza place is a local favorite located in just off Interstate 40. You'll find a diverse, inexpensive selection on the menu. Try the Vegetarian Deluxe Pizza with a mug of cold lager or a glass of wine out on the small patio. ⊠ *1901 Needles Hwy.* ☎ *760/326–9191.*

¢

▦ **Best Western Colorado River Inn.** The country-western style rooms at this reliable chain are spartan, but they're decorated in rich colors. **Pros:** good rates; clean rooms. **Cons:** town's dead at night; occasional train noise. ⊠ *2371 Needles Hwy.* ☎ *760/326–4552 or 800/780–7234* ⊕ *www.bestwestern.com* ⌁ *63 rooms* ⚹ *In-room: a/c, Internet (some). In-hotel: pool, laundry facilities, some pets allowed* ⦿ *Breakfast.*

¢
☾

▦ **Fender's River Road Resort.** This funky little 1960s-era motel is one of the best-kept secrets in Needles. **Pros:** on the river; clean rooms. **Cons:** several minutes from the freeway; bare-bones amenities. ⊠ *3396 Needles Hwy.* ☎ *760/326–3423* ⊕ *www.fendersriverroadresort.com* ⌁ *10 rooms, 27 campsites with full hookups* ⚹ *In-room: a/c, kitchen. In-hotel: beach, laundry facilities.*

LAKE HAVASU CITY, AZ

Hwy. 95, 43 mi southeast of Needles in Arizona.

In summer Angelenos throng to Lake Havasu. This wide spot in the Colorado River, which has backed up behind Parker Dam, is accessed from its eastern shore in Arizona. Here you can swim; zip around on a Jet Ski; paddle a kayak; fish for trout, bass, or bluegill; or boat beneath the London Bridge, one of the desert's oddest sights. During sunset the views are breathtaking.

Once home to the Mohave Indians, this riverfront community (which means "blue water") was settled in the 1930s with the construction of Parker Dam.

GETTING HERE AND AROUND

Shuttle operators from Las Vegas can get you here and back, but as is the case with every site in this chapter, traveling by car is the only practical way to go. **Havasu Area Transit** (☎ *928/453–7600*) runs public buses among the city and surrounding communities.

WHERE TO EAT

$$
AMERICAN
★

✕ **Shugrue's.** This lakefront restaurant, a favorite of locals and tourists, serves up beautiful views of London Bridge and the English Village. Heavy on fresh seafood, and steak, the restaurant is also known for such specials as Bombay chicken and shrimp, served with spicy yogurt sauce and mango chutney. ⊠ *1425 McCulloch Blvd.* ☎ *928/453–1400* ⊕ *www.shugrues.com/lhc.*

SPORTS AND THE OUTDOORS

Docked at the London Bridge, the **Dixie Bell** (☎ 928/453–6776 ⛟ $16) offers a leisurely way to spend an afternoon. The two-story, old-fashioned paddle-wheel boat, with air-conditioning and a cocktail lounge, takes guests on a one-hour narrated tour around the island. Tours are given daily at noon and 1:30.

Right on the beach, **London Bridge Watercraft Tours & Rentals** (✉ *1534 Beachcomber Blvd., Crazy Horse Campground* ☎ *928/453–8883* ⊕ *www.londonbridgewatercraft.com*) rents personal watercraft such as Jet Skis and Sea-Doos.

OWENS VALLEY

Along U.S. 395 east of the Sierra Nevada.

In this undervisited region, the snow-capped Sierra Nevada range abruptly and majestically rises to the west and the high desert whistles to the east.

LONE PINE

30 mi west of Panamint Valley via Hwy. 190.

Mt. Whitney towers majestically over this tiny community, which supplied nearby gold- and silver-mining outposts in the 1860s. In more recent decades—especially the 1950s and '60s—the town has been touched by Hollywood glamour: more than 300 movies, TV shows, and commercials have been filmed here. The Lone Pine Film Festival now takes place here every October.

GETTING HERE AND AROUND

Get here via scenic Highway 395 from the north or south, or Highway 190 from Death Valley National Park. There is no train and no regularly scheduled bus service.

ESSENTIALS

Visitor Information Lone Pine Chamber of Commerce (✉ *126 S. Main St., Lone Pine* ☎ *760/876–4444 or 877/253–8981* ⊕ *www.lonepinechamber.org*).

EXPLORING

Alabama Hills. Drop by the Lone Pine Visitor Center for a map of the Alabama Hills and take a drive up Whitney Portal Road (turn west at the light) to this wonderland of granite boulders. Erosion has worn the rocks smooth; some have been chiseled to leave arches and other formations. The hills have become a popular location for rock climbing. There are three campgrounds among the rocks, each with a stream for fishing. ✉ *Whitney Portal Rd., 4½ mi west of Lone Pine.*

★ **Mt. Whitney.** Straddling the border of Sequoia National Park and Inyo National Forest–John Muir Wilderness, Mt. Whitney (14,496 feet) is the highest mountain in the continental United States. A favorite game for travelers passing through Lone Pine is trying to guess which peak is Mt. Whitney. Almost no one gets it right because Mt. Whitney is hidden behind other mountains. There is no road that ascends the peak, but you can catch a glimpse of the mountain by driving curvy Whitney Portal Road west from Lone Pine into the mountains. The pavement ends at the trailhead to the top of the mountain, which is also the start of the 211-mi John Muir Trail from Mt. Whitney to Yosemite National Park. At the portal, a restaurant (known for its pancakes) and a small store mostly cater to hikers and campers staying at Whitney Portal Campground. You can see a waterfall from the parking lot and go fishing in a small trout pond. The portal area is closed from mid-October to early May; the road closes when snow conditions require.

WHERE TO EAT AND STAY

¢ ✕ **Alabama Hills Café & Bakery.** Locals flock to this breakfast and lunch
AMERICAN eatery just off the main drag. The extensive menu includes many vegetarian items. Portions are huge, which is good news for anyone who is fueling up for a walk in the Sierra range looming to the west. ⊠ *111 W. Post St.* ☎ *760/876–4675* ⊗ *Closed Tues.*

$$$ ✕ **Seasons Restaurant.** This inviting, country-style diner serves all kinds
AMERICAN of upscale American fare. For a special treat, try the medallions of Cervena venison, smothered in port wine, dried cranberries, and toasted walnuts; finish with the Baileys Irish Cream cheesecake or the lemon crème brûlée for dessert. Children's items include a mini–sirloin steak. Customers consistently praise the extensive wine selection. ⊠ *206 S. Main St.* ☎ *760/876–8927* ⊗ *No lunch. Closed Mon.*

¢ ▥ **Dow Villa Motel and Hotel.** Built in 1923 to cater to the film industry, Dow Villa is in the center of Lone Pine. **Pros:** historic property; recently updated; nice views. **Cons:** feels a bit dated; road noise. ⊠ *310 S. Main St.* ☎ *760/876–5521 or 800/824–9317* ⊕ *www.dowvillamotel.com* ⤶ *91 rooms* ♿ *In-room: a/c, Internet. In-hotel: pool, spa.*

MANZANAR NATIONAL HISTORIC SITE

U.S. 395, 11 mi north of Lone Pine.

GETTING HERE AND AROUND

There's no public transportation here; virtually everyone arrives by private car. There's a big parking lot a few hundred feet west of Highway 395.

★ **Manzanar National Historic Site.** A reminder of an ugly episode in U.S. history, the remnants of the Manzanar War Relocation Center have been designated the Manzanar National Historic Site. This is where some 10,000 Japanese-Americans were confined behind barbed-wire fences between 1942 and 1945. Manzanar was the first of 10 such internment camps erected by the federal government following Japan's attack on Pearl Harbor in 1941. In the name of national security, American citizens of Japanese descent were forcibly relocated to these camps, many of them losing their homes, businesses, and most of their possessions in the process. Today not much remains of Manzanar but a guard post, the auditorium, and some concrete foundations. But you can stop at the entrance station, pick up a brochure, and drive the one-way dirt road past the ruins to a small cemetery, where a monument stands as a reminder of what took place here. Signs mark where structures such as the barracks, a hospital, school, and fire station once stood. An outstanding 8,000-square-foot interpretive center has exhibits and a 15-minute film. ⓓ *Manzanar Information, c/o Superintendent: Death Valley National Park, Death Valley 92398* ☎ *760/878–2932* ⊕ *www. nps.gov/manz* ✉ *Free* ☉ *Park daily dawn–dusk. Center Apr.–Nov., daily 9–5:30; Nov.–Apr., daily 9–4:30.*

CERRO GORDO GHOST TOWN

20 mi east of Lone Pine.

GETTING HERE AND AROUND
Reach here by turning north off Highway 190. You can't visit Cerro Gordo without a car, and due to the rocky, steep roads you can't expect to make it here safely with a low-clearance undercarriage.

★ **Cerro Gordo Ghost Town.** Discovered by Mexican miner Pablo Flores in 1865, Cerro Gordo was California's biggest producer of silver and lead, raking in almost $13 million before it shut down in 1959. Today it's a ghost town, home to many original buildings, including the circa-1871 American Hotel, the fully restored 1904 bunkhouse, the 1868 Belshaw House, a bullet-riddled saloon, and Union Mine and General Store, which now serves as a museum and outlook point over the majestic Sierra mountains and Owens Dry Lake.

The Sarsaparilla Saloon inside the hotel serves up its own Cerro Gordo Freighting Company Root Beer, bottled in nearby Indian Wells (proceeds go back to restoring and maintaining the ghost town). You'll have to time your visit for summer (usually early June through mid-November), as its 8,300-foot elevation means that the steep road into the town is impassable in winter. A four-wheel-drive vehicle is recommended at all times. A day pass is $5 per person, which includes a tour if arranged in advance. Guests are forbidden to take artifacts from the area or explore nearby mines. ⓓ *Box 221, Keeler 93530* ☎ *760/876–5030* ⊕ *www.cerrogordo.us.*

INDEPENDENCE

U.S. 395, 5 mi north of Manzanar National Historic Site.

Named for a military outpost that was established near here in 1862, Independence is small and sleepy. But the town has some wonderful historic buildings and is certainly worth a stop on your way from the Sierra Nevada to Death Valley (⇨ *Chapter 12*).

GETTING HERE AND AROUND
Greyhound does pass through town, but most travelers arrive by car on Highway 395.

ESSENTIALS
Visitor Information Independence Chamber of Commerce (✉ *139 N. Edwards, Independence* ☎ *760/878–0084* ⊕ *www.independence-ca.com*).

EXPLORING
☻ **Mt. Whitney Fish Hatchery.** As you approach Independence from the north, you'll pass the Mt. Whitney Fish Hatchery, a delightful place for a family picnic. The hatchery's lakes were full of hefty, always-hungry breeder

A memorial honors the 10,000 Japanese-Americans who were held at the Manzanar War Relocations Center during World War II.

trout until a devastating mudslide in July 2008 prompted an expensive and extensive rebuilding project that took a year to complete. Built in 1915, the hatchery was one of the first trout farms in California, and today it produces fish that stock lakes throughout the state. ⊠ *Fish Hatchery Rd., 1 mi north of Independence* ☎ *760/878–2272* 🖼 *Free* ⊙ *Thurs.–Mon. 10–4.*

Eastern California Museum. The Eastern California Museum provides a glimpse of Inyo County's history. Highlights include a fine collection of Paiute and Shoshone Indian basketry, an exhibit about the Manzanar internment camp, and a yard full of agricultural implements used by early area miners and farmers. ⊠ *155 N. Grant St.* ☎ *760/878–0364* ⊕ *www.inyocounty.us/ecmuseum* 🖼 *Donations accepted* ⊙ *Daily 10–5.*

WHERE TO STAY

For expanded hotel reviews, visit Fodors.com.

¢ 🖼 **Winnedumah Hotel Bed & Breakfast.** This 1927 B&B has the best— and most famous—digs in town: celebrities such as Roy Rogers, John Wayne, and Bing Crosby all stayed here while filming nearby. **Pros:** historic property; clean rooms. **Cons:** no television. ⊠ *211 N. Edwards St.* ☎ *760/878–2040* ⊕ *www.winnedumah.com* 🛏 *24 rooms, 14 with bath* ⚄ *In-room: a/c, no TV. In-hotel: some pets allowed* ¶⊙¶ *Breakfast.*

BISHOP

U.S. 395, 43 mi north of Independence.

One of the biggest towns along U.S. 395, Bishop has views of the Sierra Nevada and the White and Inyo mountains. First settled by the Northern Paiute Indians, the area was named in 1861 for cattle rancher Samuel Bishop, who established a camp here. Paiute and Shoshone people reside on four reservations in the area.

GETTING HERE AND AROUND

In order to fully enjoy the many surrounding attractions, you must get here by car. Arrive and depart via scenic Highway 395 or, from Nevada, Highway 6. **The Eastern Sierra Transit Authority** (☎ *800/922–1930*) has limited service to nearby tourist sites.

ESSENTIALS

Visitor Information Bishop Chamber of Commerce (⊠ *690 N. Main St., Bishop* ☎ *760/873–8405* ⊕ *www.bishopvisitor.com*).

EXPLORING

Laws Railroad Museum. The Laws Railroad Museum is a complex of historic buildings and train cars from the Carson and Colorado Railroad Company, which set up a narrow-gauge railroad yard here in 1883. Among the exhibits are a self-propelled car from the Death Valley Railroad and a full village of rescued buildings, including a post office, an 1883 train depot, the 1909 North Inyo Schoolhouse, and a restored 1900 ranch house. ⊠ *U.S. 6, 3 mi north of U.S. 395* ☎ *760/873–5950* ⊕ *www.lawsmuseum.org* ⊠ *$5 suggested donation* ⊙ *Daily 10–4.*

WHERE TO EAT AND STAY

¢ SCANDINAVIAN ★ ✕ **Erick Schat's Bakkerÿ.** A popular stop for motorists traveling to and from Mammoth Lakes, this shop is chock-full of delicious pastries, cookies, rolls, and other baked goods. But the biggest draw here is the sheepherder bread, a hand-shaped and stone hearth–baked sourdough that was introduced during the gold rush by immigrant Basque sheepherders in 1907. In addition to the bakery, Schat's has a gift shop and a sandwich bar. ⊠ *763 N. Main St.* ☎ *760/873–7156* ⊕ *www.erickschatsbakery.com.*

$ AMERICAN ★ ✕ **Whiskey Creek.** Since 1924, this Wild West–style saloon, restaurant, and gift shop has been serving crisp salads, warm soups, and juicy barbecued steaks to locals and tourists. Warm days are perfect for sitting on the shaded deck and enjoying one of the many available microbrews. ⊠ *524 N. Main St.* ☎ *760/873–7174* ⊕ *www.whiskeycreekbishop.com.*

$ **Best Western Creekside Inn.** The nicest spot to stay in Bishop, this clean and comfortable mountain-style hotel is a good base from which to explore the town or go skiing and trout fishing nearby. **Pros:** nice pool; spacious and modern rooms; all rooms are nonsmoking. **Cons:** pets not allowed. ⊠ *725 N. Main St.* ☎ *760/872–3044 or 800/273–3550* ⊕ *www.bishopcreekside.com* ➴ *89 rooms* ⌂ *In-room: a/c, kitchen (some), Wi-Fi. In-hotel: pool* ⦿ *Breakfast.*

Death Valley National Park

WORD OF MOUTH

"It is a vast park, awesome and unique and otherworldly. You can see plant and animal life that has adapted to the extreme climate and lack of water. One fascinating example is at the Salt Creek boardwalk where you can view the pupfish which can live in an inch of hot water."

—Elnap 29

WELCOME TO DEATH VALLEY NATIONAL PARK

TOP REASONS TO GO

★ **Weird science:** Death Valley's Racetrack is home to a moving boulder, an unexplained phenomenon that has scientists baffled.

★ **Lowest spot on the continent:** Stand on the lowest spot on the continent at Badwater, 282 feet below sea level.

★ **Wildflower explosion:** During the spring, this desert landscape is ablaze with greenery and colorful flowers, especially between Badwater and Ashford Mill.

★ **Ghost towns:** Death Valley is renowned for its Wild West heritage and is home to dozens of crumbling settlements including Ballarat, Cerro Gordo, Chloride City, Greenwater, Harrisburg, Keeler, Leadfield, Panamint City, Rhyolite, and Skidoo.

★ **Natural wonders:** From canyons to sand dunes to salt flats and dry lake beds, Death Valley serves up plenty of geological treasures.

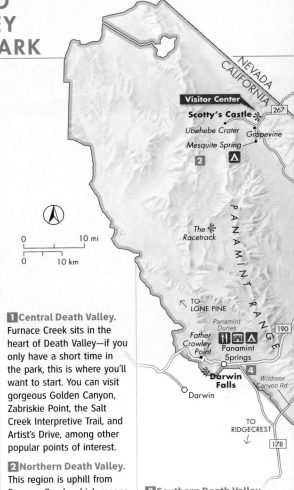

1 Central Death Valley. Furnace Creek sits in the heart of Death Valley—if you only have a short time in the park, this is where you'll want to start. You can visit gorgeous Golden Canyon, Zabriskie Point, the Salt Creek Interpretive Trail, and Artist's Drive, among other popular points of interest.

2 Northern Death Valley. This region is uphill from Furnace Creek, which means marginally cooler temperatures. Be sure to stop by Rhyolite Ghost Town on Highway 374 before entering the park and exploring Moorish Scotty's Castle, colorful Titus Canyon, crumbling Keane Wonder Mine, and jaw-dropping Ubehebe Crater.

3 Southern Death Valley. This is a desolate area, but there are plenty of sights that help convey Death Valley's rich history. Don't miss the Dublin Gulch Caves, or the famous Amargosa Opera House, where ballerina Marta Becket, now in her eighties, still wows the crowds.

4 **Western Death Valley.**
Panamint Springs Resort
is a nice place to grab a
meal and get your bearings
before moving on to quaint
Darwin Falls, smooth rolling
sand dunes, beehive-shaped
Wildrose Charcoal Kilns,
and historic Stovepipe Wells
Village. On the way in, stop
at Cerro Gordo Ghost Town,
where you can view restored
buildings dating back to
1867.

GETTING ORIENTED

Death Valley National Park
covers 5,310 square mi,
ranges from 6 to 60 mi
wide, and measures 140
mi north to south. Within
the park, the Panamint
Range parallels Death
Valley to the west, the
Amargosa Range to the
east. Nearly the entire
park lies in southeastern
California, with a small
eastern portion cross-
ing over into Nevada.

12

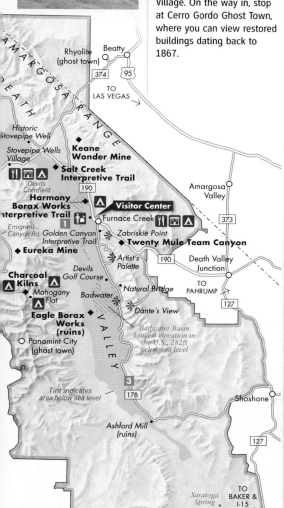

Updated by Sura Wood and Reed Parsell

The desert is no Disneyland. With its scorching summer heat and vast, sparsely populated tracts of land, it's not often at the top of the list when most people plan their California vacations. But the natural riches of Death Valley—the largest national park outside Alaska—are overwhelming: rolling waves of sand dunes, black cinder cones thrusting up hundreds of feet from a blistered desert floor, riotous sheets of wildflowers, bizarrely shaped Joshua trees basking in the orange glow of a sunset, tiny pupfish that enthrall youngsters, and a silence that is both dramatic and startling.

PLANNING

WHEN TO GO

Most of the park's one million annual visitors still come between late fall and early spring, taking advantage of moderate temperatures and the lack of rainfall. During these cooler months you will need to book a room in advance, but don't worry: the park never feels crowded. If you visit during summer, believe everything you've ever heard about desert heat—it can be brutal, with temperatures often topping 120°F. The dry air wicks moisture from the body without causing a sweat, so drink plenty of water. Bring sunglasses, a hat, and sufficient clothing to block the sun's rays and the wind. Flash floods are common; sections of roadway can be flooded or washed away. The wettest month is February, when the park receives an average of 0.3 inch of rain.

GETTING HERE AND AROUND

It can take more than three hours to cross from one side of the park to another, so it's important to choose an entrance point that makes sense for what you want to see. If you're driving from Los Angeles, enter through the western portion along Highway 395; enter from the north at Beatty, Nevada, or via the central entrance at Death Valley Junction if you're coming from Las Vegas. Travelers from Orange County, San Diego, and the Inland Empire should access the park via I–15 North at Baker.

12

Much of the park can be toured on regularly scheduled bus tours, but these often don't allow time for hikes to sites not seen from the road, such as Salt Creek, Golden Canyon, and Natural Bridge. The best option is to drive to a number of the sites, get out of the car, and walk.

When driving in Death Valley, reliable maps are a must, as signage is often limited. Other important accessories include a compass, a mobile phone (though these don't always work in remote areas), and extra food and water (3 gallons per person per day is recommended, plus additional radiator water). If you're able to take a four-wheel-drive vehicle, bring it: many of Death Valley's most spectacular canyons are otherwise inaccessible.

The **California State Department of Transportation Hotline** (☎ *916/445–7623 or 800/427–7623* ⊕ *www.dot.ca.gov*) has updates on Death Valley road conditions. The **California Highway Patrol** (☎ *760/ 255-8750 near Barstow, 760/872–5900 near Bishop* ⊕ *cad.chp.ca.gov*) offers the latest traffic incident information.

WHAT IT COSTS					
	¢	$	$$	$$$	$$$$
RESTAURANTS	under $10	$10–$15	$16–$22	$23–$30	over $30
HOTELS	under $90	$90–$120	$121–$175	$176–$250	over $250

Restaurant prices are for a main course at dinner, excluding sales tax. Hotel prices are for two people in a standard double room in high season, excluding service charges and tax.

PARK ESSENTIALS

ADMISSION FEES AND PERMITS
The entrance fee is $20 per vehicle and $10 for those entering on foot, bus, bike, or motorcycle. The payment, valid for seven consecutive days, is collected at the park's entrance stations and at the visitor center at Furnace Creek. (If you enter the park on Highway 190, there is no entrance station; remember to stop by the visitor center to pay the fee.) Annual park passes, valid only at Death Valley, are $40.

A permit is not required for groups of 14 or fewer, but if you're planning an overnight visit to the backcountry, complete a registration form at the Furnace Creek Visitor Center. Backcountry camping is allowed in areas that are at least 2 mi from maintained campgrounds and the main paved or unpaved roads, and ¼ mi from water sources. Most abandoned mining areas are restricted to day use.

ADMISSION HOURS
Most facilities within the park remain open year-round, daily 8–5.

EMERGENCIES

For all emergencies, call 911. Note that cell phones don't work in many parts of the park.

PARK CONTACT INFORMATION

Death Valley National Park ⌂ *P.O. Box 579, Death Valley 92328* ☏ *760/786–2331* ⊕ *www.nps.gov/deva.*

EXPLORING

HISTORIC SITES

Fodor's Choice
★
Keane Wonder Mine. The tram towers and cables from the old mill used to process gold from Keane Wonder Mine are still here, leading up to the crumbling mine, which is a steep 1-mi hike up the mountain. A nearby path leads north to Keane Wonder Spring. ⊠ *Access road off Beatty Cutoff Rd., 17½ mi north of Furnace Creek.*

☼
★
Scotty's Castle. This Moorish-style mansion, begun in 1924 and never completed, takes its name from Walter Scott, better known as Death Valley Scotty. An ex-cowboy, prospector, and performer in Buffalo Bill's Wild West Show, Scotty always told people the castle was his, financed by gold from a secret mine. In reality, there was no mine, and the house belonged to a Chicago millionaire named Albert Johnson, whom Scott had finagled into investing in the fictitious mine. Despite the con, Johnson and Scott became great friends. The house functioned for a while as a hotel and still contains works of art, imported carpets, handmade European furniture, and a tremendous pipe organ. Costumed rangers, to varying degrees of enthusiasm, re-create life at the castle circa 1939. Check out the Underground Mysteries Tour, which takes you through a ¼-mile tunnel in the castle basement. ⊠ *Scotty's Castle Rd. (Hwy. 267), 53 mi north of Furnace Creek Interpretive Trail* ☏ *760/786–2392* ⊕ *www.nps.gov/deva* ⊠ *$11* ☉ *Winter: Daily 8:30–5:30; Summer: 9-4:30, tours daily 9–5.*

SCENIC STOPS

★
Artist's Palette. So called for the contrasting colors of its volcanic deposits, this is one of signature sights of Death Valley. Artist's Drive, the approach to the area, is one way heading north off Badwater Road, so if you're visiting Badwater, come here on the way back. The drive winds through foothills of sedimentary and volcanic rocks. About 4 mi into the drive, a short side road veers right to a parking lot that's a few hundred feet before the "palette," whose natural colors include shades of green, gold, and pink. ⊠ *11 mi south of Furnace Creek, off Badwater Rd.*

★
Badwater. At 282 feet below sea level, Badwater is the lowest spot on land in the Western Hemisphere—and also one of the hottest. Stairs and wheelchair ramps descend from the parking lot to a wooden platform that overlooks a sodium chloride pool, a small but remarkably persistent reminder that the valley floor used to contain a lake. You can continue past the platform on a broad, white path that peters out after a half-mile or so. Badwater is one of the most popular and easily accessible sites within the park. From this lowest point, be sure to look

across to Telescope Peak, which towers more than 2 mi above the valley floor. ⊠ *Badwater Rd., 19 mi south of Furnace Creek.*

Fodor'sChoice
★
Dante's View. This lookout is more than 5,000 feet up in the Black Mountains. In the dry desert air you can see across most of 110-mi-wide Death Valley. The view is astounding. Take a 10-minute, mildly strenuous walk from the parking lot toward a series of rocky overlooks, where with binoculars you can spot some of Death Valley's signature sites. A few interpretive signs point out the highlights below in the valley and across, in the Sierra. Getting here from Furnace Creek takes an hour—time well invested. ⊠ *Dante's View Rd., off Hwy. 190, 35 mi from Badwater, 20 mi south of Twenty Mule Team Canyon.*

Devil's Golf Course. Thousands of miniature salt pinnacles carved into surreal shapes by the desert wind dot this wildly varied landscape. The salt was pushed up to the earth's surface by pressure created as underground salt- and water-bearing gravel crystallized. Get out of your vehicle and take a closer look; you'll see perfectly round holes descending into the ground. ⊠ *Badwater Rd., 13 mi south of Furnace Creek. Turn right onto dirt road and drive 1 mi.*

★
Racetrack. Getting here involves a 27-mi journey over a rough and almost nonexistent dirt road, but the trip is well worth the reward. Where else in the world do rocks move on their own? This phenomenon has baffled scientists for years. No one has actually seen the rocks in motion, but theory has it that when it rains, the hard-packed lake bed becomes slippery enough that gusty winds push the rocks along—sometimes for several hundred yards. When the mud dries, a telltale trail remains. The trek to the Racetrack can be made in a passenger vehicle, but high clearance is suggested. ⊠ *27 mi west of Ubehebe Crater via dirt road.*

Sand Dunes at Mesquite Flat. These dunes, made up of minute pieces of quartz and other rock, are ever-changing products of the wind-rippled hills, with curving crests and a sun-bleached hue. The dunes are the most photographed destination in the park, and you can see them at their best at sunrise and sunset. Keep your eyes open for animal tracks— you may even spot a coyote or fox. Bring plenty of water, and note where you parked your car: it's easy to become disoriented in this ocean of sand. If you lose your bearings, climb to the top of a dune and scan the horizon for the parking lot. ⊠ *19 mi north of Hwy. 190, northeast of Stovepipe Wells Village.*

★
Titus Canyon. Titus Canyon is a popular 28-mi drive from Beatty south along Scotty's Castle Road. Along the way you'll pass Leadville Ghost Town, petroglyphs at Klare Spring, and spectacular limestone and dolomite narrows at the end of the canyon. Toward the end, a two-section of gravel road will lead you into the mouth of the canyon. ⊠ *Access road off Scotty's Castle Rd., 33 mi northwest of Furnace Creek.*

★
Zabriskie Point. Although only about 710 feet in elevation, this is one of Death Valley National Park's most scenic spots, overlooking a striking panorama of wrinkled, multicolor hills. It's a great place to watch the sunrise, but it can be bustling any time of day. Pair it with a drive out to magnificent Dante's View. ⊠ *Hwy. 190, 5 mi south of Furnace Creek.*

VISITOR CENTERS

Furnace Creek Visitor Center and Museum. The exhibits and artifacts here provide a broad overview of how Death Valley formed; you can pick up maps at the bookstore run by the Death Valley Natural History Association. This is also the place to sign up for ranger-led walks (available November through April) or check out a live presentation about the valley's cultural and natural history. The center offers 12-minute slide shows about the park every 30 minutes. Your children are likely to receive plenty of individual attention from the enthusiastic rangers. ✉ *Hwy. 190, 30 mi northwest of Death Valley Junction* ☎ *760/786–3200* ⊕ *www.nps.gov/deva* ☽ *Daily 8–5.*

Scotty's Castle Visitor Center and Museum. If you visit Death Valley, you'll likely make a stop here at the main ticket center for Scotty's Castle living-history tours. Here you'll also find a nice display of exhibits, books, self-guided tour pamphlets, and displays about the castle's creators, Death Valley Scotty and Albert M. Johnson. Fuel up with gasoline, sandwiches, or souvenirs before heading back out to the park. ✉ *Rte. 267, 53 mi northwest of Furnace Creek and 45 mi northwest of Stovepipe Wells Village* ☎ *760/786–2392* ⊕ *www.nps.gov/deva* ☽ *Visitor's center8:30–5:30; tours 9–5.*

SPORTS AND THE OUTDOORS

BIRD-WATCHING

Approximately 350 bird species have been identified in Death Valley. The best place to see the park's birds is along the Salt Creek Interpretive Trail, where you can spot ravens, common snipes, killdeer, spotted sandpipers, and great blue herons. Along the fairways at Furnace Creek Golf Club, you can see kingfishers, peregrine falcons, hawks, Canada geese, yellow warblers, and the occasional golden eagle—just remember to stay off the greens. Scotty's Castle attracts wintering birds from around the globe who are attracted to its running water, shady trees, and shrubs. Other good spots to find birds are at Saratoga Springs, Mesquite Springs, Travertine Springs, and Grimshaw Lake near Tecopa. You can download a complete park bird checklist, divided by season, at ⊕ *www.nps.gov/deva/naturescience/birds.htm*. Rangers at Furnace Creek Visitor Center often lead birding walks through Salt Creek between November and March.

FOUR-WHEELING

Maps and SUV guidebooks for four-wheel-drive and other backcountry roads (including the popular Cottonwood/Marble canyons, Racetrack, Eureka Dunes, Saratoga Springs, Warm Springs Canyon) are offered at the Furnace Creek Visitor Center. Remember: never travel alone and be sure to pack plenty of water and snacks. Driving off established roads is strictly prohibited in the park.

HIKING

Plan to hike before or after midday in the spring, summer, or fall, unless you're in the mood for a masochistic baking. Carry plenty of water, wear protective clothing, and keep an eye out for tarantulas, black widows, scorpions, snakes, and other potentially dangerous creatures.

Some of the best trails are unmarked; if the opportunity arises, ask for directions.

EASY

Fodor's Choice
★
Darwin Falls. This lovely 2-mi round-trip hike rewards you with a refreshing waterfall surrounded by thick vegetation and a rocky gorge. No swimming or bathing is allowed, but it's a beautiful place for a picnic. Adventurous hikers can scramble higher toward more rewarding views of the falls. ⊠ *Access the 2-mi graded dirt road and parking area off Hwy. 190, 1 mi west of Panamint Springs Resort.*

Natural Bridge Canyon. A 2-mi access road with potholes that could swallow basketballs leads to a parking lot. From there, set off to see interesting geological features in addition to the bridge, which is ¼-mi away. The one-way trail continues for a few hundred meters, but scenic returns diminish quickly and eventually you're confronted with climbing boulders. ⊠ *Access road off Badwater Rd., 15 mi south of Furnace Creek.*

Salt Creek Interpretive Trail. This trail, a ½-mi boardwalk circuit, loops through a spring-fed wash. The nearby hills are brown and gray, but the floor of the wash is alive with aquatic plants such as pickerelweed and salt grass. The stream and ponds here are among the few places in the park to see the rare pupfish, the only native fish species in Death Valley. Animals such as bobcats, fox, coyotes, and snakes visit the spring, and you may also see ravens, common snipes, killdeer, and great blue herons. ⊠ *Off Hwy. 190, 14 mi north of Furnace Creek.*

★
Titus Canyon. The narrow floor of Titus Canyon is made of hard-packed gravel and dirt, and it's a constant, moderate uphill walk. Klare Spring and some petroglyphs are 5½ mi from the mouth of the canyon, but you can get a feeling for the area on a shorter walk.

MODERATE

Mosaic Canyon. A gradual uphill trail (4 mi round-trip) winds through the smoothly polished walls of this narrow canyon. There are dry falls to climb at the upper end. ⊠ *Access road off Hwy. 190, ½ mi west of Stovepipe Wells Village.*

DIFFICULT

Fodor's Choice
★
Keane Wonder Mine. Allow two hours for the 2-mi round-trip trail that follows an out-of-service aerial tramway to this mine. The way is steep, but the views of the valley are spectacular. Do not enter the tunnels or hike beyond the top of the tramway—it's dangerous. The trailhead is 2 mi down an unpaved and bumpy access road. ⊠ *Access road off Beatty Cutoff Rd., 17½ mi north of Furnace Creek.*

Telescope Peak Trail. The 14-mi round-trip begins at Mahogany Flat Campground, which is accessible by a very rough dirt road. The steep and at some points treacherous trail winds through pinyon, juniper, and bristlecone pines, with excellent views of Death Valley and Panamint Valley. Ice axes and crampons may be necessary in winter—check at the Furnace Creek Visitor Center. It takes a minimum of eight hours to hike to the top of the 11,049-foot peak and then return. Getting to the peak is a strenuous endeavor; take plenty of water and only attempt it

Flora and Fauna

There's a general misconception that Death Valley National Park consists of mile upon endless mile of flat desert sands, scattered cacti, and an occasional cow skull. Many people don't realize that across the valley floor from Badwater—the lowest point in the Western Hemisphere—Telescope Peak towers at 11,049 feet above sea level. The extreme topography of Death Valley is a lesson in geology. Two hundred million years ago seas covered the area, depositing layers of sediment and fossils. Between 3.5 million and 5 million years ago faults in the Earth's crust and volcanic activity pushed and folded the ground, causing mountain ranges to rise and the valley floor to drop. The valley was then filled periodically by lakes, which eroded the surrounding rocks into fantastic formations and deposited the salts that now cover the floor of the basin.

Most animal life in Death Valley (51 mammal, 36 reptile, 307 bird, and 3 amphibian species) is found near the limited sources of water. The bighorn sheep spend most of their time in the secluded upper reaches of the park's rugged canyons and ridges. Coyotes can often be seen lazing in the shade next to the golf course and have been known to run onto the fairways to steal a golf ball. The only native fish in the park is the pupfish, which grows to slightly longer than 1 inch. In winter, when the water is cold, the fish lie dormant in the bottom mud, becoming active again in spring. Because they are wary of large moving shapes, you must stand quietly over a pool at Salt Creek to see them.

Botanists say there are more than 1,000 species of plants here (21 exist nowhere else in the world), though many annual plants lie dormant as seeds for all but a few months in spring, when rains trigger a bloom. The rest congregate around limited sources of water. Most of the low-elevation vegetation grows around the oases at Furnace Creek and Scotty's Castle, where oleanders, palms, and salt cedar grow. At higher elevations you will find pinyon, juniper, and bristlecone pine.

in fall unless you're an experienced hiker. ⊠ *Off Wildrose Rd., south of Charcoal Kilns.*

EDUCATIONAL OFFERINGS

GUIDED TOURS

Death Valley Explorer Tour. Look Tours hosts this 11-hour luxury motor-coach tour of the park passes through its most famous landmarks. Tours include lunch and hotel pickup from designated Las Vegas–area hotels. ☏ *Death Valley Tours, 800/566–5868 or 702/233–1627 Look Tours* ✉ *$239* ⊙ *Tues., Thurs., at 5:45 am.*

Furnace Creek Visitor Center tours. This center has the most tour options, including a weekly 2-mi Harmony Borax Walk and guided hikes to Keane Wonder Mine, Mosaic Canyon, and Golden Canyon. Less strenuous options include wildflower walks, birding walks, geology walks, and a Furnace Creek Inn historical tour. The Furnace Creek

Visitor Center is where you hop aboard a distinctive, pink four-wheel-drive vehicle with **Pink Jeep Tours Las Vegas** (☎ *702/895–6777 www. pinkjeep.com*), to visit places—the Charcola Kilns, the Racetrack, and Titus Canyon among them—that your own vehicle might not be able to handle. Pink Jeep tours last two hours and cost $65. The visitor center also offers orientation programs every half hour, daily from 8 to 6. ⊠ *Furnace Creek Visitor Center, Rte. 190, 30 mi northwest of Death Valley Junction* ☎ *760/786–2331.*

Gadabout Tours. Take multiday trips through Death Valley from Ontario, California, in February, March, and November. ⊠ *Sheraton Ontario Airport, 428 N. Vineyard Ave., Ontario* ☏ *1801 E. Tahquitz Canyon Way, Palm Springs 92262* ☎ *760/325–5556 or 800/952–5068* ⊕ *www. gadabouttours.com.*

PERFORMING ARTS

Marta Becket's Amargosa Opera House. An artist and dancer from New York, Becket first visited the former railway town of Amargosa while on tour in 1964. Three years later she returned to town and bought a boarded-up theater that sat amid a group of run-down mock–Spanish colonial buildings. To compensate for the sparse audiences in the early days, Becket painted a Renaissance-era Spanish crowd on the walls and ceiling, turning the theater into a trompe l'oeil masterpiece. Now in her mid 80s, Becket performs her blend of ballet, mime, and 19th-century melodrama to sellout crowds. After the show you can meet her in the adjacent gallery, where she sells her paintings and autographs her books. There are no performances mid-May through September. Reservations are required. ⊠ *Rte. 127,608 Death Valley Junction 92328* ☎ *760/852–4441* ⊕ *www.amargosa-opera-house.com* ⌨ *$15* ☾ *Oct.– May (through Mother's Day weekend).*

WHERE TO EAT

$$
CAFÉ
☾ ✕**Forty-Niner Cafe.** This casual coffee shop serves typical American fare for breakfast, lunch, and dinner. It's done up in a rustic mining style with whitewashed pine walls, vintage map-covered tables, and prospector-branded chairs. Past menus and old photographs decorate the walls. ⊠ *Furnace Creek Ranch, Hwy. 190, Furnace Creek* ☎ *760/786–2345* ⊕ *www.furnacecreekresort.com.*

$$$$
AMERICAN
Fodor's Choice
★
✕**Furnace Creek Inn Dining Room.** Fireplaces, beamed ceilings, and spectacular views provide a visual feast to match the inn's ambitious menu. Dishes may include such desert-theme items as crispy cactus, and simpler fare such as salmon, free-range chicken, and lamb chops. For vegetarians, there's squash lasagna and polenta. An evening dress code (jeans are OK, but no T-shirts or shorts) is enforced. Lunch is served October–May only, but you can always have afternoon tea, an inn tradition since 1927. Breakfast and Sunday brunch are also served. ⊠ *Furnace Creek Inn Resort, Hwy. 190, Furnace Creek* ☎ *760/786– 2345* ⊕ *www.furnacecreekresort.com* ⌂ *Reservations essential* ☾ *No lunch June–Sept.*

"I'd always wanted to photograph this remote location, and on my drive into Death Valley I was rewarded at Zabriskie Point with this amazing view." —photo by Rodney Ee, Fodors.com member

$$$
AMERICAN

✕ **Toll Road Restaurant.** There are wagon wheels in the yard and Old West artifacts on the interior walls at this restaurant in the Stovepipe Wells Village hotel. A stone fireplace heats the dining room. A full menu, with steaks, chicken, fish, and pasta, is served October–mid-May; breakfast and dinner buffets are laid out during summer. Quench your thirst in the full-service saloon. ✉ *Hwy. 190, Stovepipe Wells* ☎ *760/786–2604.*

WHERE TO STAY

During the busy season (November–March) you should make reservations for lodgings within the park at least one month in advance.

For expanded hotel reviews, visit Fodors.com.

$$$$
Fodor's Choice
★

▦ **Furnace Creek Inn.** This is Death Valley's most luxurious accommodation, going so far as to have valet parking. **Pros:** refined; comfortable; great views. **Cons:** a far cry from roughing it; expensive. ✉ *Furnace Creek Village, near intersection of Hwy. 190.* ⌂ *P.O. Box 190, Death Valley 92328* ☎ *760/786–2345* ⊕ *www.furnacecreekresort.com* ⇆ *66 rooms* ⚒ *In-room: a/c, Internet, Wi-fi, In-hotel: restaurant, room service, bar, tennis courts, pool* ☾ *Closed mid-May–mid-Oct.*

$

▦ **Panamint Springs Resort.** Ten miles inside the west entrance of the park, this low-key resort overlooks the sand dunes and peculiar geological formations of the Panamint Valley. **Pros:** slow-paced; friendly; there's a glorious amount of peace and quiet after sundown. **Cons:** far from the park's main attractions. ✉ *Hwy. 190, 28 mi west of Stovepipe Wells* ⌂ *P.O. Box 395, Ridgecrest, 93556* ☎ *775/482–7680* ⊕ *www.*

OUTFITTERS AND EXPEDITIONS

Reserve well in advance for all tours.

FOUR-WHEELING

The 10-hour **Death Valley SUV Tour** (*Death Valley Tours* ☎ *800/719–3768* ⊕ *www.deathvalleytours.net*) departs from Las Vegas and takes you on a fully narrated whirl through Death Valley in a four-wheel-drive Jeep. Tours ($255.95 per person; slightly less if booked through the Internet) departs daily, Sept. through May at 7:45 am and include free pickup from designated hotels. Bottled water and snacks are provided, and camera rentals, tripods, and film are available for an additional fee.

HIKING

Join an experienced guide and spend six days exploring Death Valley's most popular sights with **Death Valley National Park and Red Rock Hiker** (*Escape Adventures* ☎ *800/596–2953 or 702/596–2953* ⊕ *www.escapeadventures.com*). The tour ($1,290), offered October and February–April, also spends two days in Red Rock Canyon National Conservation Area. For an additional fee, you can rent, tents, sleeping bags, ground pad, and pillow in a kit for $90, The price includes a night in the Bonnie Springs Inn.

HORSEBACK AND CARRIAGE RIDES

Set off on a one- or two-hour guided horseback or carriage ride ($45–$60) from **Furnace Creek Stables** (⊠ *Hwy. 190, Furnace Creek* ☎ *760/614–1018* ⊕ *www.furnacecreekstables.net*). The rides traverse trails with views of the surrounding mountains, where multi-color volcanic rock and alluvial fans form a background for date palms and other vegetation. Evening carriage rides take passengers around the golf course and Furnace Creek Ranch. Cocktail rides, with champagne, margaritas, and hot spiced wine, are available. The stables are open October–May only.

deathvalley.com/psr ⤳ *14 rooms, 1 cabin* ♿ *In-room: a/c (some), no phone, no TV, Wi-Fi. In-hotel: restaurant, bar, some pets allowed.*

$ 🏨 **Stovepipe Wells Village.** If you prefer quiet nights and an unfettered view of the night sky and nearby sand dunes, this property is for you. **Pros:** intimate, relaxed; no big-time partying; authentic desert community ambience. **Cons:** isolated; a bit dated; can feel a bit dodgy after dark. ⊠ *Hwy. 190, Stovepipe Wells* ✉ *P.O. Box187, Death Valley 92328* ☎ *760/786–2387* ⊕ *www.escapetodeathvalley.com* ⤳ *83 rooms* ♿ *In-room: no phone, no TV (some). In-hotel: restaurant, bar, pool, some pets allowed.*

Camping in Death Valley

⚠ **Furnace Creek.** This campground, 196 feet below sea level, has some shaded tent sites. Pay showers, a laundry, and a swimming pool are at nearby Furnace Creek Ranch. Reservations are accepted for stays between mid-October and mid-April; at other times sites are available on a first-come, first-served basis. Two group campsites can accommodate 40 people each. **Pros:** inexpensive; central to park's main attractions; many tent-only sites have trees for limited shade. **Cons:** the campground often is full or parts of it are closed; tent-only sites are hard and pebbly; RV spots have no shade. ⊠ *Hwy. 190, Furnace Creek* ☎ *301/722–1257, 800/365–2267 reservations* ⇨ *136 tent/RV sites* ⚍ *Flush toilets, dump station, drinking water, fire grates, picnic tables, public telephone, ranger station* ⊟ *Credit cards accepted for reservations only.*

⚠ **Panamint Springs Resort.** Part of a complex that includes a motel and cabin, this campground is surrounded by cottonwoods. The daily fee includes use of the showers and restrooms. **Pros:** at an elevation of 1,000 feet, it's cooler than the valley floor; has water and electricity. **Cons:** road to it has many potholes; some reports of rude hosts. ⊠ *Hwy. 190, 28 mi west of Stovepipe Wells* ☎ *775/482–7680* ⇨ *11 RV sites, 26 tent sites, 30 water-only RV sites* ⚍ *Flush toilets, full hookups, partial hookups (water), dump station, drinking water, showers, fire grates, picnic tables, public telephone, general store, service station (gas only).*

⚠ **Stovepipe Wells Village.** This is the second-largest campground in the park. This area is little more than a giant parking lot, but pay showers and laundry facilities are available at the adjacent motel. It's first-come, first-served. **Pros:** creature comforts are nearby, including a saloon; near the sand dunes; lots of socializing possibilities. **Cons:** nothing special as a camping experience, as there's no shade or frills inside the campground. ⊠ *Hwy. 190, Stovepipe Wells* ☎ *760/786–2387* ⇨ *190 tent sites, 14 RV sites* ⚍ *Flush toilets, full hookups, dump station, drinking water, public telephone, general store, swimming (pool)* ⊟ *No credit cards for tent sites* ⊘ *Mid-Oct.–mid-Apr.*

The Central Valley

HIGHWAY 99 FROM BAKERSFIELD TO LODI

WORD OF MOUTH

"We have many rivers that can be rafted. The closest river to Southern California and one of the best is the Upper Kern near Bakersfield. This was a fun day in June!"

— photo by Kim Brogan, Fodors.com member

WELCOME TO
THE CENTRAL VALLEY

TOP REASONS TO GO

★ **Down under:** Forestiere Underground Gardens is not the flashiest tourist attraction in California, but it is one of the strangest— and oddly inspirational.

★ **Grape escape:** In the past 15 years, Lodi's wineries have grown enough in stature for the charming little town to become a must-sip destination.

★ **Port with authority:** Stockton has long been a hub for merchandise that is being transferred from roadway to waterway—or vice versa. Watch some of that commotion in commerce from the riverfront downtown area.

★ **Go with the flow:** White-water rafting will get your blood pumping, and maybe your clothes wet, on the Stanislaus River near Oakdale.

★ **Hee haw!:** Kick up your heels and break out your drawl at Buck Owens' Crystal Palace in Bakersfield, a city some believe is the heart of country music.

1 **Southern Central Valley.** When gold was discovered in Kern County in the 1860s, settlers flocked to the southern end of the Central Valley. Black gold— oil—is now the area's most valuable commodity; the county provides 64% of California's oil production. Kern is also among the country's five most productive agricultural counties. From the flat plains around Bakersfield, the landscape grows gently hilly and then graduates to mountains as it nears Kernville, which lies in the Kern River valley.

2 **Mid-Central Valley.** The Mid-Central Valley extends over three counties—Tulare, Kings, and Fresno. Historic Hanford and bustling Visalia are off the tourist-traffic radar but have their charms. From Visalia, Highway 198 winds east 35 mi to Generals Highway, which passes through Sequoia and Kings Canyon national parks (⇨ see Chapter 16). Highway 180 snakes east 55 mi to Sequoia and Kings Canyon. From Fresno, Highway 41 leads north 95 mi to Yosemite National Park (⇨ see Chapter 15).

3 **North Central Valley.** The northern section of the valley cuts through Merced, Madera, Stanislaus, and San Joaquin counties, from the flat, abundantly fertile terrain between Merced and Modesto north to the edges of the Sacramento River delta and the fringes of the Gold Country. If you're heading to Yosemite National Park (⇨ see Chapter 15) from northern California, chances are you'll pass through (or very near) at least one of several small gateway communities, which include Mariposa and Oakdale.

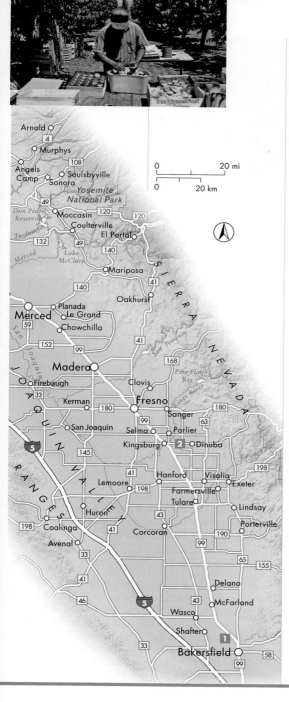

GETTING ORIENTED

California has a diversity of delicious vacation possibilities. Among its many outstanding regions, however, the Central Valley is arguably the least inviting. This flat landscape, sometimes blistery hot and smelly, contains no famous attractions beyond its bountiful farmland, which few would regard as scenic except perhaps just before harvest. For many vacationers, it is a region to drive through as quickly as possible on the way to fabulous Sequoia, Kings Canyon, and Yosemite national parks (⇨ see Chapters 15 and 16). For those who have an extra day or two, whose tourism tastes don't demand Disneyland-level excitement, it can represent a pleasant diversion and provide insights into an enormous agricultural region. The valley is the vast geographical center of California, and from a breadbasket perspective, its proverbial heart.

Updated by
Reed Parsell

Among the world's most fertile working lands, the Central Valley is important due to the scale of its food production but, to be honest, it lacks substantial appeal for visitors. For most people, the Central Valley is simply a place to pass through on the way to greater attractions in the north, south, east, or west. For those willing to invest a little effort, however, California's heartland can be rewarding.

The agriculturally rich area is home to a diversity of wildlife. Many telephone posts are crowned by a hawk or kestrel hunting the land below. Vineyards, especially in the northern valley around Lodi, and almond orchards, whose white blossoms make February a brighter month, are pleasant sights out motorists' windows. In the towns, historical societies display artifacts of the valley's eccentric past; concert halls and restored theaters showcase samplings of contemporary culture; and museums provide a blend of both. Restaurants can be very good, whether they be fancy or mom-and-pop. For fruit lovers, roadside stands can be treasure troves. Country-music enthusiasts will find a lot to appreciate on the radio and on stages, especially in the Bakersfield area. Summer nights spent at one of the valley's minor-league baseball parks—Bakersfield, Fresno, Modesto, Stockton, and Visalia have teams—can be a relaxing experience. Whether on back roads or main streets, people tend to be proud to help outsiders explore the Central Valley.

PLANNING

WHEN TO GO

Spring, when wildflowers are in bloom and the scent of fruit blossoms is in the air, and fall, when the air is brisk and leaves turn red and gold, are the best times to visit. Many of the valley's biggest festivals take place during these seasons. (If you suffer from allergies, though, beware of spring, when stone-fruit trees blossom.) Summer, when temperatures often top 100°F, can be oppressive. June through August, though, are the months to visit area water parks and lakes or to take in the air-conditioned museums. Many attractions close in winter, which can get dreary. Thick, ground-hugging fog is a common driving hazard November through February.

GETTING HERE AND AROUND

The 225-mi Central Valley cuts through Kern, Tulare, Kings, Fresno, Madera, Merced, Stanislaus, and San Joaquin counties. It's bounded on the east by the mighty Sierra Nevada and on the west by the smaller coastal ranges.

Fresno Yosemite International Airport is serviced by Alaska, Allegiant, American and American Eagle, Delta, Horizon, Mexicana, United, United Express, and US Airways. Kern County Airport at Meadows Field is serviced by United Express and US Airways. United Express flies from Los Angeles and San Francisco to Modesto City-County Airport, and US Airways flies from Las Vegas to Visalia Municipal Airport.

Greyhound provides service among major valley cities. Orange Belt Stages provides bus service, including Amtrak connections, to many valley locations.

Amtrak's daily *San Joaquin* travels among Bakersfield, San Jose, and Oakland, stopping in Hanford, Fresno, Madera, Merced, Turlock, Modesto, and Stockton.

Highway 99 is the main route between the valley's major cities and towns. Interstate 5 runs roughly parallel to it to the west but misses the major population centers; its main use is for quick access from San Francisco or Los Angeles. Major roads that connect I–5 with Highway 99 are highways 58 (to Bakersfield), 198 (to Hanford and Visalia), 152 (to Chowchilla, via Los Banos), 140 (to Merced), 132 (to Modesto), and 120 (to Manteca).

ESSENTIALS

Airport Contacts Kern County Airport at Meadows Field (✉ *1401 Skyway Dr., Bakersfield* ☎ *661/391–1800* ⊕ *www.meadowsfield.com*).

Bus Contact Greyhound (☎ *800/231–2222* ⊕ *www.greyhound.com*). **Orange Belt Stages** (☎ *800/266–7433* ⊕ *www.orangebelt.com*).

Road Conditions California Department of Transportation hotline (☎ *800/266–6883 or 916/445–1534*).

Train Contact Amtrak (☎ *800/872–7245* ⊕ *www.amtrakcalifornia.com*).

TOUR OPTIONS

Central Valley Tours provides general and customized tours of the Fresno area and the valley, with special emphasis on the fruit harvests and Blossom Trail.

Contacts Central Valley Tours (☎ *559/276–4479* ⊕ *www.angelfire.com/poetry/inc/valleytours.html*).

RESTAURANTS

Fast-food places and chain restaurants dominate valley highways, but away from the main drag, independent and family-owned eateries will awaken your taste buds. Many bistros and fine restaurants take advantage of the local produce and locally raised meats that are the cornerstone of California cuisine. Even simple restaurants produce hearty, tasty fare that often reflects the valley's ethnic mix. Some of the nation's best Mexican restaurants call the valley home. Chinese, Italian, Armenian, and Basque restaurants also are abundant; many serve massive, several-course meals.

HOTELS

The Central Valley has many chain motels and hotels, but independently owned hotels and bed-and-breakfasts also can be found. There's a fair selection of upscale lodgings, Victorian-style B&Bs, and places that are simply utilitarian but clean and comfortable.

WHAT IT COSTS					
	¢	$	$$	$$$	$$$$
Restaurants	under $10	$10–$15	$16–$22	$23–$30	over $30
Hotels	under $90	$90–$120	$121–$175	$176–$250	over $250

Restaurant prices are for a main course at dinner, excluding sales tax of 7%–10% (depending on location). Hotel prices are for two people in a standard double room in high season, excluding service charges and 8%–13% tax.

SOUTH CENTRAL VALLEY

BAKERSFIELD

110 mi north of Los Angeles via I–5 and Hwy. 99; 110 mi west of Ridgecrest via Hwy. 14 south and Hwy. 58 west.

Bakersfield's founder, Colonel Thomas Baker, arrived with the discovery of gold in the nearby Kern River valley in 1851. Now Kern County's biggest city (it has a population of 334,000, which includes the largest Basque community in the United States), Bakersfield probably is best known as Nashville West, a country-music haven closely affiliated with performers Buck Owens (who died here in 2006) and Merle Haggard (who was born here in 1937). It also has a symphony orchestra and two good museums.

GETTING HERE AND AROUND

Arrive here by car via Highway 99 from the north or south, and via Highway 58 from the east or west. Amtrak and Greyhound also have regular train and bus service here. In town, the Golden Empire Transit District (☎ 661/869–2438 ⊕ *www.getbus.org*) serves the area's commuters.

ESSENTIALS

Bus Contact Orange Belt Stages (☎ 800/266–7433 ⊕ www.orangebelt.com).

Visitor Information Greater Bakersfield Convention & Visitors Bureau (✉ 515 Truxton Ave., Bakersfield ☎ 661/325–5051 or 866/425–7353 ⊕ www. bakersfieldcvb.org). **Kern County Board of Trade** (✉ 2101 Oak St., Bakersfield ☎ 661/500–5376 or 800/500–5376 ⊕ www.visitkern.com).

The Central Valley

NEVADA
CALIFORNIA

5
99
Lodi
Jackson
49
88
Lockeford
San Andreas
Arnold
Murphys
4
88
26
Stockton
Angels Camp
Sonora
Soulsbyville
108
Bridgeport
Yosemite National Park
Lathrop
205
4
Manteca
Escalon
Knights Ferry Recreation Area
108
Oakdale
Waterford
Don Pedro Res.
Moccasin
120
167
Mono Lake
Lee Vining
80
Ripon
Salida
Modesto
132
Turlock
Delhi
49
Coulterville
49
El Capitan
Half Dome
395
Patterson
Merced River
Lake McClure
140
El Portal
Mammoth Lakes
Newman
5
Livingston
Atwater
140
Mariposa
41
Lake Crowley
Gustine
152
Merced
Planada
Le Grand
Oakhurst
SIERRA
Los Banos
59
Chowchilla
152
99
41
San Joaquin River
NEVADA
Dos Palos
Madera
168
Kings Canyon National Park
Firebaugh
33
Kerman
180
Clovis
Pine Flat Res.
Panoche
J1
San Joaquin
Sanger
Kings River
Wilsonia
198
Fresno
see detail map
99
145
Selma
Parlier
63
5
Kingsburg
Dinuba
COAST
198
Lemoore
41
Coalinga
198
Huron
Hanford
Visalia
198
Three Rivers
RANGES
101
Farmersville
Kaweah Oaks Preserve
Exeter
Sequoia National Park
43
Tulare
Lindsay
Avenal
33
Corcoran
99
41
Porterville
190
190
SAN JOAQUIN VALLEY
Colonel Allensworth State Historic Park
65
155
155
Paso Robles
46
Delano
Kernville
101
46
McFarland
Lake Isabella
178
Wasco
5
178
Lake Isabella
Shafter
33
43
Bakersfield
McKittrick
119
99
58

0   20 mi
0   20 km

EXPLORING

California Living Museum. A combination zoo, botanical garden, and natural-history museum, the emphasis here is on the zoo. All animal and plant species displayed are native to the state. Within the reptile house lives every species of rattlesnake found in California. The landscaped grounds—in the hills about a 20-minute drive northeast of Bakersfield—also shelter captive bald eagles, tortoises, coyotes, black bears, and foxes. ⊠ *10500 Alfred Harrell Hwy.; Hwy. 178 east, then 3½ mi northwest on Alfred Harrell Hwy.* ☎ *661/872–2256* ⊕ *www.calmzoo.org* ⊠ *$9* ☉ *Mar.– Oct., daily 9–5; Nov.–Feb., daily 9–4.*

> ### LOCAL LITERARY LEGENDS
>
> The Central Valley's cultural diversity and agricultural roots have woven a textured social fabric that has been chronicled by some of the country's finest writers, including Fresno native William Saroyan, Stockton native Maxine Hong Kingston, and *Grapes of Wrath* author John Steinbeck.

Kern County Museum and Lori Brock Children's Discovery Center. The 16-acre site is one of the Central Valley's top museum complexes. The indoor-outdoor Kern County Museum is set up as an open-air, walk-through historic village with more than 55 restored or re-created buildings dating from the 1860s to the 1940s. "Black Gold: The Oil Experience," a permanent exhibit, shows how oil is created, discovered, extracted, and transformed for various uses. The Lori Brock Children's Discovery Center, for ages eight and younger, has hands-on displays and an indoor playground. ⊠ *3801 Chester Ave.* ☎ *661/852–5000* ⊕ *www.kcmuseum. org* ⊠ *$10* ☉ *Wed.–Sun. 10–5.*

WHERE TO EAT

$ ✕ **Jake's Original Tex Mex Cafe.** Don't let the cafeteria-style service fool
MEXICAN   you; this is probably the best lunch place in Bakersfield. The chicken burritos and the chili fries (with meaty chili ladled on top) are superb; the coleslaw is a favorite, too. For dessert, try the chocolate cake, which locals rave about—with good reason. It's open for dinner, too. ⊠ *1710 Oak St.* ☎ *661/322–6380* ⊕ *www.jakestexmex.com* ⊅ *Reservations not accepted* ☉ *Closed Sun.*

$$ ✕ **Uricchio's Trattoria.** This downtown restaurant draws everyone from
ITALIAN   office workers to oil barons—all attracted by the tasty food and casual atmosphere. *Panini* (Italian pressed sandwiches, served at lunch only), pasta, and Italian-style chicken dishes dominate the menu; the chicken piccata outsells all other offerings. Reservations are recommended. ⊠ *1400 17th St.* ☎ *661/326–8870* ⊕ *www.uricchios-trattoria.com* ☉ *Closed Sun. No lunch Sat.*

NIGHTLIFE AND THE ARTS

Buck Owens' Crystal Palace. Buck Owens is Bakersfield's local boy made good, and this venue named in his honor is a combination nightclub, restaurant, souvenir store, and showcase of country-music memorabilia. Country-and-western singers perform here, as Owens did countless times before his death in 2006. A dance floor beckons customers who can still twirl after sampling the menu of steaks, burgers, nachos, and gooey desserts. Entertainment is free on most weeknights; on Friday and Saturday nights, there's a cover charge (usually $8 to $15) for some of the more well-known entertainers. ✉ *2800 Buck Owens Blvd.* ☎ *661/328–7560* ⊕ *www.buckowens.com* ☾ *Closed Mon.*

KERNVILLE

50 mi northeast of Bakersfield, via Hwys. 178 and 155.

The wild and scenic Kern River, which flows through Kernville en route from Mt. Whitney to Bakersfield, delivers some of the most exciting white-water rafting in the state. Kernville (population 1,700) rests in a mountain valley on both banks of the river and also at the northern tip of Lake Isabella (a dammed portion of the river used as a reservoir and for recreation). By far the most scenic town described in this region, Kernville has lodgings, restaurants, and antiques shops. The main streets are lined with Old West–style buildings, reflecting Kernville's heritage as a rough-and-tumble gold-mining town once known as Whiskey Flat. (Present-day Kernville dates from the 1950s, when it was moved upriver to make room for Lake Isabella.) The road from Bakersfield includes stretches where the rushing river is on one side and granite cliffs are on the other.

GETTING HERE AND AROUND

You get here from Bakersfield via Highway 178, and Highway 155 connects the town to Delano. There's no train line or regularly scheduled bus service.

ESSENTIALS

Visitor Information Kern County Board of Trade (✉ *2101 Oak St., Bakersfield* ☎ *661/500–5376 or 800/500–5376* ⊕ *www.visitkern.com*).

WHERE TO EAT AND STAY

$ ✕ **That's Italian.** For northern Italian cuisine in a typical trattoria, this
ITALIAN is the spot. Try the braised lamb shanks in a Chianti wine sauce or the linguine with clams, mussels, calamari, and shrimp in a white-wine clam sauce. ✉ *9 Big Blue Rd.* ☎ *760/376–6020.*

$$$ ⊡ **Whispering Pines Lodge Bed & Breakfast.** Perched on the banks of the Kern River, this 8-acre property gives you a variety of overnight options. **Pros:** rustic setting; big breakfasts; great views; very clean. **Cons:** bungalows are quite pricey; town is remote. ✉ *13745 Sierra Way* ☎ *760/376–3733 or 877/241–4100* ⊕ *www.kernvalley.com/ whisperingpines* ⇆ *17 rooms* ♨ *In-room: a/c, kitchen (some), Internet. In-hotel: pool* ⦿| *Breakfast.*

SPORTS AND THE OUTDOORS

BOATING AND The Lower Kern River, which extends from Lake Isabella to Bakersfield
WINDSURFING and beyond, is open for fishing year-round. Catches include rainbow trout, catfish, smallmouth bass, crappie, and bluegill. Lake Isabella is popular with anglers, water-skiers, sailors, and windsurfers. Its shoreline marinas have boats for rent, bait and tackle, and moorings. **North Fork Marina** (☎ *760/376–1812*) is in Wofford Heights, on the lake's north shore. **French Gulch Marina** (☎ *760/379–8774*) is near the dam on Lake Isabella's west shore.

WHITE-WATER
RAFTING

The three sections of the Kern River—known as the Lower Kern, Upper Kern, and the Forks—add up to nearly 50 mi of white water, ranging from Class I (easy) to Class V (expert). The Lower and Upper Kern are the most popular and accessible sections. Organized trips can last from one hour (for as little as $35) to more than two days. Rafting season usually runs from late spring until the end of summer.

Kern River Tours (☎ 800/844–7238 ⊕ www.kernrivertours.com) leads several rafting tours from half-day trips to three days of navigating Class V rapids, and also arranges for mountain-bike trips.

Mountain & River Adventures (☎ 760/376–6553 or 800/861–6553 ⊕ www.mtnriver.com) gives calm-water kayaking tours as well as white-water rafting trips, leads mountain bike excursions, and has a campground. In the wintertime, M&R has snowshoe and cross-country ski rentals. Half-day Class II and III white-water rafting trips are emphasized at **Sierra South** (☎ 760/376–3745 or 800/457–2082 ⊕ www.sierrasouth.com), which also offers kayaking classes and calm-water excursions.

MID-CENTRAL VALLEY

Flat and odor-challenged (there are countless cow operations here), this region's small towns offer oases of low-key urban pleasures, with decent restaurants and pleasant parks. Colonel Allensworth State Historic Park is its quietest but most worthy attraction.

COLONEL ALLENSWORTH STATE HISTORIC PARK

45 mi north of Bakersfield on Hwy. 43.

GETTING HERE AND AROUND

A major passenger rail line runs right by the park, but stops only on special occasions. Getting here is easiest and best by private automobile, on Highway 43, about 15 minutes from major Central Valley corridor Highway 99.

★ **Colonel Allensworth State Historic Park.** A former slave who became the country's highest-ranking black military officer of his time founded Allensworth—the only California town settled, governed, and financed by African-Americans—in 1908. After enjoying early prosperity, the town was plagued by hardships and eventually was deserted. Its scattering of rebuilt buildings reflects the few years in which it thrived. Festivities each October commemorate the town's rededication. Amtrak occasionally stops here (group travel with advanced reservations), which makes the park a potential side trip for those taking the train between Los Angeles and San Francisco. At this writing the park was closed to cars except Friday through Sunday, but accessible to visitors on foot daily; call for the latest information. ✉ 4129 Palmer Ave. ☎ 661/849–3433 ⊕ www.cal-parks.ca.gov 🎟 $6 per car ☉ Daily sunrise–sunset, visitor center open on request, buildings open by appointment.

VISALIA

40 mi north of Colonel Allensworth State Historic Park on Hwy. 99 and east on Hwy. 198; 75 mi north of Bakersfield via Hwy. 99 north and Hwy. 198 east.

Visalia's combination of a reliable agricultural economy and civic pride has yielded the most vibrant downtown in the Central Valley (not that competition in the category is too fierce). A clear day's view of the Sierra from Main Street is spectacular, if sadly rare due to smog and dust, and even Sunday night can find the streets bustling with pedestrians.

Founded in 1852, the town contains many historic homes; ask for a free guide at the **visitor center** (⊠ *220 N. Santa Fe St.* ☎ *559/734–5876* ☉ *Mon. 10–5, Tues.–Fri. 8:30–5*).

GETTING HERE AND AROUND

Highway 198, just east of its exit from Highway 99, cuts through town (and proceeds up the hill to Sequoia National Park). Greyhound stops here, but Amtrak trains get no closer than Hanford, 20 mi to the west. Visalia Transit (☎ 559/713–4300) buses run between Visalia, Goshen, Farmersville, and Exeter.

ESSENTIALS

Airport Contacts Visalia Municipal Airport (⊠ *9501 W. Airport Dr., Visalia* ☎ *559/713–4201* ⊕ *www.flyvisalia.com*).

Bus Contact Orange Belt Stages (☎ *800/266–7433* ⊕ *www.orangebelt.com*).

Visitor Information Visalia Chamber of Commerce and Visitors Bureau (⊠ *220 N. Santa Fe St., Visalia* ☎ *559/334–0141* ⊕ *www.visaliachamber.org*).

EXPLORING

Chinese Cultural Center. Housed in a pagoda-style building, the center mounts exhibits about Asian art and culture and documents the influx of Chinese workers to central California during the gold rush. Today, people of Chinese descent make up less than one half of 1% of the city's population. ⊠ *500 S. Akers Rd., at Hwy. 198* ☎ *559/625–4545* ⊡ *Free* ☉ *By appointment only.*

Kaweah Oaks Preserve. Trails at this 324-acre wildlife sanctuary off the main road to Sequoia National Park (⇨ *see Chapter 16*) lead past majestic valley oak, sycamore, cottonwood, and willow trees. Among the 134 bird species you might spot are hawks, hummingbirds, and great blue herons. Lizards, coyotes, and cottontails also live here. ⊠ *Follow Hwy. 198 for 7 mi east of Visalia, turn north on Rd. 182, and proceed ½ mi to gate on left side* ☎ *559/738–0211* ⊕ *www.sequoiariverlands. org* ⊡ *Free* ☉ *Daily sunrise–sunset.*

Mooney Grove Park. Amid shady oaks you can picnic alongside duck ponds, rent a boat for a ride around the lagoon, and view a replica of the famous *End of the Trail* statue. The original, designed by James Earl Fraser for the 1915 Panama-Pacific International Exposition, is now in the Cowboy Hall of Fame in Oklahoma. ⊠ *27000 S. Mooney Blvd., 5 mi south of downtown* ☎ *559/733–6291* ⊡ *$7 per car, free in winter (dates vary)* ☉ *Late May–early Sept., weekdays 8–7, weekends 8 am–9*

Each spring the fruit orchards along the Blossom Trail, near Fresno, burst into bloom.

pm; early Sept.–Oct. and Mar.–late May, Mon., Thurs., and Fri. 8–5, weekends 8–7; Nov.–Feb., Thurs.–Mon. 8–5.

Tulare County Museum. This indoor-outdoor museum contains several re-created environments from the pioneer era. Also on display are Yokuts tribal artifacts (basketry, arrowheads, clamshell-necklace currency) as well as saddles, guns, dolls, quilts, and gowns. A $1.45 million replacement building opened in 2009. ✉ *Mooney Grove Park, 27000 S. Mooney Blvd., 5 mi south of downtown* ☎ *559/733–6616* 🔖 *Free with park entrance fee of $7* ☉ *Weekdays 10–4, weekends 1–4.*

WHERE TO EAT

$
MEXICAN

✕ **Henry Salazar's.** Traditional Mexican food with a contemporary twist is served at this restaurant that uses fresh ingredients from local farms. Bring your appetite if you expect to finish the Burrito Fantastico, a large flour tortilla stuffed with your choice of meat, beans, and chili sauce, and smothered with melted Monterey Jack cheese. Another signature dish is grilled salmon with lemon-butter sauce. Colorfully painted walls, soft reflections from candles in wall niches, and color-coordinated tablecloths and napkins make the atmosphere cozy and restful. ✉ *123 W. Main St.* ☎ *559/741–7060* ⊕ *www.henrysalazars.com.*

$$$
CONTINENTAL
Fodor'sChoice
★

✕ **The Vintage Press.** Built in 1966, this is the best restaurant in the Central Valley. Cut-glass doors and bar fixtures decorate the artfully designed rooms. The California–Continental cuisine includes dishes such as crispy veal sweetbreads with a port-wine sauce, and a bacon-wrapped filet mignon stuffed with mushrooms. The chocolate Grand Marnier cake is a standout among the homemade desserts and ice creams. The wine list has more than 900 selections. ✉ *216 N. Willis St.* ☎ *559/733–3033* ⊕ *www.thevintagepress.com.*

HANFORD

20 mi west of Visalia on Hwy. 198; 43 mi north of Colonel Allensworth State Historic Park on Hwy. 43.

Founded in 1877 as a Southern Pacific Railroad stop, Hanford had one of California's largest Chinatowns—the Chinese came to help build the railroads and stayed on to farm.

GETTING HERE AND AROUND

Amtrak trains stop here several times daily as they roll between the Bay Area and Bakersfield. Otherwise, drive here from the east or west via Highway 198 or from the north or south via Highway 41. For buses, Kings Area Rural Transit (☎ 559/584–0101 ⊕ *www.mykartbus. com*) operates among Hanford, Armona, Avenal, Corcoran, Fresno, Grangeville, Hardwick, Kettleman City, Laton, Lemoore, Stratford, and Visalia.

ESSENTIALS

Bus Contact Orange Belt Stages (☎ *800/266–7433* ⊕ *www.orangebelt.com*).

Visitor Information Hanford Visitor Agency (✉ *200 Santa Fe Ave., Suite D, Hanford* ☎ *559/582–5024* ⊕ *www.visithanford.com*).

EXPLORING

Hanford Carnegie Museum. Visitors here encounter fashions, furnishings, toys, and military artifacts that tell the region's story. The living-history museum is inside the former Carnegie Library, a Romanesque building dating from 1905 that is on the U.S. National Register of Historic Places. ✉ *108 E. 8th St.* ☎ *559/584–1367* ⊕ *www.hanfordcarnegiemuseum.org* 🖙 *$3* ☺ *Tues.–Sat. 11–4.*

Hanford Conference & Visitors Agency. You can take a self-guided walking tour with the help of a free brochure, or take a driving tour in a restored 1930 Studebaker fire truck ($35 for up to 15 people). One tour explores the restored buildings of Courthouse Square, whose art-deco Hanford Auditorium is a visual standout; another heads to narrow China Alley. If you have specific interests, a tour can also be designed for you. ☎ *559/582–5024* ⊕ *www.visithanford.com*

Taoist Temple. A first-floor museum in this 1893 temple displays photos, furnishings, and kitchenware from Hanford's once-bustling Chinatown. The second-floor temple, largely unchanged for a century, contains altars, carvings, and ceremonial staves. You can visit as part of a guided tour at noon on the first Saturday of the month, or by appointment. ✉ *12 China Alley* ☎ *559/582–4508* 🖙 *Free; donations welcome.*

WHERE TO EAT AND STAY

¢ ✕ **La Fiesta.** Mexican-American families, farmworkers, and farmers all
MEXICAN eat here, polishing off traditional Mexican dishes such as enchiladas and tacos. The Fiesta Special—for two or more—includes nachos, garlic shrimp, shrimp in a spicy red sauce, clams, and two pieces of top sirloin. ✉ *106 N. Green St.* ☎ *559/583–8775.*

13

$$ ✗ **The Purple Potato.** This locally
AMERICAN   owned, colorful restaurant—with purple walls, not surprisingly—has become what locals say is the best restaurant in town. The broad menu, which includes steaks, pasta, and poultry, draws raves for its shrimp scampi and pan-seared scallops. The wine list is extensive. ⊠ *A few blocks west of downtown, 601 W. 7th St.* ☎ *559/587–4568* ⊙ *No lunch weekends.*

¢   ⌂ **Irwin Street Inn.** Four tree-shaded, restored Victorian homes have been converted into spacious accommodations with comfortable rooms and suites. **Pros:** big rooms and bathrooms; funky decor; very unlike chain hotels. **Cons:** musty; mattresses can be uncomfortable; not much to do in town. ⊠ *522 N. Irwin St.* ☎ *559/583–8000* ⟿ *24 rooms, 3 suites* ⌂ *In-room: a/c, Wi-Fi. In-hotel: restaurant, pool* ⫚⚬⫙ *Breakfast.*

> **BLOSSOM TRAIL**
>
> The 62-mi self-guided **Blossom Trail** driving tour takes in Fresno-area orchards, citrus groves, and vineyards during spring blossom season. Pick up a route map at the Fresno City & County Convention and Visitors Bureau (⊠ *848 M St., Fresno* ☎ *559/233–0836 or 800/788-0836* ⊕ *www.gofresnocounty.com*). The Blossom Trail passes through small towns and past rivers, lakes, and canals. The most colorful and aromatic time to go is from late February to mid-March, when almond, plum, apple, apricot, and peach blossoms shower the landscape with shades of white, pink, and red.

FRESNO

35 mi north of Hanford via Hwys. 43 and 99 north.

Sprawling Fresno, with more than 470,000 people, is the center of the richest agricultural county in the United States. Cotton, grapes, and tomatoes are among the major crops; poultry and milk are also important. About 75 ethnic groups, including Armenians, Laotians, and Indians, call Fresno home. The city has a vibrant arts scene, several public parks, and an abundance of low-price restaurants. The Tower District—with its chic restaurants, coffeehouses, and boutiques—is the trendy spot (though like the rest of Fresno it can look drab on a cloudy day). Pulitzer Prize–winning playwright and novelist William Saroyan (*The Time of Your Life, The Human Comedy*) was born here in 1908.

GETTING HERE AND AROUND

Highway 99 is the biggest road through town; other thoroughfares are Highway 41 (which continues north toward Yosemite National Park) and Highway 180 (which heads east to Kings Canyon National Park). Amtrak trains from points north and south stop here more than a dozen times daily. **Fresno Area Express** (☎ *559/621–7433)* is the local bus service, with multiple routes around town as well as to and from the suburbs. Taxis are easy to come by, too.

ESSENTIALS

Airport Contacts Fresno Yosemite International Airport (⊠ *4995 E. Clinton Way, Fresno* ☎ *559/621–4500* ⊕ *www.fresno.gov/discoverfresno/airports*).

Fresno Area

13

Visitor Information Fresno City & County Convention and Visitors Bureau
(⊠ *848 M St., Fresno* ☎ *559/445–8300 or 800/788–0836* ⊕ *www.fresnocvb.org*).

EXPLORING

☺ **Forestiere Underground Gardens.** Sicilian immigrant Baldasare Forestiere
★ spent four decades (1906–46) carving out this rather odd place, a sub-
terranean realm of rooms, tunnels, grottoes, alcoves, and arched passageways that once extended for more than 10 acres between Highway
99 and busy, mall-pocked Shaw Avenue. Only a fraction of Forestiere's
prodigious output is on view, but you can tour his underground living
quarters, including bedrooms (one with a fireplace), the kitchen, living
room, and bath, as well as a fishpond and auto tunnel. Skylights allow
exotic full-grown fruit trees, including one that bears seven kinds of
citrus as a result of grafting, to flourish more than 20 feet belowground.
The gardens are renovated each year. ⊠ *5021 W. Shaw Ave., 2 blocks
east of Hwy. 99* ☎ *559/271–0734* ⊕ *www.undergroundgardens.com*
🎟 *$14* ⊙ *Tours weekends 11–2 Mar.–Nov.; also Fri. in summer. Call
for other tour times.*

Fresno Art Museum. Find American, Mexican, and French art here; highlights of the permanent collection include pre-Columbian works and
graphic art from the postimpressionist period. The 152-seat Bonner
Auditorium is the site of lectures, films, and concerts. ⊠ *Radio Park,*

2233 N. 1st St. ☎ 559/441–4221 ⊕ www.fresnoartmuseum.org ▧ $5; free Sun. ⊙ Tues., Wed., and Fri.–Sun. 11–5, Thurs. 11–8.

Kearney Mansion Museum. The drive along palm-lined Kearney Boulevard is one of the best reasons to visit the museum, which stands in shaded 225-acre **Kearney Park.** The century-old home of M. Theo Kearney, Fresno's onetime "raisin king," is accessible only by taking a guided 45-minute tour. ⊠ 7160 W. Kearney Blvd., 6 mi west of Fresno ☎ 559/441–0862 ▧ Museum $5; park entry $5 (waived for museum visitors) ⊙ Park 7 am–10 pm; museum tours Fri.–Sun. at 1, 2, and 3.

Legion of Valor Museum. Military-history buffs of all ages will enjoy this museum. It has German bayonets and daggers, a Japanese Namby pistol, a Gatling gun, and an extensive collection of Japanese, German, and American uniforms. The staff is extremely enthusiastic. ⊠ 2425 Fresno St. ☎ 559/498–0510 ⊕ www.legionofvalor.com ▧ Free ⊙ Mon.–Sat. 10–3.

Meux Home Museum. Inside a restored 1889 Victorian, "the Meux" displays furnishings typical of an upper-class household in early Fresno (Thomas Richard Meux was a doctor for the Confederate army during the Civil War, and subsequently was a family practitioner out West). Guided tours proceed from the front parlor to the backyard carriage house. ⊠ Tulare and R Sts. ☎ 559/233–8007 ⊕ www.meux.mus.ca.us ▧ $5 ⊙ Fri.–Sun. noon–3:30.

☙ **Roeding Park.** Tree-shaded Roeding Park is a place of respite on hot summer days; it has picnic areas, playgrounds, tennis courts, horseshoe pits, and a zoo. The most striking exhibit at **Fresno Chaffee Zoo** (☎ 559/498–2671 ⊕ www.chaffeezoo.org ▧ $7 ⊙ Feb.–Oct., daily 9–4; Nov.–Jan., daily 10–3) is the tropical rain forest, where you'll encounter exotic birds along the paths and bridges. Elsewhere at the zoo you'll find tigers, grizzly bears, sea lions, tule elk, camels, elephants, and hooting siamangs. Also here are a high-tech reptile house and a petting zoo. A train, little race cars, paddleboats, and other rides for kids are among the amusements that operate March through November at **Playland** (☎ 559/233–3980 ⊙ Wed.–Fri. 11–5, weekends 10–6). Children can explore attractions with fairy-tale themes at **Rotary Storyland** (☎ 559/264–2235 ▧ $5 ⊙ Weekdays 11–5, weekends 10–6), which is also open March through November. ⊠ Olive and Belmont Aves. ☎ 559/498–1551 ▧ $1 per vehicle at park entrance, Playland rides require tokens, Storyland $5.

★ **Woodward Park.** Woodward Park, the Central Valley's largest urban park with 300 acres of jogging trails, picnic areas, and playgrounds in the northern reaches of the city, is especially pretty in spring, when plum and cherry trees, magnolias, and camellias bloom. Outdoor concerts take place in summer. The **Shinzen Friendship Garden** has a teahouse, a koi pond, arched bridges, a waterfall, and Japanese art. ⊠ Audubon Dr. and Friant Rd. ☎ 559/621–2900 ▧ $3 per car Feb.–Oct.; additional $3 for Shinzen Garden ⊙ Apr.–Oct., daily 7 am–10 pm; Nov.–Mar., daily 7–7.

WHERE TO EAT AND STAY

$$ ✕ **Tahoe Joe's.** This restaurant is
STEAKHOUSE known for its steaks—rib eye, strip,
or filet mignon. Other selections
include the slow-roasted prime rib,
center-cut pork chops, and chicken
breast served with a whiskey-pep-
percorn sauce. The baked potato
that accompanies almost every dish
is loaded tableside with your choice
of butter, sour cream, chives, and
bacon bits. Tahoe Joe's has three
Fresno locations. ⌧ *7006 N. Cedar
Ave.* ☎ *559/299–9740* ⌧ *2700
W. Shaw Ave.* ☎ *559/277–8028*
⊕ *www.tahoejoes.com* ⌦ *Reserva-
tions not accepted* ◔ *No lunch.*

> ### OLD TOWN CLOVIS
>
> Old Town Clovis (⌧ *Upper Clovis
> Ave., Clovis*) is an area of restored
> brick buildings with numerous
> antiques shops and art galler-
> ies (along with restaurants and
> saloons). Be warned, though—not
> much here is open on Sunday. To
> get here, head east on Fresno's
> Herndon Avenue about 10 mi,
> and then turn right onto Clovis
> Avenue.

13

$$ ⛶ **Piccadilly Inn Shaw.** This two-story property—the best in the area—has
7½ attractively landscaped acres and a big swimming pool. **Pros:** big
rooms; nice pool; best lodging option in town. **Cons:** some rooms are
showing mild wear; neighborhood is somewhat sketchy. ⌧ *2305 W.
Shaw Ave.* ☎ *559/226–3850* 🖷 *559/226–2448* ⊕ *www.piccadillyinn.
com/shaw* ⬳ *194 rooms, 5 suites* ⬧ *In-room: a/c, Internet. In-hotel:
restaurant, pool, gym, laundry facilities.*

NIGHTLIFE AND THE ARTS

The **Fresno Philharmonic Orchestra** (☎ *559/261–0600* ⊕ *www.fresnophil.
org*) performs classical concerts at the recently renovated **William Sar-
oyan Theatre** (⌧ *700 M St.*) September through June. **Roger Rocka's Dinner
Theater** (⌧ *1226 N. Wishon Ave.* ☎ *559/266–9494 or 800/371–4747*
⊕ *www.rogerrockas.com*), in the Tower District, has been staging
Broadway-style musicals since 1978. The **Tower Theatre for the Performing
Arts** (⌧ *815 E. Olive Ave.* ☎ *559/485–9050* ⊕ *www.towertheatrefresno.
org*) has given its name to the trendy Tower District of theaters, clubs,
restaurants, and cafés. The restored 1930s art-deco movie house presents theater, ballet, concerts, and other cultural events year-round.

SPORTS AND THE OUTDOORS

Kings River Expeditions (⌧ *211 N. Van Ness Ave.* ☎ *559/233–4881 or
800/846–3674* ⊕ *www.kingsriver.com*) arranges one- and two-day
white-water rafting trips on the Kings River. **Wild Water Adventures**
(⌧ *11413 E. Shaw Ave., Clovis* ☎ *559/299–9453 or 800/564–9453*
⊕ *www.wildwater.net* ⌫ *$27, $17 after 3 pm*), a 52-acre water park
about 10 mi east of Fresno, is open from late May to early September.

NORTH CENTRAL VALLEY

Agriculture on a massive scale is the trademark of this flat region is all about. The vineyards around Lodi provide a more sophisticated vibe.

MERCED

50 mi north of Fresno on Hwy. 99.

Thanks to a branch of the University of California opening in 2005 and an aggressive community redevelopment plan, the downtown of county seat Merced is coming back to life. The transformation is not yet complete, but there are promising signs: a brewpub, several boutiques, a multiplex, the restoration of numerous historic buildings, and foot traffic won back from outlying strip malls.

GETTING HERE AND AROUND

The most scenic approach to Yosemite National Park, at least from the west, is via Highway 140 as it rambles through and past Merced. Drivers get here mostly via Highway 99, but Amtrak also stops several times daily. In town, The Bus (☎ 800/345–3111) gets local people who know what they're doing where they want to go.

ESSENTIALS

Visitor Information Merced Conference and Visitors Bureau (✉ *710 W. 16th St., Merced* ☎ *209/384–2791 or 800/446–5353* ⊕ *www.yosemite-gateway.org*).

EXPLORING

Merced County Courthouse Museum. Even if you don't go inside, be sure to swing by this three-story former courthouse. Built in 1875, it's a striking example of Victorian Italianate style. The upper two floors are a museum of early Merced history. Highlights include ornate restored courtrooms and an 1870 Chinese temple with carved redwood altars. ✉ *21st and N Sts.* ☎ *209/723–2401* ⊕ *www.mercedmuseum.org* 🎫 *Free* ⊙ *Wed.–Sun. 1–4.*

Merced Multicultural Arts Center. The center displays paintings, sculpture, and photography. The Big Valley Arts & Culture Festival, which celebrates the area's ethnic diversity and children's creativity, is held here in late September or early October. ✉ *645 W. Main St.* ☎ *209/388–1090* ⊕ *www.artsmerced.org* 🎫 *Free* ⊙ *Weekdays 9–5, Sat. 10–2.*

WHERE TO EAT AND STAY

$$ ✕ **The Branding Iron.** Do not bother coming here if you are a vegetarian
STEAKHOUSE   or vegan; beef is what this restaurant is all about. It's a favorite among farmers and ranchers looking for a place to refuel as they travel through cattle country. Try the juicy cut of prime rib paired with potato and Parmesan-cheese bread. California cattle brands decorate the walls, and when the weather is nice, cooling breezes refresh diners on the outdoor patio. ✉ *640 W. 16th St.* ☎ *209/722–1822* ⊕ *www.thebrandingiron-merced.com* ⊙ *No lunch weekends.*

$$$ ✕ **DeAngelo's.** This restaurant, which recently moved from downtown
ITALIAN   to about 2 mi away, is one of the best in the Central Valley. Chef Vincent DeAngelo, a graduate of the Culinary Institute of America, brings his considerable skill to everything from basic ravioli to calamari

steak topped with two prawns. Half the restaurant is occupied by Bellini's, a bar-bistro with its own menu, which includes brick-oven pizza. The delicious crusty bread comes from the Golden Sheath bakery, in Watsonville. ✉ *2000 E. Childs Ave.* ☎ *209/383–3020* ⊕ *www. deangelosrestaurant.com* ☾ *No lunch weekends.*

$$ ⊡ **Hooper House Bear Creek Inn.** This 1931 neocolonial home stands regally at the corner of M Street; rooms are appointed with well-chosen antiques and big, soft beds. **Pros:** historic charm; friendly staff; good breakfast. **Cons:** front rooms can be noisy. ✉ *575 W. N. Bear Creek Dr., at M St.* ☎ *209/723–3991* ⊕ *www.hooperhouse.com* ☞ *3 rooms, 1 cottage* ⚲ *In-room: a/c, Internet* ⑷ *Breakfast.*

13

SPORTS AND THE OUTDOORS

At **Lake Yosemite Regional Park** (✉ *N. Lake Rd. off Yosemite Ave., 5 mi northeast of Merced* ☎ *209/385–7470* ☜ *$6 per car late May–early Sept.*), you can boat, swim, windsurf, water-ski, and fish on a 387-acre reservoir. Paddleboat rentals and picnic areas are available.

MODESTO

38 mi north of Merced on Hwy. 99.

Modesto, a gateway to Yosemite (⇨ *see Chapter 15*) and the southern reaches of the Gold Country, was founded in 1870 to serve the Central Pacific Railroad. The frontier town was originally to be named Ralston, after a railroad baron, but as the story goes, he modestly declined—thus the name Modesto. The Stanislaus County seat, a tree-lined city of 207,000, is perhaps best known as the site of the annual Modesto Invitational Track Meet and Relays and birthplace of film producer-director George Lucas, creator of the *Star Wars* film series.

GETTING HERE AND AROUND

As is the case with most Central Valley cities, Highway 99 is the major traffic artery. Highway 132 heads from here east toward Yosemite National Park. You also can arrive via Amtrak, with several stops daily. Modesto Area Transit (☎ *209/521–1274*) is the local public bus service.

ESSENTIALS

Airport Contacts Modesto City-County Airport (✉ *617 Airport Way, Modesto* ☎ *209/577–5319* ⊕ *www.modairport.com*).

Visitor InformationModesto Convention and Visitors Bureau (✉ *1150 9th St., Suite C, Modesto* ☎ *209/526–5588 or 888/640–8467* ⊕ *www.visitmodesto. com*).

EXPLORING

Blue Diamond Growers Store. You can witness the everyday abundance of the Modesto area with a visit here; on offer are tasty samples, a film about almond growing, and many roasts and flavors of almonds, as well as other nuts. ✉ *4800 Sisk Rd.* ☎ *209/545–6230*

International Heritage Festival. The prosperity that water brought to Modesto has attracted people from all over the world. The city holds a well-attended International Heritage Festival in early October that

The Central Valley is California's agricultural powerhouse.

celebrates the cultures, crafts, and cuisines of many nationalities. ☎ *209/521–3852* ⊕ *www.internationalfestivalmodesto.org*

★ **McHenry Mansion.** A rancher and banker built the 1883 McHenry Mansion, the city's sole surviving original Victorian home. The Italianate mansion has been decorated to reflect Modesto life in the late 19th century. Its period-appropriate wallpaper is especially impressive. ⊠ *15th and I Sts.* ☎ *209/577–5341* ⊕ *www.mchenrymuseum.org* ▨ *Free* ⊙ *Tours Sun.–Thurs. 12:30–4.*

McHenry Museum. A repository of early Modesto and Stanislaus County memorabilia, the museum's displays include re-creations of an old-time dentist's office, a blacksmith's shop, a one-room schoolhouse, an extensive doll collection, and a general store stocked with period goods such as hair crimpers and corsets. ⊠ *1402 I St.* ☎ *209/577–5366* ⊕ *www. mchenrymuseum.org* ▨ *Free* ⊙ *Tues.–Sun. noon–4.*

Modesto Arch. The Modesto Arch, one of the broadest and most striking "welcome to downtown" signs you'll see, bears the city's motto: "Water, Wealth, Contentment, Health." ⊠ *9th and I Sts.*

WHERE TO EAT AND STAY

$ ╳ **Hero's Sports Lounge & Pizza Co.** Modesto's renowned microbrewery
AMERICAN makes Hero's (formerly St. Stan's) beers. The 14 on tap include the delicious Whistle Stop pale ale and Red Sky ale. The restaurant is casual and serves good corned-beef sandwiches loaded with sauerkraut as well as a tasty beer-sausage nibbler. ⊠ *821 L St.* ☎ *209/524–2337* ⊙ *Closed Sun.*

$$$ ╳ **Tresetti's World Caffe.** An intimate setting with white tablecloths and
AMERICAN contemporary art draws diners to this eatery—part wineshop (with 500-plus selections), part restaurant—with a seasonally changing menu.

For a small supplemental fee, the staff will uncork any wine you select from the shop. The Cajun-style crab cakes, served for lunch year-round, are outstanding. ⊠ *927 11th St.* ☎ *209/572–2990* ⊕ *www.tresetti.com* ☾ *Closed Sun.*

¢ ⊡ **Best Western Town House Lodge.** The downtown location is the primary draw for this hotel. **Pros:** perfect location; updated. **Cons:** staff's knowledge of town is sometimes limited. ⊠ *909 16th St.* ☎ *209/524–7261 or 800/772–7261* ⊕ *www.bestwesterncalifornia.com* ⟿ *59 rooms* ⚹ *In-room: a/c. In-hotel: pool, parking* ☈ *Breakfast.*

13

OAKDALE

15 mi northeast of Modesto on Hwy. 108.

Oakdale was founded as an orchard community and, in a real stretch, calls itself the Cowboy Capital of the World.

WHEN TO GO

If you're in Oakdale—formerly home of a Hershey's chocolate factory—the third weekend in May, check out the **Oakdale Chocolate Festival** (☎ *209/847–2244* ✉ *$4*), which attracts 50,000 to 60,000 people each year. The event's main attraction is Chocolate Avenue, where vendors proffer cakes, cookies, ice cream, fudge, and cheesecake.

GETTING HERE AND AROUND

Reach Oakdale via Highway 108 from Modesto, about 15 minutes to the southwest. If you are really determined to take public transportation in town, look into Riverbank Oakdale Transit Authority (☎ *209/869–7444* ⊕ *www.rotabus.com*).

EXPLORING

☾ **Knights Ferry Recreation Area.** The featured attraction is the 355-foot-long
★ Knights Ferry covered bridge. The beautiful and haunting structure, built in 1863, crosses the Stanislaus River near the ruins of an old gristmill. The park has camping, picnic, and barbecue areas along the riverbanks, as well as three campgrounds accessible only by boat. You can hike, fish, canoe, and raft on 4 mi of rapids. ⊠ *Corps of Engineers Park, 17968 Covered Bridge Rd., Knights Ferry, 12 mi east of Oakdale via Hwy. 108* ☎ *209/881–3517* ✉ *Free* ☾ *Daily dawn–dusk.*

Oakdale Cheese & Specialties. You can sample the wares at this spot, which has tastings (try the aged Gouda) and cheese-making tours. There's a picnic area and a petting zoo. ⊠ *10040 Valley Home Rd.* ☎ *209/848–3139* ⊕ *www.oakdalecheese.com.*

SPORTS AND THE OUTDOORS

Rafting on the Stanislaus River is a popular activity near Oakdale. **River Journey** (⊠ *14842 Orange Blossom Rd.* ☎ *209/847–4671 or 800/292–2938* ⊕ *www.riverjourney.com*) will take you out for a few hours of fun. To satisfy your white-water or flat-water cravings, contact **Sunshine River Adventures** (☎ *209/848–4800 or 800/829–7238* ⊕ *www.raftadventure.com*).

STOCKTON

29 mi north of Modesto on Hwy. 99.

California's first inland port—connected since 1933 to San Francisco via a 60-mi-long deepwater channel—is wedged between I–5 and Highway 99, on the eastern end of the Sacramento River delta. Stockton, founded during the gold rush as a way station for miners traveling from San Francisco to the Mother Lode and now a city of 290,000, is where many of the valley's agricultural products begin their journey to other parts of the world. The city has attempted to spruce up its riverfront area downtown, including building a spiffy minor-league baseball park for the Stockton Ports, but there remains much room for improvement.

ASPARAGUS FEST

If you're here in mid-April, don't miss the **Stockton Asparagus Festival** (☎ *209/644-3740* ⊕ *www.asparagusfest.com*), at the Downtown Stockton Waterfront. The highlight of the festival is the food, with more than 500 vendor booths; organizers try to prove that almost any dish can be made with asparagus.

GETTING HERE AND AROUND

Highway 99 (on the city's eastern side) and Interstate 5 (on the western side) are connected through downtown by Highway 4, so you can zip from place to place pretty efficiently via freeways. Amtrak comes here from the north (Sacramento), west (Oakland), and south (Bakersfield). San Joaquin Regional Transit District *(⊕ www.sanjoaquinrtd.com)* buses shuffle people about town and the suburbs.

ESSENTIALS

Visitor Information Stockton Visitors Bureau (✉ *46 W. Fremont St., Stockton* ☎ *209/547-2770 or 888/778-6258* ⊕ *www.visitstockton.org*).

EXPLORING

★ **Haggin Museum.** In pretty Victory Park, the Haggin has one of the Central Valley's finest art collections. Highlights include landscapes by Albert Bierstadt and Thomas Moran, a still life by Paul Gauguin, a Native American gallery, and an Egyptian mummy. ✉ *1201 N. Pershing Ave.* ☎ *209/940–6300* ⊕ *www.hagginmuseum.org* 🖼 *$5* ☉ *Wed.–Sun. 1:30–5; open until 9 on 1st and 3rd Thurs.*

WHERE TO EAT

$$$$
CONTINENTAL
✕ **Le Bistro.** This upscale restaurant serves modern interpretations of classic French cuisine—steak tartare, Grand Marnier soufflé—and warms hearts with a romantic atmosphere. ✉ *Marina Center Mall, 3121 W. Benjamin Holt Dr., off I–5, behind Lyon's* ☎ *209/951–0885* ⊕ *www.lebistrostockton.com* ☉ *No lunch weekends.*

¢
CHINESE
✕ **On Lock Sam.** This Stockton landmark (it's been operating since 1898) is in a modern pagoda-style building with framed Chinese prints on the walls, a garden outside one window, and a sparkling bar area. One touch of old-time Chinatown remains: a few booths have curtains that can be drawn for complete privacy. A change in ownership in late 2009 provoked disgruntlement among some longtime patrons. ✉ *333 S. Sutter St.* ☎ *209/466–4561.*

LODI

13 mi north of Stockton and 34 mi south of Sacramento on Hwy. 99.

Founded on agriculture, Lodi was once the watermelon capital of the country. Today it's surrounded by fields of asparagus, pumpkins, beans, safflowers, sunflowers, kiwis, melons, squashes, peaches, and cherries. It also has become a wine-grape capital of sorts, producing Zinfandel, Merlot, Cabernet Sauvignon, Chardonnay, and Sauvignon Blanc grapes. For years California wineries have built their reputations on the juice of grapes grown around Lodi. Now the area that includes Lodi, Lockeford, and Woodbridge is a wine destination in itself, boasting about 40 wineries, many offering tours and tastings. Lodi still retains an old rural charm, despite its population of nearly 70,000. You can stroll downtown or visit a wildlife refuge, all the while benefiting from a Sacramento River delta breeze that keeps this microclimate cooler in summer than anyplace else in the area.

> **HOUSEBOAT RENTALS**
>
> Several companies rent houseboats (of various sizes, usually for three, four, or seven days) on the Sacramento River delta waterways near Stockton. **Herman & Helen's Marina** (⊠ *15135 W. 8 Mile Rd.* ☎ *209/951–4634*) rents houseboats with hot tubs and fireplaces. **Paradise Point Marina** (⊠ *8095 Rio Blanco Rd.* ☎ *209/952–1000*) rents a variety of watercraft, including patio boats.

13

GETTING HERE AND AROUND

Most of Lodi lies to the west of Highway 99, several miles east of Interstate 5. Amtrak trains and buses stop here frequently. Although the Grape Line (☎ *209/333–6806*) can get you around town and to many of the wineries, you are better off with your own vehicle.

ESSENTIALS

Visitor Information Lodi Conference and Visitors Bureau (⊠ *2545 W. Turner Dr., Lodi* ☎ *209/365–1195 or 800/798–1810* ⊕ *www.visitlodi.com*).

EXPLORING

★ **Jessie's Grove.** One of the standout wineries in the area is Jessie's Grove, a wooded horse ranch and vineyard that has been in the same family since 1863. In addition to producing outstanding old-vine Zinfandels, it presents blues concerts on various Saturdays June through October. ⊠ *1973 W. Turner Rd.* ☎ *209/368–0880* ⊕ *www.jessiesgrovewinery. com* ☉ *Daily 11–5*

Lodi Wine & Visitor Center. Stop by the Lodi Wine & Visitor Center to see exhibits on Lodi's viticultural history, pick up a map of area wineries, and even buy wine. ⊠ *2545 W. Turner Rd.* ☎ *209/365–0621* ⊕ *www. lodiwine.com*

☾ **Micke Grove Regional Park.** This 258-acre, oak-shaded county park is 5 mi north of Stockton off Highway 99; it includes a Japanese tea garden, picnic areas, children's play areas, softball fields, an agricultural museum, and a water-play feature. (Micke Grove Golf Links, an 18-hole course, is next to the park.) Geckos and frogs, black-and-white ruffed lemurs, and hissing cockroaches found only on Madagascar inhabit "An

Lodi Lake Park is a great place to escape the Central Valley heat in summer.

Island Lost in Time," an exhibit at the **Micke Grove Zoo** (☎ *209/953–8840* ⊕ *www.mgzoo.com* ✉ *$4* ⊙ *Daily 10–5*). California sea lions, Chinese alligators and a walk-through Mediterranean aviary are among the highlights of this compact facility. Most rides and attractions at the park's **Fun Town at Micke Grove** (☎ *209/369–7330* ⊙ *Mid-May–Labor Day, daily 11–dusk*), a family-oriented amusement park, are geared toward children. ✉ *11793 N. Micke Grove Rd.* ☎ *209/953–8800* ✉ *Parking $5.*

Phillips Farms Michael-David Winery. At its homey facility, kid-friendly Phillips Farms Michael-David Winery offers tastings from its affordable Michael-David vineyard. You can also cut flowers from the garden, eat breakfast or lunch at the café, and buy Phillips' and other local produce. ✉ *4580 W. Hwy. 12* ☎ *209/368–7384* ⊕ *www.lodivineyards.com.*

Woodbridge Winery. At the Woodbridge Winery, you can take a free 30-minute tour of the vineyard and barrel room. The label's legendary founder, Robert Mondavi, died in 2008 at age 94. ✉ *5950 E. Woodbridge Rd., Acampo* ☎ *209/365–8139* ⊕ *www.woodbridgewines.com* ⊙ *Tues.–Sun. 10:30–4:30*

WHERE TO EAT

$ ✕**Habañero Hots.** If your mouth can handle the heat promised by the res-
MEXICAN taurant's name, try the tamales. If you want to take it easy on your taste buds, stick with the rest of the menu. ✉ *1024 E. Victor Rd.* ☎ *209/369–3791* ⊕ *www.habanerohots.com.*

$$$ ✕**Rosewood Bar & Grill.** In downtown Lodi, Rosewood offers fine din-
AMERICAN ing without formality. Operated by the folks at Wine & Roses Hotel and Restaurant, this low-key spot serves American fare with a twist,

such as meat loaf wrapped in bacon, and daily seafood specials. The bar has a full-service menu, and live music on Friday and Saturday. ⊠ *28 S. School St.* ☎ *209/369–0470* ⊕ *www.rosewoodbarandgrill.com* ⊗ *No lunch.*

WHERE TO STAY

For expanded hotel reviews, visit Fodors.com.

$$ 🔲 **The Inn at Locke House.** Built in 1865, this B&B was a pioneer doctor's
★ family home and is on the National Register of Historic Places. **Pros:** friendly; quiet; lovely. **Cons:** remote; can be hard to find. ⊠ *19960 N. Elliott Rd., Lockeford* ☎ *209/727–5715* ⊕ *www.theinnatlockehouse. com* ⇨ *4 rooms, 1 suite* ⚬ *In-room: a/c, no TV* ⦿*Breakfast.*

$$ 🔲 **Wine & Roses Hotel and Restaurant.** Set on 7 acres amid a tapestry
★ of informal gardens, this hotel has cultivated a sense of refinement typically associated with Napa or Carmel. **Pros:** luxurious; relaxing; quiet. **Cons:** expensive; isolated; some guests have said the walls are thin. ⊠ *2505 W. Turner Rd.* ☎ *209/334–6988* ⊕ *www.winerose.com* ⇨ *47 rooms, 4 suites* ⚬ *In-room: a/c. In-hotel: restaurant, bar, spa* ⦿*Breakfast.*

SPORTS AND THE OUTDOORS

Even locals need respite from the heat of Central Valley summers, and **Lodi Lake Park** (⊠ *1101 W. Turner Rd.* ☎ *209/333–6742* ⊠ *$5*) is where they find it. The banks, shaded by grand old elms and oaks, are much cooler than other spots in town. Swimming, bird-watching, and picnicking are possibilities, as is renting a kayak, canoe, or pedal boat ($2 to $4 per half hour, Tuesday through Sunday, late May through early September only).

student must feel at ease in each, and daily seafood specials. The bar has a full service menu and live music on Friday and Saturday ⋈ 28 A St., oef St. ☎ 1206/fo9-0910 ☎ www.com.bardaryly.com ⊙ No lunch.

WHERE TO STAY

For romantic, river forest, and indifference.

$55 **The Inn at Lucks House.** Built in 1887, this B&B is a spacious, homey * family home and is on the National Register of Historic Places. Frosty friendly, quiet hotels. Guest rooms can be hard to find. ⋈ 1990 N. Elliott Rd., Lakeford ☎ 200/2-277 ⊕ www.inncombedandina.com ⥅ 4 rooms, 1 suite ⊙ In-room: no-TV. ⎍ AE, V, MC.

$55 **Wine & Roses Hotel and Restaurant.** Set on the acre amid a tapestry * of manicured gardens, this hotel has cultivated a sense of refinement typically associated with Napa or Carmel. Frou luxurious, relaxing, quiet. Cozy screened / animal-more rugs have said the walls are thin. ⋈ 2324 W. Turner Rd. ☎ 206/-2-3001 ⊕ www.inncombedandina.com ⥅ 47 rooms, 4 suites ⊙ In-room: a/c. In-hotel: restaurant, bar, spa. ⎍ AE,D,MC,V.

SPORTS AND THE OUTDOORS

Even locals need respite from the heat of Central Valley summers, and * **Lodi Lake Park** (☎ 7101 W. Turner Rd. ☎ 206/3-3-6067-233.55) is where they find it. The banks, shaded by grand old oaks and oaks, are much cooler than either spot in town. Swimming, bird watching, and picnicking are possibilities, as is renting canoes, kayaks, and pedal boats (5⊙ to $4 per half hour). Day-use hours vary daily. Late May through early September only.

The Southern Sierra

AROUND SEQUOIA, KINGS CANYON, AND YOSEMITE NATIONAL PARKS

WORD OF MOUTH

"Sitting on the edge of [the] Sierra Nevada Mountains, Mono Lake is an ancient saline lake. It is home to trillions of brine shrimp and alkali flies. You can see many limestone formations known as Tufa Towers, such as this, rising from the water's surface. Mono Lake is visited by millions of migratory birds each year."

—photo by Randall Pugh, Fodors.com member

WELCOME TO THE SOUTHERN SIERRA

TOP REASONS TO GO

★ **Take a hike:** Whether you walk the paved loops in the national parks (⇨ Chapter 15, Yosemite National Park, and Chapter 16, Sequoia and Kings Canyon National Parks) or head off the beaten path into the backcountry, a hike through groves and meadows or alongside streams and waterfalls will allow you to see, smell, and feel nature up close.

★ **Hit the slopes:** Famous for its incredible snow-pack—some of the deepest in the North American continent—the Sierra Nevada has something for every winter-sports fan.

★ **Mammoth fun:** Mammoth Lakes is eastern California's most exciting resort area.

★ **Old-world charm:** Tucked in the hills south of Oakhurst, the elegant Château du Sureau will make you feel as if you've stepped into a fairy tale.

★ **Go with the flow:** Three Rivers, the gateway to Sequoia National Park, is the launching pad for white-water trips down the Kaweah River.

1 **South of Yosemite National Park.** Several gateway towns to the south and west of Yosemite National Park (⇨ Chapter 15), most within an hour's drive of Yosemite Valley, have food, lodging, and other services.

2 **Mammoth Lakes.** A jewel in the vast eastern Sierra Nevada, the Mammoth Lakes area lies just east of the Sierra crest, on the back side of Yosemite and the Ansel Adams Wilderness. It's a place of rugged beauty, where giant sawtooth mountains drop into the vast deserts of the Great Basin. In winter, 11,053-foot-high Mammoth Mountain provides the finest skiing and snowboarding in California—sometimes as late as June or even July. Once the snows melt, Mammoth transforms itself into a warm-weather playground, with fishing, mountain biking, golfing, hiking, and horseback riding. Nine deep-blue lakes are spread through the Mammoth Lakes Basin, and another 100 lakes dot the surrounding countryside.

3 **East of Yosemite National Park.** The area to the east of Yosemite National Park (⇨ Chapter 15) includes some ruggedly handsome, albeit desolate, terrain, most notably around Mono Lake. The area is best visited by car, as distances are great and public transportation is negligible. U.S. 395 is the main north–south road on the eastern side of the Sierra Nevada, at the western edge of the Great Basin. It's one of California's most beautiful highways; plan to snap pictures at roadside pullouts.

GETTING ORIENTED

The transition between the Central Valley and the rugged Southern Sierra may be the most dramatic in California sightseeing; as you head into the mountains, your temptation to stop the car and gawk will increase with every foot gained in elevation. Although you should spend most of your time here in the national parks ⇨ be sure to check out some of the mountain towns on the parks' fringes—in addition to being great places to stock up on supplies, they have a variety of worthy attractions, restaurants, and lodging options.

14

4 South of Sequoia and Kings Canyon: Three Rivers. Scenic Three Rivers is the main gateway for Sequoia and Kings Canyon National Parks (⇨ Chapter 16).

Updated by
Reed Parsell

Vast granite peaks and giant sequoias are among the mind-boggling natural wonders of the Southern Sierra, many of which are protected in three national parks.

*(⇨ Chapter 15, Yosemite National Park, and Chapter 16, Sequoia and Kings Canyon National Parks).*Outside the parks, pristine lakes, superb skiing, rolling hills, and small towns complete the picture of the Southern Sierra. Heading up Highway 395, on the Sierra's eastern side, you'll be rewarded with outstanding vistas of dramatic mountain peaks, including Mt. Whitney, the highest point in the contiguous United States, and Mono Lake, a vast but slowly vanishing expanse of deep blue—one of the most-photographed natural attractions in California.

PLANNING

GETTING HERE AND AROUND

Fresno Yosemite International Airport (FYI) is the nearest airport to the national parks; Reno–Tahoe is the closest major airport to Mammoth Lakes.

Airports Fresno Yosemite International Airport (⊠ *5175 E. Clinton Ave., Fresno* ☎ *559/621–4500 or 559/498–4095* ⊕ *www.flyfresno.org*). **Reno–Tahoe International Airport** (⊠ *U.S. 395, Exit 65B, Reno, NV* ☎ *775/328–6400* ⊕ *www. renoairport.com*).

From San Francisco, interstates 80 and 580 are the most efficient connecting routes to Interstate 5 and Highway 99 on the western side of the Sierra Nevada range. To best reach the eastern side from the Bay Area, take Interstate 80 to Highway 395, then head south.

To get to Mammoth Lakes in summer and early fall (or whenever snows aren't blocking Tioga Road), you can travel via Highway 120 (to U.S. 395 south) through the Yosemite high country; the quickest route in winter is Interstate 80 to U.S. 50 to Highway 207 (Kingsbury Grade) to U.S. 395 south; either route takes about seven hours.

Contacts California Road Conditions (☎ *800/427–7623* ⊕ *www.dot.ca.gov/ hq/roadinfo*).

RESTAURANTS

Most small towns in the Sierra Nevada have at least one restaurant; with few exceptions, dress is casual. You'll most likely be spending a lot of time in the car while you're exploring the area, so pick up snacks and drinks to keep with you. With picnic supplies on hand, you'll be able to enjoy an impromptu meal under giant trees.

HOTELS

If you're planning to stay on the Sierra's western side, book your hotel in advance—especially in summer. Otherwise, you may end up driving pretty far to find a place to sleep. Thanks to the surge in hotel development in Mammoth Lakes, making an advance reservation is not as critical on the Sierra's less-traveled eastern side. Wherever you visit, however, be prepared for sticker shock—rural and rustic does not mean inexpensive here.

14

BOOKING A ROOM

If you'd like assistance booking your lodgings, try the following agencies: **Mammoth Lakes Visitors Bureau Lodging Referral** (☎ *760/934–2712 or 888/466–2666* ⊕ *www.visitmammoth.com*). **Mammoth Reservations** (☎ *800/223–3032* ⊕ *www.mammothreservations.com*). **Three Rivers Reservation Center** (☎ *866/561–0410 or 559/561–0410* ⊕ *www.rescentre.com*).

WHAT IT COSTS					
	¢	$	$$	$$$	$$$$
Restaurants	under $10	$10–$15	$16–$22	$23–$30	over $30
Hotels	under $90	$90–$120	$121–$175	$176–$250	over $250

Restaurant prices are for a main course at dinner, excluding sales tax of 7.25%–7.75% (depending on location). Hotel prices are for two people in a standard double room in high season, excluding service charges and 9%–10% tax.

SOUTH OF YOSEMITE NATIONAL PARK

People heading to Yosemite National Park, especially those interested in seeing the giant redwoods on the park's south side, pass through Oakhurst and Fish Camp on Highway 41.

OAKHURST

40 mi north of Fresno and 23 mi south of Yosemite National Park's south entrance on Hwy. 41.

Motels, restaurants, gas stations, and small businesses line both sides of Highway 41 as it cuts through Oakhurst. This is the last sizeable community before Yosemite (⇨ *Chapter 15*) and a good spot to find provisions. There are two major grocery stores near the intersection of highways 41 and 49. Three miles north of town, then 6 mi east, honkytonky Bass Lake is a popular spot in summer with motorboaters, Jet Skiers, and families looking to cool off in the reservoir.

GETTING HERE AND AROUND

Sitting at the junction of highways 41 and 49, Oakhurst is not near any freeways and is a solid hour's drive north of Fresno. It's the southern gateway to Yosemite, so many people fly to Fresno and rent a car to get here and beyond. In town, there's no public transportation system of any consequence.

ESSENTIALS

Visitor Information **Yosemite Sierra Visitors Bureau** (⌂ 41969 Hwy. 41, Box 1998, Oakhurst 93644 ☎ 559/683–4636 ⊕ www.yosemitethisyear.com).

DRIVING TIPS

Keep your tank full. Distances between gas stations can be long, and there's no fuel available in Yosemite Valley, Sequoia, or Kings Canyon ⇨ If you're traveling between October and May, rain on the coast can mean heavy snow in the mountains. Carry tire chains, know how to put them on (on Interstate 80 and U.S. 50 you can pay a chain installer $30 to do it for you, but on other routes you'll have to do it yourself), and always check road conditions before you leave. Traffic in national parks in summer can be heavy, and there are sometimes travel restrictions.

WHERE TO EAT

$$$
AMERICAN

✕ **Ducey's on the Lake.** For great views of Bass Lake and food that consistently impresses locals and tourists alike, make your way a few miles east of Oakhurst to this steakhouse-style restaurant, operated within The Pines Resort. Be sure to try the mashed potatoes. Alcoholic drinks are notably strong, so consider spending the night! ✉ 39255 Marina Dr. ☎ 559/642–3131 ⊕ www.basslake.com ⌕ Reservations recommended ⊘ Brunch Sun.

$$$$
CONTINENTAL
Fodor's Choice
★

✕ **Erna's Elderberry House.** Austrian-born Erna Kubin-Clanin, the grande dame of Château du Sureau, has created a culinary oasis, stunning for its elegance, gorgeous setting, and impeccable service. Crimson walls and dark beams accent the dining room's high ceilings, and arched windows reflect the glow of candles. The seasonal six-course prix-fixe dinner can be paired with superb wines, a must-do for oenophiles. When the waitstaff places all the plates on the table in perfect synchronicity, you know this will be a meal to remember. Premeal drinks are served in the former wine cellar. ✉ 48688 Victoria La. ☎ 559/683–6800 ⊕ www.elderberryhouse.com ⌕ Reservations essential ⊘ No lunch Mon.–Sat.

WHERE TO STAY

For expanded hotel reviews, visit Fodors.com.

$
☺

▦ **Best Western Yosemite Gateway Inn.** Oakhurst's best motel has carefully tended landscaping and rooms with attractive dark-wood American colonial–style furniture and slightly kitsch hand-painted wall murals of Yosemite. **Pros:** pretty close to Yosemite; clean; comfortable. **Cons:** chain property; some walls may seem thin. ✉ 40530 Hwy. 41 ☎ 559/683–2378 or 888/256–8042 ⊕ www.yosemitegatewayinn.com ⌨ 121 rooms, 16 suites ⌕ In-room: a/c, Wi-Fi. In-hotel: restaurant, bar, pools, laundry facilities.

$$$$
Fodor's Choice
★

▦ **Château du Sureau.** This romantic inn, adjacent to Erna's Elderberry House, is straight out of one of Grimm's fairy tales: From the moment you drive through the wrought-iron gates and up to the enchanting castle, you feel pampered. **Pros:** luxurious; stunning spa; spectacular property. **Cons:** you'll need to take out a second mortgage to stay here. ✉ *48688 Victoria La., Oakhurst* ☎ *559/683–6860* ⊕ *www. elderberryhouse.com* ↝ *10 rooms, 1 villa* ♿ *In-room: a/c, Wi-Fi. In-hotel: restaurant, bar, pool, spa, some age restrictions* ⑩ *Breakfast.*

$$ ⊞ **Homestead Cottages.** If you're looking for peace and quiet, Homestead
★ is the place, because serenity is the order of the day at this secluded getaway in Ahwahnee, 6 mi west of Oakhurst. **Pros:** remote; quiet; friendly owners. **Cons:** remote; some urbanites might find it *too* quiet. ✉ *41110 Rd. 600, 2½ mi off Hwy. 49, Ahwahnee* ☎ *559/683–0495 or 800/483–0495* ⊕ *www.homesteadcottages.com* ↝ *5 cottages, 1 loft* ♿ *In-room: a/c, kitchen.*

FISH CAMP

57 mi north of Fresno and 4 mi south of Yosemite National Park's south entrance.

As you climb in elevation along Highway 41 northbound, you see nothing but trees until you get to the small settlement of Fish Camp, where there's a post office and general store, but no gasoline (for gas, head 10 mi north to Wawona, in the park, or 17 mi south to Oakhurst).

GETTING HERE AND AROUND

Arrive here by car via Highway 41, from Yosemite National Park a few miles to the north, or from Oakhurst (and, farther down the road, Fresno) to the south. Unless you're on foot or a bicycle, cars are your only option.

EXPLORING

☺ **Yosemite Mountain Sugar Pine Railroad.** A narrow-gauge steam train chugs through the forest, following 4 mi of the route the Madera Sugar Pine Lumber Company cut through the forest in 1899 to harvest timber. The steam train, as well as Jenny railcars, runs year-round on fluctuating schedules; call for details. On Saturday (and Wednesday in summer), the Moonlight Special dinner excursion (reservations essential) includes a picnic with toe-tappin' music by the Sugar Pine Singers, followed by a sunset steam-train ride. ✉ *56001 Hwy. 41* ☎ *559/683–7273* ⊕ *www. ymsprr.com* ⛁ *$18 steam train; Jenny railcar $14.50; Moonlight Special $48* ☉ *Mar.–Oct., daily.*

WHERE TO STAY

For expanded hotel reviews, visit Fodors.com.

$$ ⊞ **Narrow Gauge Inn.** All of the rooms at this well-tended, family-owned
★ property have balconies (some shared) and great views of the surrounding woods and mountains. **Pros:** close to Yosemite's south entrance; well appointed; wonderful balconies. **Cons:** rooms can feel a bit dark; dining options are limited (especially for vegetarians). ✉ *48571 Hwy. 41* ☎ *559/683–7720 or 888/644–9050* ⊕ *www.narrowgaugeinn.com* ↝ *26 rooms, 1 suite* ♿ *In-room: no a/c (some), Internet, Wi-Fi (some). In-hotel: restaurant, bar, pool, some pets allowed* ⑩ *Breakfast.*

$$$$ ⊞ **Tenaya Lodge.** One of the region's largest hotels, the Tenaya Lodge is
★ ideal for people who enjoy wilderness treks by day but prefer creature

comforts at night. **Pros:** rustic setting with modern comforts; good off-season deals. **Cons:** so big it can seem impersonal; few dining options. ✉ *1122 Hwy. 41* ☏ *Box 159, 93623* ☎ *559/683–6555 or 888/514–2167* ⊕ *www.tenayalodge.com* ⟿ *244 rooms, 6 suites* ⌂ *In-room: a/c, Wi-Fi. In-hotel: restaurants, bar, pool, gym, children's programs.*

EL PORTAL

14 mi west of Yosemite Valley on Hwy. 140.

The market in town is a good place to pick up provisions before you get to Yosemite (⇨ *Chapter 15*). There's also a post office and a gas station, but not much else.

GETTING HERE AND AROUND
The drive here on Highway 140 from Mariposa and, farther west, Merced, is the prettiest and gentlest (in terms of steep uphill and downhill portions) route to Yosemite National Park. Much of the road follows the Merced River in a rugged canyon. The Yosemite Area Regional Transportation System (YARTS; ⊕ *www.yarts.com*) is a cheap and dependable way to go between Merced and Yosemite Valley; all its buses stop in El Portal, where many park employees reside.

WHERE TO STAY
For expanded hotel reviews, visit Fodors.com.

$$$ **Evergreen Lodge at Yosemite.** Near Hetch Hetchy on Yosemite National Park's northwest side, this recently renovated, 22-acre property is a dream come true for families. **Pros:** near the underrated Hetch Hetchy; family atmosphere; clean cabins. **Cons:** about an hour's drive from Yosemite Valley. ✉ *33160 Evergreen Road* ☎ *209/379–2606 or 888/935–6343* ⊕ *www.evergreenlodge.com* ⟿ *90 cabins* ⌂ *In-hotel: restaurant, bar, laundry facilities, some pets allowed.*

$$ **Yosemite View Lodge.** The motel-like design aesthetic is ameliorated by its location right on the banks of the boulder-strewn Merced River and its proximity to the park entrance 2 mi east. **Pros:** huge spa baths; great views; friendly service. **Cons:** air-conditioning inconsistent; restaurant can get crowded; can be pricey. ✉ *11136 Hwy. 140* ☎ *209/379–2681 or 888/742–4371* ⊕ *www.yosemiteresorts.us* ⟿ *335 rooms* ⌂ *In-room: a/c, kitchen (some). In-hotel: restaurant, bar, pools, laundry facilities, some pets allowed.*

MAMMOTH LAKES

30 mi south of eastern edge of Yosemite National Park on U.S. 395.

Much of the architecture in Mammoth Lakes (elevation 7,800 feet) is of the faux-alpine variety. You'll find increasingly sophisticated dining and lodging options here. International real-estate developers joined forces with Mammoth Mountain Ski Area and have worked hard to transform the once sleepy town into a chic ski destination. The Village at Mammoth (⇨ *below*) is the epicenter of all the recent development. Winter is high season at Mammoth; in summer room rates plummet. Highway 203 heads west from U.S. 395, becoming Main Street as it

Twin Lakes, in the Mammoth Lakes region, is a great place to unwind.

passes through the town of Mammoth Lakes, and later Minaret Road (which makes a right turn) as it continues west to the Mammoth Mountain ski area and Devils Postpile National Monument.

GETTING HERE AND AROUND

The best way to get here, no surprise, is by private automobile. The town is a couple of miles west of Highway 395; take one of two exits to get here. The Yosemite Area Regional Transportation System (YARTS; ⊕ *www.yarts.com*) has once-a-day service between here and Yosemite Valley. The Eastern Sierra Transit Authority (☎ 800/922–1930 ⊕ *www. easternsierratransitauthority.com*) operates shuttle buses among Mammoth Lakes, Bishop, and nearby tourist sites.

ESSENTIALS

Visitor Information **Mammoth Lakes Visitors Bureau** (⊠ *Along Hwy. 203, Main St., near Sawmill Cutoff Rd., Box 48, Mammoth Lakes* ☎ *760/934–2712 or 888/466–2666* ⊕ *www.visitmammoth.com*).

EXPLORING

Mammoth Lakes Basin. The lakes, reached by Lake Mary Road off Highway 203 southwest of town, are popular for fishing and boating in summer. First comes Twin Lakes, at the far end of which is Twin Falls, where water cascades 300 feet over a shelf of volcanic rock. Also popular are Lake Mary, the largest lake in the basin; Lake Mamie; and Lake George. Horseshoe Lake is the only lake in which you can swim.

Minaret Vista. The glacier-carved sawtooth spires of the Minarets, the remains of an ancient lava flow, are best viewed from the Minaret Vista, off Highway 203 west of Mammoth Lakes.

☺
Fodor'sChoice
★
Panorama Gondola. Even if you don't ski, ride the gondola to see Mammoth Mountain, the aptly named dormant volcano that gives Mammoth Lakes its name. Gondolas serve skiers in winter and mountain bikers and sightseers in summer. The high-speed, eight-passenger gondolas whisk you from the chalet to the summit, where you can read about the area's volcanic history and take in top-of-the-world views. Standing high above the tree line atop this dormant volcano, you can look west 150 mi across the state to the Coastal Range; to the east are the highest peaks of Nevada and the Great Basin beyond. You won't find a better view of the Sierra High Country without climbing. Remember, though, that the air is thin at the 11,053-foot summit; carry water, and don't overexert yourself. The boarding area is at the Main Lodge. ⊠ *Off Hwy. 203* ☎ *760/934–2571 Ext. 2400 information, Ext. 3850 gondola station* ⊐ *$21 in summer* ☉ *July 4–Oct., daily 9–4:30; Nov.–July 3, daily 8:30–4.*

Village at Mammoth. The overwhelming popularity of Mammoth Mountain has generated a real-estate boom, and a huge new complex of shops, restaurants, and luxury accommodations, called the Village at Mammoth, has become the town's tourist center. Parking can be tricky. There's a lot across the street on Minaret Road; pay attention to time limits.

WHERE TO EAT

$$$
AMERICAN
✕ **Petra's Bistro & Wine Bar.** Other restaurateurs speak highly of Petra's as the most convivial restaurant in town. Its lovely ambience—quiet, dark, and warm—complements the carefully prepared meat main dishes and seasonal sides, and the more than two dozen California wines from behind the bar. The service is top-notch. Downstairs, the Clocktower Cellar bar provides a late-night, rowdy alternative—or chaser. ⊠ *6080 Minaret Rd.* ☎ *760/934–3500* ⊕ *www.petrasbistro.com* ⊲ *Reservations essential* ☉ *No lunch.*

$$$$
AMERICAN
✕ **Restaurant at Convict Lake.** Tucked in a tiny valley ringed by mile-high peaks, Convict Lake is one of the most spectacular spots in the eastern Sierra. Thank heaven the food lives up to the view. The chef's specialties include beef Wellington, rack of lamb, and pan-seared local trout, all beautifully prepared. The woodsy room has a vaulted knotty-pine ceiling and a copper-chimney fireplace that roars on cold nights. Natural light abounds in the daytime, but if it's summer, opt for a table outdoors under the white-barked aspens. Service is exceptional, as is the wine list, with reasonably priced European and California varietals. ⊠ *2 mi off U.S. 395, 4 mi south of Mammoth Lakes* ☎ *760/934–3803* ⊲ *Reservations essential* ☉ *No lunch early Sept.–July 4.*

$$$$
FRENCH
✕ **Restaurant LuLu.** The sunny, sensual, and assertive flavors of Provençale cooking—think olive tapenade, aioli, and lemony vinaigrettes—are showcased here. At this outpost of the famous San Francisco restaurant, the formula remains the same: small plates of southern French cooking

served family-style in a spare, modern, and sexy dining room. Standouts include rotisserie meats, succulent roasted mussels, homemade gnocchi, and a fantastic wine list, with 50 vintages available in 2-ounce pours. Outside, the sidewalk café includes a fire pit where kids will love do-it-themselves s'mores. LuLu's only drawback is price, but if you can swing it, it's worth every penny. The waiters wear jeans, so you can, too. ⊠ *Village at Mammoth, 1111 Forest Trail, Unit 201* ☎ *760/924–8781* ⊕ *www.restaurantlulu.com* ♤ *Reservations essential.*

$ ✕ **Side Door Café.** Half wine bar, half café, this is a laid-back spot for an
CAFÉ easy lunch or a long, lingering afternoon. The café serves grilled panini sandwiches, sweet and savory crepes, and espresso. At the wine bar, order cheese plates and charcuterie platters, designed to pair with the 25 wines (fewer in summertime) available by the glass. If you're lucky, a winemaker will show up and hold court at the bar. ⊠ *Village at Mammoth, 1111 Forest Trail, Unit 229* ☎ *760/934–5200.*

$ ✕ **The Stove.** A longtime family favorite for down-to-earth, folksy cook-
AMERICAN ing, this is the kind of place you take the family to fill up before a long car ride. The omelets, pancakes, huevos rancheros, and meat loaf won't win any awards, but they're tasty. The room is cute, with gingham curtains and pinewood booths, and service is friendly. Breakfast and lunch are the best bets here. ⊠ *644 Old Mammoth Rd.* ☎ *760/934–2821* ♤ *Reservations not accepted.*

WHERE TO STAY

For expanded hotel reviews, visit Fodors.com.

$ 🏨 **Alpenhof Lodge.** The owners lucked out when developers built the fancy-schmancy Village at Mammoth right across the street from their mom-and-pop motel. **Pros:** convenient for skiers; good price. **Cons:** could use an update; rooms above the pub can be noisy. ⊠ *6080 Minaret Rd., Box 1157* ☎ *760/934–6330 or 800/828–0371* ⊕ *www.alpenhof-lodge.com* ⇆ *54 rooms, 3 cabins* ♤ *In-room: no a/c, kitchen (some), Wi-Fi. In-hotel: restaurant, bar, pool, laundry facilities.*

$ 🏨 **Cinnamon Bear Inn Bed and Breakfast.** In a business district off Main Street, this bed-and-breakfast feels more like a small motel, with nicely decorated rooms, many with four-poster beds. **Pros:** quiet; afford-able; friendly. **Cons:** a bit tricky to find; limited parking. ⊠ *113 Center St.* ⌂ *Box 3338, 93546* ☎ *760/934–2873 or 800/845–2873* ⊕ *www.cinnamonbearinn.com* ⇆ *22 rooms* ♤ *In-room: no a/c, kitchen (some), Wi-Fi. In-hotel: bar* ⍾ *Breakfast.*

$$$ 🏨 **Double Eagle Resort and Spa.** You won't find a better spa retreat in the eastern Sierra than the Double Eagle, which is in a spectacularly beautiful spot under towering peaks and along a creek, near June Lake, 20 minutes north of Mammoth Lakes. **Pros:** pretty setting; generous breakfast; good for families. **Cons:** expensive, remote. ⊠ *5587 Hwy. 158, Box 736, June Lake* ☎ *760/648–7004 or 877/648–7004* ⊕ *www.doubleeagleresort.com* ⇆ *16 2-bedroom cabins, 16 cabin suites, 1 3-bedroom cabin* ♤ *In-room: no a/c, kitchen (some), Internet. In-hotel: restaurant, bar, pool, gym, spa, some pets allowed.*

$$$ ▥ **Juniper Springs Lodge.** Tops for slope-side comfort, these condominium-style units have full kitchens and ski-in ski-out access to the mountain. **Pros:** bargain during summer; direct access to the slopes; good views. **Cons:** no nightlife within walking distance; no a/c; some complaints about service. ✉ *4000 Meridian Blvd.* ⬡ *Box 2129, 93546* ☎ *760/924–1102 or 800/626–6684* ⊕ *www.mammothmountain.com* ⬂ *10 studios, 99 1-bedrooms, 92 2-bedrooms, 3 3-bedrooms* ⬕ *In-room: no a/c, kitchen, Internet. In-hotel: restaurant, bar, golf course, pool, laundry facilities.*

$$$ ▥ **Mammoth Mountain Inn.** If you want to be within walking distance of the Mammoth Mountain Main Lodge, this is the place. **Pros:** great location; big rooms; a traditional place to stay. **Cons:** can be crowded in ski season; won't be around for many more years. ✉ *Minaret Rd., 4 mi west of Mammoth Lakes* ⬡ *Box 353, 93546* ☎ *760/934–2581 or 800/626–6684* ⊕ *www.mammothmountain.com* ⬂ *124 rooms, 91 condos* ⬕ *In-room: no a/c, kitchen (some), Internet. In-hotel: 2 restaurants, bar, pool, laundry facilities.*

$$ ▥ **Tamarack Lodge Resort & Lakefront Restaurant.** Tucked away on the

Fodor'sChoice
★ edge of the John Muir Wilderness Area, where cross-country ski trails loop through the woods, this original 1924 lodge looks like something out of a snow globe, and the lake it borders is serenely beautiful. **Pros:** rustic but not run-down; plenty of eco-sensitivity; tons of nearby outdoor activities. **Cons:** thin walls; some main lodge rooms have shared bathrooms. ✉ *Lake Mary Rd., off Hwy. 203* ⬡ *Box 69, 93546* ☎ *760/934–2442 or 800/626–6684* ⊕ *www.tamaracklodge.com* ⬂ *11 rooms, 35 cabins* ⬕ *In-room: no a/c, kitchen (some), no TV. In-hotel: restaurant, bar.*

$$$ ▥ **Village at Mammoth.** At the epicenter of Mammoth's dining and nightlife scene, this cluster of four-story timber-and-stone condo buildings nods to Alpine style, with exposed timbers and peaked roofs. **Pros:** central location; clean; big rooms; lots of good restaurants nearby. **Cons:** pricey; can be noisy outside. ✉ *100 Canyon Blvd.* ⬡ *Box 3459, 93546* ☎ *760/934–1982 or 800/626–6684* ⊕ *www.mammothmountain.com* ⬂ *277 units* ⬕ *In-room: no a/c, kitchen (some), Internet. In-hotel: pool, gym, laundry facilities, parking.*
The Village at Mammoth hosts events and has several rockin' bars and clubs.

SPORTS AND THE OUTDOORS

For information on winter conditions around Mammoth, call the **Snow Report** (☎ *760/934–7669 or 888/766–9778*). The **U.S. Forest Service ranger station** (☎ *760/924–5500*) can provide general information year-round.

BICYCLING

Mammoth Mountain Bike Park (✉ *Mammoth Mountain Ski Area* ☎ *760/ 934–3706* ⊕ *www.mammothmountain.com*) opens when the snow melts, usually by July, with 70-plus mi of single-track trails—from mellow to super-challenging. Chairlifts and shuttles provide trail access, and rentals are available. Various shops around town also rent bikes and provide trail maps, if you don't want to ascend the mountain.

FISHING

Crowley Lake is the top trout-fishing spot in the area; Convict Lake, June Lake, and the lakes of the Mammoth Basin are other prime spots. One of the best trout rivers is the San Joaquin, near Devils Postpile. Hot Creek, a designated Wild Trout Stream, is renowned for fly-fishing (catch-and-release only). The fishing season runs from the last Saturday in April until the end of October.

Kittredge Sports (✉ *3218 Main St., at Forest Trail* ☎ *760/934–7566* ⊕ *www.kittredgesports.com*) rents rods and reels and also conducts guided trips.

To maximize your time on the water, get tips from local anglers, or better yet, book a guided fishing trip with **Sierra Drifters Guide Service** (☎ *760/935–4250* ⊕ *www.sierradrifters.com*).

HIKING

Hiking in Mammoth is stellar, especially along the trails that wind through the pristine alpine scenery around the Lakes Basin. Carry lots of water; and remember, you're above 8,000-foot elevation, and the air is thin. Stop at the **U.S. Forest Service ranger station** (✉ *Hwy. 203* ☎ *760/924–5500* ⊕ *www.fs.fed.us/r5/inyo*), on your right just before the town of Mammoth Lakes, for a Mammoth area trail map and permits for backpacking in wilderness areas.

HORSEBACK RIDING

Stables around Mammoth are typically open from June through September. **Mammoth Lakes Pack Outfit** (✉ *Lake Mary Rd., between Twin Lakes and Lake Mary* ☎ *760/934–2434 or 888/475–8747* ⊕ *www.mammothpack.com*) runs day and overnight horseback trips, or will shuttle you to the high country. **McGee Creek Pack Station** (☎ *760/935–4324 or 800/854–7407* ⊕ *www.mcgeecreekpackstation.com*) customizes pack trips or will shuttle you to camp alone. Operated by the folks at McGee Creek, **Sierra Meadows Ranch** (✉ *Sherwin Creek Rd., off Old Mammoth Rd.* ☎ *760/934–6161*) conducts horseback and wagon rides that range from one-hour to all-day excursions.

SKIING

June Mountain Ski Area. In their rush to Mammoth Mountain, most people overlook June Mountain, a compact, low-key resort 20 mi north of Mammoth. Snowboarders especially dig it. Two freestyle terrain areas are for both skiers and boarders, including a huge 16-foot-wall super pipe. Best of all, there's rarely a line for the lifts—if you want to avoid the crowds but must ski on a weekend, this is the place. And in a storm, June is better protected from wind and blowing snow than Mammoth Mountain. (If it starts to storm, you can use your Mammoth ticket at June.) Expect all the usual services, including a rental-and-repair shop, ski school, and sports shop, but the food quality is better at Mammoth. Lift tickets run $69, with discounts for multiple days. ✉ *3819 Hwy. 158, off June Lake Loop, June Lake* ☎ *760/648–7733 or 888/586–3686* ⊕ *www.junemountain.com* ⟳ *35 trails on 500 acres, rated 35% begin-*

14

ner, 45% intermediate, 20% advanced. Longest run 2½ mi, base 7,510 feet, summit 10,174 feet. Lifts: 7.

Fodor'sChoice   **Mammoth Mountain Ski Area.** If you ski only one mountain in California,
★   make it Mammoth Mountain Ski Area. One of the West's largest and best ski areas, Mammoth has more than 3,500 acres of skiable terrain and a 3,100-foot vertical drop. The views from the 11,053-foot summit are some of the most stunning in the Sierra. Below, you'll find a 6½-mi-wide swath of groomed boulevards and canyons, as well as pockets of tree-skiing and a dozen vast bowls. Snowboarders are everywhere on the slopes; there are three outstanding freestyle terrain parks of varying technical difficulty, with jumps, rails, tabletops, and giant super pipes (this is the location of several international snowboarding competitions). Mammoth's season begins in November and often lingers into May. Lift tickets cost $65. Lessons and equipment are available, and there's a children's ski and snowboard school. Mammoth runs free shuttle-bus routes around town and to the ski area, and the Village Gondola runs from the Village complex to Canyon Lodge. However, only overnight guests are allowed to park at the Village for more than a few hours. Warning: The main lodge is dark and dated, unsuited in most every way for the crush of ski season. Within a decade, it's likely to be replaced. ⊠ *Minaret Rd., west of Mammoth Lakes* ☎ *760/934–2571; 800/626–6684; 760/934–0687 shuttle* ⌖ *150 trails on 3,500 acres, rated 30% beginner, 40% intermediate, 30% advanced. Longest run 3 mi, base 7,953 feet, summit 11,053 feet. Lifts: 27, including 9 high-speed and 2 gondolas.*

Trails at **Tamarack Cross Country Ski Center** (⊠ *Lake Mary Rd., off Hwy. 203* ☎ *760/934–5293 or 760/934–2442* ⊕ *www.tamaracklodge.com*), adjacent to Tamarack Lodge, meander around several lakes. Rentals are available.

SKI RENTALS

★   When the U.S. Ski Team visits Mammoth and needs their boots adjusted, they head to **Footloose** (⊠ *3043 Main St.* ☎ *760/934–2400* ⊕ *www.footloosesports.com*), the best place in town—and possibly all California—for ski-boot rentals and sales, as well as custom insoles (ask for Kevin or Corty).

Advanced skiers should rent from **Kittredge Sports** (⊠ *3218 Main St.* ☎ *760/934–7566* ⊕ *www.kittredgesports.com*). **Mammoth Sporting Goods** (⊠ *1 Sierra Center Mall, Old Mammoth Rd.* ☎ *760/934–3239* ⊕ *www. mammothsportinggoods.com*) rents good skis for intermediates, and sells equipment, clothing, and accessories.

EAST OF YOSEMITE NATIONAL PARK

Most people enter Yosemite National Park from the west, having driven out from the Bay Area or Los Angeles. The eastern entrance on Tioga Pass Road (Highway 120), however, provides stunning, sweeping views of the High Sierra. Gray rocks shine in the bright sun, with scattered, small vegetation sprinkled about the mountainside. To drive from Lee

Vining to Tuolumne Meadows is an unforgettable experience, but keep in mind the road tends to be closed for at least seven months of the year.

LEE VINING

20 mi east of Tuolumne Meadows via Hwy. 120 to U.S. 395; 30 mi north of Mammoth Lakes on U.S. 395.

Tiny Lee Vining is known primarily as the eastern gateway to Yosemite National Park (summer only; ⇨ *Chapter 15*) and the location of vast and desolate Mono Lake. Pick up supplies at the general store year-round, or stop here for lunch or dinner before or after a drive through the high country. In winter the town is all but deserted, except for the ice climbers who come to scale frozen waterfalls. You can meet these hearty souls at Nicely's restaurant, where the climbers congregate for breakfast around 8 on winter mornings.

GETTING HERE AND AROUND

Lee Vining is on Highway 395, just north of the intersection with Highway 120 and on the south side of massive Mono Lake. Greyhound can get you here from Reno and the Yosemite Area Regional Transportation System (YARTS; ⊕ *www.yarts.com*) from Yosemite Valley, but you're much better off with a car.

ESSENTIALS

Visitor Information Lee Vining Chamber of Commerce (⌂ *Box 130, Lee Vining 93541* ☏ *760/647–6629* ⊕ *www.leevining.com*). **Mono Lake** (⌂ *Box 49, Lee Vining 93541* ☏ *760/647–3044* ⊕ *www.monolake.org*).

To try your hand at ice climbing, contact **Sierra Mountain Guides** (☏ *760/648–1122 or 877/423–2546* ⊕ *www.themountainguide.com*).

EXPLORING

★ **Mono Lake.** Eerie tufa towers—calcium carbonate formations that often resemble castle turrets—rise from impressive Mono Lake. Since the 1940s, the city of Los Angeles has diverted water from streams that feed the lake, lowering its water level and exposing the tufa. Court victories by environmentalists in the 1990s forced a reduction of the diversions, and the lake has since risen about 9 feet. From April through August, millions of migratory birds nest in and around Mono Lake. The best place to view the tufa is at the south end of the lake along the mile-long **South Tufa Trail.** To reach it, drive 5 mi south from Lee Vining on U.S. 395, then 5 mi east on Highway 120. There's a $3 fee. You can swim (or float) in the salty water at Navy Beach near the South Tufa Trail or take a kayak or canoe trip for close-up views of the tufa (check with rangers for boating restrictions during bird-nesting season). You can rent kayaks in Mammoth Lakes. The sensational **Scenic Area Visitor Center** (⊠ *U.S. 395* ☏ *760/647–3044*) is open daily from June through September (Sunday–Thursday 8–5, Friday and Saturday 8–7), and the rest of the year Thursday–Monday 9–4. Its hilltop and sweeping views of Mono Lake, along with its interactive exhibits inside, make this one of California's best visitor centers. Rangers and naturalists lead walking tours of the tufa daily in summer and on weekends (sometimes on cross-country skis) in winter. In town, the **Mono Lake**

14

Committee Information Center & Bookstore (✉ *U.S. 395 and 3rd St.* ☎ *760/647–6595* ⊕ *www.monolake.org*) has more information about this beautiful area.

EN
ROUTE

Heading south from Lee Vining, U.S. 395 intersects the **June Lake Loop** (✉ *Hwy. 158 W*). This gorgeous 17-mi drive follows an old glacial canyon past Grant, June, Gull, and other lakes before reconnecting with U.S. 395 on its way to Mammoth Lakes. The loop is especially colorful in fall.

WHERE TO EAT AND STAY

$ ✕ **Tioga Gas Mart & Whoa Nelli Deli.** Near the eastern entrance to Yosem-
DELI ite, Whoa Nelli serves some of Mono County's best food, including lobster taquitos, pizzas, and enormous slices of multilayered cakes. But what makes it special is that it's in a gas station—possibly the only one in America where you can order cocktails (a pitcher of mango margaritas, anyone?)—and outside there's a full-size trapeze where you can take lessons (by reservation). This wacky spot is well off the noisy road, and has plenty of shaded outdoor tables with views of Mono Lake; bands play here on summer evenings, and locals love it, too. ✉ *Hwy. 120 and U.S. 395* ☎ *760/647–1088* ☉ *Closed mid-Nov.–mid-Apr.*

$$ ⌂ **Lake View Lodge.** Lovely landscaping, which includes several inviting and shaded places to sit, is what sets this clean motel apart from its handful of competitors in town. **Pros:** attractive; clean; friendly staff. **Cons:** could use updating. ✉ *51285 U.S. 395* ☎ *760/647–6543 or 800/990–6614* ⊕ *www.lakeviewlodgeyosemite.com* ⇥ *76 rooms, 12 cottages* ⌂ *In-room: no a/c, kitchen (some).*

BODIE STATE HISTORIC PARK

23 mi northeast of Lee Vining via U.S. 395 to Hwy. 270 (last 3 mi are unpaved).

GETTING HERE AND AROUND

You need to get here by private car. About 15 mi north of Lee Vining (7 mi south of Bridgeport), look for signs pointing you east toward the ghost town, another 13 mi via Highway 270. The last 3 mi are unpaved, and possibly treacherous depending on erosion and the weather.

EXPLORING

Fodor'sChoice ○ **Bodie Ghost Town.** Old shacks and shops, abandoned mine shafts, a
★ Methodist church, the mining village of Rattlesnake Gulch, and the remains of a small Chinatown are among the sights at fascinating Bodie Ghost Town. The town, at an elevation of 8,200 feet, boomed from about 1878 to 1881, as gold prospectors, having worked the best of the western Sierra mines, headed to the high desert on the eastern slopes. Bodie was a mean place—the booze flowed freely, shootings were commonplace, and licentiousness reigned. Evidence of the town's wild past survives today at an excellent museum, and you can tour an old stamp mill and a ridge that contains many mine sites. Bodie, unlike Calico in Southern California near Barstow, is a genuine ghost town, its status proudly stated as "arrested decay." No food, drink, or lodging is available in Bodie. Though the park stays open in winter, snow may close

Highway 270. Still, it's a fantastic time to visit: rent cross-country skis in Mammoth Lakes, drive north, ski in, and have the park to yourself. ⊠ *Museum: Main and Green Sts.* ☎ *760/647–6445* ⊕ *www.bodie.net* ☜ *Park $3, museum free* ☉ *Park: late May–early Sept., daily 8–7; early Sept.–late May, daily 8–4. Museum: late May–early Sept., daily 9–6; early Sept.–late May, hrs vary.*

SOUTH OF SEQUOIA AND KINGS CANYON: THREE RIVERS

200 mi north of Los Angeles via I–5 to Hwy. 99 to Hwy. 198; 8 mi south of Ash Mountain/Foothills entrance to Sequoia National Park on Hwy. 198.

In the foothills of the Sierra along the Kaweah River, this sparsely populated, serpentine hamlet serves as the main gateway town to Sequoia and Kings Canyon national parks (⇨ *Chapter 16, Sequoia and Kings Canyon National Parks*). Its livelihood depends largely on tourism from the parks, courtesy of two markets, a few service stations, banks, a post office, and several lodgings, which are good spots to find a room when park accommodations are full.

GETTING HERE AND AROUND

From Memorial Day through Labor Day, you can ride the city of Visalia's Sequoia Shuttle (☎ 877/404–6473 ⊕ *www.ci.visalia.ca.us*) to and from Three Rivers, up to and down from Sequoia National Park. You probably should count on driving here yourself, however, via Highway 198. The town is slender and long, and to walk from your hotel to a restaurant might take longer than you think.

WHERE TO EAT AND STAY

¢ ✕ **We Three Bakery.** This friendly, popular-with-the-locals spot packs
ECLECTIC lunches for trips into the nearby national parks; they're also open for breakfast. ⊠ *43688 Sierra Dr.* ☎ *559/561–4761.*

$$ ⊞ **Buckeye Tree Lodge.** Every room at this two-story motel has a patio facing a sun-dappled lawn, right on the banks of the Kaweah River. **Pros:** scenic setting; clean. **Cons:** could use an update. ⊠ *46000 Sierra Dr., Hwy. 198* ☎ *559/561–5900* ⊕ *www.buckeyetree.com* ⇗ *11 rooms, 1 cottage* ⅋ *In-room: a/c. In-hotel: pool, some pets allowed* ⅋⊙⅋ *Breakfast.*

RAFTING

Kaweah White Water Adventures (☎ *559/561–1000 or 800/229–8658* ⊕ *www.kaweah-whitewater.com*) guides two-hour and full-day rafting trips in spring and early summer, with some Class III rapids; longer trips may include some Class IV.

Yosemite
National Park

WORD OF MOUTH

"I don't really have a favorite park, but we all agreed that Yosemite definitely gets the prize for waterfalls. I thought that Columbia River Gorge couldn't be beat, but it doesn't come close to Yosemite for waterfalls."

—spirobulldog

WELCOME TO YOSEMITE NATIONAL PARK

TOP REASONS TO GO

★ **Feel the earth move:** An easy stroll brings you to the base of Yosemite Falls, America's highest, where thundering springtime waters shake the ground.

★ **Tunnel to heaven:** Winding down into Yosemite Valley, Wawona Road passes through a mountainside and emerges before one of the park's most heart-stopping vistas.

★ **Touch the sky:** Watch clouds scudding across the bright blue dome that arches above the High Sierra's Tuolumne Meadows, a wide-open alpine valley ringed by 10,000-foot granite peaks.

★ **Walk away from it all:** Early or late in the day, leave the crowds behind and take a forest hike on a few of Yosemite's 800 mi of trails.

★ **Powder your nose:** Winter's hush floats into Yosemite on snowflakes. Wade into a fluffy drift, lift your face to the sky, and listen to the trees.

1 Yosemite Valley. At an elevation of 4,000 feet, in roughly the center of the park, beats Yosemite's heart. This is where you'll find the park's most famous sights and biggest crowds.

2 Wawona and Mariposa Grove. The park's southeastern tip holds Wawona, with its grand old hotel and pioneer history center, and the Mariposa Grove of Big Trees, filled with giant sequoias. These are closest to the South Entrance, 35 mi (a one-hour drive) south of Yosemite Village.

3 Tuolumne Meadows. The highlight of east-central Yosemite is this wildflower-strewn valley with hiking trails, nestled among sharp, rocky peaks. It's a two-hour drive northeast of Yosemite Valley along Tioga Road (closed mid-October–late May).

4 Hetch Hetchy. The most remote, least-visited part of Yosemite accessible by automobile, this glacial valley is dominated by a reservoir and veined with wilderness trails. It's near the park's western boundary, about a half-hour drive north of Big Oak Flat Entrance.

GETTING ORIENTED

Yosemite is so large that you can think of it as five parks. Yosemite Valley, famous for waterfalls and cliffs, and Wawona, where the giant sequoias stand, are open all year. Hetch Hetchy, home of less-used backcountry trails, closes after the first big snow and reopens in May or June. The subalpine high country, Tuolumne Meadows, is open for summer hiking and camping; in winter it's accessible only via cross-country skis or snowshoes. Badger Pass Ski Area is open in winter only. Most visitors spend their time along the park's south-western border, between Wawona and Big Oak Flat Entrance; a bit farther east in Yosemite Valley and Badger Pass Ski Area; and along the east–west corridor of Tioga Road, which spans the park north of Yosemite Valley and bisects Tuolumne Meadows.

15

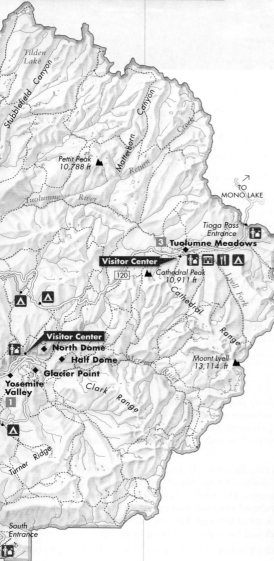

By Sura Wood and Reed Parsell

By merely standing in Yosemite Valley and turning in a circle, you can see more natural wonders in a minute than you could in a full day pretty much anywhere else. Half Dome, Yosemite Falls, El Capitan, Bridalveil Fall, the meadows, Sentinel Dome, the Merced River, white-flowering dogwood trees, maybe even bears ripping into the bark of fallen trees or sticking their snouts into beehives—it's all in the Valley.

In the mid-1800s, when tourists were arriving to the area, the Valley's special geologic qualities, and the giant sequoias of Mariposa Grove 30 mi to the south, so impressed a group of influential Californians that they persuaded President Abraham Lincoln to grant those two areas to the state for protection. On Oct. 1, 1890—thanks largely to lobbying efforts by naturalist John Muir and Robert Underwood Johnson, the editor of *Century Magazine*—Congress set aside 1,500 square mi for Yosemite National Park.

PLANNING

WHEN TO GO

During extremely busy periods—like the 4th of July—you may experience delays at the entrance gates. ■ TIP→ For less crowds, visit midweek. Or come mid-April through Memorial Day or mid-September through October, when the park is only a bit busy and the days are usually sunny and clear.

Summer rainfall is rare. In winter, heavy snows occasionally cause road closures, and tire chains or four-wheel drive may be required on the roads that remain open. The road to Glacier Point beyond the turnoff for Badger Pass is closed after the first major snowfall; Tioga Road is closed from late October through May or mid-June. Mariposa Grove Road is typically closed for a shorter period in winter.

The temperature chart below is for Yosemite Valley. In the high country, it's cooler.

GETTING HERE AND AROUND

Roughly 200 mi from San Francisco, 300 mi from Los Angeles, and 500 mi from Las Vegas, Yosemite takes a while to reach—and its sites and attractions merit much more time than what rangers say is the average visit: four hours. Most people arrive via car or tour bus, but public transportation (courtesy of Amtrak and the regional YARTS bus system) also can get you here.

Of the park's four entrances, Arch Rock is the closest to Yosemite Valley. The road that goes through it, Route 140 from Merced and Mariposa, is a scenic western approach that snakes alongside the boulder-packed Merced River. Route 41, through Wawona, is the way to come from Los Angeles. Route 120, through Crane Flat, is the most direct route from San Francisco. The only way in from the east is Tioga Road, which may be the best route in terms of scenery—though due to snow accumulation it's open for a frustratingly short amount of time each year (typically early June through mid-October).

However you get to the Valley, once you're there you can take advantage of the free shuttle buses, which make 21 stops, and run every 10 minutes or so from 9 am to 6 pm year-round; a separate (and also free) summer-only shuttle runs out to El Capitan. Also during the summer, from Yosemite Valley you can pay to take the morning "hikers' bus" to Tuolumne or the bus up to Glacier Point. Bus service from Wawona is geared for people who are staying there and want to spend the day in Yosemite Valley. Free and frequent shuttles transport people between the Wawona Hotel and Mariposa Grove. During the snow season, buses run regularly between Yosemite Valley and Badger Pass Ski Area. For more information, visit ⊕ *www.nps.gov/yose/planyourvisit/bus.htm* or call ☎ *209/372–1240.*

There are few gas stations within Yosemite (Crane Flat, Tuolumne Meadows, and Wawona; none in the Valley), so fuel up before you reach the park. From late fall until early spring, the weather is unpredictable, and driving can be treacherous. You should carry chains. For road condition updates, call ☎ *800/427–7623 or 209/372–0200* from within California or go to ⊕ *www.dot.ca.gov.*

WHAT IT COSTS

	¢	$	$$	$$$	$$$$
RESTAURANTS	under $10	$10–$15	$16–$22	$23–$30	over $30
HOTELS	under $90	$90–$120	$121–$175	$176–$250	over $250

Restaurant prices are for a main course at dinner, excluding sales tax. Hotel prices are for two people in a standard double room in high season, excluding service charges and tax.

FLORA AND FAUNA

Dense stands of incense cedar and Douglas fir—as well as ponderosa, Jeffrey, lodgepole, and sugar pines—cover much of the park, but the stellar standout, quite literally, is the *Sequoia sempervirens*, the giant sequoia. Sequoias grow only along the west slope of the Sierra Nevada

GOOD READS ON YOSEMITE

■ The Photographer's Guide to Yosemite, by Michael Frye, is an insider's guide to the park, with maps for shutterbugs looking to capture perfect images.

■ John Muir penned his observations of the park he long advocated for in The Yosemite.

■ Yosemite and the High Sierra, edited by Andrea G. Stillman and John Szarkowski, features beautiful reproductions of landmark photographs by Ansel Adams,

accompanied by excerpts from the photographer's journals written when Adams traveled in Yosemite National Park in the early 20th century.

■ An insightful collection of essays accompany the museum-quality artworks in Yosemite: Art of an American Icon, by Amy Scott.

■ Perfect for beginning wildlife watchers, Sierra Nevada Wildflowers, by Karen Wiese, indentifies more than 230 kinds of flora growing in the Sierra Nevada region.

between 4,500 and 7,000 feet in elevation. Starting from a seed the size of a rolled-oat flake, each of these ancient monuments assumes remarkable proportions in adulthood; you can see them in the Mariposa Grove of Big Trees. In late May the Valley's dogwood trees bloom with white, starlike flowers. Wildflowers, such as black-eyed Susan, bull thistle, cow parsnip, lupine, and meadow goldenrod, peak in June in the Valley and in July at higher elevations.

The most visible animals in the park—aside from the omnipresent western gray squirrel—are the mule deer. Though sightings of bighorn sheep are infrequent in the park itself, you can sometimes see them on the eastern side of the Sierra Crest, just off Route 120 in Lee Vining Canyon. You may also see the American black bear, which often has a brown, cinnamon, or blond coat. The Sierra Nevada is home to thousands of bears, and you should take all necessary precautions to keep yourself—and the bears—safe. For one, do not feed the bears. Bears that acquire a taste for human food can become very aggressive and destructive and sometimes must be put down by rangers.

Watch for the blue Steller's jay along trails, near public buildings, and in campgrounds, and look for Golden eagles soaring over Tioga Road.

PARK ESSENTIALS

ADMISSION FEES AND PERMITS

The admission fee, valid for seven days, is $20 per vehicle or $10 per individual.

If you plan to camp in the backcountry, you must have a wilderness permit. Availability of permits, which are free, depends upon trailhead quotas. It's best to make a reservation, especially if you will be visiting May through September. You can reserve two days to 24 weeks in advance by phone, mail, or fax (✉ P.O. Box 545, Yosemite, CA 95389 ☎ 209/372–0740 🖷 209/372–0739); a $5 per person processing fee is charged if and when your reservations are confirmed. Requests must include your name, address, daytime phone, the number of people in your party, trip date, alternative dates, starting and ending trailheads, and a brief itinerary. Without a reservation, you may still get a free permit on a first-come, first-served basis at wilderness permit offices at Big Oak Flat, Hetch Hetchy, Tuolumne, Wawona, the Wilderness Center (in Yosemite Village), and Yosemite Valley in summer; fall through spring, visit the Valley Visitor Center.

ADMISSION HOURS
The park is open 24/7 year-round. All entrances are open at all hours, except for Hetch Hetchy Entrance, which is open roughly dawn to dusk. Yosemite is in the Pacific time zone.

PARK CONTACT INFORMATION
Yosemite National Park ⌂ *Information Office, P.O. Box 577, Yosemite National Park, CA 95389* ☎ *209/372–0200* ⊕ *www.nps.gov/yose.*

SAFETY
In an emergency, call 911. You can also call the Yosemite Medical Clinic in Yosemite Village at 209/372–4637. The clinic provides 24-hour emergency care.

15

EXPLORING YOSEMITE NATIONAL PARK

HISTORIC SITES

★ **Ahwahnee Hotel.** Gilbert Stanley Underwood, the architect for Grand Canyon Lodge on the North Rim in Arizona, also designed the Ahwahnee. Opened in 1927, it is generally considered to be his best work. The Great Lounge, 77 feet long with magnificent 24-foot-high ceilings and all manner of Indian artwork on display, is the most special interior space in Yosemite. You can stay here (for $459 or more a night), or simply explore the first-floor shops and perhaps have breakfast or lunch in the lovely Dining Room. ⊠ *Ahwahnee Rd., about ¾ mi east of Yosemite Valley Visitor Center, Yosemite Village* ☎ *209/372–1489.*

Ahwahneechee Village. This solemn smattering of re-created structures, accessed by a short loop trail, is an imagination of what Indian life might have resembled here in the 1870s. One interpretive sign points out that Miwok referred to the 19th century newcomers as "Yohemite" or "Yohometuk," which have been translated as "some of them are killers." ⊠ *Northside Dr., Yosemite Village* ☎ *Free* ☉ *Daily sunrise–sunset.*

Pioneer Yosemite History Center. Some of Yosemite's first structures—those not occupied by American Indians, that is—were relocated from various parts of the park and placed here in the 1950s and 1960s. You can spend a pleasurable and informative half-hour walking about them and reading the signs, perhaps springing for a self-guided-tour pamphlet (50¢) to further enhance the history lesson. Wednesdays through Sundays in the summer, costumed docents conduct free blacksmithing and "wet-plate" photography demonstrations, and for a small fee you can take a stagecoach ride. ⊠ *Rte. 41, Wawona* ☎ *209/375–9531 or 209/379–2646* ☐ *Free* ☉ *Building interiors are open mid-June–Labor Day, Daily 9–5.*

★ **Wawona Hotel.** One can imagine an older Mark Twain relaxing in a rocking chair on one of the broad verandas of Yosemite's first lodge, a whitewashed series of two-story buildings from the Victorian era. Across the road is a somewhat odd sight: Yosemite's only golf course, one of the few links in the world that does not employ fertilizers or other chemicals. The Wawona is an excellent place to stay or to stop for lunch, but be aware that the hotel is closed in January. ⊠ *Rte. 41, Wawona* ☎ *209/375–1425.*

SCENIC STOPS

★ **El Capitan.** Rising 3,593 feet—more than 350 stories—above the Valley, El Capitan is the largest exposed-granite monolith in the world. Since 1958, people have been climbing its entire face, including the famous "nose." You can spot adventurers with your binoculars by scanning the smooth and nearly vertical cliff for specks of color. ⊠ *Off Northside Dr., about 4 mi west of the Valley Visitor Center.*

Fodor's Choice **Glacier Point.** If you lack the time, desire, or stamina to hike more than
★ 3,200 feet up to Glacier Point from the Yosemite Valley floor, you can drive here—or take a bus from the Valley—for a bird's-eye view. You are likely to encounter a lot of day-trippers on the short, paved trail that leads from the parking lot to the main overlook. Take a moment to veer off a few yards to the Geology Hut, which succinctly explains and illustrates how the Valley looked like 10 million, 3 million, and 20,000 years ago. For details about the summer-only buses, call ☎ *209/372–1240.* ⊠ *Glacier Point Rd., 16 mi northeast of Rte. 41.*

★ **Half Dome.** Visitors' eyes are continually drawn to this remarkable granite formation that tops out at more than 4,700 feet above the Valley floor. Despite its name, the dome is actually about three-quarters "intact." You can hike to the top of Half Dome on an 8.5-mi (one-way) trail whose last 400 feet must be ascended while holding onto a steel cable. Park officials now require a permit to climb above the subdome mid-May to mid-October ($1.50). Permits must be scheduled in advance. Call the main line for reservations (☎ *209/372–0200*). To see Half Dome reflected in the Merced River, view it from Sentinel Bridge just before sundown. But stay for sunset, when the setting sun casts a brilliant orange light onto Half Dome, a stunning sight.

Hetch Hetchy Reservoir. When Congress green-lighted the O'Shaughnessy Dam in 1913, pragmatism triumphed over aestheticism. Some 2.4 million residents of the San Francisco Bay Area continue to get their water from this 117-billion-gallon reservoir, although spirited efforts are being made to restore the Hetch Hetchy Valley to its former, pristine glory. Eight miles long, the reservoir is Yosemite's largest body of water, and one that can be seen up close from several trails. ⊠ *Hetch Hetchy Rd., about 15 mi north of the Big Oak Flat entrance station.*

★ **Mariposa Grove of Big Trees.** Of Yosemite National Parks' three sequoia groves—the others being Merced and Tuolumne, both near Crane Flat well to the north—Mariposa is by far the largest and easiest to walk around. Grizzly Giant, whose base measures 96 feet around, has been estimated to be the world's 25th largest tree by volume. Perhaps more astoundingly, it's about 2,700 years old. On up the hill, you'll find

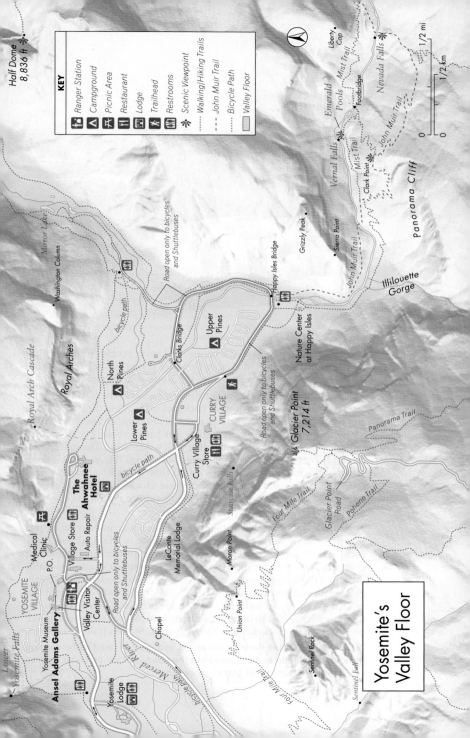

Yosemite's Valley Floor

KEY

Ranger Station	Walking/Hiking Trails
Campground	John Muir Trail
Picnic Area	Bicycle Path
Restaurant	Valley Floor
Lodge	
Trailhead	
Restrooms	
Scenic Viewpoint	

Half Dome
8,836 ft

Liberty Cap
Mist Trail
Nevada Falls
John Muir Trail

Emerald Pools
Footbridge
Vernal Falls
Mist Trail
Clark Point
Panorama Cliff

Mirror Lake
Washington Column

Grizzly Peak
Sierra Point

Illilouette Gorge

1/2 mi
1/2 km

Road open only to bicycles and Shuttlebuses

bicycle path

Clarks Bridge

Upper Pines

Happy Isles Bridge

Nature Center at Happy Isles

John Muir Trail

Royal Arch Cascade
Royal Arches

North Pines

Lower Pines

Road open only to bicycles and Shuttlebuses

CURRY VILLAGE

Glacier Point
7,214 ft

Panorama Trail

bicycle path

The Ahwahnee Hotel

Curry Village Store

Staircase Falls

Four Mile Trail

Glacier Point Road

Pohono Trail

Medical Clinic
P.O.
Village Store
Auto Repair

LeConte Memorial Lodge

Moran Point

YOSEMITE VILLAGE
Yosemite Museum
Ansel Adams Gallery

Valley Visitor Center

Road open only to bicycles and Shuttlebuses

Chapel

Union Point

Lower Yosemite Falls

Yosemite Lodge

Bicycle Path
Merced River

Sentinel Rock

Four Mile Trail

Sentinel Fall

"This is us taking a break before conquering the top of Lembert Dome, while enjoying the beautiful view over Yosemite's high country." —photo by Rebalyn, Fodors.com member

many more sequoias, a small museum, and fewer people. Summer weekends are especially crowded here. Consider taking the free shuttle from Wawona. ⊠ *Rte. 41, 2 mi north of the South Entrance station.*

★ **Tuolumne Meadows.** The largest subalpine meadow in the Sierra (at 8,600 feet) is a popular way station for backpack trips along the Pacific Crest and John Muir trails. The setting is not as dramatic as Yosemite Valley, 56 mi away, but the almost perfectly flat basin, about 2½ mi long, is intriguing, and in July it's resplendent with wildflowers. The most popular day hike is up Lembert Dome, atop which you'll have breathtaking views of the basin below. Keep in mind that Tioga Road rarely opens sooner than June and usually closes by mid-October. ⊠ *Tioga Rd. (Rte. 120), about 8 mi west of the Tioga Pass entrance station.*

WATERFALLS

Yosemite's waterfalls are at their most spectacular in May and June. When the snow starts to melt (usually peaking in May), almost every rocky lip or narrow gorge becomes a spillway for streaming snowmelt churning down to meet the Merced River. By summer's end, some falls, including the mighty Yosemite Falls, dry up. They begin flowing again in late fall, and in winter they may be hung dramatically with ice. Even in drier months, the waterfalls can be breathtaking. If you choose to hike any of the trails to or up the falls, be sure to wear shoes with good, no-slip soles; the rocks can be extremely slick. Stay on trails at all times.

■ **TIP→** Visit the park during a full moon, and you can stroll in the evening without a flashlight and still make out the ribbons of falling water, as well as silhouettes of the giant granite monoliths.

Bridalveil Fall. The filmy waterfall of 620 feet is often diverted as much as 20 feet one way or the other by the breeze. It is the first marvelous view of Yosemite Valley you will see if you come in via Route 41. ✉ *Yosemite Valley, access from parking area off Wawona Rd.*

Nevada Fall. Climb Mist Trail from Happy Isles for an up-close view of this 594-foot cascading beauty, the first major fall as the Merced River plunges out of the high country toward the eastern end of Yosemite Valley. If you don't want to hike, you can see it—distantly—from Glacier Point. ✉ *Yosemite Valley, access via Mist Trail from Nature Center at Happy Isles.*

Ribbon Fall. At 1,612 feet, this is the highest single fall in North America. It's also the first valley waterfall to dry up in summer; the rainwater and melted snow that create the slender fall evaporate quickly at this height. Look just west of El Capitan from the Valley floor for the best view of the fall from the base of Bridalveil Fall. ✉ *Yosemite Valley, west of El Capitan Meadow.*

Vernal Fall. Fern-covered black rocks frame this 317-foot fall, and rainbows play in the spray at its base. You can get a distance view from Glacier Point, or hike to see it close up. ✉ *Yosemite Valley, access via Mist Trail from Nature Center at Happy Isles.*

Fodors Choice ★ **Yosemite Falls.** Actually three falls, they together constitute the highest waterfall in North America and the fifth-highest in the world. The water from the top descends a total of 2,425 feet, and when the falls run hard, you can hear them thunder all across the Valley. When they dry up—usually in late summer—the Valley seems naked without the wavering tower of spray. ■ **TIP→** If you hike the partially paved, mile-long loop trail to the base of the Lower Falls during the peak water flow in May, expect to get soaked. You can get a view of the falls from the lawn of Yosemite Chapel, off Southside Drive. ✉ *Yosemite Valley, access from Yosemite Lodge or trail parking area.*

VISITOR CENTERS

Le Conte Memorial Lodge. This small but striking National Historic Landmark, with its granite walls and steeply pitched shingle roof, is Yosemite's first permanent public information center. Step inside to see the cathedral-like interior, which contains a library and environmental exhibits. To find out about evening programs, check the kiosk out front, look in the park's newspaper, or visit ⊕ *www.sierraclub.org.* ✉ *Southside Dr., about ½ mi west of Curry Village* ☉ *Memorial Day–Labor Day, Wed.–Sun. 10–4.*

Valley Visitor Center. At this center—which was overhauled in 2007—you can learn how Yosemite Valley was formed and about its vegetation, animals, and human inhabitants. Don't leave without watching the superb *Spirit of Yosemite*, a 23-minute introductory film that runs every half-hour in the theater behind the visitor center. ✉ *Yosemite Village* ☏ *209/372–0200* ⊕ *www.nps.gov/yose* ☉ *Late May–early Sept., daily 9–7; early Sept.–late May, daily 9–5.*

SPORTS AND THE OUTDOORS

BICYCLING

There may be no more enjoyable way to see Yosemite Valley than to ride a bike beneath its lofty granite monoliths. The eastern valley has 12 mi of paved, flat bicycle paths across meadows and through woods, with bike racks at convenient stopping points. For a greater challenge, you can ride on 196 mi of paved park roads—but bicycles are not allowed on hiking trails or in the backcountry. Kids under 18 must wear a helmet.

You can get **Yosemite bike rentals** (✉ *Yosemite Lodge or Curry Village* ☎ *209/372–1208* ⊕ *www.yosemitepark.com* 💳 *$9.50/hour, $25.50/ day* ☽ *Apr.–Oct.*) from either Yosemite Lodge or Curry Village bike stands. Bikes with child trailers, baby-jogger strollers, and wheelchairs are available.

BIRD-WATCHING

Nearly 250 bird species have been spotted in the park, including the sage sparrow, pygmy owl, blue grouse, and mountain bluebird. Park rangers lead free bird-watching walks in Yosemite Valley one day each week in summer; check at a visitor center or information station for times and locations. Binoculars are sometimes available for loan.

The Yosemite Association sponsors one- to four-day **birding seminars** (☎ *209/379–2321* ⊕ *www.yosemite.org* 💳 *$82–$254* ☽ *Apr.–Aug.*) for beginner and intermediate birders.

HIKING

The staff at the **Wilderness Center** (☎ *209/372–0655*), in Yosemite Village, provides free wilderness permits, which are required for overnight camping (advance reservations are available for $5 and are highly recommended for popular trailheads from May through September and on weekends). The staff here also provide maps and advice to hikers heading into the backcountry. From April through November, **Yosemite Mountaineering School and Guide Service** (✉ *Yosemite Mountain Shop, Curry Village* ☎ *209/372–8344*) leads two-hour to full-day treks.

EASY

★ **Yosemite Falls Trail.** This is the highest waterfall in North America. The upper fall (1,430 feet), the middle cascades (675 feet), and the lower fall (320 feet) combine for a total of 2,425 feet and, when viewed from the valley, appear as a single waterfall. The ¼-mi trail leads from the parking lot to the base of the falls. Upper Yosemite Fall Trail, a strenuous 3½-mi climb rising 2,700 feet, takes you above the top of the falls. ✉ *Trailhead off Camp 4, north of Northside Dr.*

MODERATE

★ **Mist Trail.** More visitors take this trail (or portions of it) than any other in the park other than Lower Yosemite Falls. The trek up to and back from Vernal Fall is 3 mi. Add another 4 mi total by continuing up to 594-foot Nevada Fall; the trail becomes quite steep and slippery in the final stages. The elevation gain to Vernal Fall is 1,000 feet, and to Nevada Fall an additional 1,000 feet. Merced River tumbles down both falls on its way to a tranquil flow through the Valley. ✉ *Trailhead at Happy Isles.*

★ **Panorama Trail.** Few hikes come with the visual punch that this 8½-mi trail provides. The star attraction is Half Dome, visible from many intriguing angles, but you also see three waterfalls up close and walk through a manzanita grove. Before you begin, look down on Yosemite Valley from Glacier Point, a special experience in itself. ⊠ *Trailhead at Glacier Point.*

DIFFICULT

Fodor's Choice
★
John Muir Trail to Half Dome. Ardent and courageous trekkers can continue on from the top of Nevada Fall, off Mist Trail, to the top of Half Dome. Some hikers attempt this entire 10- to 12-hour, 16¾-mi round-trip trek from Happy Isles in one day; if you're planning to do this, remember that the 4,800-foot elevation gain and the 8,842-foot altitude will cause shortness of breath. Another option is to hike to a campground in Little Yosemite Valley near the top of Nevada Fall the first day, then climb to the top of Half Dome and hike out the next day; it's highly recommended that you get your wilderness permit reservations at least a month in advance. Be sure to wear hiking boots and bring gloves. The last pitch up the back of Half Dome is very steep—the only way to climb this sheer rock face is to pull yourself up using the steel cable handrails, which are in place only from late spring to early fall. Those who brave the ascent will be rewarded with an unbeatable view of Yosemite Valley below and the high country beyond. ⊠ *Trailhead at Happy Isles.*

HORSEBACK RIDING

Reservations for guided trail rides must be made in advance at the hotel tour desks or by phone. For overnight saddle trips, which use mules, go online to ⊕ *www.yosemitepark.com* and fill out a lottery application for the following year. Scenic trail rides range from two hours to a full day; six-day High Sierra saddle trips are also available.

Tuolumne Meadows Stables (⊠ *Off Tioga Rd., 2 mi east of Tuolumne Meadows Visitor Center* ☎ *209/372–8427* ⊕ *www.yosemitepark.com*) runs two-, four-, and eight-hour trips—which cost $53, $69, and $96, respectively—and High Sierra four- to six-day camping treks on mules, beginning at $625. Reservations are essential. **Wawona Stables** (⊠ *Rte. 41, Wawona* ☎ *209/375–6502*) has two- and five-hour rides, starting at $53. Reservations are essential. You can tour the valley and the start of the high country on two-hour and four-hour rides at **Yosemite Valley Stables** (⊠ *At entrance to North Pines Campground, 100 yards northeast of Curry Village* ☎ *209/372–8348* ⊕ *www.yosemitepark.com*). Reservations are required for the $60 and $80 trips.

RAFTING

Rafting is permitted only on designated areas of the Middle and South Forks of the Merced River. Check with the Valley Visitor Center for closures and other restrictions.

The per-person rental fee at **Curry Village raft stand** (⊠ *South side of Southside Dr., Curry Village* ☎ *209/372–8319* ⊕ *www.yosemitepark. com* ☞ *$20.50* ☼ *Late May–July*) covers the four- to six-person raft, two paddles, and life jackets, plus a shuttle to the launch point on Sentinel Beach.

DID YOU KNOW?

Yosemite's granite formations provide sturdy ground for climbers of all skill levels. The sheer granite monolith El Capitan—simply "El Cap" to climbers—is the most famous, climbed by even Captain Kirk (if you believe the opening scene of *Star Trek V: The Final Frontier*), but climbers tackle rocks up in the mountains, too.

ROCK CLIMBING

Fodor's Choice   The one-day basic lesson at **Yosemite Mountaineering School and Guide**
★   **Service** (✉ *Yosemite Mountain Shop, Curry Village* ☎ *209/372–8344*
⊕ *www.yosemitepark.com* 🖃 *$117–$300* ☉ *Apr.–Nov.*) includes some
bouldering and rappelling, and three or four 60-foot climbs. Climbers
must be at least 10 (kids under 12 must be accompanied by a parent
or guardian) and in reasonably good physical condition. Intermediate
and advanced classes include instruction in belays, self-rescue, summer
snow climbing, and free climbing.

ICE-SKATING

Curry Village ice-skating rink. Winter visitors have skated at this outdoor rink for decades, and there's no mystery why: it's a kick to glide
across the ice while soaking up views of Half Dome and Glacier Point.
✉ *South side of Southside Dr., Curry Village* ☎ *209/372–8319* 🖃 *$8
per 2 hrs, $3 skate rental* ☉ *Mid-Nov.–mid-Mar. afternoons and eve-
nings daily, morning sessions weekends; 12–2:30 pm on weekends as
well (hrs vary).*

SKIING AND SNOWSHOEING

Badger Pass Ski Area. California's first ski resort has five lifts and 10
downhill runs, as well as 90 mi of groomed cross-country trails. Free
shuttle buses from Yosemite Valley operate during ski season (December
through early April, weather permitting). Lift tickets are $42, downhill
equipment rents for $31, and snowboard rental with boots is $35. The
gentle slopes of Badger Pass make

    Yosemite Ski School (☎ *209/372–8430*) an ideal spot for children and
beginners to learn downhill skiing or snowboarding for as little as $35
for a group lesson. The highlight of Yosemite's cross-country skiing
center is a 21-mi loop from Badger Pass to Glacier Point. You can rent
cross-country skis for $23.00 per day at the

    Cross-Country Ski School (☎ *209/372–8444*), which also rents snow-
shoes ($22.00 per day), telemarking equipment ($29), and skate-skis
($24).

    Yosemite Mountaineering School (✉ *Badger Pass Ski Area* ☎ *209/372–
8344* ⊕ *www.yosemitemountaineering.com*) conducts snowshoeing,
cross-country skiing, telemarking, and skate-skiing classes starting at
$30. ✉ *Badger Pass Rd., off Glacier Point Rd., 18 mi from Yosemite
Valley* ☎ *209/372–8434.*

EDUCATIONAL PROGRAMS

CLASSES AND SEMINARS

Art Classes. Professional artists conduct workshops in watercolor, etch-
ing, drawing, and other mediums. Bring your own materials or purchase
the basics at the Art Activity Center, next to the Village Store. Call to
verify scheduling. ✉ *Art Activity Center, Yosemite Village* ☎ *209/372–
1442* ⊕ *www.yosemitepark.com* 🖃 *Free* ☉ *April.–early Oct., Tues.–
Sat., 10 am–2 pm.*

Yosemite Outdoor Adventures. Naturalists, scientists, and park rangers lead multi-hour to multiday educational outings on topics from

woodpeckers to fire management to pastel painting. Most sessions take place spring through fall, but a few focus on winter phenomena. ⊠ *Various locations* ☎ *209/379–2321* ⊕ *www.yosemite.org* 🖃 *$82–$465.*

RANGER PROGRAMS

Junior Ranger Program. Children ages 3 to 13 can participate in the informal, self-guided Little Cub and Junior Ranger programs. A park activity handbook ($8) is available at the Valley Visitor Center or the Nature Center at Happy Isles; once your child has completed the book, a ranger will present him or her with a certificate and a badge. ⊠ *Valley Visitor Center or the Nature Center at Happy Isles* ☎ *209/372–0299.*

Ranger-Led Programs. Rangers lead walks and hikes and give informative and entertaining talks on a range of topics at different locations several times a day from spring through fall. The schedule is reduced in winter, but most days you can usually find a ranger program somewhere in the park. In the evenings at Yosemite Lodge and Curry Village, lectures by rangers, slide shows, and documentary films present unique perspectives on Yosemite. On summer weekends, Camp Curry and Tuolumne Meadows Campground host sing-along campfire programs. There's usually at least one ranger-led activity each night in the Valley; schedules and locations are posted on bulletin boards throughout the park and published in the *Yosemite Guide* you receive when you enter the park.

TOURS

★ **Ansel Adams Photo Walks.** Photography enthusiasts shouldn't miss these two-hour guided camera walks that are offered four mornings each week—Monday; Tuesday, Thursday, and Saturday—by professional photographers. Some walks are hosted by the Ansel Adams Gallery, others by Delaware North; meeting points vary. All are free, but participation is limited to 15 people. Reservations are essential. To reserve a spot, call up to 3 days in advance or visit the gallery. ☎ *209/372–4413 or 800/568–7398* ⊕ *www.anseladams.com* 🖃 *Free.*

DNC Parks and Resorts. The main concessionaire at Yosemite National Park, this organization operates several guided tours and programs throughout the park, including the **Big Trees Tram Tour** of the Mariposa Grove of Big Trees, the **Glacier Point Tour,** the **Grand Tour** (both Mariposa Grove and Glacier Point), the **Moonlight Tour** of Yosemite Valley, the **Tuolumne Meadows Tour,** and the **Valley Floor Tour.** ☎ *209/372–1240* ⊕ *www.yosemitepark.com* 🖃 *shuttle buses, free; tours $26–$83, check Web site exact prices.*

WHERE TO EAT

RESTAURANTS

$$$$
CONTINENTAL
✕ **Ahwahnee Hotel Dining Room.** Rave reviews about the dining room's appearance are fully justified—it features floor-to-ceiling windows, a 34-foot-high ceiling with interlaced sugar-pine beams, and massive chandeliers. Although many continue to applaud the food, others have reported that they sense a recent dip in the quality both in the service and what is being served. Diners must spend a lot of money here, so perhaps that inflates the expectations and amplifies the disappointments. In

CLOSE UP

Camping in Yosemite

The 464 campsites within Yosemite Valley are the park's most tightly spaced and, along with the 304-site campground at Tuolumne Meadows, the most difficult to secure on anything approaching short notice.

The park's backcountry and the surrounding wilderness have some unforgettable campsites that can be reached only via long and often difficult hikes or horseback rides. Delaware North operates five High Sierra Camps with comfortable, furnished tent cabins in the remote reaches of Yosemite; rates include breakfast and dinner service. The park concessionaire books the extremely popular backcountry camps by lottery; applications are due by late November for the following summer season. Phone ☎ 801/559–4909 for more information, or check for current availability by navigating from ⊕ www.yosemitepark.com to the High Sierra Camps pages.

To camp in a High Sierra campground you must obtain a wilderness permit. Make reservations up to 24 weeks in advance first by visiting the park's Web site (⊕ www.nps.gov/yose/

planyourvisit/backpacking.htm) and checking availability. For a $5 nonrefundable fee, you can make reservations by phone (☎ 209/372–0740) or by mail (⊠ P.O. Box 545, Yosemite, CA 95389); make checks payable to "Yosemite Association."

Reservations are required at most of Yosemite's campgrounds, especially in summer. You can reserve a site up to five months in advance; bookings made more than 21 days in advance require prepayment. Unless otherwise noted, book your site through the central **National Park Service Reservations Office** (⊠ P.O. Box 1600, Cumberland, MD 21502 ☎ 800/436–7275 ⊕ www.recreation.gov ⊗ Daily 7–7.

Delaware North Companies Parks and Resorts (⊠ 6771 N. Palm Ave., Fresno, CA 93704 ☎ 801/559–5000 ⊕ www.yosemitepark.com), which handles most in-park reservations, takes reservations beginning one year plus one day in advance of your proposed stay. Or, you can roll the dice by showing up at the front desk and asking if there have been any cancellations.

---

any event, the Sunday brunch ($49) is consistently praised. Reservations are always advised, and for dinner, the attire is "resort casual." ⊠ *Ahwahnee Hotel, Ahwahnee Rd., about ¾ mi east of Yosemite Valley Visitor Center, Yosemite Village* ☎ *209/372–1489* ⚭ *Reservations essential.*

$$$
AMERICAN
★
✕ **Mountain Room.** Though good, the food becomes secondary when you see Yosemite Falls through this dining room's wall of windows—almost every table has a view. The chef makes a point of using locally sourced, organic ingredients, so you can be assured of fresh greens and veggies here. The Mountain Room Lounge, a few steps away in the Yosemite Lodge complex, has a broad bar with about 10 beers on tap. ⊠ *Yosemite Lodge, Northside Dr. about ¾ mi west of the visitor center, Yosemite Village* ☎ *209/372–1281* ⊗ *No lunch.*

$$
AMERICAN
✕ **Tuolumne Meadows Lodge.** At the back of a small building that contains the lodge's front desk and small gift shop, this restaurant serves hearty American fare at breakfast and dinner. Let the front desk know

in advance if you have any dietary restrictions, and the cooks will not let you down. ⊠ *Tioga Rd. (Rte. 120)* 🕾 *209/372–8413* ⌕ *Reservations essential* ⊘ *Closed late Sept.–Memorial Day. No lunch.*

$$$$
AMERICAN
★

✕ **Wawona Hotel Dining Room.** Watch deer graze on the meadow while you dine in the romantic, candlelit dining room of the whitewashed Wawona Hotel, which dates from the late 1800s. The American-style cuisine favors fresh California ingredients and flavors; trout is a menu staple. ⊠ *Wawona Hotel, Rte. 41, Wawona* 🕾 *209/375–1425* ⌕ *Reservations essential* ⊘ *Closed Jan.–mid-March.*

PICNIC AREAS

Considering how large the park is and how many visitors come here— some 3.5 million people every year, most of them just for the day—it is somewhat surprising that Yosemite has so few formal picnic areas, though in many places you can find a smooth rock to sit on and enjoy breathtaking views along with your lunch. The convenience stores all sell picnic supplies, and prepackaged sandwiches and salads are widely available. Those options can come in especially handy during the middle of day, when you might not want to spend precious daylight hours in such a spectacular setting sitting in a restaurant for a formal meal. None of these spots have drinking water available; most have some type of toilet. Good spots to hit include Cathedral Beach, Church Bowl, Swinging Bridge, and Yellow Pine.

15

WHERE TO STAY

■ TIP→ Reserve your room or cabin in Yosemite as far in advance as possible. You can make a reservation up to a year before your arrival (within minutes after the reservation office makes a date available, the Ahwahnee, Yosemite Lodge, and Wawona Hotel often sell out their weekends, holiday periods, and all days between May and September).

For expanded hotel reviews, visit Fodors.com.

$$$$
Fodor'sChoice
★

🏨 **The Ahwahnee.** A National Historic Landmark, this hotel is constructed primarily of concrete and sugar-pine logs. **Pros:** best lodge in Yosemite (if not all of California); concierge. **Cons:** expensive; some reports that service has slipped in recent years. ⊠ *1 Ahwahnee Rd., about ¾ mi east of Yosemite Valley Visitor Center, Yosemite Village* 🕾 *209/372–1407 or 801/559–5000* ⊕ *www.yosemitepark.com* ➾ *99 lodge rooms, 4 suites, 24 cottage rooms* ⌂ *In-room: a/c, Wi-Fi. In-hotel: restaurant, room service, bar, pool.*

$$

🏨 **Curry Village.** Opened in 1899 as a place where travelers could enjoy the beauty of Yosemite for a modest price, Curry Village has plain accommodations: standard motel rooms, cabins, and tent cabins, which have rough wood frames, canvas walls, and roofs. **Pros:** comparatively economical; family-friendly atmosphere. **Cons:** can be crowded; sometimes a bit noisy. ⊠ *South side of Southside Dr., Yosemite Valley* 🕾 *801/559–5000* ⊕ *www.yosemitepark.com* ➾ *18 rooms, 527 cabins* ⌂ *In-room: no a/c, no phone, no TV. In-hotel: restaurants, bar, pool.*

$$$

🏨 **Wawona Hotel.** This 1879 National Historic Landmark sits at Yosemite's southern end, a 15-minute drive (or free shuttle bus ride) from the Mariposa Grove of Big Trees. **Pros:** lovely; peaceful atmosphere; close

to Mariposa Grove. **Cons:** few modern in-room amenities; half of the rooms have no baths. ⊠ *Hwy. 41, Wawona* ☎ *801/559–5000* w*www. yosemitepark.com* ➟ *104 rooms, 50 with bath* ⚬ *In-room: no a/c, no phone, no TV. In-hotel: restaurant, bar, golf course, tennis court, pool* ⊙ *Closed Jan. 2–Apr. 6; Nov 27–Dec. 14; call ahead to check for seasonal closures.*

$ 🍴 **White Wolf Lodge.** Set in a subalpine meadow, White Wolf offers rustic accommodations in tent cabins. **Pros:** quiet; convenient for hikers; good restaurant. **Cons:** far from the Valley; not much to do here other than hiking. ⊠ *Off Tioga Rd. (Rte. 120), 25 mi west of Tuolumne Meadows and 15 mi east of Crane Flat 95389* ☎ *801/559–5000* ➟ *24 tent cabins, 4 cabins* ⚬ *In-room: no a/c, no phone, no TV. In-hotel: restaurant* ⊙ *Closed mid-Sept.–early June.*

$$$ 🍴 **Yosemite Lodge at the Falls.** This lodge near Yosemite Falls, which dates from 1915, looks like a 1960s motel-resort complex, with numerous brown, two-story buildings tucked beneath the trees, surrounded by large parking lots. **Pros:** centrally located; dependably clean rooms; lots of tours leave from out front. **Cons:** can feel impersonal; appearance is little dated. ⊠ *Northside Dr. about ¾ mi west of the visitor center, Yosemite Village95389* ☎ *DNC reservations line: 801/559–5000; direct line: 209/372–1274* ⊕ *www.yosemitepark.com* ➟ *245 rooms* ⚬ *In-room: no a/c, Wi-Fi. In-hotel: restaurant, bar, pool.*

Sequoia and Kings Canyon National Parks

WORD OF MOUTH

"At the south end of Sequoia, Giant Forest is the best area for viewing the Big trees. . . . At the edge of Giant Forest, there are amazing views down into the valley . . . The best view is from the top of Moro Rock."

—Sequoia370

WELCOME TO SEQUOIA AND KINGS CANYON NATIONAL PARKS

TOP REASONS TO GO

★ **Gentle giants:** You'll feel small—in a good way—walking among some of the world's largest living things in Sequoia's Giant Forest and Kings Canyon's Grant Grove.

★ **Because it's there:** You can't even glimpse it from the main part of Sequoia, but the sight of majestic Mount Whitney is worth the trek to the eastern face of the High Sierra.

★ **Underground exploration:** Far older even than the giant sequoias, the gleaming limestone formations in Crystal Cave will draw you along dark, marble passages.

★ **A grander-than–Grand Canyon:** Drive the twisting Kings Canyon Scenic Byway down into the jagged, granite Kings River Canyon, deeper in parts than the Grand Canyon.

★ **Regal solitude:** To spend a day or two hiking in a subalpine world of your own, pick one of the 11 trailheads at Mineral King.

1 **Giant Forest–Lodgepole Village.** The most heavily visited area of Sequoia lies at the base of the "thumb" portion of Kings Canyon National Park and contains major sights such as Giant Forest, General Sherman Tree, Crystal Cave, and Moro Rock.

2 **Grant Grove Village–Redwood Canyon.** The "thumb" of Kings Canyon National Park is its busiest section, where Grant Grove, General Grant Tree, Panoramic Point, and Big Stump are the main attractions.

3 **Cedar Grove.** Most visitors to the huge, high-country portion of Kings Canyon National Park don't go farther than Roads End, a few miles east of Cedar Grove on the canyon floor. Here, the river runs through Zumwalt Meadow, surrounded by magnificent granite formations.

4 **Mineral King.** In the southeast section of Sequoia, the highest road-accessible part of the park is a good place to hike, camp, and soak up the unspoiled grandeur of the Sierra Nevada.

5 **Mount Whitney.** The highest peak in the Lower 48 stands on the eastern edge of Sequoia; to get there from Giant Forest you must either backpack eight days through the mountains or drive nearly 400 mi around the park to its other side.

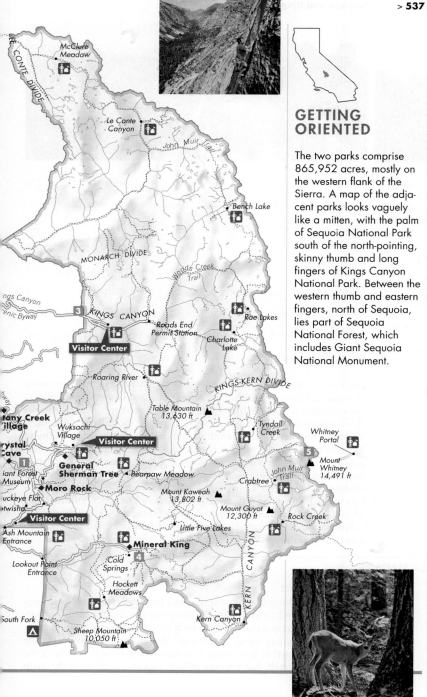

McClure
Meadow

LE CONTE DIVIDE

Le Conte
Canyon

John Muir Trail

GETTING
ORIENTED

The two parks comprise
865,952 acres, mostly on
the western flank of the
Sierra. A map of the adjacent parks looks vaguely
like a mitten, with the palm
of Sequoia National Park
south of the north-pointing,
skinny thumb and long
fingers of Kings Canyon
National Park. Between the
western thumb and eastern
fingers, north of Sequoia,
lies part of Sequoia
National Forest, which
includes Giant Sequoia
National Monument.

16

Bench Lake

MONARCH DIVIDE

Woods Creek
Trail

Kings Canyon
Scenic Byway

3 KINGS CANYON

Rae Lakes

Roads End
Permit Station

Charlotte
Lake

Visitor Center

Roaring River

KINGS-KERN DIVIDE

Table Mountain
13,630 ft

Tyndall
Creek

Whitney
Portal

Tony Creek
Village

Wuksachi
Village

Crystal
Cave

Visitor Center

1

**General
Sherman Tree**

Bearpaw Meadow

Mount
Whitney
14,491 ft

5

John Muir
Trail

Crabtree

Giant Forest
Museum

Moro Rock

Mount Kaweah
13,802 ft

Mount Guyot
12,300 ft

Rock Creek

Buckeye Flat

Potwisha

Little Five Lakes

Visitor Center

KERN CANYON

Ash Mountain
Entrance

Mineral King

4

Lookout Point
Entrance

Cold
Springs

Hockett
Meadows

South Fork

Sheep Mountain
10,050 ft

Kern Canyon

Updated by
Sura Wood
and Reed
Parsell

Although *Sequoiadendron giganteum* is the formal name for the redwoods that grow here, everyone outside the classroom calls them sequoias, big trees, or Sierra redwoods. Their monstrously thick trunks and branches, remarkably shallow root systems, and neck-craning heights are almost impossible to believe, as is the fact they can live for more than 2,500 years. Many of these towering marvels are in the Giant Forest stretch of Generals Highway, which connects Sequoia and Kings Canyon national parks.

Next to or a few miles off the 43-mi road Generals Highway are most of Sequoia National Park's main attractions and Grant Grove Village, the orientation hub for Kings Canyon National Park. The two parks share a boundary that runs west–east, from the foothills of the Central Valley to the Sierra Nevada's dramatic eastern ridges. Kings Canyon has two portions: the smaller is shaped like a bent finger and encompasses Grant Grove Village and Redwood Mountain Grove (the two parks' largest concentration of sequoias), and the larger is home to stunning Kings River Canyon, whose vast, unspoiled peaks and valleys are a backpacker's dream. Sequoia is in one piece and includes Mount Whitney, the highest point in the Lower 48 states (although it is impossible to see from the western part of the park and is a chore to ascend from either side).

PLANNING

WHEN TO GO

The best times to visit are late spring and early fall, when temperatures are moderate and crowds thin. Summertime can draw hoards of tourists to see the giant sequoias, and the few, narrow roads mean congestion at peak holiday times. If you must visit in summer, go during the week. By contrast, in wintertime you may feel as though you have the parks all to yourself. But because of heavy snows, sections of the main park roads can be closed without warning, and low-hanging clouds can move in and obscure mountains and valleys for days. Check road and weather conditions before venturing out mid-November to late April.

Temperatures in the chart below are for the mid-level elevations, generally between 4,000 and 7,000 feet.

GETTING HERE AND AROUND

Sequoia is 36 mi east of Visalia on Route 198; Kings Canyon is 53 mi east of Fresno on Route 180. There is no automobile entrance on the eastern side of the Sierra. Routes 180 and 198 are connected by Generals Highway, a paved two-lane road that sometimes sees delays at peak times due to ongoing improvements. The road is extremely narrow and steep from Route 198 to Giant Forest, so keep an eye on your engine temperature gauge, as the incline and congestion can cause vehicles to overheat; to avoid overheated brakes, use low gears on downgrades.

If you are traveling in an RV or with a trailer, study the restrictions on these vehicles. Do not travel beyond Potwisha Campground with an RV longer than 22 feet on Route 198; take straighter, easier Route 180 instead. Maximum vehicle length on Generals Highway is 40 feet, or 50 feet combined length for vehicles with trailers.

16

Generals Highway between Lodgepole and Grant Grove is sometimes closed by snow. The Mineral King Road from Route 198 into southern Sequoia National Park is closed 2 mi below Atwell Mill either on November 1 or after the first heavy snow. The Buckeye Flat–Middle Fork Trailhead Road is closed mid-October–mid-April when the Buckeye Flat Campground closes. The lower Crystal Cave Road is closed when the cave closes in November. Its upper 2 mi, as well as the Panoramic Point and Moro Rock–Crescent Meadow roads, are closed with the first heavy snow. Because of the danger of rockfall, the portion of Kings Canyon Scenic Byway east of Grant Grove closes in winter. For current conditions, call ☎ *559/565–3341 Ext. 4.*

WHAT IT COSTS				
¢	$	$$	$$$	$$$$
Restaurants	under $10	$10–$15	$16–$22	$23–$30	over $30
Hotels	under $90	$90–$120	$121–$175	$176–$250	over $250

Restaurant prices are per person for a main course at dinner. Hotel prices are per night for two people in a standard double room in high season, excluding taxes and service charges.

PARK ESSENTIALS

ADMISSION FEES AND PERMITS

The admission fee is $20 per vehicle and $10 for those who enter by bus, on foot, bicycle, motorcycle, or horse; it is valid for seven days in both parks. U.S. residents over the age of 62 pay $10 for a lifetime pass, and permanently disabled U.S. residents are admitted free.

If you plan to camp in the backcountry, you need a permit, which costs $15. One permit covers the group. Availability of permits depends upon trailhead quotas. Advance reservations are accepted by mail or fax beginning March 1, and must be made at least two weeks in advance (⊙ *Sequoia and Kings Canyon National Park, Wilderness Permit Reservations, 47050 Generals Hwy. #60, Three Rivers, CA 9327* ☎ *559/565–3766* 📠 *559/565–4239*). Without a reservation, you may still get a permit on a first-come, first-served basis starting at 1 pm the day before you plan to hike. For more information on backcountry camping or travel with pack animals (horses, mules, burros, or llamas), contact the Wilderness Permit Office (☎ *559/565–3761*).

ADMISSION HOURS

The parks are open 24/7 year-round.

EMERGENCIES

Call 911 from any telephone within the park in an emergency. Rangers at the Cedar Grove, Foothills, Grant Grove, and Lodgepole visitor centers and the Mineral King ranger station are trained in first aid. National Park rangers have legal jurisdiction within park boundaries: contact the closest ranger station or visitor center for police matters. For nonemergencies, call the parks' main number (☎ *559/565–3341*).

PARK CONTACT INFORMATION

Delaware North Park Services (⊙ *P.O. Box 89, Sequoia National Park, CA 93262* ☎ *559/565–4070 or 888/252–5757* ⊕ *www.visitsequoia.com*). This concessionaire operates the lodgings and visitor services in Sequoia, and some in Kings Canyon. **Kings Canyon Park Services** (⊙ *P.O. Box 909, Kings Canyon National Park, CA 93633* ☎ *559/335–5500 or 866/522–6966* ⊕ *www.sequoia-kingscanyon.com*). Some park services, including lodging, are operated by this company. **Sequoia and Kings Canyon National Parks** (✉ *47050 Generals Hwy. [Rte. 198], Three Rivers, CA 93271–9651* ☎ *559/565–3341* ⊕ *www.nps.gov/ seki*). **Sequoia Natural History Association** (⊙ *HCR 89 P.O. Box 10, Three Rivers, CA 93271* ☎ *559/565–3759* ⊕ *www.sequoiahistory.org*). The SNHA operates Crystal Cave and the Pear Lake Ski Hut, and provides educational materials and programs. **U.S. Forest Service, Sequoia National Forest** (✉ *900 W. Grand Ave., Porterville, CA 93527* ☎ *559/338–2251* ⊕ *www.fs.fed.us/r5/sequoia*).

SEQUOIA NATIONAL PARK

EXPLORING

SCENIC STOPS

Crescent Meadow. John Muir called this the "gem of the Sierra." Take an hour or two to walk around, and see if you agree. Wildflowers bloom here throughout the summer. ✉ *End of Moro Rock–Crescent Meadow Rd., 2.6 mi east off Generals Hwy.*

★ **Crystal Cave.** One of more than 200 caves in Sequoia and Kings Canyon national parks, Crystal Cave is unusual in that it's composed largely of marble, the result of limestone being hardened under heat and pressure. It contains several impressive formations, even more visible now that an environmentally sensitive relighting project has completed. Unfortunately, some of the cave's formations have been damaged or destroyed by early 20th-century dynamite blasting. The standard tour will give you 45 minutes inside the cave. ⊠ *Crystal Cave Rd., 6 mi west off Generals Hwy.* ☎ *559/565–3759* ⊕ *www.sequoiahistory.org* 🎫 *$11* ⊗ *Mid-May–mid-Oct., daily 10–4.*

★ **General Sherman Tree.** Neither the world's tallest nor oldest sequoia, General Sherman is nevertheless tops in volume—and it is still putting on weight, adding the equivalent of a 60-foot-tall tree every year to its 2.7 million-pound mass. ⊠ *Generals Hwy. (Rte. 198), 2 mi south of Lodgepole Visitor Center.*

Mineral King. This subalpine valley sits at 7,800 feet at the end of a steep, winding road. The trip from the park's entrance can take up to two hours. This is the highest point to which you can drive in the park. ⊠ *End of Mineral King Rd., 25 mi east of Generals Hwy. (Rte. 198), east of Three Rivers.*

★ **Moro Rock.** Sequoia National Park's best non-tree attraction offers panoramic views to those fit and determined enough to mount its 350-ish steps. In a case where the journey rivals the destination, Moro's stone stairway is so impressive in its twisty inventiveness that it's on the National Register of Historic Places. The rock's 6,725-foot summit overlooks the Middle Fork Canyon, sculpted by the Kaweah River and approaching the depth of Arizona's Grand Canyon. ⊠ *Moro Rock–Crescent Meadow Rd., 2 mi east off Generals Hwy. (Rte. 198) to parking area.*

Tunnel Log. This 275-foot tree fell in 1937, and soon a 17-foot-wide, 8-foot-high hole was cut through it for vehicular passage that continues today. Large vehicles take the nearby bypass. ⊠ *Moro Rock–Crescent Meadow Rd., 2 mi east of Generals Hwy. (Rte. 198).*

VISITOR CENTERS

Foothills Visitor Center. Exhibits focusing on the foothills and resource issues facing the parks are on display here. You can also pick up books, maps, and a list of ranger-led walks, and get wilderness permits. ⊠ *Generals Hwy. (Rte. 198), 1 mi north of the Ash Mountain entrance* ☎ *559/565–4212* ⊗ *Oct.–mid-May, daily 8–4:30; mid-May–Sept., daily 8–5.*

Lodgepole Visitor Center. Along with exhibits on the area's geologic history, wildlife, and longtime American Indian inhabitants, the center screens an outstanding 22-minute film about bears. You can also buy books and maps here. ⊠ *Generals Hwy. (Rte. 198), 21 mi north of Ash Mountain entrance* ☎ *559/565–4436* ⊗ *June–Oct., daily 7–6; Closed from Nov.–May.*

Mineral King Ranger Station. The small visitor center here houses a few exhibits on the history of the area; wilderness permits and some books and maps are available. ⊠ *End of Mineral King Rd., 25 mi east of East Fork entrance* ☎ *559/565–3768* ⊗ *Late May–mid-Sept., daily 8–4:30.*

16

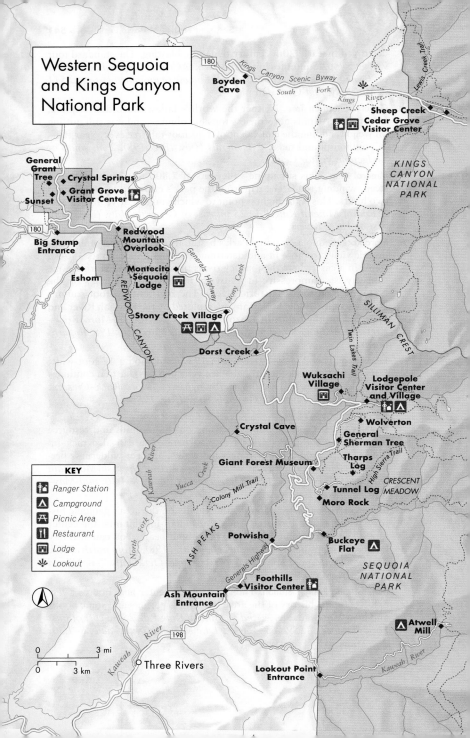

Western Sequoia and Kings Canyon National Park

180
Boyden Cave
Kings Canyon Scenic Byway
South Fork
Kings River
Lewis Creek Trail

Sheep Creek
Cedar Grove Visitor Center

KINGS CANYON NATIONAL PARK

General Grant Tree
Crystal Springs
Grant Grove Visitor Center
Sunset

180
Big Stump Entrance

Redwood Mountain Overlook

Eshom

Montecito Sequoia Lodge

REDWOOD CANYON

Generals Highway

Stony Creek

Stony Creek Village

Dorst Creek

SILLIMAN CREST

Twin Lakes Trail

Wuksachi Village

Lodgepole Visitor Center and Village

Crystal Cave

Wolverton

General Sherman Tree

Giant Forest Museum

Tharps Log

Kaweah River

Yucca Creek

Colony Mill Trail

High Sierra Trail

CRESCENT MEADOW

Tunnel Log

Moro Rock

KEY

North Fork

ASH PEAKS

Potwisha

Buckeye Flat

SEQUOIA NATIONAL PARK

Generals Highway

Foothills Visitor Center

Ash Mountain Entrance

Atwell Mill

0   3 mi
0   3 km

198
Three Rivers

Kaweah River

Lookout Point Entrance

Kaweah River

Flora and Fauna

The parks can be divided into three distinct zones. In the west (1,500–4,500 feet) are the rolling, lower elevation foothills, covered with shrubby chaparral vegetation or golden grasslands dotted with oaks. Chamise, red-barked manzanita, and the occasional yucca plant grow here. Fields of white popcorn flower cover the hillsides in spring, and the yellow fiddleneck flourishes. In summer, intense heat and absence of rain cause the hills to turn golden brown. Wildlife includes the California ground squirrel, noisy blue-and-gray scrub jay, black bears, coyotes, skunks, and gray fox.

At middle elevation (5,000–9,000 feet), where the giant sequoia belt resides, rock formations mix with meadows and huge stands of evergreens—red and white fir, incense cedar, and

ponderosa pines, to name a few. Wildflowers like yellow blazing star and red Indian paintbrush, bloom in spring and summer. Mule deer, golden-mantled ground squirrels, Steller's jays, mule deer, and black bears (most active in fall) inhabit the area, as does the chickaree.

The high alpine section of the parks is extremely rugged, with a string of rocky peaks reaching above 13,000 feet to Mt. Whitney's 14,494 feet. Fierce weather and scarcity of soil make vegetation and wildlife sparse. Foxtail and whitebark pines have gnarled and twisted trunks, the result of high wind, heavy snowfall, and freezing temperatures. In summer you can see yellow-bellied marmots, pikas, weasels, mountain chickadees, and Clark's nutcrackers.

16

SPORTS AND THE OUTDOORS

The best way to see Sequoia is to take a hike. Unless you do so, you'll miss out on the up-close grandeur of mist wafting between deeply scored, red-orange tree trunks bigger than you've ever seen. If it's winter, put on some snowshoes or cross-country skis and plunge into the outscale woodland swaddled in snow. There are not too many other outdoor options: no off-road driving is allowed in the parks, and no special provisions have been made for bicycles. Boating, rafting, and snowmobiling are also prohibited.

BIRD-WATCHING

More than 200 species of birds inhabit Sequoia and Kings Canyon national parks. Not seen in most parts of the United States, the white-headed woodpecker and the pileated woodpecker are common in most mid-elevation areas here. There are also many hawks and owls, including the renowned spotted owl. Species are diverse in both parks due to the changes in elevation, and range from warblers, kingbirds, thrushes, and sparrows in the foothills to goshawk, blue grouse, red-breasted nuthatch, and brown creeper at the highest elevations. Ranger-led bird-watching tours are held on a sporadic basis. Call the park's main information number to find out more about these tours.

Contact the **Sequoia Natural History Association** (HCR 89, P.O. Box 10, Three Rivers, CA 93271 ☎ 559/565–3759 ⊕ www.sequoiahistory. org) for information on bird-watching in the southern Sierra.

CROSS-COUNTRY SKIING

Pear Lake Ski Hut. Primitive lodging is available at this backcountry hut, reached by a steep and extremely difficult 7-mi trail from Wolverton. Only expert skiers should attempt this trek. Space is limited; make reservations well in advance. ⊠ *Trailhead at end of Wolverton Rd., 1½ mi northeast off Generals Hwy. (Rte. 198)* ☎ *559/565–3759* ⊠ *$38* ☉ *Mid-Dec.–mid-Apr.*

Wuksachi Lodge. Rent skis here. Depending on snowfall amounts, instruction may also be available. Reservations are recommended. Marked trails cut through Giant Forest, just 5 mi south of the lodge. ⊠ *Off Generals Hwy. (Rte. 198), 2 mi north of Lodgepole* ☎ *559/565–4070* ⊠ *$15–$20 ski rental* ☉ *Nov.–May (unless no snow), daily 9–4.*

HIKING

The best way to see the park is to hike it. The grandeur and majesty of the Sierra is best seen up close. Carry a hiking map—available at any visitor center—and plenty of water. Check with rangers for current trail conditions, and be aware of rapidly changing weather. As a rule of thumb, plan on trekking 1 mph.

EASY

★ **Congress Trail.** This easy 2-mi trail is a paved loop that begins near General Sherman Tree and winds through the heart of the Sequoia forest. You'll get close-up views of more big trees here than on any other Sequoia hike. Watch for the clusters known as the House and Senate. ⊠ *Trail begins off Generals Hwy. (Rte. 198), 2 mi north of Giant Forest.*

★ **Crescent Meadow Trails.** John Muir reportedly called Crescent Meadow the "gem of the Sierra." Brilliant wildflowers bloom here by midsummer, and a 1.8-mi trail loops around the meadow. A 1.6-mi trail begins at Crescent Meadow and leads to Tharp's Log, a cabin built from a fire-hollowed sequoia. ⊠ *Trail begins end of Moro Rock–Crescent Meadow Rd., 2.6 mi east off Generals Hwy. (Rte. 198).*

MODERATE

Tokopah Falls Trail. This moderate trail follows the Marble Fork of the Kaweah River for 1.75 mi one way and dead-ends below the impressive granite cliffs and cascading waterfall of Tokopah Canyon. It takes 2½ to 4 hours to make the 3.5-mi round-trip journey. The trail passes through a mixed-conifer forest. ⊠ *Trail begins off Generals Hwy. (Rte. 198), ¼ mi north of Lodgepole Campground.*

DIFFICULT

Mineral King Trails. Many trails to the high country begin at Mineral King. The two most popular day hikes are Eagle Lake and Timber Gap, both of which are somewhat strenuous. At 7,800 feet, this is the highest point to which one can drive in either of the parks. Get a map and provisions, and check with rangers about conditions. ⊠ *Trailhead at end of Mineral King Rd., 25 mi east of Generals Hwy. (Rte. 198).*

HORSEBACK RIDING

Trips take you through redwood forests, flowering meadows, across the Sierra, or even up to Mt. Whitney. Costs per person range from $25 for a one-hour guided ride to around $200 per day for fully guided trips for which the packers do all the cooking and camp chores.

Grant Grove Stables is the stable to choose if you want a short ride. ⊠ *Rte. 180, ½ Mi north of Grant Grove Visitor Center, near Grant Grove Village, Gran Grove* ☎ *559/337–2314 mid-June–Sept., 559/337–2314 Oct.–mid-June*

Horse Corral Pack Station. Hourly, half-day, full-day, or overnight trips through Sequoia are available for beginning and advanced riders. ⊠ *Off Big Meadows Rd., 12 mi east of Generals Hwy. (Rte. 198) between Sequoia and Kings Canyon national parks* ☎ *559/565–3404 in summer, 559/564–6429 in winter* ⊕ *www.horsecorralpackers.com* ☎ *$35–$145 day trips* ☉ *May–Sept.*

Mineral King Pack Station. Day and overnight tours in the high-mountain area around Mineral King are available here. ⊠ *End of Mineral King Rd., 25 mi east of East Fork entrance* ☎ *559/561–3039 in summer, 520/855–5885 in winter* ⊕ *mineralking.tripod.com* ☎ *$25–$75 day trips* ☉ *July to late Sept. or early Oct.*

SLEDDING AND SNOWSHOEING

The Wolverton area, on Route 198 near Giant Forest, is a popular sledding spot, where sleds, inner tubes, and platters are allowed. You can buy sleds and saucers, starting at $8, at the **Wuksachi Lodge** (☎ *559/565–4070*), 2 mi north of Lodgepole. You can also rent snowshoes for $15–$20. Naturalists lead snowshoe walks around Giant Forest and Wuksachi Lodge, conditions permitting, on Saturdays and holidays. Snowshoes are provided for a $1 donation. Make reservations and check schedules at **Giant Forest Museum** (☎ *559/565–4480*) or **Wuksachi Lodge.**

EDUCATIONAL OFFERINGS

CLASSES AND SEMINARS

Evening Programs. In summer, the park shows documentary films and slide shows, and has evening lectures. Locations and times vary; pick up a schedule at any visitor center or check bulletin boards near ranger stations. ☎ *559/565–3341.*

★ **Seminars.** Expert naturalists lead seminars on a range of topics, including birds, wildflowers, geology, botany, photography, park history, backpacking, and pathfinding. Some courses offer transferable credits. Reserve in advance. For information and prices, pick up a course catalogue at any visitor center or contact the **Sequoia Natural History Association** (☎ *559/565–3759* ⊕ *www.sequoiahistory.org*).

Sequoia Sightseeing Tours. The only licensed tour operator in either park offers daily interpretive sightseeing tours in a 10-passenger van with a friendly, knowledgeable guide. Reservations are essential. They also offer private tours of Kings Canyon. ☎ *559/561–4189* ⊕ *www. sequoiatours.com.*

RANGER PROGRAMS

Free Nature Programs. Almost any summer day, half-hour to 1½-hour ranger talks and walks explore subjects such as the life of the sequoia, the geology of the park, and the habits of bears. Giant Forest, Lodgepole Visitor Center, Wuksachi Village, and Dorst Creek Campground are frequent starting points. Check bulletin boards throughout the park for the week's offerings.

Junior Ranger Program. This self-guided program is offered year-round for children over five. Pick up a Junior Ranger booklet at any of the visitor centers. When your child finishes an activity, a ranger signs the booklet. Kids earn a patch upon completion, which is given at an awards ceremony. It isn't necessary to complete all activities to be awarded a patch. ☎ *559/565–3341.*

KINGS CANYON NATIONAL PARK

SCENIC DRIVES

★ **Kings Canyon Scenic Byway.** About 10 mi east of Grant Grove Village is Jackson View, where you'll first see Kings River Canyon. Near Yucca Point, it's thousands of feet deeper than the much more famous Grand Canyon. Continuing through Sequoia National Forest past Boyden Cavern, you'll enter the larger portion of Kings Canyon National Park and, eventually, Cedar Grove Village. Past there, the U-shaped canyon becomes broader. Be sure to allow an hour to walk through Zumwalt Meadow. Also, be sure to park and take the less-than-five-minute walks to the base of Grizzly Falls and Roaring River Falls. The drive dead-ends at a big parking lot, the launch point for many backpackers. Driving the byway takes about one hour each way (without stops).

16

EXPLORING

Kings Canyon National Park consists of two sections that adjoin the northern boundary of Sequoia National Park. The western portion, covered with sequoia and pine forest, contains the park's most visited sights, such as Grant Grove. The vast eastern portion is remote high country, slashed across half its southern breadth by the deep, rugged Kings River Canyon. Separating the two is Sequoia National Forest, which encompasses Giant Sequoia National Monument. The Kings Canyon Scenic Byway (Route 180) links the major sights within and between the park's two sections.

HISTORIC SITES

★ **Fallen Monarch.** This Sequoia's hollow base was used in the second half of the 19th century as a home for settlers, a saloon, and even to stable U.S. Cavalry horses. As you walk through it (assuming entry is permitted, which has not always been the case in recent years), check out how little the wood has decayed, and imagine yourself tucked safely inside, sheltered from a storm or protected from the searing heat. ⊠ *Trailhead 1 mi north of Grant Grove Visitor Center.*

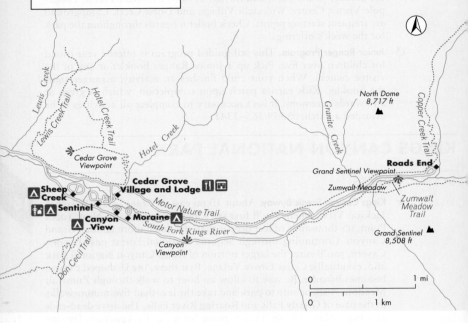

Kings Canyon's Cedar Grove Area

Lewis Creek

Lewis Creek Trail

Hotel Creek Trail

Hotel Creek

Cedar Grove
Viewpoint

Granite Creek

Copper Creek Trail

North Dome
8,717 ft

Roads End

Grand Sentinel Viewpoint

Sheep
Creek

Cedar Grove
Village and Lodge

Zumwalt Meadow

Zumwalt
Meadow
Area

Sentinel

Moraine

Motor Nature Trail

Grand Sentinel
8,508 ft

Canyon
View

South Fork Kings River

Don Cecil Trail

Canyon
Viewpoint

0   1 mi

0   1 km

SCENIC STOPS

Canyon View. There are many places along the scenic byway to pull over for sightseeing, but this special spot showcases evidence of the canyon's glacial history. Here, maybe more than anywhere else, you'll understand why John Muir compared Kings Canyon vistas with those in Yosemite. ⊠ *Kings Canyon Scenic Byway (Rte. 180), 1 mi east of the Cedar Grove turnoff.*

★ **Redwood Mountain Grove.** If you are serious about sequoias, you should consider visiting this, the world's largest big-tree grove. Within its 2,078 acres are 2,172 sequoias whose diameters exceed 10 feet. Your options range from the distant (pulling off the Generals Highway onto an over-look) to the intimate (taking a 6- to 10-mi hike down into its richest regions, which include two of the world's 25 heaviest trees). ⊠ *Drive 5 mi south of Grant Grove on Generals Hwy. (Rte. 198), then turn right at Quail Flat; follow it 1½ mi to the Redwood Canyon trailhead.*

VISITOR CENTERS

Cedar Grove Visitor Center. Off the main road and behind the Sentinel Campground, this small ranger station has books and maps, plus infor-mation about hikes and other things to do in the area. ⊠ *Kings Canyon Scenic Byway, 30 mi east of park entrance* ☎ *559/565–3793* ☉ *mid-May–late September, daily 9–5.*

Grant Grove Visitor Center. Acquaint yourself with the varied charms of this two-section national park by watching a 15-minute film and perusing the center's exhibits on the canyon, sequoias, and human history. Books, maps, and free wilderness permits are available, as are updates on the parks' weather and air-quality conditions. ✉ *Generals Hwy. (Rte. 198), 3 mi northeast of Rte. 180, Big Stump entrance* ☎ *559/565–4307* ☉ *Summer, daily 8–6; mid-May–late Sept., daily 9–4:30; winter, daily 9–4:30.*

SPORTS AND THE OUTDOORS

CROSS-COUNTRY SKIING

Roads to Grant Grove are easily accessible during heavy snowfall, making the trails here a good choice over Sequoia's Giant Forest when harsh weather hits.

HIKING

You can enjoy many of Kings Canyon's sights from your car, but the giant gorge of the Kings River Canyon and the sweeping vistas of some of the highest mountains in the United States are best seen on foot. Carry a hiking map—available at any visitor center—and plenty of water. Check with rangers for current trail conditions, and be aware of rapidly changing weather.

If you're planning to hike the backcountry, you can pick up a permit and information on the backcountry at **Road's End Permit Station** (✉ *5 mi east of Cedar Grove Visitor Center, at the end of Kings Canyon Scenic Byway* ☎ *No phone* ☉ *Late May–late Sept., daily 7–3:30*). You can also rent or buy bear canisters, a must for campers. When the station is closed, you can still complete a self-service permit form.

EASY

Fodor'sChoice
★ **Zumwalt Meadow Trail.** Rangers say this is the best (and most popular) day hike in the Cedar Grove area. Just 1.5 mi long, it offers three visual treats: the South Fork of the Kings River, the lush meadow, and the high granite walls above, including those of Grand Sentinel and North Dome. ✉ *Trailhead 4½ mi east of Cedar Grove Village turnoff from Kings Canyon Scenic Byway.*

MODERATE

★ **Big Baldy.** This hike climbs 600 feet and 2 mi up to the 8,209-feet summit of Big Baldy. Your reward is the view of Redwood Canyon. The round-trip hike is 4 mi. ✉ *Trailhead 8 mi south of Grant Grove on Generals Hwy. (Rte. 198).*

★ **Redwood Canyon Trail.** Avoid the hubbub of Giant Forest and its General Sherman Tree by hiking down to Redwood Canyon, the world's largest grove of sequoias. Opt for the trail toward Hart Tree, and you'll soon lose track of how many humongous trees you pass along the 6-mi loop. Count on spending four to six peaceful hours here—although some backpackers linger overnight (wilderness permit required). ✉ *Trail begins off Quail Flat* ✛ *Drive 5 mi south of Grant Grove on Generals Hwy. (Rte. 198), then turn right at Quail Flat; follow it 1½ mi to the Redwood Canyon trailhead.*

16

DIFFICULT

★ **Hotel Creek Trail.** For gorgeous canyon views, take this trail from the canyon floor at Cedar Grove up a series of switchbacks until it splits. Follow the route left through chaparral to the forested ridge and rocky outcrop known as Cedar Grove Overlook, where you can see the Kings River Canyon stretching below. This strenuous 5-mi round-trip hike gains 1,200 feet and takes three to four hours to complete. For a longer hike, return via Lewis Creek Trail for an 8-mi loop. ⊠ *Trailhead at Cedar Grove pack station, 1 mi east of Cedar Grove Village.*

HORSEBACK RIDING

One-day destinations by horseback out of Cedar Grove include Mist Falls and Upper Bubb's Creek. In the backcountry, many equestrians head for Volcanic Lakes or Granite Basin, ascending trails that reach elevations of 10,000 feet. Costs per person range from $25 for a one-hour guided ride to around $200 per day for fully guided trips for which the packers do all the cooking and camp chores.

Take a day or overnight trip along the Kings River Canyon with **Cedar Grove Pack Station** (⊠ *Kings Canyon Scenic Byway, 1 mi east of Cedar Grove Village* ☎ *559/565–3464 in summer, 559/337–2314 off-season* ✉ *Call for prices* ☉ *May–Oct.*). Popular routes include the Rae Lakes Loop and Monarch Divide. A one- or two-hour trip through Grant Grove leaving from **Grant Grove Stables** (⊠ *Rte. 180, ½ mi north of Grant Grove Visitor Center* ☎ *559/335–9292 mid-June–Sept., 559/337–2314 Oct.–mid-June* ✉ *$40–$60* ☉ *June–Labor Day, daily 8–6*) is a good way to get a taste of horseback riding in Kings Canyon.

SLEDDING AND SNOWSHOEING

In winter, Kings Canyon has a few great places to play in the snow. Sleds, inner tubes, and platters are allowed at both the Azalea Campground area on Grant Tree Road, ¼ mi north of Grant Grove Visitor Center, and at the Big Stump picnic area, 2 mi north of the lower Route 180 entrance to the park.

Snowshoeing is good around Grant Grove, where you can take naturalist-guided snowshoe walks on Saturdays and holidays mid-December through mid-March as conditions permit.

MOUNT WHITNEY

At 14,494 feet, Mt. Whitney is the highest point in the contiguous United States and the crown jewel of Sequoia National Park's wild eastern side. Despite the mountain's scale, you can't see it from the more traveled west side of the park, because it is hidden behind the Great Western Divide. The only way to access Mt. Whitney from the main part of the park is to circumnavigate the Sierra Nevada via a 10-hour, nearly 400-mi drive outside the park. No road ascends the peak; the best vantage point from which to catch a glimpse of the mountain is at the end of Whitney Portal Road. (Whitney Portal Road is closed in winter.)

Hiking in the Sierra mountains is a thrilling experience, putting you amid some of the world's highest trees.

WHERE TO EAT

$$ ✕**Cedar Grove Restaurant.** For a small operation, the menu here is sur-
AMERICAN prisingly extensive, with dinner entrées such as pasta, pork chops, and
steak. For breakfast, try the biscuits and gravy, French toast, pancakes,
or cold cereal. Burgers (including vegetarian patties) and hot dogs domi-
nate the lunch choices. Outside, a patio dining area overlooks the Kings
River. ⊠ *Cedar Grove Village* ☎ *559/565–0100* ⊙ *Closed Oct.–May.*

$$$ ✕**Grant Grove Restaurant.** In a no-frills, open room, you can order basic
AMERICAN American fare such as pancakes for breakfast or hot sandwiches and
chicken for later meals. Vegetarians and vegans will have to content
themselves with a simple salad. Take-out service is available. ⊠ *Grant
Grove Village* ☎ *559/335–5500.*

¢ ✕**Lodgepole Market and Snack Bar.** The choices here run the gamut
CAFÉ from simple to very simple, with the three counters only a few strides
apart in a central eating complex. For hot food, venture into the
snack bar. The deli sells prepackaged sandwiches along with ice cream
scooped from tubs. You'll find other prepackaged foods in the market.
⊠ *Next to Lodgepole Visitor Center* ☎ *559/565–3301* ⊙ *Closed early
Sept.–mid-Apr.*

$$$ ✕**Wolverton Barbecue.** Weather permitting, diners congregate on a
BARBECUE wooden porch that looks directly out onto a small but strikingly ver-
dant meadow. In addition to the predictable meats such as ribs and
chicken, the all-you-can-eat buffet has sides that include baked beans,
corn on the cob, and potato salad. Following the meal, listen to a ranger
talk and clear your throat for a campfire sing-along. Purchase tickets at
Lodgepole Market, Wuksachi Lodge, or Wolverton Recreation Area's

office. ✉ *Wolverton Rd., 1½ mi northeast off Generals Hwy. (Rte. 198)* ☎ *559/565–4070 or 559/565–3301* ◷ *Open in summer only, seven days a week.*

$$$
AMERICAN
★

✕**Wuksachi Village Dining Room.** Huge windows run the length of the high-ceilinged dining room, and a large fireplace on the far wall warms both the body and the soul. The diverse dinner menu—by far the best in the two parks—includes filet mignon, rainbow trout, and vegetarian pasta dishes, in addition to the ever-present burgers. The children's menu is economically priced. Breakfast and lunch also are served. ✉ *Wuksachi Village* ☎ *559/565–4070* 🥢 *Reservations essential.*

WHERE TO STAY

For expanded hotel reviews, visit Fodors.com.

$$$

🏨**John Muir Lodge.** This modern, timber-sided lodge is nestled in a wooded area in the hills above Grant Grove Village and offers year-round accommodations. **Pros:** common room stays warm; it's far enough from the main road to be quiet. **Cons:** check-in is down in the village. ✉ *Kings Canyon Scenic Byway, ¼ mi north of Grant Grove Village* ⌖ *Sequoia Kings Canyon Park Services Co., P.O. Box 907, Suite 101, Kings Canyon National Park CA 93633* ☎ *559/335–5500 or 866/522–6966* ⊕ *www.sequoia-kingscanyon.com* ⇱ *36 rooms* ⌂ *In-room: no a/c, no TV.*

$$$
Fodor'sChoice
★

🏨**Wuksachi Lodge.** The striking cedar-and-stone main building here is a fine example of how a man-made structure can blend effectively with lovely mountain scenery. **Pros:** best place to stay in the parks; lots of wildlife. **Cons:** rooms can be small; main lodge is a few minutes' walk from guest rooms. ✉ *Wuksachi Village* ☎ *559/565–4070 front desk, 888/252–5757 reservations* ⊕ *www.visitsequoia.com* ⇱ *102 rooms* ⌂ *In-room: a/c (some), Internet, Wi-Fi. In-hotel: restaurant, bar.*

Travel Smart
Southern
California

WORD OF MOUTH

"Yes, the distances here in California are huge. As you'll be spending many hours in the car, make sure that you get one that's not going to be too cramped. You ought to carry bottled water with you all the time, but especially when you're driving through the desert."

—Barbara

GETTING HERE AND AROUND

Wherever you plan to go in Southern California, getting there will likely involve driving (even if you fly). With the exception of San Diego, major airports are usually far from main attractions. (For example, four airports serve the Los Angeles area—but three of them are outside the city limits.) Southern California's major airport hub is LAX in Los Angeles, but satellite airports can be found around most major cities. When booking flights, it pays to check these locations, as you may find cheaper flights, more convenient times, and a better location in relation to your hotel. Most small cities have their own commercial airports, with connecting flights to larger cities—but service may be extremely limited, and it may be cheaper to rent a car and drive from L.A.

There are two basic north–south routes in California: I–5, an interstate highway, runs inland most of the way from the Oregon border to the Mexican border; and Highway 101 hugs the coast for part of the route from Oregon to Mexico. (A slower but much more scenic option is to take California State Route 1, also referred to as Highway 1 and the Pacific Coast Highway, which winds along much of the California coast and provides an occasionally hair-raising, but breathtaking, ride.) From north to south, the state's east–west interstates are I–80, I–15, I–10, and I–8. Much of California is mountainous, and you may encounter winding roads, frequently cliff-side, and steep mountain grades. In winter, roads crossing the Sierra east to west may close at any time due to weather, and chains may be required on these roads when they are open. Also in winter, I–5 north of Los Angeles closes during snowstorms. The flying and driving times in the following charts are best-case scenario estimates, but know that the infamous California traffic jam can occur at any time.

FROM LOS ANGELES TO:	BY AIR	BY CAR
San Diego	45 minutes	2 hours
Death Valley		6 hours
San Francisco	1 hour 25 minutes	6 hours 30 minutes
Monterey	1 hour 10 minutes	5 hours 45 minutes
Santa Barbara	45 minutes	1 hour 45 minutes
Big Sur		5 hours 40 minutes
Sacramento	1 hour 20 minutes	6 hours 30 minutes

▌ AIR TRAVEL

Flying time to California is about six hours from New York and four-and-a-half hours from Chicago. Travel from London to Los Angeles is 11 hours and from Sydney approximately 14. Flying between San Francisco and Los Angeles takes about 90 minutes.

AIRPORTS

Southern California's gateways are Los Angeles International Airport (LAX) and San Diego International Airport (SAN). Other Los Angeles airports include Long Beach (LGB), Bob Hope Airport (BUR), LA/Ontario (ONT), and John Wayne Airport (SNA).

Airport Information Bob Hope Airport (☎ 818/840–8840 ⊕ www.burbankairport. com). **John Wayne Airport** (☎ 949/252–5200 ⊕ www.ocair.com). **LA/Ontario International Airport** (☎ 909/937–2700 ⊕ www. flyontario.com). **Los Angeles International Airport** (☎ 310/646–5252 ⊕ www.lawa.org/ lax). **Long Beach Airport** (☎ 562/570–2619 ⊕ www.lgb.org). **Oakland International Airport** (☎ 510/563–3300 ⊕ www.flyoakland. com). **San Diego International Airport** (☎ 619/400–2404 ⊕ www.san.org).

FLIGHTS

United, with hubs in San Francisco and Los Angeles, has the greatest number of flights into and within California. But most national and many international airlines fly here. Southwest Airlines connects smaller cities within California, often from satellite airports near major cities.

Airline Contacts Air Canada (☎ 888/247–2262 ⊕ www.aircanada.com). **Alaska Airlines/Horizon Air** (☎ 800/252–7522 ⊕ www.alaskaair.com). **American Airlines** (☎ 800/433–7300 ⊕ www.aa.com). **British Airways** (☎ 800/247–9297 ⊕ www.britishairways.com). **Cathay Pacific** (☎ 800/233–2742 ⊕ www.cathaypacific.com). **Continental Airlines** (☎ 800/523–3273 for U.S. and Mexico reservations, 800/231–0856 for international reservations ⊕ www.continental.com). **Delta Airlines** (☎ 800/221–1212 for U.S. reservations, 800/241–4141 for international reservations ⊕ www.delta.com). **Frontier Airlines** (☎ 800/452–2022 ⊕ www.frontierairlines.com). **Japan Air Lines** (☎ 800/525–3663 ⊕ www.jal.com). **JetBlue** (☎ 800/538–2583 ⊕ www.jetblue.com). **Qantas** (☎ 800/227–4500 ⊕ www.qantas.com.au). **Southwest Airlines** (☎ 800/435–9792 ⊕ www.southwest.com). **Spirit Airlines** (☎ 800/772–7117 ⊕ www.spirit.com). **United Airlines** (☎ 800/864–8331 for U.S. reservations, 800/538–2929 for international reservations ⊕ www.united.com). **US Airways** (☎ 800/428–4322 for U.S. and Canada reservations, 800/622–1015 for international reservations ⊕ www.usairways.com).

▋ BOAT TRAVEL

CRUISES

A number of major cruise lines offer trips that begin or end in California. Most voyages sail north along the Pacific Coast to Alaska or south to Mexico. California cruise ports include Los Angeles, San Diego, and San Francisco.

Cruise Lines Carnival Cruise Line (☎ 305/599–2600 or 800/227–6482 ⊕ www.carnival.com). **Celebrity Cruises** (☎ 800/647–2251 or 800/437–3111 ⊕ www.celebritycruises.com). **Crystal Cruises** (☎ 310/785–9300 or 800/446–6620 ⊕ www.crystalcruises.com). **Holland America Line** (☎ 206/281–3535 or 877/932–4259 ⊕ www.hollandamerica.com). **Norwegian Cruise Line** (☎ 305/436–4000 or 800/327–7030 ⊕ www.ncl.com). **Princess Cruises** (☎ 661/753–0000 or 800/774–6237 ⊕ www.princess.com). **Regent Seven Seas Cruises** (☎ 954/776–6123 or 800/477–7500 ⊕ www.rssc.com). **Royal Caribbean International** (☎ 305/539–6000 or 800/327–6700 ⊕ www.royalcaribbean.com). **Silversea Cruises** (☎ 954/522–4477 or 800/722–9955 ⊕ www.silversea.com).

▋ BUS TRAVEL

Greyhound is the major bus carrier in California. Regional bus service is available in metropolitan areas.

Bus Information Greyhound (☎ 800/231–2222 ⊕ www.greyhound.com).

▋ CAR TRAVEL

Three major highways—I–5, U.S. 101, and Highway 1—run north–south through California. The main east–west routes are I–15, I–10, and I–8 in Southern California.

FROM LOS ANGELES TO:	ROUTE	DISTANCE
San Diego	I–5 or I–15	120 mi
Las Vegas	I–10 to I–15	265 mi
Death Valley	I–10 to I–15 to Hwy. 127 to Hwy. 190	304 mi
San Francisco	I–5 to Hwy. 156 to Hwy. 101	403 mi
Monterey	Hwy. 101 to Salinas, Hwy. 68 to Hwy. 1	334 mi
Santa Barbara	Hwy. 101	95 mi
Big Sur	Hwy. 101 to Hwy. 1	297 mi
Sacramento	I–5	386 mi

GASOLINE

Gasoline prices in California vary widely, depending on location, oil company, and whether you buy it at a full-serve or self-serve pump. It's less expensive to buy fuel in the southern part of the state than in the north. If you're planning to travel near Nevada, you can save a bit by purchasing gas over the border. Gas stations are plentiful throughout the state. Most stay open late (24 hours along major highways and in big cities), except in rural areas, where Sunday hours are limited and where you may drive long stretches without a chance to refuel.

ROAD CONDITIONS

Rainy weather can make driving along the coast or in the mountains treacherous. Some of the smaller routes over mountain ranges and in the deserts are prone to flash flooding. When the rains are severe, coastal Highway 1 can quickly become a slippery nightmare, buffeted by strong winds and obstructed by falling debris from the cliffs above. When the weather is particularly bad, Highway 1 may be closed due to mud and rock slides.

Road Conditions Statewide Hotline (☎ 800/GAS–ROAD [800/427–7623] ⊕ www.dot.ca.gov/hq/roadinfo).

Weather Conditions National Weather Service (☎ 805/988–6610 Los Angeles area, ☎ 858/675–8700 San Diego area ⊕ www.weather.gov).

ROADSIDE EMERGENCIES

Dial 911 to report accidents on the road and to reach the police, the California Highway Patrol (CHP), or the fire department. On some rural highways and on most interstates, look for emergency phones on the side of the road. In Los Angeles, the Metro Freeway Service Patrol provides assistance to stranded motorists under nonemergency conditions. Call #399 on your cell phone to reach them 24 hours a day.

RULES OF THE ROAD

Children under age 6 or weighing less than 60 pounds must be secured in a federally approved child passenger restraint system and ride in the back seat. Seat belts are required at all times and children must wear them regardless of where they're seated (studies show that children are safest in the rear seats). Unless otherwise indicated, right turns are allowed at red lights after you've come to a full stop. Left turns between two one-way streets are allowed at red lights after you've come to a full stop. Drivers with a blood-alcohol level higher than 0.08 who are stopped by police are subject to arrest, and police officers can detain those with a level of 0.05 if they appear impaired. California's drunk-driving laws are extremely tough—violators may have their licenses immediately suspended, pay hefty fines, and spend the night in jail. The speed limit on many interstate highways is 70 mph; unlimited-access roads are usually 55 mph. In cities, freeway speed limits are between 55 mph and 65 mph. Many city routes have commuter lanes during rush hour.

Those 18 and older must use a hands-free device for their mobile phones while driving, while teenagers under 18 are not allowed to use mobile phones or wireless devices while driving. "Texting" on a wireless device is illegal for persons of all ages while driving in California. Smoking in a vehicle where a minor is present is an infraction. For more information refer to the Department of Motor Vehicles driver's handbook at ⊕ www.dmv.ca.gov/dmv.htm.

CAR RENTAL

When you reserve a car, ask about cancellation penalties, taxes, drop-off charges (if you're planning to pick up the car in one city and leave it in another), and surcharges (for being under or over a certain age, for additional drivers, or for driving across state or country borders or beyond a specific distance from your point of rental). All these things can add substantially to your costs. Request car seats and extras such as GPS when you book.

Rates are sometimes—but not always—better if you book in advance or reserve through a rental agency's Web site. There are other reasons to book ahead, though: for popular destinations, during busy times of the year, or to ensure that you get certain types of cars (vans, SUVs, exotic sports cars).

■TIP➔ Make sure that a confirmed reservation guarantees you a car. Agencies sometimes overbook, particularly for busy weekends and holiday periods.

A car is essential in most parts of California. In sprawling cities such as Los Angeles and San Diego, you'll have to take the freeways to get just about anywhere.

Rates statewide for the least expensive vehicle begin at around $52 a day and $209 a week (though they increase rapidly from here). This does not include additional fees or tax on car rentals, which is 9.75% in Los Angeles and 8.75% in San Diego. Be sure to shop around—you can get a decent deal by carefully shopping the major car rental companies' Web sites. Also, rates are sometimes lower in San Diego; compare prices by city before you book, and ask about "drop charges" if you plan to return the car in a city other than the one where you rented the vehicle. If you pick up at an airport, there may also be a facility charge of as much as $12 per rental; ask when you book. When you're returning your rental, be aware that gas stations can be few and far between near airports.

In California, you must have a valid driver's license and be 21 to rent a car; rates may be higher if you're under 25. Some agencies will not rent to those under 25; check when you book. Non-U.S. residents must have a license with text that is in the Roman alphabet that is valid for the entire rental period. Though it need not be entirely written in English, it must have English letters that clearly identify it as a driver's license. In addition, most companies also require an international license; check in advance.

Specialty Car Agencies In San Francisco and Los Angeles **Specialty Rentals** (☏ 800/400-8412 ⊕ www.specialtyrentals.com); in Los Angeles (several locations), **Beverly Hills Rent a Car** (☏ 800/479-5996 ⊕ www.bhrentacar.com), or in Los Angeles (several locations) **Midway Car Rental** (☏ 800/824-5260 ⊕ www.midwaycarrental.com).

Major Rental Agencies
Alamo (☏ 800/462-5266 ⊕ www.alamo.com). **Avis** (☏ 800/331-1212 ⊕ www.avis.com). **Budget** (☏ 800/527-0700 ⊕ www.budget.com). **Hertz** (☏ 800/654-3131 ⊕ www.hertz.com). **National Car Rental** (☏ 800/227-7368 ⊕ www.nationalcar.com).

▌ TRAIN TRAVEL

One of the most beautiful train trips in the country is along the Pacific Coast from Los Angeles to Oakland via Amtrak's *Coast Starlight,* which hugs the waterfront before it turns inland at San Luis Obispo for the rest of its journey to Seattle. (Be aware that this train is frequently late arriving at and departing from Central Coast stations.) The *Pacific Surfliner* connects San Diego and San Luis Obispo via Los Angeles and Santa Barbara with multiple departures daily; and the *Sunset Limited* runs from Los Angeles to New Orleans via Arizona, New Mexico, and Texas.

Information Amtrak (☏ 800/872-7245 ⊕ www.amtrak.com).

ESSENTIALS

■ ACCOMMODATIONS

The lodgings we list are the cream of the crop in each price category. We always list the facilities that are available, but we don't specify whether they cost extra; when pricing accommodations, ask what's included and what costs extra. ⇨ *For price information, see the planner in each chapter.*

Most hotels require you to give your credit-card details before they will confirm your reservation. If you don't feel comfortable e-mailing this information, ask if you can fax it (some places even prefer faxes). However you book, get confirmation in writing and have a copy of it handy when you check in.

BED-AND-BREAKFASTS

California has more than 1,000 bed-and-breakfasts. You'll find everything from simple homestays to lavish luxury lodgings, many in historic hotels and homes. The California Association of Bed and Breakfast Inns has about 300 member properties that you can locate and book through their Web site.

Reservation Services Bed & Breakfast.com (☏ 512/322–2710 or 800/462–2632 ⊕ *www.bedandbreakfast.com*). **Bed & Breakfast Inns Online** (☏ 310/280–4363 or 800/215–7365 ⊕ *www.bbonline.com*). **BnB Finder.com** (☏ 646/205–8016 or 888/547–8226 ⊕ *www.bnbfinder.com*). **California Association of Bed and Breakfast Inns** (☏ 800/373–9251 ⊕ *www.cabbi.com*).

■ COMMUNICATIONS

INTERNET

Internet access is widely available in California's urban areas, but it's usually more difficult to get online in the state's rural areas. Most hotels offer some kind of connection—dial-up, broadband, or Wi-Fi (which is becoming much more common). Most hotels charge a daily fee (about $10) for Internet access. Cybercafés are also located throughout California.

Contacts Cybercafés (⊕ *www.cybercafes.com*).

■ EATING OUT

California has led the pack in bringing natural and organic foods to the forefront of American cooking. Though rooted in European cuisine, California cooking sometimes has strong Asian and Latin influences. Wherever you go, you're likely to find that dishes are made with fresh produce and other local ingredients.

The restaurants we list are the cream of the crop in each price category. ⇨ *For price information, see the planner in each chapter.*

CUTTING COSTS

■ TIP➜ If you're on a budget, take advantage of the "small plates" craze sweeping California by ordering several appetizer-size portions and having a glass of wine at the bar, rather than having a full meal. Also, better grocery and specialty-food stores have grab-and-go sections, with prepared foods on par with restaurant cooking, perfect for picnicking (remember, it rarely rains between May and October). At resort areas in the off-season (such as San Diego in January), you can often find two-for-one dinner specials at upper-end restaurants; check local papers or with visitor bureaus.

RESERVATIONS AND DRESS

Regardless of where you are, it's a good idea to make a reservation if you can. We only mention them specifically when reservations are essential (there's no other way you'll ever get a table) or when they are not accepted. For popular restaurants, book as far ahead as you can (often 30 days), and reconfirm as soon as you arrive. (Large parties should always call ahead to check the reservations policy.) We mention dress only when men are required to wear a jacket or a jacket and tie.

Online reservation services make it easy to book a table before you even leave home. OpenTable covers most states, including 20 major cities, and has limited listings in Canada, Mexico, the United Kingdom, France and elsewhere. DinnerBroker has restaurants throughout the United States.

Contacts OpenTable (⊕ www.opentable.com). **DinnerBroker** (⊕ www.dinnerbroker.com).

▌HEALTH

Do not fly within 24 hours of scuba diving.

Smoking is illegal in all California bars and restaurants, including on outdoor dining patios in some cities. Hotels and motels are also decreasing their inventory of smoking rooms; inquire at the time you book your reservation if any are available. In addition, a tax is added to cigarettes sold in California, and prices can be as high as $6 per pack. You might want to bring a carton from home.

▌HOURS OF OPERATION

Banks in California are typically open weekdays from 9 to 6 and Saturday morning; most are closed on Sunday and most holidays. Smaller shops usually operate from 10 to 6, with larger stores remaining open until 8 or later. Hours vary for museums and historical sites, and many are closed one or more days a week, or for extended periods during off-season months. It's a good idea to check before you visit a tourist site.

▌MONEY

Los Angeles and San Diego tend to be expensive cities to visit, and rates at coastal and desert resorts are almost as high. A day's admission to a major theme park can run upward of $70 a head, though you may be able to get discounts by purchasing tickets in advance on line. Hotel rates average $150 to $250 a night

(though you can find cheaper places), and dinners at even moderately priced restaurants often cost $20 to $40 per person. Costs in the Death Valley/Mojave Desert region are considerably less.

CREDIT CARDS

Record all your credit-card numbers—as well as the phone numbers to call if your cards are lost or stolen—in a safe place, so you're prepared should something go wrong. Both MasterCard and Visa have general numbers you can call if your card is lost, but you're better off calling the number of your issuing bank, since MasterCard and Visa normally just transfer you to your bank; your bank's number is usually printed on your card.

Reporting Lost Cards American Express (☎ 800/992–3404 in U.S., 336/393–1111 collect from abroad ⊕ www.americanexpress. com). **Discover** (☎ 800/347–2683 in U.S., 801/902–3100 collect from abroad ⊕ www. discovercard.com). **Diners Club** (☎ 800/234–6377 in U.S., 303/799–1504 collect from abroad ⊕ www.dinersclubinternational. com). **MasterCard** (☎ 800/622–7747 in U.S., 636/722–7111 collect from abroad ⊕ www. mastercard.com). **Visa** (☎ 800/847–2911 in U.S., 410/581–9994 collect from abroad ⊕ www.visa.com).

▌SAFETY

Southern California is a safe place to visit, as long as you take the usual precautions. In large cities ask the concierge or desk clerk to point out areas on your map that you should avoid. Lock valuables in a hotel safe when you're not using them. (Some hotels have in-room safes large enough to hold a laptop computer.) Keep an eye on your handbag when you're out in public. Security is high (but mostly invisible) at theme parks and resorts.

▌TAXES

Sales tax in California varies from about 8.25% to 9.75% and applies to all purchases except for food purchased in a grocery store; food consumed in a restaurant is taxed but take-out food purchases are not. Hotel taxes vary widely by region, from 10% to 15%.

∎ TIME

California is in the Pacific time zone. Pacific daylight time (PDT) is in effect from mid-March through early November; the rest of the year the clock is set to Pacific standard time (PST).

∎ TIPPING

Most service workers in California are fairly well paid compared to those in the rest of the country, and extravagant tipping is not the rule here. Exceptions include wealthy enclaves such as Beverly Hills and La Jolla as well as the most expensive resort areas.

TIPPING GUIDELINES FOR CALIFORNIA	
Bartender	$1 per drink, or 10%–15% of tab per round of drinks
Bellhop	$1–$5 per bag, depending on the level of the hotel
Hotel Concierge	$5 or more, if he/she performs a service for you
Hotel Doorman	$1–$2 if he/she helps you get a cab
Valet Parking Attendant	$2 when you get your car
Hotel Maid	$1–$2 per person, per day; more in high-end hotels
Waiter	15%–20% (20% is standard in upscale restaurants); nothing additional if a service charge is added to the bill
Skycap at Airport	$1–$3 per bag
Hotel Room-Service Waiter	$1–$2 per delivery, even if a service charge has been added
Taxi Driver	15%–20%, but round up the fare to the next dollar amount
Tour Guide	10% of the cost of the tour

∎ TOURS

Guided tours are a good option when you don't want to do it all yourself. You travel along with a group (sometimes large, sometimes small), stay in prebooked hotels, eat with your fellow travelers (the cost of meals is sometimes included in the price of your tour, sometimes not), and follow a schedule.

But not all guided tours are an if-it's-Tuesday-this-must-be-Belgium experience. A knowledgeable guide can take you places that you might never discover on your own, and you may be pushed to see more than you would have otherwise. Tours aren't for everyone, but they can be just the thing for trips to places where making travel arrangements is difficult or time-consuming.

Whenever you book a guided tour, find out what's included and what isn't. A "land-only" tour includes all your travel (by bus, in most cases) in the destination, but not necessarily your flights to and from or even within it. Also, in most cases prices in tour brochures don't include fees and taxes. And remember that you'll be expected to tip your guide (in cash) at the end of the tour.

INDEX

PHOTO CREDITS

and bottom), Robert Holmes. 378, iStockphoto. 382, William Royer/iStockphoto. 393, David Falk/ iStockphoto. 410, Brett Shoaf/Artistic Visuals Photography. Chapter 10: Joshua Tree National Park: 417, Eric Foltz/iStockphoto. 418 (top), Loic Bernard/iStockphoto. 418 (bottom), Eric Foltz/iStockphoto. 419 (top), Justin Mair/Shutterstock. 419 (bottom), Mariusz S. Jurgielewicz/Shutterstock. 420, Eric Foltz/iStockphoto. Chapter 11: The Mojave Desert: 425, Robert Holmes. 426, amygdala imagery/ Shutterstock. 427, Robert Holmes. 428, San Bernardino County Regional Parks. 435, Merryl Edelstein, Fodors.com member. 441, Robert Holmes. 451, Paul Erickson/iStockphoto. Chapter 12: Death Valley National Park: 453, Rodney Ee, Fodors.com member. 455 (top), Igor Karon/Shutterstock. 455 (bottom), iofoto/Shutterstock. 456, Paul D. Lemke/iStockphoto. 462-63, James Feliciano/iStockphoto. 466, Rodney Ee, Fodors.com member. Chapter 13: The Central Valley: 469, Kim Brogan, Fodors.com member. 470, Gary Allard/ iStockphoto. 471–92, Robert Holmes. Chapter 14: The Southern Sierra: 495, Randall Pugh, Fodors.com member. 496, Craig Cozart/iStock-photo. 497 (top), David T Gomez/ iStockphoto. 497 (bottom left and bottom right), Robert Holmes. 498, christinea78, Fodors.com member. 503, moonjazz/Flickr. 510, Douglas Atmore/iStockphoto. Chapter 15: Yosemite National Park: 513, Sarah P. Corley, Fodors.com member. 514, Yosemite Concession Services. 515 (top), Andy Z./ Shutterstock. 515 (bottom), Greg Epperson/age fotostock. 516, Doug Lemke/Shutterstock. 522, Rebalyn, Fodors.com member. 525, Nathan Jaskowiak/Shutterstock.527, Greg Epperson/age fotostock. 532-33, Katrina Leigh/Shutterstock. Chapter 16: Sequoia and Kings Canyon National Parks: 535 and 536, Robert Holmes. 537 (top), Greg Epperson/age fotostock. 537 (bottom) and 538, Robert Holmes. 545, urosr/Shutterstock. 551, Robert Holme

NOTES

NOTES

ABOUT OUR WRITERS

Native Californian **Cheryl Crabtree**—who updated the Central Coast and Monterey Bay Area chapters—has worked as a freelance writer since 1987. She has contributed to *Fodor's California* since 2003 and has also written for *Fodor's Complete Guide to the National Parks of the West*. Cheryl is editor of *Montecito Magazine*. She currently lives in Santa Barbara with her husband, two sons, and Jack Russell terrier.

A Northern California resident for 17 years, **Reed Parsell** has traveled extensively throughout the region and written hundreds of newspaper travel stories based on his experiences. A part-time copy editor and travel writer for the *Sacramento Bee*, Parsell also writes a "going green" column for *Sacramento* magazine and was the primary writer for *Fodor's InFocus Yosemite, Sequoia and Kings Canyon National Parks*. He updated our Central Valley, Southern Sierra coverage.

Freelance writer **Christine Vovakes**—who updated the Travel Smart Southern California chapter—has also contributed to *Fodor's National Parks of the West* and *Essential USA*. Her travel articles and photographs have also appeared in many other publications, including *The Washington Post, The Christian Science Monitor, The Sacramento Bee,* and the *San Francisco Chronicle.*

Sura Wood is a San Francisco-based writer who has covered the Bay Area arts and lifestyle scene in particular and the film industry in general. Her profiles, reviews, and features have appeared in *The Hollywood Reporter,* the *San Jose Mercury News, San Francisco Arts Monthly,* and many other publications. For this edition, she fact-checked our National Parks chapters, including Channel Islands, Joshua Tree, Death Valley, Yosemite, Sequoia and Kings Canyon, and Redwood National Park.

Bobbi Zane—who updated the Experience Southern California, Inland Empire, and Palm Springs chapters for this edition—grew up in Southern California, watching the region grow from its mostly rural roots into one of the most exciting places in the world. Her articles on Palm Springs have appeared in the *Orange County Register* and *Westways* magazine. She has contributed to *Fodor's Complete Guide to the National Parks of the West, Fodor's San Diego,* and *Escape to Nature Without Roughing It.* A lifelong Californian, Bobbi has visited every corner of the state on behalf of Fodor's.